THE IRON AGE OF MARS

The Author wishes to extend his thanks and gratitude to the Mainwaring Archives Foundation for its support of his research. At the same time, he would acknowledge the affectionate collaboration of Anne-Marie Hueber de Grazia, his wife.

Copyright 2005 by Alfred de Grazia
All rights reserved

Second Edition, March 2009
Metron Publications
P.O. Box 1213
Princeton, NJ 08542-1213
USA
Metronax
B.P. 60062
74003 LA FERTE-BERNARD Cedex
FRANCE

ISBN: 978-160377-077-4

Library of Congress Control Number:
2009901917

Cover: *Front:* One of the statuettes of the god Reshef found by Claude Schaeffer in the ruins of Enkomi-Alasia. Reshef is identified with Mars and Nergal (p.434) *Back:* Tithonium Chasma and Ius Chasma, Western part of Valles Marineris, Mars. Photo: European Space Agency/DLR/FU Berlin (G. Neukum).

Alfred de Grazia

The Iron Age of Mars

Speculations on Quantavolution and Catastrophe in the Greater Mediterranean Region of the First Millennium B.C.E.

metron

To Paul Rafael

"Let me tell you, said Mercier, before you go any further, I haven't an answer to my name. Oh there was a time I had, and none but the best, they were my only company, I even invented queries to go with them. But I sent them all packing long ago."

Samuel Beckett, Mercier and Camier *

*French edition 1970, Grove Press English language edition (1975) with Samuel Beckett's own copyrighted translation (1974), p.87.

Table of Contents

Foreword   15

1. The Iron Age Quantavolution   19
2. The Q Paradigm Applied   30
3. Spheres of Change   59
4. Earth and Heaven: Conjoined and Interactive   80
5. Heroic Scholars: Old and New   95
6. Ruination of Trade, Lands and Peoples   130
7. Vagrants of the Phantom Age   160
8. Mars and Its Doppelgaengers   175
9. Mars Brings Iron to Earth   196
10. Hebrews of the Iron Age   220
11. The Fabled Holy Land   254
12. The Arabian Alternative   268
13. Changed Ideologies   287
14. The Extermination of Volsinium   307
15. The Wolf of Rome   338
16. The Burning of Troy   350
17. Profiles of Many Destructions   378
18. An Atlantis Connection   436
19. A Society in Shock   447
20. A Neurosis of Concerned Scholars   488
21. Near and Far Future Defenses   516

Figures   *516*

Bibliography   *554*

About the Author and Appreciations   *601*

Endnotes   *603*

Table of Contents
(Including Subheadings)

Foreword — 15

1. The Iron Age Quantavolution — 19
- *Predecessors* — 20
- *Holospheric Quantavolution* — 21
- *Explaining the Phantom "Dark Age"* — 27
- *Switching from ~-1250 to ~-850* — 28

2. The Q Paradigm Applied — 30
- *Defining Quantavolution* — 30
- *Measuring and Indexing Quantavolutions* — 31
- *Principles of Quantavolutio* — 36
- *Convention vs Quantavolution* — 49
- *C-Q Test* — 52

3. Spheres of Change — 59
- *Holism* — 60
- *The Spheres of Quantavolution Defined* — 61
- *The Three Errors of Iron Age Timing* — 62
- *Work of Edwin Schorr* — 65
- *Earth Sciences* — 66
- *The Behavior of Sky Systems* — 67
- *Biosphere and Cultural Spheres* — 72
- *The Alphabet* — 74

4. Earth and Heaven: Conjoined and Interactive — 80
- *Downgrading Planets to Comets* — 81
- *Iron Age Disasters Known Worldwide* — 85
- *The Mobile Heavens* — 87

5. Heroic Scholars: Old and New — 95
- *Schaeffer's Magnum Opus* — 96
- *A Warm Relationship Develops* — 99
- *Schaeffer Reads Velikovsky's Work* — 101
- *Schaeffer's Extensive Objections to 'Ages in Chaos'* — 105
- *A Grazian Intervention* — 123
- *Israel Finkelstein* — 126
- *Kamal Salibi Enters the Lists* — 128

6. Ruination of Trade, Lands and Peoples — 130
No City or Village Left Standing — *132*
Ashes, Flames and Fires — *134*
The History of Peat Deposits — *137*
The Number and Extent of Mars Visitations — *141*
Expert Explanations of the Destructions — *142*
International Trade within the Ambit of Amber — *144*
The Plagues: Local, Worldwide and Exoterrestrial — *148*
Earthquakes — *149*
Exoterrestrial and Terrestrial Catastrophe — *151*
Placement of Ramses III and Medinet Habu — *154*
Our Revised Calendar — *156*
Summary of Reasons for Displacing Ramses III — *158*

7. Vagrants of the Phantom Age — 160
Blood Genes and Farming — *161*
Jewish Descent — *162*
Need for Maps of Migrations — *163*
"Peoples of the Sea" Stand for Universal Vagrancy — *166*
Thucydides on Wild Early Greece — *172*

8. Mars and Its Doppelgaengers — 175
Earth, Moon and Mars Scenarios — *177*
Patten-Windsor Theory — *178*
History of the Quantavolution of Mars — *183*
God by Any Other Name... — *186*
Recent Geological Marks on Mars — *189*
Historical Indications of the Mars-Earth Interaction — *191*
Astrophysical Agonies of Mars — *194*

9. Mars Brings Iron to Earth — 196
Strange Patterns of Bolides — *197*
Mascons of Iron — *198*
Banded Iron Formations — *199*
Chemical Processing of Iron in Nature — *200*
Iron Foundries — *202*
The Word "Iron" and Myth — *204*
Lightning Transfers — *205*
Soft Landings of Meteorites — *208*

Interplanetary Welding	*211*
Fall-Outs of Poisons and Germs: Arsenic	*217*
Iron and the Ocean Bottoms	*218*

10. Hebrews of the Iron Age — 220
Where did the Hebrews Come From? — *221*
Finkelstein's Scope and Method — *223*
Ignoring Catastrophe and Amnesia — *225*
Failure to decipher Myth and Legend — *226*
Joshua's Legend and the United Monarchy — *228*
King Hazael or Mother Nature? — *229*
Hillbilly Hebrews — *231*
Jerusalem's Mice — *234*
Robert Forrest's Exacting Critique — *236*
The Jews as Planet-Worshipers — *239*
Remembering Horrors Poorly — *241*
Bible as a History of Blame and Punishment — *242*
The Judges as Condottieri — *243*
Isaiah's Madness — *246*
Charity and Welfare in the Bible — *247*
Limiting Hostilities Among Archaeologists of the Bible — *249*
Deconstructing the Bible — *250*

11. The Fabled Holy Land — 254
"King David the Nebbish" — *254*
'Der Spiegel' Collects the Minimalists — *256*
The Little Struggling Kingdoms — *260*
The Monotheism Project of King Josiah — *260*
Scandalous Religious Practices — *262*
Like Falsifying Medieval Monks — *264*
The Hebrews Born an Iron Age People — *266*

12. The Arabian Alternative — 268
The Background and Thesis of Salibi — *269*
Toponymics — *271*
Opposition to the Arabian Scenario — *272*
Beginning the Defense of the Arabian Thesis — *273*
Arabia Deserta — *274*
The Promised Land — *278*
Moving the Peoples North to "Priori-Palestine" — *278*

The Erasure of Ubar   279
A Confusion of Places: the Wabar Craters   280
A Literal Bible Meets a Topsy-Turvy Geography   282
The Babylonian Experience from Arabia   283
Asura Mazda and Yahweh   285

13. Changed Ideologies   **287**
Résumé: Meanwhile, in the Sky...   288
Was Yahweh a Doppelgaenger?   290
"A Plague on All Ye God-Names..."   292
David in His Martian Role   294
The Messiah Idea, from David to Jesus, and Astrology   296
The Human-Mind Turns into Pre-Socratic Philosophy   300
Martian Theater and Martian Engineering   303
The Divine Succession: Jesus, Christ   305

14. The Extermination of Volsinium   **307**
From Villanovans to Etruscans   308
The Volsinium Story   309
Pliny's Relevant Comments on Astro-Catastrophe   310
Conjuring Lightning   311
Lightning Geology   313
Etruria Dating Less Obsessively Askew   315
Orvieto Not the Center of the Volsinii   316
Lightning and Ashes of Etruria   318
Changed Moods in Art, Culture and Rituals   321
Chronometry, Vulcanism, Topography   323
An Asteroid Impact?   326
A Tunguska Blast Scenario   327
Lightning Storm Scenario   328
A Martian Gas Cloud and Particle Storm   330
Hercules and the Monster Volta Active at Volsinium   332
Conclusion: Destruction by Bolide and Lightning-Fire Shower   334
A List of Matters for Investigation in a Further Program
Concerning the Volsinium Quantavolution   335

15. The Wolf of Rome   **338**
A Founding Date of -747   338
2000 Years of Virgil   342

Peroni's Problem With the Old Early Date	*343*
Aeneas Lands at Sol Indiges and Names it Troy	*345*
The Trojans Stop at Carthage	*346*
Did Aeneas Quit Troy Early?	*347*

16. The Burning of Troy — 350

The Burnt City of Troy	*352*
Discovery of the Treasure of Priam	*353*
The Puzzle of the Scorched Treasure	*356*
A Catastrophe Without Warning	*357*
A Natural Force Helped to Devastate Hisarlik-Troy	*359*
A New Interdisciplinary Method	*364*
Salvaging the Ashes and Debris for Analysis	*365*
The Lack of Geo-Mythology	*368*
Testing the Metals and Calcinated Debris	*370*
Postscript of November, 1983	*372*
Troy of the Trojan War since the Blegen Expeditions	*374*

17. Profiles of Many Destructions — 378

Thebes	*379*
The Tsunami of Euripides	*380*
Prototype: the Mycenae Model	*381*
The Phantom Age Spanned in Athens	*386*
Pylos	*389*
Asia Minor, Anatolia, West Asia	*392*
Nisyros	*394*
A Focus on Syria-Palestine	*397*
Tel Rehov	*399*
Peter James on Lachish and Ramses III	*401*
Italy	*407*
Lago Albano	*408*
Sicily	*411*
Crete (Tarshish)	*412*
Thera-Santorini and the Cyclades	*416*
Phrygians, Cimmerians, Scythians and Ethiopians	*419*
Egypt	*422*
The Founding of Carthage	*426*
Central and Celtic Europe	*427*
Enkomi	*428*
Ugarit	*434*

18. An Atlantis Connection — 436
My Earlier View to be Amended — *437*
Helgoland, the Crash Scene of Phaethon — *438*
The Eddas and Fenris-Wolf — *441*
Felice Vinci's Troy in Finland — *441*
The Amber Trade — *445*
Spanuth's Work Attracts Disgraceful Support — *446*

19. A Society in Shock — 447
Q-Shock — *448*
Iron Shortens Life Variously — *449*
Isaiah and the Hebrew Prophets — *467*
Humanity Shocked Beyond Recall — *472*
King Nabopolassar's Stress and Shock — *473*
Collective Shock.Response — *474*
High-Energy Shocking Forces — *475*
Did God Call in "Katrina" to Destroy New Orleans? — *479*
Why Societies Collapse — *480*
Inventiveness in the Iron Age — *483*
Changes, in Greek and Jewish Societies, and in General — *485*

20. A Neurosis of Concerned Scholars — 488
Professional Hazards — *489*
The Zionist Dilemma of the Western Scientist — *491*
What Makes a Yalie into an Archaeologist — *493*
Anxieties Peculiar to Archaeology — *494*
Aesthetics Respond to Quantavolution — *496*
The Broad-Gauged Archaeologist — *498*
Paradigm Paralysis — *499*

21. Near and Far Future Defenses — 508
A Radical Approach to Applied Science — *508*
Providing for Short-Run Defense — *511*
Far Future Sky Defense — *513*

Figures — 516
Bibliography — 554
About the Author and Appreciations — 601
Endnotes — 603

Foreword

*"Damn the torpedoes!..Go ahead!..
Full speed!"*

Admiral David Farragut
Battle of Mobile Bay, 5 August 1864

I seek in this book to apply the theory of quantavolution to events in the Greater Mediterranean world of the First Millennium B.C.E., describing how a set of sudden, intensive changes enveloped that region owing to erratic proximate movements of planet Mars and to other astrophysical phenomena. Every sphere of nature and human behavior was radically affected, producing effects that, while subsiding, became and remain part of modern nature and culture.

Granting your right to judge for yourself what I have achieved, I believe that these several propositions will prove to be useful and important.

A holistic paradigm that we call "Quantavolution" may help the arts and sciences to understand history, both human and natural. It can be shown to compete successfully with the propositions of conventional science in this task. Holistic means to us all-enveloping; a paradigm means to us a pattern of how things function.

During a two-centuries passage from the historical ages that are termed Bronze and Iron, roughly in the years 850 to 650 B.C.E., there occurred an immense set of happenings to the Earth and its People. Every sphere of existence was demonstrably affected suddenly and intensively.

The exoterrestrial origin of this undeniable quantavolution can be argued plausibly and, furthermore, attributed to the planet Mars in large part. Not simply but profusely, it is iron that conditions the Iron Age and it is of Mars, conveyed catastrophically to Earth.

Every quantavolution, of which at least five occurred from the recent birth of the human species up to this Martian Age, or Martia, has introduced a sudden, intensive change in all aspects of existence covering measurably the whole Earth. The entire Jovean planetary system becomes involved, including an actively transforming plasmasphere.

In the Greater Mediterranean Region upon which we focus our study -- a Region that coincides roughly with the Roman Empire at its height -- all basic spheres of natural and human activity are obviously impacted. The astrosphere, the geosphere, the anthroposphere, the psychosphere, and the theosphere are among them. Change was holistic.

Scarcely any landscape or village, including its inhabitants, escaped ruin from the material and gaseous fall-outs, the lightning, the fires, the earthquakes, the volcanism, the tsunami and flooding, the land's rising and sinking, the climatic changes, the hurricanes, and the plague. Those humans who survived changed or remade their gods. A majority of people were forced to migrate or chose to wander. They fought countless battles for territory, for possessions, for their culture and gods, and out of sheer madness.

The peak period of the quantavolution of Mars occupied, according to the method of reckoning that we have adopted and its calendar, the ninth to seventh centuries B.C.E., roughly 850 to 650 B.C.E.. Conventional scholars continue to number this calendar as roughly 1250 to 650 BCE, and call the period the Dark Age (of Greece). As I move along, I cannot help but address and repair this injurious conduct, which amounts practically to a neurosis. I sometimes call the spurious Dark Age the "Phantom Age" to help specify and clarify the discussion.

To illustrate and amplify the radical holospheric

change that occurred, we shall concentrate upon a number of sites that have been subjected to scientific investigation. Several cases will be extensively discussed: Troy, Israel, Rome, Encomi, and Volsinium (Etruria). I have a special chapter advancing the theory that the Hebrews and most of their Bible material had their origins in the Asir region of Western Arabia. Unexpectedly this moderates a preceding special chapter that exposes the recent devastating deflation of the Bible and Hebrew history. Other famous cases of Iron Age quantavolution will be put forward in lesser detail: Mycenae, Pylos, Ugarit, Encomi-Alesia, Athens, Egypt, Crete.

And more cases will be briefly treated: Nisyros, the Scythians, the Swiss-Italian Lake villages, Sicily, and so forth, with a few words of the quantavolution's work in Northwestern Europe. Another score of places will simply be named and granted a paragraph or two. Additional cases could be counted in, still far fewer than should be available for study and comparisons. The Late Bronze Age of the Greater Mediterranean Region hosted myriads of settlements. Their excavation lies in the future. But they should be explored with a better theory and methodology than has been the case in the past.

In two volumes, written in the 1970's, I merged a new theory of human origins with the paradigm of quantavolution. The human species was called homo sapiens schizotypus, homo schizo for short. In the present study, I show how homo schizo was stressed and shocked in the Iron Age into new cultures and outlooks. I inquire as well whether the psychology of archaeologists has been reacting neurotically against the quantavolution paradigm.

In the end I express my concern for the future. The bewildering advances of the specialized sciences provide both despair and hope. Everybody knows this. Perhaps a way may be invented to cope with quantavolutions and lesser catastrophes and with the world that they bring into being. We need especially a new kind of belief-system, if we are to control ourselves and our environment, and in order to meet a forbidding future with equanimity.

Try as I may, I cannot expect to solve the complex

and controversial problems that I have encountered. At best I can set up a paradigm and a mode of thought that should produce good results in good time. I shall have to question and contradict established authorities and specialists who have sweated (literally, in many cases) over the problems discussed. I do so regretfully, for I would rather have learned effortlessly all about these matters from those in charge.

So be it: my speculations are being published, claiming the first contemporary definition of the *Oxford (Unabridged) Dictionary:* **Speculation:** *"The contemplation, consideration, or profound study of some subject"* and I should add the implication: *"...with trepidation."*

Please sympathize with the bear who is causing a disturbance in the cook-house.

Alfred de Grazia
Island of Naxos,
Thanksgiving Day, November 2005

Chapter One

The Iron Age Quantavolution

Between the Late Bronze Age and the Iron Age comes what has been and still is called by many Classical scholars the Greek Dark Ages (or Dark Age), marking a dreadfully long passage between civilizations. My position has been and remains that the Dark Ages hardly existed, although they were even more dreadful than conceived. For they marked a holospheric change in the world, so much change in every sphere – astrosphere, geosphere, biosphere, historisphere, etc – that they altogether amounted to a quantavolution, which is defined as an immense event of wide scope, great intensity and stunning suddenness. It was a catastrophe; still, it carried with it the seeds of classical Greece and the Roman Empire, wonders of humanity to this day. Also, though I find the task difficult, I may be able to detect in Iron Age events the spores of Judaism, and therefore of Christianity and Islam. It is fairly possible, too, that Mars was forced to cast upon Earth millions of tons of iron, for which element the planet was anciently known.

This Martian quantavolution, initiating a period that I term Martia, was not the first and last of quantavolutions to beset the Earth. The most immediate and still influential quantavolution was the preceding one, of the mid-second millennium, beginning circa 1450 B.C.E., that brought into play the planet Venus.[1] I cannot pause on this story, and must ask the reader, before judging its actuality, to read the works of Dr. Immanuel Velikovsky, as well as my own that support him on the subject.[2] I might add here that Venus did not exit gracefully from the near skies but occasionally, every 52 years perhaps, came within unreasonable bounds of Earth. But then, after intercourse with Mars as well as Earth and Moon, Venus moved out of bounds to its present circular orbit.

Predecessors

That is to say, my scenario with respect to quantavolutions has been argued before – most directly in my quantavolution series and several articles of twenty years ago -- but originally by Immanuel Velikovsky in his works at the turn of the Nineteen Fifties. Alongside and coming out of a French-Alsatian archaeological tradition, and at the same time as Velikovsky, whose background was Jewish-Russian-German-Israeli-American, was Claude Schaeffer, of Alsatian-French origin, Professor at the College de France. Late in life the two men came to know, respect and sympathize with each other, and I came to know the former well and the latter by personal acquaintance and from his works.

In a work entitled *The Velikovsky Affair*, I organized, edited, co-authored, financed and published a full defense of the theses of Velikovsky. Though a psychoanalyst, a polymath in fact, Velikovsky, who was not academically entrenched, was more vulnerable to disbelief and attack than Schaeffer. Claude Schaeffer was by contrast a refugee from the Germans and the French occupation authorities; he joined General Charles De Gaulle in England, spent most of World War II there, and so carried back with him enlarged prestige and respect in French academia. He had done notable research in the Near East and had become Professor of Archaeology at the famous College de France. Furthermore, because he ignored the skies in his explanations of catastrophe, he escaped being identified as was Velikovsky (incorrectly so) with the Christian and Jewish Bible fundamentalists who followed their God in the astrosphere.

So, when Schaeffer reported in his large study, *Stratigraphie Comparée*, his findings of universal settlement destructions on several occasions of the Bronze Age, he was not condemned and maligned, but was damned with faint praise in France, and hardly read in England, if only because few Englishmen would bother to learn French and devote themselves to his thick volume about catastrophes. When a generation later a *Festschrift* was finally composed in his honor, another massive volume was published, containing several score articles; but not a single one defended his thesis as a whole and hardly a one paused to detail or praise it.[3] Almost without exception, the contributions were descriptive, highly specialized, and concerned with patterns of culture traits. The sky did not exist for them, nor even the possibility of widespread concurrent destruction of civilizations, whatever the cause. I am to say something about this neurosis of archaeologists farther along in this book.

Holospheric Quantavolution

The forces of nature were in the Iron Age immensely destructive and concurrently so. The atmosphere, for example, was active and poignantly significant to peoples everywhere. This was the age when Heraclitus concluded that "Lightning steers the universe," a fragment of his rare preserved thoughts.

The 'Agents of Catastrophe' of which much will be said, can be mentioned here as Earth and sky, winds and fire, water-tides-floods-tsunamis, plague and radiation, thunderbolts, human destroyers, divine delusions viewed as animations of reality and natural forces, civil war, economic collapse – in short, the Martian Quantavolution, like all others, worked on the ironic "Murphy's Law" – "If anything can go wrong, it will."

We must worm our way into all parts of the holosphere of existence. Linguistics tells us not only cute derivations, for example, but also connects spheres of existence as affected by quantavolutionary forces. Thus, for 'thunderbolt" the Hebrew apparently has *la-haziz qolot*, literally 'for the lightning of the voices', *qol* or 'voice' being a common word for "thunder." Thunderbolts must be heard to speak and be understood.

So all other spheres of existence were exponentially affected. The quantavolution would be total in its effects upon the different elements of being: cultural, genetic, biological, geographical and geological, and climatic. I name and define and exemplify thirteen of these spheres below in Chapter Three.

First, however, I would introduce my general view of the catastrophic events of the Iron Age, which can be paraphrased from my manuscript of 1979, then published in Bombay, India, in 1982, as *Chaos and Creation*. We return to the abovementioned major question concerning the "Greek Dark Ages" that are supposed to have occupied the years between the Thirteenth and Seventh centuries, between the fall of the Mycenaean cities and the advent of the archaic Greeks.

Edwin Schorr, using sometimes the pen name Israel Isaacson, a graduate student and research assistant to Velikovsky, drove nails into the coffin designed by Velikovsky to contain the Greek "Dark Ages."[3] Velikovsky's own work on the subject awaited publication indefinitely, until it was published on the Internet in 2000. Both men have shown how Mycenaean civilization moved directly into the archaic and classical Greek culture with little lapse of time.

The centuries hitherto assigned to the Dark Ages are fictions aimed at accommodating an incorrectly dated Egyptian chronology to a Greek chronology that was only correctly figured after the seventh century BCE. Mycenaean ruins and art, as with the remains of all of the Near East civilizations, have been tied to the Egyptian dating, which, for reasons exposed fully by Velikovsky with contributions by independent scholars such as Chervil and Dayton, was made out to be far too old.

It is noteworthy that the collapse of Mycenaean civilization around the Aegean Sea has been believed to correspond in time to the "Invasions of the Sea Peoples" throughout the Near East, that is, the falsely acclaimed 13th century B.C. In fact, both the Mycenaean collapse and the Near East ruination were events of the same period. It was not the 13th century but the 8th and 7th centuries. The cause was not "the Sea Peoples," who did not exist as such, but the raging sky-god Mars, and its antagonist, Venus.

Once the reconceptualization of the events and time was accomplished, the reconstruction of the separate pieces of Near East history, including its mysteries, could become routine. Thus when the *Cambridge Ancient History* publishes tablets inscribed on the very doomsday of Pylos, the city of old King Nestor on the western Peloponnesus, it reports that a tablet, apparently the last, written in haste, "immediately before the destruction which baked them and rendered them durable," details how troops were sent to watch the sea.[4] Again, far to the East, the last documents of Boghazköy and Ugarit, reported by M. C. Astour and J. T. Hooker, appear to describe defense preparations, after which there is nothing but destruction and ruins to await the modern excavator.

The revision in these cases, and in many excavation reports, is simple: for "invaders" or "people of the sea," read Mars-Ares-Nergal etc. For defense preparations, read universal portents, alerts, rescue parties, mobilization, sacrifices, propitiations, exodus. A people in readiness for cosmic catastrophe behave, at least in the prejudiced eyes of an archaeologist, like people organized to defend themselves against foreign enemies.

Claude Schaeffer, famed excavator of Ugarit and practically the sole systematic and clear-sighted surveyor of Bronze Age reports in the archaeological profession, published his findings as early as 1948. Absolute and completely, they showed a set of disasters marking off the ages. In 1968, Prof. Schaeffer was impelled to point out to his still uncomprehending colleagues that the disasters were the same and to be found everywhere. The response was respectful indifference and a continuation of the same kind of individual excavation reporting that dares not conjecture beyond the description of the ruin and its contents. Yet, in 1948, he had been required, by the authoritatively accepted chronologists of Egypt, to mark a limit to the latest excavations of many sites of the Near East at about 1200, labeling them as destruction by "Peoples of the Sea."

In 1977, Velikovsky published *Peoples of the Sea*. But here the iconoclast was undertaking the task of showing that Ramses III, and certain successors were of the time of the

Persian conquests, that is, of the fourth century B.C. instead of the conventionally dated thirteenth century. An absolute and authoritative chronology was off by 800 years! (The vagrant peoples of the Iron Age were definitely not the "Peoples of the Sea," of which Ramses III tells, though historians and archaeologists have given them this name, an unfortunate connection that has confused most scholars.)

Also in 1977, Velikovsky published *Ramses II*, whereupon a large chunk of the pseudo-historical plastering covering the "Dark Ages" -- that connected with the "Hittite" Empire -- cracked. The Hittites evidently were Chaldeans, and their time was of the beginning of Martia.

The Greek "Dark Ages", too, was intended for early publication, but this did not occur in his lifetime. Meanwhile, should the scholar wish to view the reconstructed history, it is to be found on the Velikovsky web site. There, too, old "discredited" studies are revived, such as Krickenhaus' work on Tiryns, for example, where fire destroys the Mycenaean palace, and a new temple of Greek style is promptly built over it No five centuries of "Dark Ages Gaposis" in between!

In these two books, Velikovsky did not delve into the many other "Peoples of the Sea" cases. These, as stated above, fell not into the thirteenth century, not into the fourth century, but into the eighth and seventh century Martian catastrophes. That is why, in Schaeffer's comparative studies, it can be observed that, following this period of disasters, settlements were either absent or, if present, were of proto-classic or even classic type.

Extensive and systematically presented documentation is available in Schaeffer's work. Below one meter of Troy's soil, all remains are prehistoric except a "few Roman sherd fallen from above." Below begins Troy VII B prehistorically with ruins caused by "Peoples of the Sea," dated ~-1150 B.C. Archaeological science has taught its students for generations that the site of Troy was abandoned. But Maoris wrote that the site was a source of violent contention for some centuries because of its position to command the commerce between Asia and Europe that passed through the Dardanelles. He is so cited in *The Burning of Troy*. If so, such a long-term desolation cannot be.

Yet we find the same disconsolate conclusions reached at the many other sites: Ras Shamra, nothing after ~-1200 [~-800 by my dating]; Byblos, final destruction ~-1200 [~-800] Chagar Bazar, nothing from ~--1350 [~-950] onwards; Hama, Mycenaean at ~-1300 [~-900] and nothing thereafter; Beit Mirsim, Jericho, Bei'an, Megiddo, Tell el Hesi, Tars – all finished by the "Peoples of the Sea," *ca* ~-1200 [~-800]; Alana Huyuk, where first level of culture begins at ~-1300 [~-900]; Alishar Huyak, ~-1150 [~-850]; Cyprus, Iron Age at [~-1150 [~-850], then nothing; Tepe Giyan, last level ends at ~-1200 [~-800]; Talyche, Agha-Evlar, etc. in Persia, end at ~-1150 [~-750]; the Caucasus sites, no re-beginning after ~-1200 [~-800]; Luristan, nothing after Recent Bronze set at ~-1450 [~-1000]. No man-made catastrophe then could be so bad as all this. The uniformitarian chronologists, unwittingly leagued with mistaken Egyptian chronologues, have produced a 400-to-500-year artificial extension of catastrophe throughout the Old World - in order (consciously or unconsciously) to deny it.

The New or Late Bronze Age did not end because of some new use of metal, or the advent of some enlightened monarch, or the desire of some people to intrude upon another people's habitat. It marked a new celestial stage. A cosmic catastrophe destroyed cultures to the extent that the newly created cultures were distinctive. The world moved into an age of Mars, during which the fortunes of the Earth and human race followed a path of exponentially declining destruction, violence and madness. Finally, as the effects of Martia wore off or were assimilated to the human mind and culture, a period that we might call Solarian began. This would have been around the time of Jesus Christ.

I took Martia to be the seventh great quantavolution of mankind, and Solaria, our own age, would be the Eighth. This is a kind of cyclical or helical history of the ages. Egyptian priests told Herodotus that this was our Fifth Sun after four destructions of the celestial order. The Aztecs told the Spanish priests the same. The Hindu *Bhagavata Purana* puts us in the fifth age also. But the Buddhist *Visuddhi-Magga* allows seven destructions. Rabbinical authorities claimed six reconstructions, placing us in the seventh. Hesiod was the first reporter of Greek beliefs, and counted the ages in metal, almost as today: the golden, the silver, the bronze and the iron.

Thus, many cyclic theories of the ages exist. Why do they never (perhaps) exceed ten; why are they never one or even two? Or even three, the favorite categorical fixation of scholarship since Plato? Cumont wrote that "The idea of seven ages attached to the seven planets is common to a number of religions. Tentatively, for convenience, we place ourselves today in the eighth period of the Holocene epoch and of humanity, the Solarian Period, following seven quantavolutions. These I call, too, by the planets, the Uranian, Lunarian, Saturnian, Jovean, Mercurian, Venusian, and Martian Periods. My reason is that each planet was the principal actor on a quantavolution that introduced another planet.

In the Iron Age phantom centuries have already been introduced. Merely to begin the game, about four centuries must be cut out of the calendar so that the year ~-1200 becomes ~-800. But, once this is done, the quantavolution fits into place. The events of the Iron Age thenceforth proceed more understandably.

I may mention that Peter James and others of the larger Velikovsky circle decided that he had not been consistent and had given too much time to the Dark Age that lasted, in their opinion, about 250 years, and they point out that he himself would be the first to profit from giving back 150 years of time to the Egyptian chronology, since this would coordinate better the disastrous events and the peculiar catastrophized behavior of the Assyrian, Egyptian and other rulers of the early Iron Age.[5] I cannot discuss the "disagreement among friends" here because of its large complexity.

However, archaeologists, seeing the extreme changes between the Late Bronze Age and the Iron Age, and being evolutionists culturally as well as biologically, rest satisfied with the Egyptian chronology handed to them, for it gives them several hundred years to work with, parceling out the changes. Not until my next to last chapter do I go seriously into this strange behavior of scientists who are increasingly dismayed at the contradictions evidenced by the absence of true finds in their digs of the Phantom Dark Ages between ~-1200 and ~-800.

Explaining the Phantom 'Dark Age'

Practically every work that attempts to bridge the Gaposis of four to five centuries between the end of the Mycenean Civilization (and every other culture both East and West, we should add) and the uncouth civilizations, which credibly can be shown to develop into classical antiquity, wallows in half-truths, ellipses of logic, incomplete statements, and cavities. Yet, when it comes to changing the chronology of the ages, all of this weakness becomes as nothing because of the strength of dogma. Every scholar who denies the Dark Ages can expect one or more of the many tricks of academic discrimination to be employed against him or her.

Perhaps this explains why the immense bibliographic resources near at hand offer few supporting citations to the scholar needing help. I have looked at some works that cite other works and altogether have analyzed over a hundred studies that speak directly of excavations that carry from one level to another from the Late Bronze into the Iron Age and therefore are in a position to expose a direct transition with no sign of a large temporal gap, and that bear evidence calling for the ghostly "passage of several centuries." In short, an internal contradiction. Far from finding none at all, I find nothing but such contradictions.

In advance of a severe criticism of the failure of practically every scholar producing studies of the period to adopt and use the revised chronology, I would give them two sympathetic excuses. One is that they were under the heavy hand of the establishment of the old British Empire, Egyptian scholars, and a world press that blew up to giant proportions the achievements and marvels of ancient Egypt. The United States, just beginning to amount to something in the world of cultural science, backed up the Anglo credo.

A second excuse is that at the end of the Bronze Age there was a enormous gap of sites and material and a world of change. Greek and Near East and Italian archaeology found itself having to fill this gap with time and did so in makeshift years, pseudo-Egyptian years in our revision. This appeared all the more logical since they were part of the uniformitarian world of science, with an ideology of gradualism and evolution by normal social change. This was the ideology of Herbert Spencer, Charles Lyell, and Charles Darwin, of Victorian complacency. Remote as it may appear, and this is typical of the application of ideological analysis to history, the effects of this socio-political outlook was to smoothen over intimations of disaster in ancient times.

Switching from ~-1250 to ~-850

It may be well to fix again here the chronological problem and its solution as adopted in this book. The Bronze Age was blown apart throughout the world, including of course our center of attention in the Mediterranean, and replaced by an Iron Age, and this Explosive change will appear understandable if we take it as given that the Iron Age was more than just finding pieces of iron that had been laying about all the while, and that they had their source in exoterrestrial activities extending particularly from Planet Mars.

If we can bear this in mind, the rest of the book and the events of the Iron Age everywhere will be easier to comprehend. The Bronze Age ended in a holospheric set of events, exoterrestrially provoked, that occupied rather less than two centuries of real time, between 850 and 650 B.C.E.. These dates should be substituted for the dates from and between ~-1250 to ~-650 whenever these latter are encountered in reading practically all work discussing the Iron Age. The Iron Age then subsided with negative exponentialism into a set of great classical ages around much of the world. Mankind was not cured, nor has he been yet; he behaved less traumatized and mad. Importantly, he was permitted by a subsidence of catastrophe in nature to redress his civilizations.

How certain can we be that we would be on the right track of ancient history if we proceed accordingly? Fairly so, but as I have subtitled my book, using the word "speculations," I feel that I have given our reader fair warning in the unlikely event that I am wrong in this connection, and for that matter in regard to the other major and minor theses of my book. Philosophy and the sciences are rushing along, a turbulent stream of ideas and practices. The quantavolution paradigm swims abreast of it.

Chapter Two

The Q Paradigm Applied

Long experience at conferences, in classrooms, and as an editor, has taught me that the word 'catastrophism' is readily accepted because the persons using it believe that they know what it is all about, from horror stories and popular news media. Often one does not pause to consider that quantavolution (that is, the scientific fullness of catastrophism) is a complicated viewpoint opposed to much of conventional (accepted, establishment, textbook) science. For this reason, it may be well to move deeply and heavily into the perspectives and beliefs common in the field. The Iron Age is not simply a label attached to a period of time. In order to address the transition between the Bronze and Iron Ages we need to understand and apply the paradigm of quantavolution.

Defining Quantavolution

A quantavolution, we have said, may be usefully defined as an abrupt, profound, and large-scale set of changes in the world system. (Etymologically: *quanta* signifies *packets* and *volution* signifies a *turn*.) We use the term because it does not prejudge the changes as being completely negative, which the word 'catastrophes' implies. An example would be the Cretaceous-Tertiary boundary set of events of conventionally 100 million years ago, that affected deeply every part and sphere of existence on Earth – that is, affected the world *holistically*. The shift thereupon from a reptile-dominated to a mammal-dominated vertebrate fauna may be, in retrospect, preferred.

A quantavolution enters the world, statistically, as a steep exponential curve that carries with itself all the components of the great event. It takes effect, with a duration that must vary greatly but does not maintain its peak for very long and then begins to subside according to some negative exponent. It draws out its effects, it tails off endlessly until in a model, it will become a flat curve, whose components, however, are differently fashioned. The world is not nor will ever be the same again.

Depending upon the scales set to define their dimensions, a full roster of quantavolutions (of Tunguska size) could well exceed one hundred in number over the past 25,000 years. Indeed, an idea that would have appeared impossible a generation ago would now be accepted by many scientists and scholars: that the preponderant changes in all aspects of the Earth's history have occurred as quantavolutions.

Measuring and Indexing Quantavolutions

Gauging (Measuring) Quantavolutions is a first step, a faltering one, I might add, inasmuch as no one has gone about the task in any systematic -- should we say, scientific? -- way. Was Pompeii-Herculaneum (79 C.E.), was Tunguska (1908), was Krakatoa (1883), or its predecessor of the Sixth Century C.E, was Hurricane Ivan, was the disaster-filled Fourteenth Century in Eur-Asia: were Alexander, Attila, Tamurlane, Jesus, Mahomet, Napoleon Buonaparte, Hitler quantavolutions? Always in mind, of course, is our case of Mars. We assume that it was a quantavolution, and perhaps this book will have ample evidence to demonstrate it. Perhaps we have recognized all the candidates for Q until now. But Professor David Keyes recently found evidence, which, as we shall show, make an event of about 535 C.E. a likely candidate for the Q honor.

We may note how Velikovsky was pursuing the idea that, conventional opinion to the contrary, there must have been occasions for Egyptian-Israelite contacts in the Middle Bronze Age, then found a document (Ipuwer Papyrus) from the end of the Middle Bronze Age that gave an account of disasters seemingly in accord with the Bible's account of the Plagues of Egypt and the circumstances of the Exodus, and from there went in two directions, toward revising Egyptian chronology, and toward demonstrating that a great body in the sky was disrupting Earth (later identified as Planet Venus). The events were such as to provide, if accepted as partial fact or more, an actual holospheric quantavolution.

Let me go only so far back as the sixth century to where the Krakatoa event occurred in Indonesia. What I should do is to summarize the event, or let a well-equipped person do it for me, and cull all the manifestations that add up to a quantavolution. Actually I counted from a document by a reputable author and accessible to all, and list below, thirty-nine aspects of the event. We could use this list as the standard for a minimum Q. Let us say, 1 on a scale of 5. The exponential form of Q is multifariously demonstrated. The 'tailing off' effect is shown, too, in consequences that may be delayed by many many years, a century or two, and indefinitely.

The Environmental Catastrophe that Remade History
by Gar Smith

> *"In AD 535-536, [humankind] was hit by one of the greatest natural disasters ever to occur. It blotted out much of the light and heat of the sun for 18 months and the climate of the entire planet began to spin out of control."* - David Keyes, *Catastrophe* (Ballasting Books, 1999)

In an extraordinary new book, British historian David Keys convincingly traces many disparate threads of modern history back to a single (and quite literally Earth-shaking) event [1]- the explosion of a "supervolcano" in the third decade of the sixth century.

The explosion tore through the same South Pacific region that later gave rise to the Krakatoa eruption in 1883. The earlier convulsive detonation created the islands of Sumatra and Java and left behind a gap that is now known as the Sunda Straits.

The eruption's aftermath was felt worldwide "Crops failed in Asia and the Middle East as global weather patterns radically altered. Bubonic plague, exploding out of Africa [as the climate change increased rodent populations , wiped out entire populations in Europe. Floods and drought brought ancient cultures to the brink of collapse. In a matter of decades, the old order died and a new world - essentially the modern world as we know it today - began to emerge." [8,9]

The 100 years following the eruption marked the beginning of the

Dark Ages. During the cold years that enveloped the ash-clouded Earth, the Roman Empire began to collapse. Yellow dust fell like snow over the dying croplands of Asia. A 32-year drought clutched at the throat of Central America, prompting a popular uprising that toppled the great pyramid-building empire of the Aztecs.

The evidence has been there all along, waiting for someone to piece it together. Over a period of four years, Keys did just that. Keys visited more than 1,000 archeological sites in 60 countries and he discovered clues everywhere - buried in the rings of trees, hidden in polar ice cores, and lost in the forgotten jottings of ancient scribes.

In the cellulose records encoded in the tree trunks of the world's forests, Keys discovered that a sudden, calamitous chill in the mid-Sixth Century had stunted tree growth everywhere on Earth.

Ice cores drilled deep into the frozen Arctic turned up the black signature of volcanic ash. Ice cores sunk into the icepick of Antarctica turned up the same long-buried traces.

In the year 535 CE, the journals of the Roman historian Prosopis recorded "a most dread portent ... [The sun gave forth its light without brightness like the moon during this whole year. " From that day on, Prosopis wrote, "men were not free from war, nor pestilence, nor anything leading to death."

In Japan, an Imperial edict lamented that "yellow gold and ten thousand strings of cash cannot cure hunger ... [when a country is] starving of cold."

In China, Keys found an entry in the ancient History of the Southern Dynasties that referred to a great explosion that rocked the world in February 535 when "there twice was the sound of thunder."

Finally, in an obscure Indonesian chronicle, the Pustaka Raja Purwa (The Book of Ancient Kings), Keys found this chilling passage:

"[A] great glaring fire, which reached to the sky came out of the mountain... There was a furious shaking of the earth, total darkness, thunder and lightning . Then came forth a furious gale, together with torrential rain, and a deadly storm darkened the entire world ... [W]hen the waters subsided, it could be seen that the island of Java had been split in two, thus creating the island of Sumatra."

Keys reasons that the 535 eruption was "one of the largest volcanic events of the past 50,000 years." His reconstruction of the event paints a hellish vision of "molten magma [shooting] into the air at up to 1,500 miles per hour, reaching heights of perhaps 30 miles. The sound of this explosion would have broken the eardrums of most humans and animals living within a 15-mile radius ... [After the blast] car-sized chunks of the mountain ... would have fallen back to earth within a radius of three to seven miles. The microfragments, however, would have been carried skyward by powerful convection currents.

"A hot, poisonous wall of destruction, more than 1,000-feet high, would have moved outward ... at up to 250 mile per hour, killing anything in its path," Keys theorizes. A mushroom cloud ascending from the 1,650-degree-Fahrenheit heart of the volcano would have rained ash on villages and forests a thousand miles distant, while a six-foot-deep blanket of floating pumice would have coated the seas.

Keys believes that the eruption, and the climatic destabilization that followed, "resynchronized world history."

1. Global seismism
2. Altered morphology
3. Global crop failures
4. Altered global weather patterns
5. Bubonic plague
6. Rodent proliferation
7. Flood
8. Collapsing cultures
9. Abruptness
10. Deep cold
11. Global ash clouds
12. Dust fall-outs
13. Drought
14. Civil rebellion
15. Stunted bio-growth
16. Ice formation
17. Spectres
18. Prolonged darkness
19. Increased warfarring
20. Mass Starvation
21. Great thundering
22. Column of fire
23. Heavy earthquake
24. Lightning
25. Hurricanes

26. Torrential rains
27. Jets of Magma
28. Deafness
29. Heavy-debris fall-out
30. Poisoned blasts
31. Exponentialism of charge
32. Pumice-coated seas
33. Negative exponentialism of charge
34. Destabilized great cultures
35. Countless dead by explosion, famine, hurricane, drowning, conflicts
36. Destruction of thousands of towns (implicit)
37. Exo-terrestrial agencies and forces (??)

Keys does not allow any exoterrestrial forces such as mega-lightning, solar storms, plasma pressures, bolides, comets, or planetary influences, whereas, we, in this book, are attentive to any indications of exoterrestrial influences during the Mars period.

As revealed in the mega-disaster of the Indonesian tsunami of 2004, the tectonic plates separated by the great fractures of the ocean-girdling fracture system are in continuous motion and can have caused (precipitated) the upwelling and explosion of magma. This phenomenon is to be watched for in the Mediterranean Region as well.

Other classes or types of effects will be noted of the Martian period that may not have occurred in the Krakatoa I or may not have been observed or considered.

Our studies at the University of Bergamo, of the literature of science over the past century, have demonstrated, as one might by now have come to expect, an exponential increase in studies that pertain to or describe quantavolutions. For example, sixty years ago, when Velikovsky was finishing the composition of his book *Worlds in Collision,* scientific and scholarly articles and books dealing with specific quantavolutions or the subject in general (ignoring religious discussions of the Apocalypse, the Biblical Deluge and other dogmatic materials), were few in number. Today they number in the hundreds each month.

What we call the Conventional ideology is that of

our grandfathers, of a century ago, of an age fast losing its grip on the mind, while holding tightly to the establishments of science and education. By contrast, there is growing fast an ideology which we call quantavolution. Within the realms of these two ideologies and in the vast spaces in between are all kinds of beliefs and theories of world history. We do not deny these world views. We do say that we refuse them when they are less useful than ours and when, in our perspectives, they threaten mischief and harm to the public.

So these two ideologies, the Conventional and the Quantavolutional, are two major ways of making sense out of the cosmos, in the name of truth. And to them this book addresses itself.

Principles of Quantavolution

A dozen 'Q' (for quantavolution) principles, with their derivative principles and most important examples, command the contents of this book. I set them forth below, with some sharpness. We can contrast them with conventional principles that are most starkly opposed. We number them for convenience. The list of principles is not shared completely by quantavolutionists nor is the set of quantavolutionary items in the test that is demonstrated a few pages down. No doubt but that in time, as the paradigm develops, propositions will be modified, possibly removed, while others may be added.

1. The Conventional prescription for natural and human history calls for a world that has changed almost entirely by small-scale, incremental transactions of small scope over billions of years. That is: one observes everywhere, and in all things, differences between them when viewed first at time A and then at time B, and these differences are almost always minute in relation to the total shape of things. But, owing to the accumulation of small changes over long periods of time, there occur vast differences between what was A and what is B.

By contrast, the Q prescription depicts a world that has changed mostly by large-scale and abrupt jumps from the earliest times. A cold climate will suddenly become warm, a species of animal will abruptly disappear, man will speak.

Quantavolution refers to great changes of both inorganic and organic realms of existence happening swiftly, powerfully, and on a large scale. Several thousand years ago, a great flood descended upon what are called the Washington State Scablands today and drastically altered the topography and biota of many thousands of square miles. Such are the catastrophes, and not the major catastrophes of which we speak. But they can be constructive as well as destructive.

If you prefer mammals to dinosaurs as your pets, then possibly you would regard the sky forces, meteoroids or whatever, that struck the Earth at the end of the Cretaceous period, exterminating the dinosaurs and most other species, as a stroke of good luck, as a quantavolution that was on the whole favorable for the mammals and from the human point of view.

If we choose to believe that a future humanity with qualities and life styles far removed from our own is to be preferred and sought for, then we have to be alarmed by catastrophes and be driven to control them, or escape them, always in the direction of the ideal humanity we envision.

Essentially, change refers to a detectable difference in anything between Time 1 and Time 2 . By the world is meant the universe and all that it may contain, including its motions and events.

By **most** is meant something not much less than entirely, and what is left over consists of changes that are local and gradual.

Large-scale applies to spaces and things and behaviors that rather arbitrarily we would envision as at least the size and features of Russia or South America or the Caribbean Sea. The **change would occur abruptly,** which we define as time durations from an instant to a century in which 50% of the total physical transformation happens. Terms used for quantavolution, "development by packets", include catastrophism, neocatastrophism, saltation (a jump), revolution, apocalypse and punctuated equilibrium. A salient argument against the use of the term "catastrophism", we have said earlier, is that it denotes a total misfortune, whereas a moment's reflection will persuade one that a great part of the fortunate inheritance of the world comes from the same catastrophes -- including the quantavolution or abrupt evolution of the human being.

If we may play a game for a moment, we could imagine an Earth that was assembled from a nebula of the Sun, then went into several billion years of uniform small changes, nothing to excess. A thin cloak of dust would cover the globe and the life upon it would be viral, bacterial, and wormy. The worm's eye view of the world would be uninspiring unless a god were to turn it upon its back to view the universe above, which, however, might have been forever unchanging shade. The world today, for all its faults, is vastly different and improved to our way of thought because, like our observing selves, the world has been quantavoluted on numerous occasions to the point of chaos. And if, one day, we shall be extincted, we will have had meanwhile a good run for our money.

2. When a quantavolution occurs, the phenomena of air, water, earth, and forms of being change sharply. Logically, then, every science is concerned with quantavolutions, past and future. Every sphere of being is affected, so we can say that Q is holospheric.

In the Krakatoan case, it seems likely that every sphere of existence was affected, although not conveyed in the list. For instance, were languages spoken, read, written, and verbalized differently afterwards, and if so, where and how much?

Languages are highly vulnerable to physical and mental changes. Too every language is loaded with ancient words of disaster and electricity and punishing gods. A study by Hugh Crosthwaite tells us that about 15% of the words of ancient Hebrew, Latin, Greek, and Egyptian were connected in some fashion with electricity.

Conventional science tends to study isolated effects. Changes concerning one area of scientific observations are normally observed by themselves and studied and reported by themselves. And, associated with this practice is a common view that changes are normally weakly discernible in other areas and ecologies and effects transfer into them slowly. There is no general rush of many things to change.

Thousands of plant and animal species extincted with the famous dinosaurs. The stratigraphy of much of the Earth changed. The atmosphere changed. The motions of the Earth changed -- how much we do not yet know. As a matter of fact, we know very little yet about the events and changes that took place when the dinosaurs and everything else on Earth felt the disastrous effects of falling bodies from outer space. But name any field of learning, and it is easy to foresee a number of doctoral dissertations in that field on questions of quantavolution.

Thus: if a meteor (or comet) of ancient times strikes at "Chassenon, France" and is 1.5 km in diameter, striking with a speed of 20 k/second, coming from the Northwest, it will burst open, within seconds, a great crater, and shoot up a towering column of fire, gas, and debris, a terrestrial tsunami whose swells will become arcs of hills, and all forms of rocks for 20 km around will be metamorphosed, while practically all life forms will be extincted up to a radius of 500 km, and most habitats around the world and the atmosphere everywhere will be affected to different degrees but markedly. A new world will be soon established over the vast area , and when humans come to inhabit it a long time afterwards, they will not recognize its nature and learned scientists will call it a volcano, until they finally realize that the strange rocks providing the natives with beautiful stone for building are not sedimentary.

Finally, 17 years after a book called *Worlds in Collision* raises a hullabaloo, knowing nothing about Chassenon, a leading French scientist (perhaps having no awareness of said book) will visit colleagues in Germany at the Ries crater; he will change his mind about Chassenon, and initiate 27 years of research, while persuading other scientists that they are dealing with an exoterrestrial meteoritic phenomenon . In 1994 a conference called specially for the purpose, gives its certificate of authenticity to the site as housing a cosmic catastrophe, and in 1995 a geological map of the area is produced.

The earlier tale of the discovery of the catastrophic origin of the horrendous scablands of Washington State by Professor J. H. Bretz, and the acceptance of his findings, took several decades. Similar stories can be told about an increasing number of places around the world. Old volcanoes are turning into meteor craters.

I wondered for many years whether many geologists could be wrong in regarding Lago di Bolsena, North of Rome, as a typical extinct volcano crater, or only as such. The Roman encyclopedist, Pliny, had said that it was the spot where a Jovian thunderbolt had destroyed the rich Etruscan city of Volsinium. Practically all geologists disagree, but a compromise view may be possible, as I try to show in Chapter Fourteen below. We encounter a heavy incidence of lightning disasters and destroyed settlement sites of the eighth to seventh centuries in the region; according to Pliny again, no group could build a fortress on any eminence because it would be promptly struck and burned by mega-lightning bolts. The Etruscans identified and possessed religious rites for some thirty different types of lightning. Volsinium, now nothing but ruins, if indeed we can be sure of where it was at that time, might well have suffered an intense electrical bombardment or lightning fireball that erased it.

Today one can introduce these matters without being absolutely contradicted. Fifty years ago, if I raised them before a respectable audience, I would be regarded as a strange character who belongs at the fringes of outer space. When Immanuel Velikovsky published his *Worlds in Collision* in 1950, after many years of research, he was roundly denounced or coldly ignored by leaders of every branch of science. Today there is scarcely a one of his theses of natural history and ancient history that goes begging for study by scholars. But not in his name or accredited to him. Too, both friendly and hostile scholars have gone behind him to search out his predecessors and sources and these have been found to be many.

Still, the C paradigm is very much in control of minds and resources, while the Q scholars are largely forced to collect their water from the many leaks in the communications of Conventional scientists. Quantavolution must build upon Conventional science wherever it can. The materials of C are incomparably more abundant. Very often they are carefully and fully done, and understandable by critical readers who are not however experts of the field (for very few are those in number who can read much less appraise the contents of a typical article submitted for publication in a scientific journal or delivered at a scientific conference).

3. Conventional science has tended to accord the Earth a high degree of autonomy. It is believed that the Earth has developed its physical and vital forms from internal sources of materials and energy. That is: Practically all that is present on Earth has evolved solely under the influence of combinations of ingredients and forces that preceded it on Earth and which in turn and ultimately go back to the earliest ages of the Earth.

But Q finds that the ultimate source of quantavolutions has been exoterrestrial. The Earth was itself formed from exoterrestrial elements, an obvious deduction, but the fact leads to a realization that probably at no time in its existence has the Earth been out of touch with the exosphere. From its beginnings, the Earth had no internal force or energy that was not exoterrestrial in origin. Its volcanism, earthquakes, hurricanes, and floods have been compelled by exoterrestrial bodies composed of perhaps every kind of mineral and gas, and of every degree of density.

According to one branch of Q theory, the solar system originated and developed to this day as an often violent process of transactions between the Sun and a solar-exploded body. Explaining the solar system is readily accomplished by introducing a theory of binary stars, ever more frequently observed, in which the explosion (nova) of a heavily charged sun expels a mass of debris whose largest portion, though a small fraction of the sun, acts as an electrical pole exchanging charge with the sun along a current of electric fire, which also serves to create a vast electromagnetic plenum in which planets, with their own electrical properties, develop. Conditions for the growth of life forms are often favorable and persist until the electrical axis and the tube around it practically expire, whereupon the planets are "on their own," so to speak. Although the theory of solaria binaria is unique to my small group of Q students, it can easily entertain other quantavolutionary theories that have been developing in recent years, which portray the solar system as undergoing a series of explosive and high energy events.

4. Poly-episodic Catastrophes. Quantavolutions (usually referred to pejoratively as catastrophes) have been experienced on sundry occasions and have been unequal in intensity. Geological, astronomical, paleontological, legendary, and archaeological research has settled upon more than one and conjectured up to a score of global catastrophes in natural history, such that it is possible now to hypothesize a quantavolution at the end of and beginning of every major section of the geological column and every cultural period of the bronze and iron age.

Among the greatest in effect have been, among geologists, those associated with the global fracture system circling the world, among paleontologists, those associated with the disappearance of the dinosaurs, and the flowering of life forms in the Cambrian period, and among ancient historians those deemed by the ancients to be connected to the conduct of the planets and affording evidence in the wholesale destruction of ancient civilizations repeatedly.

A quantavolution need not be a single shot occurrence. The interacting bodies may be several, their interaction repeated, and a single body may return for a second or more rounds of exchanges. One theory of Venus has the planet as a comet disrupting the air space of Earth several times over fifty-two year periods. Similarly, Mars has been seen -- the point will be discussed -- to divide at least two critical centuries of the Iron Age by 15-year close-in incursions.

Extant species have simultaneously on occasion been drastically reduced in numbers and type or extinguished while new species were being generated and old ones modified by holistic mutated gene leadership. The scale and intensity of Q implies the decimation of species, and palaeontology increasingly locates and admits to the catastrophic ending of species. At the same time, C theory will not admit the sudden creation of new species in the same conditions of catastrophe, whereas the Q theorists can claim that the same conditions allowed the springing forth in quick time of new families and species. Q theory accounts for the persistence of species as well as the destruction and creation of species to produce the puzzling array of flora and fauna of today.

5. Disturbed Geological Columns. Most Q scholars would agree that every geological column on Earth is idiosyncratically disturbed. If one were to dig anywhere in the world, one would find practically everywhere an incomplete series of rock types and periods, with no two such drillings being alike. This claim goes counter to the prevailing belief in conventional science that a normal deep drilling to basic rock usually would produce mineral and fossil layers in their proper chronological order with few or no layers or ages missing.

6. Lunar Explosions with Global Fracture. Scientists divide unevenly into a majority who believe that the Moon was captured by the Earth billions of years ago, and a minority who believe that the Moon separated from the Earth at an equally early date. Most of these experts grant that the event was catastrophic and quantavolutionary. After more than a century of argument, astronomers seem to have come over to the side of those, who like the present author, believe that the Moon emerged from the Earth, but they put the event at a time so remote and so undetailed and unevidential that one could hardly call such scholars quantavolutionary except by default. The thesis of a few contemporary Q scholars, however, is that quite recently, perhaps some twelve thousand years ago, the explosion of Moon from Earth, and the global fracture accompanying it, produced the present basic volume and morphology of Earth. The present author devised this hypothesis and expounded it in Chaos and Creation *and other works.*

In September of 2002, *Der Spiegel* magazine published the claim of a paleontological team that three billion years ago an object smashed into the Earth, burst out the Moon, and started up the tectonic movements of the plates. In several volumes of the Quantavolution Series of two decades ago, this theory, without the unimaginable old dating, was broached and developed by the present author. Briefly said, there is no reason why the scenario which I propounded might not have taken place in geologically quite recent times. Short of exploding, the planet Earth and other planets can absorb immense alterations and changes. Expelling the Moon-sized material from the now - Pacific Basin could have been the most traumatic physical incident of Earth history.

Evidence points to the Pacific Ocean Basin as the source of the crust that was wrenched from the Earth by an electrically attractive passing body, coincidentally with a fracture that shot around the world as the continents that were coming now into existence swung in a great gravity slide to fill the basin. Besides the mainly crustal loss of the Moon-gathering, the fully-encrusted Earth lost additional material as debris into farther space, and swelled in volume as its charge diminished. Or such is my speculation.

Evidence of the Moon material being Earth-born continues to aggregate. In July 2005 a Japanese team claimed evidence of the carbon dioxide of Earth's atmosphere being responsible for the abundance of the gas on the Moon and said that it was carried there onetime when the Earth's magnetic field was out of order, warning that the same event could occur again.

Probably this Moon-crash team that I refer to above, if it believed in its own work, would score modestly as quantavolutionists, if only because they already are convinced of vast changes being brought about at least in one instance shockingly deep, fast and widespread in effects. If you were to argue that the chronology is to be dismissed, that the split-up occurred when Luna exploded from the now Pacific Basin in the time of man, then you would be even more Q, and might even be a top-scorer (For the most extreme of Q views is that the age of the Earth is drastically shorter than is alleged by Conventional scientists.)

7. Schizoid Humanization. During a quantavolution, Homo Sapiens originated in a sudden gestalt as a schizoid species controlling multiple selves, and preferably to be called Homo Sapiens Schizotypicalis.

Several Q theories of the birth of man are possible. One is indicated here. A gestalt is a sudden complex perception and cognition of a large body of mental material that has hitherto been disassembled and unknowledgeable. In a suddenly new natural environment and atmospheric state and in a minor genetic change from the hominid, a new being emerged with a delayed instinctive apparatus, connected with the bilateralism of brain hemispheres and functioning, such that a microdelay in the transmission of mental operations ensued, sufficient to expand the destinations around the brain of stimuli and the awareness of doubt about the meaning of the stimuli and a fearful need to control the multiple selves that were groping "thoughtfully" with the disparate end-locations of the stimuli. The mentation and behavior of the new animal is diagnosable today as a general schizophrenia, with its basic symptoms of shock, aggression, compulsion, and displacement.

8. Mass Amnesia and Sublimation. Primeval Homo Sapiens experienced a traumatic suppression of memory and acquired a sublimatory psychological complex. The instinct- delay cerebral system genetically or permanently demanded by a new environmental constant quickly installed a memory blockage or amnesiac system to limit the flood of fears and doubts and contradictory demands on the new person. The amnesiac system allowed, or was compelled by overload problems to bring about, an amorphous unconscious.

The unconscious fostered a random, partially controlled, and imaginative surfacing of materials that were the source both of aesthetic creations and hypotheses, which, when subjected to demands to restore the more comfortable if less competent instinctive system of the hominid, also developed logic, calculation, science, and, in a word, rationality.

9. Cultural Hologenesis. Homo Sapiens promptly developed a poly- faceted language and full- function culture. Speech and variegated behaviors emerged promptly and spontaneously with the poly-ego and its talking to itself.

Transfer of first epithets, imprecations, and commands to the greatest powers known, the happenings in the sky and the responses of the earth, would impregnate catastrophe in the language as it developed for mundane use. The same would characterize the swiftly developing culture -- with rites, priests, magic, acoustical and electrical performances, fire-control and cuisine, etc. This hologenetic Q- theory stands alone perhaps to contend with conventional theories of linguistic and cultural genesis.

10. Divine Succession. Originally gods were idealized by the human mind, and their basic traits and functions proceeded through all successive major gods and families of gods.

Practically all religions, although some exceptional persons will claim the opposite, are in the line of descent from the primordial religiousness. With the illusory establishment of the first gods and of delusory devices to control them, the basic elements of religious practices from then until now were fixed: appeasement, obsessive forms of divine communication, sacrifice, basic artistic forms, authoritative ideologies, institutional imitations of the sky and earth- connected divine illusions. Successive quantavolutions repeated the same types of physical disasters and fell upon peoples that were inclined to fortify their old religions rather than to devise new ones, but at the same time would often rename the old and condemn them to try their fortunes with new, more powerful gods.

At least one branch of Q theory questions the roots of so-called rationality, yet accepts the newer logic and linguistics as its only tools for arriving at "truth." It accepts experiments and the scientific method generally and it guards the method by psychosociological analysis of the processes. It is not mystic nor magical nor religious nor populist. The Q paradigm reconstructs the historical and scientific world with the historical and scientifically defensible weapons of science.

11. Cross-validation of Time and Events. *Quantavolutions, since the solar nova that instituted the solar system, occupied brief periods of time, while intervals between them were also brief, measurable in thousands running back to a million years. This thesis can be termed microchronism.*

The evolution of the solar system, Earth, and life forms, according to the Conventional view is that the whole of evolution has taken up about five billion years, of which the last several million were required to produce human beings with their advanced societies. That is: although only rough estimates of the age of the Earth and the several periods of its organic and inorganic evolution can be obtained, continued progress in chronometry has moved the age of the earth and its epochs to ever longer times, allowing thus adequate time for all of the observed transformations to have taken place.

The conventional view holds that dozens of distinct measures and correlations have mutually supported macrochronism and, with the theory of evolution, have proven the singular correctness of the historical path of science. To take an example of a common test, we may go to radiocarbon dating. That is: radioactive decay, occurring at constant rates over enormous periods of time, has been measured in association with its environment, organic and inorganic, and these have been shown to have ages generally much greater than geological measures alone have produced, showing the latter to have been partly conjectural, even if vastly longer than biblical time had been. Different radio chronometries are highly correlated when applied to the same objects, and variations have been successfully accommodated to settle differences. With the development of dendrochronology, dating from layered ice cores, radiocarbon dating, thermoluminescence dating, and other chemical, thermal, and historical methods, few lengthy gaps remain in the geological and biological record that are unapproachable scientifically.

Archaeologists and ancient history scholars have striven mightily to correlate historical dates and radiocarbon dates, with a bare success. Or so it may be amply argued.

For, basically, radiocarbon calls for the stable concentration of carbon in the atmosphere and to a lesser extent, in water, land, and life forms.

Some Q theorists have attempted to preserve the appearances and save a great many reputations by staging their quantavolutions in accord with the present billions of years of "proven" earth history. Such would be, for instance, the theory of "punctuated equilibrium," an awkward euphemism promoted by paleontologist Stephen Jay Gould, as well as a scarcely justified faith in the swollen periods given to the past, now approaching 5 billion years. The problem of erasing these billions is easy when it comes to traditional geological measurements of time that employ stratigraphy, that apply uniform erosion rates of today to the past, et al. The problem is more difficult when it comes to measurements by radioactive decay of chemical elements, but here, too, uniformitarian assumptions can be brought into question: electromagnetic conditions of the past, far different than those of today, could eradicate the great stretches of time claimed by conventional scientists.

Let me here introduce a caveat: Different calendars may result from different methods of calculating the passage of time, but they may also result from inaccuracies in employing the same method. Much of this book is impeded by what I consider to be both an improper method and inaccurate measurement. In regard to specifying dates, I try to be helpful to my readers in three situations, at a hopefully small cost in patience and mental adjustment:

1. I have gotten rid of the 'nth century' as a marker because it confuses the ordinary reader (and me, too). All dates are numerical, not 'early 7th century' BCE, but ~-690 to 680, for example.

2. I have guessed at some dates, e.g., Volsinium extermination, ~- 650, because figuring closer would require an elaboration of several alternative guesses, or because no date is to be found.

3. I have presumptively 'corrected' every date given by the old Egyptian calendar with the settings provided by a revised calendar, almost always by 400 years, so that, for

instance, '1200 BPE' becomes more properly '[-800]'.

The general reader will find these settings to be gratifying. The specialist historian and archaeologist will be boggled at first but will soon become accustomed to them and may even in some cases adopt them.

12. *The paradigmatic, that is, the methods which a paradigm employs to arrive at its truths of conventional and quantavolutionary science are consonant.*

Despite a much greater stress by 'Q' theory upon electromagnetic forces in all natural and vital events, the experiences (including experiments) and logic employed in constructing and proving the quantavolution paradigm are homologous with those of the conventional paradigm of scientific method.

Convention vs. Quantavolution

Having called up the major principles on which this book is founded, we find ourselves in a position to draw up and administer a test on the subject of who believes how strongly in the Conventional ideology, while opposing the Quantavolution al ideology. We can do so if we generalize the prescription for quantavolution, thus becoming slightly more precise and mathematical. Quantavolution is not a theory that I can express mathematically. It is a cognitive theory, or perhaps only a heuristic theory. I can write it in signs, as if it were a formula. This might help in remembering it.

$$Q = C(HIS)^{ex} \geq k$$

Q = Quantavolution
C = Change in the parenthetical effects
H = Holistic (affecting most aspects of reality)
I = affecting them with great Intensity or effect
W = over a wide Scope
S = Suddenly, abruptly
^{ex} = an Exponential Rising and Subsiding of the

effects
> = greater than
k = a defined level of Change deemed useful for purposes of study.

    In the formula, it will be noted that some element of quantification is hinted at and allowed. We can go so far as to compose a test of the extent to which a person adheres to the ideas of C and Q. We could treat the concept of Q as a plastic, scalable idea, reflecting operations and pragmatism. There would be the premise that all changes (and therefore the belief in changes) can be registered by a score, not an absolute, belief. Then upon taking the test, you would be scored as more or less tending to think and believe as a Conventionalist or a Quantavolutionary. A large advantage of this method is in providing you with self-awareness. You will know where you stand on great issues of science and cosmology.

    For example, you hear arguments that the dinosaurs expired abruptly, within a century or two. With all the associated changes, this would be indeed a Q. Do you believe this strongly, as a fair probability, as quite undecided, as improbable or as untrue. These can be seen as five degrees of your possible C-Q ideology. If you mark the item as 1, you are on you way to demonstrating an ideology of Q. If we concocted a test of 20 such scalable opinions, and you scored yourself as 1 or 2 on this item, you would be unquestionably Q in your ideology. If, however, you began to waver in your responses to similar questions in other fields, you would perhaps get an average score of 3 whereupon you would be a person who is tending in both directions, Q and C, perhaps because of a divided type of education, misunderstanding of items, or some other reason. However, should you end up with a score of nearly 100 on the test, you would have to be a confirmed Conventional thinker (unless you are devoted to one of the many peripheral ideologies, cults, philosophies that I mentioned are found in the interstices of the C-Q perspectives.

    A report, hitherto unpublished, on a preliminary administration of the Q-C test, will help distinguish the spread of ideas around the population. The research was performed at the *CENTER FOR QUANTAVOLUTION STUDIES,* University of Bergamo, at Bergamo, Italy.[6]

We were able to gather responses from 462 respondents, 316 of which were Italian, 101 Bulgarian, and 36 American. They represent an interesting sampling of scientific opinions - quantavoluntary or conventional - among three groups issuing from markedly different educational systems: European, American, and Eastern European/ex-Communist. The participating Bulgarian group was generally older and of a higher educational level than the participating Italian group.

The protocol is presented here:

[illegible script]

C-Q TEST

The C-Q Test[7] is an exploration of beliefs and attitudes, not a competitive test nor a test of knowledge. It is designed to discover the partiality of the respondent to two large approaches to science respecting natural and human history. These two approaches are termed Conventional and Quantavolutional. Your cooperation and that of others in completing the test will cast a welcome light upon some major trends in contemporary professional and public perspectives on the science.

Instructions: There follow twenty-two pairs of statements, each statement being preceded by a short name in boldface. Please react to each pair by checking the box of the one statement that you prefer, as being, in your opinion, more correct. Please do not skip any pair. And please do not check both boxes of any pair. If you are unclear or uninformed about the items, mark your best guess or your intuition as to which you think may be correct, or, and this is important to remember, mark if you must the statement that you would prefer to be correct. The average time taken by persons holding a college degree to complete the test is 19 minutes, but time is not considered in scoring the test.

Begin now here below:

☐1. **Relativity.** There is no such thing as absolute science.
☐2. **Progressivism.** Science of all kinds is progressing rapidly.

☐3. **Gradualism**. The world has changed almost entirely by small-scale, incremental transactions of small or large scope from earliest to present times.

☐4. **Quantavolution**. The world has changed mostly by large-scale and abrupt jumps or saltations or quantavolutions from earliest to present times.

☐5. **Independent Effects**. Changes in one field of scientific observation normally are weakly discernible in other areas and transfer into them slowly.

☐6. **Holospherics**. Every quantavolution was holospheric such that, what became in late times human morals and science, were affected in their every branch by its remnant evidence and its contemporary effects.

☐7. **Exoterrestrial Genesis**. The ultimate source of quantavolutions has been exoterrestrial.

☐8. **Terrestrial Isolation**. From earliest times, Earth has developed its physical and vital forms from internal sources of materials and energy.

☐9. **Solaria Binaria**. The solar system originated and developed to this day as an often violent process of transactions between the Sun and a solar-exploded body.

☐10. **Gravitational Accumulations**. The solar system originated in gravitational condensations from a gigantic dust cloud surrounding a young Sun.

☐11. **Poly-episodic Catastrophes.** Quantavolutions (usually referred to pejoratively as catastrophes) have been experienced on sundry occasions and have been unequal in intensity

☐12. **Elaborative Polymorphism**. Great variations of all inorganic and organic forms occurred by lawful, regular processes of nature.

☐13. **Lunar Capture**. The Moon formed during the condensation of gases and dust that originated the solar system and came within the gravitational grasp of the Earth.

☐14. **Lunar Explosions with Global Fracture**. The explosion of Moon from Earth, and the global fracture accompanying it, produced the present basic volume and morphology of Earth.

☐15. **Disturbed Geological Columns**. Every geological column on Earth is ideosyncratically disturbed.

☐16. **Perennial Geological Flux**. In due course, the Earth's surface has been altered by the gradual limited and calculable play of natural forces: waters, winds, pressures, and heat.

☐17. **Uniformitarianism**. Inorganic and organic nature have transmuted, with minor exceptions, at low, uniform rates for all of Earth history.

☐18.**Exponential Apocalypses.** Every quantavolution has taken the form of an exponential catastrophic curve with a sharp ascent and a negatively exponential descent, tailing off toward uniform change.

☐19. **Evolution.** The present species of life have unexceptionally developed from ever earlier forms that themselves originated by environmental adaptation in isolation and occasional successive chemical mutations.

☐20. **Species Mass Changes and Extinction.** Extant species have simultaneously on occasion been drastically reduced in numbers and type or extinguished while new species were being generated and old ones modified by holistic mutated gene leadership.

☐21. **Schizoid Humanization.** During a quantavolution, Homo Sapiens originated in a sudden gestalt as a schizoid species controlling multiple selves, and preferably to be called Homo Sapiens Schizotypicalis.

☐22. **Homo Sapiens Sapiens.** In the course of evolution, natural selection, working at every vital level, eventuated in a being of high intelligence, capable of deliberate, rational decisions.

☐23. **Evolution.** Whether fast or slow, evolution by definition must occur in natural history.

☐24. **Differences.** There is in fact very little fundamental difference between quantavolution and conventional science.

☐25. **Increasing Consciousness and Self-awareness.** Gradually humans developed a sense of history that let them order their lives presently and for their future, and learned to exercise advanced faculties for pleasure.

☐26. **Mass Amnesia and Sublimation.** Primeval Homo Sapiens experienced a traumatic suppression of memory and acquired a sublimatory psychological complex.

☐27. **Cultural and Institutional Invention.** Bit by bit, cultural traits were evolved in all of the various aspects of life, and could be placed ever higher upon a ladder of complexity and utility.

☐28. **Cultural Hologenesis.** Homo Sapiens promptly developed a poly-faceted language and full-function culture.

☐29. **Divine Succession.** Originally gods were idealized by the human mind, and their basic traits and functions proceeded through all successive major gods and families of gods.

☐30. **Religious Sophistication.** From primitive fear and ignorance, gods were imagined, and afforded sacrifices, but eventually higher religions, with a benign, single god and simple rites, prevailed.

☐31. **Microchronism.** Quantavolutions, since the solar nova that instituted the solar system, occupied brief periods of time, while intervals between them were also brief, measurable in thousands up to a million years.

☐32. **Macrochronism.** The evolution of the solar system, Earth, and life forms, took up about five billion years, of which the last several million years were required to produce human beings with their advanced societies.

☐33. **Gravitation.** Newton's laws of gravitation are sufficient to explain physical processes of bodily interaction, and to control them insofar as is possible.

☐34. **Electromagnetic dominance.** From the smallest to the largest settings of nature and existence, electromagnetic processes are the most effective producers of change.

☐35. **Consonant logic and method.** Despite a much greater stress upon electromagnetic forces in all natural and vital events, the experiences (including experiments) and logic employed in constructing and proving the quantavolution paradigm are homologous with those used in pursuing the conventional paradigm of science.

☐36. **Cross-validation of Time and Events.** Dozens of distinct measures and correlations have mutually supported macrochronism and, with evolution theory, have proven the singular correctness of the conventional historical path of science.

☐37. **Acceptance.** Conventional science is more a matter of etiquette of science than it is a set of accepted theories.

☐38. **Contrast.** There is in fact very little chance of accommodating catastrophic theory to conventional theory in the sciences.

☐39. **Rationality.** Humans are rational animals.
☐40. **Non-rationality.** Humans are non-rational animals.

☐41. **Leader genes.** Genes have an ability to test on large organ components of a body various mutations that will have quantavolutionary effects extending far beyond the original

signaled change.
☐42. **Limited genes**. Genetic mutations are narrowly defined and just as narrowly effective in changing other gene or larger behavior.

End of test

Note on scoring: A fully conventional configuration on the test would be in accord with the following statements: 2, 3, 5, 8, 10, 12, 13, 16, 17, 19, 22, 23, 24, 25, 27, 30, 32, 33, 36, 38, 39, 42. (22 items). A fully quantavolutional score would then be 1, 4, 6, 7, 9, 11, 14, 15, 18, 20, 21, 23, 24, 26, 28, 29, 31, 34, 35, 37, 40, 41. (22 items)

C-Q TEST: Scores of informants and percentages approving each of 40 items.

The average Q-score is 7 out of a possible 20. This is also close to the median score, which is somewhat below 7. More than half of the respondents therefore scored below 7 on the Q-scale. Only 88 respondents (19%) reached scores equal or superior to 10.

We notice immediately that our survey comprises one question - number 12: "On occasion, living species have simultaneously been drastically reduced in numbers and type or extinguished while new species were being generated and old ones modified" - which collects a very high rate of Q-favorable answers (90%!) - meaning, that it carries the support of a great number of rather C- tending opinions (those being in the majority). Question 4 ("Catastrophes have produced a large variety of inorganic and organic forms occupying a great many ecological niches,") and question 9 ("Every catastrophe is holospheric, meaning that all branches of human morals and science are affected by its residual and contemporary effects") receive an almost equally high rate of Q-favorable answers (over 80%). Remarkably, this is so in all three national groups, and irrespective of age!

The lowest agreement with the Q paradigm go to questions number 5 ("Homo Sapiens originated abruptly as a species with strong self-awareness") and 10 (over 80% of respondents agreeing with the Conventional proposal that "The features of the Earth's surface are accounted for by a gradual limited play of natural forces of waters, winds, pressures, and heat.") These results would be expected. We may point out that for question 5 the agreement between the three national groups is inexistent: the (alas, all too small) American group is in much higher agreement (over 40%) with the proposal than the Italian (less than 10%). Only 1 in 5 of the scientifically well-educated Bulgarian group are ready to go with Alfred de Grazia's theory of Homo Schizo! Of course, they had not received an explanation of the theory. However, Question 10 would tend to show an almost similar rate of Bulgarians disagreeing with the Conventional statement about the geology of the Earth's surface. The Bulgarians (at 60%) also overshoot the two Western-educated groups (at ca. 35%) in believing that "Homo Sapiens, when splitting from hominoids, promptly developed a poly-faceted language and a full-function culture, which he thereafter elaborated." Other patent national discrepancies (like the answer to question 5 - also pertaining to the Homo Schizo hypothesis) seem to me suspicious, but still worthy of further investigation.

Question number 3 ("An explosion of Moon from Earth, and the global fracture accompanying it, produced the present basic volume and morphology of Earth") offers a highly quantavolutionary formulation, and represents a theory which in recent years has become generally admissible by the scientific community. Yet it draws only a relatively small percentage overall (20%) of answers in agreement - even from respondents who tend to high Q scores. This seems to show a general lag in scientific education - particularly evidenced by the younger Italian group (15% only in agreement). The finger of blame must be pointed at the teachers, whose percentage of agreement with question number 3 is only 13.64% overall, resulting in a percentage of 16.39% among students, whereas scientists show a percentage of agreement of 42.65% (among those, a look at individual responses shows an even higher agreement on the part of physicists and mathematicians).

Another example - bordering on the absurd - of the divorce between teachers and scientists is represented by question number 4, where 76.47% of scientists agree with the statement that "Catastrophes have produced a great variety of forms, organic and inorganic, which have occupied many ecological niches," whereas only 3.68% of the teachers do. 76% of the students agree with the scientists, probably intuitively for the greatest part, and because of information received outside school or university, most likely from the media culture. It is possible that the use of the word "catastrophe" may have triggered, in some kind of "knee-jerk" response, the excessive rejection reaction of the teachers - which would be in itself a significant revelation.

The highest scorers on the Q scale are scientists. Of the 9 respondents who achieve a score equal or superior to 13, six (75%!) are scientists. Of the 46 respondents whose score is equal to or higher than 11, thirteen (28%) are scientists. Scientists are over-represented in our sample, making up 14% of the respondents, and it must be pointed out that the majority of scientists score low, even quite low, on the Q scale, as is to be expected. (The lowest score is 2, obtained from 3 respondents

- all three scientists!) The finding is nevertheless significant.

In all, despite its want of American responses, the administration of the Q-C test provided relevant findings, explainable within the frame of what we known to have been historically the attitudes towards quantavolutionary ideas. It shows trends toward the quantavolutionary paradigm, and does not go counter to what we perceive to be the general trend in the sciences over the twenty years that have passed since the publication of the Quantavolution Series. However, its being mentioned here is not so much to validate the test as to contrast the ideas of convention and quantavolution. And to show how the paradigm may be made the basis for surveys of scientific attitudes of different reference populations.

Chapter Three

Spheres of Change

The Greater Mediterranean Region, including its star performer, the Mycenean Period, moved directly into the Iron Age. Attempting to bridge the gap between the Egyptian and Greek histories, scholars *en masse* have laid claim to flimsy evidence as of a Dark Age of Greece. We insist that nothing existed in the period roughly given in their works as from 1250 BCE to 800 BCE. It is understandable that a century and a half of deep disturbances to all spheres of existence marked the transition from Late Bronze to Iron Age. We fill this first part of the Iron Age partly with events that many scholars place in the years assigned to the Late Bronze Age and for the rest out of their Iron Age I.

The categories of events of existence we refer to as spheres. How might the major spheres of existence be defined and exemplified?

Various categories can be set up to handle the areas in which quantavolutions are active. Here I would offer a group of thirteen spheres that would amply cover the range of natural (and human) events and operations that one could expect to be activated by the forces of quantavolution,

Ian Tresman, the most prominent bibliographer and compiler of studies of Quantavolution, uses conventional terms such as biology rather than biosphere, or astronomy rather than astrosphere (though here we have the denigration of astrology that came in with the earliest scientific presumption, and so it had to be wiped out diligently).

Why would we prefer to use the suffix *'-spheres'* instead of the suffix *-logies* ? Because *-logies* implies a science and knowledge of a kind of event. Sphere would refer to the events themselves. It does not pretend to knowing the event, but only to the happening of an event. The event occurs whether or not we know much about it in the way of laws, propositions and even hypotheses. The use of the term or ending *sphere* implies correctly that we begin with an event and then proceed to define it and make valid and reliable statements about it.

Holism

If we are studying quantavolutions generally, we are perforce studying them *holistically*. All aspects of the cosmos, of existence, are to be included. We divide the cosmos into spheres. A sphere is defined as an enclosure of transacting events. The enclosure is deemed useful for methodological, heuristic, and practical purposes. It is serviceable both for conventional studies and for quantavolution studies.

We may conveniently divide the holosphere of existence into thirteen special spheres, intending to find whatever behaviors and consequences are associated with a sphere in the course of natural history. A citation exemplifying the Bronze-Iron Age Quantavolution (BIAQ) is provided in each case, preliminary to its being taken up with several similar cases later on. The total evidence of the Bronze and Iron Ages histories and their crucial transitional Quantavolution could be subdivided in a completely different way by assigning to its appropriate sphere each bit of the myriad data brought forward.

An instance would be afforded by the writing falling into a linguistic sphere subtended from the cultural subsphere of the anthroposphere

I quote Velikovsky's unpublished remarks on Linear B and follow with a comment.

> The reading of these tablets in the Greek language raised the question: How could a literate people in the fourteenth century become illiterate for almost five centuries, to regain literacy in the eighth century? Thus the problem already answered in *Ages in Chaos* was brought into relief, and a heretical idea crept into the minds of a few scholars: is there some mistake in the accepted timetable? In the last century a Dark Age of five centuries' duration between the Mycenaean and the Ionian ages was forced upon the scholars of the Greek past by students of Egyptology, and in three quarters of a century this notion, first bitterly opposed, became as bitterly defended by the new generation of classical

scholars, only to be confronted with the riddle of the Mycenaean tablets written in Greek more than five hundred years before the oldest known Greek inscription in alphabetic characters adapted from the Hebrew-Phoenician script.

The solution of Linear B as being Greek constitutes evidence that the Dark Age did not exist as traditionally formulated, but that, in the course of the catastrophic exchange from one civilization to another, from Bronze Age to Iron Age, an alphabetizing of Greek became readily possible. Quantavolution signifies revolutionary change in every sphere, including the linguistic.

The Spheres of Quantavolution Defined

We shall be watching for these spheres as we move from one locale to another. I may venture to claim that whenever a competent quantavolutionist, whether formally or informally educated to a sphere, sets himself to unearth evidence of characteristic events of his given sphere in a given quantavolution, he will succeed.

1. The **Holosphere of Quantavolution.** Holistic Theory of the spheres is intersdisciplinary science *par excellence..* The interdependence of and transactions among all elements of the spheres adds up readily to a useful general paradigm of theory and knowledge. We could picture the materials of this book as a large chart interrelating the bits of evidence from the Iron Age in each sphere to achieve the meaning and utility of holosphere.

2. **Chronosphere**: Time consists of defined Intervals between the succession of events. The calculation of time by various methods so as to interrelate absolutely and relatively the processes of existence follows. A theme of this work is that the rash presumption of a long interval of time between two sets of events can practically wreck the possibility of intelligible recitation of the events and useful historical understanding.

Three Errors of Iron Age Timing

Three gross errors of conventional chronology are exposed and despatched in this book. They account for much of the uncertainty and confusion and slow progress in the history of the Iron Age.

First, we arrive at the proper beginning of the Iron Age only after having shortened by some 400 years the time of arrival of Pharaoh Thutmose III of Egypt upon the stage of history. It was he who destroyed Israel's best attempt at empire, the heritage left by King Solomon.

Second, we must emphatically dispense with the dating of almost all Mediterranean events, moving them from the 13th century to the ninth century, and correspondingly, the twelfth to the eighth and the eleventh to the seventh. (The confusion is such, however, that we should better think in looser figures about these phantom centuries.)

The third chronological devastator of the Iron Age of Mars is the conventional imposition of Pharaoh Ramses III in the 13th century or thereabouts instead of placing him in the fifth-fourth centuries, 800 years later, and with him, a recalibrated group of Egyptians rulers both following Ramses II at the beginning of the Iron Age and alongside and following Ramses III as the Iron Age has subsided into the regime of Alexander of Macedon. The queer historiography of the Iron age is only another indication of the queer history itself.

Throughout this work, then, a difference of about 400 years is maintained between the conventional chronology and quantavolution chronology. Such that the base date of 1200 BCE, ordinarily used to assemble end-events of the Bronze Age becomes 800 BCE. Originally, in the 1960's, we thought that our young dates would soon win the chronological content by the employment of the new technology of carbon-dating and then later of dendrochronology and afterwards of ice core analysis. For reasons lengthily historical and highly technical, we found all three of these technologies unsuited for relating catastrophic events of the Iron Age and before

For instance, the famous explosion of the Island of Thera-Santorini has been dated by conventional laboratories and scholars using the new chronology to have occurred on several dates from 1750 BCE to 1200 BCE. (We date it at about 1450 BPE largely because it would seem to fit the pattern of destruction occurring in the Venusian Quantavolution. Drs. Blöss and Niemitz have published their study in German, *C-14 Crash!* In several works and drawing upon other quantavolutionaries such as Melvin Cook, Ralph Juergens, and Earl Milton, I have satisfied myself that I may speculate that the solar system needs no more than a million years to have produced itself as it is today from an initial supernova of the sun, that a period of 14,000 years suffices to encompass the quantavolution and history of homo sapiens, and that subsequently the history of mankind can be most usefully divided into several quantavolutionary periods, the latest of which was to be the Iron Age of Mars.

Wherever quantavolution theory can fit, great gaps of time suddenly seem to appear, and have to be dissolved or transferred else. We have translated a page here from the book, *C-14 Crash,* by Christian Blöss and Hans-Ulrich Niemitz (1997), to show the puzzle introduced by conventional science as soon as it "went Q" at the end of the Cretaceous Period.

> The idea that a fauna would not fossilize under normal conditions to begin with, and that fossil finds, as far as they could be found "en masse," should rather be seen as witnesses to a single, abrupt event, could not establish itself for, while the new theory of Alvarez et al. was catastrophic, the methodical equipment of the geologists remained as actualistic and uniformitarian as before. The theory of asteroid impacts was only able to impose itself against all actualistic objections because it did not put forward any arguments of a nature pertaining to geological systems or to evolution theory (or directed against them), but to the contrary, it relied principally upon systematically foreign physical theories (the physics of isotopes) and newly developed models based on computer technology. Catastrophism won, therefore, because spectroscopic processes which had hitherto remained unused were brought into play, and high-powered computers were available and put to work. This is one of the reasons why the traditional geological methodological thinking remained practically untouched and could therefore continue to be used unceasingly.

Because of the big changes noted, the transition was typically given all the time "needed" for species to "evolve."

Nevertheless, in one fell swoop, the time period which was supposed up to now to mark the passage from the Cretaceous to the Tertiary, and which was habitually made to last even longer than the Tertiary itself, was disposed of once and for all. Simultaneously, there occurred a virtual space during which up to now the evolution of mammals, who were to be found in the Tertiary layers, was supposed to have taken place. If the Tertiary had left behind enormous amounts of sediments in which the relevant evolutionary successions sequences could be followed, there would exist a legitimacy to the concept of an epochal structure of the Tertiary. However, Tertiary finds occur merely as localized, single intrusions, 6464which, if taken individually, have nothing to show in the way of substantial, transmissible evolutionary sequences and whose chronological, epochal order could only arise out of the application of a specific bio-stratigraphic evolutionary form of thought.

With our reflections we would associate also a plea for the interpretation of Tertiary and Quaternary finds as snapshots of one or several large catastrophic events. We show [..here] that an absolute chronology for the Tertiary could only arise because the existence of a Tertiary epoch in the order of 60 million years of length was understood and misused as a certainty, never liable to questioning.

Velikovsky never saw fit to argue over ages beyond the Saturnian Deluge of around 4000 BPE, and seemed to believe in long durations even while being skeptical of longtime evolutionary Darwinism. His great contribution was to pull down 'the three pillars' of ancient Egyptian chronology, and to build an alternative thereto. The first of these was the reliance upon an often errant Dynastic list of Manetho, to which erroneous corrections were made. A star-based Sothic Period was calculated that was baseless and this was fitted artfully into the Manetho list. Calculations of reigning dates of the Eighteenth and Nineteenth Dynasties were computer using lunar festivals for the most part. The final chronology of Egypt was then handed around and down.

"The specialists in astronomical chronology made their calculations and announced their expert results. The specialists in pottery took the results of the specialists in Sothic computation as a firm base on which to build. Specialists in the history of art, the history of religion, philology, and history in general followed. Difficulties were swept away and the findings of the specialists corroborate one another, and so they have scientific proof that their systems are constructed with precision and are well fortified on all sides. The readers of cuneiform borrow dates from the readers of hieroglyphics; the Bible exegetes from the archaeologists; the historians from all of them. Thus there came into existence an elaborate, entrenched system that bears very little resemblance to the real past.

"The Sothic system of ancient chronology is rooted in a fallacy; Menophres is unknown, if he is anyone at all; Manetho's list of dynasties is a bewildering maze. Yet the chronology of Egypt is erected up these three 'pillar' and the history of the world is built upon this chronology."

It is barely possible that when all is said and done, the pieced-together quantavolutions may give better shape to ancient chronology than the accepted norms.

Work of Edwin Schorr

A key to the Iron Age has long been sought in the darkness of the Homeric Age. Here I would show how Edwin Schorr brilliantly exposed the need for the dating we have adopted in this work, the Eighth Century.

Literary critics have, as we noted for tripods, engaged in the same tug of war for over 2000 years now. Contemporary philologists, employing linguistic criteria in an attempt to determine the precise date of Homer's allusions, and thereby resolve the debates of their colleagues, find themselves as perplexed as the other disputants, since they cannot neatly separate the manifestations of eighth-century Greek from those which they judge to be 500 years older, and find numerous cases of "Mycenaean" language describing late material and late language describing Mycenaean material.

The philologists, trying to aid the archaeologists to establish dates, readily confess their consternation that "'older' and 'younger' elements (whether archaeological, linguistic, or social) interlock," and that those same components, which "differ in age by more than half a millennium . . . are inextricably blended"—a fact which they term "most bewildering," and for dating purposes, even "fatal." Since the linguists' attempts to separate the elements into distinct strata has met with failure,[14] they send the problem back to the archaeologists. As Snodgrass remarked, the whole matter is "a sorely vexed question, but it cannot be shirked. It remains as true today [1971] as it has been for some years past, that there are only two positively and widely identifiable historical 'strata' in the world described in the Homeric poems," the LH III period and the eighth century. For temples specifically, and for each of a number of other items, he saw "a pattern. . . emerging," wherein they belonged either to the thirteenth-twelfth centuries or the eighth-seventh, but not between. "

The dating controversy still rages over temples and an astonishing number of other matters, with the recent discoveries of Mycenaean temples encouraging those who prefer to see all of Homer's references as genuine Mycenaean memories rather than eighth-century anachronisms. But two gnawing questions arise: how did the LH III and eighth-century elements become so "inextricably blended" in the poems, if the epics grew through accretion; and why are those the only two periods in evidence? The second question goes to the very heart of the notion that oral poetry sustained Mycenaean memories through 500 years of illiteracy. If the epics in their original form were so sacrosanct that no poet, who transmitted them, altered them for centuries, why did an eighth-century hard feel that he could insert language, customs and objects of his own day in such a pervasive manner? On the other hand, if it is true that no oral poet memorizes another bard's songs verbatim, or even sings his own tale twice the same way, then one should expect that those transmitting enormous, unwritten secular sagas for 500 years would gradually omit or alter many of the Mycenaean details, which would only have confused or had no meaning to themselves or their audience during the Dark Age; one would further expect that the bards between the LH III period and the eighth century would have added contemporary language and references to make their epics more relevant and comprehensible to their own day and their own listeners: yet they seem to have done neither of those things. Consequently, for Homer's temples, as for other matters, the "tug of war" across a 500-year chasm continues, and the entire situation remains "most bewildering."

There is much to be said later on concerning the possibility of relocating the peoples of Iron Age Palestine in West Arabia. Dating controversy is rife over all dating activity of the times. Several of the problems of dating there and elsewhere are revealed in the procedures for dating Wabar, a crater complex in the remote desert of Central Arabia (see Chapter Twelve).

Earth Sciences

3. **Geosphere:** Here we treat data serving the earth sciences, a broader term than "geology". Quantavolution particularly studies major features of the Earth's surface as products of impacts, fall-outs, and interrupted motions. The

hydrosphere may be included. Reports are legion of earthquake (hundreds of instances), land rising and sinking, great floods, tsunamis. Cyprus evidences all of these, including as Thompson reports the perfectly empirical understanding of Babylonian astrologers: "When the Earth quakes continually, there will be an invasion of the enemy."

Land sinks are common in the Southeastern Argolid, Southwestern Anatolia, and the shores of the Black Sea. Myriads of wells went dry overall. Settlements of Lake Dwellers, whether on or alongside the shores, were drowned, as in Scandinavia so in Central Italy, Switzerland and Germany. According to Sernander, when the villages were destroyed around -800, they were never to be reconstructed. Gams and Nodhagen agree that at this date, the lakes were tilted.

Further, the Earth's magnetic field is often perceived to reverse itself, if one can judge from the reverse orientations of a great many lavas of the world (The most common crustal surface is igneous rock.) Glaciers have been growing and melting, usually at a pace not provided for by uniformitarianism. The Iron Age is a pivotal point in this recent history.

The Behavior of Sky Systems

4. **Astrosphere:** Astronomy and astrophysics deal with the complex, regular and erratic behaviors of sky system components. We note, for instance, the Hebrew prophets and their insistence upon the aberrations of the sun. Velikovsky, among others, advances the argument: The North Celestial Pole was once in the Great Bear, but since the eighth century the North Celestial Pole has been in the Little Bear. The change was sudden. If true, this axial tilt alone would bring about a quantavolution of worldwide dimensions. And this is only one of many extraordinary happenings in the skies above.

The astrosphere extends to space falls — bolides, meteorites, comets, dust, metals. Very recently cosmic impact craters have been discovered in Italy, Bosnia and Iraq. The search for such craters has become worldwide and a popular kind of exploration. It is likely that in the end the

Earth will be shown to have been struck as frequently as the Moon and Mars, and as sporadically. It has enough rainfall and vegetation to smoothen its complexion and mask its true face.

Early in the Iron Age, probably even long before, the association of eclipses with earthquakes was noted. This correlation presently is rejected, although persons expounding this hypothesis, as that of sun spots with earth tremors, will at least be given a fairly calm hearing. There seemed to be little doubt of this thesis in Martian times, for we have Thucydides, Herodotus and others making the connection. Ordinarily this combination would be a *casus belli*, but an eclipse during a struggle between Medes and Lydians that had lasted five years brought both parties to the peace table in 585 BPE.

We plead for a liberty in examining the movements of astronomical bodies whether the 'system', the planets, comets, meteoroids or plasmas: we cannot be brought before the bar for loose dealing with them. It has happened that scholars, diligent and trained, have spent their lives in the past generation on one of a number of mechanical gravitational and electrical models of how it could happen that the expostulations of legends, early philosophers, and ancient historians regarding their movements could be worked out in mathematical form or in a way to suit the known laws of physics and electrodynamics. Not only do we lack the knowledge and dedication for such exercises, which we would so relish to have done by others, but we gesture at the present output of scientific eccentricities, where the anomalous, as soon as discovered, is converted by computer hardware and programs into a systematic alternative to existing formulae of astrophysics.

5. **Electrosphere:** Electricity is a universal sculptor of transactions and forms on all scales. See *Fig. 2*. The **plasmasphere**, which is a variety of intricate mixtures of electrically composed and behaving and uncharged matter is the stuff of space, internal and external, cosmic and physiological, and its activity. Ultimately it composes over 99% of all that can be perceived as matter or substance in the universe. Significantly, it was in the discovery of natural

philosophy in the Iron Age that Heraclitus, whose works come down to us unfortunately in a few fragments, observed, "Lightning steers the Universe." Only in the past generation has mankind, because he is creating ever more powerful charges and discharges of electricity, and also at the same time discovering the immense operations of electricity in the upper atmosphere and space, become able to imagine what the ancients could be experiencing with the thunderbolts of Jupiter, of Yahweh, of Mars. We see why they could assign to thunderbolts and sheets of lightning the destruction of cities, living forms, and lands. The case of Volsinium will be presented in some detail in Chapter Fourteen.

6. **Atmosphere:** The gaseous envelopes above the Earth's surface, extending outwards from earth indefinitely to where a measuring instrument would discover the least of whatever component of the atmosphere is being observed. Darkness, brought on by widespread volcanic emanations from Thera and many other sources is evidenced, in the Martian period. *Fig. 2* diagrams the levels of the atmosphere up to the Ionosphere and mentions the main forms in which great electric manifestations take place, embodying huge energies. Electric phenomena can be searched into the ionosphere and further space, and even emanating from the planets, and, of course, comets and meteoroids: all of these are to be found in plethora during the Mars period in the guise of myth, legendary history, written references, and effects.

Climate is a function of atmospheric conditions, no more amenable to analysis and prediction than the atmosphere. W.B.Wright's *Quaternary Ice Ages* was already able to generalize some eighty years ago that during geological history, including the very recent, including, we think, the Iron Age, there have been many changes of climate a number of which were undoubtedly attributable to the displacement of the poles or an axial tilt of the Earth.

The Australian astrophysicist Bowen discovered upon regular observation that a month after a meteoric shower, there were heavy falls of rain and snow worldwide. He surmised that the meteors and precipitation were connected, and that the interval of time was required to let meteoric dust layers pass from the ionosphere down to the cloud-bearing atmospheric levels. Using a high-flying aircraft of the U-2 type and flying at a height of 23,000 meters above the oceans and the South Pole, he trapped a quantity of fine dust that turned out to be of the constituents of meteors, that is, iron, chromium, and rock dust. Thus, the far heavens bring probably the heaviest rains and snows upon Earth.

If this ordinarily occurs, the effects can average out to periods corresponding to the incidence of meteoric high and low activity. Other causes of changes in climate may be more absolute and bring fairly abrupt ecological and cultural changes. The readiest if less acceptable cause up to this time would be the occasional changes in ocean levels, and axial tilts of the globe. Both of these occurred in connection with the Iron Age, as will be hypothesized in due course. Even so, although causes may not be known, effects are evident. Along with worldwide climate changes, the Mediterranean region underwent sharp alterations within a generation. Claude Schaeffer in his *magnum opus* (p. 360) talks about climatic changes.

> "...we arrived the conclusion that the climate in the Age of Bronze was less humid than at the Hallstatt period... In Switzerland, by comparison with the neolithic, the level of lakes had then decreased considerably and had forced the fishermen to build new palaffites farther in the dried up shores. In the Upper Alps, the man of the Bronze Age establish himself up into altitudes where before, and also today, agriculture is impossible, or which are even constantly covered with snow. Littered with finds, passes and passages attest to their frequentation during the Bronze Age, whereas today they are often obstructed by glaciers. Also in Alsace, Bronze Age finds are not rare on the summits of the Vosges. In the marshes of Central and Northern Europe, they lie in obviously desiccated layers characterized by plants adapted to a continental climate.
>
> At the beginning of the Hallstatt period, a return of a cooler and wetter Atlantic climate forced populations to move out of the forests. In the habitations bordering the Swiss lakes, one notices that new layers of floor were put on top of the old ones in order to combat excessive humidity of the soil. In the end, dwellings had to be abandoned, and men retired to shores higher up. In the Upper-Alps, remains of the Hallstatt period are completely missing; the same is true of the Upper Vosges. In the marshes of central and Northern Europe, the dry layers of the

Bronze Age are covered with thick humid strata abounding with a vegetation preferring the more humid Atlantic climate.

The change of climate at the end of the Bronze Age and at the beginning of the Hallstatt therefore affected all of Central and Northern Europe. It probably affected the whole Eurasian continent. We notice now, at Enkomi, that the effects of this perturbation were felt, probably in a weaker degree, all the way into the Mediterranean region, towards which the migrations of numerous peoples were headed in the search of new land.

The change of climate at the end of the Bronze Age and at the beginning of the Iron Age coincides with the ethnic movements which characterize this period....If the climate of the Bronze Age has favored cattle-raising and brought about a greater mobility of the populations, the return of an Atlantic climate at the beginning of the Iron Age should have inclined towards a return to agriculture. Yet, it is precisely at this time that the most important migrations were triggered, among which those of the Peoples of the Sea constitute only the southern or Mediterranean endpoint. The explanation of this phenomenon must probably be sought in the fact that the return of an Atlantic climate, according to all available clues, happened in a rather sudden manner, so that adaptation could not occur, early on, rapidly enough.

On the other hand, one has observed that in proto-historical Europe these migrations coincide, as they do on Cyprus, with an increase in mining activity and the apparition of the first tools and weapons made of iron.

Our findings and observations in the layers of Cypriot Iron I, and in particular in those of the beginning of the XII century BCE [~-700] at Enkomi, furnish therefore the studies of migrations at the end of the Bronze Age and the beginning of the Iron Age, with a very useful chronological marker. The latest evaluations based on archaeological inquest place these migrations between 1300 and 900 BC, [~-900 to ~-500] whereas the geologists have situated the return of the Atlantic climate, characterized, at its beginning by a phase of rapid deterioration and strongly increased rainfall, towards around 1150 BCE [~-750]. This date is remarkably precise when compared to that now obtained at Enkomi, where the struggle against inundations, according to our stratigraphic observations, falls into the period between about 1150 to 1100 BCE [~-750].[8]

Schaeffer's dates tend to confuse, and we might help to clarify if we say that drastic climatic changes, various migrations, and a pronounced increase in the use of iron mingle, over the space of a century and more, from the transition from the Bronze Age to the Iron Age, with the quantavolution climaxing at that time. All of this occurs in a vast territory that includes Central Europe with the Greater Mediterranean Region.

Biosphere and Cultural Spheres

7. **Biosphere:** The origins and development of life forms and ecospheres or habitats. Sudden extinction and origination of species. Droughts of continental proportions are reported. Mars is a leading god of pestilence; the mystery of the apparent sudden drop in Mediterranean populations in the finale of the Bronze Age is partially solved with this fact and its many associations.

Whether man existed or not alongside now extinct animal species is a settled issue. He did indeed. He built villages of the ivory of the mammoths he hunted. Probably, too, he witnessed, and was an unlucky small part of, the immense waves of animal destruction conveyed over long distances by waters and winds. A favorite time assigned to such catastrophes, when they are discovered, is 'the end of the Ice Ages.' And this particular time can be as late as 2700 years ago: that is, great floods of water and ice would have been used to deep-freeze animal assemblages and a single earth tilt, as is supposed by some to have occurred at that time, would suffice to slaughter, transport and preserve until now the victims in a large number of lockers in beds of peat, in caverns, quarries and deserts, now to be found on occasion of the search for minerals and metals or the making of infrastructures for modern industry and communications. Or even upon the hypotheses of archaeologists. A long time favorite of catastrophists has been the Hippopotamus bones, strings of tissue hanging on, that are stuffed into fissures in English rocks.

8. **Theosphere:** The traditionally discussed realms of existence of gods and spirits and their operations in the natural and living world. The origins, changes in, and persistence of religions in quantavolutions. In accord with this author's major thesis of *The Divine Succession,* gods and divine systems change with every quantavolution, but claim to be the hitherto unrecognized elements of the old gods or

new elements and sometimes claims (historically unfounded) for a brand-new god. Here, from a past as an agricultural god in some religions, Mars becomes everywhere in his many guises a leading god to be feared and worshiped.

A proof of exoterrestrial intervention in the world may be the fact, so evident, so widespread, in the Iron Age, that the theosphere houses the most radically changed modes of behavior. In a Q crisis, gods invariably order, according to the most trusted purveyors of the word of god, the massacre or other punishment of our enemies, whether foreign, domestic, or ourselves. The exalted Prophets of Israel are among the worst offenders when it comes to translating natural and psychological events into human behavior. Actually, human crisis has been forever misgoverned by divine commands. If this crisis conduct is to be controlled, the gods and their helpers must be stopped.

9. **Mythosphere:** The formulations of beliefs from the earliest to the present times that present the world in non-logical, non-scientific form. The shadowing and reflection of quantavolutions in the bodies of myth. Hercules, the god-hero, becomes the subject of innumerable stories, most of them recognizable as part of the catastrophized environment.

10. **Anthroposphere:** The origins and development of humans, their traits and cultures. Man as created by and respondent to quantavolution. The prompt hologenesis of language is apropos. The alphabet changes or is adopted suddenly. Linear B Greek is replaced suddenly by the modified Phoenician alphabet. Again, the rich range of Mycenean representational art is promptly reduced to a bare pictorial terra cotta medium. Further, we may ask why should the style of the Mycenean Period be followed by the very different Geometric style in Greek pottery and other *objects d'art*; can it occur that the Geometric style has traits that relate to ironwork, the troubled heavens, and catastrophe?

Mycenean Greece of the Late Bronze Age, borrowing at first from the Levant, became a rich center of ivory carving. Many representations, abstract and realistic, were worked by highly trained artisans. Trade was brisk around the Mediterranean. With the Iron Age break ivory carving ceased in all Mycenean centers but also in all other centers of ivory working. Then the art resumed, but with the phantom period intervening such that scholars were thrown into confusion. They realized that the later work resembled almost indistinguishably the earlier. Some imagined the later to be heirlooms 500 years old. Others put the ivory in the eighth and still others in the thirteenth century, wherever it seemed to fit and did not attack publicly the discrepancy. One suggested that maybe in the interval the artisans turned to wood or textiles before returning to ivory later on. The anguish of many scholars is apparent, yet beginning with the British authority of a century ago, A.S. Murray, they would rather suffer doubt that have their reputations smeared. Murray was attacked by Arthur Evans and the British Museum: they then simply pushed his dates back 500 years to fit the emerging Egyptian chronology. 'Gaposis' triumphant!

Jeremy Rutter is one of a band of scholars who have tried to fill the gap of dead time, to no avail. He speculates that the Palace culture collapsed following a period of growing unrest (undescribed), and that a simpler life followed. Writing was gone but representational art remained, whose barbarous style could be defended for revealing a freeing of art forms. The media of artists and artisans were many fewer, and technologies disappeared.

The Alphabet

A guiding light should be the development of the alphabet in the Iron Age. Yet it too has succumbed to obfuscation and broken links. The alphabet was fully precedented; it was not invented entirely in the Iron Age. The Q-event of the Iron Age produced the state of mind that could dismiss the old order and the writing that subtended from it. The line of descent is from an original form of counting and gaming, based upon an ancient Sumerian square, according to Livio Stecchini and Samuel Kramer, holding 4 x 4 compartments, containing in all 16 characters, at first numbers, much later letters, then computations, lists and communications. The board became an abacus and the numbers could be quickly figured. Letters were produced, also in an order.

Stecchini discovered that from its origins in the Middle East in the Old Bronze Age (I would imagine in connection with the clearing of the skies after the Saturnian Deluge, about 4200 BPE, when numberless stars were exhibited in various combinations and permutations of groupings) that the farther from the source in the Middle East (therefore in Korea and Ireland, for instance), the more clearly the alphabet in use reveals the original primitive form.

For ideological and political reasons, the alphabet of disengaged characters is not needed, where hierarchy, prevails and the wish for the liberty of expression has yet to come with the arts, philosophy and the invention of linguistic possibilities.

Cyrus Gordon writes that in the time of the new order of the Iron Age with natural disasters and warring, Minoans of Northwestern Semitic origin, known as Arameans, established city states at Damascus, Aleppo, Carchemish and elsewhere. They brought in and developed the proto-alphabet. "The alphabet owes more to the Arameans than to any other source." The first full alphabet, 29 or 30 letters, corresponding to the length of the lunar month, emerged from Ugarit.

In 1929 on the tell of Ras Shamra, a French archaeological expedition had uncovered the ruins of the ancient city of Ugarit. There they found writing not known before, which could be called Ugaritic Aramean. Much data of interest came forth with its translation. For instance, one text says: "The heavens rain oil, the wadis run with honey." Perhaps the age when manna and ambrosia fell from Heaven had not gone forever. The Gods, to listen to Homer and the other retailers of divine deeds, enjoyed their ambrosia in many ways: as perfumes, fodder, ointments, enveloping oneself in a cloud bath, nectar, pastry, heavenly dew.

The signs of Ugaritic were cuneiform, like all the systems of the region, but they revealed something quite new, an alphabet. We would expect important things to come out of Ugarit, pondering the mixed ethnic groups thereabouts, the individualism that came with Martian survivorship and vagrancy, the coinage of money, and the proliferation of the sciences – hence why not the alphabet?

Although it will not be until a much later chapter that I present the full case, I will say here that I accept the theory of Kamal Salibi of the birth of the Bible in Western Arabia, and thence I reconstruct the situation as follows: Yes, the Arameans developed the alphabet (and Aramean significantly and ultimately became the lingua franca of the vast Persian Empire and took over the Bible in translation from the practically dead Hebrew language).

But the Arameans did not originate, as Gordon would have it, in Crete. They originated, like the Phoenicians, Canaanites, Philistines, and Hebrews in West Arabia, from the South tip of the Gulf of Aqaba, weeks of march north of Mecca, down through Hijaz as far as Yemen, and East about two hundred kilometers deep into the peninsula over and beyond the volcanic coastal range.

The alphabet probably developed, if it did not originate, there. It is possible, even more likely than not, that Moses, leading his bedraggled people south from Egypt, was a modernizer and inventor of the alphabet. Or so I speculated in *Moses and the Management of Exodus*. This may have been centuries before the Iron Age. And the alphabet would then have incubated in Asir and the coastal region of Arabia until the Iron Age brought its waves of destruction and opening of minds. (West Arabian archaeology is practically nil.) The Arameans numbered, says Genesis, the Uncle of Jacob, Laban, who spoke Aramean, as did Jacob. The tribe of Jacob may have been controlling the northern passes between Hijaz and Northern Asir and then migrated deeply into Asir, merging with the Hebrews of the region.

We can pick up the story again with Moses' return with the slave workers from Egypt. The Iron Age introduced a new wave of movement. First the Arameans left for the North of Palestine and Westernmost Syria, then the Phoenicians followed (called Canaanites even after their residence in Palestine), then the Philistines, and the Hebrews. The Hebrews counted among themselves literate priests and officials who were ready, if they had not already done some part of the job in Arabia, to write down or largely compose the Bible. They could claim joint or triple invention of the alphabet.

Ugarit and its related Aramean cities were already employing an alphabet when the Phoenicians and Hebrews arrived in Palestine. (All of these immigrations to the North took place more or less as small groups, unofficial, often individual, flights and adventures.)

Cadmus was a son of the King of Phenicia. He was probably forced into exile by an invading army; legend has him wandering, looking for his sister Europa. He does find Europe, Boeotia, and a site that he names Thebes, after the capital of Pharaoh Akhnaton, that is in throes of destruction after Akhnaton's downfall. He must have been an ally of Akhnaton. Myth has him recruiting his fierce warriors by sowing the seeds of a dragon he killed; more likely they were typical of the crazed heroes of Homer's epics. The Thebes they founded and raised to magnificence met with destruction and did not participate in the Trojan War.

He introduced the alphabet to the Greeks, who called it the Phoenician alphabet and proceeded to use it magnificently. Adoption of this kind of geometric and manipulatable small set of symbols suited the intellectual side of the crazy warrior mentality that pervades Greek, Homeric, and other Martian societies. The earliest instance of an alphabetic inscription in the Greek language has been credited to the mid-Eighth Century, time of the first Olympic perhaps, and not long before the Trojan War.

So we should put aside the idea that the alphabet came to Greece in the Fourteenth, Thirteenth, or Ninth Century, and also the idea that the Greeks had been illiterate for five hundred years of the Dark Age, for having lost the art of writing with the fall of the Mycenean palaces. In the confusion and admixtures of the Martian quantavolution, organized systems -- intellectual, industrial, demographic, political, were torn apart. However, the transition to the Iron Age culture of Homer came rapidly, not over centuries. The Greeks were not without writing for any extended period of time, although the number of writers and readers must have been drastically reduced by catastrophe.

A most subtle connection between philology and catastrophe was fashioned by J. Pokorny.

I myself have hypothesized that the Germanic sound-shift can be explained in purely physiological terms by assuming that following the catastrophic change in climate in the Baltic area, people, in order to protect themselves from the cold and damp air, closed their mouths more tightly when drawing the breath in; this naturally resulted in a stronger outbreath, and a narrowing of the frictional surface of the air stream... if one remembers that the Germanic sound-shift coincidences more or less with the beginnings of the Nordic Iron Age, and the climatic drop, then the conclusion is almost forced upon one, that there must have been some connection between these events.[9]

11. **Historisphere:** The records of all of the world, made available in written documents through all time, as they have been used and misused in relation to quantavolutions. At the beginning of the Iron Age, records and documentation suddenly curtailed to the point of disappearance. What should be one of the greatest sources of documentation, Phoenicia, gives us nothing.

12. **Psychosphere:** The mental operations of humans from earliest time to the present. What the distinctive properties of the human species and mind, such as rationalization and sublimation, owe to quantavolutions. Pre-Socratic Greek philosophy, for instance, represents a radical transformation in Greek and regional mentation. So do the prophets of Israel. Why should the geometric style in Greece follow the Mycenean style of decoration? Could it signify not only a complete artisan class turnover, but also a drastic change in mentality and a fatal attraction to an imposing set of sky images, plasma figures rather than social settings? We have much to say on these questions in later pages.

13. **Paedeiasphere.** The development of transmission of culture, including science. There are numerous methods of pedagogy, experiment, scientific logic, the Socratic method, group brainstorming, and so on.

The **Linguisphere** is closely related. Too, the cultivation of language overlaps other spheres. In regards to the Chronosphere, for instance, it is significant that, following upon its decipherment, a recent and accepted theory regards Mycenean Greek to be as advanced (or, as 'up-to-date') as the Ionian and other Dialects of Greek, rather than as 'backward' as it would be if four hundred years had elapsed between Mycenean and the Greek language of the eighth century.

With the diminution of chaos, formal private education is born and sets itself the task of interpreting the world rationally. The pedagogy of quantavolution considers how quantavolution might be fitted into and taught in the universities and schools of the future and how libraries of quantavolution relevance can be set up.

The change from writing systems of the Bronze Age to the alphabetic systems of the Iron Age would qualify as a quantavolutionary effect. A secularizing and abstracting sharpness brought along alphabetizing, it may be conjectured, a divorce of thought and things, at least for the manipulation of both thought and things.

Rarely, archaeologists have tried to explain what they have noticed as a primitivization of cultures between Bronze and Iron Ages. One has called this phenomenon 'democratization,' another, 'miscegenation.' I gather sometimes the feeling, rarely expressed by field archaeologists or even ancient historians, because it is too far from present-day history, that there occurred a bolshevik rebellion whereby the upper classes of the regimes, the palaces, were dissolved or overturned, and a revolutionary proletariat took over. This may not be far from the truth, though painted with a broad brush.

There should be a relationship between the radical change in writing systems and the radical transformation of the theoretical part of theocracy into scientifically framed natural philosophy. The matter requires much study. Not only here but in all spheres evidence must, and possibly can be, increasingly found out.

Chapter Four

Earth and Heaven: Conjoined and Interactive

Professor (Admiral) Harry Hess, famed for his oceanography, especially regarding sea-mounts, and Chairman of the Princeton University Department of Geology, was a *rarissimo* establishment sympathizer of our work in quantavolution in the 1960's. He asked his classes to read Velikovsky's "Earth in Upheaval." He might well have recalled how in the 1930's any hint of connection between heaven and earth was strictly for church on Sunday.

Still, Hess, with Paul McClintock, in 1935[10] (*Science,* April 3rd, 1936) tackled the conventional theories of mud-flows and ice cap forming and melting, bringing to bear new explorations revealing the configuration of many sunken valleys that extended rivers along the sea-bottoms. They could argue that the valleys were very young, even post-Mousterian (e.g. Congo River). Further, the same sculpturing was world-wide and done abruptly.

So they postulated that a sudden slow-down of the Earth's rotation would pull the waters to the poles, giving the rivers a chance to cut valleys, before the waters returned. As to what slowed the Earth? "While of course we do not know what could have caused the sudden change in rotation, it is conceivable that a collision with a small extra-terrestrial body could be competent to produce the effect. The grave difficulty of changing the earth's rate of rotation is readily admitted. The authors would welcome any suggestions of other means by which the ellipticity of sea-level might be changed."

I explained the submarine canyons almost fifty years later, as follows:

I think that we have progressed far enough along in this book [*Lately*

Tortured Earth] to dispose readily of the submarine canyon problem. The canyons were instantly created great river courses that rushed down, first, precipices, then, steep slopes, then gradual slopes, into the ocean basins that were only partly filled with water. Drainage of the water-logged continents and successive deluges filled the ocean basins to overflowing. As the seas encroached upon the rivers, the rivers were also receiving far less water to give to the sea. The underseas box-like, sluice-like channels ended their careers as turbulent rivers within perhaps two thousand years...

A generation still later, the problem is supposed to be unsolved. The basic reason for this is the scientoid resistance against taking a total quantavoluntary view of the earth sciences.

Alarmed by their own boldness, Hess and McClintock "submitted the idea of slowing down the Earth's rotation to Prof. H. N. Russell for criticism." Russell suggested omitting the passage, because the Earth was so hard to budge. The authors, however, plucked up their courage and their last sentence is "we feel, however, that it can do no harm, and might bring forth some discussion of other possibilities."

The "caution" sign is still posted. Yet, hundreds of studies postulating heaven-earth connections have entered the scientific literature in the past seventy years, advancing scores of different types of relationships and encounters. Major contributors were often outside of academia, like Charles Bruce, an electrical engineer, I. Velikovsky, a medical doctor, Ralph Juergens, a civil engineer, David Talbott, a farmer, and Anthony Perratt, a plasma physicist of NASA.[11] They were rarely mainstream scientists, and more likely were failed scholars, or high-school teachers, or hand-to-mouth students pathetically reminiscent of Francois Villon at the University of Paris in the 1400's. Then very late, in the mid-1980's, the regular academic scientists began to catch on. Still, seldom is an encounter of sky and earth forces discussed, where mythology has to be matched with the earth sciences or astronomy.

Downgrading Planets to Comets

Meanwhile, as ever, worldwide, peoples (the masses),

speaking through the voice of their authorities, assert that the world has been repeatedly destroyed and recreated, invariably with a new 'sky' or new 'sun'. Babylonian astronomers claimed that Nergal-Mars had unhinged the Earth. Isaiah the Hebrew prophet, declared that "the Earth moved exceedingly" on one occasion in his times and that she moved "out of her place while huge earthquakes occurred."[12] Unless conventional science manages to deconstruct this ancient and global consensus, we must continue to entertain it as a possibility, not a nullity.

A few words on the issue of whether planets were really active performers in ancient history may be pertinent here. Readers of astrology who believe that they and the world are governed by the planets are infinitely more numerous than astronomers and their scientific followers. These astrologists may or may not belong to religious cults, practically all of which have many beliefs about God and Heavens, but which separate their religious beliefs to some extent from their faith in astrology.

Scientists are today almost all convinced that the planets have been moving on course for hundreds of millions of years. Quantavolutionists are ready to discover that the planets have not been so correct in their movements. More and more conventional scientists are edging toward them. In between the conventionals and the planet-movers are comet-movers. These are quantavolutionists who believe that the planets have been stable but have been pummelled on occasion by a few of the millions of comets and meteoroids that have moved about the solar system.

Here now if one is to believe Pliny, lightning of the Planet Mars struck the Earth, and if all the other stories and histories that claim a catastrophic period for Earth in the eighth and seventh centuries BCA hold substance, then the Planet Mars must be considered to have been on a different course or an erratic journey at this period of time.

Taking the path of least resistance, while seeking advanced standing, a few scientists and a number of neo-catastrophists or quantavolutionists opt for comets as the means of accomplishing the obvious, the destruction by sky bodies and forces of significant portions of Earth. They are helped by the recent discovery (one might argue for "postulation") of two large sets of comets, a Kuiper Belt and an Oort Cloud, named after their discoverers or postulators. These offer almost unlimited numbers of invisible bodies, that, individually or in groups, might put in a sudden appearance, to the misfortune of Earth.

The British astronomers, Victor Clube and William Napier, are prominent in this regard and the most active and prestigious of societies of amateurs of quantavolution science, the British Society for Interdisciplinary Studies, which was originally founded forty years ago to support work along the planetary lines of Immanuel Velikovsky, has divided over the past twenty years into partisans of planets and those preferring comets as instruments of catastrophes, with especial reference to historical times.

In connection with the present work, which invites both meteoroids and planets to participate in events, the major actor who would need to be dispensed with in order to present a solely cometary or non-planetary scenario would be the god Mars in all of his names, forms and manifestations. This might seem to be an easy concession, but in practice it would be like removing Napoleon Bonaparte from the history of 19th century France.

Planets can move anomalously, and the reader here may be assured that a considerable respectable literature has gone into demonstrating how this has been possible, given the laws of gravitation and electromagnetics. An event of December 2004, only weeks before the writing of these lines, may give pause. South Asia and its conglomerate of islands saw its coasts ravaged, and half a million persons killed or injured by a tsunami emerging from an earthquake in the southern Bay of Bengal, near Sumatra. This would not be classified as a quantavolution, although it brought holospheric changes. Simply, it was not enough of a catastrophe to qualify. Yet the whole Globe, or perhaps the continental crust of some part of the Earth, a tectonic plate probably, was actually shifted by some 30 meters.

Interactions may be profoundly disturbing or less so by degrees. For example, fireballs (non-impacting bolides) can cause a disturbed atmosphere at several of its levels. Electromagnetic pulses can generate through or around the world when the Earth's geomagnetic field is pushed or penetrated by pulses or blows from foreign sources. If the invading body contains iron, the intensity of interaction would be multiplied.

The cosmology of quantavolution requires a continuous permanent conjunction and interaction. The myths of all nations have assured us so, and then, after a period of denial of catastrophes that has exceeded the past couple of centuries, we are back to a modern advanced scientific theory that lets us picture the universe as a single entity, whose elements are never separated by more than a thin active plasma. No empty space exists, in a pure sense, but rather a succession of densities that can be separated into sub-entities of existence according to various useful measures.

We are intrigued by a sentence in *De Cometis* from the Roman Stoic philosopher and dramatist, Seneca, citing various sources: "When a planet enters upon conjunction with another one, they conjoin their lights into one light and they have the appearance of an elongated star... The interval which separates them is illuminated by both of them; it inflames and transforms into a trail of fire."

In the *Aeneid* [VIII, 24ff] of Virgil, as my colleague, Hugh Crosthwaite, quotes to me, we come upon a scene where

> The Cyclopes, Brontes the Thunderer, Steropes the Lightner, and Pyrakmon the Fire-Anvil, were making a thunderbolt. They had given it three spokes of twisted rain, three of rain-cloud, and three of red fire and winged South wind. Now they were mixing in it terror-flashes, thunderclaps and fear, and rage, with flames that pursue. Elsewhere they were working on a chariot for Mars with the flying wheels with which he inflames men and cities: also the aegis that fills with horror, the weapon of angry Pallas.... They were competing to polish it with golden scales of serpents, with snakes intertwined, and on the breast of the goddess the Gorgon's Head rolling its eyes.

The *Aeneid* is an epic of events of the Age of Mars, as I shall later on demonstrate. The image conveys several of the plasma spectacles and mega-effects of the Mars incursions.

Iron Age Disasters Known Worldwide

The present book is confined to what probably happened in the Iron Age to that part of the earth called the Mediterranean region, and to some extent the adjoining areas, also referring to Persia, India, Britain and Northern Europe on occasion. As for the rest of Earth, greater Asia, Eastern Europe, sub-Sahara Africa, China, and the South Seas, much of the same was happening at the same time. For 'Nature was in Charge,' and indications are that the Mediterranean region was representative of events in the rest of the world.

A Chinese Taoist of the Martian Age, Wen-Tze, wrote:

> When the sky, hostile to living beings, wishes to destroy them, it burns them; the sun and the moon lose their form and are eclipsed; the five planets leave their paths; the four seasons encroach one upon another; daylight is obscured; glowing mountains collapse; rivers are dried up; it thunders then in winter; hoarfrost falls in summer; the atmosphere is thick and human beings are choked; the state perishes; the aspect and the order of the sky are altered; the customs of the age are disturbed; ...all human beings harass one another."[13]

Herodotus tells us of the Egyptian record that on four occasions since the time of the first king of Egypt, the sun had changed its position of rising and setting – it could be a tilt or reversal of the globe's rotation. His words might coincide with two Biblical statements.[14] On the day when King Ahaz was buried, it was said, the Earth's motion was disturbed, and the sun set early. In the days of his son, Hezekiah, the Assyrian army of King Sennacherib invaded Judah and appeared before Jerusalem for a showdown. His army suffered a catastrophe. Shortly thereafter, another cosmic disturbance occurred. This time the sun backed up Eastward before resuming its journey to the West. This might be one of the four, with biblical reports of what might be a second earlier change, and a third much earlier. In both cases, the tilt was of 10 degrees and the 'reporter' was the prophet Isaiah. The Bible and rabbinical literature as relayed by Velikovsky is the source of the tales.

Charming though it be, it may also be true. King

Atreus was fighting against Mycenae, Seneca tells us in his tragedy of *Atreus*, and the sun set shockingly early. The dates may have been identical in one of the cases. Another version of the same story, however, has the sun retarding rather than speeding up. So says Apollodorus.[15] Psychic compression, we might say, in the Greek case.

But, looking into the reversal again, Velikovsky affords us the following: Hebrew tradition says the event took place on the night of Passover in early Spring of -687. Chinese records say that in the same year and on March 23, "during the night the fixed stars did not appear, though the sky was clear. In the middle of the night, stars fell like rain."[16]

We return to Rome. The 23rd was the greatest holiday of the God Mars. Ovid says that King Romulus, a contemporary of Hezekiah and the founder of Rome, soared to the stars on the steeds of Mars, amidst a general panic, with a vanishing sun and a flaming sky, while "the poles shook and Atlas lifted the burden of the sky..."[17] [Metamorphoses..] The flight, if we are to credit the ancients with any portion of their terrorized testimony, was believed to truly end on the Planet Mars. Romulus went "to join his father." It was not a metaphor in their minds.

A quantavolution of world-wide proportions occurred in the 9th to 7th centuries B.C.E. and this work is given over to existence in the Greater Mediterranean Region under its circumstances. A constellation of events, problems and issues needs discussion, using the Revised Q Chronology. This is the Chronology established by Immanuel Velikovsky and modified by associated or kindred scholars, including the present scholar to a small degree. Velikovsky, working between 1940 and 1979, published extensively, yet left a considerable body of work available in his archive and on the Web.

I have followed his ideas wherever I felt compelled by them and in conscience. Major differences open up between us respecting quantavolution, as well as in several spheres of knowledge where he and I were professionally disengaged, such as political sociology in my case and calendrics in his case. They are considerable, yet not irreconcilable, inasmuch as I have developed my own models so as to have the possibility of adjusting mine to his or his to mine. It is exceedingly difficult to determine the source of basic ideas and their detailed development; the major theory that I derived from Velikovsky, along with many cited details in support of it, was the historically and scientifically demonstrable occurrence of major instabilities and eccentricities of solar system movements, including those of Earth. This - and the nerve to attempt and proceed with the holistic development of the paradigm of quantavolution.

The Mobile Heavens

Velikovsky was assaulted from every quarter of physics and astronomy for writing that the heavens were mobile and that the planets might have lived up to their ancient reputation as 'wanderers.' I cannot, in these limited pages, put forward his position *in extenso*, nor mine, for that matter. The debate that was kindled has continued. Now the issue appears less that the planets have moved, than when and how they have moved.

Ford, Lystad and Rasio[18] report with regard to many of the planets around nearby stars, "many of their orbits are highly eccentric; all planets in our solar system are on nearly circular orbits, as is expected if they formed by accretion processes in a post-stellar disk..." In one case an eccentric perturbation occurs that is thought to return to circularity every 6,700 years. Various theories are offered, with impulsive forces from one or another of the planets as one possibility.

We will allow ourselves another instance of extra-solarity. Thus, in 2005 Canadian astronomers reported upon a remarkable planetary system where a giant close-in planet is forcing its binary to rotate in lock-step with the planet's orbit.[19] "Tail wags dog," quipped the leader of the group. The planet, tau Bootis-b is large, but its mass is only 1% of that of the star's mass and yet its effect appears to be enormous: the same face of the star illuminates the planet; the two magnetic fields are entangled; the star wobbles; and the star's output of light varies slightly.

Tendencies of this kind lead us to speculate that in

times gone by the planets of our solar system may also have been close-in. But, even more important to our theory, they may have affected severely one another and showed such effects, but the effects may be indistinct, if only because we are used to them, today.

Bertrand Russell, the great reformer and mathematical philosopher, quotes approvingly the equally great physicist John Eddington in his article on 'relativity' of the *Encyclopedia Britannica* (1926 ed.) That "the net result of relativity theory is to show that the traditional laws of physics, rightly understood, tell us almost nothing about the course of nature, being rather of the nature of logical truisms." Whatever we know is some human working of history -- artificial history by experiment, news, rather recent, or decidedly ancient happenings.

With the docile help of ever-faster and exponentially powerful computers, scientists, both social and natural, have run wild with theoretical speculations.[20] (It is only their dealing in billions of years that permits them to cavort so comfortably on the fringes of science.) The most weighty difference between the most heretical and most acceptable presentation is in the elegance of the equipment and the access to research assistance and publishing media of the acceptable offerings. Too, they claim to stand on the shoulders of giants. Further, they bask in the blessings of the most privileged of the present hierarchy.

Thus, a USA NASA-Italian-French-University of Arizona team figured out that as the solar system was aborning, Jupiter's great gravity gathered together bunches of asteroids and hurled them into unstable orbits. These were planetary embryos (as evidenced by the deuterium - to-hydrogen ratio of comets), and when they struck Earth, they filled its ocean basins..[21] *Voila!*

Violent electrical disturbances in the Earth's upper atmosphere have positive correlations, not yet charted well, among the planets and sun, as these assume sundry configurations. The planets, moon and sun are electrically charged , as units as in their complex components. Radio frequencies (and therefore all that they may represent and correlate with) respond vigorously to these constellations. Robert Adler has speculated that gamma ray blasts triggered lightning storms as grand as the solar system, which fused dust grains into chondrules that in turn seeded the formation of Earth and other planets 4.6 billion years ago.[22] (Our two books, *Chaos and Creation* (1980) and *Solaria Binaria* [1982] provided a plenum that would invite this theory to coalesce.)

What this has to do with Mars and the Iron Age is, that neither GRB 's nor dust nor chondrules are rare today. The surface of Mars is covered with them, but also with chondrites, so that the primordial processes continue, though in less profusion.

If quantavolution theory is correct, as I see it, there existed a plenum of plasmas of practically an infinity of types when the planet and life generated, but this plasma had been thinning over the millennia so that the long-distance mega-thunderbolts, once experienced in abundance, are confined to the upper reaches of the atmosphere today.

Astronomy Professor Lawrence Dixon has sought a solution to the possible close-interaction of Earth-Moon, Venus, Mars, and asteroids on occasion in the past few millennia, and finds five systems of interactive orbits, each of which has problems such that still another has to be sought, probably in non-gravitational physics, which to me indicates electrical theory.[23]

Professor Walter Baltensberger, considering the plasticity of the Earth, calculated that a relaxation time of a few hundred days or more is adequate in the event of a frequently propounded North Pole shift from Baffin Bay to its present position. "Earth's rotation is stabilized by the equatorial belt. The shift is made possible by the one per one thousand stretching deformation of the Earth in an oblique direction. This could be produced by a tidal action of a mass like that of Mars passing at a distance of less than 15,000 kilometers. The gyroscope Earth then performs a tumbling motion, while its shape relaxes to an equilibrium with a displaced equatorial belt."[24] (The closely similar scenario of Peter Warlow[25] is to be borne in mind here, too.)

Admiral Flavio Barbiero, accepting in effect my definitions of quantavolution, pictures a sudden shift of the poles, given the threshold energy of impact of a an asteroid of only one kilometer in diameter. Besides the many effects attribute to such a collision, Barbiero calls attention to the

Coriolis component that would bring orogenesis on the latitudinally displaced masses, and new patterns of circulation in the subcrustal sima.[26]

Professor T.Y.H. Ma of the National Taiwan University in Formosa claimed in 1955 that changes measured in sedimentary strata of the Atlantic and Pacific ocean bottom in recent times (giving 2700 years ago [our Martia] as the time of one recent event) must be attributed to "changes in latitude due to the sudden total displacements of the solid earth shell and the intermittent readjustments."[27]

Professor Vladimir Damgov, a most prominent "chaos theory" expert, writes that "cosmic chaos has been present and is present everywhere in the Solar system, especially in the history of its internal planets."[28] But, he adds, resonance and gravitational tidal relations among the planets render the solar system stable.

At all times, we bear in mind that the quantavolution is to be described and explained by evidence of the radical transformation of the many spheres of Earth events in the course of employing the new revised chronology. Here we stress the contradictions of archaeological and historical research. Then, we must bring in the external causes of the quantavolution, which are never so convincing as when they are directly connected with astronomical events, in the case of this quantavolution centering upon the planet Mars.

The conventional and traditional and, I should add, most stubborn consistency of viewpoint of the involved sciences – ancient history, archaeology, anthropology, geography, the earth sciences, astronomy – asserts and has done so for the past hundred years that nature has behaved very much as it does nowadays, and humans do so as well.

If troubles were experienced, the cause lay with an extraordinary number of invading enemies, and sometimes earthquakes and volcanos burgeoning from the Earth's mantle. However, it is well to rid ourselves of this notion that earthquakes and volcanos are fundamentally indigenous to Earth. They may be unexceptionally products of recent or long-past exoterrestrially-provoked quantavolutions. The earthquakes of the Martian period and Iron Age numbered myriads. The surface of the world did not settle down to their present incidence for some centuries.

Almost all scholars do admit one thing: there was a disastrous decline in civilization – but then they hitch themselves to the incorrect Egyptian chronology and posit a Dark Age of long duration in Greek culture, and related Near East cultures. Very few of the thousands of scholars of the region have extended their studies of disasters in time and space and delved into their origins. By my reckoning here, their Dark Age devolves from some ~4.5 centuries to only one, plus a prelude and an aftermath of fifty years, and then a long-lasting tailing off.

A striking case of professional specialization, leading to the ignoring of major factors in explaining nature and human behavior, would be the failure of archaeologists to discuss the possible connection with sky events of any of their subject-matter – whether it be ruins, architecture, artistic production, migrations, or in fact more than one or two of the many spheres in which historical events occurred. One would think that scientists would look keenly for evidences in excavations of attention to and relationships with gods and religion. If I am wrong, I am not far wrong. No one of the Establishment has made his reputation as a specialist on the religious angle of excavations.

In 1963 we published studies by Livio Stecchini showing that a crisis in Babylonian astronomy occurred in the 8th century, that the old records have become unreliable, and that the heavens now had a new order, the Era of Nabonassar, it was called, beginning in -747 with new reckonings that have continued.[29] The pioneering expert on Babylonian astronomy, Xavier Kugler (1862-1929), afforded him backing. Kugler also had sought to confirm, with some success, the flight and crash of comet Phaeton seven hundred years earlier along with sunlike behavior of the planet Venus-Athena, and the founding of Athens. At this same time seven hundred years before the Mars Quantavolution, Kugler and Stecchini placed the deluge of Deucalion and Ogyges.

In his monumental treatise entitled in English translation, *Astronomical Science and Astronomical Observations at Babylon*, Kugler devoted a chapter to "Positive Proofs for the Absence of a Scientific Astronomy before the Eighth Century, B.C."[30] He showed that the Babylonian astronomers, who by all indications, were masters of their art and science, appeared to be numerologists and astrologers rather than true scientists, but suddenly, beginning with the otherwise undistinguished "Era of Nabonassar" in -747, began to make systematic and correct measurements of astral behavior.

Kugler failed to follow his own lead, wrote Stecchini, which would have interpreted the mistaken numerology not as a fault of the astronomers but as true deviations of the sky bodies, which refused to provide continuously uniform measurements in space and time. As we move through the present volume, we shall find a number of significant dates that confirm important sky occurrences at or around this date.

For instance, it is notable that the Greeks later on gave the date of -776 to the first Olympiad (which was prompted by and dedicated to the order of the skies). They gave the same date to the beginning of historical times (the *historikon*), coming out of the mythological times (*mythikon*).[31] The heavy implication of the change, which could be called quantavolutionary, is that now with one could base accounts of events on a reliable calendar and, perforce, a stable solar system.

Citing five sources, Velikovsky tells us that "the stone on which the Temple of Solomon was built – Eben Shetiya, or fire stone – is a bolide that fell in the beginning of the tenth century, in the time of David, when a comet, which bore the appearance of a man with a sword, was seen in the sky." (It is probable that this whole period of the Holocene experienced active skies and atmospheres; it is possible, too, that the Mars bombardments of Earth could have begun as early as the tenth century, although it would have been more welcome to our theory if the bolide had struck the temple a century later.) Mars was seen elsewhere in the Iron Age as itself a sword in the sky, as well as a chariot, as a wolf, and as a mouse. Man continuously, pitifully, sought to imitate and interpret the skies via the materials and beings at hand.

Human wars were inspired by sky wars, so he thought, and waged in conjunction with them. Not a culture known but that conducts some of its warfare and describe its history by the way of celestial phenomena. (U.S. Air Force chaplains in WWII liked to preach, "God is our Co-pilot.") Yahweh was a persistent interloper of Jewish wars. The Hellenic region had its Homer with its scenes to match the descent from the Bronze into the Iron Age. But so did the Nordic peoples, and Finns, and so too the Mexicans, and, in 100,000 couplets, seven times the size of the epics of Homer, so did the Hindus.

Their *Mahabaratha*, like the Wars of Troy, contained many elements that were composed in their final form during the Iron Age of Mars. It, too, centered around a great and prolonged war (centering about the Battle of Kurukshetra, which, unlike Troy, is a known geographical place) that involved the gods with all their good and evil conduct. It was fashioned in the period of transition from the heavily sacrificial Vedaic religions to the forms of individualized worship that were most pronounced in new sects, the most significant of which may have been Buddhism and Jainism. Like the Greek epics, the *Mahabaratha* was a tremendous unifying and acculturating instrument of the separate and rather distinct groups. Still in neither case did it bring about a prompt unification. The chaos of Mars was prolonged and disjunctive.

Greek philosophers and the general elite of the associated cultures consciously accredited this function to the "Divine Homer." We had many related peoples milling about and menaced by assimilation to giant states – Egypt, Assyria, Persia – or migrant hordes, Celts, Teutons, horsemen of the steppes. Ultimately, their culture found armed champions, Alexander, in the East, and the Roman Republic in the West, Ares and Mars.

Caught in the proliferation of confusing bits of evidence, I find it difficult yet compelling to prove that the great epics were a reflection of Iron Age chaos that used the tools that had been invented or diffused by the Iron Age, literacy, the alphabet, and the concept of the epic itself as a novel conglomeration of cultural anthropology. I must use the propositions of sociology and social psychology, not only on the behavior of the ancients, but perhaps also on the present-day historians of ancient history, the vast majority of whom claim to be uniformitarians.

Venus, we have argued elsewhere, was the protagonist of an immense quantavolution of the Second Millennium BPE. There are indications that the Venus catastrophes were grander than the Martian ones that concern us here. It is also to be shown that Venus was not absent from the Martian proceedings, but indeed played a crucial role in the end by chasing both Mercury and Mars toward their present orbits. For example, Venus (Uzza) continued to play a large part in the history of the Jews, as Greenberg and Sizemore showed in a study of almost 40 years ago,[32] and moved its influence also over to the Christians. Or to take another example, during the crisis of Venusia, a great fall-out of ambrosia or manna was experienced in many areas of the world. In the Martian period, the gods were still on a diet of ambrosia, but it had not lately fallen. Nor did the sky drop the vast quantities of petroleum elements that appear to have been part of the Venusian Quantavolution.

Yet to come, however, is the discussion of a great contribution of iron that Mars made to Earth. Other materials came down as well. Who in the next generation of scholars will make a strict and more richly researched comparison of the aerial contributions of different astral bodies to Earth?

Chapter Five

Heroic Scholars: Old and New

Eager for support, Immanuel Velikovsky went to distinguished men to inquire how they would handle his theses and to get their help. Hess, Einstein, Schaeffer, Shapley, Kallen...and others of high professional stature.[33] He avoided, on the other hand, associations, whether in person, name or ideas, with well-known marginal scholars and scientists. He abhorred Hoerbigger, avoided Charles Hapgood, skirted Donnelly, snubbed Donald Patten, missed seemingly Melvin Cook, ignored Beaumont and Baker, and contemned Daniken.[34]

At the same time he fostered disciples who lacked significant distinctions, degrees or reknown, who could be useful and, if necessary, discarded. He sought to be defended and substantiated, not to be appraised judiciously. Though vastly egotistic, or perhaps because of it, he never hesitated to ask scholars and publicists for help. He was fiercely dedicated, charismatic, prompt to a rebuttal, and tireless.

He was an excellent lecturer – imposing of appearance, calm, firm, of sonorous voice, and hardly dependent on script or notes. (His lectures have been listed by his heirs on his web site.) He gave only two courses in his lifetime. One consisted of half-a-dozen lectures delivered to a general scholarly audience at the New School for Social Research in New York City. The second was conducted as a seminar in the studio of ancient studies at the University of the New World of Valais, Switzerland, which I founded with several students in 1971. Of his lectures, most of those delivered around the country occurred after my publication of *The Velikovsky Affair* in 1963. Before then, he lectured to local Jewish circles in Princeton, to University students, where Professor Hess' backing was helpful. Whenever he spoke, his opponents became annoyed, all the more because he made converts, and they were often vocal.

In 1966 University Books Publishers brought out in

book form, with some additions, the special issue of my magazine, *The American Behavioral Scientist*, of September, 1963, entitled *The Velikovsky Affair*. The seven thousand copies of the journal, judiciously distributed among the international intelligentsia, and the several thousand copies of the book that were sold, became a major lesson in the history of prejudices and aberrations in the sciences. A copy of the book went to Claude Schaeffer, who had already been alerted by Velikovsky to the controversy.

Schaeffer's Magnum Opus

It appears, from a study of the gifted copy itself,[35] that Schaeffer felt no need to study the scandalous incident, still very much continuing, but zeroed in on the appendix to the book that contained some examples of "correct prognosis" that Velikovsky had been gathering. He noted the confirmations, some obviously news to him, and then signifies with a question mark a passage in which Velikovsky refers to him and claims his support for the catastrophic termination of the Egyptian Middle Kingdom. He was not yet persuaded and never would be, that a grave set of happenings must have ended especially that age.

Claude Schaeffer was Professor at the College de France, *École des Hautes Études*, at Paris. Schaeffer was fortified in his eminent post for having joined General Charles De Gaulle in England in World War II. There, although working at Intelligence for the Free French, where his bilingualism in German was most welcome, he composed a massive study, published only in 1948, and only in French, by foundations working with the Oxford Press. It has not yet been translated into another tongue. This was called *Stratigraphie Comparée et Chronolgie de l'Asie Occidentale*.

He had before the War excavated in the pre-history of his native province Alsace, and won fame for his many years and publications ensuing from expeditions to Ras Shamra, ancient Ugarit, in Syria.[36] His work was studied by Velikovsky and employed in *Ages in Chaos* to help establish the theory that a quantavolution (a term not yet coined) had occurred ~-1500 (accepting the Velikovsky chronological reconstruction of Near East and Western history), at the end of the Middle Bronze Age, and again around the year -800, marking the beginning of the Iron Age. Significantly, his use of the Ras Shamra materials was as a ploy to demonstrate the contradictions of scholars trying to adjust to Egypto-chronism. He came upon Schaeffer's masterwork tardily.

Schaeffer had independently invented a neo-catastrophism for the Aegean and Near East, based upon concurrent Earthquakes. He indicated general quantavolutions at the end of the major periods of the Bronze Age, and finally of the transition between the Bronze and Iron Ages (his 12th, our 8th century).

Points of heavy destruction between one age and another may be mentioned, using my dates.[37]

Schaeffer's starting point was the stratigraphy of Ras Shamra, a tell on the North Syrian coast, almost directly opposite the eastern tip of Cyprus. He identified as main strata: Ugarit Recent, Middle, and Ancient, each again subdivided into three layers numbered III, II and I.

Schaeffer found that ancient Ugarit was finally destroyed and then abandoned at the end of the Late Bronze Age (Ugarit III).(-1200 ~-800 BCE)

Immediately below late Ugarit II was another destruction level, late Ugarit II. Schaeffer established that it stemmed from an earthquake. (~- 850)

Below Late Ugarit I, Schaeffer discerned a hiatus or break in occupation, which he estimated to be of the order of 100 to 150 years. (His dating ~-1350 to -1200.)

In the next occupation level -- Middle Ugarit I -- the ruins of Early Ugarit III had been levelled to build temples to Baal and Dagon on a yellow clay soil. Below this was a sterile layer of some one to one and a half meter's thickness in which a thick layer of ash was covered by blackish soil mingled with bricks or fragments of bricks hardened by the fire which had destroyed the city. (~-1700 his dating)

There is another level of destruction between Early Ugarit III Early Ugarit II. (~- 1900 his dating)

Strata at other Syrian sites such as Byblos and Qualsat er Souss in which objects similar to those discovered at Early Ugarit III were found, and almost certainly contemporary with it, had also been destroyed by fire. In

Egypt, the Old Kingdom collapsed. In Syria, the temple of Byblos and the city of Hama were destroyed; in Palestine, Beth Shan was destroyed (but Beit Mirsim, Tell el Ajjul, Beth Shemesh, Gezer, Tell Hesi and Ashkelon were founded). Cultural changes took place in Cyprus; breaks in occupation at Chagar Bazar, Tell Brak and Tepe Gawra in Northern Mesopotamia and at Tepe Hissar and Giyan in Persia. Similar breaks occur in the Caucasus and between the Early Dynastic (Ur) and Agade periods in Southern Mesopotamia. In Anatolia, thick layers of ash at Alaça Hüyük, Alishar, Tarsos and the second city of Troy.

The end of the Middle Bronze Age was marked by violent destructions at many sites. Alaça Hüyük; Alishar and Bogazhköy in Anatolia; Tepe Gawra in Mesopotamia; Jericho, Bethel, Hazor, Beit Mirsim and Iachish in Palestine were all destroyed by fire. Moreover, at every site described by Schaeffer in his study, even where there is no evidence of physical destruction, there is a long hiatus or break in occupation of varying duration but estimated by him to have lasted 100 and 200 years. These events are associated with ethnic movements similar to those which marked the end of the Early Bronze Age. Egypt was invaded by the Hyksos; in Southern Mesopotamia the incursion of the Hittite King Mursilis I was followed by the fall of the First Dynasty of Babylon and the Kassite conquest; in Anatolia the Hittite Old Kingdom came to an end. Schaeffer points out that there is evidence for epidemics and famines as far afield as Palestine, Asia Minor and Cyprus.

It seems to us that the downfall of Akhnaton may have been caused by the failure attributed to his One God to forestall general natural disaster.[38] For the next general upheaval noted by Schaeffer occurred during the Amarna period, during the reign of Akhnaton (Amenhotep IV). Destructions are in evidence at Boghazköy, Tarsos and Troy VI in Anatolia; Alalakh (Tell Atchana) in Syria; and at Beit Mirsim, Beth Shan, Megiddo, Tell Hesi, Beth Shemesh, Lachish and Ashkelon in Palestine. Schaeffer synchronised these events with the earthquake which destroyed Late Ugarit II. Chagar Bazar and Tell Brak in Northern Mesopotamia appear to have been abandoned at about the same time.

Finally, the late Bronze Age city of Ugarit was destroyed at about the same time as numerous other cities throughout Western Asia. There were destructions at Boghazköy, Tarsos and Troy VIIa in Anatolia; at Byblos in Syria; and at Beit Mirsim, Beth Shan, Megiddo and Tell Hesi in Palestine. Schaeffer found no evidence for attributing these final destructions to natural causes and inclined to see in them the handiwork of the "Sea Peoples" (We shall be reshaping the phenomenon of the so-called Peoples of the Sea in due course below.)

On page 561 of his book, Schaeffer writes of chronological complexities encountered in his comparative studies:

> In sum, the examination of objects and the stratigraphic analysis of a single site permits one only rarely to arrive at a satisfying chronological precision. Urban centers whose careers continued without interruption across the centuries are rare in the Near East. Most often the stratigraphic sequence and the chronology present gaps. Our comparative method permits almost always a way to arrange them. Moreover, it lets one recognize an important fact, that the stratigraphic constitution of the principal archaeological sites present certain similarities that are highly significant for the chronology of the Bronze Age throughout this vast region.

A Warm Relationship Develops

And, of course, Velikovsky was elated to have the catastrophic conclusion of the ages attested to by an authority. In a note, unpublished until after his death, he wrote:

In concluding his book, Schaeffer epitomized: "Our inquiry has demonstrated that these repeated crises which opened and closed the principal periods...were caused not by the action of man. Far from it – because, compared with the vastness of these all-embracing crises and their profound effects, the exploits of conquerors and all combinations of state politics would appear only very insignificant. The philosophy of the history of the antiquity of the East appears to us singularly deformed" namely, by describing the past of nations and civilizations as the history of dynasties, rather than as a history of great ages, and by ignoring the role that physical causes played in their sequence.

He admits Schaeffer to the exclusive club of one person - "the almost superhuman enterprise of unraveling the manifold ramifications of the recent tribulations of this planet was not committed all to one scholar." Still, he insists that while his accord with Schaeffer is nearly miraculous, it does not extend to the calendar of absolute dates.

In *Ages in Chaos*, however, before he knew of the grand comparative study, Velikovsky was using Schaeffer's special studies of Ras Shamra (Ugarit)as a foil for his chronological reconstruction. Either the Biblical dates and events, adhered to by Velikovsky, were five centuries earlier than he believed, or vice versa the Ras Shamra dates were set too early. He chose and proved the latter. "Even in minute details the life in Ras Shamra of the fifteenth century and the life in Jerusalem some six or seven hundred years later were strikingly similar."[39] He could point to parallel alphabetical writings, closely similar expressions between the Ugaritic and the Psalms and Proverbs of the Bible, almost identical religious rites and offices, circumcision common to both cultures, taboos and correspondingly much enjoyed culinary dishes (calf boiled in its mother's milk), corresponding medical prescriptions and practices, equal weights for the talent money measure in the Bible and in Ras Shamra, similar gold jewelry, similar funeral practices, and so on. The cultural correlations are so astonishing that I attempted to hypothesize that the Bible was a total lie, in that its composers of the seventh century purloined wholesale. My hypothesis collapsed. The two cultures – Ugarit (Ras Shamra) and the Judaic were so close as to be of the same Canaanite - Phoenician larger culture. Indeed, it led me to reflect more favorably upon the Salibi thesis that these peoples had followed one another out of Western Arabia in the preceding couple of centuries.

All of these correlations of objects, style, rituals, writing, measures, apparel and jewel had to place Ugarit (Ras Shamra) in the eighth or ninth century, except that Ugarit was forcibly placed according to Egyptian and misconnected Mycenean chronology in the fifteenth and fourteenth centuries. There was simply no way out of these contradictions for Schaeffer nor the whole archaeological profession.

Schaeffer reads Velikovsky's Work

Not until 1956 did acknowledgment and praise of Schaeffer's grand work occur to Velikovsky, and this was by way of sending Schaeffer a copy of his work on catastrophes in the Earth Sciences, *Earth in Upheaval*. Schaeffer replied in a four-page densely written letter, expatiating its merits: "I finished reading your book with the greatest interest and much profit." We have also located the presentation copy itself at the Cyprus-American Archaeological Research Institute where the Schaeffer library is held. Soon thereafter, Schaeffer was given a copy of *Worlds in Collision* and read that thoroughly as well.

Both books are extensively marked in Schaeffer's hand, nearly on every page. Most of these markings consists of single lines drawn along one margin of the page, as one would do in the process of reading. We decided to interpret these lines as representing a favorable attitude of Schaeffer towards the ideas contained in the passages so enhanced. We think that this decision is correct, as reactions of doubt, or opposition on the part of Schaeffer are clearly marked by other means. These vertical lines should by no means be taken to mean full intellectual support, but rather that the contents in question were deemed important enough to be stressed for remembering and further reflection and also, to be found easily upon perusing again the book. In most cases they are seen as interesting to Schaeffer in themselves (facts he may not have been of aware of before, or along the lines of which he may have previously reflected himself) and visibly, as possibly providing support to Schaeffer's own theses and queries.

The reading of *Worlds in Collision* appears almost as a dialogue between Schaeffer and the author, as the marginalia are very numerous. Of 389 pages, there are 132 instances when a page bears signs of a "favorable" attitude of the reader towards the material (as defined above). In 11 cases, he enjoins himself to "look-up" certain elements, presumably for verification or for further research. In 15 instances, he expresses doubt; in 10 instances, his attitude seems to be of opposition, but most of the time these are expressed as irritation towards exaggerations, flights of extra-scientific fancy, and the like. (I attach a copy -- probably afterwards recopied -- in his handwriting, of his letter that was written after his reading of the book.)

This work was sent to him later than *Earth in Upheaval*. Perhaps Velikovsky had wanted to test the waters. Schaeffer's reading of *Oedipus and Akhnaton* gives us only a few marginal notations, eleven favorable for looking up, 4 doubts and 2 in opposition. *Ages in Chaos*, and *Ramses II and His Times* do not give us any marginal notations. It is most likely that he had read other copies of them. The relationship of the two men met a crisis when Velikovsky sent Schaeffer his reconstruction, not of the period through El Amarna, but the Iron Age, when he swung Ramses III down to the Fourth Century from the Twelfth, an eight-hundred-year move that was too much for Schaeffer.

True to his own lines of research in *Stratigraphie Comparée*, Schaeffer consistently stresses mentions of "catastrophes of a global character in historical times" and anything mentioning earthquakes. He is sympathetic to any quote of Cuvier, whom he obviously regards highly. He also stresses anything mentioning shifts of global axis, realignment of the orientation of religious buildings, etc. Clearly, the idea of an exoterrestrial cause to said global catastrophes intrigues him and he at the very least leans towards its acceptance. Arguments in favor of such a thesis are almost all stressed. Also, Schaeffer (whose claim to fame rests in the discovery of the most ancient tablets in alphabetic writing) never misses marking mention of the loss of the literary record caused by upheavals and catastrophes.

The doubts expressed by Schaeffer are as consistent as his approval. He does not like any attempt at bringing Atlantis together with Crete. He doubts any attempts at chronologically connecting the Flood of Ogyges or Deucalion with Exodus. He is not comfortable with a connection between the birth of Athena and Exodus. Nor does he like overly sweeping statements by Velikovsky which pretend to connect events far apart in time and space or in time-scale (like large movements of populations, settling of lands, etc.) with the catastrophes of Venus and Mars. He reproaches Velikovsky for wanting to explain "everything" through his own discoveries. He expresses strong doubts about Velikovsky's explanation of the destruction of Volsinium and doesn't fail to point out cases of negligence on V's part.

In two places Schaeffer expresses a gentle irony at the Zionism of Velikovsky, really a Jewish sympathy that is actually gigantic and needs not these little exposures, for the whole of Velikovsky's work to its farthest reaches is inspired by Jewish indignation -- politely, inspirationally, firmly, doggedly, radically expressed.

Next, one can say that Schaeffer fully enjoyed the reading of *Earth in Upheaval*. His "favorable" marks (always according to the definition above) run along whole pages, and many of them in succession. No fewer than 230 pages (out of the book's 301) bear such marks. 17 times he feels compelled to further research some of the facts. The story of the flash-frozen mammoths seems to enthrall him. So does anything connected with the ices ages in general, particularly their end. He painstakingly marks anything concerning earthquakes, as he did in *Worlds in Collision*. Schaeffer's doubts are mildly expressed - sometimes a little remark that some statement of the author is merely a conjecture. He occasionally suggests that less drastic catastrophic events could explain certain changes, like changes in climate. (Not seeing climate changes as possibly caused by exo-terrestrial events.)

Interestingly, though, Schaeffer expresses strong doubts about Velikovsky's theories in those matters which are closest to his, Schaeffer's, expertise. Particularly Cnossos and Crete, and also the destruction of Troy are sources of disagreement. He distances himself from Velikovsky's interpretation of his, Schaeffer's, own work: he finds the way Velikovsky reports on his findings to be one-sided and exaggerated. As in *Worlds in Collision*, he strongly disagrees with Velikovsky's chronology: emphatically, he denies that the end of the Middle Kingdom in Egypt occurred simultaneously with the Venus catastrophes and was caused by it. He even urges upon himself to verify his own quotes from *Stratigraphie Comparée*, as reported by Velikovsky. Nor is he amenable to any catastrophic explanation of the destruction of Homeric Troy, such as I shall be discussing in Chapter 16 below.

This sudden negative attitude is not unexpected: his emotional and scientific investment is bigger in these areas and he feels more threatened. Nor should one entirely discount that, being indeed an expert, he has necessarily a more detailed knowledge than Velikovsky, the sum of which could tend to invalidate Velikovsky's broader, theoretical views. One would probably get the same reaction from an expert on the extinction of mammoths, otherwise open-minded when it comes to dating the Exodus or the end of the Middle Kingdom...

It is a pity that the volume of *Ages in Chaos*, present in the collection, with a dedication by Velikovsky, seems not to be the copy that Schaeffer read, because it is unmarked. It is impossible that Schaeffer's opposition to Velikovsky's chronological reconstruction, of which he got his first inklings in the preceding books, prevented him from further readings. For we have letters expressing his criticisms, not only of *Ages in Chaos I,* but on the second volume, which Velikovsky sent him in perhaps an unfortunate burst of enthusiasm in 1957, although the manuscript was practically unchanged from a decade of waiting for its turn to be published, and in fact never was published as such, but rather replaced by the two books on *Ramses II and his Times* and Ramses III *(Peoples of the Sea).*

Also Schaeffer's copy of *Oedipus and Akhnaton* has some marginal notes. They are less numerous than for the two preceding books, and also seem more negative. He agrees with Velikovsky's analysis of the succession of Akhnaton and of the probable events surrounding the life of Tutankhamen. No psychoanalyst he, and clearly a man of narrower interests than Velikovsky, he disagrees on principle with Freud and the Oedipus complex. Interestingly, he comments on the description of a blood-bath perpetrated by the Goddess Hathor that it reminds him of a similar blood-bath perpetrated by the Goddess Anat in the tablets of Ugarit. The wording is similar (p. 34 of *Oedipus and Akhnaton*).

Schaeffer finally did not accept new dating or

exoterrestrial theories, a repetition of the Velikovsky-Einstein friendship. He never wrote directly and publicly on the propositions of Velikovsky as put to him by Velikovsky and also by De Grazia. So Schaeffer did little publicly to promote or to postpone the controversial reconstruction. Privately he may have defended and even supported to some extent quantavolutionary activity and research. If so, we have found no mark of it. He did not write any reviews of Velikovsky's books, nor comment openly on the treatment tendered him by the archaeological profession. Unquestionably Schaeffer did much less than he might have done to help Velikovsky's reputation, and we may suppose that he did not help much mainly because of his wariness concerning the ripping apart of the established chronology and the intervention of exoterrestrial events.

He had independently invented a neo-catastrophism for the Aegean and Near East, based upon concurrent Earthquakes. He indicated general quantavolutions at the end of the major periods of the Bronze Age, and finally of the transition between the Bronze and Iron Ages (his 13th, our 9th century).

In a respectful and totally relevant manner, Velikovsky upset the whole chronological basis of Schaeffer's works, both the main corpus of pre-WWII excavation studies, principally of Ras Shamra, and of the relative chronological specifics of the great comparative study done after the War. It remains to be seen later on in this book how this can be confirmed by studies of Schaeffer and all of the archaeologists who treaded on this ground after the War.

Schaeffer's Extensive Objections to Ages in Chaos

By 1957, Velikovsky and Schaeffer had become friends, their wives included. However, Velikovsky was not ready to withdraw any of his criticisms of the Enkomi-Ugarit work of Schaeffer and, as expected, was ready to down-date the whole Schaeffer chart of the Bronze Ages.

The crisis came and tested their warm friendship that had been formed by correspondence and by visits together in Switzerland, Athens and Paris. Having passed off to

Schaeffer *Worlds in Collision, Earth in Upheaval,* and *Chaos in Creation* (vol. I through the El Amarna letters), with many expressions of pleasure and respect from Schaeffer, he sent Schaeffer the outdated proofs of *Ages in Chaos II.* Here it was patent that Egyptian chronology would go down younger by another 400 years in the Late Bronze Age and then another 400 years in the middle Iron Age. This was too much for Schaeffer.

There occurred one of the most remarkable exchange of letters in the history of science. Cushioned by their friendship, the strenuous debate brought no break in relations. But Schaeffer had nowhere to go, and Velikovsky went storming along. There was no large productive exchange or cooperation between the two men afterwards. De Grazia tried to generate a new cooperation, without success; his idea was simply to help Schaeffer to bring all of the new excavations since 1946 into the data bank for facilitating comparisons and measurement and testing Schaeffer's findings. Velikovsky asked Schaeffer in a letter to do something about excavating at El Arish (believed by him to cover the capital of the Hyksos-Egyptian early Late Bronze of Avaris). The Foundation for Studies of Modern Science (FOSMOS), a group of close supporters of Velikovsky, led by Bruce Mainwaring, Alfred de Grazia and Richard Holbrook made an abortive attempt to organize an expedition to Avaris as well. The story is briefly told in my *Cosmic Heretics*.

Here was the happening as perceived by Velikovsky, written in his memoires and not released until after his death, by which time Schaeffer, too, had deceased. Elisheva was controlling the reins, Jan Sammer was helping her, Lynn Rose was advising Elisheva, there was some quarreling about what to do next. I was standing by, visiting Sheva and Jan, writing the *Quantavolution Series.*

I neither asked nor was offered access to the archive, which was being bundled for sale or gift to Princeton University and the Hebrew University of Jerusalem. (The originals ended up in Israel, a copy at Princeton.) A web site was started up, and in time held useful manuscripts and letters. Books were finished and published, including the *Ages in Chaos II* volume which actually appeared as two books, *Ramses II and His Times* and *Peoples of the Sea* (with Ramses III included), bringing the whole reconstruction of chronology up to the conquest of Egypt by Alexander.

All of this was water over the dam that was built up in the two letters that follow. I would present first the excerpt from Velikovsky marking the incident, then the letter of Schaeffer, and finally the response of Velikovsky, both of which were discovered and kindly released to me for reproduction by the Mudd Library of Princeton University.

> When I was away came a long letter from Claude Schaeffer, and it was so completely negating my reconstruction, that Elisheva spent many sleepless nights, not being able to face the situation: How will she ever be able to let me see Schaeffer's letter. In that letter he was intemperate; and instead of giving arguments, invoked his own and his colleagues' authority, even more his own position in learned institutions, than authority. Cannot be, is not, impossible, with these words he strafed all my identifications. Schaeffer asked Elisheva to show me his letter only after I shall recover, because he was by then acquainted with my breakdown. But his letter almost broke completely Elisheva and she cried in the night and kept the letter hidden under her mattress. To me she would not show the letter, saying she misplaced or destroyed it -- but finally, upon my insistence, about a week after my return home, showed it to me. I took it, to her surprise, very calmly, and then I wrote a long answer to Schaeffer. He was probably also personally hurt because his work in Alasia was not accounted by me (he forgot that I had my mss of Ages 2 set in 1951). "I beseech you" not to publish my work for the sake of my reputation and his friendship for me. But I was not disheartened.

The Schaeffer letter that caused Elisheva such grief was this one:

Parkhotel, GUNTEN (Lac de Thun), Switzerland 11th July 1958

Dear Mrs. Velikovsky,

My letter sent from Raveno on July 1st crossed the ocean, when you wrote me on the next day, letter for which I thank you and which reached me here, where we are staying for some ten days before going off to Vitznau.

I am disturbed by the news that your husband is again not feeling well and I very much hope he is better now. But it is certain that *he must be careful and restore completely his health before going on working*. My previous letter told you and him that it was simply the pressure of work which prevented me from writing earlier and answering his letter of May 16th.

I am sorry that I gave you by my silence doubt on my willingness to read the proofs of Ag. in Ch. I and to give my opinion on the problems raised in that volume. The first remarks have already reached you. And my visit to Raveno was favorable to my going on reading the proofs and I am going to finish them here.

Gunten, 14 July 1958

This part of my letter is confidential to you as long as Em. is not entirely recovered from his fatigue. Please do not cause him any strain or worry and this will inevitably be the case by what I have to say him and you [*sic*], now after having carefully read the rest of the proofs and looked into the problem of the main thesis of Ages in Ch. II. It is with great sorry that I have to do my duty as a real friend to Dr. Velikovsky, for I cannot do it in the ambiguous way of Dr. Pfeiffer who wrote on the jacket of vol. I: "If Dr. Velikovsky is right, this vol. is the greatest contribution to the investigation of ancient times ever written." But he never made it clear in writing and publishing with his titles [bibles?] if he believes that following the reduction of the "Short centuries" from Egyptian chronology according to E., the textbooks of ancient history have to be radically rewritten and 600 years to be deducted from oriental and near eastern history.

My friendship with Em. is probably much more recent than his with Prof. Pfeiffer. But it became rapidly sincere and profound and I was attracted by the sincerity of E. convictions and his sometimes prophetical force with which he expressed them. Because I am convinced of the genuineness of E.'s endeavor to pursue scientific truth and after having found that in his volumes of the historicity of some of the major global disturbances, he is on the right way, I accepted to give my opinion on A. in Ch. II. And I am willing to sign my opinion with my title of Professor at the College de France, excavator of Ras Shamra and Enkomi and author of many archaeological works, one of which: Stratigraphy Comparée I having been used by Em. in his propre research. And there cannot be any uncertainty about my opinion when I have to say now: No, dear friend, your chronology *is not possible*, your rearrangement of Egyptian history, your comparisons with events of Jewish or Assyrian and Babylonian times are impossible. There may be some correction necessary in the chronology of the XVIIIth - XXth dynasties, of some 50 to 100 years perhaps. But in the main lines the events happened as in the conventional history they are written and Mycenaean, Hittite, Palestinian and Syrian archaeology are standing where they are chronologically speaking: between 1500 and 1000 B.C. in round figures.

Now, perhaps you will ask me how it is possible that more than 300 pages carefully worked and studied [?] and wrote down by Em. can be considered wrong by me. It is like with Galilei: either he was right by saying the earth turns around itself & around the sun, or he was mistaken. In the first case all or practically all what he wrote about the same subject is right. In the second case, all was to be considered wrong. It is tragic that Em. selected a physical catastrophe which probably happened as he supposed and identified it with the happenings at the time of the exodus. In order to do that he had to lower down the Egyptian chronology by 600 or more years, or to displace the exodus on the chronological scale. But the example was wrongly chosen. From this starting point, with persistence and enthusiasm, he went on to reconstruct the political & cultural history of the Ancient East, Egypt & the eastern Mediterranean countries. And such was his conviction of the correctness of his theory, that instead of carefully testing it with the help of stratigraphical archaeology, of philological considerations, he selected unconsciously ancient and doubtful data which could be, with some effort, brought in accord with his theory. So he operates with the scarab of Thutmoses III found in the palace of Samaria, a stray find which can be interpreted in different ways; he misunderstands the significance of the Lacerta [?] finds; he refers to the isoriage sherals [isolated sherds??] found in the disturbed filling of the Ahiram tomb of Byblos and writes such exaggerations as (p. 103) "the Cyprian pottery that covered the floor of Ahiram's tomb . . ."; he opposes the old interpretations of about 100 years concerning the Jazelihaza [?] rock carvings against some more recent ones which do not fill the purpose, but leaves out those he chose when the results of the recent research using more perfected methods (Bittel, Laroche, etc.); he makes use of the very bad observed strata of Alishar [?] which have been mixed up as it has been established long ago especially in my Stratigraphie Comparée; he denotes as a "chaos of opinions" some minor difficulties in my Baghazkeny [?] finds which can only be disentangled by some one who has real experience in digging and stratigraphical research; he mixes there Phrygian pottery with older finds, because the archaeologists there don't know; without having been at Tanis and seen the finds, without making use of the recent finds of Moditet [?] he questions the identification & topographical results arrived at there; without having any stratigraphical and archaeological experience, without having seen probably any excavations he undertakes to use archaeological evidence " in support of the case for assailing the conventional history of the ancient world as an impostor" (p. 275), these are hard words from an author who after presenting theory after theory goes on to pretend: "Summing up the evidence (!) we see that it has been presented in proof (!) that, with the fall of the Middle Kingdom and the Exodus synchronized, events in the histories of the peoples of the ancient world coincide all along the centuries"; we have a french saying here: "il prend ses désirs pour des réalités"; he excavates long abandoned errors as that of Ramsay (1888!) about the Phrygian origin of the Mycenaean lion jade of Mycenae, in order to eliminate these objections; he returns to Murray's inadequate methods during his first excavations at Eukorin [Enkomi?] and rejects the corrections of the more modern researchers (the Swedish Expedition and my own work there) by saying simply "simple and great questions are eclipsed by nomenclature" and "in recent years French & French-British campaigns in Tukorce [?] have failed to solve the problems left by the British Museum excavations of

1896", their mistake being "the finds are still evaluated by Egyptian chronology", but nothing is said by the aslvese [?] observations by which Murray's lack of experience & mistaken conclusions have long since been eliminated (p. 279 ss); he remembers Furtwangler & Doeppeld's Merite quarrels and uses the discussions for his purpose; and here he comes to some ironical remarks about younger scholars "properly trained in the science of archaeology ..."; ici Firgus he uses the mixed upper layers when Mycenaean and geometric ware are in contacts to conclude that they are contemporaneous (p. 293); he tries to discredit strati graphical research in general (p. 298) by referring to some doubtful interpretations, but does not refer to the numerous facts where Assyrian and seco-Babylonian strata are clearly separated & later from the XIVth-XIIIth c. strata, thus hiding before the inexperienced reader a wealth of facts and material which opposes his "revolutionary chronology" and this he does again without intending it, simply by looking only for confirmations and eliminating hostile remarks; that Palestinian archaeology is at some sites "a confused terrain very [?] upside down", may be true in some older research, but in the whole research there has corrected itself and certainly does not warrant the conclusion: "(p. 306) the Mycenaean ware is thought to be a product of the pre-Israelite period whereas actually it denotes the period between Salomon and Aezekial". When he must refer to a meaning of strati graphical research which does not submit to his interpretations, he corrects it dogmatically (p. 308 Beth-Ihan); that site [?] was known long before the iron age (which only means the time of iron as a current material).

It is an old story and no archaeologist takes these terms in the sense in which they are used to question the general validity "bronze before iron" (p. 320); reference is made to iron objects found at Ras Thacuza [?], but it is not said that during the "bronze age" they occur as valuables, in the neobabylonian times they were found there in form of ordinary objects (p. 527); there does not exist an archaeologist so stupid than the one who would make the mistake suggested in p. 328.--

The use of epigraphical and philological material is also in many cases seriously inadequate and it would take me many more pages to show how subjective here too is his method of investigation.

I would therefore sum up by referring only to the archaeological and strati graphical data used by Em. Thirty years of independent research in that field with no regard to conventional ideas, having learned through excavations in France, Syria, Cyprus, and Turquie and by studying on the spot all archaeological sites excavated or in process of examination in the Mediterranean and Near & Middle Eastern sector, the "language" of the archaeological soil, I must say: there is not the slightest possibility that Em.'s assumption of a 600 years error in Egyptian chronology and thus in the dependant chronologies of the neighbouring civilizations can be correct. It is impossible to identify Seti the Great with Psammeltesh of Herodotus, Ramses II with Necho II and make him the contemporary of Nebuchadnezzar of Babylon; Horemheb was not an appointee of Jesurachezib or Esashaddon, Carchemish has nothing to do with Kadesh [?].

The use of the Hittite texts from Baghazkemy in a context determinated by Nebuchadnezzar is an illusion, it is also impossible to identify Hattusilis with Nebuchadnezzar and it is very disturbing that in order to eliminate the adverse document, letter 41 of El-Amarna, it is simply doubted that the letter belongs to the El Amarna collection and said at the same time that this is no attempt to avoid a difficulty; there is much to be corrected in Hittite archaeology & chronology, but the Hittite Empire existed and can't be rubbed out as E. thinks possible (p. 178).

The testimony of *all* modern excavations in the Near East are against E. thesis as he can easily ascertain by studying the following well observed and recently published sites (from south to north): Jericho (Miss Kenyon), Tell Ra. (de Vaux) and Hazor (Yadin) in Palestine arabe & Israelite, Ras Thumura (Cyprus), Tarsus (Miss Goldman), Troy (Blegen), Kultepi (Ozguç), Beysultan Tepe (Lloydds) in Asia Minor and many more sites already analyzed in Stratigraphy Comparée I.

So, dear friends, *I beseech you not to publish* Ag. in Ch. II. It would certainly tarnish E. scholarly reputation and it is to be feared that, as a reaction, his valuable research on the great disturbance of the global history would be rejected for many years. And believe me that my advice is given you with all my conviction and as the service of a sincere friend who remains

Yours ever
/signed/ *C. Schaeffer*

Here, now, is the response of Velikovsky:

Princeton
August 22, 58

Dear Professor Schaeffer, my good Friend:

The time came to return to my desk and to write you before I start concentrating on my manuscripts. You will possibly remember the words with which you have parted from me in Vitznau: "I wish you twenty years of productive work." This was the best blessing; yet there were days when I feared that this would not be my lot. Less than two weeks after we parted in Athens, I became sick, went through surgery, and its after-effects plus fatigue made me think that I will have to reduce my ambitious plans and will be able to finish only a selection of planned works. Thus "Three Fires" seemed to be extinguished, though partly written in Israel.

[*Velikovsky spoke from time to time of a wish to write a book,* Three Fires, *that would tell of the lives of three great heretics burnt at the stake during the Inquisition: Giordano Bruno, first and foremost, then Diego Pirez, and Michael Servetus. When he and Schaeffer visited the tomb of Schliemann in Athens together, where Schaeffer laid flowers, Schaeffer remarked that he would like to write a book about "Three at Troy," which would deal with the interlacing lives of Schliemann, Doerpfeld, and Blegen.]*

I turned 63 in June and the best advice I can give you: don't postpone what you have to do; because I procrastinated much too much. I have still to write the natural story of earlier catastrophes – of the third and fourth millennia – a companion volume to "Worlds in Collision"; the astronomical aspect of my theory – "The Orbit"; and to bring up to date and improve "Ages in Chaos", vol. 2. Presently I retook my "Oedipus and Akhnaton", a smaller book, which covers the period of the end of the 18th dynasty, the end of Akhnaton, the struggle between Smankhkare and Thutenkhamon, the origin and role of Ay; it is appropriate to print it between the first and the second volumes of "Ages"; this gives me also a little respite to improve "Ages".

I asked Elisheva to show me your letters; she had a heavy heart when she received your second letter, thinking that it will upset me. I am not upset; I know the shortcomings of this volume, [page 2] but I believe also that I am right. This does not mean that I have not made blunders; that I have not overlooked important facts; and, on the other hand, that I have have [sic] exploited every argument for my theory: but I have not with intent, or consciously, suppressed any argument or fact.

In your criticism you have omitted to observe that the typographical set was made in 1951, seven years ago, and therefore neither your work on Cyprus, nor Miss Kenyon's work at Jericho, neither other recent excavations could find mention there; and actually the work was largely done in 1941-46, when I turned to writing "Worlds in collision." To help me to know the shortcomings of my book I asked you to read it.

I carefully read the four little pages with notes to the first 20 pages of the proofs; I can only regret that your time did not permit you to continue these notes. I never was satisfied with the beginning of the volume, exactly these twenty pages, and intended to rework them. I omit much to develop my subject there because, as I said, this period is partly illuminated by me in my book on the end of the eighteenth dynasty. My other shortcoming is that I cannot speak with authority in the field of stratigraphy: I have to rely on printed material, but it is very specialized; yet wherever I had a book-report on excavation of some site, it was hardly a case that some supporting statement for my thesis would not be found there. Yet rather regularly some explanation would be given, or in a later volume-report some retraction would be made; or various views would be presented, and more often than no, the difference in opinions would be perfectly explainable by my [page 3] thesis.

You write that I had a preconceived idea and this caused me to go astray. You return to the subject of the first volume of "Ages" when you say that I was mistaken in synchronizing the end of the Middle Kingdom with the Exodus. I challenge you to go back to the first volume.

This was the most fruitful idea of my life, when in the spring of 1940 I realized that the Exodus took place amidst a natural catastrophe. First of all this could help to establish the time of the Exodus in the Egyptian history if a similar record could be found among the Egyptian papyri or monuments. papyrus of Ipuwer and the shrine of El-Arish, hardly mentioned in books on history, convinced me that I had before me a story of the plagues described by an eyewitness, and the story of the "wirlpool" [sic] at Pi-Khiroi (Pi-ha-Khirot of the book of Exodus), where the last pharaoh of the Middle Kingdom drowned; the catastrophe was that of the end of the Middle Kingdom. This having established, I had to compare the historical texts of Biblical and Egyptian histories for many generations and see whether the collation of texts will reveal synchronism in each consecutive generation. Today, six and a half years after the publication of the first volume of "Ages" I have nothing to change there; and no critic, you included, could show me even on one single instance that the correlations of vol. 1 are not convincing. Before adjudging my entire reconstruction as erroneous, please reread the story of the plagues in vol. I: the equation of Hyksos and Amalekites; the story of the expedition to Punt; the treasuries carried by Thutmose III from Palestine and the treasures of Solomon's temple; the letters of el-Amarna and the rest.

Then I knew that I was on a true path. The belief in my being on the right path will be better understood by somebody who could follow me then, in 1940-41, in my work. I was new and ignorant when I started. I used to spend all my days in the library. If I am right, I said to myself, then the Hyksos must have been the Amalekites, whom the Israelites met on leaving Egypt; next I find that Tabari, el-Samhudi, Masudi, and many other Arab authors of the eighth-ninth centuries described in details the conquest of Egypt by the Amalekites and wrote at length about Amalekites pharaohs. If I am right, then, perchance, Queen Hatshepsut left a record of a voyage to Phoenicia? And the record was there. Again, if I am right, then Thutmose III must have sacked the temple of Solomon-Rehoboam. And I open the folios, and the record and the pictures of the furniture and vessels are there. If I am right then in Ras-Shamra texts expressions may be found known to us from prophets and psalms, ascribed by the higher criticism to late centuries; and they were found by you, only to ascribe them to a period not by six but by twelve centuries differing from the established view. If I am not on a wrong path, then in the letters of el-Amarna I will find letters of Ahab and Jehoshaphat; and I found there not only their letters and actually the prayer of Jehoshaphat at the invasion from Seir and Moab, but also letters signed by the generals of Jehoshaphat-Ben-Zichri, Jehozabad, Addaia, and others, known to us from the Scriptures. Where in the entire historical literature was brought together a collation of texts, with such an abundance, almost in thousands, of minute equations. The chapters on el-Amarna letters should suffice for every objective and careful reader to stop and re-examine his entire concept of ancient history.

I could not be on a wrong track if for hundreds of years – from the end of the Middle Kingdom to the time of Akhnaton in every generation we have a complete conformity and even straight contacts between the Egyptian and the Palestinian records, always at the proper intervals of time. Suppose some comparison is just an accident; but in this orderly sequence of events in collated texts, could be nothing but contemporaneity.

Thus it was not a blind man's march upon a preconceived route. The conventional history of the ancient world suffers from a preconceived plan.

The origin of history should have been in archaeology; but it happened so that the construction of history was ready in the time of Champollion and long before the age of archaeology; thus you and your colleagues have dug with a preconceived chronological table, arranged before cuneiform or much of the hieroglyphics were deciphered. This chronological table fits neither into ancient historians, like Herodotus, nor into collated historical written documents. History of pre-Champollion days was made a guide for archaeologists, instead of archaeologists guiding the historians. Manetho's history known as entirely worthless, especially as to the figures – or names –, was then made to a historical-chronological scheme with the help of "astronomy".

Have you read the chapter on Astronomy and Chronology in "Ages" vol. 2 and have you found out on what was built Egyptian chronology? Read it then and find that an entirely faulty interpretation of the Sothis period and a mix-up of Venus and Sirius (Star of Isis and Star of Sothis) in the reading of the Canopus Decree, a very clear document, served to put the beginning of the 18th dynasty where you find it now, and no historical or archaeological ground was a basis for it. Without reading this chapter in the proofs you may think that those who put the beginning of the New Kingdom at 1580 had some point in history or stratigraphy.

Thus it occurs that thousands of explanations are needed, [but] hardly ever needed in the reconstruction. When found in foreign countries, scarabs are usually not where they should be: they are later imitations; or ancient heirlooms; or they were dug in by later grave diggers; or the archaeologists were not careful to observe a correct stratification; or they were left by tomb violators who transferred them from other graves. But usually they are in the places where the reconstructed history expects them to be.

Why are Samarian ivories identical with those six hundred years older ones, also those in Thutenkhamon's tomb? Archaeologist is left with the only possible explanation of a late revival of a style and late imitation. Who makes him to make this conclusion? The historian, who himself is unable to say how it came that he is "absolutely certain" that the New Kingdom started in -1580; only if he searches for the basis of this certainty he discovers that it was an astronomical computation of Sothic periods that made him so certain and made him to an authority for the sweating [crossed out, and overwritten by "digging"] archaeologist.

How wrong am I by quoting different opinions on the age of Ahiram's tomb? You express yourself on this point as if I described the vases found there as originating from a late Cyprian period.. I only quoted many authorities on Ahiram's sepulcher, and the debate is not concluded.

The Israelite layer at Beth-Shan is lacking though Beth Shan played an important role in the time of Judges and Kings, alike. After Ramses II' thick layer come the Neo-Babylonian and Persian layers. This [is] what I expect: but it was not my interpretation, but of the archaeologists who digged [sic] there. That in Gordium and in Alisar identical pins were found, in layers probably seven hundred years apart, is it my interpretation, or of those who digged? And many other similar instances; and are not the chamber graves in the necropolis of Ras Shamra and similar tombs on Cyprus ascribed to two ages, divided by the expected span of time? Possibly I am wrong in this instance, so instruct me.

Why do you say that Carchemish could not be Kadesh of Ramses II' campaign? I have not supplied you with the drawing indicated in the text, but the topographical description I quoted, and the location north of Bab and Arime, mentioned by Ramses II in his annals, leave no doubt that the old identification with Tell-Nebu-Mend is absolutely mistaken [-Nebu could also be -Nebi – unclear from the overstrike in the typewritten copy]; Bab and Arime are stll [sic] existing places south of Hieropolis and Carchemish. Tell-Nabi-Mend was Riblah, and its historical name is still preserved in the name of the village a few miles away. Independent of my thesis in general, Kadesh of Ramses battle was at Carchemish, as also the pictures of the battle and many other indesputable [sic] considerations make clear. But as you know, not the mute objects but historical inscriptions on stone, clay, or papyrus, make the bulk of argument of both volumes of Ages; in their case absence of experience with field stratigraphy is hardly a hindrance.

Why do the annals of Ramses II and Jeremiah speak so similarly of the battle and of the retreat of the Egyptian army toward the north, away from their Egyptian base? How is it that for nineteen years all events of the war of Necho and of the equally long war of Ramses II are so identical, year after year and month after month? Read please pages 86-69 of the proofs and give kindly your explanation if I am wrong.

Who placed, and on the basis of what, Ramses III in the twelfth century? This was decided before the era of archaeology; he is not even mentioned in Manetho. On the reverse of his tiles are Greek letters incised by the workers before burning the tiles in the kiln. I compared his long description of the war and his picture with Diodorus' who described Nectanebo I's war against the Persians. On the picture of Ramses III the Pereset carry characteristic Persian tiaras seen also on the basrelief of the tomb of Darius. Please reread the chapter of Ramses III (you have not referred to him and this chapter in your letter) and find your own explanation to the collation of texts and pictures.

Judge my book not by its weakest argument but by its strongest. Because it is enough to establish in one point of history that Jeroboam I visited Thutmose III, or that the revolt of Mesha is many times narrated by the writers of el-Amarna letters, or that Ramses III fought with the Persians, and the entire history tumbles down for one identification.

"Hittite" pictographs will be soon read, also the stela that was found in Nebuchadnezzar's palace in Babylon. Then, not so far away, we will exchange letters on this issue: Chaldean or Hittite? Nebuchadnezzar was a Chaldean. His story in smallest details, personal and military, his portrait (Dog River Stela), his prayers, are similar up to identical with the personal and military story of Hattusilis, his only portrait (visiting Egypt) and his prayers. His father, Nabopolassar made a long protracted war against the Assyrians and Egyptians, as Merosar, in the very same places in the same sequence against the same Assyrians and Egyptians.

A passage in your letter, and only this passage, hurt me: "It is very disturbing that in order to eliminate the adverse document, letter 41 of el-Amarna, it is simply doubted that the letter belongs to the El Amarna collection and said at the same time that this is no attempt to avoid difficulty.

The letter 41 was signed by Suppiluliumas. I attributed El Amarna letters to the time of Shalmanasser III. Shalmanasser III refers to a prince or King Sapalulmi of Patina. Therefore I could have added in my chapter on Al Amarna a further proof, namely, Sapalulmi (read by scholars also Suppiluliumas) who was mentioned by Shalmaneccar and who signed the letter was one and the same. I omitted to do this, or to exploit an identity of names. This I omitted to do because of the name of the addressee of the letter – Huria, who was neither Amenhotep III, or IV, nor one of their followers. Although it was recognized that Huria, the addressee, is not a name of one of these kings, scholars compromised with the difficulty, assigning this name differently to one or another of the last kings of the 18th dynasty. Also the name of the widow of Huria – Dahamun (in Mursilis' biography of his father) is not a name of a queen of the late 18th dynasty, but of the Queen of [these last three words inserted in pencil] Tirhaka. His name was Huria. (p. 131). All of [page 10] which is only a proof of my being reticent to have a point gained when it is easy to do so but is not believed by me right to do.

Why have the Chaldeans left nothing for archaeologists to find? Did they not occupy the very same places – follow Xenophon – where the Hittite relics are found? I wrote ("Forum Lecture", October 14, 1953, before the Graduate College Forum of Princeton University) and published as a supplement to Earth in Upheaval: "In my reconstruction I come to the conclusion that there are Chaldean signs, not Hittite. I also expect unequivocal evidence that these signs were used down to the last century before the present era." At that time the latest signs were of the seventh century before the present era. Since then "Hittite" signs were found on coins from Commagene, of the first post-Christian century. In the last century it was assumed that the reference in the Bible to the Chaldean language is erroneous, since no unknown language or script was found in those parts of the East; but when about the same time pictographs were described, it was necessary to look for a people to whom they may have belonged; thus the Hittite Empire, or forgotten empire, was resurrected. At the end, it will disclose itself as the Chaldean Kingdom, people, and language.

About the same time, in the eighties of the last century, the scholars in the Hellenic past fought against the inclusion of six hundred dark years into their history; but they were left without argument when in Thebes of Amenhotep III and El Amarna of Akhnaton there was found Mycenaean ware, and these kings by Sothis computation were put in the days of Lepsius or before him into the first half of the fourteenth century. Today the Hellenic scholars would be only glad to get rid of the six dark centuries. Why and how did a literary people forget the art of writing for six hundred years? In advance of Ventris' decipherment, I said in the same lecture that Linear B would be Greek.

-- Continued on September 7th, 58 --

In the history of the ancient East I found a discrepancy of 540 years (18th dynasty), 700 years (19th dynasty), 800 years (20th dynasty). A radiocarbon test of an object 23 century old may easy disclose an error in estimate as large as 800 years. In your letter of two years ago (of 23.VII.56) which you wrote me upon reading "Earth in Upheaval", you have made me a very kind proposal (page 9 of your letter):

"You wish (p. 278) that radiocarbon analysis be made of objects dating from the New Kingdom. I offer you gladly the material I have from dated Ras Shamra levels of the time of Amenophis III, IV and

Ramses II. I could send it over to you for analysis by radiocarbon or, better, you come to collect it in Paris. Your dating thus would be proved or disproved. The lowering of the accepted chronology by 5 to 7 centuries is perhaps not impossible, but seems at the present state of our knowledge improbable. But tests made as you suggest (p. 278) would decide."

This offer so important for me made me decide, in the summer of 1957, to go to Europe. On our return from Israel, where we did not originally think to go and where we were retarded by surgery, we have not come to Paris. But you have sent some material to a new laboratory. However, I am afraid, a new laboratory will need to gather experience and also its results will not be accepted without questioning. Is it not possible to send some material for tests to the University of Chicago where the experiments with radiocarbon originated (Prof. Libby)? There it will also not take much time and I believe there is no charge for examination. It is important to select correctly the material, so that the discrepancy in dating should be pronounced. Certainly also in England's larger universities these tests are made. it is preferable to have the same test made simultaneously in more than one laboratory, without informing them of what dynasty the objects are. If this letter finds you on Cyprus or in Syria, you may send some of the new material directly from there. It is remarkable that since the invention of the method, no object from the Ancient East was tested that belongs to the time synchronical with the New Kingdom in Egypt -- nothing of the time between the Middle Kingdom and the Ptolemies. The piece of wood from beneath Alisar's city wall disclosed that the age must be reduced by 800 years, exactly as expected by the time table of my reconstruction. Here you have in your hands a way to prove me wrong or right.

My "Worlds in Collision" required a change of one thousand years in the Aztecs-Toltecs-Maya history. There, contrariwise to what I found in Egyptian chronology, the history must have been turned back. I had for [t]his a lesser reason than for the Egyptian history. These Mexican nations carried wars under the protection of Venus (Quetzalcoatl) and Mars (Witzliputzli), and this must have taken place long before the beginning of the present era. The Mexicologists were united in opposing my this [sic] statement on p. 254 of the American edition, and ascribed these happenings to a period rather late in the present era: a difference of 1000 years. I have before me an article by Dr. George Kubler, Professor at Yale and recognized authority on Meso-American civilization published in 1950 (as one article in a series of four written by him, also by a Chinologist, an Orientalist, and an Astronomer) against "Worlds in Collision": he attacked me for referring these wars to such an early period, and claimed also that "the Meso-American cosmology to which Velikovsky repeatedly appeals for proof did not originate until about the beginning of our era" and not in the eighth (or even 15th) century before the era. Recently I received from a correspondent in Rome working there in Agriculture Organization of the United Nations this excerpt from the press:

"Atomic science has been used to establish that Mexican civilization formerly dated 400-5-- A.D. are 1,000 years older than that, says the U.S. National Geographic Society. Radio-active carbon in charcoal from ancient fires at La Venta was compared with other material of known date." Since the letter with this clipping arrived only recently I had not yet a chance to look up the original literature. The Mexicologists were quite [this word added in pencil] as certain in their computations as the Orientalists in theirs.

In your last letter you write that I do not "refer to the numerous facts where Assyrian and Neo-Babylonian strata are clearly separated and later from the XIVth-XIIIth c. strata." According to my reconstruction the Neo-Babylonian strata *must* be more recent than those of the 18th dynasty. Also Assyrian strata of Sargon, Sennaherib, Esarhadon and Assurbanipal are by 100 to 200 years *younger* than the 18th Dynasty. Yet the Nineteenth Dynasty is younger than these Assyrian kings and *contemporaneous* with the Neo-Babylonian kings. Ramses III is contemporaneous with the Persians and it is no wonder that his tiles, with his emblems and cartouches on the face, have Greek letters incised on the back, and the letter Alpha has the form it acquired in the days of Plato, as was stressed by the scholars who wrote about these tiles (see my chapter on Ramses III).

Last fall you have taken upon yourself to control my time-table on a grave in Cyprus; you wrote me then that no Assyrian objects we [sic] were found in the tomb to compare with other datable objects, but that some finds required querying and that you would discuss these finds with me in Paris. I wish I knew what it was. this year you will have more occasions to control and check on my reconstruction. If you should find something of Shalmanasser III (-840) you may wonder that in the same level you may find also some datable objects from El-Amarna time. And objects of Ramses II may be found in association with Neo-Babylonian relics. And Ramses III with Persian. And Ethiopian or Lybian time in Egypt, should you find some objects of their time, will be not above but beneath the 19th and 20 dynasty levels.

Professor Robert Pfeiffer was not "equivocal." He expressed himself that not scientific reasons (since he did not know to confront me with an answer to my series of queries), but those of psychological nature are in the way of a scholar who spent his lifetime in studying and writing in accepted pattern in history, to change all concepts. I had a long correspondence with him. At first he thought that the "chronological data which are certain beyond a shadow of doubt" were disregarded by me -- this upon reading the first draft of the first two chapters (July 22. 42) [Date added in pencil.] I enclose a letter that he wrote me five years later, in 1947. At this occasion he signed his letter as head of the department at Harvard; and at a later date he permitted me to publish anything that he wrote in connection with my books. -- On other occasions he also stressed that he would like to have my work studied by his students and discussed in the classes so that the truth should emerge.

When the first week of May this year I was in Zurich I have received from you the very kind invitation to stay with you. With the same mail I have received a letter (re-addressed by you) from Mrs. Robert Pfeiffer, in which she wrote that her husband died. This sad news made me feel very unhappy, because I loved Professor Pfeiffer. The pleasure I had in reading your letter changed to mourning over the passing of a loyal friend: he was one of the best men I ever knew. The feeling of post-operative fatigue deepened that day, and we have [I think this word was crossed out] decided to change our route.

You will notice from the dates of Pfeiffer's letters mentioned here that I was not in hurry to publish my reconstruction. Yet my procrastination places on me the obligation to go through the literature of almost a decade. Together with this, I do not think that older authors were always the wrong ones. Very often a problem was in good relief when first discussed; later authors are already rich in all kinds of explanations that were offered at the sight of similar difficulties through the decades. Puchstein for instance was a very good authority on ancient art -- in his days. He was firm that Yazilikaya basreliefs originated in the 7th century. But he reversed himself when the Boghazkoi texts were read and proved to have been contemporaneous with Ramses II. The recent discoveries also [word added in pencil] coerce to tackle the problem of ghost centuries. I quote from an article by Albright in a volume dedicated to Hetty Goldman (The Aegean and The Near East) (1956?7?). He starts:

"There is a remarkable lacuna in the history of monumental art between the twelfth and eighth centuries B.C. Students of Aegean archaeology have recently been enlarging this gulf by pushing back the end of Bronze-Age Mycenae toward the middle of the twelfth century or even earlier and by lowering the end of the geometric to below the eighth century. Rhys Carpenter, Rodney Young and others have virtually refused to accept a date before the seventh century for any art objects or inscriptions, leaving practically nothing but tomb groups of pottery to bridge the gap. Carpenter holds that the Greek did not borrow their alphabet from the Phoenicians until toward the end of the 8th c. and prefers for Homer a date in the middle decades of the 7th c.

"... The same tendency appears also among students of Anatolian archaeology, where the destruction of the great Hittite Empire by Barbarians toward the end of the 13th century B.C. provides a better historical basis than elsewhere for assuming a prolonged gap in higher culture. Acc. to Ekkrem Akurgal 'in central Anatolia up to now neither Phrygian nor indeed any cultural remains of any people have come to light which might be dated between 1200 and 800 B.C."

Albright also quotes Frankfort who raised the problem of a gap, and also Frankfort's opinion that Ahiram sarcophagus belongs to the 13th c., yet the inscriptions to several centuries later; but the inscriptions say that Itobaal made the coffin for his father.

He refers also to the cultural closeness of the Mycenaean culture in the 13th c.. and the Greek of Homer, and wonders with T. Webster, (*Antiquity* no. 113, 1955, pp. 10ff) "which is all the more striking when we realize that Webster himself attributes the Homeric epics to the 8th century." (Albright refers also to Cyprus, to Cjerstad's and your work there: 'all based mainly on sequence dating and there is no stratigraphic control in Cyprus itself.")

The solution of the problem is in that the Egyptian history has pharaohs known from the Egyptian archaeological [sic] material and other pharaohs known from Greek writing authors (Herodotus and others), and some of the dynasties of the former are but historical originals of the latter. Thousands of problems disappear should the "dark ages" between the Mycenaean and the Greek ages be omitted and the dating of Mycenae should not follow the age of Amenhotep III and IV, but vice versa, and the Greek tyrants of the Argive plain should be returned to the eighth century w[h]ere they were placed by the classical scholars before the Mycenaean ware of Thebes and El-Amarna made the dark or ghost ages necessary. Most of all, the Egyptian history will profit from this.

It was not an "unfortunate idea" of synchronism of the end of the Middle Kingdom and the Exodus. It carried me to the concept of comparative folklore ("Worlds in Collision") and geology and evolution ("Earth in Upheaval") and ancient history ("Ages"); also to a new concept in celestial mechanics. I knew that I will antagonize almost all specialists in their fields. The most important conclusion of my work -- all my theories are interrelated -- was in my interpretation of the causes of the catastrophes and the consequence for celestial mechanics. I became skeptical of the concept of 1666 (*Principia* of Newton) which did not know of electrical and magnetic forces in celestial mechanics. My stand was attacked by every astronomer. For eighteen months I carried long conversations and exchanged many letters with A. Einstein: he too would adamantly oppose the idea of a charged earth and a magnetic sun. Now at the end of the first twelve months of the International Geophysical Year it is made known by the Russians and by the Americans alike, that the sun has a magnetic field more than 8000 times of what it was supposed, and the earth, absolutely neutral, according to scores of articles written by astronomers against "Worlds in Collision", now is proved to have an electrical field of immense potential high above the ground. You have probably read about it in the daily press. I was alone against all specialists. So was also one of the "Three at Troy" whom you brought flowers.

When you have discovered the signs of great catastrophes in archaeological strata all over the ancient East, the next question that should be before you: Where are the historical records of these catastrophes that occurred in the historical past? Then you would search in legends and in historical inscriptions. You would recognize that the biblical record -- Exodus, Numeri, Psalms, Prophets -- all speak of a catastrophe which is the very same that took place at the end of the Middle Kingdom, followed by the invasion of the Hyksos. Then you would stand before a *"histoire comparée"*.

We came to identical results about the catastrophes, their historical times (end of the Old Kingdom, end of the Middle Kingdom, and several more), about their wide spread and their devastating effects. Possibly you are still in isolation on this your find and interpretation; but both of us can feel secure because we worked on different material, not knowing one of the other's work, and came to {this word added in pencil] almost identical results. I hope that the future will bring us closer also in time table. You youself [sic] have written in Stratigraphie Comparée, p. 566:

"La valeur des dates absolue adoptée par nous dépend, bien entendu, pour une part, du degré de précision obtenue dans le domaine des recherches sur les documents historiques utilisables pour la chronologie ...."

As a devoted friend I would like to ask you to reconsider the idea that the migration of the "sea-peoples" in the days of Ramses III was caused by one of the catastrophes; I understood from what you told me in Vitznau that you intend to elaborate on this theme in the second volume of Stratigraphie. As recently was observed, these armies and fleet are not hordes, and certainly not refugees from catastrophic upheavals, but well organized armies and fleet. Pharnambazus the Persian and Ipicrates the Athenian organized and led them. As you see, you need carbon test, to be on a secure ground.

I spoke several weeks ago with Mr. W. Bradbury, Managing Editor of Doubleday and Co. They would be very interested to publish a volume that we have considered but only as a single volume and if I participate in it since in America I have an established circle of readers. This is not what you thought, and as to myself I must first dedicate myself to books that I must write not just can write. Therefore let us wait. Yet I would recommend that you should write a short popular exposé and this will attract attention of the general reader, will be translated, and possibly Doubleday will publish it too. Then the scientific world will be compelled to pay attention to this your idea -- and to [word added in pencil] proofs of it in *Stratigraphie Comparée*.

At the end of this long letter I wish to ask you whether you could be interested to make a try to discover Auaris at el-Arish? The identification is in *"Ages"*, vol. I, pp. 86-89.

I assume that you may still wish to read one or another part of the proofs and therefore I do not yet ask to return them. Later I will need them.

Elisheva's and my good wishes will accompany Mrs. Schaeffer and you on your new expedition. Cyprus, as also the Syrian coast, were crossroads of many cultures; there you have the chance to contemplate at a distance from all conventional views and controversial theories the past of the ancient East as it really took place. Good luck to you!

Very cordially,

[Immanuel Velikovsky]

A Grazian Intervention

Over twenty years went by. The two men tried to cut their Gordian Knot with radiocarbon tests, to no avail. All available tests were inconclusive. They went each his own way, still friends. Neither man surpassed his earlier achievements with new works. Velikovsky had only to perfect and let go of major manuscripts, Schaeffer to return and reinforce his earlier considerations of Cyprus. He still wished to update his survey of destruction sites. It is a wonder that with all of his fame and influence, he could not accomplish the rather simple task.

In March of 1978, I visited Schaeffer, with Anne-Marie Hueber, not yet de Grazia, a French novelist and my companion, at his home at St.-Germain-en-Laye, by Paris. Besides paying our respects, we had in mind to ask Schaeffer if he had been collecting in any kind of order the many excavation reports that had been issued since the publication of his own magnum opus. Would it not be possible, if so, and actually he had done so, to examine them with a mind to discovering within them evidences of disaster? He said that he would be pleased to cooperate. When I returned to the United States, I applied to the National Geographic Society for a grant-in-aid, and was turned down.

In 2004, Anne-Marie and I journeyed to Cyprus, where the Schaeffer archive had ended up. The archive was not in order to make such a search. More elaborate preparations were required. Funding and personnel were needed. The importance of the study grows with time and its fullness. Millions have been spent uncovering ruins, but a few thousands would have given answers in individual cases if not overall concerning the full extent and factors involved in the Iron Age Quantavolution.

Schaeffer had three chances to grow great, all of which he refused.

A) He could have been persuaded that the evidence of the Iron Age of Mars (much of it his own doing) indicated that exoterrestrial forces were operative in the sudden disastrous changes and behaviors of the Late Bronze-Iron Age transition.

B) He could have moved the time of his excavations to the real time instead of sticking to the phony Egyptian timetable that had never, before Velikovsky, been intelligently and acutely criticized.

C) He did not arrange for a simple, methodical, comparative compilation of destructions and survivals of the Iron Age, marking especially the highly suggestive prevalence of ashes and charring in excavations of the period.

Velikovsky's advantage over Schaeffer was that he was raised in a more romantic environment of Judaism, respect for mythology and depth psychology involving psychoanalytic theory. When young he was inspired by Albert Einstein, who was the kind of Jew that Velikovsky wished to be, and he daringly made contact with him, to be resumed many years later. He never persuaded Einstein to change from gravitation to electricity as the greatest universal moving force, but he did win the respect of Einstein and serious consideration for the role of quantavolution in universal, even human history, the importance of sudden immense, transforming events instead of uniformitarianism.

Neither he nor Einstein nor for that matter Schaeffer recognized that a kind of *vox populi* gave Velikovsky a sort of disreputable prestige that yet impressed the great ones. The force of his tiny group of reasonable and reasonably successful academicians who supported his cause counted little compared to his army of uneasy orthodox Jews, 'hard shell' Christians, irascible unorthodox Jews, insane and failed scholars, intellectual guerilas, smart publicists, intellectually venturesome businessmen, and several over-reactive reputable scientists.

In 1980, a *Festschrift für Claude F.A.Schaeffer* was published commemorating his 80th birthday on 6 March 1979. 88 articles were printed, 33 in German, 8 in French, 40 in English, 2 in Italian. None of them dealt with his work on earthquakes nor of his general theory of correspondences among the destructions of the several ages of Bronze. A glancing humorous remark was noted where one writer commented on her having been warned when she was a graduate student to beware of the earthquake fixation in Schaeffer's work. "Archaeologists of my generation, who attended university in the immediate aftermath of Schaeffer's great work (1948), were brought up to view earthquakes, like religion, as an explanation of archaeological phenomena to be avoided if at all possible. Thus it is only recently that the presence of an earthquake at Mycenae has begun to be a serious hypothesis." So begins Elizabeth B. French of the British School at Athens, in her report of a survey at Mycenae. (Significantly, Schaeffer had also mentioned plagues as a frequent accompaniment of seismism. Little was said about plagues either.)

The survey was promising but spoke restrainedly. It seems to have been an earthquake (at least one, we should say). Some, not all, destruction, was from the quake. Great monuments kept their stances: the rampant lions of the gate, the Treasury of Atreus, The Tomb of Aegisthus. I might add that the discovery of skeletons in two places is anomalous. They should have been buried by survivors.

Velikovsky was greatly concerned over the fate of his own archive. There were many problems, but major books were published and many papers were placed on the Web after his demise, practically all of them well-edited by his heirs and assistants. Velikovsky died in 1979, Schaeffer in 1981.

In 2003, I studied the disappearance of Etruscan Volsinium around 600 B.C. and revived my interest in the Iron Age and Mars. I decided to review the whole question of Iron Age events in the Mediterranean Region. I did not move far before hearing the din of battle over the Bible. I could not avoid the struggle. Too many of the events, dates, operations and dates focused upon and spread from Palestine. They always had done so.

Israel Finkelstein

Then I had to confront two major events since the long-ago years when I was reviewing Near East literature. Two new heroes had appeared upon the scene. Both published their book in the 1980's, but after the Quantavolution Series had been published, and neither author had read or would have been convinced by these works at that time. Nor may they be acceptable now. One was, if not alone in his work, creator and leader of a distinguished group of Tel Aviv University archaeologists – Prof. Israel Finkelstein. The other, quite lacking the fame of the others, except locally, was the Lebanese historian and linguist, Kamal Salibi. These two men turned the whole picture around for me, and let me treat the Iron Age of Mars not as a souped-up version of what I had thought twenty-five years ago, but as an amazing turnabout, which would require the reappraisal in part of Velikovsky's theories and of Schaeffer's work as well.

I shall introduce them in only several paragraphs here, for their time on stage will come later.

Finkelstein and company, if I may use *The Bible Unearthed* as their bible, accord mere humdrum origins to the Hebrews, make them nothing better and often lower in culture and conduct than their neighbors in Palestine, and then cut down the stature of Biblical heroes and in some cases annihilate the very personages. Doubt is cast on the historicity of the Exodus, and, if not that, then its size, importance, timing, leadership and crossing of the Red Sea, just to begin with. The Hebrews do show up, practically *deus ex machina*, descending from the Eastern hills and acquiring, as they descended upon their more cultivated Canaanite neighbors, the liberal arts and sciences. With much trouble, David and Solomon may be discovered and possibly Jerusalem, though not the Temple of Solomon.

Although the Jews did not quite manage to kill each other off, they did split into two warring states, Israel in the North and Judah in the South, which were then picked off in due time, the one by the Assyrians and sent into "never-never land," the latter taken away into a scattering of places, primarily Babylon, into the so-called Babylonian Captivity, from which they were released by Cyrus, King of Persia and new ruler of Babylon, to go home, if they could find the place. Some, then, a hard core, turned to Judah. These had a vision most pleasing to their King, and could therefore impose locally a dramatic performance that could be entitled: "The Bible as Played by Certain Recently Returned Jews of Babylon, with Audience Participation Demanded under Pain of Stoning."

Backed up in vassalage to the Persian Empire, the Act took firm grip on this small people, who kept tenaciously their land and belief-system, making it, if anything, more exclusive than called for by the playwrights, such that, after hundreds of years, they could not even be seduced or commanded by Rome, and rebelled and were dispersed and, finding Jews everywhere already, they enhanced the Diaspora, until 2000 years later they formed another exclusive club, centered in Palestine, armed with nuclear missiles, and named it the State of Israel.

There is an important reductive history in Finkelstein's view, but we shall not let his circle escape without admitting to the possibility that a massive natural destruction, maybe even Yahweh-Mars, accounts for the dismaying dearth of evidence of anything having happened in Palestine corresponding to the Bible stories. Many an ancient civilized center around the world has disappeared and cannot be ever found or certainly is difficult to find.

But there is also, admittedly, the Hollywood Factor, that peaked with Cecil B. de Mille's *Ten Commandments.* There is an unfortunate tendency of people (archaeologists not excepted) to create Hollywood settings in their minds and in their descriptions of history, especially with respect to sacral happenings. A few happily chosen words attributed to a gay young King Solomon can be exponentialized into an extravaganza of the 'most wise, most just, most resplendent monarch.' So grand a personage, then, must be surrounded by the most fantastic temples, palaces, stables, menageries, potters, wives and women, and visiting Queens of Empire.

Velikovsky certainly expresses the Hollywood View, the Judaeo-Christian celestialism, the grand romantic vision of what had been, richer tenfold than King Arthur's Court or Kubla Khan's.

Kamal Salibi Enters the Lists

However, neither Finkelstein, champion of denigration, nor Velikovsky, with his planetary catastrophism doing the work of Yahweh, is let to rest on his laurels. Finkelstein has an institution and a liberal following, no match for the believers in Moses and Machiavelli who rule the State of Israel and Jewish power centers abroad. Yet the end of reductionism of the Bible as True Religious Programming was to be imposed from an unexpected quarter, Lebanon, and from a Congregationalist Professor of History in an American - funded University. The book was called *The Bible Came from Arabia* and meant most of what it says. Kamal Salibi has suffered from the Biblical and Scientific Establishment worse than Velikovsky: Velikovsky got off the ground before being peppered with bullets; Salibi could barely take off. Undeterred, he went on to publish in 1998 *The Historicity of Biblical Israel: Studies in 1 and 2 Samuel.*

His theory is that the Hebrews and all major components of later-day Palestine originated South of Mecca in Arabia in what is today the province of Asir and the region around. Using the powerful tool of toponymics, he placed the historical events of the Bible, wherever they referred to a place, as hundreds did, convincingly in Western Arabia. (Toponymics, incidentally, is part of onomastics, which is the study of the origins and forms of words, especially of proper names and places, and of the etymology of words in general.) "Can a dozen lexicons out-manage a hundred spades?" we ask ourselves.

Salibi appears as a modest man, like many daring explorers – not everyone being so ego-evident as Velikovsky – and asserts often that he cannot use archaeology because there has been none in the region to speak of. But he adds the important skills of a linguist and life-long student of Semitic language. He analyzes reasonably the rationale of Biblical Authorities on scores of occasions. Frequently he has to let them appear puerile and foolish. He appears convincing on the movements of the peoples North into Palestine. And, I may add, he shows no signs of having considered what the Velikovsky scenario may have done to help him get along – by shortening Egyptian time, by precipitating the catastrophic factor, by the introduction of the gods as real-time 'actors.' With regard to Finkelstein's plot, one can say that Salibi transfers its origins and history of the Hebrews and Bible to a new-old location, Western Arabia.

As I proceed, in addition to my other duties, I shall be synthesizing all four of these great scholars, Velikovsky, Schaeffer, Finkelstein and Salibi. Egyptian chronology will come down, first by 400, then by another 400 years, connecting with the Hebrews and all of Palestine and the Near East, in fact. I shall correct my Moses itinerary of yore to bring him down to Mecca and points south, instead of up into Palestine via Sinai. I shall process the several major ethnic and religious groups of Western Arabia, such as the Arameans, Phoenicians, Philistines, Canaanites, and Hebrews, into Palestine. I shall endeavor, also, to show the beginnings of the collection and writing of Bible materials in Arabia and then transfer the operation to Judah in Palestine for completion by the organization of the hard core of Jews returned from Babylon. The ambuscades of Mars will drive forward the peoples, hammering at their minds and behavior.

Chapter Six

Ruination of Trade, Lands, and Peoples

The Dartmouth College Classics Department, in a memorandum to its students, advised: "Any attempt to reconstruct the course of events on the Mycenean Greek Mainland in the 13th and 12th centuries B.C. and to determine therefrom the probable causes of the destruction of the Mycenean palaces and the collapse of the highly centralized political and economic system based upon them must rely on a sound and detailed chronology." Immediately the memo makes clear that no such chronology exists. It goes even further to say that "Although slow progress is being made, it will be a long time yet before the numerous local catastrophes of the two centuries between ca. 1250 and ca. 1050 B.C. [our ~-850 to ~-650] 0can be placed with some confidence into the order in which they occurred."

And then, "Aside from problems with dating, there is in addition the problem caused by the constant proliferation of theories which purport to explain the Mycenean collapse." For 'Mycenean' they might as well say the 'Greater Mediterranean Region.' (See the maps, 00 of the Mediterranean Sea proper and 01 of the Near East and Africa extended to be included in our study.)

Our answers to both problems are spelled out in this book: "Turn up your clocks from (~-1250 to ~ -1050) to (~- 850 to ~-650), eliminating the in-between years as a Phantom Age, and your data will jump into place in most cases ." If this is not done, indeed progress will be "slow" and take "a long time."

In respect to your second problem, the proliferation of theories can be reduced drastically if you postulate the Q Paradigm: An exoterrestrially originating event-series caused sudden great regional changes in every sphere of natural and human existence. All of your now-dissociated phenomena will take their place in the order of events. They will therefore and then become understandable.

Professor James D. Muhly of the American School of Classical Studies declared several years ago, "The concept of a 'Dark Age' (or 'Ages') in Greek prehistory is still very much with us." He cites a number of major works, paying no attention to the few objecting works authored by quantavolutionists during the past generation. He adds other areas, viz., Boardman (1999) writing, "To pretend that only the Greeks had a Dark Age does little justice to the almost impenetrable gloom that surrounds the archaeology of Canaanite/Phoenician cities in the same years.."

And then Tandy: The collapse may not have been as rapid as once thought ... but its precipitousness is still certain, and by 1050 (ca ~-650) the Aegean world had hit rock bottom." Not only settlements but also virtually all temples were ruined. (We, of course, have extended the ruination of the palace cultures of the Myceneans to all peoples and cultures everywhere.)

Prof. Dever writes (p.101) : "The Bronze Age does not end in a single sudden cataclysm around 1200 B.C., as conventional portraits sometimes suggest, but rather in a series of gradual, often sudden changes, over a century or more between ca 1350 and 1250." The dating of excavation findings being what it is, one may offer the alternative hypothesis, that the disasters came, not all at once, but probably at intervals of a few, say 15 years, coinciding with the orbital motion and proximate location of planet Mars. Patten, Velikovsky, Ackerman and others have essayed this patterning mode. Most likely the same picture will present itself throughout the Mediterranean Region. Typically through the literature we find statements such as, "Tacanach is another Jezreel Valley site where the late Bronze occupation continues until the mid-twelfth century B.C., when there is finally a destruction.." Or, "when there is a final destruction."

We reiterate that the ruination signified a holistic quantavolution. We read an article by William D. Hallo. He finds great changes in literature, writing, art, with the emergence of empires in place of city-states and kingdoms. The cities are ruined, their patron deities exiled. The Iron

Age, he says, was more highly urbanized, its agricultural base much attenuated. Collecting tribute seems to have replaced a multi-faceted economy and commodity exchange system. It appears that a production economy was replaced by a predator economy.

I might quote at length the syllabus that is offered at Dartmouth College to its students of the course on Prehistoric Archaeology of the Aegean. It offers no alternatives, but it gives what we would regard as the best possible face to the modern cracked mirror of the times. Hallo dismisses the skies as a cause of change: "..notions of celestial interference in human history are too redolent of diasterism to occupy us here."

We note that the skies might as well not exist for all that they are scanned for catastrophic agencies. Authors of the Dartmouth course then take up, for instance, architecture, and describe water system failures, fires in the high citadels, abandonment, a refugee problem, hilltop settlements, possible tsunamis, and a general unrecoverable decline in culture. They have extended the period to a century and a half, thanks to recent excavations, or to about the same length of time that we are assigning to the Martian Age time of high catastrophe, the Apex of the Martian Quantavolution.

No City or Village Left Standing

Archaeologists who attempt a census of settlements in some sector of the Iron Age are commonly bewildered. Some try to ignore the problem of the innumerable destructions. Others point up some, but not all that they have come across. A few are flabbergasted by the great extent of the destruction. The list of ruined habitations and countrysides grows year by year. Whenever a new site of the period is uncovered, it may be expected to have been abandoned or destroyed.

Spanuth has summarized the extent of the destructions; he can be cited here. Others will be quoted as the occasion occurs. Spanuth also brings in German sources not well known in Anglophone countries. Wiesner in 1943 is saying that "from Troy VII to Palestine a chain of devastation can be traced." Schachermeyr in 1944 is writing of "A catastrophe which was one of the worst in world history," p.78. Lesky in 1947 wrote, "The results of these [catastrophes] make them some of the most frightful in the history of the world." (p.2)

An inscription from Ugarit reads: "The star Anat (Mars) has fallen from Heaven; he slew the people from the Syrian land."[40] Descriptions from the excavations of Assur and Hattusa state clearly that the totality of ruins were melted, merged, exploded. A human agency committing such destruction was unimaginable. Vitrification was common. All of priori-Palestine was burned to the ground before the arrival of the Philistines.

Desborough's work of 1964 and 1972 could produce a table for Greece. Messene and Triphylia give 150 known settlements for the 13th (our 9th century), 14 for known settlements of the 12th (our 8th); Laconia from 30 to 7; Argolis and Corinth north of the Isthmus 44 to 14; Boeotia 27 to 3; Pocis 19 to 3; Attica 24 to 12. What is more, many, perhaps all, of the existing settlements of the 8th century had been destroyed once or more times, and then partially rebuilt. Furthermore, since 1972 many more destruction levels and sites have been discovered.

The hypothesis for the Iron Age Apex might then well be "Not a village was left standing." Weirdly, the ratio of destroyed settlements could be applied to original populations and survivors, perhaps 20 to 1. Every organized group descended into chaos. Gods were shuffled like decks of cards. It was all tied into iron, too, somehow. Hesiod and the whole of learned and popular opinion agreed that the Iron Age that succeeded the Bronze was Hobbesian, a war of all against all when (and they meant usually 'now') life was brutish, nasty and short. No one predicted an end to it.

The Iron Age did not become in anyone's mind and voice precedent to an Age of Sweet Light, or Illumination, not in the Mediterranean Region at least until, as we shall see, some philosophers contended for men's minds, from Thales to Seneca, and far away in China the gods disappeared in favor of the ancestors, and in India the Buddhists came forward with a creed of endurance, sufferance, and reincarnation. The monotheistic Aten of

Akhnaton might be an early brief exception, perhaps too the monotheism of Zoroaster, but certainly not Yahweh, the warlike and vengeful God of the Jews. He was typically an Iron Age deity, until a few of his worshipers found a way out in a now-denominated New Testament. Glory be where good is done.

The Revised Chronology brings many found and surmised destructions into the same pattern and the same time and probably in the same event. But still the Martian Q appears to have been discontinuous, over a century or more, not all at once.

Ashes, Flames and Fires

The study of ashes in archaeology is critical yet backward. The profession, which is so handicapped by the stringency of its evidence – sherds, patterns of settlement and architecture, the comparison of successive layerings, and a few other primitive and tiresome procedures, has nevertheless not been led to the finer techniques in such matters as the analysis of ashes, or calcinology, as I once named it when I was researching the ruination of Troy, as described in Chapter 16 below. An exception, but not maximally used by any means, has to do with the detection of different chemistries of differing volcanic ash deposits.

Ashes are found in a great many excavations. They may come from hearth fires in an abandoned house-ruin or from as far away as a thousand kilometers from the site. They might even be exo-terrestrial in origin. If meteorites can fall from Mars, as most of them do these days, so can dust and ashes. Galileo's proof, bowdlerized as: a feather and a cannonball fall at the same speed in a vacuum, should apply to objects in space if they are small enough and de-electrified.

Such probabilities remain to be proven beyond doubt; they are more commonly accepted these days than not. The Tunguska bolide of 1907 provided combustion products from the sky that mixed with ash from the burnt areas of the taiga. When found in archaeological investigations no difference is sensed and ashes of any kind become the source of a cliché such as "a fire destroyed the settlement." As if to say, "so much for that."

Evidence of fire is almost always, too, assigned to enemy conquerors or to earthquakes. Earthquakes can, it is true, if grave, and supplied with methane or other super-combustibles, bring a fire that will destroy a town. The oceanographers Dimitrov, *père et fils*, explorers of the murky bottom of the Black Sea mention such a fire in their book, *The Black Sea (2004)*.

> What actually happened during the earthquake on the 11th of September 1927, known also as the Crimean earthquake? The earthquake was with magnitude of about 8 to 9 on Richter Scale. "A blaze of fire in the sea before Evpatoria was noticed at 2.48 P.M. Later, at 3.31 P.M. a fire wall – 500 m high and 1.5 miles wide was observed before Sevastopol. A similar phenomenon was seen from the Lukula observation post. The first tremor occurred on the 11th Sof September, 1927, at 10.15 P.M. "

A prominent Russian geologist, S.I. Popov, witnessed the event. He concluded, "It was an explosion of methane, thrown from fractures to [sic, at?] the bottom when [sic, from?] underwater mud volcanoes at the time of the earthquake." The authors, disposing of other explanations, point out that it is known now that numerous mud volcanoes emitting several gases sit on the bottom of the Black Sea. They scoff at popular rumors that the Black Sea might explode one day.

Imagine this happening throughout the Greater Mediterranean Region in order to appreciate the meaning of a full quantavolution. The bogs of the high Eastern Alps caught fire. The Black Forest incinerated. One scientists, K. Muller of the University of Freiburg, writes that a deliberate firing was impossible, nor could lightning [as we know it] burn a giant mountain forest, but the region was hardly inhabited.[41]

That flaming or igniting clouds of methane could fall from space or the upper atmosphere under the conditions of the Mars events remains a distinct possibility. I allude to the matter again in the chapter to come on Volsinium.

As for conquerors, the burning of a town is a tedious and even arduous job, hardly what the victors wish to be put up with. Looting, yes, killing, yes, letting a fire burn itself out, sometimes, if valuables are not threatened. Mainly a fire would be set to assure that the scattered population would not have a home to return to and renew their threat, or that no other potential enemy would profit by its occupancy. (This may have been the main reason for the heavy fire-bombing of Dresden, Germany, by 800 planes of the Western Allies, two days after the boundaries of the zones of occupation of Germany were affirmed by the heads of state meeting at Yalta on February 4-11, 1945; Dresden was to be occupied by the Soviet Union.) Or for the mad joy of watching a large fire.

Olive oil was worthwhile preserving and transporting or selling on the spot. Wood, cut and shaped, had its considerable value, too. Grain and seed, favorites for carbon-dating, would also have value, and would usually be ignited accidentally. Sheer malevolence, even at cost to oneself, has to be sometimes the case. Napoleon I burned Moscow in 1812, to little effect. The British burned Washington, D.C., a little later. Both had practical effect of modest value to the invaders.

The biggest and most effective fires are set by nature, as a forest or grass fire moves into a town, or, and we have had small experience of this in recent times, a ruinous lightning shower can burn down a town, and from what we are developing in the way of a catastrophic scenario in these pages, it seems more likely than any means suggested so far, that some phenomenon that we know little about in these non-quantavolutionary times – megalightning storms from the far atmosphere and outer space, and profuse fall-outs of flammable gases – would have caused most of the ash and fire levels encountered by the excavators of sites in the Martian period of which we speak. I have reported in some detail the situation worldwide in regard to natural fire, in *The Lately Tortured Earth*.

There is a strong implication of planetary intrusion in many fires on Earth. Over a century ago, Donnelly conjectured that the City of Chicago and the Pestigo area forests, both of which suffered great damage from fires of mysterious origin and ferocity, were ignited thanks to gaseous (I would surmise electrified) filaments drifting down from Comet Biela that was passing near to Earth. The latest news about comets (September 2005) comes from the deliberate impacting of Comet Tempel I by an instrumented projectile (NASA mission Deep Impact). The five-mile-long comet turned out to be 75% empty space and to have "the strength of lemon meringue."[42] Ice, silicates, clay carbonates, olivine, iron-bearing compounds and aromatic hydrocarbons were noted in the exploded debris, gases, and dust. Forthcoming information may reveal more instant and explosive flammables, such as methane. Since Tempel I does not orbit in far space, as does Halley's Comet, for instance, the chances of detecting important differences in electric potentials are small.

Practically all natural science writers of antiquity believed in the historicity of flames shooting down from heaven, as megalightning or accompanying bolides and gases. Hebrew uses for the word thunderbolt *la-haziz qulot*, for the lightning of the voices, *qol* or 'voice' being a common word for thunder. Thus thunder must be heard to speak and needs to be understood. Etruscans held similar views.

The archaeological study of Eastern and Central Europe has lagged behind the study of the Mediterranean region. Recently, a Bulgarian gold hoard the size of and rather similar to the famous gold hoard that Schliemann located at "Troy-Hisarlik" was exposed, its date estimated at somewhat earlier than Schliemann's "Burnt City." But the Martian Quantavolution is to be readily discovered there too. Typically in the niches and interstices of conventional geophysical and anthropological studies, one finds quantavolution support.

The History of Peat Deposits

Thus, adverting to the subject of peat, which has long been found in situations divulging catastrophic effects as in Germany, we can go to carefully done articles on peat in the Balkans, in Greece for example, where the University of Patras geology group has been active.

Typically in the niches and interstices of conventional geophysical and anthropological studies, one finds quantavolution support. The fens of Philippi are one major instance of this. On this scene of the Battle between the Roman armies of Brutus and Cassius on the one side and the army of Octavian and Mark Anthony on the other side, following the assassination of Julius Caesar, there exists a fen, carrying perhaps the largest deposit of peat in the world, as large as the island of Elba and up to 200 meters deep. Drilling down to some 15 meters into the peat uncovered three different levels of volcanic tephra, the first two dated at around 13,000 y by C14, and possibly of the same set of events sourced from Thera-Santorini tephra (ca 1300 BPE) with a third 23Ky tephra that held the various signatures of the Italian volcanoes of the Vesuvius so-called Phlegean volcanic region. See *Fig. 5*.

The authors, in concluding their article, write:

> The B3300 yr "Minoan" or Z-2 tephra of Thera has been reported on-land from Kos (Keller,1981), Rhodes (Doumas and Papazoglou,1980),Crete (Warren and Puchelt,1990) and from the Nile delta (Stanley and Sheng,1986). It is also known from numerous studies of cores of deep-sea sediments in the Eastern Mediterranean Sea (summarized in Eastwood et al.,1999). From early deep-sea sediment core work, a south-easterly dispersal axis was initially suggested by Ninkovich and Heezen (1965). Recent discoveries from terrestrial records implied an easterly dispersal (Sullivan,1988, 1990; Pyle,1990), but the presence of Minoan tephra sediments of the Black Sea (Guichard et al.,1993)suggests a dispersal axis for the Minoan tephra fallout toward a northeasterly direction. Previous research on the Cape Riva and Minoan eruptions of Santorini suggests that tephra from Hellenic Arc volcanic centers had the potential to reach locations as far away as Philippi. Tephra unit PhT1 is most likely the product of a hitherto unknown Theran eruption and future research should focus on ascertaining a complete inventory of the tephra deposits on Santorini.[43]

The absence of Thera ashes or tephra for some "13,000 years" bespeaks one of three possibilities to this writer's mind. First, the radiocarbon dating, though conscientiously and repeatedly performed, was quite off the mark of 3400 years ago or so, by ten thousand years!

Second, the ashes and tephra had been there, as they were everywhere else – in the Black Sea Region, the Levant, Rhodes, Crete, Egypt and the islands all around the Aegean – but they were washed away by a tsunami of the time or of a later date, such as during one of the Mars incursions. Notably, Philippi is only a few kilometers from the sea and several types of land fill that separate it from the sea on other sides are composed of quite recent stone, possibly filled in later.

The whole setting is fascinating. The dates of the deposits of peat, and below it lignite, (a harder form of the same and a forerunner of coal) could be merely deceptive. Catastrophe could have laid down great volumes of water-soaked vegetation in one or a set of closely related incidents. Velikovsky was the first to my knowledge whose theory of peat formation and coalification explained helpfully the previously most perplexing problem of sourcing of these fossil fuels.

In the third place, a cyclone or hurricane or meteoroid blast of 300 kph would have stripped the tephra and some peat layers off the surface. We note that all three explanations could be tied together and explain the geological configuration. That is, a complex convulsion could have knocked out the radiocarbon clock in the atmosphere, picked up and washed into the shore vast quantities of vegetative and animal material, clays and sand, providing an instant bog, and clipped off any cap of tephra from the Thera explosion.

A kindred team explored the fen of Keri, Greece, and Kimon Christianis, Geology Professor at the University of Patras, Greece described their work in a conference on quantavolution at the University of Bergamo, Italy. Herodotus, writing 2500 years ago, tells of a fen deep in peat and bubbling usable asphalt from springs below the fen. ...I myself saw pitch drawn from the water of a pool in Zakynthos." There were many pools affording the pitch. "Whatever thing falls into the pool is carried under ground and appears again in the sea, which is about four furlongs distant from the pool..." The springs are still gushing asphalt.

The Keri Peat Fen gives a date of about 2700 BCE, a Martian date. Examination of the layering of peat shows thousands of years of accumulation at slow rates . Prof. Christianis writes this author, "Ash-rich peat , as well as inorganic layers intercalating with peat are very common in the fens. This inorganic material is washed-out from the surrounding rocks and is fluxed into the fen. Which is the topographically lowest part in a sedimentary basin." *(Letter of 23 Feb 2005)*

He adds that to his knowledge, concerning the hundreds of excavations of which he knows, no analyses have been made of any ashes found, seeking, for instance, fullerenes containing so-termed 'noble gasses.'

Although the Keri peat is determined to go back several thousand years, there is no indication in it of Thera tephra. This would confirm that either the peat is less than 3400 years old or that its top layers have been washed or blown away.

The cases of Philippi and Keri may be instructive vis-a-vis the ice-core exponents who claim that examination of the cores of Greenland and Antarctica disprove the occurrence of catastrophes in the Holocene period. The opponents of the Q paradigm, who often use these ice cores, said to go back even 100,000 years, argue that no evidence of catastrophes exists at the times when they were supposed to occur, such as -1450 and -800. The fens of Philippi seem to offer an explanation, the same that has been offered by me elsewhere in the case of ice core dating but independently so. They show that for the past 15K yrs or so there has been no sign of the gigantic volcanic ash explosions of Thera and the Venusian and Martian period events. Climate does not affect directly the peat deposits, so one must posit that the peat that corresponded to the years of the catastrophes was blown or washed away as part of the catastrophes or later.

When it came my time to take up an interest in quantavolutions, I read in Schaeffer of the beds of ashes at Hisarlik-Troy and analyzed them as best I could, publishing the results of my study, which, if it neither proved or disproved the location of the Trojan War, provided a modicum of enlightenment to a field that I named calcinology, or the study of beds of ashes, with special reference to ancient cultures in my case. As happened with Schaeffer, my interest was not decried; it was simply ignored, and the science of calcinology in archaeology has hardly developed from that date.

The excavations at Troy-Hisarlik revealed the findings common to Iron Age destruction sites, and in a later chapter here will be quoted at length; the culture there moves directly from Bronze Age Mycenean cultures into the

Troy of the Iron Age.

The Number and Extent of Mars Visitations

Writers differ as to the number of visitations by the planet Mars troubled the Earth, Ackerman following the Vedas with over one hundred, Patten the Bible with several, Velikovsky with three. Whom shall we support? Basically we need two or more for our theory here. Isaiah the Prophet exclaims that the Messenger of God, by which he must mean Gabriel, by which is meant planet Mars, will visit at 15-year intervals.

Why do we welcome evidence of two approaches? We do so because we are of the opinion that not all of the destroyed centers of the period were ruined at the same time; so, repeated collisions of energies are required. If Mars were in close and eccentric orbit, then we might envision several or more close encounters. If archaeology were in a position around the world to give us a more or less correct chronology of the first millennium BCE, we would be able to conclude how many approaches actually occurred.

This is not an impossible expectation. That is, I do not expect this to be the last pertinent book and the final defense of the thesis that planet Mars damaged planet Earth. For instance, it may soon be possible to add a list of Black Sea destructions. Kondratov mentions that Bulgarian researchers have discovered and mapped many sunken settlements along the Black Sea Coast, which happened, according to their calculations, in the Eighth to Fifth Centuries BCE. The Western Mediterranean region has not seen the number of Iron Age excavations witnessed in the East and Mideast. There, a number of major geological transformations may have occurred in connection with the Mars quantavolution.

The principal question would deal with the creation of the Sahara Desert, enquiring whether its 'Triton Sea,' which is a complex of seas stretching from the Atlantic Ocean to the Red Sea, where we have many neolithic and possibly later evidences of human occupation, could have become desiccated in a sudden shift of geological strata or Earth tilt that poured its waters into the Mediterranean and

Black Seas and Atlantic Ocean.

Rhyss Carpenter is a specialized quantavolutionist, one might say, inasmuch as he relies upon climate change, followed by drought, famine and plague to do the job of the Martian Iron Age catastrophes. Sometime before ~-1200 [our ~-800], "a northward shift of the Saharan drought zone into southern Europe occurred, with the resulting famine causing the abandonment of large areas..." The out-pouring of these huge offshoots of the ancient Tethyan Sea would have the same effects as moving the desert dryness northward -- desiccation, drought, famine.

Expert Explanations of the Destructions

Let us turn now to several explanations offered by specialists in the area for the widespread destructions.

For instance Professor James Weinstein, pondering the causes of the Egyptian imperial collapse, says that "its demise was not a gradual process which transpired over the course of 25-50 years, but a fairly quick and decisive event." He believes that while the Empire was in a parlous state at home, military conflict in western Asia was the direct cause of the collapse there. The Sea Peoples, he says, take part of the responsibility but so, too, other inland parties. Moreover, says he, the Egyptians in retreat may have destroyed some of their own garrison towns and settlements. In one case, many valuables were left behind; in another case extensive looting occurred. Mutinies of the Egyptian armed forces should not be discounted. By far, the greatest part of this explanation is cut out of whole cloth.

Professor L.H. Lesko discounts Ramses III as a plagiarizer of the mortuary temple of Pharaoh Merneptah (-1213 to -1203, but sixth century in Velikovsky's plausible revision), because of numerous peculiarities of the Medinet Habu Temple, and the Papyrus Harris account of the boasts of Ramses III. (That is, it is not enough to say that Ramses III boasted grandly, because he talked of impossible and unknown events!)

Other bizarre facts cast doubt upon the Ramses III pretensions, so solidly entrenched. The conventional time given him is -1182 to -1151. His temple of Medinet Habu would fall in this period. So would Khonsu. Medinet Habu is in surprisingly good condition, suspiciously, almost impossibly so had it been so old and considering the destructions wrought by nature, the Assyrian invaders and Persian conquerors. Incongruously, the temples of Philae (5th century B.C.) (Denderah (~-115 to ?), Edfu (third century B.C., and Kom Ombo (~-15o to ~217), bear strong similarities to Medinet Habu with respect to their pylon-portal entrances and a number of textual inscriptions. Medinet Habu might conceivably have been in bad shape and throughly reconstructed according to fourth century models, with the original inscriptions poorly copied. A renowned original excavator, the architect of the Breasted Oriental Institute expedition, raised this possibility. I do not offer this explanation except in desperation on behalf of the 150 years of scholars who have lived by the date.

There may be no end to Ramses III contradictions. A cartouche of his at Medinet Habu is carved and set in front of the seated monarch, who is of heroic size. But it resembles in concept and a dozen details a large carving in relief of Persian King Darius (-521 to -485). The cartouche is of inferior workmanship. Obviously it is impossibly late according to the consensus; it should have been done centuries before the Darius creation.

To summarize the various theories offered for the near simultaneous destruction of so many sites in the Mediterranean region in the early Iron age, we would put forward the following, all of which except the astrophysical have been offered by scientists in the field:

1. Exhaustion of natural resources over the whole region. The cutting and burning of forests, the wasting of the soil, the taking away of crops and livestock in endless wars among the states.

2. Change of climate from desiccation and cooling or warming. This would be the Carpenter thesis that we have reported earlier in these pages.

3. Destructive levies of tribute and spoils upon conquered foes. An example would be the vaunted expeditions of

Thutmoses III in Late Bronze that destroyed and despoiled the Near East and Western Arabia. Velikovsky went to great lengths to identify the hundreds of items pictured on the Pharaoh's walls as properties of the sacked Temple of Solomon in Jerusalem (Jeroboam, son of Solomon being the vanquished ruler then). Considering the downgrading of the magnificence of Solomon and his Temple on the part of one school of Biblical archaeology, one must say that in spite of everything these archaeologists are wrong, or having viewed the walls of Thutmoses III, the Seventh Century Biblical creation editors in Judah sent a team of draftsmen to copy and list the objects on the walls in order to beef up the Bible image of the reign of Solomon. One is left with the impression that Jerusalem was stripped bare.

It is still possible that a ruined Jerusalem sits far deeper down in debris than ever suspected. Or, too, that this settlement, whether or not it was called Jerusalem, could be 'New Jerusalem, and was far distant from the original Jerusalem, identified by Salibi as sitting in Western Arabia, although this, too, has no surface indications of magnificence or even of a flourishing town. But, then, there has no excavating here nor available aerial survey. Moreover, Salibi brilliantly theorizes that Jerusalem was actually a village-cluster occupying considerable space.

4. Over-taxation. This actually would have little effect except sometimes to depress an economy. That overtaxation would occur throughout the great Mediterranean Region is quite unlikely.

International Trade Within the Ambit of Amber

5. Cessation of international commerce. To quote Muhly, "In the course of the Late Bronze Age.. Palatial administrations dominated the world of the Eastern Mediterranean and the Near East. Centered at sites such as Mycenae, Tiryns, Pylos and Thebes, at Knossos, Aiya Triadha, . And Hania, at Boghazköy, Masad Hoyuk, and Alaca Hoyuk, at Ugarit and Emar, Megiddo and Hazor, these administrations worked together to create a system of intellectual and commercial exchange unlike anything that

had ever existed before." The system and all that depended upon it died out. No one has come up with an acceptable theory.

The cessation of trade and commerce may be covering up all too well in other regards the Greater Mediterranean Region that preceded it. An important thesis of our work will deal with the transference of Hebrew and Bible history in great part from Palestine to Western Arabia. One reason for doubting this geocultural switch is the blank in our minds concerning the richness of trade routes and products of the Southern part of the Region. We lack, unfortunately, the world trade volumes of statistics of today. But, it is fairly certain that the southern routes through Arabia and up the Red Sea and Persian Gulf were carrying more valuable products than the north, in greater variety, abundance, and intrinsic value. The high value and commercial consequences of the amber trade coming from the North is matched several times over by the valuable objects of commerce from the South, and this is to be suggested when imagining the busy state of Western and Southwestern Arabia economy in the Late Bronze Age.

In the far North of Europe, a clear and significant disaster overcame the trade in amber. Amber was found close to the sea, under the sea, on the beaches. It was found in drops or chunks. It was close to gold in value. Amber had many uses; it was not only a jewel, but a chemical, a medicament, a perfume and fumigator, a sculptural material, and so on. It was used to decorate temples. It was magnetic (amber means "the saffron that attracts"). It softens and melts easily. It came from a singular region where there had to have been a catastrophic drowning of pine forests. "A cuneiform inscription from Assur, now in the British Museum, mentions caravans that were sent from 'the island of Kaptara, where the pole star stands at the zenith, and amber... is fished out of the sea." Spanuth covers the story briefly but well.

There are three great routes of the Amber trade. See *Fig. 7*. It is important to note that the two routes of the West were ended in a quantavolution, probably not the Martian, but the preceding Venusian. The third route halted and then picked up again in the later Iron Age and Roman times. The amber of the first two routes simply disappeared beneath the wave as the land of the northwest seas submerged.

"For this precious material, the object of a trade network which reached as far as Egypt, vanished suddenly and totally from the market after 1200 B.C.E. (~ -850) and was not known again for centuries."[44]

Three authorities will suffice: "This lively north-south trade continues all through the northern Bronze Age, only to break off suddenly" (Behn, 1948, 161). "..the article in the Pauly-Wissowas *Realenzyklopädie* (1899) spoke of a 'centuries-long stoppage in the amber supply' to the Mediterranean lands. The Hungarian archaeologist Pál Patay said of the time between 1200 and 500 BC: 'Even the economically very important amber trade from the North Sea through the western part of Hungary to Greece was then interrupted'". One writer thought that the migrating Celts had cut the amber routes, which, together with a climatic crisis "explains the impoverishment of the Germanic peoples at the time of the transition to the Iron Age culture."(S. Guttenbrunner, 1939, 31)

No one would connect the words *orichalcon, (mountain droppings of heaven), electron,* and *amber* altogether properly. The Old German word *'glass'* meant amber, too, and old traditions of the region talk of the city, mountain, towers, etc. of amber that were sunk. That the Heliades sisters wept amber tears for their dead brother, Phaeton, who was zapped by Jupiter, was suggestive, of course. That insects were found in drops of amber was also suggestive: instant fossilization under catastrophic conditions. Vast sunken pine forests manufactured the amber. As I explain in *Chaos and Creation,* (1981, 72-3), geologists must be many millions of years too old on this phenomenon. Phaeton, who can be placed well within the memory of man, possibly ~-1500, possibly ~-850, as a major Marut, exploded around the North Sea-Danish-Heligoland region and flooded a vast area, with permanent changes in land levels, and by terrifically destructive tsunamis.

The impact crater, even though, *à la* Tunguska, there need not have been one, has not been pronounced as having been found. However, a candidate, in my opinion, suddenly appeared in the course of petroleum seismic soundings in the North Sea during 2002, when, between central Britain and Denmark, a sizeable crater was discovered with concentric rings (unusually well-defined for a sea-impacted bolide). It is called Silverpit Crater. The crater is 2.4 km across and with the usual assumptions the impactor may have had a 120 meter diameter, about half the estimation of the bolide of Tunguska. (Stewart SA, Allen PJ (2002). A 20-km-diameter multi-ringed impact structure in the North Sea. *Nature 418 (6897): 520-3, PMID 12152076,* and see, more generally, *Wikipedia Encyclopedia* on the Internet. The bolide may have been, on the other hand, a comet, with somewhat different configuration.

As part of his argument on behalf of finding in this region the location of Atlantis, Spanuth mentions conscientiously two facts about the Atlantis account of Plato: Earthquake is not given as a cause, but merely it is said, "the island of Atlantis was similarly swallowed up by the sea and vanished," and he also adds that the North Atlantic is not an earthquake zone. In my several books I advance the theory that the Atlantic Ocean Basin was fissured in human times, and then expanded and on more than one occasion provided with gigantic infusions of water. I implicated the planets Uranus and Saturn in the creation of the oceanic basins in great part, and Saturn especially in the Deluge of Noah, so-called, around -4000. The drowning of the northern lands and the formation of amber might have happened then, and the amber dug up or collected in the Bronze Age, and afterwards from Baltic Sea sources in the Iron Age. This theory, however, does not preclude the superimposing of the Bronze-Iron Age theory of Spanuth (except that for his date of ~-1200, as usual I substitute my preferred date of ~-850.

6. Decline of technology. The destruction of trade and commerce meant the cessation of production in most instances and the substitution therefor, if at all, of local primitively-constructed devices and concoctions. The advent of iron was for a time an unrealized potential, even a tabu element, taking the place of bronze and wooden implements, not moving into many new designs and inventions.

7. Breakup of the Egyptian Empire left a power vacuum and invited mutual warfare of small states.

8. Collapse of 'top-heavy' centralization in the palaces and elsewhere. The state organization broke down. But this is taken two ways. In one view, a bureaucracy simply wound down the energies of the country, discouraged initiatives, inflicted too many laws and penalties, and otherwise ran the gamut of faults of which today people accuse the agencies of state. In another view, this orderly administration was somehow broken down and when such happened, production and commerce followed suit. Also related is the theory of "diminishing margin returns::" As a society invests in ever more complex operations, the costs increase beyond the increased profitability.

9. Peoples of the Sea (a term that should be replaced by "vagrant peoples") and will be discussed later on. This term may have been at fault, I am inclined to believe, in placing Ramses III far back in time, where the chaos of the Iron Age witnessed numbers of peoples of the sea in motion. It appeared that his inscriptors coined the term "Peoples of the Isles" and modern scholars leaped to a facile but false connection with the earlier vagrant peoples.

J.D. Muhly writes: "Long regarded as the foundation for all studies of events at the end of the Late Bronze Age, the records from Medinet Habu now also have their detractors," and he quotes approvingly the Egyptologist Leonard Lesko, when Lesko writes that he "...would prefer to regard the entire Sea Peoples account of Ramses III as anachronistic and suggest that this record was probably also borrowed from Merneptah's mortuary temple."

The Plagues: Local, Worldwide and Exoterrestrial

10. Plague.

Direct reports of plague in the Mediterranean Iron Age are uncommon. Yet severe population declines everywhere suggest plague, as in the bubonic plague of the 14th century in Europe, and it could occur so throughout a large region. Mars, Apollo, and other gods of pestilence are hovering about. Too, a possibility of exoterrestrial gases and radiation storms existed as a threat to humans and animals alike. Therefore, often, archaeologists reasonably connect the severe depopulation noticed throughout the Mediterranean with plague.

A simple process of elimination by common knowledge would persuade one that warfare would not cause such widespread and enduring depeopling, that earthquakes would neither be so gigantic and widespread as to cause more than a temporary diminution, that volcanism and huge smoke clouds could not manage the job. Could plagues be so completely and lengthily destructive?

Under extreme plague circumstances, as with the American Indians suffering from European-induced smallpox, or as with the Euro-Asiatic region in the 14th century, a third of the population may die in a single generation. In the case of the Indians, the disease, the shock, forcible aggression by Euro-Americans, and the abuse of alcohol combined to initiate what ultimately came to near annihilation – but not in Central and South America! Lacking systematic studies of the plagues of the Iron Age, we must retain it as a useful hypothesis.

We should be aware, at the same time, that plagues, according to the astro-physicist Fred Hoyle and others, can come from microbial or poisonous chemicals from outer space. We should also remember that the plagues of Exodus, of ancient Athens, and of the near-East city states can be with some reason attributed to the direct and indirect consequences of the proximity or crash of exoterrestrial bodies. Planet Mars, as we shall be explaining, was a god of pestilence, too. The close association of arsenic and iron is suggestive.

Earthquakes

11. Earthquakes. Adding to what we said above, weaknesses of earthquake theory exist. With hardly a persuasive idea of their own, professors often have warned their students against the concurrent seismic theory of Schaeffer. They are told to stick to their site . For, as Paul Astrom of Goteborg University advised, "When an archaeologist tries to make a larger synthesis he may be too

biased by his own site, as for example C.A.F. Schaeffer was in his monumental book Stratigraphie Comparée in 1948, where he imposed the events of Ras Shamra on other sites in the Eastern Mediterranean.. The distinguished excavator suffered from what may called a site syndrome, specifically a Ras Shamra syndrome."[45] The same author, incidentally, explains the etymologies and meanings of the words catastrophe and disaster without alerting us to the fact that the terms denote a downfall of stars (as well as a climactic downturn of a drama) and a deviation (dys)-aster of stars.

Ambraseys labored to count the earthquakes occurring in the Near East from AD 10 to AD 1699. He concluded that the three thousand quakes that he found mentioned in the records and literature followed a curve that if anything brought more earthquakes in modern times. There occurred one or two earthquakes per year. His record may be invalid and unreliable in that historical earthquakes, even of great intensity, continue to be discovered in geography and described in legend and proven to have happened. In any case, the earthquake frequency of the Martian period is far beyond Ambraseys figures, and their intensity on the average would seem to be much greater.

Students of earthquakes usually do not ask whether earthquakes can be prepared and triggered by forces such as volcanism and exoterrestrial electrical atmospheric changes. Evidence mounts to this effect, and there is no reason to deny a great abundance of earth shocks in Martian times. Pliny, the natural philosopher, could not have been speaking nonsense when he noted that the Rome of his times had been shaken by scores of seismic shocks in a single year.

On the other hand, it is well to consider that only a high intensity earthquake accompanied by invasion and conflagration is likely to discourage survivors from beginning all over again. We see this happening on many occasions in the Iron Age, but what is more impressive is the high number of cases where earthquakes are followed by the abandonment of a town, palace, or temple. Here would be conceivably a mighty earthquake going beyond the highest calibration of the Celsius and Mercalli scales used today. Or a rain of fire that wiped out the population and their possessions. Or also by a tsunami following upon an earthquake elsewhere. A study of Phanouria Dakaronia from Lamia Castle, 14th Ephoreia, of the locale of Kynos on the North Eubean Gulf finds two Martian period destructions, both indicating earthquake, the second followed by fire of unknown origin, and the scattered debris and marine fossils indicating that a tsunami stuck. Later construction was poorer and inferior. It is notable that Kastraki, a nearby site, is considered to have enjoyed a continued occupation until Byzantine times.

Exoterrestrial and Terrestrial Catastrophe

12. Exoterrestrial forces. As insistently put forward in this book, but nowhere in the conventional and authoritative literature, these are numerous and can take the form of direct impacts, close encounters, accelerations of the Earth, tilts of the Earth, poisonous down-drafts, Maruts (asteroidal companions of Mars in the Vedas), debris bombardment, mega-lightning, and fire-storms.

Toting up the Score: If a quantavolution is a sudden intensive wide-scale set of changes in all spheres of life, does the Iron Age of Mars qualify as a quantavolution? Unquestionably. Every sphere of existence is deeply affected within a brief time.

When I conceived of quantavolution, I thought of the phenomenon as inextricably connected with astrophysical events. I believe still that the great cases of Q will follow this course from Sky to Earth, but perhaps room should be made to include grave misadventures of mankind, such as a nuclear war discharging several hundred missiles, or a plague or poison warfare that has worldwide serious effects. (A 2005 inventory of nuclear explosives, prepared by the Institute for Science and International Security, estimates that the material in readiness or in potential could furnish or fashion 300,000 nuclear bombs.)

We have far to go before scoring the events of the Iron Age in full, but reviewing the list just offered above, and positing a scale of 1 to 10 for the fulfillment of the demand upon each item to make it reach the quantavolution boundary, we would have to consider the Iron Age a quantavolution. Knowing what is to come, I would score the

Iron Age in terms of effects, in the holosphere of change, as a 6. Rather than explain this by moving from 1 upwards, I would score it backwards, that is, denoting the extent to which a given force did not place the events as a quantavolution.

Routinely but naively, we are challenged, after all is said and done, "Where are your reliable accounts of the direct impact and explosion of a bolide?" This is asking too much. Who has given but an indirect account with the help of theory and gauges of what happens in a nuclear furnace? Any meteoroid crash of over a ton far exceeds because of its speed the explosive force in a nuclear furnace.

Further, with our many indicators of a catastrophic event having taken place, we scarcely should be put upon for eye-witnessing. Is it not enough to witness the geological markers, the fossil markers, the chemical markers, the human accounts of precedent (burning and nearing sky body, e.g.) happenings, the numerous agglutinated changes in the living and earthen environment?

To witness means to observe and record and report. This is asking much, considering the acoustics, the brilliance, the blackness, the blast and concussion – all occurring in a microsecond. All witnesses are exterminated before their right hemisphere of the brain has time to cross over to tell the left hemisphere it is happening.

But what of the extreme and therefore quiet margins of the event, like the ripple from a far off wave? Were this to be, one would know little to report besides the ripple. Or one would be in the dark and would know little else for the moment at least. The results of collisions may be directly sensed and misinterpreted sometimes, too, by persons on the fringe, as with the shaking of the earth, or the rumble of distant 'thunder'. In sum, a witness and reporter from the fringe would not recognize the phenomena he is witnessing and would be unreliable. The effects of the event are erratically sensed: does plague come before or after an invading horde of desperate aggressors?

"But what of your theory of 'soft landings?'" A 'soft landing' is an integrated body-fall that hardly penetrates the ground. But the conditions of heat, wind, concussion, and light will still be deadly. No exoterrestrial fall is likely to be as gentle as a hailstorm. A large body will certainly only be known to people beyond eyesight and then, it they approach the scene later on, they are reporting history, based upon the usual types of indirect, inferred, logical, pieced-together evidence of which history is usually composed.

In his book on *Early Anatolia*, Seton Lloyd alleges against Schaeffer that "it is in fact difficult to admit the theory which he proposes that so many centers far removed from one another were affected at one and the same time. It is generally known that the force of an earthquake diminishes proportionately to the distance from the epicentre. His hypothesis would accordingly postulate some extraordinary seismic phenomena without parallel in the known periods of history."

Exactly. An atypical form of seismism was operational. What would it be? A shift in the Earth's crust? A tilt of the Earth? A glitch in the Earth's rotation? A number of close encounters?

How could Schaeffer answer Lloyd's objection except to say that it may not have happened on the same day, but at close intervals and owing to the same causes.? In the 1940's Schaeffer could not have known the theory of quantavolution, nor the evidence that the Mars quantavolution was a complex of repeated encounters. Velikovsky, Patten and Ackerman claim approaches by Mars at fifteen-year intervals. On two occasions at least, it interacted with a close-in Venus as well as with Earth and Moon. All of the destruction needed not have occurred on one occasion nor need the destruction have been evenly spread over the globe. (It is to be noted that astronomers accept the repeated visits of a comet. Near-Earth objects, too, have been known to skip in the upper atmosphere and glance off into outer space, to return perhaps another day. The highly differentiated morphology of the Earth adds to the different speeds of the intruder many differing kinds of target – oceans, mountains, ice fields, etc. Given the youth of the Q paradigm, a panoply of scales, tests, measures to gauge the event, even if we could obtain basic data about it (which is not the case) is unavailable. For instance, we know that Pylos and Tiryns were destroyed in the same period of time, but not whether they were simultaneously destroyed.

Placement of Ramses III and Medinet Habu

An important by-product of our research into destructions of the Iron Age concerns the placement of Pharaoh Ramses III in time and activity. We reversed our position twice. First, it was and is the universal position of archaeologists that Ramses III was an important Pharaoh following in the footsteps of Ramses II and dated in the 13th century. So we thought too.

Then, Velikovsky, in reconstructing the chronology of Egypt placed him not only along with the whole of New Kingdom rulers four hundred years later than conventionally affirmed, but by himself, so to speak, 800 years later than Egyptian chronologists had him, that is, in the Fourth Century BCE, smack into Persian times. But as I read the inscriptions that accompanied said Ramses III at Medinet Habu temple and the script of the Harris Papyrus inscribed soon after him, I was impressed by the disasters that appeared to surround him and by his words "Peoples of the Isles" or "Peoples of the Sea," a phrase that was adopted by the archaeologists and ancient historians as apparently confirming notices of disorders at the end of the Bronze Age. So I rejected the Velikovsky chronology and was pleased to add the bloody experiences of Ramses III to all the others showing the general ruination of the flourishing Late Bronze Age.

But then, restudying Velikovsky and the inscriptions and papyrus, I once more changed my mind and now am persuaded that the total Ramses story, as Velikovsky tells it, is the solution: Ramses was known as Nectanebo I to the Greeks of the Fourth Century, titled himself as Ramses III, and fought against the Libyans and against the reoccupation of Egypt by the Persians who had invaded the Delta of the Nile with Greek mercenaries and Asia Minor vassals.

There is therefore no longer a problem for me, although the conventional view continues to spread confusion. The whole story of Ramses III and his successors makes sense in the international world of the fourth century BCE. And there is ample and indeed total destruction during the century of the nearest approaches of Mars in connection with Moon, Mercury and Venus, as we shall later set forth. So we do not need the scenes of warfare and reports of destruction of the time of Ramses III in order to provide a holistic quantavolution beginning four centuries earlier than Ramses III.

For instance, an extensive article on the "Collapse of the Egyptian Empire," merges the Thirteenth and Fourth Centuries sites of Palestine and struggles mightily through the resulting confusion.[46]

"It has long been recognized that Ramses III's claims to Syrian conquests in the Papyrus Harris I lack historical validity" and that the Syrian claims of Ramses III at Medinet Habu are also quite false. Since they are ahead of the Pharaoh by 800 years, there is reason for the Syrian lacunae.

Again the same author describes "the demise of the Egyptian Empire in Palestine: Beth-Shan, Lachish, Tell esh-Shariça, and Megiddo. The first three provide archaeological testimony for Egyptian activity during the reign of Ramses III and its termination at the end of his reign or shortly thereafter. The fourth site, Megiddo, may also fall in this category.." All of them came to a fiery end, according to our reading of the beginning of the Iron Age. Typically nothing came thereafter, just as in other parts of the Mediterranean region, or perhaps some poor primitive village. The paragraphs that follow are confused in the attempt to tie in Ramses III. The author turns to other excavators of his material and finds them in trouble as well. At Beth-Shan,

> Yadin discovered that a violent destruction, inexplicably missed by the Pennsylvania excavators [at work 1921 to 1933], brought an end to this Egyptian occupation... The succeeding level — Yadin's Stratum III, also not recognized by the American team (unless it is part of an ephemeral phase they labeled Late Level VI) — represents a poor settlement consisting mostly of pits, ovens, and some flimsy walls... After Level VI, Egyptian activity ceased altogether at Beth-Shan. It is difficult to fix a precise termination date for Level VI, since regnal years are not mentioned on any inscribed artifacts from this stratum. It is unlikely, though, that the garrison lasted much past the reign of Ramses III. This king is mentioned on a number of objects from Beth-Shan.

So Ramses III is actually named in these old digs of the Bronze Age — perhaps? Yes and no. Were these objects from rubbish heaps? Other objects were. The Palestinian excavations may be among the worst offenders in containing mixed-up levels and objects. Most disturbing of all, were the levels of occupation mistakenly identified to begin with, such that these sites were given dates far too old? There is a presumption favoring hard-digging archaeology as opposed to inscriptions, legends, scriptures and documents. But archaeology can be as inaccurate, improperly assessed, misread, and barren as these other sources of history. Many scientists and hoi polloi believe that when material evidence is scanty and prone to mislead, then theory, especially broad theory, is all the more untrustworthy, whereas the opposite is the case. The less the senses supply, the more the mind must provide.

What is sometimes to be suspected is that strata which scholars believe to be contemporary with Ramses III are actually of the end of the Bronze and the beginning of the Iron Age. They can hardly help themselves. It has been given to them as such, first 400 extra years and now 800. He turns inevitably to the inscriptions of Medinet Habu and the Harris Papyrus, believing that these are 13th century strata when they are in fact fourth century.

To conclude this discussion of Ramses III, I shall proceed by placing him practically out of the picture, up in the Fourth Century. I would grant a possibility of error. However, the theses of this book are not affected by his dates or activities. Whatever destructions are implied or declared in his descriptions are made up for by the original destructions in the very same places, such as Megiddo. We do not need Ramses III or his happenings to demonstrate that these destructions happened in the Iron Age Apex of the revised chronology, that is, -850 to -650. So far as concerns the Peoples of the Sea, this term, mistakenly carried over by archaeology and history from Ramses III to all manner of destruction everywhere, by land and by sea, we shall treat them in the forthcoming chapter on Vagrant Peoples.

Our Revised Calendar

I can summarize at this point the revised calendar

that I have been and will continue to follow. It is the reconstructed calendar brought forth by Velikovsky:

a. -1450 to -1020. The Middle Kingdom of Egypt ends in a quantavolution, and the Hyksos, Arabians, take over the Empire for four centuries.

b. -1020 to -830. Under the onslaught of Kamose and Ahmose of Thebes, Egyptian local rulers, and of Saul, King of Israel, the Hyksos are expelled from Egypt. The Theban dynasty that includes Thutmoses and Amenhotep follows A brief interval sees Akhnaton as absolute ruler.

c. -830 to -720. Sosenk and Osorkous provide Egypt with a Libyan Dynasty.

d. -720 to -663. Ethiopian Dynasty. It is interrupted by intermittent conquests of the country by Sennacherib the Assyrian (who crowned Haremhab as vassal ruler of Egypt), Esarhaddon, and Assurbanipal, who crowned Necho I as vassal ruler (he being called Necho I in Greek and also Ramses I, soon killed in battle with the Ethiopians.

e. -663 to -525. The Tanitic Dynasty centered at Tanis in the Nile Delta begins with Seti (Psammetich to the Greeks) son of Ramses I. Ramses II follows (Necho II to the Greeks). Then Merneptah (called Apries by Herodotus and Hophra by Jeremiah). He is overthrown by a General, Amasis, who rules for 40 years.

f. -525 to -332. Persian rule by 7 kings, beginning with Cambyses. Now begins, too, a series of intermittently autonomous rulers, "Native Kings" or the "Sebennytic Dynasty". These include Nepherites, Acoris, Nectanebo I (a Greek appellation of Ramses III), Tachos, and Nectanebo II, who is cast out by the Persians in -343, and, then, a decade later, in -332 Alexander of Macedon invades and conquers Egypt. Between -420 and -300 there exists also a Priestly Dynasty in Libya, set up by the Persians. So goes our Chronology of Egypt that displays abundantly connections with the outer world and the Bible, whether the Bible speaks from Palestine or Western Arabia..

Ramses III appears here, then, in the Fourth Century, probably a General who has effectively rid the country of Persian rule temporarily, and defeated an attempt to recapture the country, as depicted on the walls of his temple at Medinet Habu. And to summarize Velikovsky's reasons for placing him in the Fourth Century, far removed from the Bronze Age transition into the Iron Age, as even Ramses II, now of the later relaxation of the Martian Iron Age intrusions.

Summary of Reasons for Deplacing Ramses III

The case for placing Ramses III out of reach of the Apex of Mars can be briefed here.

1. Ordinary cemeteries connected with his ruins are late in style and contents (even to containing late Hellenistic and Roman objects in the tombs). Here Griffiths (back by Petrie and Albright) outgunned the French archaeologist Naville, who agreed to disagree from his colleague in the excavating, Griffiths.

2. A great many tiles from Medinet Habu, found in the temple compound, carried Greek letters on their backs, while their faces resembled strongly Persian designs of the period.

3. Greek authors wrote copiously of a famous Nectanebo I, who so closely resembled Ramses III that he was almost surely the same person.

4. The battles boastfully described – but basically correct – in the inscriptions of Ramses III were also described as those of Nectanebo I by Diodorus, the Sicilian historian and other Greek authors.

5. There was no clear line of descent from Ramses II to Ramses III. Ramses II could be held in place in the sixth century or thereabouts, already several centuries later than the conventional chronology, and there sense can be made of his activities. But Ramses III appears to have been a General prior to seizing power.

6. The art and architecture throughout the structures of Ramses III were of a degraded character and quite unlike the work of the times of Ramses II.

7. The "Peoples of the Isles ," to which Ramses or his inscribers independently gave names of unknown peoples (possibly vassals of the Persians called upon to help invade Egypt by sea), were, if the inscribed murals were realistic, typical Persian troops and Greek mercenaries of a late age.

(Not part of the argument in these days, but worth mentioning to accent the confusion behind the Ramses III inscriptions, is the belief of H.H. Breasted, the most famous Egyptologist of his age and translator of the inscriptions, that the wars with the People of the Isles there portrayed, took place in Syria rather than in the Egyptian Delta! (Vol.4, pp 3-85 of his *Ancient Records of Egypt*, 1906,, Chicago, U of Illinois press, 2001.) He uses the word "harbor-mouths" rather than "Delta."

One would conclude that the vaunted ruins attributed to Ramses III do not belong to or lead to a better understanding of the Early Iron Age. They might be considered as evidence that wandering and warfaring were still going on, centuries after the Apex of the Iron Age. But gross natural destruction does not appear to be part of the picture.

Chapter Seven

Vagrants of the Phantom Age

Professor William W. Hallo is concerned about our underestimating what we would call the quantavolutionary character of the Iron Age. Besides technological change [iron-making] and natural upheavals, "what further factor could account for the quantum leap that precipitated the 'crisis years' of the 12th century?" His answer: migrations. The migrations "include not only the seaborne movements along the littoral and islands of the Mediterranean, but also the equally momentous, if less spectacular displacements in all the hinterlands, from Anatolia to the Syro-Arabian desert." He terms it a "population explosion such as had most probably stimulated the agricultural revolution of ca. 8000 B.C. and the urban revolution of ca. 3000 B.C."[47]

Here we might differ, since I am working on a calendar of quantavolutions and the nearest I have to what could have caused the agricultural revolution was the Saturnian Golden Age, introduced by the change in the Uranian skies when, true, the population had increased everywhere, and it would be the Jovean or Jupiter quantavolution that would have encouraged the building of urban centers.[48] Still, in our opinion he is on the right path, and he would do well to pursue his own counsel "that the great transitions of human history do after all have a certain coherence to them, that the isolated findings of scattered regions can add up to a pattern," and scholars should collaborate in 'the search for interconnections on an interregional scale."

The issue is not often faced squarely: Were the takeovers fast or slow? We vote usually and generically for fast takeovers, but would allow trickles, bands, and individuals to find their way in early and leave early. Cyprus is a proper case. There, Vassos Karageorgis writes: "What is known as the 'Achaean colonization' of Cyprus was a long and slow process" of a century or more. We cannot argue. The Greeks may have come in waves or bands. Finally, the Greek language began to dominate. He says, though, that there was a collapse in Cyprus, and probably that the Greeks and Cypriotes long struggled for supremacy.[49]

Blood Genes and Farming

The famed authors at work on migrations, Luigi Lucca Cavalli-Sforza[50] and his self-appointed nemesis, Bryan Sykes,[51] manage to bring the peoples across half of Asia and all the way to Britain without recourse to earthquakes, much less quantavolutions, over a long period of time, by means of tracings of blood lines and genetic DNA sampling.

Cavalli-Sforza mapped the probable migration of agriculture from the Fertile Crescent to the British Isles, and also an apparent regression of the Rh- blood type and B gene types to the West, 'pursued' by the agriculturalists who carried Rh+ and lacked the B gene. In a system of statistical multiple correlation originated by Harold Hotelling, Cavalli-Sforza's team produced a primary or principal component found in a collection of 95 genes and plotted them on a map of the greater Mediterranean and North European areas, finding a significant differentiation of genes as the measure is taken going North West. See *Fig. 8* and *9*.

The Cavalli-Sforza group is strongly uniformitarian. It is Darwinian, but seeks to find a place not only for the neo-Darwinism of genetic drift but also for migration. It would do well to use quantavolutions to explain the geographical progression of certain genetic and blood types from the Asian East to the European Far West, especially because not only is there a general statistical trend from East to West, but there are also a number of "islands" of different blood and gene types. No great catastrophes mix up the march westwards and northwards.

We are all groping in the dark, of course, searching for *when did who go where in what numbers*. The group, rightly we think, believes that people carried their new systems and tools of production to new areas. It is not that the "Anglophone" theory of Childe is incorrect in maintaining that the inventions went 'by themselves,' that is, with individual traders and travelers.[52] Both went on. It is seriously important that absolute propositions be admitted only carefully.

Several Teutonic peoples traversed the whole of the Roman Empire in less than a century. The Huns from Far Asia raced on their ponies across a vast territory in a lifetime; they left contingents in Hungary who became fine horsemen. The Arabs did as well or better several centuries later. See how the Indian Americans and their vast territories were take over or removed -- by Columbus, Cortez, Pizzarro, John Smith, William Penn, individuals, small parties, gold-seekers, buccaneers, religious cults, military expeditions, corporations, governments, dissidents, escaped criminals and slaves, and miscegenating traders. There is little reason to claim a less varied assortment of social groups and types for the vast migrations of the Martian Apex period.

Almost three centuries in all were required, but the regions were continental-sized and 300 years are not 3000 years. That is, referring again to the map purporting to show the progress of agriculture from Asia to the British Isles, the datings probably lack much meaning. A neolithic ship-wrecked crew or a fugitive band from the Near East would not revert completely to fishing and hunting, giving no thought to the agricultural skills its members might contribute to the commonweal. Agriculture probably spread like the plague, jumping hither and yon, regardless of the neat progression of the centuries or millennia. The iron slash and cut sword took only several generations to be made and found everywhere in the vast Euro-Asian region. The flange-hilted sword swept from northwestern Europe down to Egypt and Asia Minor in less than a century.

Jewish Descent

Cavalli-Sforza's studies report the genetic constitution of Jews, to show how miscegenation has had noticeable affects on Jewish genomes wherever they have settled down for any length of time. Basically, the migrations of the Jews whether in personal emigration or in groups, have differentiated them genetically in due course. The great many who have joined in religious or secular miscegenation are lost to the counting, which has been done on those asserting themselves to be Jews. (Let us trust that the illogic of counting as Jews persons who have "Jewish" genes was avoided.) The closest relationship of the largest proportion of Jews wherever they are tested in the world is with the Arabs, and the closest here, with non-Jewish Palestinians.

    If Salibi is correct, then we would expect this to be the case, for we would have the Jews, descending from the Hebrews who were genetically, culturally, and geographically associated with other Semitic Arabian tribes and confederations of the Iron Age and before. This would also hold true if the Finkelstein group is correct, drawing the Hebrews from the sleepy hollows of the back mountains of Palestine, and practically asserting that they were Canaanites, regardless of what the Bible said. (It should be stated and borne in mind that the Hebrews were only one of many Arabic tribes who settled down and could call themselves kingdoms, and who had commerce and fought wars with one another, just as the American Indian nations went about clubbing and arrow-shooting each other, when they were not smoking the pipe of peace.)

    As Salibi says, "Such being the proximity between Canaanite-speakers and Aramaic -speakers in Biblical West Arabia, the Israelites, I would suggest, were at a loss to which group they originally belonged."

    However, their shared traditions, legends, and histories did not produce a Common Bible. Whether their histories and fortunes were happier than those of the People of the Book over the succeeding 2500 years cannot be convincingly judged.

Need for Maps of Migrations

    It would be useful to possess a map of the Greater Mediterranean Region, dotted with all of its Iron Age sites, destroyed or not, and it would be equally useful to have a map of the known and surmised migrations of the Iron Age peoples. Our gift list of systematic data would also include an intensity and extensity scaling of the destructions and a code of their causes, at the same time denoting the number of people and size of groups making their different journeys, plus the time plot of each routed group. (I appreciate that I am speaking of a dozen or so monographs or dissertations.)

A more modest beginning could consist of drawing upon other people's maps, those of Cavalli-Sforza and Salibi, for instance. We should then indicate upon them any idea that is received of people that we have encountered in the Iron Age: is it recently settled, has it lost or sent a considerable number of its peoples to other regions, or even to a new settlement a few miles uphill or down? One of these possibilities would generally be the case.

Look to the large cities. Nineveh swelled and was destroyed. Jerusalem may or may not have been large, but it cannot be found, and if found, cannot have been large. It was probably a scattering of related settlements, a central town with satellite villages, as Salibi seems to demonstrate. Thebes in Egypt persisted, but lost people and acquired contingents of other people from Asia and Africa. Babylon experienced a coming and going of various immigrant types. Cyprus exchanged contingents and individuals with Syria and Mycenean Greece. Phrygians and Cimmerians trekked down from the Northeast. Greek city-states founded many Ionian coastal cities, settled many Aegean Islands, went west to Sicily, Italy, France. Phoenicians migrated to Africa and Greece. Scandinavians (Were they of another race, non-Viking, then?) walked and rowed South along a broad belt of territory from the Volga to the Oder. Libyans and Ethiopians moved into Egypt.

If amber trade routes ran from the North Sea and Baltic Sea coastal areas down to the Mediterranean, they must certainly have been walked, ridden, and sailed by people capable of miscegenation, carrying or protecting or accompanying the amber party. Granted 2000 years of the trade, an exchange of 2,000,000 genomes would be minimal. (And then one must count the branching out of these.) In times of catastrophe, the numbers of migrants and vagrants would have increased many-fold.

Who inhabited Palestine the full length of the Mediterranean East Coast at the dawn of history is not known. Giants would be an odd guess, but so went one fable. The stone ages give up remains and bones of no special flavor that would lead to an ethnic identification later on. We assume here that all the well-known peoples came to Palestine during the Iron Age. Possibly they found there a wasteland, lately ruined.

The Philistines may have been the first to arrive, since the coastal region is named for them. (But America is not called Indiana.) The Phoenicians and the Canaanites followed, the Arameans and Moabites as well, to the East of the others. They all were prompted to emigrate as individuals and groups earliest by commerce, then by natural destruction, then by pressures and invasions from Ethiopia, Egypt and Assyria, later from Babylonia and Persia. The Hebrews felt these incentives as well, and recalled in a tradition not strong in the other areas, a long sojourn in Egypt of much of their population. Furthermore, ten of their twelve tribes (Israel) were finally defeated and captured by the Assyrians, and were dispersed far to the North, as far as the Caucasus. Most of Judah's people were captured in war with the Babylonians later on and some third of these perhaps were sent to Babylon, whence, after a time, they were allowed to disperse to Judah and other locations once again. The tight little kingdom of Judah now led its own life for some time, as a vassal state to be sure, and at some brief interval under the Herods amounted to a significant force in the Near East, but then was crushed and dispersed by the Romans, and, except for exciting a mean interest from Christian Crusaders for being the Holy Land, was not in a socio-demographic sense Jewish until the year 1948 and the proclamation of a State of Israel.

Salibi speaks thus from the West Arabian hypothesis: "As an imperial people the ancient Egyptians were keenly interested in bringing West Arabia and its trade routes under control. So were the Assyrians and Babylonians in their time. In the wake of every imperial invasion, from whatever direction, a new wave of migration from West Arabia to other lands such as Palestine must have taken place." When the Egyptians were in trouble, at the beginning of the Iron Age, the Israelite Kingdom of Saul, David and Solomon displayed strength, only to decline and split into two kingdoms when the Egyptians once more collected their forces.

The Queen of Sheba, whose kingdom lay not far south in the powerful Kingdom of Sheba (Saba), probably did visit King Solomon, contradicting Velikovsky, who would have her be Queen Hatshepsut. But Hatshepsut, being ruler of Egypt and Ethiopia, may also have ruled Saba. Saba was perhaps the most powerful of the West Arabian nations in the full Iron Age, a focal transition between the Indian Ocean and the Near East. Ethiopian pressures on Judah, as on Egypt, weakened the country. The persistent tradition that King Menelik I of Ethiopia was the son of the Queen of Sheba and Solomon, and made off with the original Ark of Moses (which would have been in the Temple of Solomon) should not be dismissed offhand.

The vast panorama of migrations over about three centuries would tend to induce cultural metamorphosis everywhere and to bring about ethnic and religious mixing. Too, a country might change capitals -- Egypt engaging its government now at Thebes, then at Memphis, then at Tanis, not to mention the brief spell at Akhetaton (Amarna), and in the sixth century to autonomous rulers, particularly important being the Saitic priesthood of the Libyan oases; too, one should count the heavy bureaucratic and military exchange with each conquest and occupation by a foreign power, Assyria, Babylon, Libya, Ethiopia, Persia. Independent invention and diffusion of objects and practices were both accelerated during the Iron Age, and did not slide into a normal flat curve of innovation until the second century CE of the Roman Empire.

"Peoples of the Sea" stands for Universal Vagrancy

Where did term "Peoples of the Sea" come from? I have made the point earlier. Strange that rulers, writers, priests etc who knew the geography and peoples of the world would have to use this non-ethnic term for a large period of widespread transgressions. Or did they? We might recall that Immanuel Velikovsky provides us with the following thesis: The "Peoples of the Sea" who fought in Egypt were not twelfth-century wanderers or Bronze-Iron Age transition groups but fourth-century mercenaries, mostly from Asia Minor and Greece, of the days of Plato. These mainly Greek mercenaries were in the service of the Persians invading Egypt, but because practically their only specific mention as Peoples of the Sea comes in relation to the annals of Ramses III, they are pushed down the ladder of time to the 4th century, along with this ruler of Egypt, who is generally ascribed to the 12th century B.C., To quote him further:

> According to the reckoning of modern historians, Ramses III started to reign in the year [-1200 ~-460] before the present era, or only a short time later. The major event of his reign was the successful opposition to the armies coming from the north. In their sweep of conquest, the northern hordes came to the very gates of Egypt, the greatest and most glorious of kingdoms. In all ages conquerors have made Egypt their goal- Esarhaddon and Assurbanipal the Assyrians, Cambyses the Persian, Alexander the Macedonian, Pompey the Roman, Omar the Arab, Selim the Turk, and Napoleon; and some unidentified leader or group of leaders, before any of these, led armed troops to drink water from the Nile. But Ramses III rose to the occasion. He battled the invaders on land and sea and turned back the tide that threatened to envelop Egypt.
>
> This war is known as the war against the Peoples of the Sea, or the Peoples of the Isles, by which names Ramses III referred to them. Historical texts and extensive illustrations cut in stone, which illuminate this war and the pharaoh's ultimate victory, are preserved in Egypt. But of the sweep of the invading troops across the lands of the Near East before their arrival at the frontier of Egypt nothing is known from any historical source, literary or archaeological. It is only by inference that the conclusion is made: Mycenaean Greece, the Hittite Empire, and many lesser kingdoms were swept out of existence by the wandering and conquering Peoples of the Sea. This inference is made on the basis of the fact that all these kingdoms and empires were found to have been terminated in about -1200[~-850]. For the next four or five centuries there is no record and no relic of their existence and scarcely any vestige of the surviving population in these lands.
>
> What can Greece and the isles, Crete included, show for the period between - 1200 and - 750 or even - 700? After the end of the Mycenaean Age and the fall of Troy darkness envelops the history of these places and the first rays of light penetrate into the area with the beginning of the Greek, or Ionic, Age about - 700. Suddenly, as if out of nothing, comes the Homeric poetry, and the intimate familiarity displayed by the poet with the smallest details of the' life of the Mycenaean Age, five to ten centuries earlier, is a persistent cause for wonder among scholars, a theme for incessant debate.
>
> The centuries from -1200 to - 750 are called Dark Ages. They were not dark in the sense in which this term is applied to the period of European history between the end of the Roman Empire in +475 and

the end of the Crusaders' wars in the East: these centuries from the end of the fifth to the middle of the thirteenth of the current era represent a regression in learning, in commerce, in administration and law, when compared with the time of the Roman Empire, but they abound in historical relics and literary testimonies; whereas the Dark Ages between - 1200 and - 750 before the present era are dark because no document survived from that time in Greece, in Crete, in the Aegean world, or in Asia Minor. [It would be more correct to limit the European Dark Age to ~500 to ~800 – Charlemagne – or, depending upon criteria and extent of the region as defined, ~1200.]

This scheme of things is never questioned; however, its acceptance raises a great many difficult problems either not resolved or resolved at the cost of creating additional difficult problems... Ramses III enumerates the single tribes of which the Peoples of the Sea were composed, and efforts have been made to identify them with various Achaean tribes of early times.

Troy's fall was followed by migrations echoed in the wandering of Odysseus of the Achaean camp and of Aeneas from among the Trojan survivors. Although Odysseus visited an Egypt unruffled by war, it is conjectured that some great migratory wave of Achaeans carried them by land and sea to the kingdom on the Nile.

Besides the Peoples of the Sea, the other important people who took part in the war in Egypt were richly clad warriors named Pereset. They are referred to by this name and they are recognizable by their attire. Apparently they were the leaders of the expedition, the Peoples of the Sea being the mercenaries.

No ancient document, but only the inscriptions of Ramses III calls these warriors by this special name. Yet for the two centuries or so, archaeologists have increasingly used the term. And now, with the increasing fashion of treating the end of the Bronze Age as a universal disaster, and with nothing beyond invasions, tumult, ethnic movements and earthquakes to blame it on, in their frame of reference, the Peoples have been graduated into farther antiquity. What better place to put them than into a box of time called Dark Ages. Why not call them people *from* the sea, people *by* the sea, people *traveling by sea,* and why peoples instead of *people?* What did those have to do with the sea who showed up in the far regions of Anatolia, and elsewhere well inland, without boats? Prof. J.D. Muhly traces some of the Northern invaders of Greece by land, probably through Epirus, and "for the most part these northern invaders returned home, especially home to Rumania."[53] There they invented or developed a new forging technology. The age was, expectably, the transition from Bronze to Iron.

Cyrus Gordon describes many avenues of cultural diffusion around the Greater Mediterranean and regular trade routes that he calls Late Bronze Age "Internationalism."[54] Then, not crediting the great destructions, he has the Region proceeding directly to "colonialism." This is hardly permissible, since colonialism is a sharply different social species from internationalism, this being, in fact, his major finding.

When Ramses III speaks of "Peoples of the Sea" he specifies the Tjeker, the Shekelesh, the Teresh, the Weshesh, and the Sherden (or Sardan); he specifies the Denien as "Peoples of the Isles." But many other peoples (known and unknown as these) have been considered to belong to the category. The *Encyclopedia Britannica* defines them as "any of the groups of aggressive seafarers who invaded eastern Anatolia, Syria, Palestine, Cyprus, and Egypt toward the end of the Bronze Age, especially in the 13th century B.C.E.. They are held responsible for the destruction of old powers such as the Hittite Empire. Because of the abrupt break in ancient Near Eastern records as a result of the invasions, the precise extent and origin of the upheavals remain uncertain. Principal but one-sided evidence for the Sea Peoples is based on Egyptian texts and illustrations; other important information comes from Hittite sources and from archaeological data."

Still the Encyclopedia takes a stab at identification and goes on to say:

> Tentative identifications of the Sea Peoples listed in Egyptian documents are as follows: Ekwesh, a group of Bronze Age Greeks (Achaeans; Ahhiyawa in Hittite texts); Teresh, Tyrrhenians (Tyrsenoi), known to later Greeks as sailors and pirates from Anatolia, ancestors of the Etruscans; Luka, a coastal people of western Anatolia, also known from Hittite sources (their name survives in classical Lycia on the southwest coast of Anatolia); Sherden, probably Sardinians (the Sherden acted as mercenaries of the Egyptians in the Battle of Kadesh, 1299 BC); Shekelesh, probably identical with the Sicilian tribe called Siculi; Peleset, generally believed to refer to the Philistines, who perhaps came from Crete and were the only major tribe of the Sea Peoples to settle

permanently in Palestine.

Further identifications of other Sea Peoples mentioned in the documents are much more uncertain."

Much of this article is probably wrong, and it is certainly misleading.

I would propose that the Peoples of the Sea were not of a culture or kind, except as adventurers jostling desperate refugees from the countless destroyed settlements and countryside of the late Bronze Age. They were given no fixed name because they might come from anywhere, nearby or a thousand kilometers away. They could have been Sicanians (Sicilians, Siculi) from the regions of Mt. Vesuvius and Mt. Etna that were exploding in the eighth century as they had never exploded before. They might have come from Mycenean areas where all the towns were cast down, incinerated usually as part of the actions of nature. Or from Central Europe, even from Scandinavia, likely the Dorians as anyone else, the Heraclids of Hercules, also incorporated in Mars (even carrying with them the epics later to become the chants of Homer in the thesis of Felice Vinci's *Homer in the Baltic*).

Those who had been attached to the land and hardly knew the sea might be called Peoples of the Sea if they were churned into terrified and violent motion by tsunamis that during this period were frequent. They then probably could travel endlessly overland. Peoples from the Sea could also actually come from marine settings that had been uplifted and left their survivors high and dry but helpless, though in this age, marine transgressions were more common than marine regressions.

I submit that the term Peoples of the Sea is useless, precisely because it is used to refer to all those surviving uprooted persons who before and after the major electrical and mechanical contacts of Earth with Mars, Venus, bolides, plasmas, and solar flares, and the secondary volcanic, atmospheric, seismic, radiative, biological, and aquatic effects, could appear at any time and at any place in the ancient world. The waters of the world would have something to do with their being where they were, or finding themselves where they were, and their being desperately aggressive to secure the nearest possible stopping place.

Authorities - both ancient witnesses, and contemporary archaeologists and geographers, tell us that the lands rose and fell, the ocean levels went up and down for periods of time, ashes were to be found everywhere, where they burned first, where they fell from the skies, exoterrestrially as well as conveyed thousands of kilometers from explosions around the world. The conventional authorities – who in their own chosen arena achieve an openness to the newest methods of detecting movements of people – provide for the most ancient migrations of the framers and shepherds from East to West in the stone ages, but do not ponder that this Euro-Mediterranean world was thoroughly stirred up by as many as seven world-shaking quantavolutions, and that each one sent people flying in all directions, carrying their genomes with them.

Although the 'Sea Peoples' of Ramses III caused the gathering together of this whole concept of the movement of peoples in the Iron Age, especially the early Iron Age, they were a mistake. They were, as Velikovsky found out, mercenaries, vassals and soldiers of the Persian Empire. Some of course will be "Peoples Invading from the Sea." In any event, these Ramses III enemies are not needed to buttress the fact of the many movements of many diverse kinds of groups and people at the Apex of the Iron Age. We have plenty of peoples moving about by land and by sea. Simply to address the gravity of the migrations, I would venture the guess that in the Greater Mediterranean Region, 92% of the population lost their lives or were displaced during the century of the Iron Age apex.

Even the Achaeans or Danaans or Homeric Greeks were but a congeries of individuals and groups from a scores of places rising and responding to the call, on the barest (sic) pretext, to attack, kill, rob, rape and burn a city that did them no harm. Such were the crazed Achaean heroes, typical of the times. The same Achaeans and their kin are found to have settled in Cyprus and in the Western Mediterranean. It is possible, even probable, that the Myceneans left directly from their ruined and plagued palaces and farms to rumored safer, richer, healthier, well-watered, weaker or even deserted targets of opportunity for new settlement. Probably Troy

(Hisarlik or the Real Troy) was one of their targets, only to be destroyed both by the 'gods' or by nature and by the Achaeans themselves. As we shall see, in the earlier Venusian quantavolution of ~-1450, the Hebrews in Exodus passed and skirmished with the Hyksos or Amalekites on their flight from Egypt while the latter were fleeing Western Arabia, so the ended up, survivors both, by exchanging places.

The typical movement was often local, involving a flight to the hills to escape floods and tsunamis, and flight to the plains to escape lightning storms.

In both places the settlements were primitive by comparison with the Late Bronze Age centers. People lacked the time and the resources to build up decent habitats. But they learned to use the seas:

Thucydides on Wild Early Greece

The first great scientific historian, Thucydides, is crisp, dry and non-partisan. Early in his *History of the Peloponnesian War* he gives us the following information about early Iron Age Greece:[55]

> ... it is evident that the country now called Hellas had in ancient times no settled population; on the contrary, migrations were of frequent occurrence, the several tribes readily abandoning their homes under the pressure of superior numbers. Without commerce, without freedom of communication either by land or sea, cultivating no more of their territory than the exigencies of life required, destitute of capital, never planting their land (for they could not tell when an invader might not come and take it all away, and when he did come they had no walls to stop him), thinking that the necessities of daily sustenance could be supplied at one place as well as another, they cared little for shifting their habitation, and consequently neither built large cities nor attained to any other form of greatness. The richest soils were always most subject to this change of masters; such as the district now called Thessaly, Boeotia, most of the Peloponnese, Arcadia excepted, and the most fertile parts of the rest of Hellas. The goodness of the land favoured the aggrandizement of particular individuals, and thus created faction which proved a fertile source of ruin. It also invited invasion. ...
>
> For in early times the Hellenes and the barbarians of the coast and islands, as communication by sea became more common, were tempted to turn pirates, under the conduct of their most powerful men; the motives being to serve their own cupidity and to support the needy. They

would fall upon a town unprotected by walls, and consisting of a mere collection of villages, and would plunder it; indeed, this came to be the main source of their livelihood, no disgrace being yet attached to such an achievement, but even some glory. An illustration of this is furnished by the honour with which some of the inhabitants of the continent still regard a successful marauder, and by the question we find the old poets everywhere representing the people as asking of voyagers- "Are they pirates?"- as if those who are asked the question would have no idea of disclaiming the imputation, or their interrogators of reproaching them for it. The same rapine prevailed also by land....

The whole of Hellas used once to carry arms, their habitations being unprotected and their communication with each other unsafe; indeed, to wear arms was as much a part of everyday life with them as with the barbarians....

Even after the Trojan War, Hellas was still engaged in removing and settling, and thus could not attain to the quiet which must precede growth. The late return of the Hellenes from Ilium caused many revolutions, and factions ensued almost everywhere; and it was the citizens thus driven into exile who founded the cities. Sixty years after the capture of Ilium, the modern Boeotians were driven out of Arne by the Thessalians, and settled in the present Boeotia, the former Cadmeus; though there was a division of them there before, some of whom joined the expedition to Ilium. Twenty years later, the Dorians and the Heraclids became masters of Peloponnese; so that much had to be done and many years had to elapse before Hellas could attain to a durable tranquillity undisturbed by removals, and could begin to send out colonies, as Athens did to Ionia and most of the islands, and the Peloponnesians to most of Italy and Sicily and some places in the rest of Hellas. All these places were founded subsequently to the war with Troy.

Writing of the vases found of Aegean provenance, the Dartmouth College group speaks of:

...a substantial number of vases from a surprisingly wide variety of sites that depict ships. The vessels appearing on a pyxis found in the Tragana tholos in Messenia, on a small stirrup jar from a chamber tomb at Asine, and on a larger stirrup jar from the island of Skyros all lack people, were all found in funerary contexts, and just possibly were all produced for such a purpose. By contrast, a magnificent series of kraters found recently by Dakoronia (1987) at Kynos-Livadhates in coastal Locris and now on display in the Lamia Museum show warships and on-board combat, as probably do a number of more fragmentarily preserved kraters from Kos. These kraters illustrate ships for the first time ever on the Greek mainland [aside from the stern cabins, or {ikria}, decorating a wall in the palace at Mycenae that have been published by M. Shaw (1980)]; in the islands, these are the first ship depictions since the LC I examples decorating the walls of Room 5 in the West House at Akrotiri on Thera and a somewhat later building at Ayia Irini on Keos. Like the abandonment of body shields and boars'-tusk helmets, this sudden popularity of ships has much to say about the nature of warfare in this period, especially when taken in combination with the prevalence of hilltop refuge sites in both the islands and on Crete.

I shall mention in connection with Troy that Homer's characters seem never to partake of seafood. Yet the invading fleet numbered over 1100 ships. Fibs in both regards? Or perhaps half-truths. Heroes were newly-taught how to sail boats, but still ashamed to eat but meat.

As for the presence of Greeks (Danaans) at Troy, they were not strangers to Asia Minor. According to Mervyn Popham, their settling of the Coast in the "Ionian Migration" involved Aeolians, Dorians and others as well. "This event, tradition seems to place very early in the Iron Age."

Spanuth, Nielsson, Vinci and others speak of migrations from the far North of proto-Greeks, but I ask the reader's patience to let me postpone their opinions - and mine - of this particular mass vagrancy until the later chapter about Atlantis.

Chapter Eight

Mars and Its Doppelgaengers

Planet-Mars is tightly bound in ancient peoples' minds with gods who are paramount warriors, destructive heroes, crushers of towns and armies, dispatchers of plagues, and depicted as red in color. Many, if not all, nations worshiped the planet-Mars and the god-Mars, under their national names for both of them. In Babylonia he was Nergal, in Mexico Tezcatlipoca, for example.

Hundreds of Mars identities around the world came into prominence at the same time. India has Indra, for example, but also the planet Mars is named Mangala, which is possessed by a war-god named Karttike, who was the son of Shiva and Parvati. He rode a peacock and had six heads with twelve arms. The Mayan god paralleling Mars was a long-nosed creature descending to various depths from sky to earth , a segmented, banded sky serpent.

One count of Ares-Mars in Greek literature, thanks to David Talbott and Ev Cochrane, produced 110 archetypes and nicknames. In a linear B tablet of Knossos, Ares was a common noun meaning war and modifying a God Enyalios. But later in the *Iliad* Ares is the god modified by Enyalios, who is a minor cult hero. In the *Iliad* Ares ran off to his father Zeus when hurt or wounded. Why so? We may conjecture that here is a picture of Mars distancing outward rapidly after a disturbing encounter with Earth or Venus. The sons of Ares were Phobos , Demos, and Enyo, and his retinue included Pain, Panic, Famine, and Oblivion.

Many rituals, legends, superstitions, related fears, and heavy sacrifices attended the god-planet under its many names. We quote Ev Cochrane on some of this material:[56]

Erra was identified with Mars in Babylonian astronomical texts. Erra-like characteristics, moreover, were associated with the planet Mars in Mesopotamian thought, the forbidding nature of the red planet being everywhere apparent. Babylonian skywatchers described Mars as the "erratic star," the "disaster bringer," the star of evil, rebellion, and misfortune. Consistently associated with the phenomena of war, Mars was the warrior-planet *par excellence*. ...Consider the name *harabu*, signifying "to ravage, devastate, lay waste." This term is not only consistent with the ancient traditions associated with the planet Mars, it would appear to be cognate with the Semitic root **hrr*, "to scorch," that regarded by Roberts as the root in Erra. The phrase *mustabarru mutanu*, understood by the Babylonians as "swollen with pestilence," was applied to the planet Mars. And in light of Roberts' suggestion that the name of Erra derives from a root meaning "scorcher," it is significant to note that a name of Nergal/Mars in Babylonian texts was *sarrapu*, "scorcher." Indeed, Mars was viewed as the "fiery" planet throughout the ancient world. The Babylonian skywatchers called it the "firebrand." A Hellenistic name for Mars – *Pyroeis*, "Fiery Star" -- indicates that similar conceptions prevailed among the Greeks. In China, likewise, Mars was the fire-star, said to portend "bane, grief, war, and murder."

Crosthwaite gives us clues from linguistics:

> The Latin *dolabra*, axe or he, is similar to *tlabrys*, axe, a word which occurs in the language of Lydia, a country in Asia Minor which has Etruscan connections. Initial *t* and initial *s* which are sometimes dropped, so we have in *tlabrys*, the Lydian version of *labrys*, double axe, Latin *dolabra*, which symbolizes lightning and gave its name to the labyrinth.
>
> Dolabra is *ar falando*, sky fire. *Falando* is an Etruscan word meaning iron, and the sky whence iron falls in the form of meteorites. One may compare the Etruscan *falando*, sky, the Latin *palatium*, and the Hebrew *palda* iron. The fall of meteorites led some thinkers of the ancient world to the belief that the sky was made of iron.

The Romans were the people of Mars, *par excellence*, as is widely known. The Etruscans worshiped Mars, and a superior lightning God Tinia, corresponding to Jupiter and Thor, also lightning gods. All of the Etruscan gods were lightning gods, it seems, so obsessed were these people with lightning.

If, as we surmise, Mars approached closely to Earth in the Iron Age on several occasions, it might well change its figure to suggest what its names and its myths conveyed. John Ackerman is probably correct in saying that ugly protuberances would swell Mars grotesquely and give rise to myths that are incomprehensible otherwise.[57] The frightening distortions of Hercules (and, elsewhere worldwide, of the other famous god-heroes) come to mind --

of his face and stature, his red colors, his shooting fire and surrounding flames, his boiling of waters (Lord of Hot Springs) and boiling in water.

The most apt explanation of the repulsive, terrifying and painful experiences of the god heroes (for which descriptions see especially Ev Cochrane's book), is that actually they were seen, that the planet Mars underwent frightful experiences. For these heroes and gods were worshiped, they were immensely powerful in suggesting imitative behaviors, they were deemed immortal, they were cherished, feared, propitiated. How could the extremely handsome Ares, Greek God of War, of Aphrodite, become so atrociously repulsive and tortured, if what befell him was entirely a concoction of only his most devoted followers?

Thus we seek to account for the changing ugly bulges and tortures of fire, and for the giantism and then the astonishing rendering of the same gods as midgets from time to time. We are forced to imagine that, possibly as Mars approached Earth, it became a giant, and as it drew away from Earth, the planet diminished in apparent size. The Bible spoke of a tribe of giants and an individual giant. Giants are a favored theme of myth everywhere. Possibly these giants had a place in the human mind crowded by frightful images. Perhaps such giants even were perceived to drop their own images. Mesabi, the world's most productive range of iron mountains, means "the giant" in Menominee Minnesota Indian language.

It is famous that Mars is accompanied by two small moons. With the Vedas in mind, we can call them the Maruts, but the Maruts were many bodies. Jerry Ziegler and Donald Patten, among others, have found numbers of references to and descriptions of the behavior of the late principal Maruts, unmistakably the satellites Demos and Phobos, Rout and Terror, which, although not seen by modern observers until Hall's report of 1887, were well known to the ancients of many countries.

Earth, Moon and Mars Scenarios

Aside from my own treatment of the subject in *The Disastrous Love Affair of Moon and Mars,* Donald Patten, Jerry

Ziegler, Ev Cochrane, and John Ackerman have been the most radical – or perhaps one should say outspoken – in describing the movements of the planets that would have to be witnessed if near collisions were occurring. Actually these four accounts have much in common. Perhaps another hundred briefer studies would be found to add here as similar models, Velikovsky certainly, who discovered the Mars quantavolution as such, and ending with the work of Hans Bellamy at about the same time.

Ackerman is especially pertinent to the present work because he draws what I need out of Mars, namely the abundance of iron ore that has given mankind first the Iron Age, and then 2000 years of the material basis of civilization – actually until the age of plastics that started up about a century ago.

Ackerman, following closely the Vedas, counts over a hundred close encounters of Earth and Mars, over a 3000-year period, before it was brusquely despatched upon its present course by planet-Venus. He was the first (and until now, I suspect, the only) scholar to claim that Mars actually lost its prior iron core into space, in what became essentially planet Mercury. The major indicator of this event is the great bulk of the iron of Mercury as measured by its high density, and the surprisingly low density of Mars.

Patten-Windsor Theory

Donald Patten and his small circle of scientists have independently studied the recent history of Mars for many years.[58] They have given full weight to geology, astrophysics and proto-history in their research. They have also been deeply involved in reconciling natural history and the Bible. To their understanding of events, Planet Mars was struck by a body the size of Pluto several thousands of years ago and propelled into an orbit periodically threatening Earth, and in fact causing some damage, each to the other, for many centuries until, nudged into a new orbit by the wayward Planet Venus, it swung into the motions that we have been seeking to report in this book, exceedingly destructive in nature.

The original explosion and crash of much of the

body that they call "Astra" also originated, in their opinion, the innumerable asteroids, thousands of which might be designated Earth-threatening on a low or higher level of probability. (There is a similarity of scenarios, in that I designated in *Chaos and Creation* a missing planet in the present-day asteroid belt as Apollo, the same as the god Apollo, and other students, too, have conjectured a missing planet in the same region in order to explain the asteroid belt.)

The huge rift of Valles Marineris, the Tharsis Bulge of the size of Europe, and the immense volcanoes discovered on Mars occurred catastrophically in the weakest portion of the Martian crustal rocks, through the upwards thrust resulting from the crash of the hypothetical large Astra fragment they name "Hellas."

We can note the difference between the Ackerman and Patten scenarios. Both depict Mars as knocked from its prior orbit to approach Earth perilously. (Also, Velikovsky and I do so by utilizing the proto-Planet Venus, recently expelled from Jupiter, to propel Mars toward Earth.) Both have Mars in the vicinity of Earth for a millennium and more, I for a short time, although open to alternatives. Both Patten and Ackerman expel the requisite material from Mars to explain the great rift and volcanoes. I rather agree with Ackerman's view that a body the size of Mercury could have emerged from Valles Marineris, and we agree also that it was drawn out electro-gravitationally rather than kicked out by underlying forces. Both use Planet Venus to kick Mars into its present orbit. So do I.

Both Ackerman and the Patten team insist that their theories rest upon possibilities derivable from astrophysics. They also stress the coincidence of their scenario with the testimony of ancient witnesses – Babylonian, Chinese, Hebrew (Isaiah *et al.*), Greek (Hesiod, e.g.), and others. I do the same. A chasm exists between ourselves and conventional science brought on by its consensus against moving its theories into the social, psychological and historical sciences, even including archaeology.

The conventional view is not certain of itself, but appears to believe that Valles Marineris was created by a sinking of the large stretch of crust over a long period of time, as magma was siphoned off beneath it and conveyed to supply the magma that was blowing off in the gigantic explosions of the volcanoes so clearly evident even from Earth. A million cubic miles of lava was exuded in the process. I shall not proceed further with this discussion but point out, as does Patten, "Where, then, are the wrinkles in the Valles that would accompany its shrinkage?"

Obviously I support either or both hypotheses as superior to the conventional one, with regard both to the mechanism that created the phenomena and the recency of the events involved. Further, they derive much support legitimately from mythology and ancient testimony. My model, as presented in this book and elsewhere, seems to be accommodating to either of the other quantavolution models, with a certain advantage or favor accruing to Ackerman in our eyes for drawing down to Earth large amounts of iron ore from Mars and in the process expelling the small planet of Mercury, whose composition appears to be so preponderant in iron.

I had previously suggested that the Planet Mercury seemed to appear ~-2300,[59] and entitled the period from then until the takeover of the skies by Venus ~_1450 as Mercuria. I deduced then, and still have an investment in the conjecture, that there had existed a prior planet "Apollo," which exploded to produce Mercury and the asteroid belt. Several scientists, beginning in the early 1800's, have also hypothesized a destroyed planet in the asteroid space between Mars and Jupiter.

In accord with Velikovsky, Juergens, Earl Milton and others of our circle, however, I assumed that the Mars incursions were only several in number, not one hundred, and took place in the period ~-800 to ~-650. We all agreed that repeated episodes occurred at 15-year intervals, basing this idea upon little more than reasonable reports in the Bible. In the end, we concluded, Mars was released into its present orbit by a perilous conjunction.

The best alternative hypothesis as to how the ancients could observe their behavior, if they were not close in to Earth and Moon, would be the telescope. Yet none has been found in ruins nor pictured or reported. There would have to be many telescopes, inasmuch as the phenomenon is reported from around the world, and it is highly unlikely that not a single one would be reported or preserved.

Languages from around the word have developed many scores of words derived from the god-word for Mars. In English alone, Patten has counted and lists 369 words that are connected etymologically with the root of Mars, Ares, Bel, Indra, Tyr and other Martian gods. Practically all of them connote bad actions or feelings or experiences. Both the ancient and the modern characters for Mars in Chinese mean the 'fire star'. (Catastrophe is usually defined to mean the denouement of a tragic drama, but basically signifies a "a downfalling star.")

Skipping among the 369 words that Patten connects to Mars and its doppelgaengers, we give as examples from different languages finding their way into English the following: March, morose, martial, Tuesday, tremble, belligerent, typhoon, Aryan, army, arsenic, demonic, dementia, phobia, horror, Indian, cherub, Iran. The aspects of Mars disperse in every direction.

The Latin *robigo* means redness or rust. Its key consonants, *rbg*, when read backwards (this happens often, as Crosthwaite and others have shown) give *gbr*. *Gibor* is Hebrew for a "hero" or "leader." Gibor may give *gibor el*, divine warrior, and Gabriel is the Hebrew divine warrior sent by Yahweh on trips to wipe out Sennacherib's army and other enemies.

We seem to be able to go on indefinitely, grasping at straws often. Thus the woodpecker was important in augury in Etruria and Rome. It represented Mars. Why? Red, standing for Mars, plus its rapid tapping that suggests a rain of pebbles such as Mars was famously using for showering the Earth. Thus goes Crosthwaite. Straws, yes, but millions of houses are built of trillions of straws, until the builders afford better.

The watch for life from and on Mars proceeds apace, – and no longer shamefacedly. Professors Fred Hoyle and Wickramasinghe[60] have presented (and not alone) the thesis which argues the probability of a birth, proliferation, and fall of viral and bacterial matter from outer space, causing some of the major plagues that have afflicted humanity. A number of archaeologists have suspected that the abandonment of cities and countryside in the Iron Age may have been effected by plagues. Indeed, it may constitute a kind of proof of plague, when we find no evidence of enemies, earthquakes, or ashes to mark a ruin.

Sponsored by the Carnegie Institution, a Norwegian-led consortium in 2005 reported the discovery deep in the ice of a volcano vent at Svalbard, Norway, "both living and fossilized organisms, which is the kind of evidence we 'd been searching for on the Red Planet." The volcano was dated at 1my. The carbonate rocks lifted from the drill hole resemble the carbonate rosettes found in the Martian meteorite ALH84001. The organisms were found both in the ice and on the surface and surrounding rocks and crevices.

We can anticipate that a Mars explorer will soon find a tectonically similar spot with a sizeable chance of discovering there life forms. In *Chaos and Creation* I modeled an enormous plenum of gases and plasmas that once enveloped the solar system, in which a biotic soup would have afforded chances for life to develop. The newest findings relating to Mars and Earth are apropos.

If this chain of creation were to be valid, we would always have to expect the bad with the good. In the Iron Age, when Mars' surface was heated violently and transferred material of various types to Earth, there would be included organisms of strange and altered species, some poisonous, as well as some of benefit or inconsequential.

Copiously exemplified by Ev Cochrane, in his study of legends of Mars, are the several qualities and behaviors of Mars and his doppelgaenger sky bodies and god-heroes. It is submitted that these characterize the quantavolution of the Iron Age. Several volumes might readily be taken up with details. Here, though, we mention a few of the more salient legends:

1. The paragon of Mars is afflicted on occasion with ugly diseases and agonies.
2. The paragon at times grows gigantic, bulking formidably against the sky.
3. He enters the belly of a giant dragon.
4. He is consumed by flames.

5. He brings diseases and epidemics to mankind.
6. On occasion he becomes a dwarf.
7. He becomes incandescent and is plunged into water, both boiling and cold.
8. He is compelled to wander, hated by all humanity, and carrying evils with him.
9. He disturbs the heavens and the sun-god.
10. He shrinks and withers as he climbs the ladder to heaven to join the gods.
11. He is above all a bloody cruel warrior, a slayer of myriads, a destroyed or nations.

Given all of these behaviors, how could people around the Great Mediterranean Region have come to worship such a polynomenal creature? Possibly we shall learn more as we proceed. But an admonition in advance may help: the human being venerates naked power, a projection upon the world of the absolute power he wishes upon himself in all the worst forms that he would hope to reduce, and mollify, by imitation, by prayers, by magic. Thus the real conduct of Planet-Mars is absorbed into the human character.

History of the Quantavolution of Mars

Before combing a maze of names, we offer a description of the general scene of planetary misbehavior in the Iron Age, a paraphrase of my work of twenty-five years ago.

In a passage that is perilously close to the truth, E. Richardson writes of the ancient Etruscans of present day Tuscany :

> The last quarter of the eighth and the first half of the seventh centuries were evidently lively times in the Near East...Farther West, in Central Italy, the Oriental style broke like a tidal wave over the simple, if competent, civilization of the Villanovans. Here, it was not a question of occasional Villanovan traders or mercenaries coming home with new goods in a new style, not even a question of Greek traders sailing west.. but there must have been an actual shift of population from the old world of the East to the relatively uncluttered new world of the West. Almost any of the events we have chronicled above, or something we

have yet to discover might have caused such a shift during those turbulent seventy-five years.

The "something we have yet to discover" was shared by East and West, a state of affairs sometimes unbeknown to the uprooted ones -- the "something" that Rilli found mysterious in the ashes piled upon Etruscan settlements, and the ancient encyclopedist Pliny had reported as a bolt of Jupiter destroying the rich city of Volsinium – was the work of cosmic forces.

Vesuvius exploded in the eighth century and Etna in the seventh century B.C.E. The Sicani fled Eastern Sicily because of seismism and volcanism. Italy was rent by fissure seismism connecting with volcanoes along its entire length. The number of rivers reported to have disappeared was far beyond the record of later solarian times. (Ellen Semple cites some of the cases in her book on Mediterranean geography.) Many Phoenician and Greek colonies were founded in the western Mediterranean, especially in Sicily, during the Martian period.

It is possible, too, that the Etruscans settled in Italy not long before the Romans, carrying a highly developed culture from Asia Minor where, traditionally, they had been forced out by a great famine. Their blood type is similar to the Urartu people of Lake Van; their mostly undeciphered language is found upon Lemnos, favorite island of Hephaistos (blacksmith god), and is related to the Hittite(which may be Chaldean); and they are distinguishable from their Villanovan predecessors in culture and separated from them by a layer of catastrophic debris. In some cases the two cultures were intermingled.

The Etruscans were especial worshipers of Jupiter and lightning, to the point where they could be mistaken for Yahweh-sect descendants of Noah. Planet Mars, already long known to mankind as a moving star, was precipitated onto its disastrous course lasting nearly a century (-776 B.C.E. to -687 B.C.E.) when proto-planet Venus spiraled near to it . Spectacular celestial events were observed from Earth. The unsettled body invaded the orbit of Earth, and repeatedly, roughly at fifteen years intervals, it approached Earth closely, causing new disasters.

The highly developed Etruscan and rude Latin civilizations were devastated. Although Rome was born amidst the turmoil (- 753?), it gloried in the planetary god that bore the name Mars. Mycenaean civilization in Greece was largely destroyed through the same agency, there called Ares, God of War and embodiment of sheer destruction. Herakles seem to have represented the planet as well and classicists will recall that the Heraclids were identified with the Dorian invasion of Greece. In his study of *Discontinuities in Greek Civilization*, Carpenter helps one across the dizzying chasm between evolutionary and quantavolutionary thought. The Dorians were the Heraclids who were "professed linear descendants of tribal followers of the legendary hero-god Herakles..."

They came upon a destroyed civilization, "the greatest still unsolved problem in Mediterranean history.... The calendar time is 1200 B.C.E." [In fact, it is not, It is around 850 B.C.E.] "and Mediterranean man has begun to suffer the most severe cultural recession which history records or archaeology can determine. Great kingdoms have collapsed without apparent adequate reason; and the eastern sea shores are overrun by fugitives seeking to force their way into lands less smitten by disaster. In Greece the well-fortified Mycenaean palaces are burned and abandoned; but none seems to know who burned them."

[And more and worse, but Carpenter has an answer] "*famine*... And by famine I do not mean an occasional failure of several consecutive harvests, but such an enduring and disastrous destruction of the annual yield as only a drastic climatic change could have occasioned."

He then proves famine, which is usually part of a catastrophe, we have noted. The Edomite bedouin were even then migrating into Egypt "to avoid famine," says Bimson. A change in the prevailing winds is given as a cause : African wet winds changed to African dry winds. But what changes prevailing winds? And around the world? We recognize today a growing belief of meteorologists that great changes in climate originate in the celestial sphere. One Greek civilization was destroyed and another took its place. Climatic change was part of the action, and the transition period probably lasted two centuries ~ -850 to ~ - 650, not five centuries. Carpenter believed in the Dark Ages.

God by Any Other Name...

Mesopotamia suffered greatly, too; in the typical collective madness, delusion, and psychological projection that gave birth to all astral gods, the Babylonians elevated and celebrated Nergal. Nergal was Era who was Ares who was Mars. The insane human devastator of the Middle East, King Nebuchadnezzar, called himself by its name: "I am Nergal. I destroy, I burn, I demolish, leaving nothing behind me."

Nergal's deeds are described as part of solicitations for leniency: The world was "moved exceedingly" and "became moved from its place." The planet-god Nergal, "the heavens he makes dark, he moves the earth off its hinges"..."Nergal...on high stills the heavens...causes the earth to shudder." He was the"raging fire god. He was also called Sharappu, "the burner" and the "light that flames from heaven," and "lord of destruction." (Thus Velikovsky, quoting Böllenbrucher, Langdon, and Schaumberger.)

Again the gods in heaven carry on their wars through their human agents. It was Ares versus Athene again, Mars against Venus, in his march into Palestine. "From the philological, theological, and historical data, there is no question that, in both name and substance, Jerusalem was indeed the 'City of Venus.' The reign of the 'Queen of Heaven' was an uneasy one, however, and did not go unchallenged. In the end, the Venus Star yielded to a resuscitated Yahwism and relinquished its hierarchical position, but only after centuries of protracted politico-religious struggle and not until Jerusalem itself lay trampled and ruined beneath the Chaldean war-machine of Nebuchadnezzar."

The Jews commemorated the new active agency in the cosmos by the appellation Kesil Maadin, and Gabriel, and typically rendered these as inspired by their single divinity. So in the days of Uzziah there was a grand commotion (~ -747 B.C.E.) and also when Ahaz was buried in ~ -717 B.C.E. On the same day the sun dial changed about 10° (*ca* 40 minutes). According to Velikovsky, the Earth's axis shifted and twilight was hastened. This story, writes Velikovsky, "is related also in the records and told in the traditions of many peoples. It appears that a heavenly body passed very close to the Earth, moving, as it seem, in the same direction as the Earth on its nocturnal side."

The prophet Isaiah preached about 701 B.C.E. It was he who said *(22:13)*, in the midst of the Martian terrors, "Let us eat and drink, for tomorrow we shall die." "According to *Isaiah* XXI.8, the heavens were most anxiously scanned at the conjunction times, by day and by night, for the 'grievous vision' of a 'treacherous dealer' and 'destructive spoiler' (*Isa* XXI.2) According to *Jer.* I.13f, the dreaded phenomenon looked somewhat like a 'seething pot', and when it appeared in the heavens 'an evil broke forth out of the north upon all the inhabitants of the land.' These calamities happened periodically. Thus (*Jer.* L1,146) 'in one year, and after that in another year, and then there was always violence in the land, and ruler fought against ruler.'" In ~ -687 B.C.E., the restless Earth wobbled on its axis, electrical exchanges occurred, and the army of Sennacherib was destroyed by a great blast of gas.

Mars appeared as lean, wolfish, foolhardy, hot, fiery, and ardent among widely dispersed people. Mars had many names, newly coined, around the world. It was called the "wolf-star" by the Chinese, Scandinavians, and others. The Mars-obsessed Romans believed that a wolf bitch had suckled the foundling twins, Romulus and Remus, who established Rome. Mars was the "sword-star" to the Scythians, and the Romans made their new short swords integral to the equipment and maneuvers of the invincible legion. It was Marut and Rama to the Hindus, and Huitzilopochtli, high God of the Aztecs. In dispersed parts of the world occur myths that the Moon is chased by dogs or wolves and, upon eclipses, they desperately beat drums and raise a tumult to frighten off the devourer of the Moon. The Aztec Huitzilopochtli appears to have held also the names Tetzahuitl and Tezcatlipoca. Quetzalcoatl, the Plumed Serpent God, "wise and sympathetic," was "vanquished in the struggle with his contrary and enemy, Tezcatlipoco, the god who carried on his forehead a smoking mirror, who spread discord and transformed mankind into monkeys, just as Quetzalcoatl changed them into birds."

"Expelled from his city, he took the road to Yucatan, announcing, however, that he would return to his homeland. Arriving at the shore of the sea, he erected a pyre and offered himself to the flames. A few days later he reappeared transformed into the planet Venus." Thus goes the principal Mexican story pertaining to planet Mars and planet Venus in celestial combat.

The Romans worshipped their first ruler, Romulus, for having joined his father, Mars, in heaven on the occasion of a cyclonic outburst. That the Romans had a longer history somewhere, perhaps indeed at Troy, is indicated by their adoration of the whole Olympic family, and the impregnation of their institutions by them. For instance, the Roman consuls served for a Venusian-length year.

Greeks who survived the disorders of sky and planet chanted of the battle of the gods, in the language of Homer. Among the principal figures who engaged in conflict at Troy under the aegis of Zeus were Athena-Odysseus-Venus, Ares-Paris-Mars, and Aphrodite-Helen-Moon. Troy was only one of the many cities destroyed in this period, nor was this the first destruction of that city over the millennia. The Spartans made human sacrifices to Ares, and sacrificed dogs as well, in nocturnal offerings, to his *alter ego*, Enyalius.

As happened in climactic celestial events of earlier times, the Martian period brought a change of calendars around the world. Nabonassar, an obscure king of Babylon, gave his name to a new era of the calendar in the year ~ -747. The first Olympic Games marked a reassembly of Greeks and may have occurred ~ -776. The founder of the games was reputedly none other than Hercules, *alter ago* of planet Mars.

Romulus, says Ovid, brought the Romans a calendar of 10 months which made the year just the length of a woman's pregnancy, that is, 280 days. But shortly thereafter, about - 715, two months were added. Bentley, reporting on India, connects the end of the war of gods and giant there with the war of the gods in the *Iliad* of Homer and with the Era of Nabonassar.

Two Dutch scientists have reviewed the radiocarbon, tree ring, and varve studies of this period and conclude that the statistics point to a considerable lengthening of the solar year, from perhaps 280 to 365 days, ~ -780. This is the century, too, when Seuss' carbondating research suggested shifts in the magnetic poles and abrupt changes of climate.

Carli, the early scientific catastrophist (1780), believes (I think mistakenly) that Italy was covered by swamps for millennia after the flood of Ogyges (~ -4000 in his estimation). He quotes a report by Denis of Halicarrnassos that Oenotrus, son of Lycaon, having gone to settle in Italy with a colony, found the country deserted and uncultivated and was obliged to search for habitation on the mountains. Great swamps persisted in the north until the time of Hannibal. Taken together with the desolate situation of the South and Sicily in the early period of Greek colonialization, with the evidence of the destruction of the high Etruscan civilization and the coming of the Romans, this would seem to be the aftermath of the war of the gods.

The Spartans were among the most disciplined and dedicated warriors of the classical world, but whenever the earth trembled they would scuttle for home. Said Ellen Churchill Semple, "If earthquakes would break the nerve and nullify the life-long training of Spartan troops, there must have been abundant reason." She sets forth the exceptional seismicity of Laconia and much of the known world then, but in true uniformitarian fashion, never ventures that natural disasters were worse then, or had been unbelievably worse a couple of centuries earlier, when all the settlements of the Mycenaeans were wiped out, and the Spartans, as Dorian survivors and sons of Herakles, took over the area.

Recent Geological Marks on Mars

Like Venus and the Moon, Mars shows the severe effects of its recent space encounters. The geological evidence for large-body encounters with Mars in a recent time can be summed up in nine points :

1. Argon, an important ingredient of Mars' atmosphere, is also found in unexpectedly large amounts in the clouds of

Venus and in the Moon's surface rocks.

2. The surface of Mars is rent by canyons and craters of prodigious size. exhibiting both gravitational and electrical disruption.

3. The polar caps of Mars are composed of solid carbon dioxide (CO_2) and possibly ice. This must be a very recent freeze, following acquisition of CO_2 from Venus.

4. Sets of laminated spherical caps lay near the polar areas. These are meltings of the surface. They are irregularly laminated, one upon another [88]. They occurred perhaps when the polar axes heated up from interplanetary encounters with Earth or Venus, involving electrical discharges. The near side of the Moon and the surface of Mercury evidence the same type of molten-looking splotches.

5. The present poles of Mars are far off the laminated electric melts of the old poles (or the old magnetic poles when Mars rotated within the magnetic tube). This would indicate an axial tilt.

6. Hot spots, perhaps of volcanism, surface contortion and radioactivity exist. These are signs of recent externally produced disturbances.

7. No erosion has occurred on the many great cracks, rilles and canyons of the surface. These are electrical in origin, therefore, and not products of turbulent water (although E. J. Opik thinks that they may be radiating lines of craters exploded from external agents.)

8. A complex of a canyon, Coprates (now named Valles Marineris), exists that is 2000 miles long, up to 300 miles wide, and over 4 miles deep. It is likely to have been produced by a single instant unzippening of the surface by a passing body, possibly Venus.

9. The crater Nix Olympica is 300 miles wide and has a 100-mile-high peak. It is not volcanic but the result of an electrical-gravitational explosion.

Donald Patten has also listed, and discussed, details of the physical scars of Mars. His list includes:

1. The fragmentation of Astra on the Roche Limit of Mars
2. Evidence that Mars has put on 1.5% more weight

(doubtful in view of its loss of iron)
 3. The resulting genesis of the asteroids
 4. The sudden genesis of the former Martian ring system
 5. The numerous pitlets on both Deimos and Phobos
 6. The numerous pitlets also on tiny Gaspra
 7. The crater distribution on Mars, 93% on one side
 8. The rim where the Martian hemisphere of craters ends
 9. The genesis of its two bulges, Tharsis and Elysium
 10. The birth of its giant rift system, Valles Marineris
 11. The birth and infancy of the giant volcanoes of Mars
 12. The dry river beds on Mars (but without any canals)
 13. The cause of twin spin axis tilts -- Mars and Earth
 14. The genesis of the ancient icy cometary tail of Mars

According to Patten, the nearest approach to Earth of Mars and his doppelgaengers, the perigee, was 27,000 miles, with a diameter ostensibly of 17.24 times that of the Moon, taking up 69% more of the sky than did the Moon, Reflectance, if full, would have been 69+ times greater than the Moon's. Oceanic tides and magmatic (sub-crustal) tides were 5,900 times the normal lunar tides. The planet came within a perilous 16,000 kilometers of the Roche Limit, where it would have shattered. Patten adduces the testimony of Isaiah, citing the Old Testament *Isaiah 38, 11 Kings* and *11 Chronicles*. He also cites and interprets ingeniously Hesiod's poem *The Shield of Hercules* (The Disc of Ares) to describe the presence and horror of the near approach of the planet.

Historical Indications of the Mars-Earth Interaction

The historical evidence may also be summarized : Hebrew, Roman, Mexican, Greek, Hindu, Babylonian and other nations and tribes report heavy natural disturbances throughout the period ~ -776 to ~ -687. All of the high-energy forces of catastrophism were involved.

Mars (Ares) is then newly worshipped everywhere, with great intensity. The god is identified with the planet in many places. The behavior of the god corresponds to that of the planet. For example, in the *Iliad* which I have elsewhere assigned, not alone, to the turn of the Seventh Century, Pallas Athene (Venus) "cast her spear mightily against his nethermost belly" upon which "the brazen Ares bellowed loud as nine thousand or ten thousand warriors cry in battle, when they join in the strife of the Wargod." This may conceivably have been the occasion for the tearing open of the Valles Marineris (Coprates Canyon) on Mars.

Indra Girt by Maruts is a book consisting largely of the apotheosis of the electrical emanations of the Planet Mars in hundreds of poetic lines of the Vedas, with brief explanations by Jerry Ziegler. We use his words in what follows:

> Indra is the Hindu God planet identifiable as the planet Mars, and the tiny moons of Mars, the Maruts. The Maruts would have been the so-called Steeds of Mars, also called Terror, Rout, and Discord in the Iliad of Homer under command of the God Ares (Mars).. Nergal, the Mars of Babylonia, was seen to own giant raging demons that ran alongside him. Joel is said to be watching them; in the Old Testament he cries out at the days of darkness that have come like never before.

> *A fire devoureth before them; and behind them a flame burneth.... Nothing shall escape them... The appearance of them is as the appearance of horses: and as horsemen, so shall they run. The Earth shall shake before them: the heavens shall tremble; the sun and the moon shall be dark, and the stars shall withdraw their shining.*

The Maruts acted as fire devils, burning, darting flames and lightning, and showering stones promiscuously, hot gravel with tongues of flame -- stones that were collected, wherever found, and worshiped as tokens of the almighty God Mars. The Maruts are described in a number of forms that shower down, produce lightning in all of its forms, especially ball lightning, produce soma, slay cattle in the fields, and can be induced by the priesthood (Hindu) to come to eminences and altars where they may contribute to sacrifices, and impress the people. Nothing like this magnificent description of electrical activity exists in any other literature.

Rens van der Sluijs has listed 22 forms that lightning takes in mythology,[62] and we look for all of these, and find them, when we are searching the Martian literature. For instance, Motif #1: Lightning takes the form of a frightful weapon – a sword, arrow, mace, club, spear, axe, or hammer. #2: Lightning is an ancestral warrior, the hero god who defeated chaos monsters in ancestral times. Lightning-hero and lightning-weapon are frequently synonymous. #3 Lightning appears as a great bird or "thunderbird" with heaven-spanning wings. #4 Lichening is the flash of an "eye" in heaven. It is the destructive power of the "evil eye," destroying opposition. #5: Lightning is launched from a great wheel turning in the sky, the "chariot" of the gods. Etc., ending with Motif #22 that in the most ancient myths, lightning is the weapon of the planets.

Hamon, in Hebrew, means "noise" and is a name for Gabriel (Mars). "Assyrians of the host of Sennacherib, before they died, were permitted by Gabriel to hear 'the song of the celestials,' which can be interpreted as the sound caused by a close approach of the planet." Thus goes a Jewish legend. The God Hemen elsewhere in the Near East, is the God of Noise.

Yahweh is not to be omitted from consideration, not here, nor later on in this work. A god, any god, as I explained in the *Divine Succession* (1982), changes to match the times and the human state of mind. It may actually lose its usual name while keeping its traits. The Assyrian God Ninurta, (Nimrod), like the Roman God Mars, appears to have been originally an agricultural god, but then changed into a warrior god. Yahweh, too, is perceived by some scholars to have passed from an agricultural divinity to the Iron Age God of war, storm, fire, and pestilence. Others make him out also to have begun his Iron Age existence as a thunderbolting god.

I ask myself, "What does this have to do with the planet Mars and the Iron Age?" I answer that especially the prior portion of this period saw a great deal of activity in the skies by people who were at the same time cognizant that the interaction of the celestial and the mundane had been going on for a long time, and indeed cycling itself, so that the planet Mars, for a century or more, with Velikovsky claiming several cycles, Patton claiming more and Ackerman claiming for as many as a hundred cycles, had been the major celestial figure in their minds and behavior. Mars had led to the partial or general destruction of practically all aspects of Bronze Age civilizations.

Astrophysical Agonies of Mars

We do not know fully and never will know the exact astronomical scenarios of the century, but I would speculate in favor of something like the following set of events:

We must accept first of all a controversial set of circumstances preceding the Martian Quantavolution. The solar system had moved from one form of stabilization to another over the course of a short history of perhaps a million years, the intervening destabilizations or quantavolutions having brought the system to a state where Venus, a fairly new member of the planetary family, had proceeded on an irregular elliptical course that took it at intervals close enough to planet Mars to unsettle its motions. In the early Eighth Century , Mars was sufficiently destabilized to careen near to Earth and begin a fifteen-year cycle of close encounters.

The interaction was so severe that Mars was broken open and disgorged ultimately a large portion of itself of high density, which became in short order when it broke free, with the intervention of planet Venus, the planet Mercury (here adopting the theory of John Ackerman). For an interval of time, Mercury was the principal member of "the terrible ones" as they were referred to in the Bible and the Vedas, the Maruts in the Vedas, which toured the global skies, wreaking much damage upon Earth. Eventually, in an encounter with Venus, Mercury was whipped into roughly its present orbit, evidencing its stormy career as Hermes-Thoth-Mercury by a ruined thin surface and a huge iron interior, derived from Mars (which shows its loss by its low density and plethora of surface iron dust and pebbles).

Mercury has a magnetic field, like that of Earth. It may have carried this with it when it dissociated from Mars, whose surface rocks and meteorites measure a similar magnetism. According to Ackerman, shows that planetary magnetic fields arise from super-currents in the solid *FeH* inner cores of planets, not from the circulation of liquid iron in the outer core, as currently believed. The mere circulation of liquid cannot produce a magnetic field, which requires the circulation of electric charge."[63]

Mars had many images in legend as it underwent its

astronomical agonies. It appeared as a flaming sword on some occasions, as a chariot on various occasions. Among the other mythical indications we may underscore the biblical lines of *2 Kings 23:11*, where it is said, of the resolute monotheist King Josiah, "He removed from the entrance to the temple of the Lord the horses that the kings of Judah had dedicated to the sun. They were in the court near the room of an official named Nathan-Melech. Josiah then burned the chariots dedicated to the sun."

The phases when Mars was undergoing stresses and deformations by interaction with Earth and the disgorgement of Mercury may be the source of ancient legends that made the handsome ruddy warrior god a frightful mess, at one time with a hugely distended, monstrous head hanging down toward Earth, its hand stretching frequently down toward the multitudes of sinners. Mars had so many manifestations, indeed, that we may wonder whether the fanatical dedication of Josiah to bring about an unnameable god, following in the manner of David, a god without images, a god that was abstract in this sense, a very general god, an only god, that could not possibly be mistaken for Nergal-Mars or Baal of another or several of the named gods of the region: whether this brought about Yahweh.

Chapter Nine

Mars Brings Iron to Earth

Why would a brisk iron industry spring up around the world just when the highly developed, and in some ways ecumenical, old civilization, with its many thriving industries, collapses? The entrance upon the world stage of a new kind of work-material, intimately tied to the collapse, might help resolve this contradiction. Such was iron.

Of 86 known metals, ancient civilizations knew only seven, and their earliest use is conventionally set at: (1) Gold, (ca) 6000BC, (2) Copper,(ca) 4200BC, (3) Silver,(ca) 4000BC , (4) Lead, (ca) 3500BC ,(5) Tin, (ca) 1750BC , (6) Iron, (ca) 1500BC, (7) Mercury, (ca) 750BC . None of these dates is reliable, although relatively correct. For instance, iron would be more likely to have entered abundantly into history ~-850. We have explained the 400-year Phantom Age, which, when removed, brings the conventional -1200 date properly down.

In *The Lately Tortured Earth*, I generalize about the origin of several of the metals used by ancient peoples. I conjectured that they descended from the skies in the times and consciousness of mankind. Those first used were necessarily to be found at or near the surface. They are in fact to be found at or near the surface. Their order of descent may have been successive, in that gold preceded silver, silver preceded copper and copper was followed by nickel and iron. Planet Mars and some asteroids probably brought in the nickel and iron, which are closely associated in meteorites.

Iron-working is siderurgy, a word out of ancient Greece and Rome. It translates properly as the working of star-iron. The Greek word for anvil, on which iron was worked, was close to the word for a meteoric stone. The Eygptians called iron "the bones of Typhon" and "a gift from Seth," both names corresponding to bodies crashing into the Earth, devil-monster and devil-god. Meteoritic iron was known to the early dynasties. "The Jews called iron ore *nechoshet*, which literally means the '(droppings of the (cosmic)serpent,' a nonsensical term unless our interpretation of it is allowed."[64] The Jews forbade the use of iron in chiseling stones for the construction of an altar. "A similar taboo was observed in Greek and Roman cults, it was and still is widespread."[65]

A Strange Pattern of Bolides

I first proposed the astrophysical descend of iron in my book, *The Lately Tortured Earth* (chap. 10 [2]), and quote from it here:

A not-well-understood feature of meteoroid falls is that they can accomplish soft landings as well as hard crashes. In hard crashes, such as at Campo del Cielo (Argentina) where a number of meteoroids fell, "large masses of meteoritic iron and shale have been found in its vicinity." [66] Heide writes, "the 60-ton meteorite from the Hoba farm near Grootfontain, South West Africa, the heaviest of all known meteorites, imbedded itself in friable limestone at a depth of only 1.5 meters. The iron meteorites of Cape York in Greenland, weighing up to 30.875 tons, lay on solid gneiss rock, or were barely imbedded in moraine rubble, without any trace of an impact. Here we may guess that they fell on a thick layer of ice or snow and sank to their final location as the snow or ice melted.[67]

However, as the Mass and Velocity of the meteoroid increase, its Energy of impact increases, according to the formula $E = \frac{1}{2} mv^2$. The atmosphere cannot brake the body in time. Therefore, no iron masses of over 100 tons have been deemed to be of exoterrestrial origin; where such have actually fallen, and few doubt this, they have been vaporized by the impact.

In the face of this formula and the visible facts of meteoritic iron, it would appear that the large iron ore masses on Earth cannot have originated exoterrestrially. The negation, if any, depends upon variable velocity. If the falling iron mass is electrically charged, or gathers a charge, so as to render it less attractive to the Earth its velocity would diminish. Theoretically, it could waft down in a soft landing in one piece. If it crashed upon landing, it would possibly assemble itself into the form of an iron ore deposit as deluges of water and dust would fill the interstices. Strange objects have been found in the midst of iron ores being mined, such as wood of recent date.[68]

Mascons of Iron

> Masses of iron were found lying upon a Disco Island (Greenland) shore with a great gneiss erratic boulder and associated with the talus of a basalt cliff which itself contained similar bits of iron. All the iron was termed meteoritic which led the investigators to wonder, especially since the basalt fragments were found even embedded inside the iron of the beach, whether the meteorite shower "occurred while the basalt was in a state of pasty eruption."[69] But, too, the range itself, though immense and tall, might have been the rim of a great impact collision...

Like Bellamy, I am impressed by the fact that "there are, scattered over the Earth, a number of ore-mountains which are evidently foreign to their surroundings. At Eisenerz, in Austria, there is a huge mountain, consisting altogether of iron ore .... On the island of Elba, in Sweden, in Russia, in India, and elsewhere we find more or less considerable hills consisting of pure iron ore, mineral wonders of the world. In Orissa, India, in the jungle near the village of Sakchi, is a hill consisting of iron ore which is so rich that it yields almost 65 per cent of pure metal."[70] Elsewhere he writes that such mountains would, upon investigation, probably prove to be 'rootless.' He describes others as well:

> "At Gellivara in Sweden there are enormous deposits of iron ore whose special characteristic is that they are found in floelike masses, as if they had been 'pancaked' down. At Kirunavaara and Loussavaara, in Lapland, there are similar deposits of iron ore. The 'Kursk Anomaly' in Russia consists of a mass of iron ore estimated to contain about a cubic mile of high-grade material. In the Ural area there is Gora-Blagodat, the 'Blessed Mountain, 'an iron ore mountain 520 feet high, situated in a plain. In Russia too is the Wyssokaya Gora, a deposit of rich magnetite ore, littered over a strip 40 miles long by 9 miles wide."[71]

In Western Australia, the Hamersley Range conveys continuous individual beds of iron over hundreds of square miles in a horizontally bedded sequence of quartzite and iron ore thousands of feet thick.

All metals have their mysteries, all have references and rites pointing to celestial origins. Copper deposits were not greatly distant from iron deposits, as we shall see. "The

Celts," writes John Warren Andrew, "had the ability and desire to forge and cast copper , then bronze, and later iron from the time they left Scythia before 2000 B.C.E. through Western Europe and the Celtiberian Peninsula into Ireland and lastly into Scotland."[72] He alludes to a billion pounds of copper that had been removed from 5000 ancient mining sites of Northern Michigan. "Where this huge volume went has been a mystery."

Banded Iron Formations

Terrestrial iron is to be found in the surface dust of Earth, in pools of pellets, in beds of streams, in fragments of crater bowls, and in large deposits. We quote a conventional statement on the origin of most mundane or terrestrial iron.

> Banded iron formations are very large bodies of sedimentary rock laid down some 2.5 billion years ago. At that time, the Earth still had its original atmosphere of nitrogen and carbon dioxide. That would be deadly for us but it was hospitable to many different microorganisms in the sea, including the first photosynthesizers. These organisms gave off oxygen as a waste product, which immediately bonded with the abundant dissolved iron to yield minerals like magnetite and hematite.[73]

A newer speculation of some scientists is that the ocean held iron in solution, then in a catastrophe Earth lost its atmosphere, whereupon the iron hastened out of solution and formed its belts, and thereafter, conveniently, Earth regained its atmosphere, with a better promised land for having a sufficiency of iron.

These minerals composed themselves into layers. See *Fig. 17*. For example, one Banded Iron Formation, or BIF as they are called, will reveal striking colors in repeated layers -- dark red hematite, jasper red chert, bright golden quartz. They formed supposedly into hills, even low mountain ranges as much as 200 kilometers long. Similar formations are found elsewhere on all continents, but with some degree of relationship geographically throughout the world, as in North-central North America, Belo Horizonte in Brazil, and Western Australia. Some 80% of the immense Australian ore mascons ('mass concentrations') are found in the Hammersley range. Their clumping is almost suspicious: why were they not extruding randomly around the globe?

Chemical Processing of Iron in Nature

An exchange of letters on *Intersect*, a Web discussion group, brings us flippantly and then deeply into the chemical processes that could have formed iron, whether in a slowly-developing primordial ooze, or in a fast-developing catastrophic column such as Kelly and Dachille postulated in their book, *Target Earth*. I repeat the full exchange in commemoration of the yeoman labors of Amy Acheson, a Founder of the quantavolutionary Web magazine *Thoth* and of *Intersect*.

Re: [intersect] banded iron deposits
To: intersect@egroups.com
From: "Anthony L. Peratt" <alp@lanl.gov>Date: Sun, 7 Jan 2001 16:26:02 -0700
Amy,
My stuff is just dry physics. Don't you rather like the 'Just So' approach?
Tony
Hi, intersecters!
Here's a post from kronia
talk, along with my answer (well, most of the
answer came from Tony Peratt's book).

THIS FROM (GEOLOGIST) JULIE:
For what it is worth, there is dramatic evidence in the geological record of a massive event of iron deposition which seemed to occur all over the earth at about the same time. The huge banded iron deposits which can be observed today in Minnesota's Iron Range, the Hammersley Basin in Australia and the huge iron ore reserves in the vicinity of Belo Horizonte in Brazil seem to indicate an event in the history of the earth which resulted in a sudden and massive deposition of iron. One of the mainstream theories for these unusual sedimentary deposits is that the earth in some catastrophic (yes, sometimes catastrophes make their way into the mainstream theory!) event lost its atmosphere and the solubility of iron in the seas was reduced to nearly nul as a result. Thereafter, all the iron dumped out of solution to form these rich ore deposits.

By the way, clays are a family of hydrous aluminum silicates which are generally derived from the weathering of igneous rocks. Julie

FROM AMY: Thanks for this post, Julie. It came at an appropriate time for Mel and me to try to make a connection with Anthony Peratt's plasma cosmology. We were just reading about why Io's volcanos are depositing stuff in concentric rings from the center ... the following section is about Marklund Convection and Separation of Elements. [Of course, they are talking about galaxies, but since plasma phenomena is scalable over at least 12 magnitudes, it might provide a mechanism for your banded iron deposits, as well. It seems a bit simpler mechanism than first depleting, then restoring the Earth's atmosphere. Is there a time estimate (certainly pre-oxygen dependent life? Or is this one for the Devonian extinction event when the fossils were secreting silicon and everything took a loooooong time to recover?)]

Here's Peratt's story (from pp 167-8 of _Physics of the Plasma Universe_)"Marklund (1979) found a stationary state when inward convection of ions and electrons toward the axis of a filament was matched by recombination and outward diffusion of the neutralized plasma .... The equilibrium density of the ionized component normally has a maximum at the axis. However, because of the following mechanism, hollow cylinders, or modifications of hollow cylinders of matter, will form about the flux tubes.""Because of the radiated loss of energy, the filaments cool and a temperature gradient is associated with the plasma. As the radial transport depends on the ionization potential of the element, elements with the least ionization potential are brought closest to the axis. The most abundant elements of cosmical plasma can be divided into groups of roughly equal ionization potential as follows: He(24eV); H,O,N(13eV); C,S(11eV);and Fe, Si, Mg(8eV) .... These elements can be expected to form hollow cylinders whose radii increase with ionization potential. Helium will makeup the most widely distributed outer layer; hydron, oxygen, and nitrogen should form the middle layers, while iron, silicon and magnesium will make up the inner layers. Interlap between the layers can be expected and, for the case of galaxies, the metal-to-hydrogen ratios should be maximum near the center and decrease outward. Both the convection process and the luminosity increase with the field... "

"For the case of fully ionized hydrogen plasma, the ions drift inwards until they reach a radius where the temperature is well below the ionization potential and the rate of recombination of the hydrogen plasma is considerable. Because of this "ion pump" action, hydrogen plasma will be evacuated from the surroundings and neutral hydrogen will be most heavily deposited in regions of strong magnetic flux."

"Examples of this convection for galaxies are given in section 3.11.3. In addition, Mirabel and Morras (1984) have detected the inflow of neutral hydrogen towards our own galaxy."

Perhaps there have been two trillion tons of iron ore extracted since the beginning of iron mining. Almost all of the production of nearly a billion tons a year comes from open surface mining. In Pilbara, Australia, iron ore is carried for crushing and screening, in crudest form, by trucks loaded each with 200 tons. Then it is carried to shipping ports by trains up to three kilometers long with loads exceeding 25,000 tons.

Rarely does a mine extend below half a kilometer. The ore when found consists almost entirely of hematite, goethite, limonite, and magnetite, all running 60% of the extracted material.

We cannot, of course, know yet what BIF's lie along the ocean bottoms that stretch over three-quarters of the globe. These ocean bottoms are young (whether by my short chronology or the conventional long chronology of under 100my) that, if they do expose BIF's, these may well have come during the Iron Age. And they are igneous. That is, once again a caveat, should the continental slopes be very young and they are certainly geologically young, then, should they carry bodies of iron, the recent arrival of iron ore mascons should be heralded.

Iron Foundries

Iron foundries are found all around the world. It would not be far wrong to say that they began with the Age of Iron around 850 B.C.E. everywhere in the world. Everything was ready for the Age of Iron. There was a heavy demand for metals. There was an awareness and use of meteoritic iron, and it was highly valued, a hundred times the worth of copper. The processes of metallurgy were known, and I doubt that we should pay strict attention to the common belief that common mundane iron was too difficult to work by comparison with other metals. The mining technology was known.

Iron required no more than surface mining, like the other metals, even less so. Convenience of location was hardly an imperative. Tin from Cornwall was regularly shipped to the Near East. Copper may have been shipped from today's Michigan to today's British Isles. The need for a very high temperature for one branch of iron-working is but a weak excuse for denying a whole age whose abundance of prime material would have been obvious and obtrusive.

We conclude that the missing ingredient or process to create an Age of Iron was a large mass of the iron itself. We should add that when the iron did come from the skies, it encountered some religious obstacles – taboos, ritual processes that had to be performed, like only shiny white stones could be used for Jewish altars, no striated stones touched with or by iron.

The evidence for all of this is as yet unsatisfying. It may never be certain. Mankind was not only innocent of techniques for permanent recording until the Bronze Age, but the catastrophic conditions under which he would have observed their fall guaranteed that he would not live to testify about it. To repeat, iron came down last and there was precious little of it from meteoritic and mundane sources before the Iron Age. There could be no Iron Age because the metal itself was scarcely available.

In a typically condensed passage, Velikovsky summarizes the history of iron as it might have come to Egypt. The Iron Age in Egypt "may yet be proved to have even preceded the Bronze Age, is the opinion of one group of authors. The Iron Age began..with the end of the Middle Kingdom, is the opinion of another group, or in the time of Ramses II, according to a third group. The developed Iron Age in Egypt began in the days of Ramses III, a few scholars maintain. Many favor the date -1000 under the Libyan Dynasty... The year -700 may be considered as the beginning of the Iron Age in Egypt is a statement often made. It is also asserted that the earliest smelting in Egypt (at Naucratis) dates from the Sixth Century. Iron has had more contradictory statements made about it than any other metal."[74]

We are forced to notice that Ramses II and Nebuchadnezzar (Hattusilis) engaged in correspondence in which Ramses sought iron of better quality than was being made available to him from Egyptian mines and ovens that were being worked by Greeks. This would put the famous kings well into the Iron Age. There would have been no Greek iron-workers anywhere, much less in Egypt, if conventional dating several centuries earlier were applied to these kings.[75]

In another place,[76] Velikovsky surveys Egypt's Bronze Age dynasties and concludes that "it was not because of lack of skill that iron was not utilized to a greater extent.." He calls our attention to the fine work that was done to cut and carve granite, basalt and diorite, which must have required the equivalent of excellent steel tools. But there is a mystery as to the provenance of these tools, and certainly little iron was used generally until the Iron Age.

The Word "Iron" and Myth

The word *'bia'* means in Egyptian *metal in general* but more specifically iron, or "the metal of heaven." Iron seems to have been more sacral than bronze and silver. Its use for some purposes was taboo. ("It was said that iron was Seth's bone and that iron came from him. The second of these statements, says Hugh Crosthwaite in his book of KA, may be seen today as an inversion. We prefer to think that the presence of iron attracts Seth. The place where lightning struck was sacred and might be walled off with a puteal, or curb, such as was built around a well. Rock containing iron would be especially likely to attract the god of the thunderbolt, and this could easily have given rise to the belief that lightning was responsible for the presence of iron ore."

We are beginning to find stone-clad iron pellets in great abundance on Mars and these are found, whether only Martian or also Earth-born, on Earth. The root "gem" for precious stone has also been applied to pearls; the Russian word for pearl is , "jemchug," but the word "chug" by itself means "cast iron." Pearls of iron from the sky are suggested, conceivably from a time before the Iron Age as well as later, when iron-pearls rained from Mars.

The Old Testament mentions iron many times. The first mention, in *Genesis 4, verse 22*, probably a later insertion, states: "And Zillah, she also bare Tubel-cain, an instructor of every artificer in brass and iron, and the sister of Tubel-cain was Naamah." Tubel-cain could be considered on other evidence as a god-hero blacksmith such as is found in other mythologies.

In the 'Promised Land', says *Deuteronomy 8: 8-9*, " .. You will lack nothing, a land where the rocks are iron and you can dig copper out of the hills." In *Deuteronomy 27:5*, which may well have been written in the Iron Age when the worship of Yahweh reached a high pitch, we find "There you shall build an altar to Yahweh your God, an altar of stones: you shall lift up no iron [tool] on them." Was this sign of a fear of a new technology and its religious meanings? Was Yahweh here to be dissociated from Mars, the destructive Iron God (though Yahweh was doing his share of damage at the same moment of time)? Was Yahweh a doppelgaenger of Mars, and the profaning of a sacred material was not to be allowed in the creation of an artifact representing the material ideally? Or was it a typical fancy of crazy religions, as superficial, early atheistic anthropologists and their public still today are wont to exclaim? As with many other queries of this book, we shall have to forego answers.

Lightning Transfers

Lightning, so profuse in ancient times, is rare on Mars today, except in minuscule jolts, infinitely removed from the megabolts of old. The reason lies in its thin atmosphere. So it is with Mercury. Hence one might deduce that Mars lost atmosphere to Earth in making iron and sending it to Earth. Perhaps much atmosphere arrived in similitude to the Earth's atmosphere. But perhaps on Mars and on the way to Earth and Moon, the dusts of the atmosphere of Mars were aflame, with all their ingredients, as various legends carry the story. Its famous ability to send forth giant lightning bolts would have been lost, following its extreme activity.

Could the transfer of iron then have been the occasion also for the transfer of atmospheric elements to Earth? And what would have been transient effects and the final resultant effect on the atmosphere of Earth?

Indra is the Mars of India. He battles and destroys Vitra.

> *And soon the knell of Vitra's doom*
> *Was sounded by the clang and boom*
> *Of Indra's iron shower.*
> *Pierced, cloven, crushed, with horrid yell,*
> *The dying demon headlong fell*
> *Down from his cloud-built tower.*[77]

R.N. Iynegar[78] gives a traditional age of -1302 for the *Mahabharata*, but then admits it is too old and the fierce struggle among gods and men – very much like the *Iliad* – took place around the time of the Trojan War, around the seventh century. He conjectures that the principal event was a nova, a brightening of a star in the cluster of the Pleiades. The epic speaks of numerous impacts. It speaks of a metal sword falling upon Earth, called Vel or Sakti, of Kartikeya. All the texts agree that this event was followed by a severe famine and prolonged misery among men.

Along with a number of other writings, *The Encyclopedia Britannica* places the Mahabharata squarely in the Iron Age, among with a number of other writers. " The Several Centuries during which the epic took place were a period of transition from the religion of Vedic sacrifice to the sectarian, internalized worship of later Hinduism."

But we are edging away from the Greater Mediterranean Region, the scope of our study. Mars was par excellence the god of a metal. Athena was of the Age of Bronze, but was much more than a bronze-encrusted actress. Iron gods won out against the old gods of metals. Did iron create the god, in all or part, or did the god create the iron? Do men revise their god in order to go to war, or does god tell men to go to war? Both happen simultaneously.

In Villanovan Italy, as the Iron Age begins, we find a simple and effective oven, dating from the sixth century at Populonia. See *Fig. 16*. There the iron as soon as it emerges from the furnace is hammered to rid it of scories. Numerous hills composed of wastes have been left behind, a modest beginning of today's environmental pollution. In Rwanda at the same time, iron smelters were employed.

Even if iron had not literally fallen into use from Mars, the Iron Age would have come about because of the tremendous changes introduced by the behavior of planet Mars. This conjecture is all the more important because, had there been only a scanty fall of meteoric iron before, during, and after the Iron Age of Mars, it would be all the more obvious that great multiplex exo-terrestrial effects were occurring on Earth.

Mars exuded iron from every pore. Some 17% of its

sampled soils are iron. Robert Zubrin writes in his book, *The Case for Mars*[79]:

> By far the most accessible industrial metal present on Mars is iron. The primary commercial ore of iron on Earth is hematite ($F_2O_3 + 3CO$). This material is so ubiquitous on Mars that it gives the Red Planet its color, and thus indirectly, its name. Reducing hematite to pure iron is straightforward, and as mentioned both in the Old Testament and in Homer, has been practiced on Earth for some three thousand years. It can be produced by interaction with carbon monoxide or by the electrolysis of water.

Iron can be processed at low temperatures to become liquid and at a little higher temperature to decompose, whence, poured into a mold, it becomes pure iron. As Kelly and Dachille pointed out in their book, *Target Earth*, a great impact explosion can create a veritable chemical factory. The pockets, belts and clouds of chemical mixtures are exceedingly numerous and can end up as useful or simply variegated rocks, liquids, gases and plasmas. There are many kinds of iron, many more to be made also than can be found. The snatching and sucking up, passing through space, and descent upon Earth under many different conditions of temperature and pressure should have been adequate to produce whatever has been found in the form in which it is found. We might with some success seek out chemical, thermal, and other markings that would make Mars iron distinctively different by the time it landed on Earth.

A.S.Yen of the Jet Propulsion Laboratory has suggested that "the ferric component of the soil and Mars' characteristic color could have been produced by the impact events that introduced the meteoritic material. Partial vaporization of impactors and target material , recondensation in the atmosphere, and precipitation as soil and dust grains were likely an active process during the latter stages of planetary accretion. During these transient high temperature conditions under oxidizing atmospheres, metallic and ferrous iron can be readily converted to the ferric state."

He dismisses the basalt that is found mingled with the ferric materials by supposing the amalgamation to have occurred during the initial contact and mixing. The same would have happened on Earth to give the sometimes remarked upon great pre-biotic or pre-Cambrian ages to the iron ores. But Yen does leave room for the hypothesis that such a mixture could be quite recent. As do we, whenever the argument is brought up in a mundane context.

The surface of Mars is catastrophically worked over and much more evidently so than the surface of Earth, or at least to us earthlings who like the sight of green growths and waters. A goodly part of Mars is represented in the accompanying picture. It shows the tortuous sedimentary melts and dark fulgerite grids at the western end of Melas Chasma, which is the bottom section of the widest part of the middle of Valles Marineris.[80] Se fig. 22.

Soft Landings of Meteorites

An organized meteorite search party picked up a 4-pound, 3-ounce potato-shaped meteorite at Allen Hills, Antarctica December 27, 1984. It was theorized to have been created originally as part of the crust of Mars (-~4.5 by), to have been blasted from Mars in an impact incident (-~16my), and to have fallen to Earth (~ -13my). Suspected of holding products of biological activity, it was intensively investigated, with no certain answer to the question of life. In 2005, proof was advanced that the rock had originated from the Eos Chasma branch of the Valles Marineris.[81]

We may speculate that a ~ -13 my rock ought not to be resting on the surface; its velocity should have made it explode or penetrate many meters deep into the ground. But at any rate this soft landing of 4+ pounds of rock might as well have been a 4+ trillion -pound rock of like composition, or more if of iron. Such a deposit might actually exist, unrecognized. Galileo, counting on gravity and resistence, would probably agree, but, too, he would not have an alternative in mind, that the events could have been electrically facilitated. Mars, if close to Earth, might have been nearly in an electrical balance.

How could iron make a soft landing? By gliding in to a pancake landing. Or by a helicopter-like landing pulled-pushed down to Earth by an electrical attraction not so great as to crash the planets. The great amount of iron in Mars would have brought on the exchange of electric charges. Many of the stories and appellations and epithets given to the Martian doppelgaengers present them as wielders of thunderbolts, burners of cities and armies, most noteworthy, though denied by many authorities, the destruction of the Assyrian Army camped before Jerusalem.

One of the most striking features of Ackerman's scenario - and the one which tests a critic's credulity to the utmost - is his positioning of Mars at regular intervals upon its Earth excursions over the Himalayan Mountains. There it stands anchored, its bottom protruding and readying to give birth to Mercury, meanwhile - we presume - dropping iron ore upon the Earth. Here could be a method of providing the soft landing that we are seeking. An electrical balance, we suppose, might be obtained such that the loads of iron, like the trainloads of Australian iron ore, moved slowly downwards on an electrified railway.

As Mars' iron core would be pulled toward Earth, some of it would bleed out through the vast canyon, ever enlarging, of Valles Marineris, and be conveyed in molten form through approximately 45,000 miles of space to land on Earth. This would be repetitive and a series of drops would have occurred over a period of a long century. And all over the world, but in certain belts more than others. Craters on Earth can contain some of the iron, or expel it to their circumferences on occasion when the drop is explosive, creating several iron mines of the future.

The amount of iron dropped is very little compared with the total quantity of Earth's iron. Mars' vast iron supply was mostly pulled out, by the Ackerman theory, in a final incursion of Venus and sent off on its own to become the planet Mercury. In my book of 1980, I had placed Mercury in an earlier phase of the evolution of the solar system, as representing a quantavolution of the third millennium B.P.E., around 2300 B.P.E., which I believed to have coincided with various events in the mythology of Greece and elsewhere.[82] This theory has since been elaborated with distinction by Mandelkehr and others.

I said that a planet, which I called Apollo for various mythological reasons, was exploded, and became the origin of the great asteroidal belt Although Ackerman has worked out carefully the details of what he believes to have been the creation of planet Mercury, I might still see room for my theory, in the scenario of the flight of Mars iron to Earth (or some of it). This would mean, reverting to my theory, that the source of Mercury was a planet in the present asteroid belt that I termed Apollo because of certain coincidences and evidence tying Hermes-Mercury-Thoth to the God Apollo. A dense iron-bearing and magnetically cohesive portion of Apollo could have been exploded into an orbit that would eventuate in the present orbit of Mercury.

What might have happened on Mars would likely happen upon Earth also. So too with Moon. There, to take up another issue, the phenomenon of the mascon occurs, massive concentrations, tubes of hills pasted onto the surface. They are notable on the Mare Imbrium, Maria Serenitatis, Crisium, and other places. Mascons are notable for their gravity anomalies, which accelerate upon approach to the mascons and decelerate upon having passed them by. Basalt has been deemed to cause the phenomenon, but then dismissed as lacking by far the density required to produce it, even when a hypothetical summation of surface basalts and thinner crust below the mares is made.

Another possibility is the presence of dense iron ore in the mascons, cast down from an electro-gravitationally powerful astral body, Earth or Mars. Here one would have to explain which is the more likely, and without question, as we shall offer to explain, Mars would be the favored donor of mascons to the Moon.

And what would be true of the mascons of Moon would be as true for Earth, where a number of massive iron ore deposits are shaped like the lunar mascons and also differ in morphology and composition from the surrounding rocks. We have already named the location of some of these. Mentioned above was the supposition of some Mars geologists that the mascons were composed of dense basalt, in order to explain why they exhibited a gravity anomaly. Mineralogists in the course of describing iron deposits on Earth, ascribe pre-Cambrian ages to their creation because iron cannot be formed in the presence of oxygen, but, too, because they are found sometimes in layered formations with basaltic rock. On the other hand, on Mercury, there is a striking absence of basalt, despite most of the planet being composed of iron ore.

It may be suggested that the basalt layers accompanied in succession the iron layers, both not solid but molten, and both were soon solidified upon performing a soft or pancake landing. They would have comparable densities, which would prevent all but minor mixing in the process.

On a map of Canada, it can be indicated that there is a far-flung ring of iron ore centers along the arc of the Labrador geosyncline, which then bends southwest and keeps turning to pick up the immense ores along the North of the Great Lakes, including the Mesabi Range and its sister ranges East of Lake Superior. The ore hills or mascons diminish in number as the arc swings North, but are replaced by the great string of lakes that runs all the way from the northwestern Yukon region down Southeast to the many thousands of Carolina Bays, whose creation is increasingly accredited to a flight of bolides of ice. Overall, a comet or planetary fragment containing besides chondrites both ice and iron would do the job, with ice explosions producing lakes on its western wing, obviating the elevated rim that would otherwise form, and with iron ore spatting down upon its southern and eastern wing. Chester Davis, a quite unknown amateur geologist from Marietta, Ohio, marshaled over a lifetime of work a large collection of proofs of different types in support of the event.[83] See *fig. 19*.

It is highly improbable that this event occurred in the time of Martia, but I employ the example here to lend credence to what might have brought those iron ores that propelled Europe, the Mediterranean region and the Near East into the Iron Age, known to and so-called by the Ancients such as Hesiod and by archaeologists today. For the Canadian iron ores cry out for fruitful hypotheses.

Interplanetary Welding

Many years ago Ralph Juergens suggested that the peculiar mascons of the Moon might be formed by the process of welding.[84] A great electrical arc would bring down and paste upon the Moon a hill, possibly a hill of iron rather than chondrite, for welding is best performed with a magnetized substance. In this case the welding process might also be responsible for the emplacement of the hilly ranges of iron that are found around the world.

Besides the ranges of iron found in the great Labrador and Northern States arc, and the range of Australian deposits, we might include the iron ore hills of Texas. Iron ore deposits are found in Texas in the central mineral region as magnetic ores, and in Northwestern Texas as the brown ores of limonite, goethite and hematite. There is an "Iron Mountain" in Llano County. In fourteen counties " the ore deposits occur usually in strata forming the caprocks of low mountain ranges." Open pit mines are common.

Paul T. Craddock in his book, *Early Metal Mining and Production*, has given us an outstanding dissertation on the origins of iron ore production, without, however, having established the natural means by which the ores were produced and why they were found where they are. He points out the difficulties in distinguishing among meteoritic iron, hearth iron and telluric (earth) iron, especially after they have been worked. Iron as a sacred and precious gift or ornament was worked into a dagger around -800 (-1200 conventionally). Still, most archaeologists agree that worked iron could be found as early as a thousand years before then.

To explain why more iron was not used before the Iron Age, it is commonly argued that iron when found was unworkable. Too, it has long ago rusted away. It is argued that certain high temperature techniques used for bronze casting could not be obtained for a long time in the case of melting and working iron. Admitting that iron is a soft metal which is easy to shape by hammering, and to join by welding, it is insisted by Rehder 1992 for instance, that it could only gain a decisive advantage over copper alloys by becoming alloyed. This appears an unlikely story, given the small technical hop from one temperature to another and at least a thousand years to achieve it.

We date the Iron Age to begin around the earliest years of the ninth century [revised dates]. After that, one finds iron objects of many different kinds all over the

Mediterranean region, probably extending to Northern Europe and the British isles. Pleiner's study showed iron weapons to be popular in the Balkans in the eighth century B.C.E.. The quick spread of the metal indicate both its widespread availability – meaning to us its recent and frequent falls from the sky – its easy workability for one or more purposes and its practicality. The corrosion of iron makes the presence of the iron much less common in digs and underwater.

Craddock writes, "A clearer idea of the state of ironworking .. may perhaps be obtained from a set of 23 iron woodworking tools recovered from the dry deserts of Egypt, but found in association with two Assyrian bronze helmets which date the deposit to the seventh century BC." Several were carburized and heat-treated, supposedly late developments. Further into Africa iron-working seems to have come a few years later and on the heels of the stone age, since bronze smelting was not typically used.

A seminal history of iron-working from the early Iron Age to around 1000 C.E., written by Alan W. Pense, reports on the metallographical examination of "a range of iron artifacts. ... It is concluded that there was little change in iron manufacturing over this time span of 2000 years." By 500 B.C.E., techniques "to increase hardness both by increasing carbon content and by rapid cooling from the austenite range", were being employed.[85]

Many questions need to be resolved. There were truly great belts of iron in the Northern hemisphere, but there were also great deposits of ore along a tropical belt and in South America, and Australia has very large ore bodies. Could such factors as "innate aggressiveness" or generally advanced culture and technology have abetted the plunge into iron usage, or a regionally varying visibility during the most intense crisis phases of the planet Mars, have determined who plunged first and foremost into the Iron Age?

Ackerman brought to light a tantalizing piece of evidence on the planetary movements of the Iron Age, an epistle (see *fig. 20*):

> This drawing is from a ninth century A.D. arabic epistle which

classifies comets on the basis of planetary characteristics ... The individual drawings show the appearance of each of the planets , presumably at that time. The one of immediate interest s the depiction of Mercury, third from the left in the top row, as having a long straight tail. It is actually described in the associated text as a 'spear'. Also note that priori-Mars [a term that Ackerman uses to denote the condition of Mars before the planet retired to its present position], like Jupiter, displays a prominence, as opposed to a tail extending from the entire planet, like Mercury. This plume extends from the 'scar' where the core exited. ... The prominence on Jupiter was the great jet, which today is manifested as the Great Red Spot. The tail of Venus was due to the outgassing of this very hot, new planet. The prominence on priori-Mars was from the great wound out of which the core (Mercury) exited priori-Mars and the tail of Mercury was due to its high temperature, having been ejected from Mars' interior -- both events having taken place only 1400 years earlier.

Ackerman is led to wonder whether in fact the planets Mercury and Venus had still not settled into their present orbits by the 9th century C.E.. He posits a theory that the iron core of mars was pulled out by Earth and broke away when Venus approached, and thereupon became the Planet Mercury. The ratio of meteoric iron to chondrite in the asteroids and meteorites fallen to Earth is quite low and might indicate that the larger mass of iron detached from Mars went to Mercury, with a considerable tonnage crashing to Earth. Magnetic properties of the iron would actually diminish the number of individual chunks that would deviate on their fall to Earth.

The contributions of Ackerman by no means end here. He has to explain how Mars was bled of its iron and of material enough to compose a new planet, albeit a small one, Mercury. Mars is deficient in iron compared with Earth, while Mercury appears to be composed three-fourths of a core of iron. He proceeds by pointing to a spectacular feature of Mars, the Valles Marineris, as precisely the fit of Mercury. The lengthof Marineris – 4500 km -- is almost identical to the diameter of Mercury, 4878 km.

He makes frequent use of the Hindu Vedas to follow the history of Planet Mars. Then, too, he brings forth a beautiful hieroglyph from Egypt, called the Eye of Ra and the Eye of Horus, and compares it to a photograph of the Valles Marineris in all its enormity.[86] See *fig. 21* and *22*. The eyeball of the gods is explained by him as the great lump of

Mars' core that gleams in molten splendor as it is opened more and more upon the several approaches of Mars to Earth, and actually does sortie upon the last of the Mars incursions until it finally departs completely from its parent planet, chased away by the planet Venus.

Velikovsky was ridiculed by many scientists for playing ping-pong with the planets. Ackerman could be said to do the same, even also yo-yo, as the vision of infant Mercury popping back and forth from its womb in Mars is invoked. The unmodified mosaic is shown for reference. Although the core is no longer protruding through the opening, the canyons around the opening are still present. These are games, these analogies, surely, but from many earliest cultures came forth games that imitated the skies, as we have heavily noted elsewhere in our work. But one absurdity dances with another. Is it not also a mad game to pretend fiercely that the skies are changeless and insist that everybody play this game...or else! Bruno and Galileo well expressed our feeling in their writings, and suffered greatly for their attempts to enlighten their fellow savants.

John Ackerman lists all the surprises since the Mars became subject to the investigations of the Space Age, declaring that it is now observed as "a small, dry, frozen planet full of enigmas."[87] About the only major hypothesis about Mars that has not been admittedly upset is that the Planet has been on an orderly and well-timed journey around the sun for billions of years; such is the last redoubt of the astronomers.

For instance, a major set of findings discloses that Mars has been flooded by oceans of water and countless rains. Many rivers have flowed, whether their channels were formed electrically or by catastrophic erosion. If the hypothesis that the waters of Earth come largely from a nova of Saturn 6,000 years ago, Mars may not escaped the Deluge. Afterwards, and perhaps in the Iron Age, it might have given up its waters to Earth. Not 'old' melted ice, but new ice and rain may have raised water levels around the world in the Iron Age.

David Talbott has written in the past year in the Intersect Web group of how important it may be to develop ever more broadly electrical theory regarding Mars, inasmuch as electricity plays so large a role in quantavolution:

> I think we'd do well to begin registering predictions as to the coming surprises in Mars exploration. The NASA folks thought they had landed the rover in a dry lake bed. We knew differently, but didn't officially register our view. Perhaps we can settle immediately on certain obvious implications of our findings-- All of Mars' surface outside the polar regions will turn out to be a rubble field. NASA says it wants to see if they can find the "lake bed" beneath the surface debris. It won't be there. The rubble will not be limited to the surface, but will extend as deep as they can dig, and much, much deeper than that in most places. Up to MILES of material was excavated from Mars electrically and great volumes of dust and debris fell back to the surface, creating strata that are visible where vertical elevations involve exposed cliffs. More than once NASA scientists have been surprised to find olivine where they thought they would find evidence of water. Olivine reacts so quickly to water that it is the definitive indicator of water's absence. Given the origins of surface material in our view, we should assume that olivine is pervasive on the surface. Not that there wasn't water on the planet--once. But the removed material in the electrical excavation of Mars included vastly more deep rock than any surface layer. This volume of material would show no signs of the former presence of surface water, even if it had been there. We should expect many surprises from the NASA folks on the extent of glassification of the debris--and in wide-ranging contexts. During the millennia since the devastation of Mars, we should expect that vast regions of the planet were subject to electrostatic effects, whose remnants are the now-observed "dust devils." The best analogue for much of the constituent material would be the fulgurite. Amy Acheson tells me that the explorer landed in a site marked by enigmatic "striping" of the surface, a phenomenon that changes annually and which points to continuing electrostatic activity on Mars. We should therefore expect to find evidence of electrostatic fusing of surface dust. Exploring a more recent "dust devil" track should help to emphasize the point, showing recent and extensive fusing. Is there any hope that NASA will soon explore the mythical "sand dunes" (grooves and ridges) on Mars? These are among the best indicators of more violent and extensive regional discharge. In thousand of places, we see the parallel ridges protruding through surrounding dust and debris. The ridges should show much more than modest fusing of material. Rather, we should expect them to be as hard as the typical fulgurite. Glassification should be undeniable. Surely there's much more we could cite. "

One can scarcely doubt that research into Mars and Mars-Earth interactions according to a holospheric agenda would produce instrumental results. I conclude with an example.

Fall-outs of Poisons and Germs: Arsenic

Two distinguished astronomers, Fred Hoyle and Wickramasinghe, head a list of scientists who in recent years have, despite their long-age chronologies and opposition to the principle of catastrophic quantavolution, written copiously on the likelihood that various plagues of past times have been started by bacteria and viruses emanating from outer space plasmas taking different forms.

If Iron falls out from Mars, it will surely be accompanied by metallic arsenic. The two will be associated, whether as mixed dust or as ore. The arsenic will cause poisoning on a large scale if the fall-out is heavy. Diseases that begin appearing like leprosy develop into fatal cancers. Many millions of people today are suffering from arsenic poisoning from drinking water. If no iron has leached from underground mineral surfaces, then, quite likely, neither has arsenic leached, because both are often released into groundwater under similar low-oxygen conditions.

Sudden disaster could come from streams rushing with poisons. More likely, in Iron Age towns, the drinking water from wells would be poisoned by arsenic. The results will soon be noticeable depending upon the amount of iron-arsenic dust. I quote from the *Scientific American:*

> Arsenic doesn't flavor, color or scent the water. "It has all the sensory impressions that would say to you, 'This is good water,' " Simpson explains. And, unlike pathogenic surface water, arsenic-tainted groundwater doesn't sicken you right away. One can ingest low doses of arsenic for eight to 14 years before white or black spots, called melanosis, start mottling the skin. If the poisoning continues, scaly, leprosy-like skin lesions then encrust the palms and soles, eventually rotting into gangrenous ulcers. Finally come renal diseases, cancers-particularly of the bladder and lungs and death.[88]

After a few years -- I speak now of the ancients -- people will grasp the horrible fact that they cannot drink their water any more. Their only recourse will be to abandon their town. But where to go becomes a problem too and whole regions will be abandoned in the desperate search for clean water. Wars will begin if the refugees encounter towns where the people are healthy. The startling drop in population during the early Iron Age may be due to this arsenic poisoning among other factors; and perhaps other poisons as well may need consideration.

We note that five of the most instructed of Mars experts - Patton, Velikovsky, Juergens, Ackerman, Cochrane - combine legend and physics to detect a fifteen-year period between Martian close incursions upon Earth. Probably all five men could also be counted upon to bring the iron down to Earth from Mars. Depending upon its degree of presence in drinking water, arsenic will toxify a person and expose its symptoms exponentially after a few months of ingestion. A town's population will seem to have been infected with a kind of leprosy and will begin to die off. A passage of fifteen years and the approach of Mars will suffice to send the whole people into panic-stricken flight.

Extending the present case to the ancient past seems to be a permissible journey. An additional query can be addressed in due course, but not here: whether much of the arsenic that is now poisoning millions of people has its origin in Mars.

In order to follow the conglomerating of a continuously transforming mosaic of events called for by our Iron Age scenario, we must imagine the possibility of both the least likely and the most likely occurrences. One thing leads to another, sidewise throughout the holosphere and through time. Recently studies have argued that the large gaseous planets of the solar system formed in a brief period of time (as claimed in my books, especially *Chaos and Creation*, *The Disastrous Love Affair of Moon and Mars,* and *Solaria Binaria*), within a thousand years. A similar finding regarding the dense inner planets, including Earth, is probable.

Iron and the Ocean Bottoms

The bottoms of the oceans are supposed conventionally to be the chemical factories of iron ore. The probability is high that the bottoms of the oceans are not at all so old. Indeed the plates whose bottoms are the oceanic bottoms are nowhere more than sixty to ninety million years old even by conventional reckoning (which I emphatically deny). The 'primordial ooze' that should be many kilometers thick is on the average a kilometer thick.

Conventional earth science has another stiff problem: How does the anciently formed iron rise to the surface? Iron is of high density and therefore should adhere to the core, not rise above the lighter elements to the crust. Might an electrically attracted core let loose of bits and pieces to move to the surface? It is a long trip, even if the improbable cause is granted. The attractive body could only be an immense bolide bigger than the Earth, a huge comet or planet. A magnetic attraction is conceivable, like lifting junked cars with a magnetic lift. This is actually the electrical problem that was just dismissed.

We must conclude that the iron cannot come from below, but must come from above, the exoterrestrial sphere, or from catastrophic processes occurring in a mixed chemical fallout. In that case, there must have been an explosive propulsion elsewhere in space that sends the ore to Earth or an Iron Factory-en-route that makes the iron on the way to Earth. We prefer the probability that Earth's iron deposits were despatched ready-made, in more than one of the various chemical forms of iron, from Planet Mars.

Chapter 10

Hebrews of the Iron Age

The arguments of experts about Jewish history before and during the Iron Age are so many and so unsettled that my own speculations must appear as a foolish blemish upon the record. We find straightaway a key location, Megiddo, scarcely to be identified to anybody's satisfaction, giving us reason to date it in the Twelfth Century or in the Eighth century. But we recognize this problem right away – the Phantom Age may lie in between whatever this ruin may be, 400 years. The lower date relieves us from discovering a great deal of what is conventionally reckoned must be taking place as Hebrew history.

The Megiddo Expedition of the University of Tel Aviv does exist, whatever it may be uncovering, and I can quote their publication, 'The Chronology Debate', of 2005.

> Sparking the debate is the fact that there is not a single chronological anchor.. Between the end of the Egyptian 20th Dynasty rule in Canaan in the Twelfth Century B.C.E. and the Assyrian campaigns in the late eight century B.C.E.. This 'dark Age' of over four centuries covers most of Iron Age In, the days of the United Monarchy and most of the history of the Northern Kingdom of Israel. Though some inscriptions from this period have been discovered, such as the Mesha Stele from Dibon, the fragment of a Shishak Stele from Megiddo, or the Aramaic inscription from Tel Dan, they were not found in clear strati graphical contexts; hence they cannot provide straight forward evidence for dating pottery assemblages of the Iron II period."[89]

Most striking is the fact that this Megiddo " was annihilated in a terrible conflagration " .. which, we feel, may be at one end or the other of the 400 year Phantom Age.

Some degenerate Philistine pottery is to be found – again for us an indication of the social quantavolution that is being brought about forcibly everywhere. The destruction scene in this region is typical of everywhere we have visited and of what is to come in later chapters.

It is all so vague and yet so of a single piece. Almost randomly we check through a report of work done in the ruins of the copper industry and the fortress of Khirbet en-Nahas which is said to mark the onetime Iron Age Kingdom of Edom that ceased to exist "at the time" when other features of that kingdom make their appearance, the -600's and -700's. That is: flourishing, destruction, striking new features. As at Mycenae, so in the biblical sites.

Where the Hebrews Came From

But where did the Hebrews come from and how did their story in the Iron Age relate to the Bible? Is it, as Finkelstein would have it, that they were indigenous to the Eastern Hills beyond the Jordan [River], and for a long time their settlement ruins could be distinguished from those of their neighboring peoples mainly by the absence of pig bones?[90] Remarkably, the Arabians to the South shared the aversion to pork. The pork taboo, Finkelstein hints meaningfully, came before monotheism, the traditions of Exodus and the Covenant with Yahweh.

There are at least three ways of examining the history of the Hebrews in the Age of Iron. The first and traditional way among some 2 billion people living today is to accept a work called the Bible and believe in its contents as literally as possible without feeling foolish or uneducated. Accordingly, the same people believe that they are reading or hearing the true history of the Hebrew people, or components of them that may be called Israelites, Judeans, Jews, and Yehudi.

A second way is to treat the Bible as a largely correct and honest history of the Hebrew people and the world around them, without accepting or at least holding in reserve the many religious claims to a special relationship to a god insofar as He performs actions unproven or in violation of natural laws and the discoveries of science. Probably most scientists of the West and scientific workers take this position. So do most of the people of the world, if they have any opinion on the Bible at all.

A third way is to examine the Bible as a biased instrument of propaganda on behalf of a Hebrew cult of the Seventh Century (the -600's). Through its pages a strain of reality and truth runs that is always shaped by the conscious and unconscious wishes of the cult. Truth in this regard turns out to be a correct accident or incident that befalls the story-teller as he records his tale; he bears no grudge against truth in itself so long as it helps his cause. In fact, the raconteur often places what he believes to be true where either he thinks it belongs or where it would be convincing and illustrative of the lost or mistaken truth.

We may be permitted to call the first group fundamentalists, the second group naturalists, and the third group realists. Of the scholars working on the Bible or problems related to it, an example of the fundamentalists would be the Creationist Scientists, or the author Donald Patten. Of the naturalists, an example would be Immanuel Velikovsky. Instances of the realists would be Israel Finkelstein and the present writer. Kamal Salibi, although in a class by himself, might also find a home with us.

I have written extensively about the Exodus in *Moses and the Management of Exodus* and in some brief passages elsewhere about the Bible. Published many years ago, they are in need of revision. I have expressed my philosophy of religion in the book called *The Divine Succession*. Generally, in the present work, I find it most useful and true to parallel the work of Finkelstein and his co/author Neil Asher Silberman, of the book, *The Bible Unearthed: Archaeology's New Vision of Ancient Israel and the Origin of Its Sacred Texts*. I shall be borrowing liberally from them. While representing their case, I shall also engage my reservations and amendments to their work. Most important of these is the contrasting theory of Kamal Salibi. We present, therefore, additionally, two chapters hence, a plausible bypass, thanks to the toponymics of Professor Salibi.

A valuable article appeared in *Der Spiegel* magazine on December 21, 2002, called *The Invention of God*. It contains a rich summation of the wide range of assaults on the integrity of the Bible by contemporary theologians and archaeologists.

I shall use it as well, almost exclusively in the next chapter. At the same time I shall try to correct my own work, possibly to the point where my picture of the Iron Age includes coherently the Hebrews and their interactants.

Quantavolutions should be discoverable in all three versions of Hebrew history. And since it is my subject, so should the Iron Age of Mars. And in the version of Salibi. Actually only the first group, the true believers in the Bible, take catastrophes as a matter of course, as the Bible calls them up. (Excellent contributions to the study of quantavolution have been presented us by creationist scholars, such as I cite on occasion in my works. In the second group, although I mention Velikovsky, he is almost alone in his substantiation of the Deluge, the Plagues of Egypt, the storming of Jericho, etc., and, too the devastations occasioned by Mars. Rare as well are the scholars of the realist persuasion who find evidence of a quantavolution in the Iron Age.

Finkelstein's Scope and Method

Finkelstein (if I may use the single name to designate both of the authors and their book, with apologies to Neil Asher Silberman, co-author)) brings to bear on the Bible roughly two centuries of archaeology and exegesis, besides the collected tablets, inscriptions, linguistics, histories and legends of Palestine and its neighboring countries. The Bible here is the Old Testament, the Hebrew Bible, containing the Torah, with its Genesis, Exodus, Leviticus, Numbers and Deuteronomy, the Prophets, from Joshua to Malachi, and the Writings, containing the Poetry, Five Scrolls, the Prophecy of Daniel and the History with its Chronicles, Ezra, and Nehemiah.

Although he pretends his book to be based uniquely upon archaeology, he would not get far with that science. This is so even though he claims archaeology has been revolutionized by the application of the social sciences in the 1970's. This is not accurate. His work – like most of archaeology – does not know fully what the social sciences, including psychology, sociology, genetics, demography, simple statistics, and sophisticated anthropology can educe from poor evidence – or perhaps I should say what a proper perspective of theology and rigorous philosophy can do for his studies. He cannot help it perhaps: Bible studies will be forever Bible studies, done in a complex of ideologies and institutions of a baffling inherited environment.

In fact, he bases his study upon and stabilizes it by the liberal use of various imperial archives, legends, and quasi-history, including especially the Bible. This last despite the fact that he portrays in effect, if not in so many words, the sponsors, authors and editors of the Bible as cowardly lions, who might readily torture verbally their Northern Israelite brethren of the Ten Tribes, who had blasphemed and prospered, but were now scattered among far places by their victorious Assyrian enemies and could hardly pronounce a rebuttal. (The authors earn this right, we should say, by their own act of courage in pursuing over the years views of the Bible and Jewish history that collect hostility among Jews, Israeli, and fundamentalist Christians around the world.)

The Iron Age is set by Finkelstein at from 1150 to 586, with an Iron Age In from 1150 to 900 B.C.E., and the balance Iron Age II. (Recollect, by contrast, my view of the Iron Age as beginning around -800 with an exponential set of catastrophes that, after about -650, diminish exponentially, yet can still be observed as operative.

But nevertheless, the authors do not condemn clearly enough the ambitions, immorality, lies, and verily the obtuse, obsessive religion of the manipulators of the Bible. They excuse (in the name of religion?) all the lies, diatribes, and fantasy because these poor bright sods were trying to remake a world that never existed. (Granted that they had no license to condemn the freaky scholars, priests, popes and kings who taught a literal or misread Bible to the masses for 2700 years thereafter.)

Other complaints may be voiced, while we are at it, that the authors seem not to realize that what made the Bible so fascinating and believable enough to be assimilated by many diverse and foreign groups is the nasty thousand-year struggle (actually it still goes on) among the Judaic forces themselves, a civil war between Israel and Judah and so on, so that it cannot be read as a book of romantic fulsome praise of the Lord and his People.

Ignoring Catastrophe and Amnesia

Finkelstein has only bare, embarrassing notions of two momentous events: the agglomerate destruction of Palestine and the whole world, and the mnemonics that transfigures history into myth and legend over periods of time, beginning promptly with the event and continuing exponentially thereafter so as practically to lose itself in the ultimate swamps of human memory.

But lest In be unfair, let me quote proof that they do know of the disasters but fear to make them too important in what is after all a book that will be sold to be read and believed largely by Jews and Christian seminarians. Thus,

> In this world of order and prosperity for the Bronze Age elites, the suddenness and violence of their downfall would have certainly made a lasting impression – in memory, legend, and poetry... The view from the palaces of the city-states of Canaan may have looked peaceful, but there were problems on the horizon, problems that would bring the whole economy and social structure of the Late Bronze Age crashing down. By 1130 B.C.E., [our -1730] we see a wholly different world, so different that an inhabitant of Mycenae, or of No Amon (the capital of Egypt, today's Luxor), or of Hattusha from 1230 B.C.E. [our -830] would not be able to recognize it. By then, Egypt was a poor shadow of its past glory and had lost most of its foreign territories. Hatti was no more, and Hattusha lay in ruins. The Mycenean world was a fading memory, its palatial centers destroyed. Cyprus was transformed, its trade in copper and other goods had ceased. Many large Canaanite ports along the Mediterranean coast including the great maritime emporium of Ugarit in the North were burnt to ashes. Impressive inland cities, such as Megiddo and Hazor, were abandoned fields of ruins.

They *do* say it, then! Why do we object? First, the example they give copiously is that of Ramses III which we are ever more insistent to be all of another age. Then they have no idea of the two great catastrophes involved, one was of the century ~-1450 and call Venusian, and the other of the Martian age. Still, "this was one of the most dramatic and chaotic periods in history." And they add the Canaanite cities to the destroyed places, and the Philistine towns too.

Again, what more can they do? They could have

written this, my book. They could have ascribed the proper causes, including the astronomical ones. They could have tied the gods into the catastrophes. They hardly mention the reasons behind, nor even the usual "rationalistic" and "cult" contributions of Isaiah and the other prophets . They know the story of David is faked, as many other stories, but they fail to connect the destruction of all the Philistine cities to the quantavolution that they really know to be occurring everywhere. (The Bible-scribes may have pushed the Philistine and David material together, so as to make the catastrophism more human and divinely controlled.)

We can only end in praise, however, for Finkelstein is intent upon demonstrating, and does demonstrate, that "the early books of the Bible and their famous stories of early Israelite history were first codified (and in key respects composed) at an identifiable place and time: Jerusalem in the - 7th century."

Failure to Decipher Myth and Legend

In believe, with Finkelstein, that the early stories of human and Israelite history were combed for quality, given an order and recomposed in Jerusalem probably in the ~-600's. The stories are nowadays considered to be fictional romances, in great part, relating very loosely to the times of which they speak. There are too many gaps, too many inconsistencies, too many contradictions to what is actually known and mostly happened later, for the tales to be accepted literally. Still, already, Finkelstein, by putting so heavy a stress upon archaeology, passes up the chance to decipher from legend and myth an actuality in the sociological and natural sciences that plays about in the background.

In was able, In am confident, with unfortunately small benefit from archaeology, to compose a scenario of the Exodus in my book about *God's Fire: Moses and the Management of Exodus,* that is more likely than not to be essentially true. That is, true in the sense of reasoning and deducing the Exodus scenario correctly, given and accepting a naturalistic set of factual statements many of which may not be true. To the extent to which these statements are invalid, my treatise weakens in places and becomes a 'true romance.' In also accomplished a parallel adventure, not of the end of the Middle Bronze Age, but of the Iron Age, in the Book, *The Disastrous Love Affair of Moon and Mars*, eliciting what might have been a real set of events from a story chanted by the blind Demodocus in Homer's *Odyssey*.

However, my purpose here is to join up with the history of the Jews at the beginning of the Iron Age, rather than at the beginning of the Late Bronze, and to follow them through it, briefly. According to my chronology, King Solomon rules a united kingdom of Judah and Israel as the Late Bronze Age ends. Generally, throughout the greater region, this has been a flourishing period and his regime should not have been exceptional. We must accept its downgrading by Finkelstein, as we would the whole prior complex of Hebrew societies and their histories, but we would expect at its conclusion a Martian destruction that would possibly conceal some evidence of its modest splendor even from the sharp and skeptical scrutiny of today's archaeologists.

There is a great deal buried forever in the incredibly heavy destruction of the Bronze-Iron transition, possibly a more luxurious and complex civilization than Finkelstein believes. Finkelstein has now taught us what to look for, so that we might even visualize the splitting of the domain into the two kingdoms, Judah in the South and Israel in the North, as a consequence of general disorder and sociopolitical disorganization. Possibly around the same time, the Egyptian Empire suffered disasters and a loss of power internationally of great consequence. In the next century afterwards, the Assyrian Empire at the latest was greatly weakened.

One is permitted to ponder whether these events are also part of the general weakening and collapse of the Aegean and Near East civilizations. Finkelstein tells us that one reason for hearing nothing of David and Solomon in Egyptian and Assyrian sources is that "the period in which they were believed to have ruled (c.1005 - 930 B.C.E.) [Just before the Iron Age begins] was a period in which the great empires of Egypt and Mesopotamia were in decline."

Joshua's Conquests and the United Monarchy

Hundreds of settlements named in the Bible have remained unknown to this date, despite an intensity and extensiveness of aerial and ground surveying, and digging such as perhaps only Egypt, Greece and Rome have experienced. In am ready to accept the Finkelstein account of the descent by Joshua into Canaan, which presents not a set of full battles and unprovoked destructions by an ungainly horde, but a fairly accommodating occupation of and mingling with foreign peoples. The explanation of this, however, to my mind, is that Joshua (or his equivalent, unnamed) descended onto an area and upon peoples devastated by natural disasters, depopulated, owing to the astrally provoked events attributable to the planet Venus by Immanuel Velikovsky and a few other scholars. The "Chosen People of the Lord," that is, gained a major section of their Promised Land by aggressive scavenging.

Now, about seven hundred years later, in the Iron Age, we see the disruption of the monarchy in the Quantavolution of Mars. Also, many of the destroyed settlements, recently excavated, including principal cities such as Megiddo, alluded to by Finkelstein, appear to have been victims of Planet Mars rather than human conquerors impelled by Yahweh.

The Monarchy itself is reduced by Finkelstein and the new historians to humble status even in its hey-day – the Queen of Sheba must have gone elsewhere. The dates attrite. The Pentateuch was not produced in the time of David and Solomon, in the -10th century. The monarchs seem to have governed a poor land indeed. "From an analysis of the archaeological evidence, there is no sign whatsoever of extensive literacy or any other attributes of full statehood in Judah – and in particular, in Jerusalem -- until more than two centuries and a half later, toward the end of the eighth century B.C.E."[91]

Actually, under the United Monarchy, the eastern highlands, which were the traditional home of the Hebrew settlements, continued as such, while the Canaanite culture continued in the settlements of the valley, and powerful small nations occupied the coastal areas. Judah, the area of the southern highlands, remained poor, illiterate, pastoral, isolated and with a very small population. It seems to have supported only 20 small villages.

In the 10th century, Jerusalem was deserted. "Not only was any sign of monumental architecture missing, but so were even simple pottery shards." These are not the words of the dilettante, but of the eminent Professor Finkelstein and company.[92] The quantavolutionary asks whether this Jerusalem, so modest, had been wiped off the face of the earth by natural forces. An earthquake, of Pausanian Type 3,[93] might have buried the Holy City.

The Monarchy simply could not support any respectable military force, yet the Bible accredits King David with one after another assault upon and destruction of cities of the Philistines in the tenth century. At Tel Quasile, Benjamin Mazar uncovered a large prosperous Philistine settlement whose name was unknown in Bible accounts. "The last layer there that contained characteristic Philistine pottery and bore other hallmarks of Philistine culture was destroyed by fire. And even though there was no specific reference in the Bible to David's conquest of this area, Mazar did not hesitate to conclude that David leveled the settlement in his wars against the Philistines... and so it went throughout the country, with David's destructive handiwork seen in ash layers and tumbled stones at sites from Philistia to the Jezreel valley and beyond. In almost every case where a city with late Philistine or Canaanite culture was attacked, destroyed , or even remodeled, King David's sweeping conquests were seen as the cause."[94] And Finkelstein asks, could such a rural people as David's establish control not only over small sites such as Tel Quasile, but over the large Canaanite centers like Gexer, Megiddo, and Beth-Shean? His answer is a clear negative.

King Hazael or Mother Nature?

Finkelstein is, however, impressed with the fury of King Hazael of Syria, who seems to have been operating throughout northern Palestine and destroying as many or more centers than David is reputed to have ruined. And as with David, we are inspired to suggest to Finkelstein and company that Hazael may be a real life doppelgaenger of Mars. "Across the fertile expanses of the rich northern valleys, cities went up in flames, from Tel Rehov, to Beth-shean. To Taanach, to Megiddo. On the basis of this new evidence, the Israeli biblical historian Nadav Naaman concluded that these destruction layers represent a devastation of the northern kingdom by Hazael so severe that some of the sites never recovered."[95]

Many more sites are indicated. "But Hazael was not strong enough to annex the devastated Israelite centers further south in the Jezreel and Beth-shean valleys, which were far away from the core area of his rule. He apparently left them in ruins bringing about the desertion of many sites and the decline of the whole region for a few decades. Some of the centers of this region never recovered.."[96]

The scenario is so repetitive of the Davidian, and of many others in the larger region, that we cannot but perceive the overall operation of natural forces masquerading as human conquerors and are recalled once more to Claude Schaeffer's major conclusion, that invaders have been given far too large a role in the Bronze Age Destructions -- always with our overriding theory of the origin of these quantavolutions in the skies.

More emphatically this time, we can turn to Finkelstein and ask a question that he does not himself raise, not here, not anywhere in the book. Why, when the whole of the Near East and Aegean region was being leveled to the ground and burned, do he and his fellow Israeli investigators not look to the skies, or even to earthquakes (not even mentioned in the index) nor to the fear-struck exclamations of the prophets concerning the mad utterances and conduct of Yahweh, for an alternative that they themselves realize is needed to the strong arm of King David? Nor dare one mention that David, like Hercules, could have been a partly real character raised up to be Mars himself.

What ash layers were found in the many levels of destruction? Did the rural areas of orchards and wilderness reveal effects of fire? (The unparalleled intensive archaeological surveying of great stretches of the country should have systematically ticked off the presence or absence of such ecological ravages.) In must leave the answer to this question with the authors. In cannot provide it.

Hillbilly Hebrews

They have, indeed, supplied us with proof of a most important kind, burying it in a few sentences. It comes about in Finkelstein's honest attempts to find the origins of the first Israelites. They are a melange of hill folk. So indistinct are they, that he writes, "The early Israelites were – irony of ironies – themselves originally Canaanites."[97] He has gone into a dizzying search for their ancestors prior to saying this. They were all too close to being rootless – restless shepherds, people scattered to the highlands by war, famine, or heavy taxation, migrant laborers for the valley Canaanites or the Egyptian bosses.

Maybe they were originally the contemptible *Apiru*,[98] noting the close connection of this word to *Ibri* (Hebrew), and Egyptian sources thought they were Apiru. Manetho, a much later and not reliable chronologist of Egypt -- exposed by Velikovsky partly out of patriotic motives -- believed so, and believed that when the Hyksos oppressors were driven out of Egypt after a long rule there, they ended up in Jerusalem. A more respectable theory is that the Hebrews emigrated from the towns of Canaan to the hills, dwelled in poverty, as they returned from Egypt, were reorganized into a monotheistic cult led by followers (including Moses) of Pharaoh Akhnaton, the heretical revolutionary and monotheistic king of Egypt. Later on, they infiltrated Canaan and came to dominate portions of its lowlands.

Profiting from the possessions seized from Palestinians in the 1967 War, Israeli archaeologists went into the heartland of ancient Israel settlement and surveyed it intensively --- every ridge, valley, and slope. They found that "a dramatic social transformation had taken place in the central hill country of Canaan", no violent invasion or clearly defined ethnic invasion. "In the formerly sparsely populated highlands from the Judean hills in the south to the hills of Samaria in the north, far from the Canaanite cities that were in the process of collapse and disintegration, about two-hundred fifty communities suddenly sprang up. Here were the first Israelites."[99] To our way of thinking, these processes could have been Mars-connected, the wiping out of the cities and the miscegenate settlement of survivors in the hills above. This back and forth movement to the hills is, as we show in our book, common all over the Mediterranean Region. We need not postulate water as one of the forceful agents of change, but we would recommend investigation of floods and tsunamis at the time.

No public buildings were found in the sprawled hamlets. The settlements were tiny, self-sufficient, no records had been kept, houses were of rough stone, furnished barely, jars and pots and little else. Burials were simple and no signs of cult practices were found. Only a single bull figurine, this of Canaan origin, no fortifying, no signs of burning or sudden destruction. The villagers were pastoral and semi-nomadic.

Turning now to the Canaanite excavations below, "The apparent difference between Canaanites and Israelites was clearest in the realm of material culture. Immediately above the destruction layers at the various Late Bronze Age Canaanite cities, archaeologists regularly found a scatter of haphazardly dug pits and coarse pottery - the apparent remains of which they interpreted as the temporary tent - encampments of 'semi-nomads'. Archaeologists thought that these were displaced desert dwellers who had invaded and settled down."[100]

If the Finkelstein group could but realize it, the Mars scenario would help them escape from their contradictions: the flamboyant Bible, the destruction levels starkly contrasting, the peaceful intrusions. He himself presents the solution unconsciously and moves off abandoning it in a kind of absentmindedness. He says, the Israelites might not have had a unified army that marched into Canaan, but the signs of their arrivals are clear. In comparison with the monumental buildings, imported luxury items, and fine ceramic vessels uncovered in the levels of the preceding Canaanite cities, the rough encampments and implements of the arriving Israelites seemed to be on a far lower level of civilization than the remains of the population they replaced.[101]

Nor is the Finkelstein group acutely aware of the immense work of Claude Schaeffer, and the magisterial chart that he composed relating the collapse of civilizations in the interstices of the several ages from the Old Bronze through the Iron. To his view the Palestinian region suffered the same fate at the same time as the rest of the world, so far as his archaeological investigations had carried him.

However, it must be said that the Israelis of Tel Aviv have prepared a counterpart chart, but then, typical of archaeologists everywhere else, let the plain data escape without milking it of its significance. They point out that analogous cycles occurred in times past respecting the highlands. That most sites became deserted at the end of the Old Bronze - to which they assign dates of 2200/2000. Furthermore they report that the sites were deserted at the end of the Middle Bronze, 1550 in their calendar. Then again at the end of the Late Bronze transition to the Iron Age, there was a wave of settlement between 1150 and 900, which in our terms signifies a general destruction at the centers of the civilization. In the last case, over 800 sites could be detected around the -8th century.

What was happening in this microcosm was similar to what was occurring everywhere. The Quantavolution of Mars was destroying centers, pushing out an assortment of survivors, and then, after some time had passed, diminishing in intensity and permitting a new civilization to develop. Often ethnic and occupationally mixed groups formed a markedly new culture, which after a time caught up with the old in level of sophistication and even surpassed it when measured by some values.

There is more to be said about other spheres of quantavolution, insofar as concerns the making and role of the Bible. What gives the Bible its horrors, that have made it as popular through the ages as the latest flock of violent American movies.? Its slashing, crushing attacks upon its kin and humanity as a whole - Moses slaughtering a multitude of his companions at Mount Sinai, because for a moment they lost their faith in him and his God, for a moment of religious deviance. And King Saul killing his thousands and David killing his tens of thousands (celebrated in a monument to British machine-gunners at Hyde Square, London), the wiping out of former friends and foes, the mad turns of minds of rulers and their servitors, etc. In rhythm with the exaggerated wonders go the exaggerated sins and crimes and rationalized atrocities and exaggerated punition. But perhaps it was accurate, as the Sriptures report, that David, to woo the daughter of Saul, sent him the prepuces of 200 Philistines.

Finkelstein is too harsh on the bluster of the Bible writers and too easy with their morality. Time after time he pauses a moment to praise the literary qualities of their work. On occasion he delights in what he may rightfully be considering as the greatest work ever published. But he is remarkably restrained in his condemnation of the Bible's authors for entering upon the greatest fraud in literary history, and for creating an image of human destiny founded proudly upon terror and various animal behaviors in sex, food, luxury, procreation, deviousness, and violence. The Bible is a low-brow book, suited for popular consumption, and for imitation by thousands of popular writers of the succeeding ages, including hundreds of thousands of Ministers of the Faith. It is of the genre of historical romance. It is perhaps the main ancestor of *Gone with the Wind;* it brings to mind a typical textbook of *Readings in the History of American Society and Politics,* and John Bunyan's *Pilgrim's Progress.* More repellant, however, it is, than any of these.

Jerusalem's Mice

As part of its function and appeal, it describes a number of catastrophes that an unstable god brings upon them -- as the heavens are indeed unstable. By definition, presumptively, all except the survivors deserved their elimination by natural disaster. For some reason, Finkelstein does not choose to examine or even mention such fearful events as the many catastrophes of the Bible. He has trouble finding Jerusalem, much less Assyrian King Sennacherib, in the famous incident of the blasting of 185,000 enemy troops by the Lord, as the eighth century ended.

Assyrians were blasted, but Jerusalem must have been as well, probably like Volsinium in Italy disappeared in a blast of flame from Mars. However, supposing a much diminished city and enemy force to begin with, we would have to make additional suggestions. I have done so elsewhere, but may supplement the detail here. The actors may be the planet Mars (Yahweh would become the monotheistic substitute) closing in upon Earth at about 40,000 kilometers and shooting giant thunderbolts and flaming debris upon its target. The earth would quake and walls and structures of war tumble. Most of the Hebrews and Assyrians would be incinerated. But how could Sennacherib be so lucky as to escape, and then collect a heavy tribute thereafter?

Local and far-flung legends speak of the emergence from underground of armies of mice or gerbils who proceeded to masticate whatever remains might be found, not excluding, in a Jewish legend, the bowstrings of the archers. (Gut and leather might be the appetizing material of the strings.) Properly the God Apollo would be the darter of lightning from his quiver of infinite arrows, and he would be responsible both for plagues and mice and is given the name *Apollo Smintheus* – Mouse Apollo. (He had as female equivalent, Mouse Artemis, according to Pausanias.)

Mercury-Hermes-Thoth, also a great healer god, was often pictured with a mouse alongside his healing and measuring rod. The great Indian God Ganesh, a doppelgaenger of Mars, is presented in a statue with a gerbil by his foot. The Indian God Rudra was, like Apollo, a god of healing and diseases who was associated with the mouse.

Conceivably there is a connection between the Babylonian phrase "fire from the sky," *Arad gibil*, and the word gerbel with their common root *gbl*. This common shrew was indigenous to the Middle East. Of possible relevance is the reports that the Noise God Hamon or Nergal could have killed millions of the small animals by shock and noise alone. Nor are humans immune to death by noise and blast, though the lightning would be more important instrument.

A city in Egypt was named Leptopolis, Mouse City. The Roman historian, Strabo, reported that many places bore the name of Mouse-Apollo.

Mice were eaten as a cure for ailments of a dangerous sort. In Lincolnshire (UK) a fried mouse used to be fed to children suffering from whooping cough. From ancient times to the present, and from the Far East to Northern Scotland, partaking of cooked mice parts was a cure, especially for pneumic illnesses.[102] 'Pneumic' appears to be one detail too many, until we recollect the blast and a Jewish legend of Gabriel's blowing into their nostrils and the legendary hints of their suffocation, the taking away from the Assyrians of their breath.[103]

Herodotus the Historian related the account mentioned above, whereby a horde of rodents chewed up the Assyrian bowstrings, so disarming the soldiers that they had to retreat. But there is another story, this one Trojan by origin, wherein a party of Cretans, seeking to settle in Anatolia (it would be about this time), were counseled by an oracle to select the first place where they would be attacked by children of the earth. At Hamaxitus, in the Troad, a swarm of mice chewed up both their bowstrings and the leather of their shields. So there they made a home. There exists in the Troad a town named Smintheus.

It would be unfair to the possibilities of legends to deny all of these stories in all their detail. Mars was imaged in the sky as a chariot, as a sword, as a wolf, and as a rat. It is permitted to imagine the terrifying rat with electric whiskers, alternatively bowstrings, and the subsequent plunging blast of gases and shock that killed a great many Assyrians and Judeans alike. The invasion is known, Sennacherib returned to Assyria, he claimed victory, he was killed by his sons - hardly a prize for victory.

Robert Forrest's Exacting Critique

Robert Forrest, a conscientious and most exacting critic of Velikovsky's *Worlds in Collision*, tells us in his work on *Velikovsky's Sources*[104] the following:

Again, on WIC p.279, V writes:

"The Talmudic and Midrashic sources, which relate that the army of Sennacherib was destroyed by a blast and scourge accompanied by a terrible din on the night following the day when the shadow of the sun returned ten degrees, are more specific: the scourge was inflicted by the Archangel Gabriel 'in the guise of a column of fire.'"

One of V's references here is to Sanhedrin 95b, but this again bears little relation to what readers of WIC might expect:

"Wherewith did he (the angel) smite them ? -- R. Eliezer said: He smote them with his hand, as it is written. 'And Israel saw the great hand' (1), implying the hand that was destined to exact of Sennacherib (2). H. Joshua said: He smote them with his finger, as it is written, 'Then the magicians said unto Pharaoh, This is the finger of God' (3), implying this is the finger destined to punish Sennacherib.

R. Eliezer, the son of H. Jose, said; The Holy One, blessed be he, said to Gabriel, 'Is thy sickle sharpened (to mow down the Assyrians)?' He replied: 'Sovereign of the Universe'. It has been sharpened since the six days of Creation', as it is written, 'For they fled from the swords, Iron the sharpened sword etc'(4), R. Simeon b. Yohai said: it was the time for the ripening of fruits, so the Holy One, blessed be He, said to Gabriel, 'When thou goest forth to ripen the fruits (5), attack them, as it is written, "As he passeth (6) he shall take you: for morning by morning shall he pass by, by day and by night, and it shall be a sheer terror to understand the report."' (7). R. Papa said: Thus people say, 'In passing, reveal thyself to thine enemy.' (8)

Others say: He (Gabriel) breathed into their nostrils, and they died, as it is written, 'and he shall also blow upon them, and they shall wither' (9). R. Jeremiah b. Abbe said: He smote his hands at them, and they died, as it is written, 'I will also smite thine hands together, and I will cause my fury to rest' (10). H. Isaac the Smith said: He unsealed their ears for them, so that they heard the Shabboth(11) sing (praises to God) and they died, as it is written, 'at thine exaltation the people were scattered' (12)."

(Footnotes: "(1) Ex.14:31. (2) This is deduced from the def. art.

(3) Ibid. 8:14, (4) Is.21:15, (5) Gabriel being the angel in charge of this. (6) On his mission of ripening the fruits. (7) ibid. 28:19.

(a) Lit., 'on the way make thyself heard by the enemy,' i.e., take

revenge when the opportunity is afforded. (9) Ibid. 40:24. (10) Ezek. 21:22. (11) The celestial 'living creatures' mentioned in Ezekiel's mystic vision; v, Hack. 1 10.) (12) Is.33:3. The first half of the verse reads, 'At the noise of the tumult the people fled.' 'Tumult' is taken to refer to the song of the Shabboth in their 'exaltation' of the Lord.")

All in all, then, neither the Midrash Rabbah nor the Talmud can

be said to point unequivocally to a catastrophic planetary basis for the destruction of Sennacherib's army, especially when one recalls the tenor of the passages of the Midrash and Talmud that do refer to the planets!

Let us now turn to disruptions of the sun's movements. On WIC p.210 -- 11, V writes:

The catastrophe came on the day on which King Ahaz was buried. There was a 'commotion'. The terrestrial axis shifted or was tilted, and the sunset was hastened by several hours. This cosmic disturbance is described in the Talmud, in the Midrashim, and referred to by the Fathers of the Church."

V here refers to Sanhedrin 96a, the relevant portion of which reads thus:

"At that time, Merodach-baladan, the son of Baladan, king of Babylon, sent letters and a present to Hezekiah; (for he had heard that he had been sick, and was recovered)' (1), But just because Hezekiah had fallen sick and was recovered, he sent him letters and a present. (2) Indeed 'to enquire of the wonder that was done in the land'(3). For R. Johanan said: The day on which Ahaz died consisted of but two hours (4); and when Hezekiah sickened and recovered, the Holy One, blessed be He, restored those ten hours, as it is written, 'Behold I will bring again the shadow of the degrees, which is gone down in the sun dial of Ahaz, ten degrees backward. So the sun returned ten degrees, by which degrees it was gone down' (5). Thereupon he (Merodach-baladan) inquired of them (his courtiers), 'What is this ?' They replied, 'Hezekiah has sickened and recovered.' 'There is such a (great) man,' exclaimed he, 'and shall I not send him a greeting! Write thee to him: Peace to King Hezekiah, peace to the city of Jerusalem, and peace to the great God!'"

(Footnotes: "(1) Is.39:1. (2) Surely not! (3) II Chron.32:31. (4) i.e. it set ten hours too soon, to allow of no time for the funeral obsequies and eulogies. This was in order to make atonement for his sins, for the disgrace of being deprived of the usual funeral honours expiates one's misdeeds, as stated supra 46b & 47a. (5) Is.38:8. The return of the ten degrees is assumed to mean a prolongation of the day by ten hours, light having healing powers.")

I shall leave it up to the reader to evaluate the damage that Forrest has done to Velikovsky's brief passages. With apologies for moving on, I say for my part that myth-analysis permits Velikovsky to say what he says. Too, Forrest came too late for Velikovsky to respond. I said then, and repeat now, I believe Forrest to be a thoroughgoing honest, if carping, critic. He has done a service in reining in some of Velikovsky's more reckless readings and remarks. In my opinion Forrest asks too much. Legend and myth are suggestive, not conclusive. (So largely are histories and archaeology.)Velikovsky's knowledge of the Bible and its exegesis, of calendrics, astronomy, and psychoanalytic theory permits him to formulate situations in ways deemed conventionally impermissible.

The Jews as Planet-Worshiper

During these times, the Jews were planet-worshipers, though some were Yahwists. Both Velikovsky, in Worlds in Collision[105] and Finkelstein, who differ so strikingly, stress this condition. King Josiah had not gotten around to his purges in the name of Yahweh. Both scholars rely in part upon the words of the Bible (*II Chronicles 33:3 inter alia*), where King Manasseh "reared up altars for Baalim, and he made groves, and worshiped all the host of heaven, and served them."

Most of the destruction of the Iron Age Quantavolution was past when the editorial and writing crew got to work in the 7th century. Iron was being put to work in many ways, and found 102 mentions in the Bible.

We might be content with the well-ordered list of Torrey. *Theoma* on the Web provides us with the applicable sentences on iron from the Bible, the 102 of them, and we could make another list from a slightly different perspective, to add color; the occurrences of the word 'iron' in the Bible have to do with –

breastplates

nails

gates

hinges

table legs

chariots

a god of iron

iron-tooth animal

threshing tools

bars of iron

a crushing kingdom

feet of iron

armed with

vessels Yahweh's house

iron without number

land of iron stones

iron but as straw

ruling rod of iron

sky of iron

furnace of iron

picks and ashes

slanderers

neck of iron

instrument(club)

kingdom of clay& iron

limbs

pikes

blunt iron

shekels of iron

pen of iron

yoke of nations

iron-worker

points of iron

earth of iron

etc.

In brief, the Jews of the full Iron Age were familiar with most, if not all, of the uses of iron known to the outside world, and with a range of metaphors as well. Did this rich culture pertain to them before the Babylonian Captivity, or did it come out of Babylon with them? I do not know. It is apparent that the iron-bearing passages of the Bible pay little attention to precedence. The first mention of iron occurs in *Genesis 4:22*, where it is said: "And Zillah, she also bare Tubel-Cain, an instructor of every artificer on brass and iron, and the sister of Tubel-Cain was Naamah." An interesting sentence, to be analyzed elsewhere.

Remembering Horrors Poorly

But the memory of horrible events lingered and found its way into the history book. We should probably assign to the mentality and output of the Bible crew what Velikovsky called and wrote a book about, "collective amnesia." We speak of this, too, in a chapter to come, "The Sick Society." Collective Amnesia is the failure of memory and recall among a group with respect to traumatic experiences suffered by the group. It is analogous to individual amnesia.

A worldwide traumatic event such as the showering of Earth with bolides, flames, thunderbolts, and the subsequent hurricanes, fires, explosions, floods, collapsing of whole settlements, the emergence of vermin and sources of plague, and the presence of death and injury everywhere will produce, has produced, a great many first-hand accounts, each differing from the next according to the survivors involved, and thereupon in the next phase a blotting out of the worst and next worst recollections out of the mind, then in a third phase, the sewing together of adjoining or diffused stories, varying therefore as a statistical phenomenon as against any single absolutely true account, then in the fourth phase, which actually would have begun immediately, a searching out in the minds of the story-sharers for some account of the events that would be tolerable for rewriting history, for dreaming, for telling among adults as literature and for telling to children as fables. By far the greater portions of all of these processes occur subconsciously. Mnemology would then become the science of uncovering and curing the negative symptoms of collective amnesia – to a certain degree simply by correcting history and learning to live with the history.[106]

The Bible teams of Seventh Century Judah, before, during, and after the exile in Babylon, thus exaggerated for political purposes so as to restart a traditional engine of empire, yet at the same time were both close to the events of the early Iron Age and partly forgetful of them. Their invented portraits of life and evils in the state of Israel to the North let them displace and exercise in writing all of the guilt and aggression that they possessed for having actually had many of the same experiences as their hated brethren to the North. But really they could only hate Israel so because Israel was now gone, a memory to which traumatic events could be attached.

It felt good to this band and their King Josiah, as they began their work, to dream of the sufferings of the Ten Tribes. They would not admit, although the Finkelstein research shows it clearly, that the same Israel had enjoyed many successes, a fair wealth, some imposing architecture, even victories in battles and conquests of land that this same Judah had hardly experienced, and while Judah was tending its sheep. Furthermore, to match the crime to the punishment, all manner of evils were ascribed to their tribal kinfolk of the North in order to slough off the burden of guilt from themselves.

The furnaces of aggression were of course fired by the natural disasters suffered by all, the failure of Judah to hold together an empire, by the failure of the Judahites to get down off the hills and onto the lush Canaan plains and to the sea. Almost none of the promises of Yahweh had been fulfilled. The blame would be intolerable if one tried to keep this Yahweh God with his demands, without their grasping for scapegoats among their own kind as well as foreign cults so as to satisfy Yahweh and relieve their own pains -- the sufferings of the day, the sufferings of the century of quantavolution.

The Bible as a History of Blame and Punishment

Behind the ordered Bible is the disordered history. We examine the *Book of Judges*. Whatever the total time allocated to *Judges* (the Bible-based consensus giving 410 years), the Judaic formula is throughout the same. Israel sins; Israel is punished; Israel pleads with Yahweh for help; Yahweh sends a 'Judge' who saves the People. The People resume their sinning; the cycle repeats – *Da Capo alla Coda*.

If one were to list all the mentions of punishment in the Old Testament (is the Koran less so?), what percentage would be attributed to Yahweh, then to Yahweh indirectly? Almost all. It is significant that Yahweh does not even let the Jews punish their own so much as would have the job done by their veriest enemies, like the Assyrians. For instance, many, if not most, Jews, along with their Canaanite neighbors, worshiped the deity Mars-Aserah, for which conduct they were declared to have been punished by Yahweh through the mediation of Assyrian butchery. When Yahweh was not punishing them or making them feel guilty, he was depriving them of food, family, and freedom. Of such deprivations there were a great many, and here individuals and foreign nations played an important part. On rare occasion he was said to save them from some fate worse than death – like letting them out of Egypt into the Wilderness. Or sparing some Jews from the fate of other Jews. And he never lets them forget it!

The Judges as Condottieri

Note how the rulers of the period of Judges resemble Renaissance *Condottieri* more than regularly chosen officers of the state. Their highly eccentric terms of ascendency, defying patterning, supports our conjecture. Are they not also akin in some kind of parallelism to the periodic outbursts of Mars?

This is not incredible if we posit a series of blighting catastrophes, usually interpreted as wars or revolts. These, too, actually would be expected in a quantavolution where in so many places the same formula is to be found; the Jews were not by any means the only nation engaged in stupid repetitions on record; the formula resembles and relates, for instance, to the tyrant cycle of the Iron Age in Greek cities.

We permit ourselves a complex instance: *Judges 3:31, 4:1,5 and 5:6 (NASB)* gives us:

And after him was Shamgar,
The son of Anath, which slew of the
Philistines 600 men with an ox goad
and he also delivered Israel...

A battle of Taanach follows the Shamgar episode. It is subject of a poem in the next lines. Battles and chaos.

In the days of Shamgar the son of Anath,
In the days of Jael, the highways were deserted,
And travelers went by roundabout ways.

Shamgar can be translated also as 'sword' in Hebrew, the sky-sword of Mars-Nergal. Anath is also to be rendered Anat. She is sister and consort of God Baal, "the name of She who was the Asherah," consort of Baal, and goddess of war.

It seems strange that Shamgar, who, as the son of Anath, must be an enemy of the Israelites and a Philistine, appears here as a heroic Israelite figure. Strange, too, that the story cuts off here and does not complete the Yahwist formula of sin and renewed punishment.

No more strange, perhaps, than finding the same Anath being worshiped by the Jewish mercenaries and families who lived and served the Egyptian Pharaoh at the garrison city of Elephantine in Upper Egypt for a great many years.[107]

Before proceeding, let us tie more closely into the Battle at Taanach, referred to above:

1 On that day Deborah and Barak son of Abinoam sang this song:

...

*4 "O LORD, when you went out from Seir,
when you marched from the land of Edom,
the earth shook, the heavens poured,
the clouds poured down water.*

...

*5 The mountains quaked before the LORD, the One of Sinai,
bef*

ore the LORD, the God of Israel.

...

*19 "Kings came, they fought;
the kings of Canaan fought
at Taanach by the waters of Megiddo,
but they carried off no silver, no plunder.*

*20 From the heavens the stars fought,
from their courses they fought against Sisera.*

*21 The river Kishon swept them away,
the age-old river, the river Kishon.
March on, my soul; be strong!*

*22 Then thundered the horses' hoofs—
galloping, galloping go his mighty steeds.*

*23 'Curse Meroz,' said the angel of the LORD.
'Curse its people bitterly,
because they did not come to help the LORD,
to help the LORD against the mighty.'* ...

The heavens, the Heavenly Host, Yahweh in the heavens – all and more were exceedingly active during Iron Age Palestine.

Isaiah's Madness

The Bible was far from a textbook of astronomy. The Jews appear not to have contributed much to the new movement of scientific astronomy abroad. Possibly the Yahwists with their singular divine instrument could not develop the versatile scenarios of the Greek and Babylonian skies: multi-factorial analysis was denied them. Possibly the cult needed a blunt instrument for its local purposes. They formed certainly but a minor part of the sophisticated world of Babylonian, Assyrian, Egyptian and Greek astronomy.

Let us declare how Isaiah used religion to activate, more than to contemplate. He is bombastic, on the verge of the hysterical, stimulates wholesale panic, exhibits a devastated mind and a chaotic irrationalism. What kind of a god must operate by such a tool? We are fairly certain that the catastrophe that Isaiah proclaims is real; we speak of his manner of grappling with it and using it. (We are all the more concerned, because we have reason to believe in his reality and the behavior of his audience, when we see how, with infinitely less terrible things happening, our populace and leadership today in the Age of Science becomes readily re-catastrophized.)

Your country lies desolate,
your cites are burned with fire;
in your very presence, aliens
devour your land; it is desolate,
as overthrown by aliens.

Hesiod's depiction of mad and hostile human beings of the Iron Age might as well be applied to the Jews of Israel and Judah of the same time: angry gods, desolated lands, remnant peoples, alien incursions, surges of war, revolt, riot, interpersonal hostility

*If the Lord had not left us
a few survivors,
we should have been like Sodom,
And become like Gomorrah*

Now the prophet asks *"How long, O Lord,?"* "Yahweh replies:

*Until the cities lie waste without inhabitants,
And houses without men, and
the land is entirely desolate,...
And the Lord removes men far away,
And the forsaken places are many in the midst of the land.*

Isaiah has the Lord speak, to all humanity, for it is apparent that the disasters are universal.

Draw near, O nations, to hear, and hearken, O peoples! Let the earth listen, and all that fills it; the world, and all that comes from it.

For the L:ord is engaged against all the nations, and furious against all their host, he has doomed them, has given them over for slaughter.

..the mountains shall flow with their blood.

..All the host of heaven shall rot away, and the skies roll up like a scroll...

Charity and Welfare in the Bible

The Bible is an eccentric document, morally and generally. Alongside its frequent insults and scolding, its contempt of all persons without regard to class, sex, age, and provenance, there works away an occasional generosity and concern for justice and charity that in the Deuteronomy reaches a peak in the iteration of individual rights and obligations and prohibition of personal and official corruption.

Finkelstein, ever alert to supplement the Bible with archeological finds, comes delightedly upon a broken shard at a ruin far from Judah. A servant working in the fields had written thereon an appeal to his lord to get back for him, out of conscience or good practice, a garment that had been confiscated by the field foreman. This unique "proof" of a rule of law and human rights is hardly convincing. A field-hand writing so well? And in Hebrew, which was hardly used in this period, the seventh century? Finkelstein stretches the example beyond all reason, "as the foundation for a universal social code and system of community values that endure - even today."[108] It is most unfortunate that archaeological and historical materials are not sufficient to judge the veracity and validity of the Deuteronomic welfare promulgations.

These laws are not, as so many people believe, or wish us to believe, uniquely Jewish (and both Velikovsky and Finkelstein plus the multitude of Jews, Christians, and secularists would have it so). By the time that mankind found its new voice in the Iron Age, declarations of social conscience are to be found in Egypt, Assyria, Persia, and Rome. We find Solon in Athens pressing into law a radical program of economic and judicial reforms, perhaps a few years later than Judah. Finkelstein cannot quite get himself to say so, but he believes that Deuteronomy was originally mostly a creation of 622 B.C.E. and a transliteration of the Book of the Law that was heralded for its discovery in the Temple recesses (thus allegedly proving the historicity of King Josiah's sundry ordinances).

The Romans were employing a triple-tiered government, a republic, after chasing out their Kings. Their first written code of law was the Twelve Tables, inscribed and adopted in the 5th Century. The Spartans, like the German Nazis, were becoming all the more totalitarian as their subject peoples, seeking human rights, became more restive and rebellious. Is the demand for individualized social justice a concomitant of the Martian Quantavolution, part of the holospheric reaction, we wonder? Possibly a new kind of individualism was resulting from the breakup of the structural tightness of the previous social order. The public mattered and should be able to read the laws and rules. This appears consistent with the emerging natural and rational philosophy that has been noted by evidence extending from Italy to China.

The spread of literacy just then would encourage the voicing of altruism. Finkelstein speaks of "the sudden, dramatic spread of literacy in 7th century Judah."[109] It coincides with the writing of the Deuteronomy and its being read to the people. We note, too, the possible interrelationship between the public literacy and the new harshness being imparted by way of a written code.

Literacy may have provided the stimulus, too, for numerous social welfare provisions, probably newly written and demanded now in Deuteronomy.

Once again, it is to be realized that quantavolutions are not wholly destructive. They seize the steering wheel from man's grasp, but let him have another chance at driving at the next turn of the road.

Limiting Hostilities among Archaeologists of the Bible

It is well to appreciate that Finkelstein is not anti-semitic. He is anti-grandiosity, anti-romantic. But this to a degree. We find throughout his work praises of the Bible for its graces and its influences. It is true, however, that he does not go as far as he might. He is absolutely non-astral, and hardly praises the God of Israel. One wonders whether his praise of the Bible and a few other aspects of Hebrew history are not interposed to limit the hostility that his explanations must provoke, and did, indeed, provoke.

So we do find in his Acknowledgments, intimations of struggle and value-loaded words and sentences. " ..The archaeological battle over the Bible has grown increasingly bitter. It has sunk – in some times and places – to personal attacks and accusations of hidden motives."[110] His "official" view of the Bible in general is well-worth quoting to his enemies:[111]

> During a few extraordinary decades of spiritual ferment and political agitation toward the end of the seventh century B.C.E., an unlikely coalition of Judahite court officials, scribes, priests, peasants, and prophets came together to create a new movement. At its core was a sacred scripture of unparalleled literary and spiritual genius. It was an epic saga woven together from an astonishingly rich collection of historical writings, memories, legends, folk tales, anecdotes, royal propaganda, prophecy, and ancient poetry . Partly an original composition, partly adapted from earlier versions and sources, that literary masterpiece would undergo further editing and elaboration to become a spiritual anchor not only for the descendants of the people of Judah but for communities all over the world.

This purple prose will serve to save them from the fate of Giordano Bruno.

However, as we have already well illustrated, they leave out much (like Yahweh) from this sentence, and most of the ignominy of Hebrew history.

Judging the authors by these passages and by what they say throughout the work, as I have pointed out already, they have exchanged the grandiose notions of Velikovsky, who, in order to operate upon and prove his revision of chronology had to create an Israel that would be most appetizing for Egypt and the other external powers to deal with -- contentedly brushing off, I must add, a humble conception of the Jewish people and the little kingdoms which they created. I am reminded of Frederick Jackson Turner, the American professor of a century ago (1861-1932), who turned his back on the East Coast and European-oriented culture of the United States, and called attention to the Frontier as the true American pride, and here was followed all the way by popular America, and part of the way by scholarly America, and rather less by the elites of the East Coast.

Deconstructing the Bible

Finkelstein and Silberman conclude their prologue with attractive promises, saying, " ..our purpose, ultimately, is not mere deconstruction. It is to share the most recent archaeological insights – still largely unknown outside scholarly circles – not only on *when,* but also *why* the Bible was written, and *why* it remains so powerful today."[112] By deconstruction, they mean the reduction of the virtues, pretensions, and pontification of the Bible and the Hebrews responsible for its formulation and recital.

This they do and it is no small job; Voltaire and Nietzsche would be delighted with it were they still alive. Archaeology only helps our present authors part of the way, and hinders their perspectives as well. It makes them too skeptical, near to the point of denial, of the very existence of Moses, David and Solomon. Then, too, they hardly have learned from archaeology when it was that the Bible was written. The chronology is a complex construction adding up numerous sources of evidence and rationalization.

They cast grave doubt on the historicity of all things and events until the evidence begins to come in of a Canaanite people speaking a dialect that became Hebrew, a hillbilly people assembling into tribes and one does have to wonder what came first, the refugee camps that turned into tribes or the tribes that were taking refuge much of the time in the spinal column of Palestine. Before the Iron Age came crashing in, the Hebrews as a nation of tribes may not even have existed. Ask when the hundreds of Jewish legends generated and the answer may be that these had been and often still were the common property of the back-country folk of numerous tribal groups and clans.

Yahweh, some say, was originally a tribal god of the Hebrew Canaanites, maybe an agricultural divinity. (As was probably Mars to the Romans.) Salibi, however, sees in the origin of the compound divine name *(yahweh sẹbha'owth)*assigned to Yahweh in the Bible as "The Yahweh of Honors," also "The Yahweh of War," also "The Yahweh of Services [Welfare]," but also "The *Yahweh of Ashes* [Scorching]" especially since the Hebrews were dwelling in a great field of active volcanoes in Arabia, and we are reminded of the apparent volcanic nature of Mt. Sinai in *Exodus*. ..Yahweh was, by origin, clearly a volcano god."

So, at the least, given that the *Exodus* came in for extensive downloading and rewriting during the Iron Age, Yahweh's character is approaching the Martian syndrome. The absence of vowels and the play of genders make all of these meanings practically equivalents. Salibi even hints at a major theme of my book on *God's Fire*, when he wonders whether the Ark of the Covenant did not contain ashes.[113]

The *when* answers the question *why* the Bible was written. To the present author, the answer is simple political sociology. It was a wonderful idea that grew upon the impecunious elite of a small kingdom all the more as they thought how to make themselves into a distinctive nation and then as they gained a fuller idea in the rich environment of Babylon and then were given a small realm of a hundred thousand people whose local leadership lacked their Babylonian sophistication, and therefore where they might historicize as they pleased. The Bible was their *Eddas*, their Homeric epics, their *Mahabarathra*. They could now offer a proud and long history, equal to the many dynasties of Egypt and Assyria, going back to Genesis. It had now an alphabet to work by. It could be read. It was a first-rate social invention. One may even imagine that its portability was insurance against displacement of the whole people to where they might not consult it regularly -- a preparation for greater Diasporas to come.

Finkelstein and Silberman do not address the question "why it remains so powerful today." Perhaps the answer is so easy that they forgot to give it. Or perhaps they feel that they answered it on the several occasions when they cast forth generalities about the Bible as great literature. They were begging the question, actually. The Bible would have no more power than gypsy music or the Homeric epics had it not been adopted by the Christians, the Jewish agitators Jesus and Paul, and all who came after them. The Jews would exist, if at all, as a people, like the gypsies, in a now pleasant, now terrible, diaspora, with truncated storybooks, rather than violins. Their striking virtues, extraordinary everywhere, were preserved, developed, and practiced under the stimulus of invidious discrimination.

And thus we end this chapter – but not the topic! Now I have a large favor to ask of my reader. Please, Madam, Sir, take up the following proposition and return to the beginning of this past chapter, keeping the proposition in mind, and in its light scanning the chapter again. For in the chapter after next, you will have mentally to picture the facts in a new Locale:

"All that Finkelstein and company, with my acquiescence, assume to have happened in Palestine, actually happened in Western Arabia!"

Do not accept the proposition, at least, not yet.

For now you may wish to read the next intervening chapter, where you will discover that, far from finding Finkelstein to be the most radical revisionist of the Old Testament, there are, out there, top-notch scholars of the Bible and Archaeology, who, while remaining in Palestine, play hob with the contents and chronology of the Scriptures.

Then it is that you can turn, possibly with some anxiety, and discover all that can be said on behalf of moving the world's greatest troupe and its dramatic performance to the Western Region of the Arabian Peninsula.

Chapter Eleven

The Fabled Holy Land

The history of the Jews during the Iron Age was in significant ways typical of the universal course of events. They had factors going for them so far as an attentive audience of today is concerned. They had Yahweh, a special kind of god. They had a Book, quite a book, which, once put together, had an attraction that seemed irresistible. It became the Christian story and had been pretty much an Arabic story long before Islam, so much of it was familiar to and believable by the Muslims as well. As for the rest of the world: there the educated had known something of the Bible, if only because they were usually bossed by Bible-believers.

The Book does not mention Mars as planet or god as such but we have presented some evidence that he was quite active in Hebrew territory and history as elsewhere. In fact, when we last left the population of Jerusalem, the Archangel Gabriel, a doppelgaenger of Mars, was suppressing a terrifying invasion by an army of Assyrians. He was acting under the direct orders of Yahweh, who reminds us of the Roman God Mars from time to time, but combines the powers of the full band of Greco-Roman gods.

"King David the Nebbish"

The Book, the Bible, however, has lost most of its credibility so far as the educated classes of the twenty-first century are concerned. An article in Ha'aretz magazine, written by archaeologist Ze'ev Herzog, displayed the issue of the Bible versus Science flagrantly in 1999. I may quote Laura Miller, an Editor of *Salon Magazine* who reported the case on February 7, 2001. She entitled her article, "King David was a Nebbish." ('Nebbish' means 'a nothing' in Yiddish and the parlance of various American quarters.) The centerpiece is a book that we already know something about, the Finkelstein - Silberman book, *The Bible Unearthed.*

I quote her:

> The debate reached the general population of Israel, sending what one journalist called a "shiver" down the nation's "collective spine," in late 1999, when another archaeologist from Tel Aviv University, Ze'ev Herzog, wrote a cover story for the weekend magazine of the national daily newspaper, *Ha'aretz*. In the essay, Herzog laid out many of the theories Finkelstein and Silberman present in their book: "the Israelites were never in Egypt, did not wander in the desert, did not conquer the land [of Canaan] in a military campaign and did not pass it on to the twelve tribes of Israel. Perhaps even harder to swallow is the fact that the united kingdom of David and Solomon, described in the Bible as a regional power, was at most a small tribal kingdom." The new theories envision this modest chiefdom as based in a Jerusalem that was essentially a cow town, not the glorious capital of an empire.

The authors were now relegated to the "minimalists."

> The inflammatory implication behind the name "minimalist" (which Finkelstein and Silberman dismiss as a canard invented by the group's "detractors") is that an emotional, religious or political agenda, rather than a judicious weighing of the facts, drives their research. Their most vehement critics accuse the minimalists of being anti-Bible and anti-Israeli, for to some any attack on the historical legitimacy of the Bible, with its grand national myth of a people chosen by God to rule in the Promised Land, is a blow struck at the legitimacy of the current state of Israel.

For example, in line with our last chapter, the Megiddo of current investigations turns out not to have been a preciously rare uncovering of a major center of King Solomon, but rather a city of much later Iron Age date, and of the much less honored King Ahab, whose major achievements had included his notoriously pagan and unjustly despised Queen Jezebel. In truth, Finkelstein and company are not so radical as others, which we shall now proceed to demonstrate.

"Der Spiegel" Collects the Minimalists

One of Europe's best magazines is the vehicle for the minimalization of the Bible beyond Finkelstein. *"The Invention of God,"* Der Spiegel calls its report. We are paraphrasing it here at length. A full copy in German is available on *Der Spiegel's* web site and on www.grazian-archive.com/der Spiegel re Biblical study. Its contents could not help but reflect upon the study of the Iron Age. For it showed that the sacred history of the Jews, as the Bible tells of it, was largely the work of teams of propaganda writers for the cult of Yahweh, King Josiah and the post-exile rabbinate. Moreover, most of the history of the Jews and the Bible's telling of it took place in the Iron Age.

The problems presented are too difficult for us to solve, but it may be proper to speculate that some characteristic events of the Mars Quantavolution occurred then, which may give us to understand the holosphere of the Iron Age through a Freudian analysis of Biblical dreaming. As in a dream, everything found there is true just as it is false, a tremendous working of the sub-conscious mind of the human collectivity from then to now.

Was there a Great Kingdom of David that stretched from the Mediterranean to the Euphrates, it asks. No. *No* is the answer of the experts of the newer schools of biblical study and archaeology. Archaeological digs in the so/called "City of David" in East Jerusalem reveal the ruins of hovels from the age of David. Yet the Bible says: "Silver as much as stone..." made it up. In fact, in the Bronze Age, Jerusalem cannot have had more than 2000 inhabitants (so says Dr.Hanswulf Bloedhorn of the Evangelisches Institut für Altertumswissenschaft im Heiligen Land).

We continue for the rest of this chapter to paraphrase *Der Spiegel:*

Der Spiegel proclaims: Israel Finkelstein, Chief-Archaeologist at the University of Tel-Aviv wrote a book called: "No Trumpets at Jericho". It confirms that central tenets of the Bible are untrue:

* There never was an Exodus of Jewish tribes out of

Egypt

* Canaan was not conquered by force as is described in the Book of Joshua

* The Kingdoms of David and Solomon are myth. These Kings ruled only over "insignificant areas of border land."

The word of God appears to be fairy tale and a monumental enterprise of camouflage. Where scientists once surmised historical facts, they now discover political propaganda: "We are standing before a breaking dam..." says Dirk Kinet, Professor of Biblical languages at the University of Augsburg. For even the development of monotheism did not occur in the way the Bible purports. Archaeology shows: God started small. "He was a promoter of fertility, whose sexual representation was only slowly repressed." It also shows:

* In the temple at Jerusalem, sacred prostitution flourished.

* God had originally a naked female mate.

* In 100 BPE farmers and herders of the area still followed pagan rites.

Many humiliations found their way into the Bible -- despair and anger-born fantasies of omnipotence accumulated there. By means of a stroke of the pen its authors transformed the tower of Babel into a ruin (when it was in fact finished and towered at 90 meters).
It is ever more clear that the "Book of Books" is loaded with falsehoods. A group of falsifiers, called the "Deuteronomists," brushed over the *Realgeschichte* (contained in some earlier work), twisted truth around, got rid of inconvenient facts, and invented, like a Hollywood scenario, the story of the Promised Land. The threads of the deed all go back to the Temple of Jerusalem..
Three camps are involved in a debate over the dating of the Bible:

* The traditionalists believe that the main texts of the Bible started to be written around 1000 BCE.

* The moderates bet on 600 BCE.

* The minimalists consider the Old Testament to be a "Hellenistic work." Its main substance was written after 330 BCE – therefore after Socrates and Plato.

Bernd Joerg Diebner, for 30 years Professor of Theology at the University of Heidelberg goes even a step farther: the Torah is a "diplomatic compromise" which was possibly still being worked at in 50 AD! "a projection into the past of "Big Power" dreams..."

Abraham (supposedly flourishing in -1800) is shown using camels - yet these were not employed for transportation until -1000. (The camel may even have been an Iron Age domestication, and is attributed by one Arab tradition to the Jews of Asir.)

The existence of Moses is also suspect. It has been surmised that the author of the Sinai story lived around 950 BCE in David's palace. But still how can the Jews -- in *1. Moses, 42* -- be paying for their wheat in metal coins? The oldest coins found anywhere originated in Asia Minor in the 7th century BCE.

No question about it: the *Pentateuch* (*Torah* - The five books of Moses) is not a primary document from the Bronze age.

Especially does the *Book of Joshua* twist reality around.. The new archaeological finds show the whole extent of the deception: "The settling of Canaan happened in reality peacefully and slowly," says Finkelstein. In fact, ~-1200 Semitic pastoral tribes from the desert begin to infiltrate Jordanian mountains and settle down there. The Northern region up to above Lake Genezaret afforded them to some extent a good life. They cultivated grapes and olives on the hillsides.

Farther South, between Jerusalem and Hebron, the land was much poorer. Little water...

Population in -1000 was merely around 50,000 for the whole area. The South was very sparsely populated.

Constant trouble with the neighbors took place: ...in the fertile coastal plain the Philistines (who possibly came from Crete) [but we say probably from Arabia] had spread themselves out in large cities. Farther north, the seafaring Phoenicians were settled... But the uncontested master of the land was the Pharaoh of Egypt, who exploited the copper mines. Around -1250 [-850 by my dating, in fact even later], Ramses II built a chain of forts and water collectors along the "Road of Horus" - to be used by the Nile armies.....-1207 [-807] a stele of Merenptah mentions punishment of a tribe called Israel...Heavy tribute was extorted, also forced labor... To escape it, people took to the mountains, which were soon full of outlaws and escapees. Many experts derive the word "Hebrew" from "*hapiru*," vagabonds.

Yet it is precisely in this barren world of Canaan that the Bible conjures up flourishing monarchies. According to the Bible, "Solomon bettered in riches all the rulers of the world." All attempts to find signs of the existence of Solomon's Temple have proven unsuccessful. "We don't even have a trace on the ground for the temple," admits Bloedhorn.

No doubt that the Old Testament is affabulating. The Swiss Old Testament expert, Othmar Keel, sees the story of Solomon as an "ideal time," without historical substance.

At least four authors worked on the Books of Moses. One of them was the "Yahwist," who probably came from Jerusalem. Another probably lived in the North of the country and calls God Elohim or El.

Yet, there is remarkable work on details... 42 kings are listed with their dates. Were old chronicles and king lists used here? ...Scientists examined the cuneiform archives of Mesopotamia and found indeed five of the kings by name. The most important piece of evidence was found in 1993 in "Tell Dan," a settlement on a hilltop in the North of Israel. It is a stele with the word "House of David." The King must have had a historical existence, albeit as the head of a "minor city state" (according to Finkelstein).

In the light of new discoveries from the Negev and Samaria the obscure "time of the kings" can now be made out somewhat better. Around 950 BPE {later, we think, following the disappearance of Pharaoh Akhnaton] Egypt lost control over its vassals. In this power vacuum, the Hebrew tribe chieftains could establish themselves more solidly.

The Little Struggling Kingdoms

First appears in the North the ur-state of "Israel." In -884 a king Omri ascends the throne. The country had barely 100,000 inhabitants.

The south, below Jerusalem, was much more backward and poor. No more than 10,000 people subsisted there permanently.

With spade and mini-bulldozers, archeologists have now uncovered the modesty of these proto-Jewish states. In Samaria they found a few receipts for wine sales, in Arad some letters on clay tablets. No other trace of writing.

But even this would soon come to an end.

Assyria wanted to control the route of the caravans all the way to its end, in Gaza. In 732 BCE King Tiglatpileser III. attacked and soon reached the sea, conquering many territories. In the process, the state of Israel was swallowed up. As the province of Samaria, it became part of the Assyrian empire. Only the barren South was spared - or overlooked - at first.

Archaeologist from Giessen, Volkmar Fritz, was able to show how brutal the conquest had been. He digs in Kinneret, near Lake Genezaret. The 500 inhabitants of the village were subjected to a hail of iron arrowheads. "Then the soldiers destroyed the houses with iron bars."

Deportations were part of the policies of the attackers. 13,500 Israelites were forced to leave. A bas-relief in Nineveh shows Jews carrying heavy loads on their backs.

A flood of refugees overwhelmed the South. The population grew from perhaps 2000 to maybe 15,000 and was exposed without defences to its well-armed neighbors.

The Monotheism Project of King Josiah

It is in this threatening situation, according to the

moderate bible-critics around Finkelstein, that a miracle occurred: the birth of belief in a single God (monotheism).

The impulse for the project is supposed to have come from King Josiah (-639 to -609). In the Bible, he is feted as the one who came to purge the land of foreign cults and lead the people of Israel to redemption through a scrupulous following of the Law. He forthwith called up his priests (according to the moderates) to find a religious protector and to write the epic of the "Promised Land."

The primary goal was to strengthen the feeling of national worth and fight off threatening foreignism. An "ethnic isolation" was aimed at, according to Finkelstein. Therefore, tabus, exclusions, in large number. But Josiah also ordered metaphysical inclusions. Until then Yahweh had only been a thunder god, the local god of Jerusalem, honored on Mount Zion. Now he was transformed into a universal power.

Almost all biblical scholars suspect that the 5th book of Moses , the "Deuteronomy," reflects the results of Josiah's reform. This book is characterized by a unique language, such as doesn't appear in any other source. The work condemns the adoration of any other Gods and threatens with frightful punishment any case of non-compliance. God now appears as entirely remote and transcendent. Morever, the book pronounces an absolute interdiction: sacrifices to Yahweh must be performed in the temple of Jerusalem and nowhere else.

With such decrees, the priests of Zion were seeking a monopoly of the faith. More than anything else, they wanted to neutralize their colleagues in the Assyrian-dominated state of Israel. For they, too, were managing a Yahweh temple on top of Mt Garizim, 50km from Jerusalem.

This struggle between Judah in the South and Israel runs deeply all through the Old Testament. Whenever they could, the men from Jerusalem besmirched their neighbors to the North.

Particularly striking is this one-sided presentation in the Book of Kings. There the inhabitants of Israel appear mostly as cowardly failures. Their kings are almost all given over to sacrilege and sin. In Judah, by contrast, there dwell mostly pious and godfearing people. The Zion priests did not shrink from deceit and falsification. To give more weight to their monopolistic claims they came up with a refined plan. In the Second Book of Kings, it is told that their high-priest Hilkiah in -622 discovers during work done at the Temple in Jerusalem a "Book of Laws" of highest antiquity. In reality, the ink of this mysterious temple-find was hardly dry. It contained the newly written Deuteronomy.

From the standpoint of the "moderate" Bible experts the situation is therefore the following: around -630, the "Deuteronomists" wrote essential parts of the Bible. They invented the figures of Abraham and Moses and situated their actions into the past through sleight-of-hand.

But is even this correct? Had the idea of the invisible Yahweh already imposed itself in the 7th century? For most "minimalists," the Bible-criticism of the moderates around Finkelstein does not go far enough. Their suspiciousness with regard to the Bible is even larger - and they have solid grounds.

Historiography, ethics, political science - all are contained in this work. And all this long before Plato and Herodotus? As a matter of fact, antiquity barely took notice of the geniuses from Judah. Herodotus mentions some people in Syro-Palestine who practice circumcision - but he knows nothing of their feats. Only in the 3rd and 4th century does the echo becomes louder.

Moreover, the intellectual achievements are in striking contrast with the technical level evidenced at the time by the tiny country.

Most uncouth appears a project which the King of Jerusalem undertook in ~-720. He wanted to bring water to the city by means of an underground canal. The tunnel has more than 20 blind exits, because the workers dug time after time into the wrong direction - yet it is precisely this work which the Bible extols as a masterwork of water engineering.

Scandalous Religious Practices

The faction of Minimalists considers therefore also the cult-reform of Josiah to be an exaggeration. The story of the allegedly extremely ancient, draconically monotheistic

"Book of Laws" would be in their view an even more recent invention.

The archaeological finds which are now seeing the light of day support their view. The suppression of polytheism took far longer than was previously thought. In -600 the population of Judah was still as polytheistic as any of its neighbors. "There existed no difference between their religion and the religions of the surrounding cultures," says the Old Testament expert of Tubingen, Herbert Niehr.

Science owes important knowledge as to what was happening at the time in the isolated mountains around Jerusalem to the Swiss Old Testament expert Othmar Keel. He examined 8500 seals from the Syro-Palestinian area. His conclusion: Canaan was teeming with idols.

Hardly a mountain top stood without sacrificial altars. In front of the houses of the peasants were small limestone altars, for ancestor worship. Around -650, says Keel, the country saw a "boom in astrological cults." The gods of the Assyrian victors came in fashion.

And everywhere people "threw themselves at the feet of the thunderbolt-wielding Baal." The weather-god Baal was adored in many variants, one of which is Yahweh. "Beelzebub," the devil of the Gospels, is Baal Zevuv.

The main god was presented at the beginning with thunderbolt and spear. And he had a wife: the love-goddess Ashera. The Danish expert, Tilde Binger, calls her the "spouse" of the Lord.

Naked and wearing a curious crown, she was an icon of fertility. Even in the Temple of Jerusalem her cult-tree must have been standing. This is deduced from a sensational finding: a small pomegranate of ivory with the inscription: "holy priestly property of the Temple of Yahweh." The object, probably the tip of a sceptre, dates back to the 7th century. Pomegranates were the symbols of Ashera. They also decorated the robes of the high priests.

Nothing of this is to be read in the Bible. The temple censors suppressed and exaggerated: telling how the prophet Hoseah rode over the country ~-750 and pitilessly exterminated the idolaters. At the banks of the Kishon, he slew 450 priests of Baal in one fell swoop. Many experts accept that there was a "Yahweh-alone" movement around that time. But its devotees were "extreme marginals", who only won slowly in influence, according to Kinet.

The elite of Jerusalem had little to do with them. Around 590 BCE a rich citizen was buried. He wore a silver breastplate with an Old Testament blessing formula. But his tomb also contained an amulet of the Egyptian cat-goddess Bastet. Ezekiel called such worshippers "pieces of rot."

Even around -600 the Lord was not as invisible as Book 5 of Moses purports. Niehr is sure that "in the Temple in Jerusalem there was even then a likeness of the God," fully gold-covered... the "Lord of Honor" as he was then called.

Then in -587 occurred the event which probably brought about the success of monotheism. Nebuchadrezzar on his way to Egypt took Jerusalem. Judah also became Assyrian. The Temple was burned. Part of the elite was moved to Babylon. There, at the earliest, in the shadow of the 91.5m high Tower of Babel, an astronomical observatory, the Hebrews developed the theme of the "Promised Land" -- precisely because they no longer had one.

But also their representation of God took definite shape only then. In -539 the Persians conquered Babylon. Their prophet Zarathustra preached a religion which also knew angels and rested on the struggle between good and evil. Ahuramazda, main god of the Persians, was a being without a form. These people do not build altars, says Herodotus: "Who does so is foolish, these people say. From all evidence, they do not imagine their gods as humanlike beings, like the Greeks do." The Persians gave strong support to the Yahweh cult and in -538 allowed Jews to return home to what was called now Jehud, a province of Persia. About 30,000 people returned to Judah-Jehud, and rebuilt the temple.

Like Falsifying Medieval Monks

Nehemia, a new Mayor of Jerusalem in 445 BCE, was employed at the Court of the King, Artaxerxes. Only now, according to the minimalists, as governors of the Persian province of Jehud (30km in radius), did the radical

Jewish reformers go into full swing. Like the falsifying gangs of medieval monks, they set themselves to the task of rewriting whatever existed of Hebrew writing, inventing kings and kingdoms.

But more than anything, they fought the cult of the Goddess Ashera. There is no sign of the religious struggles of the time in the Bible. Only archeology begins to uncover the facts of this period. Particularly interesting is a find at Aswan, Egypt. On an island on the Nile there lived a group of Jewish mercenaries who kept up a regular correspondence with Jerusalem. There are letters to the Temple from the period -460 to -407. They show that, next to their God Jahu, Jews even at that time adored at least three other gods, one of them the love goddess, Anat, doppelganger for Athene and Planet Venus.

Even among conservative experts suspicions spread. Theologist Niehr recognizes a "tendency to more recent dating" among his colleagues. He proposes to read Moses' activities "through the glasses of Persian and Hellenistic times."

On route 443, north of Jerusalem, direction of Ramot, an archeological site "Nebi Samuel" - a cult place of about 1000 sqm represents hard work; almost all of the top of a mountain had been removed and made flat and smooth. It is bordered with wine presses and stables for the animal victims. In the provisional report of the excavation - available only in Hebrew - it is said that the tribes of Israel called there to heaven for rain and "executed other significant religious rituals." In the second century BCE, the place was still in use.

The Maccabees in -140 were still working at rewriting essential parts of the Bible. A little while later, the Zealots went on a military offensive and managed to overrun the hated North militarily. They destroyed the temple on Mt Garizim. It was at this historic moment, according to Diebner, that the dream of a Pan-Israelitic great kingdom was invented, which is drawn (retroactively) as a leitmotif through the whole Old Testament.

"There occurred then the destruction of the Samarian culture, that is to say, the imperialistic integration of the Samarian culture into a Judaic-dominated and integrated culture."

Only then, say the minimalists, was the fictitious story of Abraham, the founding father, invented. His wanderings through existing places comprise every place which the Maccabees claimed.

Also invented was the infamous story of the conquest of Canaan, in which God Yahweh orders His Chosen People to exterminate the autochtonous populations. It fits much better into the time of the Maccabees, who were involved heavily in territorial conflicts.

Is the Book of Joshua therefore a "programmatic writing from the second century BCE" as the Danish expert John Strange surmises? Also the Bible expert Krauss suspects: "It appears that the author of the book of Joshua intended to advise the high priests in poetic form about the kind of politics to follow with regard to pagan neighbors."

In theological faculties everywhere, uncomfortable ideas are being hatched. Jewish orthodoxy prefers to stop its ears. The moderate Finkelstein is already considered to be a nest-befouler...

The Hebrews Born an "Iron Age People"

So concludes our paraphrase of the article in *Der Spiegel*, 'The Invention of God.' I would add a comment before proceeding farther. The article reports that a stele of Merneptah whose date I guess at ~-807 mentions severe punishment of a people called Israelites. Finkelstein writes elsewhere, "The Merneptah stele contains the first appearance of the name Israel in any surviving ancient text. It again raises the basic questions: Who were the Semites in Egypt? Can they be regarded as Israelite in any meaningful sense? No mention of the name Israel has been found in any of the inscriptions or documents connected with the Hyksos period. Nor is it mentioned in later Egyptian inscriptions, nor in an extensive fourteenth century BCE (~-900, more likely) cuneiform archive found at Tell el Amara in Egypt, whose nearly four hundred letters describe in detail the social, political, and demographic conditions in Canaan at the time. ...The Israelites emerged only gradually as a distinct group in Canaan, beginning at the end of the thirteenth century BCE." [This would be about 900 BCE in our reckoning, entering the Iron Age -- *AdeG*.] The Jews may well be termed an "Iron Age People."

The birthday of the Israelites as a clan or tribe or even group of tribes may never be known. One can either guess the date as that of the first signs of settlement in the Eastern hills beyond the Jordan River, uncovered by archaeology. Or one can imagine them as a poor and insignificant set of families who kept their identity alive even though unorganized as a clan or tribe, and went back and forth to Egypt like many other Semites. And, in the quantavolution that ended the Middle Bronze Age, they gathered with other Semites under the leadership of Moses and found their way back to their ancestral home in the hills. The imposing scenario found in the Bible was written down by the propaganda team of King Josiah, flourished for 2600 years, and was only finally outdone perhaps by the present author in his book, *God's Fire: Moses and the Management of Exodus*, or, better, in the scenario of the motion picture, *The Ten Commandments*, directed by Cecil B. De Mille.

Chapter Twelve

The Arabian Alternative

The Iron Age experienced, we have seen, a universal vagrancy. Religious changes were many and religions and cults traveled as well. Perhaps we should look beyond Palestine for the origins of peoples, ideas, and events. The Arabs and Hebrews were among the many kindred semites who entered early upon the Arabian-Palestinian scene. Dalil Boubakeur, rector of the Muslim Institute of the Paris Mosque, asserts persuasively that the tradition of monotheism goes back to Adam, thence Noah and finally Abram, and through him his son Ismael...[114]

We cannot accept this dictum (or 'practical fiction' in the terminology of Hans Vaihinger) without satisfying ourselves as to where and when the Hebrews came into the picture. Nor can we immediately agree that the original temple of the single god was Ka'aba, whose location was at Mecca. Mecca or Beccah is believed to be a term of Chaldean origin, and Mecca has a score of alternate appellations. Ka'aba survived through the ages as a temple traditionally associated with a single god. Along with Mecca, it preceded the Temple of Jerusalem, which was a mere village until, or as the Bible would have it, David centered his cult there.

As Boubakeur would have it, and I see no reason to refuse his thesis, a strain of monotheism attended the birth and development of the semitic peoples. It finally grew forcibly in the Iron Age, and evolved one way into Judaism and Christianity and another way into the Muslim faith of the Prophet. It may be that monotheism did originate deep in the Middle East and through Abram of Ur in the Chaldees moved into Western Arabia, to the region of Mecca, and thence up North to Palestine.

We have a large explanation to offer. Conventional religious leaders, commentators, archaeologists and historians of the Jews and the Bible maintain that both were immersed from their beginnings in the region of Palestine. The only substantial author who has placed their origins and development elsewhere has been Kamal Salibi. In my opinion, Salibi may be right and they may all be wrong, including Albright, Velikovsky, and Finkelstein. With a courage unblinded by prejudice, with persistence, focusing upon geography, using simple tools of linguistics, and pursuing a sweeping trenchant hypothesis, Salibi appears to have overturned a massive structure of biblical scholarship. His explanation of the multiple linguistic sources of the Bible is clear and plausible. His choices among the Hebrew terms that are to be applied in his monumental toponymy appear to this amateur author to be wise.

So many are the misstatements and exaggerations, so many the lacunae of events and places, so powerful and logical the motives for deception in handling the contents of the Bible, that we should listen with especial attention when a competent expert announces an alternative scenario. Yet, stretch as they might to fit the Book into a historical frame, the traditionalists and radicals whom I have been discussing have not yet accommodated, or even considered seriously, the work of Kamal Salibi.

The Background and Thesis of Salibi

Professor Salibi is a long-time member of the faculty of the American University of Beirut and an influential member of the larger Lebanese and Jordanian communities. His great-great grandfather was first Pastor of the Free Congregationalist Church of Bhamdoun, Lebanon, of which he is an Elder. He studied Semitic languages and earned his Doctorate at London University.

Like Finkelstein and the Minimalists, he finds only, and in his own words :

"...baffling confusion that marks the Biblical account of the period between Exodus and the reign of Solomon....Only the pattern, or broad lines, may be regarded as tentatively credible: the escape of some Hebrew tribes from bondage; their desultory wanderings following their escape; their conquest and settlement of a land which they made their own; their rudimentary organization in that land as a loose confederacy of tribes at war with their neighbors and answering to the leadership of priests and tribal magistrates called *shophetiym*, or judges, and their subsequent – and initially hesitant – acceptance of a common rule by tribal superchiefs called *melakhiym*, or kings, first Saul, then David."[115]

Unlike Velikovsky, who advances other evidence in *Ages in Chaos*, he denies any extra-Biblical sources for the existence of the Hebrews during these centuries. He has, however, other evidence of these events of a geographical and toponymic nature.

Applying toponymics to the question of Jewish origins, as conveyed in large part through the Old Testament, he has sought to demonstrate that the Jews, at least from the end of the Bronze Age, were centered in an inland section of Western Arabia known today as Asir, that moves over a long ridge and onto a coastal strip called Tihamah between Lith and Jizan. See *fig. 11*. They spoke a Canaanite dialect, of which Phoenician, Moabite and Ugaritic were other versions. Aramaic became the language of official Persia and then of the Near and Middle East generally, including Palestine. Hebrew struggled to retain a place in Biblical language, whatever the version of the Bible, and there is no compelling reason to prefer any "authorized" version to the essentially pure and yet pragmatic solutions to Biblical Hebrew presented by Salibi.

Asir (the present Saudi Arabian province) was in ancient times well-watered and lush up to where it ended in the Great Eastern Desert. Its side by the Red Sea was a different kind of Canaan, in large part, but regularly useful for its ports, and it too was fertile. Asir was well-connected to all points of the compass. See *fig. 10*. Because people today are raised with political maps, showing the boundaries of present states , they are brain-hardened to visualize the Arabian Peninsula as sharply cut off from the North from West to East.

Even worse for historiography, has been the northward push of political power and therefore school-books attention. The ancient Tethyan Seas, Mediterranean

Sea lands and basin have drawn perhaps 95% of scholarly and advanced cultic work. Events of Northern Europe have been largely ignored until recently by archaeology. So have the regions below the grasp of Mediterranean powers.

In ancient history, Arabia was an integral part of the Middle East and Asia, both central and southern. India was quite accessible, and so was Egypt, along the entire line drawn from the Mediterranean to Ethiopia in the South. The Red Sea, the Indian Ocean, and the Persian Gulf were heavily traveled, as was, of course, the Mediterranean. Large rivers traversed the Peninsula until stricken by drought at a fairly recent date. A main caravan highway went from Babylon to Asir.

Toponymics

Salibi's findings were presented in 1985 in a book, *The Bible was Born in Arabia*. Additional research is reported in a book of 1998, *The Historicity of Biblical Israel: Studies in 1 and 2 Samuel*. Taking up the multitude of Biblical place names including many interpreted or presented as family names, he finds them to correlate superbly with the place names of West Arabia and only feebly with geographical sites of Palestine. His hundreds of associations are not gathered into sophisticated statistical form; he might have presented his analysis in tables as well as in prose, but the effect is convincing nevertheless. Here, quoting a few words, is how he proceeds:

> Hence, what we have is the following: a consonantal Hebrew text [of the Bible] which we may reasonably assume is accurate, and which must be carefully reread without regard to traditional vocalization; ancient Egyptian, Mesopotamian, and other records which cite Biblical place-names and must also be reread without regard to standing geographic or topographical interpretations; the works of Classical historians and geographers which can be of help; the consonantal text of the Koran, which has stood unchanged since it was first compiled and redacted [644-656 CE]; finally a West Arabian landscape heavily dotted with Biblical names, in most cases with their original Biblical form virtually unchanged, or at least clearly recognizable in the names they have today... I shall examine certain Biblical texts with a view to showing how perfectly their geography corresponds to that of West Arabia.

Opposition to the Arabian Scenario

His work was rarely reviewed and usually dismissed offhand. The usual reasons for blocking and suppressing books occur. Devout Christians, Muslims and Jews would take umbrage at it. Establishment scholars would dismiss it. Secularists and humanists would be uninterested and contemptuous, because to their minds he was a Bible freak who merely switched locations, like an Atlantis freak whose scenario called for the Sea of Azov rather than the Atlantic Ocean -- though the music would be always Plato's. The Arab ruling class had reason to fear a flood of secularizing archaeologists and journalists, not to mention a threat from land-hungry Zionists. Considering the high level of paranoia in the Middle East, it would be suggested that here could be a way to claim, explore and exploit the oil resources of Arabia.

Salibi endured, and still does so, all of Velikovsky's opposition, plus being opposed by the huge crowd of Christian fundamentalists who were alerted and enthused to Velikovsky in the first place by avn article entitled "The Day the Sun Stood Still," published for the millions of readers of the *Readers' Digest* shortly before the publication of *Worlds in Collision*, whence came the article in the first place.

Salibi will probably have to do without his "Velikovsky Affair." He aroused neither a public enthusiasm nor a following. Reviews were few and unfavorable. I need not go into the matter here, but my experience permits me to say that Salibi's work was dealt with shamefully. We might expect, for example, a correct scholarly reception for this study by the Head of a Department at the American University of Beirut, on a topic universally regarded as important, if only by a world-class newspaper, such as *Le Monde*, often jeered at for being a Jews-Harp. There was even a clue leading to a correct review, in that the book had been published in its French translation from the English by a respected publishing firm, Grasset.

Not at all. The book was handed to one Jean Louis Schlegel, who on July 8, 1987 did as nice a job of throat-cutting as Mack the Knife. Schlegel hardly discusses the method or theses of the book, and wonders whether the book was a joke, and then says that "unfortunately" it was not a joke. He pities Lebanon for having such poor intellectual representatives. He ends ironically, saying, "If Israel cannot be erased from the map of the Arab world, it can still be placed elsewhere than Palestine."

Beginning the Defense of the Arabian Thesis

Differing from the opposition, I would venture to say that, considering the ruinous state of the archaeological material of the Near Orient, amounting to a practical absence of any digs in Western Arabia, a thorough application of onomastics, particularly toponymics, to the problem of earliest Jewish origins would adduce more convincing evidence than the paltry findings of archaeology in Palestine. There, we find an absence of crucial materials, despite the application of the most intensive and modern surveys, inflamed by a desperate chauvinism, resting on top of centuries of biblical exegesis. I see no way of honestly avoiding his theory. For swarms of questions still hover over Palestine. Indeed, the very negativism of the new archaeology of Palestine invites a grand alternative.

Arabia is a constellation of peoples and nations housed on the Arabian peninsula. Arabs themselves are to be encountered everywhere. They are connected to Jews by origin and history from earliest times. Not only can they see themselves as monotheists with substantially the same god, but they have unusual genetic connections, in common gene patterns, in DNA, in respect to the cultural role of women, in ritual taboos (abstinence from pork) and ritual circumcision.

Salibi is worth much more than a brief paraphrase. For, besides its merits in diverting hugely the direction of biblical exegesis, his book, without the author's realizing it or even touching upon the matter, provides various clues to an understanding of the Iron Age of Mars. As an example of how his method works against the traditional hodgepodge of justifications of a Palestinian scenario, we might examine the two maps that depict the Pharaoh Sheshonk I's Holy Land campaign from the two viewpoints. See *Fig. 13*. (Sheshonk I is brought down in time and identified by Velikovsky as

Thutmoses III, who looted Jerusalem without destroying it, carrying off the treasures of the Temple of Solomon.)

The Arabian map appears to be more detailed and militarily plausible. A far greater number of the conquered places listed in the great inscription of Sheshonk appear in the geography of Arabia than of Palestine. After placing some thirty locations, Salibi says that Sheshonk crossed the escarpment and advanced against Al Sherim, that is, the suggested Biblical Jerusalem in the Nimas region, without entering the city.

Arabia Deserta

Arabia is mostly a desert, but it was not always so. The same is true of other great deserts and many tundra-type lands of today. Drought and flood can go on in the same age. Dessication in Arabia and elsewhere does not exclude flooding and sinking of the land at the same time in other parts of the Mediterranean Region. The Aegean Sea, central to our study, sank and formed a shallow sea of many islands possibly in the early Iron Age. All qualified writers who took up the subject are agreed on the flooding, but not as to when and through what agency. The Black Sea is involved always, whether as a basin that filled in a rush from Arctic melts and the downward rush of great North-South rivers such as the Dnieper, but also as being filled quickly by a vast flood originating in the emptying of the Gobi Lake by an Earth tilt or sizeable acceleration that sent the waters of the Gobi racing across Asia and into the Black Sea. Whence, in both cases, into the Mediterranean.

The Sahara waters are sometimes blamed for emptying into the Mediterranean Sea, overfilling the great basin, and sending waters to cut a strait between the Aegean Sea and the Black Sea. Geologists favor one and then the other solution, but neither they nor the ancient writers agree on the origin of the Black Sea. Outsized theories can compete in this confused scientific and legendary environment. Downbursts from a thick blanket of clouds, even a rainfall and snowfall, originating in outer space, or, in extremis, the legendary happening of a nova of Saturn that sent the Biblical (worldwide reported) deluge racing toward

Earth to fill up the continental margins of the continents everywhere and bring the oceans to their present levels. Both straits of Gibralter and Bosphorus are regarded now as corks and again as opened bottlenecks. At some point, the sequence of events will be acceptably drawn up.

From the standpoint of preparing for quantavolutionary theory in Arabia, several pages of Velikovsky's *Earth in Upheaval* are matchless. He relies upon A.Berthelot, H.ST.J.B.Philby, C.p.Grant, B. Moritz, C.M. Doughty, R. Schwinner, and L.J. Spencer, to help him paint his picture of the disasters and collapse of "Arabia Felix". The great peninsula was, in the time of pre-historic, and probably Bronze Age, man, traversed by three great rivers flowing from west to east across the whole width of the country. The groundwaters of Arabia now come via wadis, which today carry the rains of the wet season in torrents, and from uncommon springs or oases. Volcanic fields were active as late as the 13th century CE. The opening up of the Red Sea rift to its present width and the breaking through of the Indian Ocean through the strait of Bab-el-Mandeb between Ethiopia and Arabia possibly occurred also in civilized times. Many thousands of square miles of Arabia are covered by scorched and sharp-edged stones, such as might have fallen from the sky, rather more likely than from volcanoes. "The stones lie free," not stuck or contained by lava.

In his diary of November 7, 1940, Velikovsky writes of reading the *Book of Joshua* for the first time since his childhood and coming across Chapter 10, wherein the sun and moon halted and stones fell ".. a celestial body passed near by. I read once that in Koran there is a legend that hot stones fell on sinners (with inscribed names) – I brought this in connection. I read about Harras in Arabia, scorched by fire – I brought this is connection. I decided: a change of the movement [an Earth tilt] is possible at an impact like this. And I thought about ice age. I knew quite nothing about it. My supposition was right...."

Earth in Upheaval (p.95-8) presents his later reckoning. The score of immense fields of stones (the harrahs), blackened, sharp and therefore recent, running around and alongside the string of volcanoes that begin in

Africa and string up the Western region of Arabia gives him to believe that they mark the path of a giant comet as meteoroids or companions of the exoterrestrial traveler, possibly Python [my suggestion], priori-Venus itself, or a Martian flight of meteorites. Iron has not yet been found there in any quantity. Was Velikovsky correct, and alone, in his speculations? A dedicated expedition would help solve the problem.

Significantly, in April 1859, a conversation among German scientists and explorers was reported, in which the great Alexander von Humboldt expressed the opinion, examining specimens of "classical Traconitis" from Harrat Rájil, that the volcanism could have occurred in Biblical times (citing *Psalms* xviii and the time of David). There were then counted 28 giant harrahs or volcanic fields carrying the stones. The latest volcanism was reported near Khaybar in the 600's a few years after the death of the Prophet Mahomet. Von Humboldt "deemed it probable that the Koranic legend (chap. iv) of the Abyssinian host under Abraha destroyed by a shower of stones baked in hell-fire, referred, not to small-pox as is generally supposed, but to an actual volcanic eruption in Arabia."

A compromise of views is proper to suggest here: The harrah fields, hundreds of kilometers long from South to North in Western Arabia, may have originated from a quick succession of explosions of volcanoes as the giant comet passed overhead. The same volcanic field emerges in Africa before crossing the Red Sea which may well have also rifted wide or wider at the same time.

I would proceed with the basics of Arabian geography. The land has obviously a recently catastrophized history. It resembles in this regard Canada and Siberia for northern examples, and on the hot side the Gobi Desert, the Sahara, and Libya. The quantavolutions undergone by Arabia have been, as everywhere, several, but the surface of the land today does not give up easily the secret of when occurred the last one. It is likely, with supporting detail provided by traditions and myths, that much of the visible devastation was produced in the Iron Age.

The passage of the great comet Phaethon was subject of many writings in Roman times, and Arabia was supposed to have burnt up at that time. The Roman writer Ovid follows Phaeton's path through Arabia. My preferred source of details is the book on Atlantis of Jürgen Spanuth.[116]

But we are not certain of the date of Phaeton's wild ride; possibly it belongs to the Venusian quantavolution at the end of the Middle Bronze Age, rather than to the end of the Bronze and the start of the Iron Age. However, the latter event would have had to stress greatly the lands that had been already struck and never quite recovered from the Venusian approaches of 1500 B.C.E. and later. In the Sahara Desert we find many locations of drawings of a notable level of sophistication -- chariots, warfare, domestic animals, whereupon we might consider that the same are or were present in Arabia and might support Iron Age dates for the terrible desertification suffered. The country has always pictured as the home of many bedouins, but doubtless many of these were the Iron Age migrants that we have been talking about in this book.

Prof. Peter Magee of Bryn Mawr College is not alone in protesting the simplistic history of Arabia as a welter of wandering bedouins. He scolds Dame Kathleen Kenyon for stating in her influential textbook on *The Archaeology of the Holy Land* that "The Fertile Crescent encloses the plateau of the Arabian desert, which from the dawn of history has served as a vast reservoir of nomadic raiders upon the riches of the surrounding Crescent." He criticizes Robert Hoyland, too. (*Arabia and the Arabs. From the Bronze Age to the Coming of Islam*) Hoyland provides numerous instances "to reinforce the perception of ancient Arabia's inhabitants as relatively acephalous and immutable in their social and economic structure and susceptible to change only with foreign intervention."

Given the vacancy of archaeology and the probability that the Martian destructions were especially effective in wiping out civilized centers in this region, we can at the very least withhold judgement about what might have been there. And examine more attentively the alternative toponymic method presented us by Kamal Salibi.

The Promised Land

Salibi described the situation that he has marked out for the Jewish homeland. They are dull, but they are handy if one is to locate the spawning grounds of history's per capita most influential people. Another surprising claim of Salibi is to be discovered in the maps which show "The Promised Land" as *Genesis 15* would grant it to the descendants of Abram, and as *Numbers 34* would grant it to the Israelite followers of Moses. Both are depicted there as Salibi finds them in Western Arabia. See *fig. 12*.

The Exodus would have been toward the Promised Land, of course. It would, by Salibi's account, head South. Conventionally the route goes South as well, but then turns back to the North. Helpfully, Velikovsky kept the Exodus going Southwards until it arrives at Kadesh Barnea – a location never agreed upon by Bible experts, a holy place. But Kadesh Barnea turns out to be, according to Velikovsky, Mecca! (The Holy City of the Muslim World, Mecca, where Mahomet brought forth Islam.) The city, he says, had been abandoned by the Hyksos-Amalekites, in the wake of its natural destruction.

Velikovsky writes in "Desert of Wandering" about "autochtonous Arab traditions about the wandering tribes led by Mosaikaia, his brother Arnran, and his sister Zephira. The Hebrews stayed there for forty years, he thought, but then (Salibi *contra*) they went North to Palestine.

So we had, then, at the end of the Middle Kingdom of Egypt, what we have in the present book at the end of the Late Kingdom and Bronze Age – great desperate comings and goings. But whereas Velikovsky then brings the Hebrews back to Palestine, Salibi keeps them moving still farther South, indeed to the region of Asir, and keeps them there for quite a while.

Moving the Peoples North to "priori-Palestine"

Yet we must bear in mind that in this Late Bronze Age people move here and there for employment and trade, as well as in wars. The back country was underdeveloped, even while the cities were "melting pots," much as today's world has been becoming.

Finkelstein proposes a late date for the arrival in pre-Palestine of groups of Philistines and Jews, bringing in, somewhat earlier, the Canaanites. Salibi agrees generally and gets the groups out of Arabia in the order of Phoenician, Canaanite, Philistine and Hebrew. Too, Finkelstein asserts that Joshua had an easy time infiltrating Canaan. He believes that the Hebrews might have been a backward type of hillbilly Canaanite. This picture would fit Salibi's scenario. There, the Jews would be emigrating from Arabia later than the Canaanites.

As for David conquering the Philistines, to our view he probably did not destroy the Philistine cities so much as found that they had been destroyed by natural causes, under the influence of planet Mars; ergo David played the role of Mars. The ruins that would help establish history have not been found. They have not been searched for yet in Arabia, and they are hardly to be found in Palestine, which has been thoroughly surveyed.

Exodus and reconquest of the Promised Land had to be at the end of the Middle Bronze Age and take a long time. Meanwhile Canaanites, Phoenicians and Philistines were moving north. It must have been rather like the German tribes one after another invading the declining Roman Empire.

The Erasure of Ubar

No opportunity is offered us yet to uncover destructive processes in West Arabia. The persistence of a great many place names and actual little settlements even down to today raises questions::does this mean that there was no destruction in the Iron Age? No.

Other work is beginning to come to light. Arabian legend tells of a typically wicked King and people of a flourishing city called Ubar. It is mentioned in the Bible also. Through it passed the rich and heavy commerce of India and the South Seas, connecting with Egypt, Africa and the Eastern Mediterranean littoral on the West and North. A typical god raised his rod and blasted the city and its population into 'Kingdom Come.' Sands mercifully buried the disfiguring ruins for perhaps 2700 years. The ruins were so assimilated to the desert sands that they defied exposure until reconnaissance by satellite produced a photograph centered upon the most likely site, as deemed by earthbound calculations. Landsat imagery, using a Thematic Mapper, gave images in which one might locate surface tracks and other vague features on 30,000 square kilometers of terrain in a single shot. Southern Oman was pre-indicated, and at Ash Shisr there showed up hidden convergent caravan tracks.

Nearby were the ruins of Ubar. The city had been destroyed in a single event. The most radical guess that the earth-obsessed discoverers could offer was that the larger part of the city had collapsed into a hitherto unknown gigantic limestone cavern. Artefacts from far provenance were picked out of the rubbish. Such is, and was, the famed City of Ubar, that had not been fully investigated at this writing. The Biblical case of Sodom and Gomorrah comes to mind. Salibi believes that these cities were in the Arabian Judah area and that their names still persist there and that they were destroyed by one or more of the numerous eruptions from nearby volcanos. See *fig. 26.*

A Confusion of Places: the Wabar Craters

Velikovsky, holding to the Palestinian Judah, can find no volcano, but builds a strong case for the cities of the plain (or whatever was there) falling victim to the movements of the great rift that passes through the Dead Sea. Both stories make sense to me, even that two Sodoms and Gomorrahs existed, inasmuch as the Jews moving North from Arabia, carried their place names and imposed them frequently upon their new settlement sites.

The Biblical case of Sodom and Gomorrah comes to mind. Salibi believes that these cities were in the Arabian Judah area and that their names still persist there and that they were destroyed by one or more of the numerous eruptions from nearby volcanos. [See Map, Figure30.] Velikovsky, holding to the Palestinian Judah, can find no volcano, but builds a strong case for the cities of the plain (or whatever was there) falling victim to the movements of the great rift that passes through the Dead Sea. Both stories make sense to me, even that two Sodoms and Gomorrahs existed, inasmuch as the Jews moving North from Arabia, carried their place names and imposed them frequently upon their new settlement sites.

The search for Ubar had gone in another direction early in the 1930's by the dilettante explorer Philby, who used the name Wabar instead of Ubar, and as a by-product of his excruciating travel he came upon several craters. (It is a wonder that word of the location amidst the world's most inhuman and largest sand desert had been retained by faraway Arab 'locals.') He could not tell much about them but passed the word on, and they were rediscovered twice more before a well-equipped small team entered the premises in the early 1980's and 1990's. Two of the scientists, Jeffrey C. Wynn and Eugene M. Shoemaker (of the Jupiter comet crash fame, 'father of astrogeology'), wrote in the *Scientific American* of "The Day that the Sands Caught Fire."

Three craters huddled on a site of 500 x 1000 meters in the vast sands. Shock waves or impactite was found easily enough, certifying the craters as meteoritic. Coesite or shocked quartz was strewn about. So were 'shale balls' or iron-nickel fragments up to 10 centimeters in diameter and crumbling at the grasp. The largest chunk recovered weighs .2.43 tons and broke perhaps before impact. Two types of glass pellets were found, some white, some black, varying in size, composed 90% of local sand, 10% of iron and nickel. The impact struck only the sand and did not penetrate to bedrock. Estimates of velocity were of 11k/s entering the atmosphere at an oblique angle, striking ground at 5-7k/s, after breaking into four pieces. The original mass was estimated to have been about 3,500 tons, and the original kinetic energy amounted to about 100 kilotons of TNT explosive. The energy was close to that of the Hiroshima bomb but the Hiroshima explosion was in the air and therefore destroyed a larger ground area. Then bolide may or may not have come from Mars. San melted was 10 times the size of the meteorite. The sand from the craters rose in a mushroom cloud thousands of meters. The melted glass was to be found up to 850 meters from impact.

Samples of the glass were assayed for fission tracks at the British Museum and Smithsonian Institution. Dates around 6,400 years ago were produced. 'Field evidence' gives a shorter date. Bottoms of the craters rested upon hardened sand. The depth of the largest was 12 meters deep in 1932, 8m in 1961, and almost filled by 1982. The tallest rim was only 3 meters high in 1994-5. Sand beneath the impactite hardening, dated by thermoluminescence, suggested 450 years ago. Related meteorites passed over the city of Riyadh in 1863 or 1891 (dates given were confused), headed in the direction of Wabar. They proved upon direct analysis to be identical in composition with the Wabar meteorites. This would indicate the true date of the Wabar impact was only 142 years ago (to 2005). Here was some kind of evidence against the validity of certain dating methods within limits that threaten their usefulness. The authors passed over the dating error factor of 50 in one case, 3 in the second case. It has been estimated that bolides of the Wabar size impact every ten years or so on the average. Their effects are not trivial.

A Literal Bible Meets a Topsy-turvy Geography

It is a far cry from Wabar to the West of Arabia where our search for Judah-Israel carries us. We have surprisingly little to report on the discovery of destruction sites here. Salibi described the Jewish homeland; his specifications cannot indicate the dramatic ruins we find everywhere else, or that we might expect for the spawning grounds of history's per capita most influential people.

Still, topographically, Arabian Judah fits the Bible and its known events from beginning to end much better than does Palestine. Salibi does resemble the Biblical minimalists of Israel and Europe. He adds to minimalism a giant movement of the geographical setting. His descriptions of Hebrew, Canaanite, and other original peoples of the Bible suggest uncannily the work of the "moderate minimalists." He goes farther as when he analyzes the Bible passages on the layout of the "Promised Land," first as foretold by the Lord to Abraham, and then as viewed by Moses before his death. Salibi's map shows the two configurations, as they can be drawn on the ground in Western Arabia. Evidently Moses received a more generous concession. See *fig. 12*.

This map, convincing as it is, is not a "silver bullet." The prize is given by us to his comparison of what Moses would have seen were he to be looking upon the Promised Land from "Mt. Nebo," universally but mistakenly believed to be such, and carrying the name al-Siyaghah in Palestine, or the true Mt. Nebo, al-Nabawah, carrying the very name of Nebo. The Arabian mountain is much taller and commands a view of the Sea. Not so the conventional Mt. Nebo. Further, the view from el-Nabawah conforms more exactly in all respects to the Biblical specifications than the Palestinian mountain chosen for Moses' last look by the legions of Bible scholars and worshipers. Compare the two views in *fig. 27* and *28*.

The Babylonian Experience from Arabia

Salibi pictures the Jews as having been removed from Arabian Judah, rather than Palestinian Judah, when conquered by the King of Babylon Nebuchadnezzar and shipped off to Babylon and its environs. It may be of some significance to our story that the successor to Nebuchadnezzar, King Napodinus, for reasons no one has been able to fathom, moved his capital for a decade to a new city, Teima (Tayma) in Northern Hejaz, which is not far to the north of Arabian Judah. He might have been anticipating the onslaught of the Persians, that actually came not long after he returned to Babylon, and therefore thought to anticipate the event by shifting to a safer, more removed Capital. Or he may have anticipated the destruction of Babylon from natural causes. He was a fanatic devotee of Sin, the Moon god. There might have been some connection in his mind (guided by influential court astrologers) that the Moon had been interacting with Mars and indicated by its irregularities that a change of Capital was indicated (or at least a trial of such).

When the Jews were released from confinement to the Babylon region, they marched or straggled in several streams, to Palestine, to Arabia, to Egypt and elsewhere.

Salibi asserts that the whole number of 40,000 returned to Arabia from Persia and Mesopotamia, with their households, hoping to reconstruct their community and live there. But "unfortunately these returning Israelites were disappointed with what they found; everywhere around them were poverty and destruction seemingly beyond repair."[117] The Hebrew Bible, he says, now becomes silent. Judaism as a religion survived in remnant groups of West Arabia, but no integrated national community could be formed and the population dispersed. (This might conceivably be associated with natural destruction.)

I shall diverge at this point to more ancient history, the time of Exodus, and the dictatorship of Moses. The Revolt of Korah is one of the grimmer episodes of the Bible. An elite rebellion, while the Hebrews were still in the wilderness, it was crushed by Moses, employing Yahweh, electric shock, earthquakes and plague. Hundreds were massacred and an accompanying plague slew many thousands. Thus the story is in one fell swoop an account of a demand for shared power (the cause of Korah should be recorded in the philosophy of democracy, with Yahweh on the wrong side) and an account of both artificial and natural electrical effects of a deadly kind, and of the coincidence of earth tremors and plague that might be an exudation of poison gas from the ground or of a cloud of gas bursting down upon the scene.

The picture is impossible, but the components of the picture make a nightmare surrealism that reflects a reality of the times. The Korah incident has been dealt with in detail in my book on Moses. It seems relevant here because it is an ancient Exodus story that at the same time shows a clan at work, that later on becomes a place in the promised land and then reflects itself in the Psalms of the Sons of Korah, the folk songs of the clan of Korah (the Bible says explicitly that the offspring of Korah had not been let die in the revolt). Salibi argues rightly, I believe, that the Psalms, generally now thought to be a late addition to the Bible, were anciently songs of the peoples from around Judah, folk songs, and that numerous names found in them have been misconstrued, for they are in reality impassioned references to localities rather than personal names.

Salibi gives us some of the material, Finkelstein offers some as well, and, also, other sources, so that the theory I would bring forth here emerges from a sound basis. It is this: that the Jews, the Yehudim, who returned to the Jerusalem neighborhood rather than to Arabia or Egypt or other places when released from the confines of Babylon by the Persian King Cyrus, determined to seize the initiative over all other centers of Jewish activity and settlement, and to produce the essential and total history and documentation of the Jewish people. Thus they might assure themselves of commanding the reborn and righteous home of Judaism. The concept was ingenious: a propaganda missile loaded with every type of appeal, joining myths and factual details of history.

So every effort was bent toward an eclectic work that would leave nobody, no element, no episode, good and bad, out of the picture that could then frame all Jews no matter where they might be in the same culture, ideology and cult. The onetime homeland in Arabia was deliberately forgotten, not only half-forgotten or dimly remembered. There was every reason to wipe it out of the collective memory and to concentrate the total effort of the new remnant, bringing to bear their Persian experience, insisting upon a strict theocracy to discipline the new people, and recalling the people already in diaspora to the standard of the Lord in Jerusalem.

They could succeed in this bold stroke all the more readily because the remnant that had returned to West Arabia found a devastated and famine-stricken country from which they would themselves now emigrate to the revived center in Judea of Palestine. They were like Americans, perhaps 150 millions of them, who, after two or three generations, remember or know nothing of their ancestry.

Asura Mazda and Yahweh

They could succeed, perhaps also, for having carried explicitly from Persia the religion of Asura Mazda, the God preached by the messiah-like personage of Zoroaster. One must picture, inasmuch as direct evidence is unavailable, the influence of his monotheism upon the Jews, whose tribal god of the west Arabian hills had already, before their exile, incorporated or extirpated the many competing gods of the region. The Jews had a God who needed "filling out," so to speak. In Babylon and the larger Persian ecumenical environment, the process would be encouraged. And thereafter, in one version of Ezra at least, it could be said, "Cyrus the King built the House of the Lord in Jerusalem, where they worship him with eternal fire."

The great prophet of Mazda, Zoroaster, a Christ-like figure of the holistic seventh century, still within the destructive phase of the Martian Quantavolution, lacks the madness of the Hebrew prophets and the new science of the Greeks and Phoenicians. His example and preachments helped the Jews to defeat polytheism and virtually established Mazdaism in Persia. An inscription of Darius, King of Persia, reads:

> *There is one God, omnipotent Ahura Mazda,*
> *It is he who has created the earth here;*
> *It is he who has created the heaven there;*
> *It is he who has created mortal man.*

Mazda created the cosmos, the moral and material universe, pronounced the law and established order.

According to Zoroaster, the devil is an important universal presence, but still is as nothing compared with Lord Mazda, or as with Lord Yahweh of Judaism,. A Day of Judgement is not far off. A Savior will appear to resurrect the dead. We should perhaps assign to the trivial, fearful, inferior, and vassal condition of Jehud the source of what we regard as the dismaying, shrieking aggressiveness of the Bible toward unbelieving and uncooperative fellow-Jews and the foreign world generally. The lofty bureaucratic order of the Persian Empire could afford its own people a less immediately threatening religion.

Chapter Thirteen

Changed Ideologies

Most Bible specialists and theologians of the present generation have come to agree that a substantial portion of the Bible was created by a group of men of the nation of Judah, operating out of Judah until taken captive and despatched to Babylon, proceeding with their studies there and under the Persian regime that ousted the Babylonians, and finally, when permitted and even encouraged in some instances to return to their homeland, concluding and publishing the major part of their work. I agree with this version of biblical history. I am inclined, however, with Salibi, to push the major action down into Arabia, but would bring it up to Palestine in the Sixth Century. It is not imperative that the Jews developed out of Arabia or Palestine, one or the other.

The reasons for the shift of Jewish activity from Arabia to Palestine are several. The double presence, as one might put it, was part of the general shift of economic, political, and intellectual power from South to North. Persia was more of a northern than a southern power, witness its control over all of the northern routes – it did not need the trans-Arabian facilities. See, too, its strong attempts to dominate and conquer the Aegean and Black Sea regions.

The Bible students, and for that matter, the scholarly disciplines focusing upon Egypt and points to the East, have not applied to this change the necessary sociology, demography and economics. Nor have they tried to apply the catastrophic events of the time to these movements, in this case for want of abundant collecting of evidence in Arabia and the countries around its southern seas. Hence, the Bible and the People of the Bible, who had a lot affecting them besides religious concerns, moved North, pulled, pushed, driven.

Now once this holistic change had occurred, it was sloganized. Instead of viewing the whole process scientifically and statistically, it was transformed into a single history taking place in a single region, Palestine. The Torah, but particularly the exponents and devotees of the Bible, took up a simplified history – like those who, after hearing the words "The Roman Empire Fell," cock their ears for the crash.

The Bible came forth, a melange of legends, partly factual like all legends, and of the ideas and testimonies of persons then living and acting as contributing editors. It was now history and homilies, and influential among its small population in Yehud and the areas around. A couple of centuries passed. Bits and pieces were changed or added or removed. It first became publicly available in Egypt when a number of Hebrew translators were imported by Jewish residents of Egypt who could read Greek but not Hebrew.

To many scholars today, this translation is the only authentic version in existence. All others have been unjustifiably tampered with. The Jewish rabbinate, on the other hand, at a later time demoted the Alexandrian Bible in favor of a version that had been more favorably rendered by the Masoretes. Other versions were published here and there, down to the present. The problem need not concern us farther here; it would be beyond our resources and abilities to discover in which version and where in that version would be found evidence tending to extend or diminish our portrait of a catastrophic Martian Iron Age.

Résumé: Meanwhile, in the Sky...

But then I do ask myself, "What does this have to do with the planet Mars and the Iron Age?" I answer that especially the prior portion of this period saw a great deal of activity in the skies by people who were at the same time cognizant that the interaction of the celestial and the mundane had been going on for a long time, and indeed cycling itself, so that the planet Mars, for a century or more, with Velikovsky claiming several cycles, Patton claiming more and Ackerman claiming for as many as a hundred cycles, had been the major celestial figure in their minds and behavior. Mars had led to the partial or general destruction of Bronze Age civilizations. We do not know fully and never will know the exact astronomical scenarios of the century, but I would speculate in favor of something like the following set of events:

We must accept first of all a controversial set of circumstances preceding the Martian Quantavolution. The solar system had moved from one form of stabilization to another over the course of a short history of perhaps a million years, the intervening destabilizations or quantavolutions having brought the system to a state where Venus, a fairly new member of the planetary family, had proceeded on an irregular elliptical course that took it at intervals close enough to planet Mars to unsettle its motions. In the early Eighth Century , Mars was sufficiently destabilized to careen near to Earth and begin a fifteen-year cycle of close encounters.

The interaction was so severe that Mars was broken open and disgorged ultimately a large portion of itself of high density, which became in short order, when it broke free, with the intervention of planet Venus, the planet Mercury (here adopting the theory of John Ackerman, even though I would give equal weight to my own theory of a prior origin of Mercury out of the explosion of 'Planet Apollo'). For an interval of time, Mercury was the principal member of "the terrible ones" as they were referred to in the Bible and the Vedas, the Maruts in the Vedas, which toured the global skies, wreaking much damage upon Earth. Eventually, in an encounter with Venus, Mercury was whipped into roughly its present orbit, evidencing its stormy career as Hermes-Thoth-Mercury by a ruined thin surface and a huge iron interior, derived from Mars (which shows its loss by its low density and plethora of surface iron dust and pebbles).

Mars had many images in legend as it underwent its astronomical agonies. It appeared as a flaming sword on some occasions, as a chariot on various others. Among the other mythical indications we may underscore the biblical lines of *2 Kings 23:11,* where it is said, of the resolute monotheist King Josiah, "He removed from the entrance to the temple of the Lord the horses that the kings of Judah had dedicated to the sun. They were in the court near the room of an official named Nathan-Melech. Josiah then burned the chariots dedicated to the sun." Josiah would stop at nothing. He would have executed all non-believers in Yahwism. His was a terrorist regime.

The phases when Mars was undergoing stresses and deformations by interaction with Earth and the disgorgement of Mercury may be the source of ancient legends that made the handsome ruddy warrior god a frightful mess, at one time with a hugely distended, monstrous head hanging down toward Earth, its hand stretching frequently down toward the multitudes of sinners. Mars had so many manifestations, indeed, that we may wonder at but also understand the fanatical dedication of Josiah to bring about an unnameable god, following in the manner of David, a god without images, a god that was abstract in this sense, a very general god, an only god, that could not possibly be mistaken for Nergal-Mars or Baal of another or several of the named gods of the region.

Was Yahweh a Doppelgaenger?

Who is Yahweh? I asked this question before, in books on Moses and the Divine Succession. The answer can never be definitive, but for that matter the Bible was hardly definitive about the Lord. And when one turns from the Bible to other academic sources, one finds a complex and diversified figure of God, indeed.

In my study of Exodus I concluded that Yahweh was probably standing for, and was identifiable as a doppelgaenger for Mercury, Thoth, Hermes, and gave reasons for the connection. Like Jesus, the Son of God, it was functionally and even verbally, Moses, Son of God, and Moses was regarded as Thoth in later times and among Greco-Roman theologians, for his magic and genius, and Moses so that to all intents and purposes the Son of God.

I wrote the book, treating Moses as a full-blown actual character of history. Now I face experts who deny the very existence of Moses or put him into a minor class of legendary leaders, one who like a labor union leader led his people out on strike, and who was then locked out with them by the bosses. If I was mistaken in taking the Moses of the Bible seriously as a vibrant character, I have still created a fully consistent *persona*, a useful speculation. Something rather like all that I said there, about the disastrous times and the electrical effects in the atmosphere, and on the Ark of the Covenant, can be believed. What I set forth in the Appendix to the book, on the methods of interpreting myth, is not only defensible but can be turned fully on to extend further the interpretation of the Exodus.

In *Lately Tortured Earth,* I devote a chapter to pandemonium, acoustics, and music. There I cite numerous examples of real and legendary noises accompanying natural movements and events. Celestial noises are many. Mars-Nergal was also called "The God of Noise." Granted the near presence of giant astral bodies, the sky and atmospheric passage and downfall of vast numbers of stones, particles, electricity, and given winds of every velocity, often rushing through and around cavities and rugged morphology, both old and newly created, the claim or memory of trumpet-like sounds is plausible. Might the name Yahweh come from an impassioned exclamation – an invocation, Yo, Yah, Yow, or Yahu – at the "manifestation of the holy,' suggests the Encyclopedia Britannica.

Could Yahweh also have been a name for the manifestations of Mars? Could Yahweh have been another name for Jupiter-Zeus-Mazda, instead, or as well? The prehistorical reconstruction of Mark S. Smith has merit. He defines an astral God, El and Elohim (plural of El), who would have been the God (s) of the Hebrews in the early days in the dry back hills and deserts, whose astral family they worshiped (citing *Genesis 49 and Psalm 82*). Yahweh was present, he thinks, possibly as the son of El and as a warrior god, still a second-tier god. We tend also to agree with Salibi who, as we reported, finds Western Arabia full of gods, with probably every tribe or village laying claim to a distinctive god, yet all, as Southerners say, "kissing cousins."

The analogy of the Olympic family of the Greeks, beginning with Uranus, then following with Saturn, then

Jupiter, occurs. There developed a merger of Elohim and Yahweh, with Yahweh moving up into the highlands as a protégé of Baal, the coastal storm god. The Hebrews found themselves with a cluster of gods and as having to readjust their gods with the changing times, particularly now when the quantavolutionary period of Mars arrived. Yahweh moved up front. He began to perform the several acts of Mars. Yet if he was to be the god of a people striving for national identity, even a rather mixed people in this age of increasing restlessness, dispersion and break-up of tribes under natural disturbances, he had to be promoted and distinguished. The other gods had to be covered over, practically buried. This would be done, in legend under David, in history under Josiah.

"A Plague on all Ye God-names..."

The time of King David was the beginning of the Age of Iron. David is said by the Bible to have ordered the names of all gods to be discontinued and replaced by the name of the Lord Yahweh. This passage could conceivably mark the bringing of Monotheism for the first time to Israel. In other words, monotheism was not very old, it was not greatly popular, it had not been enforced by the laws of the tribes. It was not perhaps even an invention of Moses, although there were reasons (*cf* Akhnaton) why Moses himself and some followers might be monotheistic and Yahwist.

Monotheism might have occurred as an act of naming, then and there, as a matter of nomenclature. Banning the utterance of the true name of the Lord, of Adonis (in Greek), of Yahweh, let everyone be denied the usage of the name of any other god. The Romans worshiped, we said, over fifty of gods and goddesses; so, too, the Greeks – reducing for important purposes, of course, to the elite Olympians. Some Hebrews, Persians, and much later the Muslim, with some small Christian cults like the Unitarians, might be deemed wholly monotheistic. Behaviorally, humanity has been largely polytheistic.

The confusion in the naming of gods can be attributed in part to the loss of most of the historical record.

There might also be a fear of naming the wrong god. For the traits and conduct of the many gods led to confusion. And to give the wrong god credit or discredit would be thought to bring down the wrath of one or the other god upon oneself. The mixing of people in the shattering of populations must have brought on mixups in the usage of names and the passage back and forth of god-names. To conclude, a nameless Yahweh automatically helped produced monotheism.

Everything that exists can be regarded as an event. Nothing is nothing, Nothing can possibly become nothing. No event ever ends, whether part of a uniform series or of a quantavolution. The events of a quantavolution produce exponential changes. The effects pile up suddenly, decompose in a negative exponentiality. The memories and results of one enormity pile upon the remnants of the prior events. The effects tail off in a negatively exponential form but persist indefinitely. The efforts of the later kings to restore the imagined glories of the past, the Building of the Second Temple by Herod the Great, for example, they go on . They are proud and visible. But the effects persist also into the most humble crevices of society, sometimes with astonishing effect.

The failure of archaeologists to recover evidence of the existence of King David, except for one broken ceramic containing the words 'House of David,' has not prevented the stories, pictures and oral legends about David to accumulate into the thousands of pages and hundreds of thousands of paintings and sermons. Similarly, although no one in his right mind will insist that Hercules acted in any way conforming to the tales of his existence, the accounts of Hercules are innumerable. But we note, too, that Hercules was a Greek God, and a most important Roman God, Ares in the one case, Mars in the second case, and by various names worshiped throughout the world.

And we note, also, that the activities of Planet-Mars have provided us with a major Quantavolution, a set of changes so important that the world has never been the same in any major regard ever thereafter. It changed holospherically. The God Mars as transfigured by the Romans had one effect lasting to this day, in the invention of the Roman city-state, Republic and Empire. If gods are granted any meaning and effect, it is permitted to say, "If no Mars, then no Rome." Or "If no Yahweh, no "People of the Book."And the time at which planet-Mars was most active with respect to planet-Earth was the Iron Age during which Rome was founded and the history of Israel was largely written.

David in His Martian Role

Could the Biblical history of Israel then have been written like the history of the God Mars and the god/hero Hercules? In that case, might the god-hero and surrogate of Mars on Earth be King David? We recall (that is, the Bible tells us and billions of people acquiesce) that it was Yahweh who directly commanded that the boy David be led to succeed Saul as King of the United Monarchy of Israel. (As I said above, when David reigned supreme he compelled all divine titles, appellations and names to be subsumed under the name of Yahweh, the Lord of Israel.)

We recall that David was from his boyhood a slayer of giants (Goliath) and then the conqueror and destroyer of all the cities of the Philistines. He married the daughter of King Saul (sending him 200 Philistine prepuces as a gesture of good will.) Here, archaeology comes into play and informs us that the cities of the Philistines were destroyed simultaneously, and practically all agree that the destruction was wrought by human struggles or invasions – internecine, Egyptians, Israelites, and others – with almost nothing in the way of hard evidence as to who precisely did this terrible job. But archaeology places the coming of the Philistines to the beginning of the Iron Age and the destruction of their towns perhaps a century or so later. We place the Philistine catastrophes at one or several approaches of Mars.

We argue that, all around the great region which we are studying and at the same time as this was happening in Palestine, the planet Mars was balefully holospherically deconstructive, and perforce was establishing the kinds of people, ecology, and geography of the next age of the Earth. We know that the planetary surrogate was Hercules, for we have established many connections between the two. And so did David perform, according to the legendary Bible, the work of Mars. It was also the work of Yahweh, we are told. So we must suspect and perhaps sometime in the future, not now, bring forward proof that David was the scion of Yahweh who was akin to the Greek God, Zeus the Thunderbolter.

David, we surmise, was probably and still is psychically identified with the god-hero Hercules, among other such figures, and with the planet Mars. As did Hercules, David was said to experience numerous grave personal problems and tragedies. Collective amnesia assures that we do not recognize the association of the two figures, and that we make of David a much more humanly presentable historical character, as part of the task of molding the history of Israel to conform to myth rather than reality. And to promote Christianity and the Muslim faith.

Mogen David, the Shield of David in Hebrew, is called the Star of David ordinarily. It is the six-faceted star, composed of two overlaid equilateral triangles. It has stood for many things and ideas since ancient times, but has had especially close references to Judaism, including the present-day proud presence of the star on the flag of Israel. The shield of David has been interpreted at least since the symbolism of Jewish mystics of Medieval times as Yahweh, God being the shield of David. As the five-faceted star has since time immemorial been the symbol of planet Venus, the six-faceted star has been the sign of Mars, of King David.

Venus and Mars may have conveyed, in their close encounters of the Martian Age, battles in the sky as they appeared to be, the imagery of shields. That is, it is likely that there is more than sheer coincidence to the importance of the shields of the two gods and the semblances of two kinds of star in connection with them. The shield of Athena (Venus) with its Gorgon's head was believed to be intolerable to the human gaze and could turn a person into stone.

The Messiah Idea, from David to Jesus, and Astrology

In Jewish history, the concept of messiah has played a significant role. And passages of the Bible and other Jewish literature have adumbrated the figure. Only the so-named House of David, a linear descendant of King David, was designated to provide legitimate heirs for the messianic role. Many have been called, few have been chosen, but there has always been a great felt need for a messiah by those most closely possessed by Judaism. So when Jesus Christ appeared on the scene, perhaps 850 years after the legendary King David, it was to be expected that his followers would exclaim at the asserted fact that he was descended from the line of David.

In that case we would be led to suspect coincidences of Jesus with Mars, absurd as this idea might appear. An investigation would be worthwhile, if only to further the science of mnemology. Slight indications can be cited here.

The full concept of the Creche of the Holy Family in the stable at the Inn at Bethlehem at the birth of Jesus Christ was conceived by St. Francis of Assisi in the 12th century AD. He had spent time in Egypt and Jerusalem. His character and following were dominated by the practices of total peace, mercy and poverty. The Creche has become a commanding theme of Christianity, visible at hundreds of thousands of places in the Christmas season and in a great many paintings. In the manger, also called the nest, rests the Infant Jesus. To the left side stands the Virgin Mary. To the right side stands St. Joseph, the non-sexual legal Father of Jesus, called the Carpenter.

Praesepe, also called *Beehive*, is an open, or galactic, cluster of several hundred stars in the zodiacal constellation *Cancer* (catalog numbers NGC 2632 and M 44). Visible to the unaided eye as a small patch of bright haze, it was first distinguished as a group of stars by Galileo. It was included by Hipparchus in the earliest known star catalog, ~-129. The name *Praesepe* (Latin: *"Cradle,"* or *"Manger"*) was used even before Hipparchus' time. *Presepio* is still the word for creche in Italian. The name *Beehive* is of uncertain but more recent origin. For the ancient Christians it was the door with access to Heaven.

We have the scene portrayed in the sky. The *Praesepe Nebula* is also called the *Crib,* the *Creche,* and the *Nest.* Every so often the Planet Venus stands to the left of the *Crib*. Every two years Mars is to be found inside or near the *Nest* or *Crib.* On the right is the *Carpenter* star, so-called. Thus the birth scene of Christ as imagined has a preceding image in the sky of the Iron Age. And the two most significant planets, Venus and Mars, play about it. It is thought that St. Francis used the configuration somehow to calculate the true birth date of Jesus.

Mars is both a baleful and a beneficial star. Mars is also identified with Hercules and Gilgamish, both god-heroes. Anthropology provides a number of such instances. Actually Jesus is a god-hero and appears to see himself as such in his alternating self-appellations of Son of Man and Son of God. The tortures he will suffer are typical of god-heroes of mythology and possibly reminiscent of activity so interpreted in the sky at some points in time. Artists have vied in depicting the agonies of Christ. The painting by Matthias Grunewald, now at Colmar, Alsace, France, has an excruciating effect even upon the observer.

We may hypothesize that the creche scene, regarded as the most peaceful, endearing and promising scene of the life of Jesus Christ and the future of humanity, marks the waning and hopefully the ending of the Mars catastrophe and the capture of its positive good -- the control of human nature for the good of all. The god--hero is completing his evil tenure and assuming his benevolent nature. We may even wonder whether Jesus, the Christ, as so many persons have considered, even if not daring to express their secret thoughts, was supposed to replace the old god Yahweh. (The Oedipal complex aspects of this, with respect to the Virgin Mary, are not to be dismissed.) And, therefore, one might also ask whether some of the bitter animosity to Jesus coming from Jewish sources afterwards reflects a comprehension, hardly mentionable, that Jesus was assertedly born to combat Yahweh and propose the New Testament, that is, not to support the Old Testament, but to replace it. Jesus seems to want to say so, but also scolds those who do not obey the Law. Furthermore, to reprove both Christian and Jew, the failure of their religions is their failure to abandon entirely the doctrines and authority of the Old Testament. For this purpose, we need, of course, a non-catastrophic human mind, de-catastrophized, that is, which proceeds with a pragmatic science and morality -- a state of being few humans have achieved, nor any culture-mass of people.

Ptolemy, the ancient Astronomer, said that the nebula *praesepe* had a power akin to Mars and the Moon, while the two little donkeys which stood guard next to the manger "move like the Sun." The Sumerians called the constellation of *Cancer*, to which praesepe pertains, the *Carpenter*, and seem to have included with it the *Little Dog Star*, Procyon.

The Egyptians called Mars the *Western Horus* or the *Red Horus*. Horus was the son of Isis who is also Venus. But Horus is also Jupiter and therefore the parent of Venus in Velikovsky's and other schemes. It might well be both. In the Egyptian *Book of the Dead*, it is said in Chapter 54, 'We greet you who make the Two Worlds happy with food and lapis lazuli. Watch over the one in the nest, the Child, which will rise against you.' Guy Rachet thinks that this is a reference to Horus, who will rise against Seth and his Allies. A possible analogy occurs with Jesus.

Possibly Jesus spent significant time with the Essenes, whose very existence went unknown until the mid-20th century. They were called the Egyptian Healers, and had adopted Egyptian scientific knowledge, as well as rites and habits of Egyptian priests, while continuing to be culturally and religiously Jews. Recent research dispenses with their image as withdrawn desert troglodytes and makes them part of a flourishing general human community.

The *Constellation of Cancer* contains *Nebula 'M44'*, *Praesepe*. It was supposedly watched over by two little stars *delta* and *gamma* (which are called the Little Asses, Asellus Australis and Asellus Borealis. The Praesepe cluster is situated on or very near the plane of the ecliptic. In ancient Egypt it was called *Kenmut Tepa*, the *Ur/Mother*. Later they called it also *Seta* and represented it by a turtle. Among the Greeks it was called *Phatin,* which means first of all the manger, then a hole in a tooth, then also ceiling or awning.

Prophecy, astrology, superstition moved apace with history. When the Fatimid Caliph Muiz sent General Gawhar to seize Egypt in 969 CE, the General chose a new site for the capital to replace Fustat-Misr, to be called El Mansuriya, meaning "victorious." . Hundreds of workmen were placed about the prospective site and ordered to begin digging when bells hung upon a rope around the perimeter of the site were rung. The bells began to ring prematurely when a raven hopped upon the rope, whereupon the workers leaped to their task. The astrologers in charge, awaiting the correct signal, now foresaw disaster. El Kahira, which meant Mars, was in the ascendant! Promptly the city-to-be was renamed El Kahira, Cairo, which conveniently or perhaps beginning now had an alternative meaning of *victorious*.

In the Thirteenth Century, Dante represented Mars as the most powerful planet for the production of good as well as evil. He puts the sign of the cross in the Heavenly sphere occupied by Mars. For the Hellenists, Mars represents the Platonic *Thymos*, the positive values of courage, virility, passion, strength. Negatively, he represents anger. These are traits commonly attributed to Jesus Christ.

In a newsletter of January 2003, John Ackerman mentions a painting that he glimpsed in a gallery of the Louvre. By Antonio Campi, active in the 16th century, it is titled *Mysteries of the Passion of Christ*. "In the midst of the maelstrom surrounding the crucifixion there appears in the sky a mysterious entity or world. If this had been painted before 687 B.C., I would swear this was a depiction of priori-Mars [his term for pre-Seventh Century Mars] in the heavens as it orbited the Earth. It is complete with the column of smoke and fire extending down toward the Earth."[118]

Perhaps the least credible of recent manifestations of a remnant connection between Mars and Earth is a French scientific study of the birthdays of top-ranking athletes.[119] It found a highly significant relationship between their birthdays and the ascendency of planet Mars in astrological tables. A second skeptical study of 1,066 athletes and 85,280 persons as to their birth time and birthday did not reveal the Effect. The suspected causal nexus is thus far quite beyond anyone's plausible conjecture.

The descendants of Sem, Hebrews, and Canaanites were often associated with the donkey. Many references connect the messiah and the kings -- including Jesus entering Jerusalem riding a donkey a week before his execution -- with donkeys. For the Egyptian the donkey was connected to Seth. Many Hyksos kings chose the donkey as their hieroglyphic symbol. The Essenes probably integrated the donkey and the bull -- being culturally pro-Egyptian.

In sum, a few intimations have been set forth that Jesus was identified with Mars and was opposed to and probably expected by many persons to replace Yahweh. But the circumstances and story of Jesus are at least equally tied into the symbolism and mythology of planet Venus. The New Testament was supposed to replace the Old. And in fact, the history of Christianity often exhibits a conflict over how much of the Old Testament should be discarded, if not all.

Nor would wishing make it so. Contemporary society has nowhere near the capability to erase its collective unconscious. A psychiatry would have to be invented that would far exceed present capabilities.

For one thing, what we would regard as good and bad are so inextricably mingled in the human mind, to all degrees in every and all distinct persons, that merely to call them by name would be practically impossible. But once this were done, the task of targeting the "bad" networks of neurons and extirpating them is almost beyond conception. Indeed, the only way to do so would be to erase the preferences contained in the mind -- brainwashing -- and start all over again with a system of reinforcing a budget of desired preferences and corresponding behaviors.

The Human Mind Turns into Pre-Socratic Philosophy

Nature has its own way of transforming the mind. That is by the aforesaid quantavolutions, All minds in all sectors and on all levels of society are traumatized and in the expiring or negatively exponential stages of the quantavolution are forced to take up new outlooks, attitudes, behaviors. This is, of course, logical to expect. The survivors of quantavolution are not the same people who lived before. Nature explodes and the debris falls out in different kinds and shapes, whether we speak of atmosphere, life forms or rocks.

Applying this theory to the Iron Age, we see that a quantavolution has occurred by observing the behavior of the rocks, air, waters, species, groups and persons that survive. We see a new age of holospheric change. The world is rearranged physically and psychologically. In effect, if not flagrantly, Jesus is contra-Yahweh. Akhnaton is contra-Amon. Socrates is contra-Zeus, Buddha is contra-Shiva, Confucius is contra-T'ien.

In Greece, the reactive centuries of the Iron Age sponsored the pre-Socratic philosophers such as Thales and Heraclitus, whose interests were naturalistic. Relying upon my early studies in ideology, but particularly now upon those of Prof. William Mullen in pre-Socratic philosophy, I am ready to allow the Mars Quantavolution to rise to a climax and thereupon descend into a new environment. Thales, Anaximander, Anaximines, and Xenophanes were of the Milesian School, so-called, working in the Seventh and Sixth Century in Greek Anatolia.

The agenda included a survey of the known cosmos (the orderly arrangement of the inhabited world surrounded by regularly moving heavenly bodies); redefinitions of divinity, and theories of the natural processes, constantly in operation, by which both cosmos and divinity are to be understood. It also included explanations of phenomena most men deemed terrifying: thunder, lightning, earthquakes, eclipses, and periodic destruction of the cosmos itself. It assigned a separate set of terms of elements that by their behavior as water, rarefaction, etc., might explain and ultimately control the effects of catastrophe.

Anaximenes seems to believe that his condensing and rarefaction of air bring about the creation and destruction of worlds. No question but that the early philosophers were quantavolutionary. They should be studied if only because they were making up a secular periodicity, not a religious one. So was Hesiod, who constituted his ages of both great physical and ideological changes. The philosophers believed in cycles of cosmic history, which may have as its sub-conscious purpose to accommodate the idea of quantavolutions. We wonder whether anyone from among them had latched upon the idea that they, the philosophers themselves, were a product of the recent and still on-going though declining quantavolution of Mars. That is, they themselves were the quantavolution, or a significant part of it, a beneficent creative part.

The agony of terrible natural events was close to them. Whereas today we look upon an eclipse of the sun as a brief interesting spectacle, the eclipses of ancient times brought emotions and memories of a specific nature. Until a few years ago, we savants sneered at the apocalyptic prophets. Mullen quotes the poet Pindar, exclaiming at an eclipse:

> Ray of the Sun, O you who see many things, O mother of eyes, what are you devising as you steal away the supreme star in full daylight? Why are you rendering helpless the strength of men and the path of wisdom? Rushing along the path of darkness, are you driving forward something unheard of in the past?... Are you bringing some sign of war, or a withering of crops, or the unspeakable strength of a blizzard, or destructive civil war, or the emptying of the sea onto the plain, or a frost on the earth, or the south wind's heat flowing with angry streams? Or do you intend to flood the earth and create afresh a new race of men?

"The Milesians gave explanations, in terms strikingly different from traditional religion, of phenomena deemed terrifying by most of their contemporaries."[120] By comparison, the cosmic structure conceived by and the behavior and utterances of the roughly contemporary Jewish priests and prophets appear barbaric. While the Jewish ideologues were carrying their messages as historical incidents superintended by their Lord, the Greeks were coining abstract scientific concepts that entered upon empirical research and logical procedures. The hot, the wet, the divine, the good, the true, the beautiful: using the definite noun gave the human mind a chance to work operationally, objectively, and generally. Anaximander's *apeiron* means air, but is much more extensive, moving into all things, a materialism, a plasma, the holding of the all by an atmosphere that maintains all things. Becoming denser, air turned into wind, cloud, water, earth, or stone. By becoming finer it would turn into fire, *leptos*, a finer element melding into consciousness. Huge crushing events transformed the elements, defining entities operationally and secularly. All derives from the plenum, which I, in *Chaos and Creation,* perceived to be the great envelope or sac holding the solar world in electro-gravitational bonds.

Xenophanes wrote diatribes against heroes, warriors, centaurs, and fictions of earlier times. He wrote polemics against the gods and anthropomorphism. There exists "one God, greatest among gods and men, in no respect resembling mortals, either in body or in thought." He was the unmoved mover of all and "By the thought of his mind he shakes everything." There is but little question that the Greek philosophers had a more logical concept of gods than could be found elsewhere.

In Judah, the first phase of reaction brought up the omnipotent and dictatorial Yahweh. Some experts say that Yahweh never succeeded as the sole god of the Ten Tribes of Israel of the Northern Kingdom, but was unto the end of the kingdom in competition with Baal and other gods. Even in Judah, he may not have been himself as the Bible knows him, until he returned with the Jews from Persia whose monotheism had fitted that of the Persians -- Mazda as elaborated by the charismatic priest Zoroaster -- and who therefore received favors from Cyrus the King and a chance to return to Judah (now Yehud, a province of Persia) where, before their exile, a group that centered around Josiah the King had brought together all sources that they could find to add to their own ideas of what Yahwism should be as a religion. This post-climactic Iron Age period in Yehud developed its own limited renaissance in the scholars and priests, all propagandists for an imperial dream and for a long-dead contemporary ruler of little consequence. Now time had passed, more ideas and writings had developed in Babylonia and Persia, and new materials were added.

Martian Theatre and Martian Engineering

The case of the *Book of Job* has some interest for us

because of its unmitigated disasters befalling a virtuous god-loving man, because of the unholy character of Yahweh that it reveals, and the likelihood that it was written as a play in the style of Greek tragedy. Horace Kallen, Founding President of the New School for Social Research, proposed in detail this last idea, which had been introduced in ancient times by Theodore of Mopsuestia in the fifth century CE. Judging by the known history of Greek drama, the play of Job would have been produced in the mid-fifth century BCE. God is an Actor in the play and therefore it would have been blasphemous to the priestly elite of Yehud.

That it could have been a Jewish imitation of the Greek model is possible. That it could have been played in Jerusalem is quite unlikely. That it could have done well in the Greek cities as a spoof of the Hebrew religion and its god is most likely. But it was written in Hebrew, it seems, though the Hebrew language was hardly spoken by then and could have called out only a small audience. A Church Council of 553 CE in Constantinople determined that the *Book of Job* was and would remain a sacred document. So Satan has continued for 2500 years to nag Yahweh to maltreat in every conceivable way an impeccable man to prove to the Devil that Job's faith in his God was perfectly impervious to temptation and misfortune. Both Greek tragedy and Job address but cannot solve the problem of why human beings have to suffer so at the hands of gods.

Piece by piece the concurrent immersion in the quantavolution of the many cultures of the Region manifest themselves. As Cyrus Gordon wrote, "The same time and *Zeitgeist* evoked both the Jewish Apocalyptic books and the Greek Sibylline Oracles."

Engineering progressed steeply in the second phase of the Iron Age. Already explained are its foundations in the new natural philosophy of Anatolia and other centers of Greek thought. The marvels of Roman, East Indian, and Middle East constructions need only be mentioned in passing. The colossal structures of the Bronze Age were exceeded, in complexity and functionalism, if not in girth.

Examples are numerous in industry, warfare metallurgy of iron, shipbuilding. Superb agricultural operations were introduced, the three-tier plantation probably invented in Persia, where wheat, sorghum and date palms might practically occupy the same cultivated space. This would be fed by the system of the *falaj*, a form of extensive underground irrigation that is still practiced successfully today. It adapts well to the desiccated and repopulating areas, as the worst of the Iron Age passed Dr. Al Tikriti praises the *falaj* as "a highly mature capability based on the people's skill in engineering, water exploration, digging, and maintenance."[121]

The invention and widespread usage of coins and money occurred and would appear to be related to the individualism, the logic, the wanderings, the mathematical developments, the iron metallurgy, the egalitarianism, the growth of encounters among strangers, and the materialistic philosophies appearing. Even the need to recreate or rebuild innumerable towns and villages would encourage an abstract yet tangible medium, for payments of floods of billings.

The Divine Succession: Jesus, Christ

Rome, the city-state, the Republic, and the Empire, began and expanded in the name of Mars, encompassing finally the whole scope of the Greater Mediterranean Region. If it began with Mars, it might have ended with the death of Mars, that is, the abandonment of the worship of Mars. However, as I went to some length to demonstrate in *The Divine Succession*, great gods never die but simply go on forever in new forms, because the universal catastrophe lies beneath the history of gods and faiths. And it is not forgotten, no matter how heavily suppressed.

"In the inscriptions and literature of the first millennium BC, gods are often referred to... by titles or by new names, so that it is often difficult to ascertain their relationship to the deities of the second millennium, or indeed to determine their individuality in relation to one another."[122]

Gibbons, in his magisterial *Decline and Fall of the Roman Empire* blames the pacifism, otherworldliness, and passive resistance of the rapidly-growing Christian population for the grand tragedy. The Empire lost its morale and could not put down its invaders.

If such be the case, then Jesus, with whatever he came to stand for, was the next ruling God of the Divine Succession. He succeeded because he was young and was a doppelgaenger of God the Father. We could find but slight evidence that Jesus and God His Father had inherited the traits of Mars and Jupiter. But, too, we suspect that there may have been much more of a descent than our culture will let be exposed. In a way, we are saying that Christianity does not have its own Great God and must therefore be Judeo-Christianity. Jesus could not qualify as a Great God in himself because he did not enter the world on the wings of a quantavolution. He had to be introduced to the divine succession through agents of the Great God Yahweh, whose quantavolutionary credentials were impeccable. He recognized his limitations, when giving all credit to "the Father who art in Heaven."

Chapter Fourteen

The Extermination of Volsinium

Soon after the beginning of the Iron Age, probably in the -700s, we find the Etruscans descending upon Central Italy, a migrant people from a well-developed Late Bronze civilization, maybe in northwest Anatolia and across in Europe. Traditionally, they had been forced out by a great famine. Their blood type is similar to the Urartu people of Lake Van; their mostly undeciphered language is found upon Lemnos, favorite island of Hephaistos, and is related to the Hittite; and they are distinguishable from their Villanovan predecessors in culture and separated from them by a layer of catastrophic debris.

It is likely that the Etruscans settled in Italy not long before the Romans. They soon erected a flourishing group of towns, whose walls, architecture, and tombs resembled closely the Mycenean and Minoan counterparts, which, we know so well by now, are still being obsessively dated to the -1200s or earlier, 500 years earlier at least before the Etruscan migration. Besides, Jan Sammer has brought forward the frequent and sole presence of eighth century or later Etruscan artifacts in the "Mycenean" tombs. The Etruscan dates were tied into the Egyptian chronology nevertheless. Etruscologists had to give in to the Egyptologist power elite, at least for public purposes (though it takes only a glass of Chianti to get the truth flowing from them).

The Etruscans, it is now evident after a century of obliquity, were culturally coincident with the Myceneans. Hence, the evidence of close affinities between the two cultures indicate a chronological affinity as well, namely the eighth and seventh centuries. They built closely similar vaulted tombs, filled them with objects common to both cultures and technologies, constructed stone walls in the same way. A beautiful vase signed by a Greek master,

Aristonothos, of the mid-seventh century, was found at Cerveteri and resembles closely a famous vase called the 'Warrior Vase of Mycenae.' hitherto dated wrongly in the Egyptian manner, five hundred years too old. Famed Etruscan frescoes resemble frescoes of Bronze Age Crete. Thus, with other definitive comparisons, Velikovsky and Sammer were able to give another shove to the Dark Age of Crete, bringing it into line with the early Iron Age both West and East in the Greater Mediterranean.

From Villanovans to Etruscans

Once more, as in hundreds of other cases, a culture and people outside of Egypt is shown to act in accord with an Iron Age dating in the ~-700's rather than the -1200's.

The Iron Age was already behaving catastrophically in Italy. The Villanovan culture, which the Etruscans moved into, replaced, and displaced, resembled hardly at all the Etruscan culture. The Villanovan culture was already practically destroyed by the quantavolution. I quote one authority, translating:

"With the start of the Age of Iron, in the 9th century, the population abandoned almost all of its home sites from the preceding period to set itself up in groups of several hundreds of individuals in the zone of Veio, Tarquinia, Vulci, etc., occupying in distinct nucleoles marge plains and their adjavent hills; its connection with the early Villanovan culture lingered, whether we speak of funeral rites or material culture."

The distance between habitations is estimated to have enlarged from one tenth of a kilometer in the Late Bronze to about one kilometer in the early Iron Age. Rilli found mysterious ashes piled upon Etruscan settlements, and the ancient encyclopedist Pliny had reported upon as thunderbolts of the gods.

The Volsinium Story

Volsinium (more correctly the compound of adjoining

settlements called the Volsinii, the Volsinians) developed luxuriantly on what was already a lake and marsh, Lago Bolsena today. It is fairly certain that the whole of Volsinium was exterminated suddenly. If this really happened, we have a another victim of the Martian Quantavolution, a first degree homicide, *ipso facto*, with a total geological, environmental, biological, demographic, and cultural change -- abrupt, large-scale, intense change. But we must find the victim, the ruins themselves, the corpus delicti, and that is no simple matter.

The sole reporter is Pliny the Elder, a fairly reliable encyclopedist and Roman Admiral, whose testimony came about 700 years later. Announcing the cosmic crime, he claims that the culprit was Planet-Mars, and the weapon used was a sheet of fire from the sky. Also, everyone competent to do so -- archaeologists and geologists by the scores -- attest to the fantastic mess that exists below the smiling lake and lovely towns that border around.[123] See *fig 29* (a geological sketch of the Monti Vulsini), *fig. 30* (a map of the lake), *fig. 31*.

A hundred volcanos are all about, just to begin with. A deep round Lake that rises and falls, not only over history but also on any day of the week, oscillating in an intriguing manner, while down deep freshwater and hot water seep from springs, and often flatulent booms are to be heard. We encounter tales of monsters and witches, of times beyond recall and beyond history, with a few bones and artifacts, walls, and many tombs strewn about.

The town of Bolsena, today, is a small town on a low hill a few minutes' walk of the Lago di Bolsena. Although we speak glibly of its obliteration, we cannot find Volsinium, alias Velzna, Volsna, Volsinii, and Orvieto. A swarm of detectives and forensic specialists - historians, archaeologists, mythologists, and geologists -- has preceded us, and they have not found Volsinium either. Or, at the least, they have not been able to identify the body.

Pliny writes of ".. the burning lightning from *Mars*. And with such lightning was Volsinij (a most wealthie cittie of the Tuscanes) burnt full and whole to ashes.")[124]

It is common to defame Pliny, using the strict standards of historical research expounded, if not always followed, today. He had too much to say, too few records to go by, sources who were often undependable, and he left no extensive archives of notes, nor students who could recall the details and embellish them by painstaking research. The distinction between astronomy and astrology was uncertain, and Pliny was caught in their middle, trying to be scientific and at the same time indoctrinated by astrology. It was an age of superstition, of a limited body of science, and, importantly, of natural events that, unless we are up to the minute on scientific discoveries, we would dismiss as impossible.

Pliny's Relevant Comments on Astro-Catastrophe

Pliny gives us at least three further comments, other than the one quoted above, that lend sense to an hypothesis about exoterrestrial intervention on the scene, whether by meteoroids, by lightning, or by some other means.

1. **Destruction all around Volsinium.** Pliny speaks of the arrival of a monster and of all the country around Volsinium having been destroyed. His statement is interpreted by us to mean that the Volsinii communities had all been destroyed, rather than only a simple compact aggregation on a hill.

2. **The driving of people off the hilltops by lightning so intense that towers and forts were regularly destroyed.** Thus, we read in Book Two, *Chap. IV, of* Pliny: *In Italie betweene Tarracina and the temple of Feronia, they gave over in time of warre, to make towres and forts; for not one of them escaped, but was overthrowne with lightning.* Here we have a generalization, which as such, tends to be a little more reliable than a single statement about a single event. The area mentioned is as far south of Rome as Bolsena is North. *God's Fire*, as I called it in my study of Moses, was being deployed in many parts of Italy and indeed the world, in the centuries which concern us. For example, in Scotland and elsewhere, we encounter the impressive phenomenon of the vitrified forts, stone bastions affixed to stony hills. They were fused, not by the blow torches of kilted warriors, but by Planet Mars or an emissary thereof. Yet settlers or refugees repeatedly took to the hills, whether in Italy, Greece,

Palestine or Britain. And then were evicted by *God's Fire.*

3. The details of Etruscan lightning science are given by Pliny and other writers, old and recent. Pliny, in Chap LII of Book Two speaks "of observations as touching upon lightning."

The auncient Tuscanes by their learning doe hold, that there be nine gods that send forth Lightnings, and those of eleven sorts: for *Iupiter* (say they) casteth three at once. The Romanes have observed two of them, and no more; attributing those in the day time to *Iupiter:* and them in the night, to *Summanus* or *Pluto.* And these verily be more rare, for the cause afore-named; namely, the coldnesse of the aire above. In Hetruria, they suppose that lightnings breake also out of the earth, which they call *Infera, I.* Infernall; and such be made in mid-winter. And these they take to be terrene and earthly, and of all most mischievous and execrable: neither be those generall and universall lightnings, nor proceeding from the starres, but from a verie neare and more troubled cause. And this is an evident argument for distinction, that all such as fall from the upper skie above, strike aslant and side-wise: but those which they call earthly, smite straight and directly. But the reason why these are thought to issue forth of the earth is this; because they fall from out of a matter nearer to the earth, for as much as they leave no markes of a stroke behind: which are occasioned by force not from beneath, but comming full against. Such as have searched more subtillie into these matters, are of opinion, that these lightnings come from the Planet *Saturne,* like as the burning lightning from *Mars:* And with such lightning was Volsinij (a most wealthie cittie of the Tuscanes) burnt full and whole to ashes. Moreover, the Tuscanes call those lightnings Familiar, which presage the fortune of some race, and are significant during their whole life: and such are they that come first to any man, after he is newly entred into his own patrimonie or familie. Howbeit, their judgement is, that these private lightnings are not of importance and fore-tokening above ten yeeres; unlesse they happen either upon the day of first marriage, or of wedding. As for publicke lightnings, they be not of force above 30 yeeres, except they chaunce at the very time that townes or colonies be erected and planted.

Conjuring Lightning

And now we move his voice to Chapter LIII.

Of raising or calling out Lightnings by conjuration.

It appeareth upon record in Chronicles, that by certaine sacrifices and prayers, Lightnings may be either compelled or easily entreated to fall upon the earth. **There goeth a report of old in Hetruria, that such a** lightning was procured by exorcisms and conjurations, when there entred into the cittie Volsinij (after all the territory about it was destroyed) a monster, which they named *Volta*. Also, that another was raised and conjured by *Porsenna* their King. Moreover, *L. Piso* (a writer of good credit) reporteth in his first booke of Annales, that *Numa* before him practised the same feat many a time and often: and when *Tullus Hostilius* would have imitated him and done the like (for that he observed not all the ceremonies accordingly) was himselfe strucke and killed with lightning. And for this purpose, sacred groves we have and altars, yea and certaine sacrifices due thereto. And among the *Iupiters* surnamed *Stateres, Tonantes,* and *Feretrij,* we have heard that one also was called *Elicius*. Sundry and divers are mens opinions as touching this point, and every man according to his owne liking and fansie of his mind. To beleeve that Nature may be forced and commaunded, is a very audacious and bold opinion: but it is as blockish on the other side and senselesse, to make her benefits of no power and effect; considering that in the interpretation of Lightning, men have thus farre forth proceeded in skill and knowledge, as to foretell when they will come at a set and prescript day: and whether they will forgoe and frustrate the daungers pronounced, or rather open other destinies, which lie hidden: and an infinite sort of publicke and privat experiments of both kinds are to be found. And therefore (since it hath so pleased Nature) let some men be resolved herein, and others doubtfull: some may allow thereof, and others condemne the same. As for us, we will not omit the rest which in these matters are worth remembrance.

(We note here how Pliny struggles for objectivity and scientific method, but does not want to abandon the possible truth in legend, psychic communication, and means of controlling the vast forces of nature by magic.) The natural disasters provoked human behavior of extraordinary kinds, a pathology whose effects were registered and teach us about schizoid aspects of our own characters and situations that may well be encountered in the future. For the past half-century has seen the establishment of a field of universal study here called quantavolution, which pertains to all fields of knowledge, including theology and social planning, and allows us to analyse intelligently, scientifically, the occurrence and effects of events that change the world suddenly and intensively.

From a more purely intellectual point of view, the study of Volsinium engenders, it is hoped, an improved Etruscology. The beginnings of archaeology are the story of grave-robbers and art lovers. The tradition has been transformed into respectability over the past two centuries by amateurs and academicians, who have systematized and given legal sanction mostly to collections of art and representations of religion. Then occurred an interest in everyday existence, parallelling the rise of political democracy. Mysteries of the past kept the crowds enthralled – the pyramids, the Sphinx, Atlantis, lost cities and islands, anomalous "telescope," "giants of the Earth," and so on. The rocks and sediments and ashes did not play music for the diggers. Today the situation has changed somewhat, and geologists and ecologists have moved into the picture, in Italy partly because of the importance of volcanoes in its past and present.

The literature of Volsinium and the volcanic park around it is ample, but insufficient, in that it is inconclusive, one of the problems being that very few of the students of the subject had any notion that the skies might have anything to do with true history.

The several sciences most pertinent to the present study are geology, ancient history, archaeology, mythology, linguistics, and astro-physics. Each one has within its bounds to give a firm "Nay" or "Yea" to the Pliny thesis. None does. As yet. But then we have not yet fully advanced the thesis. It is also possible that two or more of the sciences named might uphold or deny the thesis.

Lightning Geology

On the subject of "lightning geology," I have found little besides the writings of the small quantavolution group. Add the work on the subject by conventional scientists and there is still no more than the makings of a thick anthology in a single volume. And almost nothing exists in conventional geology on heavy blast effects of lightning storms. Recently, some reports have appeared dealing with mega-lightning in the ionosphere and outer space. Just after a lightning discharge, huge quasi-static electric fields are built up in the upper atmosphere. Sprite filaments of enormous power play about the mesosphere.

Lightning plays a part in making life possible by fixing chemically the nitrogen of the atmosphere, which is the most abundant element to be found there. Nitrogen is compounded into usable form for plants and animals by bacteria in dead organic matter, soil and roots, and by fungi. A process of ammonification readies the nitrogen for assimilation. Fossil fuel emissions raised up and then rained down contribute a large portion of the fixation. Lightning striking the earth and playing about the clouds contributes about 20K tons of fixed nitrogen out of a total of about 100 million tons fixed in all, annually. The ionosphere also fixes nitrogen. This is very little relatively, but it would have been much more in the Iron Age when all indications are of extremely heavy electrical forces active everywhere. Given also the combustion of large sections of the globe, there must have been for a time a great surplus of fixed nitrogen. But when the age of lightning passed and extensive desertification succeeded the widespread devastation by fire, there might have occurred a scarcity of fixed nitrogen, which would have affected adversely the biosphere. The nitrogen cycle, that is, would have been interrupted.[125]

Increasing attention has been paid to electrical forces in explaining many phenomena and events. They work heavily in earthquakes, volcanoes, and tectonic shifting. For instance, millions of fault lines crisscross the earth's shell, both to conduct and condense electricity. Their frequent protrusion into and exposure to the atmosphere, as well as continuous contact with nitrogen, may be producing a considerable portion of the total nitrogen fixation occurring; if so, then periods of ground turbulence would generate increased quantities.[126]

Among the volcanic strata of the Vulsinii apparatus, there seem to be no fossils and only diminutive paleosol or soil layers. The time given for the volcanos to be started up and finally extincted is about 800,000 years. With the long intervals between eruptions there should have been extensive non-volcanic or disintegrated volcanic accrual. I suppose that many life forms buried in ashes that have hardened cannot be located and dug out. But how is this absence of surficial layers to be explained? If the eruptions occurred all in one period, the time would have been short and might be quite recent.

I have found no study yet that connects the heavy vulcanism of Vulsinii with the great biological extinctions of the end of the Pleistocene. There must be a connection, and the time must be at the beginning of the Holocene only about 10 to 15ka ago. This was also the acknowledged end of the Ice Ages. So there must have been a connection here, because the ice ages ended catastrophically.

Etruria Dating Less Obsessively Askew

The mistaken elaborate chronology of ancient Egypt ruined the chronology of ancient Greece, Mesopotamia and Rome -- indeed, everywhere it has touched. The necessary changes to cut from three to five centuries from the Manetho-Petri chronology of Egypt have not yet been accepted. The problem is not so acute in Etruscology because there have been no extremely old dates to tie into locally. Nevertheless, we can see that scholars here, too, have been misled because of having to appease the traditional calendarists of Egypt. Many have stuck to dates in the second millennium. Others have now been reducing the Etruscan "dark ages, " though not sufficiently so, as yet.

The tendency has been to push the Villanovans farther into the past, thus allowing plenty of room for the Etruscans to arrive earlier and in a more primitive state. I see no reason and no evidence for making of the Etruscans any less sophisticated beginning on the Italian scene than we make of the Greek settlements in Italy and Sicily. The Villanovans probably stayed on into the Etruscan period, as much as the general catastrophe and some unfriendly encounters permitted. The underwater settlements that have been uncovered in the last decades in Lago di Bolsena may not be independent Villanovan predecessors but , rather, tolerated and dominated sub-classes of Villanovans, neighborhoods of Volsinii, perhaps even of the type of San Francisco's old-time "Fisherman's Wharf," serving the richer and populous communities ashore.

Research is needed here as everywhere, even as at Rome, predicated upon an annulment of the several centuries that have been artificially inserted. For example, one study shows a paucity of the bones of animals of the centuries that quantavolution scholars believe never did exist, the period which is transitional between Villanovan and Etruscan in Italy, between the dates of ~1250 and 750, in this case 350 rather than 500 years (see *fig. 33*, , if the dates can be trusted).

Recent studies show that the larger area around Lake Bolsena had significantly fewer settlements to be uncovered than other areas of the region. Yet the land there is suitable for intensive development. This might indicate a wholesale destruction of settlements in the Volsinium region, and a catastrophic overlayering.

Alessandro Guidi has written, "Between the end of the Bronze Age and the beginning of the Iron Age the number of inhabited places of Etruria dropped by four-fifths!" To which Renato Peroni (*Enea nel Lazio*, 1981, p.92) remarks, "So rapid a process of depopulation (in some cases occurring violently, in others seemingly through abandonment) and the incorporation of the population in a few proto-urban centers will make way, in its turn, to the mechanisms of formation of a complex society, even of a 'stratal' type, at the beginnings of the Etruscan nation."

But, of course, this abrupt transition is characteristic of the Bronze-Iron Age transitions in many places – Sicily, Aegean, the Near East, the whole world.

Orvieto not the Center of the Volsinii

The site of Volsinium, as discussed by the *Encyclopaedia Britannica* is useful for preliminary work, if only because it does not settle upon Orvieto, where most authorities have congregated. It is there where one might well begin to test the soils and stones for signs of fulmination and other phenomena and materials that might have been part of its destruction(s). Later I shall provide the arguments for this choice of location. The *Encyclopedia Britannica* gives us:

> Etruscan Velzna, ancient Etruscan town on the site of present-day Bolsena (Viterbo province, Italy). At an unidentified neighbouring site was a temple to Voltumna, which was the headquarters of the 12-city Etruscan League and the site of the annual assemblies of the Etruscans. Excavations at Bolsena have uncovered huge double walls surrounding the group of small hills over which the city was built. A system of lateral walls within these enabled its defenders to cut off portions of the city and

retreat behind further positions. On the highest of the enclosed hills, the acropolis was situated; on the surrounding plateau of Mercatello was the main residential area.

The very absence of historical records, of art works, and of definitive ruins of Volsinium and the Fanum Voltumnum suggest that a queer mystery is present. Possibly out of frustration at not being able to fix upon a site to call their own, some archaeologists, historians, and geologists, and most writers, decided that the city of Orvieto would have been the Volsinium of old. Orvieto stands splendidly upon a bluff some twenty kilometers along an ancient road to the North, but shares the geology of the Lake region.

However, on the basis of the general logic and evidence brought to bear in this work, also of tours around the Lake Basin, but especially upon the summary of evidence provided in talks and writing by Alessandro Fioravanti, a Bolsena engineer, aged 86, who has spent his life at Bolsena and involved himself in many works of the area, including the creation of the Bolsena Museum, the present writer commits himself to the view that the most ancient Bolsena or Volsinium was born upon and continued to rest upon a hilltop, maximum altitude 600 meters, and its slopes, down to the shores of Lago di Bolsena today.

The earliest Etruscans to appear on the scene would have found there a location for living and work of superior quality, except for earthquakes, volcanism, and all-embracing electrical phenomena. The location of the center of town, its fortress, has always been on a hill that is defensible but not uncomfortably high, and an easy walk from the Lake. The Lake has been famous since earliest times for its abundance of fish and waterfowl and has enjoyed fertile soil on all sides (volcanic and therefore well mineralized).

Engineer Fioravanti supplies the following several arguments for preferring Bolsena to Orvieto as the site of the ancient city of Volsinium.

1. The ancient author Pseudo-Aristotle says that Bolsena contained a tall hill in the middle of the city. This is true of Bolsena, not of Orvieto.

2. The same writer speaks of a flourishing wood and

copious water both above and below the town. This bespeaks Bolsena rather than Orvieto.

3. Bolsena's walls are incomparably grander than Orvieto's, conforming to a text by the author, Joannes Zonaras, a medieval historian.

4. The full famous local talents were put to work on Bolsena constructions, as seen in the ruins.

5. The early tombs of Orvieto are not so impressive as those of Bolsena.

6. Bolsena has buried and undiscoverable fountains.

7. Bolsena has buried monuments of importance

8. The pressure put upon me (Eng. Fioravanti) and others to believe in the Orvieto story should be discounted.

I agree with Eng. Fioravanti.

Lightning and Ashes of Etruria

A map of the probable site of the destroyed Volsinii, was drawn by Architect T. F. Buchicchio of Bolsena. It is near the Lake. It reveals a complex urban center. One of the main roads of the Roman Empire, the Via Appia proceeds over a great wall of the probable Volsinii. See *fig. 35*.

The date of its destruction, we have guessed, might have been early in the Seventh Century, BC, about 2,650 years ago. (This would allow the Etruscans to arrive in Italy from their original territory somewhere in the Northeast during the 700's and build their cities.) The Trojans of Aeneas had recently landed 300 kilometres to the South, and were making peace with the King of the area, who gave his name to Latium. Their move into the area would be facilitated by some weakness in the powerful federation of Etruria that dominated the coast all the way down to where it encountered the equally powerful Greek tyrannies in today's Southern Italy and Sicily. They also might have moved there because the Etruscans were a kindred people from the East.

The Etruscans were especial worshipers of Jupiter and lightning par excellence, to the point where they could be mistaken for Yahweh- sect descendants of Noah. They were famed for their expertise in all forms of mysteries, rites, and astrology.

Lightning prefers damp areas, underground waters, towers and hilltops, metallic constituents in the soil, metal hordes (coins, weapons, iron). All of these were present in unusual abundance around Volsinium. Far off in the skies, the Planet Mars had been enjoying an abundance of fire and water, if we can believe the latest landings and surveys there. Both may have been transported to Earth if given the powered vehicle. Electric power, even gravitational attraction, will do. If, to fire and water, we add the super-abundant cosmic electricity of the times, we have strengthened our case of a disastrous event involving electrical forces. Archaeologists should not be too surprised. We are beginning to learn that, in the typical dig to reach settlements of the period, we find above them and below them beds of ashes, not merely the ashes of fires set by conquering enemies, but by lightning and volcanism, itself possibly occurring on a grand scale. We find catastrophic activity of water everywhere.

The Great Lightning Fear (*Cheravnophobia*) of the Etruscans plays a large role in their religion and conduct. How they feared and worshiped, and therefore studied all such phenomena indicates the ever-present likelihood of cosmic disaster. They gave the Romans Jupiter and Mars and the art and science of naming, predicting, and (sometimes) eliciting or preventing lightning.

They recognized many types of Lightning, like the Eskimo knows many kinds of snow. Thirty in all, declared the Etruscan authority Nicolo Rilli. They found that lightning which initiated from underground, which they ascribed to the agency of Saturn, to be particularly dangerous. Yet it was the lightning of Jupiter that they insisted exceeded all others, for it included all other forms and added three kinds of his own.

Still, it was the bolts of Mars that destroyed Volsinium. These were exceedingly hot and burning, according to Pliny. They appeared to come directly from the red planet, like hot sparks off a burning log.[127] This image is particularly suggestive of a reality. Mythologists have done their job: they have tied Mars and his namesakes to the planet and its behavior. It remains for astronomers and physicists to build as strong a case for the means by which lightning and meteoric material could have been discharged on Earth from Mars. It is by their default that interlopers from the historical, anthropological and humanistic disciplines have had to supply most of the theory and evidence thus far. Still, that partisans of an "electric universe" are gaining ground means a greater likelihood of a history of astronomy with eccentric planets.

Ashes were everywhere. All over Etruria and Italy and the rest of the world in those days, there were ashes, proof of some kind of fire everywhere, wherever it might come from. Modern scientists, careful archaeologists who brushed off the tiniest shards for their collections and their later recitations, almost always ascribed heavy ashes to the incendiarism of conquerors, if there were no active volcano nearby. Practically no one brought down the ashes from the sky or from a monstrous explosion of a meteoroid. Only rare attempts have been made to assign the huge beds of ashes to exoterrestrial cometary fall-outs or meteoroid crashes. Or to lightning storms, tornado-like, that burned and bulldozed large areas. It is hard to believe that this Martian world, fascinated and terrified by natural electricity, and with a number of settlements that fell to natural forces apart from the intervention of earthquake or volcanoes, lived in the world of nature that we experience today.

We hear of no conquering force that burned down irretrievably Volsinium, until the Romans, when they came, centuries later, defeated the Volsinian forces, first in 392, then in 311, then in 294 and 280, and then finally, because the slaves had taken over the city from its masters, the Romans intervened and sent the population into exile, presumably to Orvieto, a nearby city. Or maybe they sent them down to the shore to resettle. It would appear that some of the Volsinii returned on their own initiative or never left because there has always been a settlement called Volsinium or Bolsena. The Romans themselves built a fine city on the ruins or near the ruins of Volsinium. So we are moving closer to explanations introducing super-electrical phenomena as a possible explanation of its earlier destruction.

Changed Moods in Arts, Culture and Rituals

The ideology and motifs behind Egyptian culture are suggestive. There is a definite turnabout in the mood of Etruscan civilization from a first period of pleasant and positive outlook to a second ensuing period of obsession with death, burial, and the afterlife. Freud would call it *thanatos,* an obsession with death, an obsession that is the most visible and remarkable on record. It may allow us to hypothesize the same phenomenon for all cultures passing through this period of time, 850-600, with a tailing-off requiring hundreds of year and ending with the decline, practical death, and absorption of Etruscan civilization into the Roman.

The Etruscans were world leaders in the production of paintings, statues and sculpture generally, mechanical inventions, and personal tombs of a manageable size. Death was present in Etruscan art remarkably more than in most cultures, and more so after, rather than before, the civilization had peaked in brilliance. The grim, underworld figure of a dark god with a cudgel was encountered with distressing frequency. He is Techulka, smith-god and death-demon, who clubs victims with a giant hammer. He is accompanied by a winged demon with snakes.

The absence of art in the district of the Volsinium quantavolution complex is notable. A catalogue of art works, readily inspected, gives it far less than the one-twelfth or more of Etruscan art that one would expect to recover from what may have been the most prosperous center of Etruria. The situation remains unchanged if we count in all of the Volsinii, that is, Volsinian centers, remembering that the Volsinians were called by this name and not the name Volsinium, probably because their community extended through most if not all of what came later to be referred to as the large basin of the Latera volcanic complex. Most involved scholars of today would elect other cities, Tarquinia and Vulci, as sharing the Lake shores. But it may be that the Volsinii dominated the full Lake until "destroyed by Mars." It most likely commanded the premises of the Sanctuary of Voltumna, nearby; this too also disappeared, probably in the same catastrophe that wiped out Volsinium. It was reputed to be a supremely wealthy religious center for all twelve of the Etruscan cities.

We may also observe here the proof offered that conjuration is effective. We hear of the Monster Volta that entered the city after the countryside had been destroyed. The priests actually called down lightning upon their own heads (like infantry hard-pressed by an advancing enemy calls up artillery fire), and lightning then did destroy Volta. Volta would have been a familiar monster, as his name is practically that of the Volsinii themselves, and as Mars was a familiar but destructive god. I introduced earlier the work of Ackerman and Cochrane that brings out the horrible manifestations of Mars on its closest encounters with Earth. One description of the monster is of the form of a huge man with the head of a dog. In myth everywhere, Mars has as totem animal the wolf or dog. Heracles owns a set of myths presenting him with a monstrous physique even as a child.

Penetrating details of Etruscan electrical beliefs and practices are afforded us by Hugh Crosthwaite in two works: *Ka, and Fire without Smoke*. He points to a number of cases evidencing the Etruscan obsession and compulsions with lightning and fire, with their elaborately developed rituals for dealing with this great fear of the Etruscan psychosphere.

Or, again conceivably, a sickening radiation cloud, monstrous in form, had taken up residence above the city, many citizens were dying of radioactive illness, and bolts of lightning, conjured from the earth by static electric machines, cleared up the sky. Deadly radiation, as from the nuclear bomb over Hiroshima, and radioactivity, has been brought into quantavolution theory, especially with regard to biological extinction of the past, by several authors, among them Velikovsky, Schindewulf, Kloosterman, and myself. In April, 2003, an alarm in the scientific press was sounded giving evidence of an accelerated decline in the magnetic field of the Earth and of the storms of cosmic rays and other particles that would penetrate the atmosphere and cause "pestilence," if the magnetic field died or reversed itself.

A century ago French scientists discovered that certain Etruscan vases of the eighth century B.C., in this Martian Age, which were lined up in furnaces for burning, were marked by a magnetic field whose polarity was the reverse of the present field.[128] And one archaeologist, working on ceramics of a prior age, showed a polarity of the present time.

Chronometry, Volcanism, Topography

The dates of last volcanic eruptions in the Volsinium apparatus, as given by practically every geologist, are around 160,000y. One source gives 10,000y. One geologist, Prof. Donatella De Rita of the University of Roma, declares, however, that historical sources give the last eruption as -104 If this is so, would it be another indication of the tendency of radiochronometry to provide extremely old dates, in this case, figuring from 2000 AD, by a factor of 80?

It should be borne in mind that all dates in the literature are based upon dubious radiometry. Electricity and lightning can, by disrupting radioactivity in the elements forming the basis for measurement of parent-daughter relationships, render laboratory measurements useless. A leading light in the investigations of Bolsena has been Engineer Alessandro Fioravanti. He was, in my opinion, at one point deceived and bluffed by carbon-dating measures in the hands of experts, so that he gave up an empirically derived position that is correct, on the ages assigned to Gran Carro. We need not argue this question of dating right now, however.

The most ancient segment of crust is under the Lake and has been worn down and overflowed from various sources until it presents a flattened appearance with the Lake's crater in an approximate center. A geological sketch of the volcanic region displays the most ancient arcuate rim and shows that it is traversed by more than one newer eruption. See *fig. 30*. Many torrents, ditches, and fissures of the crater of Lake Bolsena, all of them going down the crater rim into the Lake. See *fig. 31*. All, that is, except the outlet of the River Marta (etym. "of Mars"), which probably depends upon ancient and repeated digging to help the waters find a way out.

There appears to be nothing distinctive about the lava flow except its enormity; it has not shown in any soundings to surmount foreign or crushed rock. (A suspicious reversal of layers occurs, however, in lower lava coverings, which might bear investigation.) Pyroclastics, ashes, pumice abound in expected amounts. Profiles of drillings are attached in the L. Vezzoli et al article.[129] Reports of many other drillings are available, almost all of them crudely depictive of the common few substances. Rust-colored iron dust is visible in large quantity in the soil upon ordinary walks around the Lake. There is no mention in the literature of non-volcanic stones, elements, or materials. Of course, the scientists were not looking for such.

Springs proceed from the Lake bottom and are given as the principal source of the waters, though there are many small flows and drainages into the Lake from torrents. At least one spring affords hot water. There are sulphur deposits in the vicinity, once mined. There has been drilling conducted some years ago in a search for petroleum and natural gas, without success or noteworthy incidental findings. (Recent studies connected with Oklahoma University have disclosed strong correlations between meteoroid craters and petroleum and gas deposits.) The region generally contains more than its share of metallic substances, uranium and plutonium, even if not in commercial proportions.

The Lake vibrates in a ~15 centimeter vertical span continually, a rarely encountered and not understood phenomenon. Seismism in the region is notable at a slightly abnormal level. Gravimetric measures do not appear exceptional. The pre-historic volcanism of the region has been termed on occasion explosive, including the main volcano beneath the Lake.

I have mentioned ruins of a settlement (Gran Carro) to be found several meters below the waters at a site near to present-day Bolsena. They are ascribed to the Villanovan culture that once was deemed to have preceded and been exterminated by the Etruscans, but more recently has been said to continue into the Etruscan period. The drowning of the settlement probably occurred in the events that brought the submergence of the Lake cultures of Switzerland and the Alps generally. This has been placed in the eighth or seventh centuries as part of the general quantavolution of the age. The cause may have been heavy volcanism or cosmic changes (solar activity, for instance) that melted ice caps and glaciers.

The volcanoes are presumed to be of varying but young ages. They form a nest. No one has considered whether they could have been excited by the high temperatures and explosions of a substantial comet or meteorite. In Arabia, the Western volcanoes tend to form a chain. Either of these forms is plausible, as a child who has watched a fireworks display will tell you.

A series of tests by the potassium-argon method was made of the region around Bolsena to determine the dating of their activity. At ten locations, ages ranged from 145 ka to 429 ka. The dates are not only uncoordinated and uncorrelated, but give varying gaps in activity that would, if one were to accept K-A dating as useful, that indicate great erraticism in their periodicity. We stress that activity has been claimed by other scientists for as little as four thousand years ago. With this kind of evidence, so difficult to fathom, one may be excused for an extensive imagination.

Geologists to this date appear not to have debated, but have asserted and agreed, that volcanism is the full and adequate explanation of the Volsini volcanic region and that there is little or no use in an exhaustive search and testing for anomalous chemical elements., and in any event, no resources are obtainable for the purpose without surprising new evidence to begin with. The cost to test in three sampled locations at the level just below the top soil of today, for radioactivity, hydrocarbons, iridium, methane, and combustion products, would not exceed $8,000.00. Yet even this has not been done.

The available gravimetric and magnetic measurements seem within the normal range, or at least the authors of the several studies of the subject seem not concerned over anomalies. If there had been a heavy downfall of cosmic material or air-transported material from elsewhere, there should be abnormalities.

A group, led by Prof. Biella, published in the *Periodico di Mineralogia of 1987,* cited above, an article that reported a high velocity body, possibly a piece of continental crust, of at least a 12-15 km radius, corresponding to a density of 2.8 to 3.0 gcm3, that extends under the Volsinium volcanic area with a corresponding velocity of 6.7-7.0 k/s. This underlays a lower velocity stratum usually found at a lower depth. Therefore a reversal or intrusion of strata is predicated. This finding bears further inquiry.

An Asteroid Impact?

We proceed here, however, with an asteroid scenario.

It is postulated that an asteroid headed over Volsinium from the Southwest and exploded in the air above the city and its neighborhood. With a diameter of 70 meters, if it was stony (half this if it was mostly iron) and at a height of one kilometer, pursuing an angle of 45° and a speed of 17 k/sec or less, it would have blown out the city and flattened it, shaped a crater about the size of the present Lago di Bolsena (no more than 200 m deep), slightly elliptical, dissolved the forests, vegetation and villages adjoining, and killed all exposed life. It would have bulldozed the surface strata into an arc of debris, now amalgamated and emplaced as a rim of several hundred meters in height over half the circumference and several kilometers beyond the lake to the North.

Fragments from its body would have been hurled forward -- south, east, and west -- exciting volcanism that had been already active beforetime, both in the form of erupting cones and as exuding fissure lava. The Lake water would have been blown out. Springs would have opened up in the Depression of Volsinium, and drainage from the crater slopes and rainfall would fill the basin that had been created. Thus would have been created Lago di Bolsena. The vegetation for many kilometers around would have been flattened and scorched. Unless the meteoroid had pancaked in slowly, it would most likely have wiped out a large part of the Etrurian region and therefore it would have been justly infamous. And thus would have disappeared in a cloud of particles, ash and debris the flourishing city of Volsinium.

This scenario is improbable. It cannot be entirely dismissed. And its true meaning may be partial. Expenses of further investigation would be considerable, if materials were found worth their testing. It might take some time to come upon "fracture cones," as pictured in attachment Ia, if such exist, although this would be an immediate practical proof of the meteoroid scenario. Attachment Ib shows a model simple impact crater and a melt cliff with columnar joining. I have noticed along the road near Bolsena a stunning four-meter columnar cliff, but it seems to be of a different order. The literature does not mention any such stones

A Tunguska Gas-Blast Scenario

Next we should consider a gas blast: a Tunguska Scenario. Three variations of one of several major theories endeavoring to explain the Tunguska blast bring together bolides (comet or meteorite), gases, explosion, and fires; a paragraph on each will show the kind of reasoning that is being applied to the Vulsini region.

The present author had also suggested a gas cloud for this and other cases in the first volume, *Chaos and Creation*, of the Quantavolution Series. One article by V. Svettsov refutes the importance of readily discernible debris. A comet strikes the upper atmosphere, is fragmented into a stream of very small fragments, which dissolve as they continue down, and ignite or scorch the earth as they reach ground level; no particles are discoverable until one moves out to five kilometers or more from the epicenter, and then they are minuscule.

A second theory, by Ion Nistor suggests that gas pouches forming over lowlying areas, "swamp-gas" it is often called, (or possibly from earthquake gas-issing fissures) rose to encounter a meteor that then exploded several times in succession , causing asymmetric areas of destruction. The soil becomes fluid and even picks up a wave pattern. The gases, burning high in the sky, set up bright nights for some days around part of the world (exciting numerous call-ins to the fire houses reporting North London was burning, incidentally).

A third hypothesis, by G.A.Nikolsky *et al.,* outlines much the same scenario, adding important features, such as a theory of high altitude explosions from electrical ignition of the braking of the comet, with its explosive ingredients.. This group calls the phenomenon a 'Vacuum Bomb' of cometary origin.

Lightning Storm Scenario

A lightning and fire-storm could be considered and called the Troy VII Scenario. By a lightning and fire-storm is meant a great number of lightning strokes delivered together or in rapid succession upon a limited territory, possibly carrying with them an abundant fallout of dusts and ashes. At Hisarlik, Turkey, Troy II, a huge bed of ashes covered the materials excavated by Schliemann, such as no ordinary incendiarism or accidental blazes could cause. Experts agreed to this, yet there was no true volcano nearby. The ashes must have been hot; metals were fused. Hisarlik was built of heavy stone. Volsinium was probably built of wood and clays for the most part, so that lightning and fire storms could reduce the ruins to a disappearing condition, especially if under water. Further along, the chapter on 'The Burning of Troy" describes a situation there as it might have applied to Volsinium, remarkably and expectably in the same century, and even perhaps in the same decade, upon a near approach of burning Ares-Mars..

If the ruins with heavy walls still standing north of Bolsena today were of the original Volsinium that was destroyed, they should show evidences of fire and scorching. Bits of metal should be found fused (2700 years of souvenir hunting may have disposed of this possibility). However, particles of iron are abundantly visible in the soils of the area, and should be tested to determine whether, as is most likely, they are a residue from volcanic fall-out, or whether they have a meteoritic source.

Probably Jovian Lightning and the fire-lightning storm would have worked together. Etched on Moon and Mars can be viewed the results of Jovian lightning, giant strikes that emulate the whole life of long-term volcanos within a few hours. In the case of Jovian bolts of high intensity, a great city could be blasted to smithereens, as by a hydrogen bomb. There is presently no set of criteria, such as has been developed in relation to meteoroid crashes, that could be applied to the Volsinium scene, but one could be put together. The full presence of Mars-Hercules on the scene, in legend and under myth analysis, warns against putting aside this hypothesis.

In wondering at the improbability that Jupiter or Mars, the planets, could really be close enough to Earth to send thunderbolts or meteoroids crashing in, we can only advise that a case can be argued for the proximity of these planets to Earth in ancient times. Solar storms travel ninety million miles to strike Earth. Jupiter now and then strikes its satellite Io with its thunderbolts, building and replenishing Io's volcanoes.

Velikovsky writes in an unpublished paper as follows (edited by Jan Sammer):

> Tacitus narrated that the catastrophe of Sodom and Gomorrah was caused by a thunderbolt – the plain was "consumed by lightning" – and he added: "Personally, I am quite prepared to grant that once-famous cities may have been burnt by fire from heaven." Also Josephus asserted that the cities had been "consumed by thunderbolts." Philo wrote that "lightnings poured out of heaven," destroying the cities.
>
> Since the time of Abraham was the period of Jupiter's domination that followed Saturn's and preceded that of Venus, we are led to the surmise that the thunderbolts which destroyed the plain with its cities originated from Jupiter, or from a magnetosphere or ionosphere overcharged by the nearby presence of the giant planet. Even today discharges leap between Jupiter and Io, one of its satellites. The charging of the Earth's atmosphere in the presence of Jupiter's huge magnetosphere prepared the way for a discharge: a planetary bolt struck the ground in the Valley of Sittim.
>
> On Earth the Hindu Jupiter, Brihaspati, "cleaves apart their cities," "their" being his enemies. A famous instance would have been the destructions of the cities of Sodom and Gomorrah, related briefly in the Hebrew Bible and referred to on occasion by ancient writers.

Specifically, Velikovsky presents the thesis defending Pliny:

> Pliny also says that a bolt from Mars fell on Bolsena, "the richest town in Tuscany," and that the city was entirely burned up by this bolt.
>
> Near Bolsena, or Volsinium, is a lake of the same name. This lake fills a basin nine miles long, seven miles wide, and 285 feet deep. For a long time this basin was regarded as the water-filled crater of a volcano. However, its area of 117 square kilometers exceeds by far that of the largest known craters on earth - those in the Andes in South America and

those in the Hawaiian (Sandwich) Islands in the Pacific. Hence, the idea that the lake is the crater of an extinct volcano has recently been questioned. *[But this source is not cited, despite its cruciality to the argument. AdeG.]* Moreover, although the bottom of the lake is of lava, and the ground around the lake abounds with ashes and lava and columns of basalt, the talus of a volcano is lacking.

Velikovsky speculates "that the agent of destruction was a bolt from Jupiter, or from the magnetosphere or ionosphere, overcharged by the nearby presence of the giant planet."

Taking what Pliny said of an interplanetary discharge together with what has actually been found at Volsinium, one may wonder whether the cinders and the lava and the columns of basalt could possibly be the remains of the contact Pliny mentions. Again, if the discharge was caused by Mars, it would probably have occurred in the 8th pre-Christian century.

A Martian Gas Cloud and Particle Storm

A holistic multi-phase scenario In the drawings I scrawled on Figures 41 and 42, there is depicted, as I noted in reading the pieces, the holistic multi-phase event that destroyed the city of Volsinium. The tentatively favored hypothesis of this writer is that a blazing bolide, weighing 100 tons, and measuring a diameter of 30 meters, with a slowed-down speed of 5 kilometers per second, dissolved into gas clouds as it neared the ground and exploded over Volsinium, raining down lightning and particles, and blowing out and up the waters of the Lake even while blowing down and out with fiery blasts the city of Bolsena and its surroundings. A giant tornado is not out of the question and in fact a tornado can be pictured, a tornado decorated throughout with strokes of lightning, swooping down, picking up and casting all about whatever on the ground is in its broad and long path.

Something of this scenario is hinted in the participation of Mars (Hercules, Nergal, et al) in the legends (and corresponding and not contradicting natural history). Mars-Hercules in legend was reputed to often deliver heaven-sent pestilence along with lightning. An islet of the

Lake is named Martana. The town at the mouth of the only stream leading from the Lake is called Marta. Not far away is the village of Massa Martana. The origins, names, deeds, and planetary connections of Hercules-Mars, which were presented in the works of Velikovsky and the present writer, have been strongly established in recent works by Cochrane, Ackerman, and Van der Sluisj. All around the world Mars-Hercules, both Planet and god-hero, were undergoing quantavolutions in the eighth and seventh centuries B..C. The oldest calendar of Rome began with the month of Mars and derived, as did the prominence of the God and Planet Mars, from the Etruscans.

Rens van der Sliujs, in his brief treatise about gods and lightning, concludes with a statement about Mars the lightning god, which we repeat here.

> Closer scrutiny of a small number of mythical motifs - thunder bird, double axe, lightning twins, thunder stone, lightning garment - has revealed a number of remarkable conclusions, which have hitherto never been acknowledged by students of ancient religion. First, it appears that traditional lightning lore is completely inconsistent with the modern-day phenomenon of lightning, however that may be explained. Second, the images share a common archetypal symbolism and often overlap each other, thus confirming their coherence and the intricate interwovenness of mythical motifs. An old verse relating to the Mayan deity Cucumatz, for instance, actually neatly summarises the archetypal reconstruction defended here:
>
> > *'In seven days he took upon himself the nature and form of a serpent, and again of an eagle, and of a tiger; and in seven days he changed himself into coagulated blood.'*

Third, all of these motifs are mirrored in the mythical biography of the Hero, who is likewise acting as a bird, appearing in twin form, hurling clubs and hammers, and decked in special garments. Often when these associations are obscure or not apparent the Hero is nevertheless associated with lightning in a direct way. *From these considerations it becomes very plain that Vahagn is a fire and lightning god, born out of the stalk in the heavenly (?) sea, with the special mission among other beneficent missions, to slay dragons.* Vahagn is the Armenian version of the dragon slayers Thra'taona and Indra. Some of the most ancient and central of these Heroes are identified with the planet Mars and it is strongly suspected that the complex of the mythical Hero as a whole may originally refer to the forms and movements of the red planet.

Although it has been shown in recent years that some of the most notable Heroes, such as Heracles, Gilgamesh and Indra, are identifiable as the planet Mars, it is unwise to designate every mythical Hero for this reason as 'Mars' as long as solid evidence for the identification with the red planet is not found.

Hercules and the Monster Volta Active at Volsinium

According to myth, Hercules arrived in Latium to achieve one of his famous labors. These were numbered as 18 in Etruria, twelve in another version. Others say that he came to rescue the nymphs Melissa and Amalthea. The consonants R and L are frequently exchanged in popular speech so that Amalthea may incorporate Mars. (The patron saint of the area is Santa Christina, possibly a stand-in. Her father, a pagan, attempted to drown her because of her Christian stubbornness, but she refused to sink and he was struck dead by lightning. We should note that Hercules was a transvestite at one period.) Further it may be as well to note at this point that when Alaric and his horde threatened Orvieto in the fifth century AD, lightning summoners from Vulsinium were despatched to block him with sheets of flame.)

Identifying the monster Mars-Volta as the bolide that descended and burst upon the Lake, we also are inclined to claim that such a burst would not only destroy the surroundings of the Lake, including Bolsena, but would also splash the water of the Lake into the sky and far away. So the water had to be replaced. Here is where Heracles the strongman hero, the earthly Mars, assumes the good-guy role and with thunderbolts fissuring the bottom of the Lake gives rise to many fresh and thermal springs that go toward filling the Lake once more.

To demonstrate to the inhabitants that he was really herculean, Heracles plunged his spear deeply into the ground, and when no one could satisfy his challenge to withdraw it, he did so himself. From the cleavage poured forth water in such abundance that Lago di Bolsena came into being. Perhaps Heracles, often given a monstrous form, was also Volta, and had exploded the waters of the lake just before bringing its waters back. Mars was, like all other gods, a good-bad guy who could undo immediately the misfortunes that he had just produced.

This mythological exchange of identities is discoverable once more, when we turn to the sacred headquarters of the Etruscan Confederation. Prof. Alberto Barzanò captured an important connection here. He described the aberrations of the Lago di Bolsena – its ups and downs, its gas and smokes, its hot and cold running water from below, its resounding booms, its fibrillations -- and he reasoned that to such behavior the collective mind would ascribe the workings of the divine. He then figured that this was behind the decision of the Etruscans to build their politico-religious capital, the *fanum voltumniae*, nearby.

He then writes: "After all, the name Voltumna would appear to be related to the same root as that of the monster, Volta, whose devastations of the Volsinium region I have earlier indicated as a possible mythic transference of seismic phenomena of minor importance." If called upon to edit such a statement, whose correctness is to be stressed, I would rather not refer to the phenomena as only seismic, but rather as quantavolutionary, and therefore not of minor, but of holistic importance.

That is, the whole of the region, including the inhabitants, derived their state of mind from these natural phenomena, and the historical and prospective disasters implied.

Weighing a collective trauma against the extent of displacement of the trauma into sacral, political, cultural, and indeed total conduct requires base lines and as many comparable instances as possible. Here the experiences of other places at the same period of time and a holistic consideration of the case would lead one to treat the founding of Voltumna as demonstrating that there already existed a heavy destruction effect on the Etruscans, that is, before the catastrophe of which we speak. Thereupon we would need to go back searching for heavy prior disasters bringing about the choice of location. We have the statement of Eusebius, to the effect that Volsinium was destroyed, presumably by divine causes, 700 years before the founding of Rome, but now we would be halted by the absence at that early date of Etruscans from the Volsinium scene entirely -- unless the Villanovans had been supplying both the disaster and the Voltumna sacred locale earlier and the Etruscans had taken it over from them.

Or would Voltumna have been actually built at a later time when Volsinium and the Etruscans were once again prospering? It would be so magnificently ordered to pacify the incumbent gods. In that case, the ruin of Voltumna would have to be shown to be a matter of later disasters or of prolonged disuse. But where was Voltumna? Alas, like Volsinium, its location is not certain, or if it is where we think it is, exploration of its foundations would be a challenging, arduous task.

With these last remarks, having presented the kind of configurative reasoning peculiar to myth analysis, we may conclude.

Conclusion: Destruction by Bolide and Lightning-Fire Shower

Much more investigation is needed if we are to confirm the statement of Pliny the Elder that the richest city of Etruria was erased by thunderbolting planet Mars. We can say that the flow of theory and evidence is moving in that direction. He did not say so, but we should wish to discover also whether the sacred Etruscan capital of Voltumna was destroyed simultaneously. Or whether Voltumna was a later creation of the Etruscans, which did not succeed in expiating offenses to the gods, or offer them a satisfactory standard of living.

Tentatively, we affirm that in the seventh century BCE, in a period of universal quantavolution, an Etruscan people around the Lake of Bolsena together with their flourishing city of Volsinium were suddenly and completely destroyed by a bolide from the position of Mars at the time, which bolide was accompanied by and finally broke up into a shower of lightning bolts and subsequent ground-level conflagration. The explosion emptied the Lake of its water within seconds, but fall-back and fissures began promptly to restore the Lake.

The disaster weakened for a century or more the Etruscan confederation, and enabled the Celts of the North and the Romans from the South to gather enough strength to displace them as the great culture and power of Italy. The area was repeopled, the Lake replenished, its flora and fauna moved or carried in from elsewhere, but the previous glorious and dominant city and its dependencies had been blasted into smithereens and in some part buried forever.

We are prepared to recognize how little we know about the conditions under quantavolutions occur. To this end, I have prepared the following budget of work that ought to be performed respecting Volsinium. The list Might be adapted to the many other destructions of other cities and lands. It will be obvious that not a single thoroughgoing research program has been carried out with regard to any ancient city.

A List of Matters for Investigation in a Further Program Concerning the Volsinium Quantavolution

A budget of about $700,000.00 (in 2002 dollars) is suggested for all phases.

1. A set of satellite maps of the Lago di Bolsena area should be purchased and perused.

2. Field trips and laboratory tests should be set up to perform all the tasks implied in the list attached hereto on the identification of an impact crater.

3. Further library research should be conducted on the collection of documents already on hand and on the

extensive bibliography that has been gathered. This would require work at multiple libraries in multiple cities.

4. Interview of 10 to 20 persons by telephone or in person to ask them a set of questions of whether they have ever considered quantavolution as a hypothesis in their Volsinium or Etruscan studies, what is their opinion of the Pliny and other statements, what do they think of the hypotheses put forward in the preliminary report of the Center for Quantavolution Studies of the University of Bergamo.

5. What studies of fossils have been made in the area of Volsinium, together with interviews of several paleontologists of the region.

6. Interview geologists who have worked in the area to whether they have come across paleosols that they have not mentioned in their reports and how do they explain the presence or absence or thinness or thickness of the paleosol presence.

7. Have any gravimetric anomalies been discovered (to be found by library research) and what might be their cause, if so? (Employ expert consultation.)

8. Have any magnetic anomalies been discovered (to be found by library research) and what might be their cause, if so? Employ expert consultation.

9. What is the nature of the "high velocity body" that Prof. Biella's group has reported, which is 12-15 K m radius, is reversed, and is possibly a piece of continental crust.

10. A search of the larger area for vitrified ruins and evidences of ancient calcination such as scorching, ashes, fusain, and charred wood is needed.

11. An expert on cosmic electricity and Lightnings should be consulted as evidence of the project develops.

12. Drillings and core examinations for the types of chemical and residues owing to impact events should be conducted, prior profiles notwithstanding.

13. Mythology should be pursued along the lines indicated by this text.

14. In all cases of field work, attention should be given to what geologists usually regard as very recent deposits, sediments, ashes, fissures, etc.

15. Have any fossil assemblages been found in the region?

16. Review the literature for recent work on migrations into Italy, 4000 to 200 B.C.A. Also review for linguistic developments relating to the Etruscan language. Continue to review the literature for mega-lightning references and other related topics.

Some comparable list could and should be prepared for every site undergoing or that has submitted to excavation around the world. Even if excavations and their accompanying legendary and literary sources were just sampled by culture or geographically, one in ten say, to begin with, we should have a much more valid and reliable portrait of the ages than is presently the case.

Chapter Fifteen

The Wolf of Rome

The story of Aeneas belongs shortly after the fall of Troy during the Iron Age of Mars. For a long time now, the founding of Rome was been accredited to truculent Latin rustics lost in the miasma of Eighth Century history. The more glorious legend of its establishment by Homeric heroes, particularly Aeneas, prince of Troy, has been in abeyance. This put the War far back in the ~-1300's. However, in the light of recent theory and newly uncovered fact, the two stories can be blended into a credible account.

To suggest the new history is my purpose here. It carries the Martian events of the East into the Central Mediterranean. It increases the likelihood that a period of over 400 years of accepted chronology around the Mediterranean world did not exist and should be stricken from the record. "The Aegean prehistorians", wrote J. Cadogan, "have no choice but to adapt themselves to the Egyptologists."[130] Until now the Roman prehistorians have felt that they, too, had to follow suit. Schoolchildren might smile with their teachers at the stern Romans' naivete in making up this fairy tale so as to give themselves a nobler ancestry.

A Founding Date of -747

Using as sources Roman and Jewish legends and traditions, pages out of Livy and Plutarch, adding bits from here and there, all of which add up to a fair probability, Velikovsky was able to describe a coherent sequence of the -700s.[131] The best guess for the Founding of Rome, -747, by Romulus develops to be the same as the beginning of a new astronomical age in the Middle East, an eccentric motion of the Sun, and an astrosphere disturbance called in Jewish history "the commotion of Uzziah." The birth year and death year of Romulus also witnessed heavy natural disturbances. Also in his time, "a plague fell upon the land, bringing sudden death without previous sickness," (we note a possible descent of gas clouds or lethal radiation), also "a rain of blood," (possibly iron-laden water), and other disasters, including seemingly interminable seismism. The Jewish legends gathered by Ginzberg[132] (VI, 280) include a statement that "The first settlers of Rome found that the houses collapsed as soon as built."

The case of Troy is helpfully instructive about the pseudo-time gap. As J. N. Sammer summed up the evidence, Troy-Hisarlik VIIb was the last Bronze Age city of the famous site. There followed a Greek town of the 7th century or later; no deposits intervened. Furthermore, there was an abundant continuity. Gray Minoan pottery was found in Troy VI, Troy VII, and the Greek Age Troy. The forms of settlement were identical in the Late Bronze Age (supposedly the 12th Century) and the -700 or later Greek settlement. A Late Bronze house was obviously used by 7th century Greeks. We shall deal further with this topic, in the next chapter.

The latest concord about Rome's foundation may be expressed in the words of F. Castagnoli:[133]

> Archaeological excavations have opened up new prospects: the considerable documentation of evidence of the Late Bronze Age (particularly in the zone involved directly with the legend such as Ardea and Lavinium) and the Mycenean imports in Southern Etruria, and between Reatino and southern Umbria, has reinvoked the thesis (for some time cast aside) of a true historical reality adumbrated in the legend; joined to this suggestion is the hypothesis that various manufactures of the oldest Latium civilization reflect Cretan models and finally the theory that the Latin language reveals Mycenean traces. In consequence, the coming of Aeneas to Latium may not be an artificially created myth, but instead, in a certain sense, a tradition, that is, the echo of real occurrences, the arrival of Aegeans in Latium during the period of the Trojan War.

This certainly does not go far enough to suit our views, but will do for a start.

At the magnificent bimillennial exposition honoring

Virgil in the beautiful setting of the Campidoglio in Rome in 1981, the heroine was the famous sculpture of the wolf of Rome, suckling Romulus and Remus. A small boy listened while his father explained: "She nursed the orphans, then they founded Rome." The wolf statue was fashioned alone in ancient times, possibly by an Etruscan master, and the twins were added only several centuries ago. The wolf of Rome and the Mars-Ares of Aeneas may not have been far apart.

Already in antiquity and possibly based upon the word of Herodotus alone, the Trojan wars had been placed in remote antiquity, the 12th and 13th centuries. When the Romans came to deal with this date, they found that their tradition of Romulus as founder of the city proper in the eighth century (753, 747, etc) was impossibly disconnected from the Trojans, who now seemed to have disappeared four centuries earlier. Thereupon at the end of the III century BCE, Q. Fabius Pictor, a Roman writing in Greek, first (to our knowledge) bridged the gap by inserting an Alban line of Kings: But a more recent quotation from him (see below) seems to contradict this reputed view. In contrast, Ennius and others connected Aeneas and Romulus directly, as grandfather and grandson.

F. Castagnoli tells us how skepticism discounted the tradition : The Trojan origin of the Latins was already put in doubt in the seventeenth century by the humanist Philipp Cluever, a rigorous critique of philological aspects begun in the middle of the Eighteenth Century (with Niebuhr, Klausen, Schwegler, etc.). Principally upon their work has been based the interpretation of legendary material accorded by most historians of ancient Rome.

It is understandable that, since the Romans had not been able to stabilize the history of their origins, the legendary part would fall prey to the new scientists who were bent upon sharpening their tools against superstition. Also presented was the theory that Greek writers had created the legend. Later on, the strong interest of the Etruscans in Aeneas was exposed. Then, after Mycenean connections had been liberally displayed in the archaeology of Italy, the notion of archaic elements corresponding to the myth grew up. More recently Latium has come under exploration, including especially Lavinium.

In the *Iliad* (302-8), the god Poseidon saves Aeneas from being killed by Achilles so as to preserve the house of Dardanus, beloved of Zeus, whose head will be Aeneas. Also, Aeneas is to become King of Troy, with many generations to follow. But Hera insists that Troy must be substituted for by another place. So went the logic behind the legend. This is more than mere dramatics. In the years when Virgil was writing the Aeneid, Properzio publicized him, announcing that he would revive the armed exploits of the Trojan Aeneas and the wall built upon the Lavinian strand. "Take yourselves back, Roman and Greek writers! There stands hidden something greater than the Iliad."

In the middle -600s, Ilioupersis of Arctinus and Miletus spoke of the secret flight of Aeneas from Troy up Mount Ida. Later the Homeric hymn to Aphrodite promises Aeneas a kingdom with a glorious future, a Troy restored. In the -500s a coin of the city Aineia on the Chalcidaean peninsula displays Aeneas in flight from Troy, whence to found this same settlement. That Aeneas went westward appears for the first time in the fragmentary record in a table of the Capitoline Museum illustrating the work of Stesichorus of the -600s. In one scene Aeneas leaves through a Trojan gate; in another, Aeneas, with his father, Anchises, son Ascanius, and companion Misenus board a ship *eis ten Hesperian,* "toward the west." Anchises carries the sacred idols.

A direct connection of Aeneas with Latium appears a century later, at the end of the -400s, with two Greek historians, Ellanicus of Lesbos and Damaster of Sigens. The story also appears of the burning of the Trojans' ship by their womenfolk, and of the naming of Rome after the Trojan heroine Roma, presumed to be ringleader of the group. The story told by Greeks (and no Roman history in Latin is known until much later) is seen in Italian perspective about 300 BCE, when the historian, Timaeus of Tauromenium, attests to sacred Trojan relics preserved in a sanctuary of Lavinium. Several decades later, the poet Licofronius, depending upon Timaeus, confirms him and details on the existence of the legendary Lavinium.

About the same time, Q. Fabius Pictor was writing

his history. A recently discovered and fragmented inscription says only this about him: "He enquired into the arrival of Hercules in Italy and the alliance of Aeneas and Latinus ... Not much later Romulus and Remus were born ." [134] Thus, contrary to his reputed view, Pictor (or Pictorinus as the inscription has it) carries Aeneas into the 700's.

The mention of Hercules is not odd. In *The Disastrous Love Affair of Moon and Mars*, I review the legendary ties between the good-man figure Hercules and the god Ares-Mars, and place the sons of Hercules, the Heraclids, as the invaders of Greece in the -700s, at Pylos, for example, where they fight against the Pylian kinsmen of the young Nestor, later famous as an old warrior of the Trojan War. Another case implicating Hercules-Mars and the Heraclids reminds us of the Roman case. It is introduced by Desborough in his book on *The Greek Dark Ages*. Temenos was one of the three Heraclid leaders who with the Dorians seized the Peloponnesus, according to the conventional Greek chronology, at the end of the -1100s (-650s our time).

> He had a grandson called Rhegnidas, who gained control of the little town of Philius; this would be not much later than the middle of the eleventh century. This event, as we are told by Pausanias, resulted in the departure to Samos of the leader of the opposition party in Philius, Hyppasos; and Hyppasos was the great-grandfather of "the famous sage Pythagoras." Pythagoras should then have been living at the end of the tenth century, and so one might think, one has an admirable Dark Age situation : until, that is to say, one discovers that Pythagoras belonged to the middle of the sixth century, a difference of no fewer than three hundred and fifty years.

The Heraclids are evidently of the -700s.

Two Thousand Years of Virgil

Again, in the superior guidebook to the *Bimillenario Virgiliano* at the Campidoglio in Rome, 22 September to 31 December 1981, we find the major leads needed to connect *"Enea nel Lazio"* to the larger Mediterranean framework of time and events. Hundreds of archaeological discoveries are displayed and all of the sites excavated until now are described. The distinguished editors and authors do not speak of a "Dark Ages" in Latium or Italy. They act nevertheless as if they existed.

Therefore we find that when all the artifacts can be grouped by centuries they concentrate into two groups, the first from the -1000s to the -1200s and the second from the -700s to the end of the Republic.

> The archaeological record of contacts between the Aegean world and Tyrrhenian Central Italy are few and difficult to interpret. Presently one treats with seven fragments of pottery and five fragment of bronze coming from the areas of Luni sul Mignon, San Giovenale, Monte Rovello, and Prediluco-Contigliano, none of them coastal. It is almost impossible to assign them precise form and the decoration is too generic to permit all but the broadest dating.[135]

Not only is there an absence of imported articles over the centuries between the supposed time of Aeneas and the time of the founding of Rome, but indigenous discoveries of the period are also rare (and, we argue, perforce non-existent). Hundreds of dates and artifacts mark the Bimillennial Exposition. Perhaps only a dozen are slipped into the period between the 11th and 8th centuries. The earlier objects and dates are of Italian provenance; the later ones are heavily Greek. The earlier period carries Central Italy into late Bronze and the beginnings of the Iron Age. The cultural uniformity of southern Etruria and Latium is called total already at this -1000s [-600s] boundary. Iron tools of Aeneas are attested to. Then, following the "Dark Ages", there occurs an outburst of production and trade.

> The kings and cities of Virgil become historical realities only when figured in the early Bronze Age: it is on the other hand certain that their origins need be sought in that crucial period, the Late Bronze age.[136]

Peroni's Problem with the Old Early Date

The arrival of "Aegean" people in the 13th Century, writes one authority, Renato Peroni, should have inaugurated a process of elements deriving from various fields of human activity, beginning with the material culture.

> Yet of all this, in the archaeological sources related to the period of Latium that interests us, there is no trace. It is hard to imagine a cultural

continuity, in ceramics for instance, greater than that which is presented during these centuries.[137]

Peroni, after expressing grave doubt that one could have an invasion and occupation without cultural impact, though that is what archaeology seems to reveal, repeats that in the 13th to 11th Centuries (and significantly for our argument he terms the 11th "less developed") "the cultural uniformity of southern Etruria and old Latium appears to be total."

What else can he say, so long as he believes the long chronology inherited from the Egyptologists: "The literary sources and archaeological evidence permit us to assign the destruction of Homeric Troy to the twelfth century [our -700's]. The Latium of the 'saga' of Aeneas is therefore of the period contained between the Middle Age of Bronze (XVI -XIV Century B. C.) [our -1200 to -800] and the first phase of Latin civilization (X Century)[-500s]."[138] Not so, we say: Bring down the Bronze Age dates to the tenth century or later.

He goes on to survey the town sites occupied in the Late Bronze Age, and finds a continuity of occupation going into the age of iron, such as Ardea, Ficana, Pratica di Mare, and Acqua Acetosa Laurentina. This in itself is remarkable, considering the lapsed centuries and the absence of cultural remains of the long period of time. He must be mistaken.

Also remarkable is the evidence, disclosed by us in the last chapter, that between the end of the Bronze Age and the beginning of the Iron Age the number of inhabited places of Etruria dropped by four fifths.[139] At the same time, the underpopulated regions of Latium and Sabina held their own and increased slightly their settlements.[140]

The Latins were beginning to accrete settlements. This scenario of Peroni suits exactly our theory of a period of natural catastrophes and survivors occurring in the -700s. One age disappears into another without evidence of transition. As in Greece the culture reverts to survivorship; strife is rampant. The Trojans arrive amidst a general desolation and disorganization, gain a foothold without difficulty, even welcomed in a way, and begin to expand and to found new towns, among them Rome. In Southern Italy and Sicily a similar set of events is occurring, as we shall see.

Aeneas Lands at Sol Indiges and Names it Troy

Virgil has Aeneas landing in Latium, at the mouth of the Numicus river (Sol Indiges, Troia, and by today's name Fosso di Pratica). The hero, desperate to feed his men, chases an animal for a distance of 24 stadi (4440 meters) and comes upon a herd of pigs on a hill. He sacrifices them there and founds the town of Lavinium. The names and distances between the two given by Virgil are exact today.[141]

Titus Livius remarks on the name, Troy, given to the place of landing. The Trojan altars were said to be still there at the end of the pagan era, by Pliny the Elder and Dionysius of Halicarnassus, the historian. At Lavinium, named for Aeneas' wife, Dionysius visited in the First Century B.C.E. There he witnessed relics, supposedly of Aeneas, held in a sanctuary and tomb dedicated to the Trojan hero. The preservation of the relics and the identification of the tomb might well have been impossible if they had originated in the 12th century; it is more plausible that they had lasted from the 7th or at least until the time of Timaeus of Tauromenum about 300 B.C.E., who saw them.

Recently, the "tomb of Aeneas" has been uncovered and placed in the 7th century, with remodeling into a shrine occurring in the 4th century.[142] Dionysius describes a round temple at Lavinium that housed the idols of the Trojans, which seems to have been emulated in the round temple of Vesta and the Penati of the Roman Forum. The small Lavinium temple is replicated on a coin of the Emperor Antonius Pius.

Aeneas probably rested in several places on his way to Latium, in Asia Minor, Macedonia, Crete, Carthage, and Sicily. Apollo's oracle at Delos told him to seek the land of his ancestors, and this was taken by his father, Anchises, to mean Crete. The refugees did go there, finding a desolate and abandoned settlement. They began to settle down, but were beset (significantly) by a natural disaster that made further consultation with Apollo necessary.

Luckily, a second trip to Delos was not required

because voices authorized by Apollo urged them to find the true place of their origins, and they set sail for the West.[143] Anchises could not remember Italy, hence had not been born there, but recalled that certain ancestors had come from there, Dardanus and Iasius, and had been Olustrians or Italians.

The Trojans Stop at Carthage

On the way to Italy, they stop at Carthage, which is, says Virgil, still under construction by Queen Dido, who has fled with her supporters from a berserk brother who ruled Phoenicia. Here we encounter a chronological problem; to be sure, it is not a matter of centuries, but of a generation. Dido is best placed at -804 or -803, before the dates which we accept for the Trojan War(s), which may have occurred over most of a century, at which time Aeneas would most likely have left Troy. Moreover, the dates assigned traditionally to Romulus, a grandson of Aeneas, are -772 (-771) to-717, and to the founding of Rome -747 or thereabout. Either Aeneas left upon an earlier sack of the city, or someone related to Aeneas and therefore confused with him visited Dido.

The stop itself was not unexpected. There appears to be a non-Greek connection that binds in alliance the Trojans and their Thracian and Anatolian friends, the Carthaginians, and the Etruscans. Etruria, said Herodotus, was settled by Anatolian Lydians before the Trojan War.[144] But who might have visited Carthage and could be mistaken for Aeneas? Philistos and Appios clearly give 50 years before the Trojan War as the date when Carthage was founded. Timaeus gives -814 and Josephus independently gives -826. Yet Carthage's earliest archaeological remains afford specimens of Greek material ascribed to the last quarter of the 8th century, presumably -725 to -700.

Were the Phoenician and Trojan refugees in motion a century apart? Not according to Virgil, obviously, who describes a passionate love affair between Aeneas and Dido. And not according to the traditional dates for Romulus and the founding of Rome. If Aeneas abandoned Dido at the turn of the century, he could have grand-fathered Romulus at the appropriate moment, about -772.

Arie Dirkswager, in an unpublished manuscript lent the author, offers a solution. He suggests that the king of Tros who founded Troy then moved to Italy where he founded Etruria and gave the Etruscans his name, about -815. It was he who knew Dido! Then later, the refugee party led by Aeneas would join its kinsmen about 747 B. C., when Troy burned.

Did Aeneas Quit Troy Early?

However, although we also view the Etruscans and Trojans as related, we see a later date for the Trojan wars finally to end, and one has to place Romulus and the founding of Rome into the very end of the 7th century.

We are perplexed now and have exhausted our meager supply of information. The most plausible suggestion I can afford is that the Trojan Wars were several until the city's final destruction (and we cannot confirm the site of Hisarlik -Schliemann's discovery as more than a frontier post in the struggles). Given the practices of those times, an age of colonization and restless wanderings having begun, Aeneas, Prince of Troy, led his party of refugees out at an early stage of the wars (which Homer combined into one for literary effect and from amnesiac causes), did visit Dido at the turn of the century, and so history picks up with Romulus and the founding of Rome in the middle of the next century.

We are introducing one doubt in order to relieve ourselves of several. And we should be grateful if some scholar would carry down the whole scenario by another century to place it squarely in the catastrophic 8th and 7th centuries. We have relieved ourselves of several notions: that Virgil was only glorifying Rome by mythmaking; that the "Dark Ages" existed in Italy between -1200 and -700; that Aeneas and Troy were of the 12th century; that Aeneas and Romulus were fictional characters; that were was no significance to Mars and the Wolf of Rome; that the Etruscans were long settled in Italy and were a natural and continual foe of the new Latins; that the Romans were a simple farm folk who took well to fighting; and that in the

8th century natural conditions were normally benign.

We understand better how and why the exasperating gap between Aeneas and Romulus was created: the need to integrate chronology of diverse cultures by basing it upon what was believed to be the nearly perfect chronology, the Egyptian; the scholarly skepticism of all legend until recently, especially when wolves and feral infants are tied to the mythical package, not to mention the hallucinogenic pantheon; the seeming circular confirmation of Etruscan-Greek-Roman interrelations; the ignorance and neglect of great natural disasters, such as Aeneas encountered in Crete; alternative explanations of the Dark Ages such as long-drawn-out climatic changes, restless northern tribesman, and normal decay of civilizations; the injection of artifacts and personages falsely into the gap of time; and the vanity of Roman noble families who had attached themselves genetically to the fictitious personae of the noble line of Alba Longa extending back to Lavinium, including even the Caesars. We surmise, by way of contrast to the conventional paradigm, that Aeneas was a Trojan noble, active around -800. He left a beleaguered Troy in an early stage of successive sieges, founded settlements in several places, eventually in Latium, near Etruscan relatives, and among a disastrously weakened native population.

A prompt acculturation and cultural homogenizing began, catalyzed by the disorganizing effects of a turbulent nature. His daughter Elia mothered Romulus (and one fantasizes that his godmother was Roma who led the female party which burned the Trojan ships to prevent further wanderings). The heavens were producing some of the disasters, and the planet Mars was connected with them to the point that the god could be the godfather to Romulus who eventually joined him in a cyclonic episode.

Romulus, wrote St. Augustine, was of the time of King Hezekiah of Judah, whose Jewish sources coincide with the Roman, particularly Ovid, who, in his *Fasti*, declares: "Both of the poles shook. Atlas lifted the burden of the sky...The sun vanished and rising clouds obscured the heavens...the sky was riven by shooting flames. The people fled and their King, Romulus, mounted upon his Father's (Mars') steeds soared to the stars."

The Bronze Age lurches abruptly into the Iron age in Latium.

Chapter Sixteen

The Burning of Troy

Scientists probing the subsoil in their attempts to build up the record of prehistoric and ancient humanity have paid little attention to ashes and other evidences of high heat and conflagration that they have encountered. We would agree with Claude F. A. Schaeffer who wrote in 1948 that "Our inquiry has often been made difficult by the rarity in most reports of observations on beds of destruction ... some reporters have regarded these beds as a nuisance or of little interest."[145] This sentence inspired the investigation reported in this chapter.

The chapter is not so much about the quantavolution of Mars, as it is about an earlier quantavolution, possibly of 2200 B.C.E., that struck at the end of the Early Bronze Age, which might be what I have called in several books the 'Age of Mercury,' or Thoth. The event and its explanation parallel the subsequent destruction of Troy-Hisarlik that occurred in the Late Bronze - Iron Age transition. We use it to bolster the case for developing a science of calcinology that is applicable to all ages.

Still, the last part of this chapter will summarize the Troy evidence for the Martian quantavolution, in order to elucidate its parallelism with more ancient quantavolutions, then to adjoin Troy-Hisarlik to the great many destruction sites of the Martian times.

One of the first matters to note is that the level of destruction called IIg at Hisarlik (the present village at the site generally believed to be Troy of the Iliad and Homer) was for a long time believed to be the level that contained and ended the Trojan War. It was and is dated at ~-2200. But after a century or so, the Blegen expedition renumbered the levels and relocated the site of the Trojan War at what became Level VI and this Late Bronze Age 'Troy' was dated at around -1300. However, this date is subject to our revised calendar and becomes some 20 years around ~-700 B.C.E..

The recent excavation of settlements of Minoan times, buried beneath or affected by the tephra of the exploded volcano of ancient Thera-Santorini, did possess the broader perspective that Schaeffer sought. Spiridon Marinatos and others introduced research on the far-flung effects of the disaster. Heezen and Ninkovich discovered a layer of ash on the south-eastern floor of the Mediterranean Sea that they could ascribe to the Santorini explosion. Charles and Dorothy Vitaliano followed up with analyses of tephra from scattered locations on Crete and elsewhere.[146] The search and testing are continuing.

Still, the Thera case is exceptional, and even yet far from complete. The ash coverings of settlements and their hinterlands have rarely been analyzed. We speak of overall calcination, and not so much of the bones of hearths that have lent evidence of the ecology, cuisine, and religious ceremonies of early human groups. Overall calcination has sometimes, with less than complete evidence, been interpreted as the work of torch-bearing invaders. For example, James Melaart uses the convenient phrase "Whether by accident or by enemy action" to describe the destructive combustion of Troy IIg.[147]

Earthquakes, too, are invoked with some frequency, although a determination that a fire is an effect of an earthquake is by no means simple. On rare occasions, where there exists a historical record such as Pliny the Younger's description of the eruption of Vesuvius in 79 A. D., volcanism is admitted and may lead ultimately to excavation. There are still other possible causes, as we shall see. The contention here is that reports of past excavations should now be reviewed with a revised set of questions. Moreover, and because of the ultimate inadequacy of the information typically contained in them, it is suggested that a new interdisciplinary calcinology be devised and carried into future excavations and the testing of soils and debris generally. The rich experience afforded by the excavations of Troy can serve to expose the problems that justify a new approach. Afterwards, we can define in a preliminary way the body of techniques that needs to be assembled and developed.

The Burnt City of Troy

In some exciting passages, which have unquestionably been among the most widely read of all archaeological writing, Schliemann describes how, in May of 1873, he uncovered "The treasure of Priam," King of Troy during the war between the Greeks and Trojans. (Neither his identification of the Treasure as Priam's nor of the City as the Troy of Homer is at issue here, and therefore these problems are passed over lightly. His Troy of Homer was much later labeled as Troy Level VIIg and given a date of around 2200 BCE,)

Schliemann reports[148] that the "Trojans of whom Homer sings" occupied a stratum of debris "from 7 to 10 meters, or 23 to 33 feet, below the surface. This Trojan stratum, which, without exception, bears marks of great heat, consists mainly of red ashes of wood, which rise from 5 to 10 feet above the Great Tower of Ilium, and the great enclosing Wall, the construction of which Homer ascribes to Poseidon and Apollo; and they show that the town was destroyed by a fearful conflagration." He calls this ruined level "the Burnt City," and others have used his phrase since then.

The large slabs of stone leading down to the plain from "The Scaean Gate" for 10 feet were so weakened by heat that they crumbled upon exposure, though farther on the slabs continued hard and intact. "A further proof of the terrible catastrophe is furnished by a stratum of scoriae of melted lead and copper, from 1/ 5 to 1 1/ 5 inches thick, which extends through the whole hill at a depth of from 28 to 29 1/ 2 feet. "Several visiting geologists and a construction engineer gave this opinion, and all concluded that large deposits of these existed at the time of the city's destruction.

Schliemann continues: "That Troy was destroyed by enemies after a bloody war is further attested by the many human bones which I found in these heaps of debris, and above all by the skeletons with helmets, found in the depths of the temple of Athena; for, as we know from Homer, all corpses were burnt and the ashes were preserved in urns. Of such urns I have found an immense number in all pre-Hellenic strata on the hill."

Discovery of the Treasure of Priam

Then he says: "Lastly, the Treasure, which some member of the royal family had probably endeavored to save during the destruction of the city, but was forced to abandon, leaves no doubt that the city was destroyed by the hands of enemies. I found this Treasure on the large enclosing wall by the side of the royal palace, at a depth of 27 1/ 2 feet, and covered with red Trojan ashes from 5 to 6 1/ 2 feet in depth, above which was a post-Trojan wall or fortification 19 1/ 2 feet high."

Schliemann spotted the Treasure through a protruding copper article. "On the top of this copper article lay a stratum of red and calcined ruins, from 4 3/ 4 to 5 1/ 4 feet thick, as hard as stone, and above this again lay the above-mentioned wall of fortification (6 feet broad and 20 feet high) which was built of large stones and earth, and must have belonged to an early date after the destruction of Troy." With his knife, he first withdrew this small copper shield, then a copper caldron with handles, then a copper plate to which a silver vase "had been fused ... in the heat of the fire".[149] Next came a copper vase, a bottle of gold, a cap of gold and then other vessels of pure and alloyed metals, wrought of cast-copper, silver, gold, electrum. There were useful objects, ceremonial objects, and daggers, battle-axes, and lance-heads. Various weapons had "pieces of other weapons welded onto them by fire."

"As I found all these articles together, forming a rectangular mass, or packed into one another, it seems to be certain that they were placed on the city wall in a wooden chest ... such as those mentioned by Homer as being in the palace of King Priam. This appears to be the more certain, as close by the side of these articles I found a copper key about 4 inches long, the head of which resembles a large safe-key of a bank. Curiously enough this key has had a wooden handle; there can be not doubt of this from the fact that the end of the stalk of the key is bent round at a right angle, as in the case of the daggers."

Schliemann conjectures on the scene:

> It is probable that some member of the family of King Priam hurriedly packed the Treasure into the chest and carried it off without having time to put out the key; that when he reached the wall, however, the hand of an enemy or the fire overtook him, and he was obliged to abandon the chest, which was immediately covered to a height of from 5 to 6 feet with the red ashes and the stones of the adjoining royal palace...[150] That the Treasure was packed together at terrible risk of life, and in the greatest anxiety, is proved among other things also by the contents of the largest silver vase, at the bottom of which I found two splendid gold diadems..., a fillet, and four beautiful gold ear-rings of most exquisite workmanship: upon these lay 56 gold ear-rings of exceedingly curious form and 8,750 small gold rings, perforated prisms and dice, gold buttons, and similar jewels, which obviously belonged to other ornaments; them followed six gold bracelets, and on the top of all two small gold goblets.[151]

Finally, Schliemann adds,

> The person who endeavored to save the Treasure had fortunately the presence of mind to stand the silver vase, containing the valuable articles described above, upright in the chest, so that not so much as a bead could fall out, and everything has been preserved uninjured.[152]

Schliemann says that death was risked in hastily retrieving the Treasure. Like many another digger, he was preoccupied with artifacts and architecture. And indeed there seemed to be nothing in the literature than a Greek-set fire. Furthermore, he was already reading the ancient story of the burning of Troy into his findings. He "knew" what he would find. So did the world of readers.

But there are puzzling aspects to his account. First of all, there is the immensity of the blaze. Can the burning of a stone and wood town of 5,000 or so inhabitants produce a bed of ashes that may have amounted to 15 to 20 feet on its first fall? For we read that it was reduced to several feet of thickness and was so hard that a huge stone wall nearly 20 feet tall could be built on top of it afterwards. And the whole area was so completely buried that the walls of the subsequent settlement were planned and built-in complete ignorance of the orientation of the walls and passageways below.

"The more recent walls run in all directions above the more ancient ones, never standing upon them, and are frequently separated from them by a layer of calcined debris, from 6 1/2 to 10 feet high."[153] The depth of the ashes is all the more impressive when it is observed that they formed on top of a wall. Then or afterwards, some part of the ashes would fall aerified or be blown off the top of a wall. And why would the bearers of such a Treasure, if they had even half a minute of time, leave the Treasure on top of a wall when they might at least have tipped it over onto the ground, and then fled? The ashes are spoken of as "red Trojan ashes," "ashes and stones" that buried the city, "mainly red ashes of wood." How thick a layer of ashes does a hand-burnt ancient city dissolve into? What kinds of heat would have been generated on the average outside and within houses? The answers are not now known, but might well be discovered.

Craig C. Chandler writes that he has "never seen 'red ashes of wood' unnatural fires, and the term sounds much more like a distillation residue than a combustion residue".[154] With the suggestion of a distillation, the remote possibility of an early invention of "Greek Fire" intrudes. This presently unknown, highly volatile and intense weapon was possibly of petroleum plus an accelerant, and was used by the Byzantines against their enemies for centuries. But this was more than two millennia later. Further,"Greek Fire" would not account for the huge amount of ashes.

A completely wooden and overstuffed contemporary house will leave no more than ankle-deep ashes when it burns to the ground, and then only on its own foundation. A flourishing natural forest and the ground cover is estimated to provide 200 tons organic matter per acre.[155] When reduced fully by heat, it will give up 160 tons of water, gases and other compounds to leave 20 tons of carbon residue and 20 tons of oily distillates. Further reduced to fine cinder and ash, it would weigh less and have less volume. If spread over an acre, the residue would amount to perhaps a pound per square foot; its height could scarcely measure 6 inches in its freshly fallen state.

Chandler has pointed out that forest fires of the greatest intensity do not consume more than a fraction of the living material, producing perhaps 3tons per acre of ashes. "This is an amount about 10 times as great as the fertilizer you spread on your lawn in the spring ... Ash residue from the burning of a city is measured in inches, rather than feet."[156] And we seem to be faced at Troy by perhaps 15 feet, or 30 times as much ash, even allowing for no wind to blow the cloud of city ashes off the citadel onto the plain and for no drift off the top of the city wall.

The Puzzle of the Scorched Treasure

But, to proceed, if the city were under tight siege, would not the Treasure have been carefully packed and readied for any emergency? Would it not perhaps have been buried in a safe place or carried off to a friendly town? Schliemann assumes that a Trojan custodian was transporting the box. He discovered what appeared to be a copper handle. Would not at least two persons have carried it? It was heavy. Moreover, several guards and priests would have been assigned to accompany the porters on their urgent mission. The key to the box was found, but it may have been placed inside the box; its presence does indicate haste, or else it would have been kept by a keeper of the keys or by the chief of the little group of movers and would have vanished with him. If the "Greeks" were in hot pursuit, as Schliemann implies, would they not have caught up with the Treasure and carted it off? It would have been laid down by its porters, who would have fled for their lives.

Would the "Greek"warriors have set such a blaze that they were frustrated in one of their primary objectives in capturing the city, to loot it of its valuables? Conquerors try not to burn a city before they loot it. Other treasures and valuables were located by Schliemann. Apparently the "invaders" were in some part, at least, frustrated in one of their most enjoyable missions by conflagration. We might assume that other treasures were indeed found and carried away. Their neglect of the deposits of lead and copper, an unconscionable dereliction, is puzzling; lead and copper supposedly ran in streams over the city grounds.

Schliemann found no bones or warrior's equipment at the site of the Treasure save for a small copper shield, which may have been in or on the chest. Indications are, unless his search was incomplete, that the porters separated themselves physically from the Treasure in a great hurry and that the "pursuers" were blocked from reaching it. Unlike the ashes with which Vesuvius buried ancient Pompeiians and from which Fiorelli in 1863 ingeniously extricated their images by injections of liquid plaster, the ashes of Troy were apparently hot. They fused and welded exposed metal objects. The wood chest had disappeared. Any humans would have been incinerated and would have disappeared like the box, but they would at least have left their buckles and arms, and possibly teeth or long bones.

Why did the porters try to go over the wall, instead of through the gate? Schliemann suggests that the "Greeks" commanded the gates. Possibly. But now we wonder whether, in fact, there were any Greek invaders climbing out of their famous Wooden Horse and reinforced by their returned comrades. For Schliemann does not find typically "Greek" (Achaean) utensils or weapons; therefore the conflagration could not come sometime after the foreigners had occupied the city and mingled their artifacts with those of the Trojans. Also, we should be inclined to deny that any invaders of any type were present. We are aware that contemporary scholarship assigns Schliemann's Troy to a period long before the "real" Trojan War. It is now called Troy II and Troy VIIa is the "real Troy," in one leading opinion.[157]

A Catastrophe Without Warning

A half century after Schliemann's work, a University of Cincinnati expedition returned to the site of Hisarlik. They explored painstakingly the area, employing the best archaeological techniques that the state of the art and the typically modest funding could provide. Apart from their extensive work on the other levels, the Cincinnati archaeologists, under the leadership of Carl Blegen, examined closely the ruins of the Burnt City - Level IIg by their code.

The debris over the whole site is deep, yet less deep than the debris atop Schliemann's Wall. The stratum of Troy IIg had an average thickness of more than 1 m(meter); it consisted mainly of ashes, charred matter, and burned debris. This deposit apparently extended uniformly over the great megaron and across the entire site, eloquent evidence that the settlement perished in a vast conflagration from which no buildings escaped ruin. This is the 'Burnt City' of Schliemann ... In all areas examined by the Cincinnati Expedition, it was obvious that the catastrophe struck suddenly, without warning, giving the inhabitants little or no time to collect and save their most treasured belongings before they fled. All the houses exposed were still found to contain the fire-scarred wreckage of their furnishings, equipment, and stores of supplies. Almost every building yielded scattered bits of gold ornaments and jewelry, no doubt hastily abandoned in panic flight. Most of the famous 'treasure' recovered by Schliemann may now be safely attributed to Troy IIg..."[158]

Thus writes Blegen (1963) and the evidence behind his words stacks up in several large printed volumes and a considerable archive. Blegen continues, seeking to explain the destruction: Whether the disaster was brought about by enemy action or by accident cannot be certainly stated, though there are considerations that point to each of these alternatives. If the city had been captured and razed by conquerors, some of the luckless inhabitants would surely have fallen victims to the attack, and an excavator might expect to find in the ruins remains of human skeletons. So far as is ascertainable in the archaeological records, we have actually only one instance in which a fragment of a small adult skull was definitely found in the stratum of Phase IIg. Schliemann mentions the skeletons of "two warriors" with bronze helmets, found in the burnt layer; but the stratigraphic position is not certified, and the helmets later turned out to be fragments of a bronze vessel. One might therefore conclude that the occupants of the town escaped. On the other hand, if an invading army took the city it would surely have thoroughly looted the houses before putting them to the torch; and few if any 'treasures' of gold and silver would have been left for archaeologists to recover. But again a counter-argument might hold that if all or most of the citizens had run away to safety, they would surely have returned sooner or later to recover the treasures they had left behind. Their failure to do so can only be accounted for by assuming that some powerful deterrent prevented their returning. What actually happened to bring about the burning of the whole establishment is still an unsolved mystery, but it is a fact that Troy II was totally destroyed."[159]

A Natural Force Helped to devastate Hisarlik-Troy

The mystery remains, and the range of speculation is both limited and expanded. We are compelled to put aside the Schliemann reconstruction as a rather complete fictional tale. In doing so, we are led to the alternative that some huge natural force ruined Schliemann's Troy. Enemy forces had not shown a gradual "intent" to destroy Troy, else the Treasure would have been packed and readied for transport. The disaster did not begin by slow degrees, else it would have permitted exit by the main gate. Or perhaps, to avoid panic or disorder, the Treasure was being sneaked out of town. Might it have been an earthquake followed by fire? There are few indications of fallen stones. It would not have been these that prevented the Treasure from being carried out the Gate of the city.

Although the scene that we are reconstructing was not created by a great earthquake, a mild earthquake may have occurred. If it did, it had not prompted the government to abandon the town up to this last moment of disaster. Valuable objects were strewn on the floors of numerous homes. The evidence from "the depths of the Temple of Athena," where bones and skeletons were found, is ambiguous: people, sensing an earthquake, flee from the crashing roofs and walls of their structures. A large quantity of bones was found in the debris of, and next to, adjoining apartments.[160] Were these people trapped and buried by the quake? Possibly. Or did they die of heat or suffocation and were their bones preserved freakishly while most bodies were quickly consumed by intense heat?

The main event may have been a sudden fall of ashes that began as a light warm shower and then developed into a heavy downpour of hot material. The fall would have incinerated all organic material except those people, plants and animals that were already in deep refuge where they suffocated and were later buried. It would have melted all exposed supplies of metal and partially exposed metal parts. Within a space of hours the city would have been covered and its life ended.

There would have been no survivors or enemy awaiting outside to reoccupy the destroyed city, excavate it, collect its treasures, enjoy its strategic location,[161] and carry on or provide a substitute for its culture. If there were, they would have been blasted, drowned in ashes or suffocated by gases while the city disappeared before their eyes. The destroyed setting does not support a firestorm, such as incendiary bombs, dropped en masse from airplanes, inflicted upon the cities of Dresden and Hamburg in World War II. There the ash levels were insignificant, because "firestorm winds scour the burned area clean."[162]

The setting suggests the action of Vesuvius in burying Pompeii and Herculaneum, the one in falling cinders and ashes, the other in towering lava flows. It was the falling ash and gases of Vesuvius that buried and suffocated the people whose images were recovered seventeen hundred years later. Some had chosen not to flee and took refuge in their houses; others could not flee; still others were drowned in ashes while in flight. Pliny the Elder was gassed to death as he stood, miles away, directing a rescue operation.

The destruction wrought by the explosions and collapse of the islet of Krakatoa off Java in 1883 was done largely by tidal waves.[163] Although many persons were burned severely and succumbed to exhaustion in the hot ash-laden and gas-polluted air, the fall of ashes was not great enough to bury houses. The fallout colors are not well-described; at least white, gray, black, brown, green, and red material was mentioned.

Examining the territory around Troy (modern Hisarlik), we find no active or extinct volcanoes.[164] Mount Ida, famous in Homer, is 30 miles to the southwest of Hisarlik. It is not reported as an active or extinct volcano. At 30 miles of distance, in order to have caused an ash-rain that would bury Troy, it would have had to explode in successive bursts of fury, exceeding the Krakatoan and Vesuvian (79 A. D.) disasters.

The Thera-Santorini explosion of late Minoan

culture occurred hundreds of miles away in the South Aegean Sea, and is not synchronized.[165] In any event, although it might have generated waves capable of battering the coastline of northwest Asia Minor, its ash-fall would probably not have reached so far and so heavily. Ninkovich and Heezen seem to have found that the overwhelming fallout of Thera ash occurred in the Southeastern Mediterranean Sea. Yet geologists might consider whether internal earth stresses could have induced not only the familiar cone volcanoes but also fissure eruptions, which, no matter how voluminously eruptive, leave little evidence for the unsuspecting eye once they have become extinct. A geologist might then search for some scars and volcanic products on the modern landscape.

It is well to remind ourselves that Homer, in describing at least one Trojan war, has Mt. Ida behaving in peculiar ways when the gods of heaven enter the battle of Greeks and Trojans: "From high above the father of gods and men made thunder terribly, while Poseidon from deep under them shuddered all the illimitable earth, the sheer heads of mountains. And all the feet of Ida with her many waters were shaken and all her crests, and the city of Troy, the ships of the Achaians."[166] The underworld god shrieked in terror and leapt from his throne at the prospect that "Poseidon might break the earth open." And Hera laid such a dense fog upon the battlefield that none could see to engage.

There was a veritable fire over the whole scene that "first was kindled on the plain" and parched it and burned the dead warriors, then turned to the river, boiling it and its tributaries. Hera, wife of Zeus, ordered up tempests from seaward to fan the flames, which another sky-god and also volcano god, Hephaistos (Vulcan), had started. All of this bespeaks volcanism with accompanying earthquakes, and possibly fissure volcanism too.

Here again, we should remind ourselves that a) the site of the "real Troy" may not be the Hisarlik site, b) there may have been several wars over the site through the ages, c) the war of which Homer sang was possibly an image of several partially idealized wars, and d) the final Homeric war probably occurred, if Velikovsky's reconstruction is followed (which eliminates the Greek Dark Age), in the late eighth and early seventh centuries. Troy IIg therefore existed at an earlier time, and we are quoting here passages regarding the landscape, nature forces, and effects of a later age or composite of ages. The date of destruction of the "Burnt City" is not at issue here.

The ancients were adamant concerning the activities of the great sky gods. Hence a look into the skies for the cause of the burial of Schliemann's Troy is not unreasonable. But will it be only for the effects of remote volcanism? An anomalous detail demands attention: Schliemann mentions that the stones of the road out of the gate had been heated to the point of disintegration but, a few feet further out, the stones continued in good condition.

The natural force seems here to have been selective, destroying by heat the crown of the hill, but sparing at least this part of the plain around. Alternatively the outer stones may have been relaid at a later period, or the first fires may have consumed the city premises alone, with the ash-fall coming later. Or again, at the Vitaliano's suggestion, shoulder return to an attacking force that heaped fires before the wooden gate to force an entrance; too, they may have hurled or shot many fiery brands at the gate.

The total context is indeed important to bear in mind, whatever its complexity. Lightning can be hot and selective and may focus upon elevations. Ancient lightning and fire have received little attention from archaeologists and geologists. E. V. Komarek, Sr. writes, "I believe that the reason we have so little information on ancient fire scars or lightning streaks is that apparently no one has searched for them."[167]

Seneca, the Roman author, has a character in Thyestes begging Jupiter to bring disaster upon Earth "not with the hands that seek out houses and undeserving homes, using your lesser bolts, but with that hand by which the threefold mass of mountains fell ... These arms let loose and hurl your fires.[168] Could there have been a qualitatively different kind of Jovian thunderbolt playing about the world in mythical and prehistoric times? A ramified bolt of hundreds of strokes is not impossible to imagine. The myriad lightning and fire effects in the Krakatoa disaster are worth recalling, but these occurred within a radius of a few kilometers.[169] The mysterious melted copper and lead, alluded to above, which covered a large area, according to Schliemann, might have originally been deposits that contributed to the attractiveness of the site for lightning discharges. They form a "stratum of scoriae, which runs through the greater part of the hill, at an average depth of 9 meters(29 1/ 2 feet)."

Were they stored by the Trojans, or were they "welded scoriae (Schweisschlacken)" of volcanoes; that is, fragments carried up by the powerful blast of expanding gases, ejected in a molten state, and solidifying after falling with a smacking sound back to the ground? --"upon impact, they are squashed out flat, and are welded together where they fall."[170] Volcanoes are not known to eject such scoriae to any considerable distance.

Still another possibility needs to be added: a meteoric fall or shower, Homer's "divine-kindled fire of stones." If a large meteor had passed nearby without crashing, its immense heat would have consumed and raised into the sky the ashes of countless trees and the dust of exploded and cyclonist fields. But the people appear to have had warning, however brief. A veritable deluge of meteoric particles from outer space, as from a large comet's tail, might produce and contribute to combustion and burial. A cometary or planetary near-encounter, and resulting fall of gases, hydrocarbons, burning pitch, and stones, of course, is Velikovsky's "first cause." Even metals (again the layer of copper and lead) have been reputed to fall.

Such events are unknown to modern experience but are indicated by ancient legends from many places,[171] and by various geological and biological phenomena.[172] We cannot ignore the Biblical sources that speak of "fire and brimstone(sulphur)" such as that which wiped out "the cities of the plain." The Cincinnati team writes in several places of the greenish-yellow discoloration characteristically found in the debris of streets and other once open areas.[173] Was this brimstone?

The clays are curious. Area 210 of the city shows much disintegrated clay and debris, plus pots, but no signs of burning. A house of Square A3-4 is in ruins "covered by a mass of clay more than 0.50 meters thick, which has turned red from the effects of internal heat."[174] The roofs were of clay and wood, but the depth is remarkable and so is the color. Is there more than one kind of clay in the ruins? Is this the same "red" that Schliemann reports as "the red ashes of Trojan wood?" For that matter, is it part of the omnipresent red dust that Velikovsky pursues through early references from numerous cultures in connection with the planet Venus?[175]

At this stage of research, one craves evidence that the rude Achaeans were quite stupid but were geniuses at setting great fires from above. Or that all excavators exaggerated in their reports. Barring these explanations, the evidence speaks, or rather, whispers faintly, on behalf of a regional multiple volcanic explosion of gases, hot scoriae and ashes, some element of which rained down suddenly and heavily upon Troy, burning, burying, and baking.

The Treasure of Priam would be buried atop the wall where it had been placed as its bearers cast a final despairing glance upon the abysmal world on all sides. One should be warned, however, that a theory of concurrent regional plinian eruptions would call up a search for causes of a more fundamental kind. Volcanism on a grand scale is another word for general catastrophe: What force can roil up the mantle and wrench around so much of the crust of the Earth at a single moment of time?

A New Interdisciplinary Method

The mystery of the "Burnt City" of Troy will soon be a century old, but its solution may be within grasp. It can now be reviewed in light of substantial advances in empirical technique and general additional and spectacular theories. Similar phenomena are reported for Etruria (Tuscany), Mesoamerica and elsewhere and might someday be synchronized.[176] At the time of Troy IIg, reports the *Cambridge Ancient History* (I: 2, 406), following in Schaeffer's footsteps, three-quarters of the settlements of western and southern Anatolia were permanently destroyed. Although he is a catastrophic revisionist, Schaeffer has not gone deeply into causes in the present instance. He demonstrated the hard evidence of universal destruction. He invoked earthquakes followed by fire, or where earthquakes were not in evidence, simply enormous calcination. He exculpated invaders as the destroyers of civilization in many instances, even though he employed conventional terms such as "the Peoples of the Sea" that are used to explain the abrupt termination of many civilized communities. He can point often to disturbed and unsettled human elements who came upon the sites afterward. (Significantly, Blegen had already shown that a new cultural element did not succeed Troy IIg; the Troy III culture was closely related.[177] This is remarkable because the calcinated debris of Troy IIg was never dug out and was probably unknown, yet the debris of the old city was strong enough to become the foundation of the new city walls.)

Few scholars have been ready to confront the anomalies of their own findings. One exception was Spiridon Marinatos, who plunged to his death in 1974 at the famous site of his work. His excavation of the Minoan culture of Thera-Santorini, from beneath the effects of the plinian explosion of the island, called international and interdisciplinary attention to the destruction of critical portion of Mediterranean civilization.

Salvaging the Ashes and Debris for Analysis

But Blegen of Cincinnati was also an exception; he was disposed to a cautious empiricism, but was piqued by the strange events that had befallen Minoan and Mycenaean civilization. In the voluminous published records of the Cincinnati expedition, we find the following lines: "A large collection of earth samples was also made this year. (1937). Specimens were taken from all strata of all main layers in the principle areas of digging, and the number of small bags thus collected exceeded 400. They were shipped to Cincinnati for scientific examination by specialists in geology and botany."[178]

When, in 1974, we discovered this passage, we made inquiry, only to find that the sample had never been analyzed. The long period of World War II had intervened. Personnel left, never to return. Other interests took priority.

The samples rested in their cloth bags in the attic of McMicken Hall at the University of Cincinnati. My inquiries bore fruit. Finally, in 1975, material from the bags was provided to Professor George Rapp of the University of Minnesota for eventual analysis. This material would serve for the first calcinological testing of the causes of the destruction of Troy-Hisarlik. It would perhaps form the basis of testing also the more general theories advanced as to the causes of the destruction of many ancient civilizations. *[But see my Postscript at the end of this chapter for the dismal denouement of this hopeful activity.]*

What questions should be asked of these humble sacks of debris, and, by extension, of all similar samples to be drawn from other destroyed settlements? In other words, of what should consist the science that investigates ancient destruction by combustion, calcinology? We may address this question either by taking up one by one the theories as to the origins of the combustion, or by taking up the techniques for the investigation of combustion.

In respect to the theories, one would inquire into the possibilities of one or a combination of accidental fire; "the invader's torch"; Greek Fire; seismic-caused fire; explosive local volcanism from fissures or now extinct cones; fall-out of tephra from remote, perhaps general, volcanism; ramified lightning; petroleum (bitumen, asphalt, naphtha) rain, non-volcanic and extraterrestrial; and gas explosion in the atmosphere, terrestrial or extraterrestrial by origin.

In respect to the techniques, one would speak of ambiance induction; artifact analysis; comparative historical deduction; thermal-visual examination; morphological examination; electron scanning microscopy; chemical mineralogical tests; thermo-luminescence tests; tests for paleo-magnetism. Inasmuch as individual techniques may dispose of more than one theory, it may be best to proceed by offering a few words concerning the irrelevance.

Fundamental to pursuing all causal alternatives is a careful inductive study of the ambiance of combustion. Whether performed on records of past expeditions or upon a setting itself, a skeptical and fully alert reading or examination is required. We have entertained too close a circle of interests and hypotheses; the Trojan record shows this. So do hundreds of other excavation reports.

First of all, an interdisciplinary group of scientist must set standards and criteria for entering upon a testable location. Conventional archaeology has certainly proceeded far along these lines, but new parameters need to be added, taken from geology and meteorology, as for instance, the effects of wind and the strength of building materials. The camera that has come to play an important part in contemporary investigations needs to be aimed at the hypotheses, so to speak. The pioneering work of the engineer, C. Lauraceae, in magnetomatic and radiotropic anterior probing of subsurface forms is worthy of generalization to standard practice.

Standards for measuring depth of debris, original and actual density of calcination, percentage of ash content, and architectural and object deformities should be set up. Pre-selection and logging of samples should be systematically done in the manner of the Cincinnati expedition of 1937.

The analysis of artifacts is sometimes conducted as part of a treasure hunt. To this day, objects from the Treasure of Priam have not been studied carefully to determine whether they have been fused by heat or by oxidation. Objects are described as they are found but not to the extent that a specific set of hypotheses is applied to each object as to how it might have been placed or dropped, or slipped, or fallen as a result of direct or indirect natural causes. Nor has an inductive, comparative, historical method been always conscientiously pursued. A single anomaly in a closed layer may be worth more to science than a golden chalice. To dismiss the anomaly as an "impossible" intrusion, a "similarity", and "forerunner" is all too common practice.

The attempt of the University of Cincinnati expedition to reconcile the anomalies of location of their carefully uncovered sherds in the face of the conventional Egyptian-anchored chronology is a case in point. "The discovery of these 7th-century sherds 'in several areas in the strata of Troy VIIb1 stratified below layer VIIb2', which is supposed to represent the 12th century, "presents a perplexing and still unexplained problem."[179] Fortunately the self-restraining, objective empirical techniques of the expedition simply stood even against an authoritative chronology at a later date.

One goal of calcinology is to establish a frame of analysis that can be transferred from one excavation to another both to interlock events and to serve eventual critiques of received versions of the comparative development (and destruction) of civilizations.

The Lack of Geo-Mythology

I should place in the same category of historical comparative method the application of mythology. Dorothy Vitaliano, pursuing a strict uniformitarian theory, has nonetheless exemplified the necessary marriage between myth and geology that research properly demands; to her, myth serves as a clue to past events, especially when they are extraordinarily forceful.[180]

Sometimes, as in the case of Troy, there are direct myths describing events overtaking the site. In other cases, myths may be transferred from other times and places as hypotheses. The examination of bones found in circumstances of combustion may well be expanded. Paleontology ordinarily does not address itself to the degree of heat to which human remains have been subjected, or whether the heat was searing or slow.

For example, a separate volume in the Cincinnati Troy series, its other merits aside, does not answer questions relevant to the sudden destruction of the city.[181] How much heat reached the people whose skeletons remained? Would the heat elsewhere have erased entirely any humans and animals? Contemporary arson experts can transfer their "know-how" to such queries. Contemporary fire experts and combustion chemists can also contribute useful principles for the visual examination of thermal effects. A high sensitivity to variations in color and texture is still not a prerequisite for professional archaeology. Conversations with persons concerned with combustion problems come around repeatedly to unanswerable questions of color, stains, textures, bubbles and cracks.

The morphology of combustion environments

would deal with terrain features that might have altered, of for that matter remained significantly unaltered, in the course of the destructive combustion. Earthquakes uplift and crack the earth. Volcanic and seismic fissures leave different traces. Lightning can burn and dig distinctive fissures as well. It would be useful to perform core drills in the hinterland of destroyed settlements to discover whether the ash trapped about the ruins is also present in some natural lowland areas of slow deposition, removed from human habitations.

Recently, for example, the Athens Metro project tested the subsoil to a depth of 20 meters in 228 locations for the purpose of planning subway construction. Archeological finds were noted and covered over, but the ordinary corings were not handled properly for the analysis of combustion or other natural phenomena. Almost all samples show "Athens schist," a vague term for sandstone, siltstones and the like; most of the preserved cores are disturbed and eroded by water used in the drilling.[182] (The rock cores, incidentally, show highly intense fracturing near the surface.)

Unfortunately, oil exploration does not concern itself with logging the cores brought up from the near subsurface of wells during the drilling.[183] It may be possible in the future to make a cooperative arrangement with petroleum geologists to provide such data. Apart from its usefulness to social and natural history, near subsurface samples may reveal chemical and morphological peculiarities of areas overhanging oil pools, such as distillates of hydrocarbons indicating surface origins. (Again, this would appear to be an appropriate scientific response, as there are frequent references in myth to rains of sticky substances from the sky.) This conjecture leads naturally to inquiry into the composition of shales, clays, and soils found in connection with ancient destruction.

An analysis of "samples that cover depositional chemical environments ranging from continental and coastal soils to marsh and subtidal marine deposits" of recent ages had disclosed complex polycyclic aromatic hydrocarbon assemblages (PAH) with "a high degree of similarity in the molecular weight distribution of the many series of alkyl homologs."[184] This PAH is carcinogenic and mutagenic. The soils sampled were from widely separated locations on and off the New England coastal region. Forest pyrolysis and atmospheric transport was suggested. A search for other nonbiological organic compounds was indicated. The cause of such an immense fire is conjectural, as is indeed the postulate of the fire itself.

Are we so swollen with pride that we cannot review Ignatius Donnelly's Ragnarok (1883) and not gain from it at least a doubt as to the origins of some of the world's clays? Clay is conventionally assigned to sedimentation or decomposed structural material, without inquiring as to possible volcanic or other sources. Yet a geological walk along many a Greek island beach may pass across deposits of pumice dust and of gray clay that visually suggests bentonite. Donnelly claimed a cometary origin for a heavy rain of fire and gravel that destroyed part of the globe and most of mankind.

Testing the Metals and Calcinated Debris

What does the new geology say to this? At least in regard to calcinated settlement debris and top open area subsurface nearby, what installed for is an increased resort to professional morphological, visual, and tactile examination, then to chemical mineralogical tests, and also to electron scanning microscopy. Reference was made earlier to the extraordinary layer of copper and lead scoriae found by Schliemann in the burnt city. Is this mined ore, purified metal, or ore in a natural state?

The origins of metals are not a settled matter. There is too long a stone age, too ready an access to ores, too abundant a mythology to relax in the arms of conventional theory. Sample tests are generally inexpensive and well structured; they require only small amounts of material, often only a gram. But of course, the sampling technique is critical and a manual of instructions for sampling calcination with a mind to covering all hypotheses raised by this paper is a task for the future. The idea that thermoluminescence, radiocarbon, potassium-argon, and fission-tract dating techniques can be applied to combustion studies withhold effect is natural but perhaps overly optimistic.

Of course, calcinology is interested in dating inasmuch as one of its aims is the establishment of concurrences in destruction; if two spatially separated combustion processes point to the same or related causes, then their dating will not only confirm their relationship but will also permit a more secure dating of other sites where similar combustion but insufficiently related artifacts and structures are discovered. Thermal effects encountered on calcinated sites play a large role in permitting age-determinations (as in thermoluminescence tests and fission-track dating) by providing a basal date from which calculations of age may be made, and in obscuring chronology by contaminating burned substances through mixing, as in radiocarbon dating.

However, it will be of interest to apply long-term dating techniques such as the potassium-argon method if only to check whether the test gives an impossibly old date to a recent volcanic event. Where uranium minerals have been used to give color to artifacts of glass, the fission-track technique may provide reliable dates and a check on radiocarbon dates. If an artificial glass is subjected subsequent to its manufacture to combustion temperatures of over 600 degrees centigrade, the fission-tracks may be partially or entirely erased, permitting the date of the new calcination to be determined from the tracks now present. Tracks in volcanic glass should date the eruption that produced it. Extra-terrestrial microtektites lend themselves also to fission-track dating and can be searched for in ruins.[185]

Tests for radiation levels of the debris are indicated because of the possibility that the destruction may have involved atmospheric or air- transported agents. For instance the radiation levels would vary from the norm if lightning had struck or a meteoric pass-by had greatly raised temperature levels. Lightning effects may also be indicated by magnetization of metal pieces; for this reason and also to determine whether a change in the magnetic pole had occurred, supposing a catastrophe to have been widespread, the then-exposed rocks should be tested for abnormal magnetism, and ceramic sherds of successive levels should be tested for the same and for possible reversal of direction from one level to another.

As the gamut of tests and procedures is subjected to the concerted attention of scholars of relevant fields, it may be expected that a system of producers and a battery of tests will evolve -- simpler, easier to employ, practicable given the conditions of archaeological exploration. The resultant research and testing would possibly confirm that archaeology and geophysics have overlooked some significant part of the absolutely small fund of ancient data. At that point, not too far away, we may begin to speak of a new subfield of science called paleo-calcinology.

And when this task is finished, we might turn to another new subfield, which beckoned us temptingly even as we tried to concentrate upon calcination, paleo-seismism. Here the implication is that the Mercalli scale (more relevant than the Richter Scale) may be quite inadequate to denominate thrusting, folding, and crustal rising and falling that may have occurred in the time of man, and that the present awareness of settlement sites is merely fractional; much more may have disappeared or is effectively hidden so as to lend a false perspective to the human story.

Also paleo-diluviology, the study of ancient floods and tidalism. And still another, paleo-meteorology, a study that would include the great winds that can sweep away everything down to bed rock, given the slightest faltering of the earth's rotation, or the passage of any substantial material from outer space through the atmosphere. Part of the total task, we seem to be saying, is to separate ancient real occurrences from ancient myth.

The larger task is to distinguish real ancient catastrophism from literal theology, not to denigrate theology but so as to recognize a quantavolution for what it did to shape man and his environment.

Postscript of November, 1983

The author's interest in the calcinology of Troy, expressed directly to Prof. Caskey and indirectly through third parties and memoranda, led the University of

Cincinnati authorities to propose an investigation of samples of debris that had been stored for many years at the University. Generous grants were obtained from several foundations and in 1982, the Princeton University press published *Supplementary Monograph 4 of the University of Cincinnati Excavation at Troy*, under the title of Troy: the Archaeological Geology, by George Rapp, Jr. and John A. Gifford. The present author, whose own research proposal had failed to receive support, was not consulted at any stage of this work.

However, since his original preliminary memorandum, which conforms closely to the present essay, had been made available to the investigators in the very beginning and he had called their attention to the possibilities residing in the neglected samples, there may have resulted some effect on what was done in the investigations. If so, it is not noticeable in the book just cited.

The book does not state its hypotheses. Its tests discovered only that in almost all samples, whatever the level, a reed (*Arundo donox*) occurred; the finding lacks significance since the reed is used in making bricks. In sample number 81 (p. 130) of Phase IId, burned earth was analyzed to reveal charcoal, bone, and *pelecypod* fragments. There appears to be nothing of further interest to calcinology proceeding from the entire investigation. It is a humdrum study, typical of the work of geologists in the perspective of quantavolution.

The soil samples were not, however, exhausted, and a future investigation is still possible, hopefully by means more sophisticated than those described in the published work. (My list of suggested tests was quite ignored.) The senior author, George Rapp, Jr., without serious defense of the thesis, seems to support earthquakes as the cause of destruction. ('... one earthquake of Richter magnitude greater than seven to affect the Troad about every three hundred years.' (p. 46)).

Troy of the Trojan War since the Blegen Expeditions

Layer VIIa became the stratum of the Trojan War. (I should again alert the reader to strong doubt that Hisarlik is the site of the Trojan War, and therefore the scene of the *Iliad.*)

Above VIIa was Layer VIII. Now I must quote extensively the brilliant analysis of E. Schorr:

After completing seven seasons of excavation at Troy, Carl Blegen, the chief archaeologist of the Cincinnati expedition of the 1930's, saw no break between layers VII and VIII. After several more years had elapsed, allowing additional time to reflect on the dig, to study the pottery more carefully, and especially after Mycenaean pottery dates became more firmly entrenched, it was realized that a gap of centuries should exist between the two layers. Nevertheless, even in their official publication, the excavators were so impressed by certain facts relating to the mound itself that they left open the possibility that there was no gap. By the accepted chronology there had to be a lacuna, as they acknowledged, but they hesitated on this point. Their reasons are interesting.

The new excavations showed that the locally-made pottery of Troy VIII was "obviously akin" to that of Troy VII. The local grey ware pots of Troy VII (i.e., of the Mycenaean Age) were looked upon as the "direct ancestors" of the local ware not only of Troy VIII but also of 7th-6th-century Northwestern Turkey and the off-shore island of Lesbos as well. With a 400-year gap in the evidence, how can one connect this widespread 7th-6th-century ware with that of the Mycenaean Age?

At the very time that there was supposed to be a 400-year abandonment of Hisarlik, one house seemed to show continuity between the end of layer VII and the time of VIII, as if no one had left and only a few years had passed.

In several deposits of Troy VIII there were sherds from Troy VII. There was finally, however, a more serious problem. Although the excavators were meticulous in their method of digging stratified layers and labeling and recording all finds and their provenience, in sub-strata of Troy VII that seemed to be undisturbed, sherds were found of the imported Greek pottery of the early 7th century. "The only explanation we can find is to suppose that, in spite of our efforts to isolate and certify the deposits we examined, contamination had somehow been effected and brought about the intrusion of the later wares into strata of Troy VII b". The discovery of these 7th-century sherds "in several areas in the strata of Troy VII b1" stratified below layer VII b2, which is supposed to represent the 12th century, "presents a perplexing and still unexplained problem".[186]

After all the digging by Schliemann, Dörpfeld, and Blegen at Hisarlik, only one sherd has turned up which could conceivably fall within the 400-year gap postulated for the site. Stratigraphically, however, it was not found where it should have been. A rim fragment from a "Protogeometric" cup was found "with sherds of Phase VII b I, but probably out of context." The reason it was probably out of context is that it was covered over by "two successive buildings of Phase VII b2" which of necessity belong to the 12th century B.C. The sherd beneath those two buildings is seen as part of a body of material found from Palestine to Macedonia which, beginning perhaps ca. 900 B.C., was in vogue until the 8th or 7th century B.C. It is stratigraphically impossible to have a 7th, 8th, or even 9th-century B.C. item below the floor of a 12th-century B.C. building, unless contamination occurred. "There was apparently no contamination from disturbance or later intrusions," however.

In time these "perplexing and still unexplained" problems were brushed aside, and reservations about a 400-year gap were abandoned, because, by the accepted chronology, that gap had to exist.

Actually, given the familiarity expressed in Homer's work with both Bronze and Iron Age objects and customs, it is fair to say that Homer's sources straddled the two ages. The analysis of Troy's datation by Schorr, Velikovsky, and Sammer is devastating to the conventional placement. Follow-up research on the debris and ashes of Troy has been costly but inadequate, if only because in the first place, Troy properly should be relocated in another place, maybe, as Felice Vinci has argued, even in the Baltic Region of the North. (*Homer in the Baltic*)

Spanuth has advanced us information that the name of troy-town has been discovered for several locations in the North of Europe. These Troy-towns are sacred dancing labyrinths. They include the great circles of stones and arches like Stonehenge in England; they number into the hundreds and are found all over Europe. The word *Troy* has the root (*tr*) that proto-Indo-European tongues employed to designate the meaning of *turning*. Atlantis would have been a troy-town because of its construction of huge circular moats and embankments around the central city.

The most wonderful of such labyrinthine constructions is the floor of the great French cathedral of Chartres. It is called a "troy". It is not impossible that Hisarlik, the town to which the name Troy has been applied for at least 2700 years was known for such because of a large wall that circled the city center at some distance, in which most of the people could live and work. But, since the term is most often found in the Baltic and western regions of northern Europe, it could have been applied to the town in Finland where Vinci believes the Trojan War actually took place.

Notable, as I have insisted upon in several works such as *Chaos and Creation, Homo Schizo I* and *The Divine Succession* that deal with the origins of religion in the skies, is the analogue between the fascinating revolving globe of the star-bearing heavens and the sacral circles and labyrinths being discussed here. Humans are prone to imitate on Earth what they discern in the sky.

In conclusion, we may continue to call it "Troy" – although it is probably not the real Troy where 'Achilles' killed 'Hector'. Nor is the mound the real Troy, even extended to a surrounding enclosure much enlarged, known as Hisarlik. Still, everything found there will be found at the Real Troy, if ever uncovered – and more. There, too, the earmarks of the Martian quantavolution will be found as everywhere else:

1. Baffling destruction of great intensity including amazing combustion and causes of mass death.
2. A false 400-year gap, unless our side wins, bringing a plethora of contradictions without means of reconciliation, and an illusion of gradualism in the processes of destruction.
3. Bizarre behavior of the actors on the eve of and following upon the destruction.
4. Evidence of prior quantavolutions down deep below the Martian levels, but only in exceptional cases destruction by natural causes afterwards, the intensity of the effects diminishing with time, but never altogether.
5. Vagrant peoples, individualism, crazy heroes and brigandage, crazier and often renamed and remodeled gods.

Please, note: The author wishes to acknowledge his obligation to a number of persons who kindly supplied information and advice as he was preparing the study. Among them are: C. C. Chandler, Director of Forest Fire and Atmospheric sciences Research, U. S. Department of Agriculture, Forest Service; Arthur Brown, Geological Engineer, Technical Consultant, Athens Metro Project ;Ruben G. Bullard, Department of Geology, Cincinnati Bible Seminary; J. L. Caskey, Professor of Archaeology, University of Cincinnati; Dr. Howard W.Emmons, Karman Laboratory of Fluid Mechanics and Jet Propulsion, California Institute of Technology; John Greeley, Professor of Physics, University of the Bosphorus; Billie Glass, Associate Professor of Geology, University of Delaware, Newark; W. A. Hans, Engineer, Fire Protection Department, Underwriters Laboratories Inca; John Gnaedinger, President, Soil Testing Services Inc., Northbrook, Ill; Jorg Keller, Professor of Mineralogy, University of Freiburg, West Germany; G. Marinas, Director, Department of Geology and Paleontology, University of Athens; Dr. Charles D. Ninkovich, Lamont-Diehard Geological Observatory, Palisades, N. Y.; Dr. GED Rustler, Consulting Geologist, Naxos, Greece; Eugene Vanderhoof, Archaeological photographer, American School of Classical Studies, Athens; Eddie Schorr, Archaeologist, Houston, Texas; Dorothy Vitaliano, Associate Professor of Geology, University of Indiana, Bloomington, Ind.; Dr. Immanuel Velikovsky, Princeton, N. J.

Chapter Seventeen

Profiles of Many Destructions

No place, rural or urban, in the Iron Age escaped destruction, and all too often we find ourselves baffled by the causes in individual cases. Significant questions in the many spheres of study are not being regularly asked and, even when asked, do not produce answers from the findings and reports of excavations. For example, that the region of Thebes (Greece) suffered ruin in the Martian Age is known, but the quantavolution paradigm is hardly applied; there is no scoring and scaling in comparison with a group of sites. At all times we find the 400-year time discrepancy (More if the Ramses III mixup is figured in). And from time to time we have anomalies that should be thoroughly investigated, such as the intact skeleton on top of heavy ashes in a Kadmeian ruin. (*See below.*)

Phanouria Dakoronia tells us in an incisive study of Kynos-Livanates in Central Greece that successive destructions did not stop rebuilding until they were reinforced by tsunamis and fire [-700s]. She also say, almost uniquely, that East Locris in Central Greece suffered many earthquakes, but was continuously occupied for a thousand years or more after the Bronze Age finale. The implication there is that earthquakes alone will not end an age or even a phase.

Ideally we should have at hand profiles of all excavated archaeological sites for every type of natural destruction and connected human conduct: plagues, wars, invasions, migrations, and cultural changes. We should have a description and measurement of the ashes, for example, on whatever level found of a settlement's history, including a chemical analysis of the ashes. We should have a systematic comparison of ceramics from one level to the next, their composition, style and themes. We should attempt an accounting for every sphere of events at every site. Thereupon we might determine the degree of exponentialism in the changes from one time to the next. We would also wish to compare the quantavolution index derived thus for each single excavation with indexes of all other excavations. The job is not impossible. Even if practically restricted, it would be a productive discipline. Eager acolytes are many. Funding is meager.

Thebes

Anomalously, in Kadmeia (Thebes), A. Sampson describes how a female skeleton was brought to light, uncarbonized, yet laying on top of a 0.7m of debris, mostly ashes. She had been killed by a falling beam. "Excavations in the Kadmeia commonly being to light a thick destruction layer, the natural result of a long-lasting fire. In the Mycenean building, the layer was more than 1 m thick, which is also indicative of a second floor." Could a burning ash cloud have fallen and cooled before letting her step into the second-story room or fall into the ashes without being incinerated? Earthquake is certainly indicated as a prime suspect, as it is often so, yet fire is an independent variable in catastrophes. The vast Pestigo Fire that enveloped part of the American West in the 1880's was not seismically caused. Nor was the great Tunguska Siberia meteoric or cometary blaze that scorched 18 million trees in an instant in 1907.

While we speak of Thebes, let us say more. This destruction is said to have occurred before the Trojan War, therefore in the early Iron Age. As a result Thebans were not to be counted among the troops there. Cadmus had founded Thebes preceding the destruction and war by perhaps two generations. He had to flee his Phoenician kingdom around the time of Pharaoh Akhnaton. His Phoenician refugee party brought the Phoenicians alphabet with it. It consisted then of 16 letters, to which 4 were added later on. Its earliest document in Greek extant is of ~-750.

The Tsunami of Euripides

Some huge disasters are difficult or impossible to assess or even to detect. Little is known or written of tsunamis in ancient times. There must have been enormous tidal flooding and many tsunamis. Euripides, in perhaps his greatest tragedy, *Hippolytus*, has his hero killed by what appears to be a tsunami. A Messenger who survives reports what happened: Hippolytus, the wronged and doomed youth, exclaims:

"O Zeus, now strike me dead, if I have sinned, and let my father learn how he is wronging me, in death at least, if not in life." Therewith he seized the whip and lashed each horse in turn; while we, close by his chariot, near the reins, kept up with him along the road that leads direct to Argos and Epidaurus. And just as we were coming to a desert spot, a strip of sand beyond the borders of this country, sloping right to the Saronic gulf, there issued thence a deep rumbling sound, as it were an earthquake, fearsome noise, and the horses reared their heads and pricked their ears, while we were filled with wild alarm to know whence came the sound; when, as we gazed toward the wave-beat shore, a wave tremendous we beheld towering to the skies, so that from our view the cliffs of Sciron vanished, for it hid the isthmus and the rock of Asclepius; then swelling and frothing with a crest of foam, the sea discharged it toward the beach where stood the harnessed car, and in the moment that it broke, that mighty wall of waters, there issued from the wave a monstrous bull, whose bellowing filled the land with fearsome echoes, a sight too awful as it seemed to us who witnessed it.

A panic seized the horses there and then, but our master, to horses' ways quite used, gripped in both hands his reins, and tying them to his body pulled them backward as the sailor pulls his oar; but the horses gnashed the forged bits between their teeth and bore him wildly on, regardless of their master's guiding hand or rein or jointed car. And oft as he would take the guiding rein and steer for softer ground, showed that bull in front to turn him back again, maddening his team with terror; but if in their frantic career they ran towards the rocks, he would draw nigh the chariot-rail, keeping up with them, until, suddenly dashing the wheel against a stone, he upset and wrecked the car; then was dire confusion, axle-boxes and linchpins springing into the air.

While he, poor youth, entangled in the reins was dragged along, bound by a stubborn knot, his poor head dashed against the rocks, his flesh all torn, the while he cried out piteously, "Stay, stay, my horses whom my own hand hath fed at the manger, destroy me not utterly. O luckless curse of a father! Will no one come and save me for all my virtue?"

The drama was set in Mycenean times but Euripides would have learned his details from witnesses of the Iron Age.

As with most indicators of quantavolution, tsunamis need to be clearly in the mind of excavators and scholars to be seen, analyzed and reported. Hardly any reports of tsunamis come directly to us, even though there must have been a number of such grave events.

Nevertheless, the Greater Mediterranean Region, we are almost in a position to say, does display, by the method of comparative matching, a high quantavolutionary profile rating in all indices for the Martian Age. In this chapter, we continue our research into the Iron Age of Mars by scanning briefly a score of places, indicating in each case some evidence of catastrophe from geology, digs, legends, and documents. Most ancient sites have been lost or are still covered, a significant index of catastrophe by itself. One of the least explored areas is Western Arabia, which, we have said, may be of prime importance.

Prototype: the Mycenae Model

A prominent level of destruction inside the walls of the citadel of ancient Mycenae is used to define the end of the Bronze age. So far as possible everything discovered anywhere else in excavations should be compared with and receive its stylistic and chronological place from the Mycenean model. In this citadel a fierce fire blazed, destroyed the whole area, and the palace was never reconstructed.

Practically all Argolid and Corinthian settlements were destroyed about the same time as Mycenae. At over 30 sites in a small corner of the Southeast Argolid, dated to Late Bronze, only 6 ended the Age active; of these 3 were lowland, one in a cave, and two were hilltop sites. (This one-fifth ratio of survival was marked also in Etruria at the same time.) Movements to the hilltops were generally extensive all over the Greater Mediterranean, while at the same time, possibly alternately just before, or just after, settlements descended onto the plains. In this teeter-totter settlements phenomenon, which deserves intensive research, there may be demonstrable alternate brief periods of electrical storms and devastating floods.

In the case of related Greek sites. I shall not give their dates of destruction because of the large confusion over transitional period dates. Just as I suggested earlier, that we automatically transfer conventional dates of around 1200 to around 850 BCE, here I suggest that we make no distinction between the ending of the Late Bronze Age and the Early Iron Age. All Late Bronze events are dangling from the end of the Age. We surmise that they actually met disaster at the beginning of the Iron in the exoterrestrial catastrophes that were occurring.

Midia lost all of its citadel to fire. Earthquake has been given as a cause, for lack of better, the same one as destroyed Mycenae and Tiryns.

> Iria, southeast of Naplion, was destroyed by fire.
> Berbati and Prosymna were destroyed and abandoned.
> Nemea-Tsoungiza were abandoned.
> Eutresis (Boetia) was abandoned.
> Thebes (Boetia) Most of the new palace was burnt up.
> Krisa (Phocis) was destroyed.
> Menelaion (Laconia) was destroyed by fire.
> Ayios Stephanos (Laconia) was abandoned
> Nichoria (Messenia) was destroyed.

And so forth.

In other words, a nearly complete depopulation appears to have occurred in the Argolide and Corinthia. Here, as throughout the Region, variations in dates assigned to the catastrophes may vary relatively, for the incursions of Mars inflicted damage periodically. We have an eye peeled for the absolute (average) discrepancy from the 13th to the 11th century and the 9th to 7th centuries.

In Achaea and Kefallonia some evidence of an influx of people might appear to be signaled by an increase in tombs, but one could also ask whether this did not show that death was reaching more people of an early age and they were dying of unusual causes?

In the 1970's Eddie Schorr (pen name, Israel Isaacson), while an assistant to Velikovsky was still a graduate student at the University of Cincinnati in Archaeology. His was a precarious status, given that one of his principal targets of criticism was the prolonged and renowned Troy expeditions of Prof. Blegen that were a pride of the University. Stressed and practically isolated, he finally gave up to return to private business in Texas. His several studies, commencing with the chronology of Mycenae, are impeccable, and have only lately been published by Ian Tresman on the Web. [187]

Concluding his several case studies, Schorr writes:

> If Mycenean pottery had not received its absolute dates from Egypt, then, on the basis of that and other stratigraphical sections from Prosymna, Tiryns, Pylos, Athens, Sparta (Therapne), Kythera, Crete (Vrocastro). Chios. Troy, Italy (Taranto), etc, .. LHIIIB-C pottery (1350-1100/1050 B.C. by Egyptian reckoning) [~-950 to -700/650] immediately preceded the seventh-sixth century Orientalizing ware.

His documentation is complete as of the time of research in the 1970's.

Regarding Mycenae, and the entrance to its Citadel, the eleventh layer from the bottom contained a mixture of eleventh century LH III C pottery but also significant fragments of orientalizing ware of the seventh-sixth century. This layer is supposed to represent 500 years of gathering but physically is only 1/6th of the thickness of the ten layers beneath it, that are supposed to represent 150-200 years. No pottery of the supposed years 1050 to 700 was to be found.

"If people continued to inhabit, enter, and leave Mycenae between the eleventh century and the seventh, one would expect to see some evidence of that fact in that trench near the gate, yet none does." No ashes, no wash, no debris occurred between the two widely separated centuries. Some scholars excused this phenomenon as being caused by dumping of the Bronze Age material in the upper layer.

Moving on, Schorr restudied the palace, the Grave Circles, Shaft Grave Art, Later Use of the Grave Circles, the Warrior vase, a Chariot Vase, and other LH III Figural

Pottery, Bronze Tripods, A Terracotta Figurine and Head, The Religious Center of Mycenae, Phantom Age burial practices, The Northeast Extension , Ivory carvings, Mycenean jewelry, and the Design of the Palace. The Lion Gate of Mycenae, itself, was shown to have its contradictory datings by Velikovsky, well back in the nineteen sixties, to no avail or effect upon the literature.

In every case, the excavators and experts made the fatal choice of the false early date in preference to the Seventh Century ambiance, typically after positing the proper dating when their findings first revealed themselves. That is, professional pressures went to work and turned their heads around. For instance, in 1878, an expert on the art of Greece, P. Gardner, judged the various gold finds from various graves dug up by Schliemann to be from the Geometric Age of Greek Art, and placed animal figurines also in the seventh-sixth centuries. He wrote before prehistoric Greece took over the Egyptian dates, moving back by five centuries the findings.

Immediately on top of the Bronze Age ruins in many Greek centers, temples were erected, but these showed no signs of religious activity during the Phantom-500 Age. (Mycenae, Aegina, Calauria, Crete, Delos, Samos, Epidaurus, Olympia, Perachora, Therapne, Isthmia, Brauron, Eleusis, Delphi, Pherai, Thermon, and Tegea.) The absurdity was rationalized in the conjuration of a devout set of remote descendants who wished to revive the old time religion. The new cultists would have had to wait for 500 years before deciding to build upon the sites immediately below their prospective shrines.

The designs, objects and art of the shaft graves of Mycenae "carry with them many identifications from as far as the Baltic Sea (amber), Albania, and the Minoan Empire sites...Some of the earliest Iron Age ware of Greece, with its distinctive fabric, its wheel made and handmade forms, and its incisive and painted decoration, resembles the pottery which culminated in the shaft Grave vases of Mycenae, and, at the site of Asine, less than twenty miles southeast of Mycenae, the excavators term the resemblance 'astounding.'"

With the fall of Mycenae, a profound depression and decline in jewelry-making and trading occurred, which is said to have occupied around 500 years, but again, when reestablished, carried the inescapable signs of the art of the earlier flourishing age. Apropos chariots, depicted upon vases, ~-700, the vase pictures appear to be the direct descendants of other contemporary chariots and their images. Experts debated whether the chariot persisted somehow and was dragged out after centuries of disuse. But in many areas the chariot seemed to disappear entirely for the full Phantom Age.

The Warrior Vase of Mycenae has been shown to have a close imitation in Cyprus, that is, independently by Cyprian chronology assigned to the early Seventh Century, but typically given a date five hundred years earlier to appease the Egyptological elite.

Figural pottery, which appears first at the Bronze Age LH III and then disappears for the assigned four or five centuries, occurs as eighth-seventh century art, not only in Greece but also in Sicily, Aegina, Melos, Crete, Rhodes, Cyprus and Eastern Anatolia. A common theory to explain this anomaly is that the prototypes escaped to Phoenicia with their makers; then they worked on and on, somewhat 'orientalized' and otherwise prepared for a new invasion of the aforesaid marketplaces after four or five centuries of nursing.

Tiryns is southeast of Mycenae and can also be used for the same purposes to show the failures of Egyptian chronology and the devastation of chronology elsewhere. There, the excavator Frickenhaus, following Schliemann and Doerpfeld, asserted that "the fire of the palace was followed immediately by the erection of the temple." The reference is to the many temples found immediately succeeding Mycenean palace buildings in iron age locales. Blegen offered one after another explanation until he was left with the notion that the temple after all was not even a Greek Temple. Nilsson joined the fray and denied Blegen's position, only to find himself without explanation of the phenomenon.

Tiryns was an activity center for Hercules-Ares, and its giant stones were emplaced by the one-eyed Cyclopes. It was destroyed in a vast conflagration. The one-eyed semi-divinity can be related to the readily visible Valles Marineris of Planet Mars and the Eye of Horus (see Figure). The Palace is seemingly described from actual vision or picturing for the use of Homer, so true is his description of it or its surrogate.

The monumental gate structures or propylaea are buried. Then supposedly 700 years later, their models turn up at Aegina and the Athens acropolis. So these, and triglyph altars, and Homeric temple plans, and temple votives jump the huge time gap at Tiryns or are presumed to have occurred during the phantom period.

The Phantom Age spanned in Athens

Athens is reputed to be the one place in Greece exhibiting a continuous sequence of ceramic remains from the Mycenean down to the Classical Age, therefore spanning the Dark Ages. Yet, not even in Athens does there exist a single stratification, showing the full sequence. Velikovsky pointed this out in an unpublished note.

In the 1930s, excavations by Broneer sounded a deep well. It had been dug as part of extensive preparations to withstand a siege. It was later abandoned and was discovered to be filled with sherds of late Mycenean pottery. According to Plato's *Critias,* earthquakes had caused the well to collapse. Concomitantly, it is said, human occupation of the Acropolis ceased. It was not resumed until the seventh century. The gap in time was really the terrible first part of the Iron Age, the transition period of the Martian Quantavolution.

The circumstances are telling: a vital well and spring on a sacred and military eminence goes dry. The wooden stairs down to it are broken, never to be repaired. An earthquake, explains Plato. When did it happen? At the end of the Mycenean period. Is there evidence of concomitant disaster? Yes, the Athenians were taking emergency measures to fortify the town, declares one investigator, and the stairs were part of them. Then the town was largely depopulated. The public cemeteries received no clients. (Significantly, at Tiryns, too, the underground water-supply system terminated, and became filled with large rubbish dumps of the end of the Bronze Age.)

No remains of human dwellings are found in Athens

for the Phantom Age -- only burial sites, most prominently, the cemetery of Keiramikos, at the foot of the Acropolis. Where the people lived, who were buried in the Kerameikos, remains a mystery. The Keiramikos was amply furnished in pottery of the style called "protogeometric," which is supposed to be the immediate successor of the pottery found in the well on the Acropolis. "It is a significant fact," says Broneer, "that the pottery from the fountain extends to, but does not overlap, the period represented by the early graves in the Kerameikos cemetery." The author of the article adds that protogeometric burials are inside cist-tombs of the type used in pre-Mycenean age, these tombs are not derived from, but precede Mycenean tombs, and the people buried in the Kerameikos lived in the pre-Mycenean settlements (that both tombs and settlements, therefore, were older than the pottery at the bottom of the well on the Acropolis.)

Pottery of the Geometric period is well represented in different sites in Athens (including the Kerameikos). In one site - a stratified deposit south of the Parthenon - it was found mixed together in the same stratum with Mycenean ware. Yet, the two periods are supposed to have been separated by four centuries. No proto-geometric ware, supposedly dated to these dark centuries, is found alongside it. This arrangement is not unique: late Mycenean and geometric pottery have been found together elsewhere, including on the Acropolis. Doerpfeld argued 150 years ago that Geometric and Mycenean pottery were contemporaneous. In Milos, geometric pottery was even found under Mycenean and mixed with it and with protogeometric pottery.

Schorr, reporting the findings of scholars, finds them multiply confused, but "that even though Athens was not invaded or destroyed, its palace still ceased to be occupied after the end of the Bronze Age. Neither is there any evidence that a new palace or mansion replaced the old palace, nor, in fact, that the Athenians erected any large-scale structures after the twelfth century and before the late seventh." Other kinds of evidence dispel the Phantom Age: eighth century temples resemble closely Late Helladic II throne rooms.

Athens was into its proto-geometric and even geometric period while the Mycenean culture was proceeding from its beginning to its end. Sherds of the wares of the two periods were mixed at he same levels at several excavations points as early as O. Broneer's study of the 1930's. Even the motifs and styles of certain sherds married the Mycenean to the Geometric female costumes and Mycenean chariots, for example. (Specialists, as one might imagine, interpreted such evidence as signs of the continuation of Athenian civilization through the Dark Age.) We quote the study of Eddie Schorr:

> What constantly surprises and perplexes archaeologists is that Athens, the one place where one should find continuity of culture, is the very place which, without any obvious reason, changed most drastically, abandoning its Mycenean characteristics more quickly and completely than every other region. While the old ways lingered on in the severely struck Peloponnese, Athens suddenly and inexplicably adopted a material culture and customs which scarcely resemble their immediate predecessors in Athens or their contemporary counterparts elsewhere in Greece, but which in art, architecture, dress, burial customs, standard of living, etc., seem more akin to antecedents now placed 500 years earlier. H. Robertson concluded from his study that "in Greece the greatest cities were all devastated; and even in places, which, like Athens escaped the destruction, there is no monumental building, and the tradition of the major arts..dies out. This seems to be absolutely true" throughout the Greek world.

A deserted city, a de-population, a crash of all the arts and ways of living. We are left to imagine devastating plagues, some radical change of atmosphere for a period of time, a removal of underground and above ground water supplies from whole areas and a drought of rainfall as well.

Returning to the details of pottery, the first and last resort of excavators all too often, we could go on and on. C. C. Edgar discovered the usual situation at Phylakopi on the Aegean Island of Milos. As Velikovsky said of Edgar's work, "He found Geometric pottery under Mycenean, and mixed with it until the very end of the Mycenean deposit." The same anomalous mixture was found in Troy, Olympia, Pylos and elsewhere.

To get a hint of the dimension of the ecological catastrophes which visited Athens we need only go to Plato, who has Critias describing Attica and Athens "before," in an ancient time which we must surmise to have been the Bronze Age, and "after," and ever since, when it is "a mere remnant of what it once was..." "...You are left, as with little islands, with something rather like the skeleton of a body wasted by disease; the rich, soft soil has run away leaving the lend nothing but skin and bone. But in these days the damage had not taken place, the hills had high crests, the rocky plain of Pheleus was covered with rich soil, and the mountains were covered with thick woods..." "The soil benefitted from an annual rainfall which did not run to waste off the bare earth as it does today, but was absorbed in large quantities and stored in retentive layers of clay, so that what was drunk down by the higher regions flowed downwards into the valleys and appeared everywhere in a multitude of rivers and springs. And the shrines which still survive at these former springs are proof of the truth of our present account of the country." "...The Acropolis was different from what it is now. Today it is quite bare of soil which was all washed away in one appalling night of flood, by the combination of earthquakes and the third terrible deluge before that of Deucalion..."

So much for "intact Athens..." There was a single spring in the area of the present Acropolis (see Schorr, above) which was subsequently choked by the earthquakes and survives only in a few small trickles in the vicinity..." The fact that Mycenean pottery sherds were found in abundance by Broneer at the bottom of the well suffices to date this catastrophic event and, concomitantly, should provide a strong hint for dating the destruction of Atlantis, which is the purpose of Critias' exposé in the first place. As for the survivors of these horrible events, "...they were an unlettered mountain race... for many generations they and their children were short of bare necessities, and their minds and thoughts were occupied with providing for them, to the neglect of earlier history and tradition..."

But let us turn now to Pylos.

Pylos

In my work of *Moon and Mars*, I describe the last day

of the kingdom of Pylos as follows:

It was early Springtime in Pylos, a Mycenaean town of the Peloponnesus, facing the western sea. The year was between 776 and 687 B. C. It may even have been March 23, -687. A force of 800 men was posted along 150 kilometers of shoreline. With them were liaison officers from the Palace of King Nestor. The famous old sage of the Achaean warriors himself would have been home from the siege of Troy.

A clay tablet, one of those inscribed "immediately before the destruction which baked them and rendered them durable" begins, "Thus are the watchers guarding the coastal regions." What could they be watching for? Obviously no enemy had been sighted nor could the men be in fighting formation, so thinly dispersed were they. It might be as in Jerusalem around this time, when Isaiah the Prophet was answering the call, "Watchman, what of the night?"

Another tablet may have been the last: A single large tablet bears evidence of haste and changes of mind during its writing. The retention of such an ill-written document in the archive might occasion surprise, unless it was in fact only written in the last day or two before the palace fell. The meaning of some key words is still uncertain, but there is no doubt that it records offerings to a long list of deities. The offerings are in each case a golden vessel, but the principal deities, if male, receive in addition a man, or, if female, a woman. It has been suggested that these human beings were being dedicated to the service of the deities, but the grisly possibility that they were human sacrifices cannot be lightly dismissed. At all events the offering of thirteen gold vessels and ten human beings to a whole pantheon of divinities must mark an important occasion; and what occasion more likely than a general supplication on the receipt of news of an imminent attack? The "occasion more likely" is catastrophe. Tidal waves were to be watched for, and the setting of the sun behind the flaming horizons. Matters quickly worsened. The news was bad. The gods and goddesses had taken to the skies. "The whole pantheon of divinities" was supplicated, with the richest offerings; gold and human bodies. Not a solitary god of the sea, or a single god of the hearth, or of love, or battle. All of the great sky-gods seem to have been involved.

So Pylos perished. It had led a brief life. According to tradition, only four kings had ruled from its founding to its destruction. The Palace was destroyed in a "holocaust" which "consumed everything that was inflammable within it, and even melted gold ornaments into lumps and drops of metal." The flames melted brick and stone into "a solid mass... as hard as rock." In one room two large pots were fused "into a molten vitrified layer which ran over the whole floor." Everything that a human invader might desire was reduced to shapelessness. Stone was burned into lime. No human hands and hand-set fires could have wreaked such ruin. Only blasts from the sky - electrical, gaseous or both.

It was built by Neleus, the father of Nestor, and soon for the first time destroyed "by an unexplained disaster, remembered in tradition as the destruction of Pylos by Herakles." Of Neleus' twelve sons, only Nestor survives. The city is rebuilt and Nestor succeeds Neleus. He was an old man when he joined the Greek forces against Troy - he had seen two generations of men pass, "those who had grown up with him, and they who were born to these in sacred Pylos, and he was king in the third age." He returned safely from Troy after the ten year siege and was alive and well ten years later, when Telemachus came to visit him when on the search for his father. Pylos is prosperous and peaceful "yet it is worth noting that Nestor took care to placate Poseidon the earthshaker with frequent sacrifices."

"The end of Pylos came in the second generation after Nestor." Pausanias says: "After the end of the war against Ilium and the death of Nestor after his return home, the expedition of the Dorians and return of the Heraclidae two generations afterwards drove out the descendants of Neleus from Messenia."

The Dorian bands descended on the weakened Mycenean kingdoms, taking possession of a depopulated land. The Heraclids, as their name shows, were worshippers of Mars. Having been expelled from the Peloponnese one or two generations before, they settled in Northern Greece. However, the dislocations and upheavals which marked the eighth and early seventh centuries uprooted them once again and brought them back to claim possession of their former homeland. The palace of Nestor was burned down. Pylos remained deserted and was never resettled, knowledge of the location of Nestor's palace remained lost.

In 1939 Carl Blegen rediscovered and excavated the site. The work was interrupted by World War II and taken up again with the University of Cincinnati in 1952. A huge number of clay tablets were found, mostly palace records.

They were dried, not fired, but were preserved by the conflagration which destroyed the palace and backed them. This disaster came suddenly - nothing was removed, not even the animals, but the humans all fled. There were no signs of battle, siege, occupation by people of another culture, or occupation in general.

Blegen dated the destruction at the close of Mycenean age, on the faith of Mycenean pottery found in the ruins, "sealed in by layers of ashes and debris."

Using the Egyptian time-scale according to which the pottery was calibrated, the destruction was set at 1200 BC. It was much more likely the Seventh Century.

As in other sites, other pottery, more recent, was also found: it had to be assigned to the late geometric age, which points to a date of the seventh century for the destruction to occur. The Late Geometric pottery was found on a yellowish-white clay deposit; immediately above it was an "extremely black layer." Besides the Late Geometric sherds, some pieces of glazed geometric ware were also found. If they dated from five hundred years after the destruction (when the site was uninhabited, as it had remained up to Blegen's time...) they would have had to penetrate through the mantle of vegetation, and through the compacted debris of the calcinated roof, under which they were found. The conclusion is: both the Mycenean and the geometric ware belonged to the last occupants.

Most of towns of Messenia suffered a similar fate and only a handful survived into the subsequent Archaic Age.

Asia Minor, Anatolia, West Asia

There is little reason to believe that the destruction incurred in the vast area of Asia Minor (Including Anatolia and West Asia), some 400,000 square kilometers, was less than that undergone by the Aegean region or anywhere else. As expected, the Phantom Age introduces many troubles . We shall here put forward only one general statement of the case, that by Ekrem Akurgal, which has emerged from the Velikovsky archive. The book, Die Kunst Anatoliens von Homer bis Alexander is of 1961, but its validity is unquestioned. Then two specific will move our exemplifications along.

"It is startling that until now in Central Anatolia not only no Phrygian, but altogether no cultural remains of any people, came to light that could be dated in time between 1200 and 750." He goes on to say: "In the south of the peninsula, in Mersin, Tarsus and Karatepe, in recent years important archaeological work was done...here, too, the early Iron Age, i.e. the period between 1200 and 750, is enwrapped in darkness."

On the mainland of Anatolia, and at a short distance from the sea, we come upon the ruins of Alalakh. Here Schorr reports 600 - to - 700 - year contradictions using the Egyptian chronology. A set of lion sculptures are promptly labeled with the Egyptian chronology and one scholar declares with some enthusiasm, " ..now for the first time we have a series of lion sculptures which cannot be later than the fourteenth century B.C." But H. Frankfort put the lions into the ninth century cage, saying that there are no works of art for the period from 1200 to 850 B.C.E., and, indeed, the lions may be a century or more younger.

Tantalis is a legendary city, whose existence and location in ancient Southwestern Anatolia (Magnesia)have been well settled by Peter James. He has gone so far as to nominate it as the original Lost Continent of Atlantis. Plato mentioned Tantalus, the King of this City and its surrounding kingdom of Sipylus, as having incurred the disfavor of the gods. In consequence, his city was drowned in Lake Saloe on whose banks it sat and he himself sentenced to an infinity in Hades being tantalized by delicacies and threatened by an overhanging stone.

Pausanias' famous guide to travelers in Greece holds two key items of information for us. He tells of a kind of super-earthquake and he assigns the type to the disposal of Tantalis, as confirmed later by Pliny. We quote the relevant passage from Peter James' book, *The Sunken Kingdom* (p.215):

> In his book on Achaea (the northern province of the Peloponnese), Pausanias includes an interesting digression on the nature of the extraordinary disaster that struck the Helike one winter's night in 373 BC. The city was utterly destroyed by a series of momentous earth shocks, and Pausanias analyzed the disaster in graphic detail, noting that 'the

character of the shock itself is not always the same. The original observers and persons instructed by them have been able to distinguish different classes of earthquakes . In the 'gentlest' kind of earthquake, Pausanias reported that buildings may be violently shaken by tremors, but often snap back roughly into position afterwards; 'a reverse tremor throws back what has already toppled.' The second kind of earthquake 'destroys everything that is the least unsteady: whatever it strikes it instantly overthrows, as with the blow of a battering-ram.'

But third on the Pausanias 'Richter' scale was the following:

> The deadliest kind of earthquake is illustrated by the following comparison. In an unintermitting fever a man's breathing is quick and laboured, as is shown by symptoms at various points of the body, but especially at the wrists: and they say that in the same way the earthquake dives under buildings and upheaves their foundations, just as molehills are pushed up from the bowels of the earth. It is this kind of shock that leaves not a trace of human habitation behind.

> They say that the earthquake at Helice was of this last kind, the kind that levels with the ground: and that, besides the earthquake, another disaster befell the doomed city that winter. The sea advanced far over the land and submerged the whole of Helice, and in the grove of Poseidon the water was so deep that only the tops of the trees were visible. So that between the suddenness of the earthquake and the simultaneous rush of the sea, the billows sucked down Helice and every soul in the city.

Earthquakes of this magnitude must have been rare, even in classical times, Pausanias, however, knew of an analogy from his homeland. A like fate befell a city on Mount Sipylus: it disappeared into a chasm, and from the fissure in the mountain water gushed forth, and the chasm became named Lake Saloe. The ruins of the city could still be seen in the lake until the water of the torrent covered them, finally burying them in mud..

Nisyros

Nisyros, a small island off the coast of Southwest Turkey, has been studied by Professor Papamarinopoulos, Department of Geology, University of Patras, who has delved into mythology to help explain his findings and conversely used his discoveries to substantiate some part of the myths. Alfred and Anne-Marie de Grazia also briefly surveyed the Island. Both of the men had studied the myth of Scheria in the Odyssey.

In the Odyssey, Alkinoos, King of Phaeacia, promises to sacrifice to Poseidon twelve choice bulls, if the god would not hide his city of sea-farers behind a huge encircling mountain. The Poseidon-Polyvotis legend of Nisyros bears some resemblance to this story. Polyvotis was one of the Giants who fought the Olympians and were defeated. Polyvotis' shield carries the emblem of a bull (cf. Thor - Taros - hammer).

Poseidon, chasing Polyvotis, struck the island of Kos with his trident, causing an earthquake, cutting off one end of it, then picked up the end section of the island and threw it at Polyvotis, burying him under the "encircling" rock which is the actual crater of the volcano. The volcano itself is called Polyvotis. The numerous earthquakes which shake the island are ascribed to his writhing and his moaning.

In Plato's *Critias*, Poseidon constructs the Metropolis of Atlantis by creating, from above, a double circle of land separated by a triple circle of sea. The Metropolis is associated with ten bulls, of which one is chosen for sacrifice. The Metropolis is destroyed by an earthquake and collapse of the land into the sea, possibly a tsunami, for which the Greeks lack a word.

In Homeric and classic vocabulary, the concept of volcano does not exist as such. Plato himself had observed Aetna, which erupted when he was in Syracuse. In *Critias*, Plato does not describe a volcanic eruption, even though it would have been part of his personal experience.

In the case of the Futunas, the threat of the falling "encircling" mountain is either a traumatic memory of an ancient event, or it is a "parastochastic" interpretation: a way to explain the circular shape of a mountain which had acted up in a way which we would call volcanic: a burst of lava could have petrified a ship anchored by the shore. Sailors observing the phenomenon from a distance would have feared to be buried by the mountain if it exploded.

The Poseidon-Polyvotis event on Nisyros could be explained by an exoterrestrial impact which activated seismic and volcanic activity in the Aegean. Or, if the parastochastic explanation is the right one, a volcanic activity which was interpreted as the fall of a mountain from above (rather than its birth and growth from lava from below).

In the same way, the Navajo Indians interpreted the Berringer Crater created by an impact of a meteoroid 40,000 (?) years ago as a sacred place produced by a thunderbolt hurled by a flying dragon as it passed above.

The multi-ringed structure of Atlantis as presented by Plato can point both to a multi-ringed volcano, or to an impact structure. Forsyth Gordon tends to believe that Atlantis was an invention of Plato, on the basis of his own life experiences: the spectacle of Aetna, its crater and its geophysical activity, compounded by the catastrophic destruction of the town of Helike on the Gulf of Corinth when Plato was 52 years old: it was shaken by an earthquake in 373 BC and thrown into the sea by a landslide, as detailed above. The city was dedicated to Poseidon.

A neat interpretation, it would appear, but there may have been more to the story. Plato describes a geological feature which can have been caused by an impact or by a volcano, but which does not resemble anything that could be seen in the Mediterranean. I would not agree that "flying Poseidon" was in all three cases (Scheria, Atlantis and Nisyros) an impacting meteorite, but the thesis deserves some further investigation. Informally, a number of Greek geologists entertain the notion of there existing a sizeable meteoric crater between Nisyros and Kos. The hypothesis has not yet been seriously investigated.

I think, following the parastochastic explanation, that the Schaerians came to settle an area with a pre-existing volcanic crater, but they interpreted it as having been produced by an impact from heaven (as the Navajo did with the Berringer crater). They feared the continuous seismic activity and projected it as a possibility of a new, future impact from the sky. Although the mummification of a boat with lava appeared as a threat evident enough, the major explosion was avoided. Also remark the story of the origin of the Lycabettos hill in Athens. It is supposed to have been a rock dropped from the fangs of Athena (as an owl) during some fight or battle in the sky. Note also the name: Lycos means wolf, symbol and visualization of Planet Mars in a persistent perspective.

We read further from the *3D Velocity Tomography of the Nisyros Volcano Area* (Institute of geophysics U. of Hamburg, and Inst. of Geodynamics, National Observatory, Athens. (2002):

> The Nisyros volcano has been identified as an apophytic intrusion of a much larger volcanic structure, with a caldera of 35 km diameter, extending between the southern coasts of the islands of Kos and Nisyros (therefore, largely submerged).:

> The tomography has allowed the finding of high velocity rocks intruding through the upper crust and penetrating into the volcano cones to depth of approx. 1.0km to 1.8 km. The high velocity bodies at shallow depth were identified as high-density cumulates of solidified magma intrusion in the caldera. These intrusions explain very high temperatures of 300 deg. Celsius observed in the lower aquifer of the caldera at 1,5km depths confirmed by drilling. The volcanic edifices of Kos, Yali, Nisyros and Strongilo are part of a major volcanic caldera nearly 35km in diameter. This explains the large volume of ignimbrites erupted 160,000 years ago..." [We caution against accepting datings such as this one without scrutiny of the tests by which they were figured.][188]

A Focus on Syria-Palestine

Contradiction are manifest all down the coast. Katzenstein tells us that "the trail of destruction wrought by the Sea-Peoples can be traced along the entire Mediterranean Coast, from Ugair... through Hawâm..." Writing later, Stern tells us that "neither Phenicia nor any of its main centers – was ever conquered by the Sea Peoples." Also at Ugarit, Schorr describes "a gold bowl combining Aegean, Egyptian, Mesopotamian and Levantine motifs that Frankfort pronounced an excellent example of Phoenician syncretism, half a millennium before Phoenicians in the proper sense are known."

Patricia Maynor Bikai tells the same and then

confounds matters by examining the exploits of Ramses III, as recounted at Medinet Abu and in the Harris Papyrus. The fearsomeness of a triple dyschronology is manifest. Events of Late Bronze splendor are feverishly mismatched with the Iron Age, including the usual discrepancies of the Phantom Ages, and then doomed to irresolution by incorporating the Fourth Century activities of Ramses III as if he were of the Late Bronze Age. Is it, by the way, as Bikai reveals, that Baal is revived and flourishing now as the Doppelgaenger of Ramses III. The Medinet Abu inscriptions refer to Baal sixteen times – and only once each to Atum, Anath and Astarte. Like Baal (and as Baal), Ramses III appears as a god of battle, of storms, of swords, of cries from heavens and mountain tops, of a raging bull. This is definitely not the old imperial religion of Egypt, but the ersatz composition of a heterogeneous cosmopolitan culture.

Holding to the uniformitarian interpretation of the transitional Bronze-Iron age, William G. Dever has concluded that the changes experienced by Egyptians, Canaanites, 'Sea Peoples' and proto-Israelites were gradual, lasting ca 1250-1150, and varied from site to site. Continuity between LB and IR I is much greater than previously thought, Phantom Ages notwithstanding. The major factors that account for change are so complex and vary so much from site to site that a regional approach is both possible and necessary.

> It was never explained what happened to the predominantly Canaanite population, since evidently it was not annihilated, as even Biblical accounts admit.) Now, however, it is abundantly clear that a number of sites suffered only minor disruptions. Furthermore, Canaanite presence and influence continued unabated well into the 12th and even the 11th century BC. The early phase of this "afterglow" was largely under the aegis of Egyptian rule, which as we now know extended (in Palestine at least) not only throughout the early 19th dynasty and the reign of Ramses II, but well into the 20th dynasty, down even into the time of Ramses VI (ca 1143-1136 as demonstrated conclusively by Weinstein (1981).

Evidently, toward the end of the Empire, the Egyptians attempted to reimpose direct rule over parts of Palestine, especially the Southern coastal plain. Even aft6er the collapse of the Empire, however, Canaanite culture persisted. This is evident from many LB II ceramic forms that continued throughout early Iron I, into the mid-12th century BC and even later, as several studies have shown.

Megiddo VIIA continues into the mid 12th century BC as evidenced by a cartouche of Ramses III (ca 1184-1153)- and maybe even 1143-1136 (Ramses VI cartouche, not found in situ). Only in the next phase does Iron IA Philistine ware begin.

Tel Rehov

"Iron Age Chronology in the Near East and Eastern Mediterranean Region has become a hotly debated issue," declare three authors of a *Science* article of 2003 on the subject of Tel Rehov. They must mean that it is even hotter than it was when Velikovsky blasted the conventional chronology in 1950 and 1952. (A second article concentrating like the first on Tel Rehov, generally agrees and adds to the welter of detail of the excavations.)

Archaeologists smothered the blast, and then cautiously got around to a creeping reform heading his way. The profession for the most part places Pharaoh Shishak (Shoshenq I) in the late tenth century (around - 925 BCE, the average simulated date of several radiocarbon datings.) and would quite deny our revision, that is Velikovsky's, if they paid any attention to it, that would coalesce Shishak with Thutmoses III, conventionally carried four centuries earlier. Archaeology is supposed to confirm historical studies or disprove them.

We place Thutmoses III (Shishak in the Bible) in the early First Millennium on the heels of Solomon, whose amassed treasures were carried off by Thutmose; year after year he took more until there was little left to impress one about Jerusalem (Kadesh). Velikovsky does a remarkable job of picturing the individual treasures taken from Solomon's Temple. The latest studies contest for dating over a century or two of late Iron Age I and early Iron Age II.

Finkelstein's group holds to a later, lower date, the more conservative scientists for the tenth-ninth century presence of Tel Rehov and other Israelite towns. The ceramics which they find are Greek Geometric styles. With them are Phoenicians and Cypriote as well as local fabrications. They are trying to fill up the four centuries of Phantom Ages, and one may be excused for claiming that they do so by inventing copious code names for the intervals and the levels assigned among them are numerous.

Tel Rehov is the principal excavation. It is mentioned in the list of cities conquered by Thutmose-Shishak. "The excavations reveal that Tel Rehov was a thriving city during the Iron Age I and IIA cultural periods." The city was destroyed and rebuilt several times. I do not know of any special study of the sources of the destruction, although invariably they are assigned to whoever is believed to be the principal foreign enemy at the approximate time. They conveniently give levels of settlement and charred grain, seeds, fine charcoal, and olive pits for radiocarbon dating.

In sum, the two reports, possibly representing the traditional outlook of Israeli archaeology, disregard earthquakes or sky events, putting all sudden change and destruction into the hands of enemy forces. But they also do not deduct the 800 years needed to reach the time of Ramses III.

Let us allude to other sites. All are dated four or more centuries too old. Beth Shan is not destroyed at the end of LB IIB. Egyptian houses there are said to belong to the garrison established by Ramses III. If so, we are speaking of the Fourth Century, and not expecting destruction.

Ta'nach (Jezreel Valley) LB occupation continues at least until mid-12th century BC, then there is a destruction, and a gap until the 10th century.

In the south we can now assemble a group of similar LB IIB sites that continue into the early/mid 12th century BC before being destroyed, again mostly those with strong Egyptian connections.

At Gezer the Egyptian tradition is especially strong: inscriptions of Merneptah, Ramses III, Ramses IX. (Here we would deny the Ramses III connection unless we place it in the 4th Century.)

Peter James on Lachish and Ramses III

Lachish probably remained an Egyptian stronghold until the mid-12th century BC rather than being destroyed in 1225 BC, as earlier thought. "A wealth of Egyptian remains..."

Here I take leave to publish a relevant letter on Lachish and the dating of Ramses III by the scholar and author of quantavolution studies, co-author of *Centuries of Darkness,* Peter James. He was an early strong supporter of Velikovsky and has now varied in several important respects from his former position.

Date: Mar 30 2005 - 5:37pm

Dear Alfred,

Sorry about the delay in replying. I have been having tunnel vision trying to meet a deadline on a chronology paper. I am working mainly on Archaic pottery chronology at the moment (7th-6th centuries BC), in order to then recheck backwards through the "Dark Age" styles.

Re Ramesses III, you are right to suspect the former, i.e. that he is early Iron Age. In fact this is unescapable. V tended to dismiss the importance of the scarab and other finds with his name in Levantine contexts and dismissed them all in a rather cavalier paragraph in Peoples of the Sea. It can't be done. There must be a good score of objects with the name of Ramesses III and other 20th Dynasty kings (including Ramesses IV and VI) in early Iron Age contexts in Palestine. Take Lachish for example, where
Ramesses III's cartouche occurs on a bronze found in Stratum VI. Here are the strata in descending order:

Lachish I - Contains Greek pottery, of the late 5th-early 4th centuries BC. The dates here are absolutely sound. Have just read a preprint by the Israeli excavator who has rechecked the (plentiful) Greek finds from this Stratum and the dates cluster around 400 BC for the buildings in this level.

Lachish II - Conventionally dated 701-587 BC. On the Centuries of Darkness model the dates come down to 587-c.440 BC.

Lachish III - Conventionally dated c. 750-701 BC. On the CoD model its dates come down to 701-587 587 BC.

Lachish IV - Iron Age Judahite. I would date this level to the 8th century BC.

Lachish V - Iron Age Judahite. My date 9th century BC.

Lachish VI - Bronze Age city. The destruction level contains a cartouche of Ramesses III on a bronze fitting. Conventional dating of destruction c.175 BC, CoD model c. 925 BC.

Lachish VII - Bronze Age city. The Fosse Temple. 18th-19th Dynasty objects.

So... according to Velikovsky's Peoples of the Sea model the Ramesses III should have been found in Str. I. Yet it was actually found six strata deeper. Incidentally these are all substantial strata, with massive building remains, while Lachish is probably one of the best excavated sites in Israel worked on by successive British and Israeli teams - all highly professional. V's only stab at Lachish (in Ramses II and His Time) was to try to take the Fosse Temple from Stratum VII and somehow muddle it into Stratum II. Can't be done.

So in my view Ramesses III undoubtedly follows the 19th Dynasty (there is mountains of evidence for this of other kinds). That does indeed place him close to the natural upheavals at the turn of the Bronze-Iron Ages. In archaeological terms I would date the transition to c. 940 BC (CoD date).

I'll try to send you a copy of Centuries next week when I have piled up enough packages to brave the queue in the Post Office. (Local ones have been cut from four to two!)

Hoping this finds you and Ami well and thriving. All the best, Peter

Despite the authority with which James speaks, I turned around once more and put Ramses III back into the Fourth Century.

To resume our review of some findings in the Near Levant:

Tel Sera yielded an Egyptian bowl with a date formula "in the 22nd year" - probably of Ramses III (i.e. ca 1154 BC) Also Tel Mor and Tell el Farah (cartouche of Seti II (ca 1200-1194 BC)

Jaffa V has produced a gateway with jamb blocks inscribed to Ramses II.

Telkl es Saidieh, in the Jordan Valley evidenced rich finds of Egyptian jewelry and luxury goods.

The settlements of the Sea-Peoples, William C. Dever points out, were hardly known some 40 years ago, i.e., around 1955. We had the reliefs of the battle with Ramses III, [which by my estimation is misplaced, causing extensive archaeological damage] and hints in the Bible about arrival of a new people in Palestine, the "Philistines."

A number of disturbances and actual destructions along the coast and slightly inland undoubtedly reflected the arrival of "Sea Peoples." They came in several waves by land and sea, from Anatolia down the Levantine coast, from Cyprus (probably a jumping off place) but all ultimately derived from earlier ethnic movements in the Aegean world at the end of the Late Bronze Age. In all these sites, after a generation or so, Philistine pottery appears.

Also sites more or less inland show disturbances that might be attributable to 'Sea Peoples". They also show the appearance of Philistine ware. There are other sites where there is no destruction between Late Bronze and Iron I, but where Philistine pottery nevertheless appears as well as other elements of Philistine culture, rather abruptly, in the mid-12th century or so. [That is, the key elements of quantavolution without structurally evident natural disaster.]

Archaeological investigation in Palestine, Dever correctly asserts, has long been dominated by "Biblical " archaeology, the father of which [in the U.S.A.] was W. F. Albright, and which thought to demonstrate archaeologically the veracity of the conquest of Joshua, with Israelite tribes sweeping into Western Palestine and destroying site after site of the Late Bronze Age IIB. This theory ".. has to be abandoned in the light of much newer data..."

"It is now abundantly clear that of the 'destructions'.. only Hazor XIII and perhaps LBA Bethel could possibly be attributed to incoming Israelites."

"Two LB sites that were not destroyed but may have been settled by the early Israelites are... Tel Dan VII (Canaanite 'Laish') which shows generally little or no destruction and may have been simply taken over peacefully by the Israelites. The same is true of Canaanite Shechem - a fact that accords well with the Biblical tradition that Shechem came into the Israelite confederation through treaty."

The city of Hazor, largest and richest and most powerful city of Canaan of the Late Bronze period, "came to a brutal end in the thirteenth century BCE [our ~ -850]. Suddenly, with no apparent alarm and little sign of decline, Hazor was attacked, destroyed, and set ablaze. The mud brick walls of the palace, which were baked red from the terrible conflagration, are still preserved today to the height of six feet. After a period of abandonment, a poor settlement was established in one part of the vast ruins. Its pottery resembled that of the early Isrraelite settlements in the central hill country to the south." (p.81)

It now seems that the 12th (our 7th) century BC "Proto-Israelites" ... were largely indigenous peoples of Palestine, perhaps displaced Canaanites, opening up and settling the hill country frontiers.... The dozens of early Iron I villages, associated with a sweeping shift in settlement type and relatively sudden demographic changes, are located precisely in those areas that were not heavily occupied in the 14-13th century BC [~- 900 to 700] or dominated by LBA Canaanite city-states. These villages are found primarily in the central hill country, but also to some extent in Lower Galilee and the Northern Negev." Almost all are un-walled, established de novo in the 12th [7th] century, then after several phases of occupation, abandoned.

There are about 250 such villages, almost all on hilltops, with arable lands around.

The economy, social structure and political order of these Iron I "Proto-Israelite" villages would seem to reflect a predominantly agrarian movement, accompanied by a strong "egalitarian" thrust... At all levels, one is struck by the lack of any evidence for elites in the Iron I villages.

Now, the driving force behind the Israelite ethnic movement may well have been Yahwism, as later Biblical sources maintain, or a revolutionary peasant revolt, as many biblical scholars have argued.

There remain a few sites which have been destroyed at the end of LBA, but they are not demonstrably connected to the known ethnic groups. Some tables with an undeciphered script are found, which looks rather Aegean.

The Canaanite population moved toward the hills and became more 'Israelite.' Hundreds of villages are revealed by geographic surveys. The 12 Tribes of Israel are hardly discernible to archaeologists.

Dever posted a chart of the Syrian-Palestinian excavations of the first 150 years of the Iron Age, covering the transition from the Bronze Age and carrying on for a century (-800 to -700 of our dates). "It arranges virtually all the sites we now have [1990's] in a basic stratigraphic framework. The scope is modern Israel, the West Bank, Jordan, Lebanon and much of coastal and southern Syria."

As is revealed by the chart, no site escaped unscathed. All towns are reported to have been destroyed and/or abandoned. We may remark that the indicated continuity from Bronze to Iron where it occurs may contradict the Dark Age theory, for where would the 400 years of the Phantom Age be placed? Dever says that there is no true Dark Age, just a gradual prolonged change. Actually this seems to be contradicted by most of what he has to say. The earmarks of quantavolution in all spheres and throughout the region (and a much larger region, he adds) are present.

Furthermore, one may note that these destructions are spread out over time, and we hold to the revised shortened chronology, so they must be occurring much closer together in time, even simultaneously, in some cases and in other cases separated by a few years that represent the intervals between successive approaches of planet Mars.

Egyptian control declined. The rule had been heavy-handed, exacting heavy taxes in commodities and manpower; public building projects benefitted only to the Egyptian administrators and the puppet princes. "These abuses - the competition for scarce resources, the class conflict, and the pathetic socio-economic situation they created - are all vividly portrayed in the Tell el-Amarna letters written from Palestine to the court of Akhnaton."

Around 1200 BC [-850], there occurred a cessation of imports of Mycenean-Cypriot ceramics to Palestine - but also of Egyptian luxury goods which had dominated the entire Bronze Age. Finally Syrian imports ceased as well. It was the end of "entrepreneurism..." There were no means to import raw materials, no market. These indicators support a quantavolution, though again Dever maintains that continuity was the rule.

It is almost as if Prof. Dever had been foreordained to visualize continuity and peaceful exchanges of whole peoples, even while his materials were signaling quantavolution. He could be easily rescued from this attempt to alter by pacifism the Biblical bloodiness of the descent upon Canaan of the Hebrews according to Albright, if he would surrender the several centuries between his dates of -1350 to -1100 in favor of -800 to -650.

Italy

The Bronze Age ended in Italy in general disaster. The Alpine lake settlements, the palafitte, were drowned or abandoned. The Po River plains region, the terramare, was abandoned. The usual reasons are given, peaceful emigration to the South or the uplands, invasions by unknown "Peoples of the Sea," climatic deterioration, epidemics, flooding. The form of social organization of *gentilizio-clientare*, a noble-client system such as would occur with the collapse of law and order appears to have become prominent with the advent of the Iron Age. (This, I would suggest, is an equivalent of the Danaans' chieftain-led gangs in the war against Troy.)

A widespread practice of hill stockades and forts, *incastellamento,* occurred with the Late Bronze, but then declined with the Iron Age, as we would expect in an age of lightning when, as Pliny said, no hilltop constructions could endure. (I have conjectured elsewhere that the Scottish hill forts went through the same fiery experience, melting into the cliffs on which they sat.) Volcanism raged in the South.

I have already delved into the circumstances of the founding of Rome, but I may conjecture at this point that the great dedication and devotion tendered Mars in Rome and elsewhere may be connected with the role of Planet Mars in ridding the skies of the immediate threat of planet Venus. Even though mankind seems to have an unlimited capacity to revere his celestial and imaginary divine torturers, he does also have a capacity for gratitude, which can mitigate the otherwise nearly total deprivations visited upon him by his god.

Mycenean connections disappear with the close of the Bronze Age. There are vague indications that transalpine European cultural contacts persisted, perhaps even migrations wherever conditions seem to permit, whether from North to South or vice versa or both. It would seem, indeed, that the Etruscans and Celts found immigration to Northern and Central Italy often scarcely opposed, when they ventured there during the middle Iron Age.

Lago Albano

Lago Albano, Southeast of Rome, was subject to a theoretical investigation by Prof. Alberto Barzano. It is known from numerous sources in antiquity that a King of Alba Longa (his name varies according to the sources) was a victim of a natural disaster, interpreted by all as a punishment for his impiety. The story occurs in Diodorus, Dionysius of Halicarnassos, Dion Cassius/Zonara and the *"Origo gentis Romanae."*

All sources concur that the King (variously called Arramulio Silvio, Allodio, Amulio, Romolo Silvio, or Aremulo Silvio) reigned for a period of 19 years, and that he was "superbus," (arrogant) towards the gods, especially towards Jupiter. He even was "a monster of tyranny," odious to men as well to the gods. The major trespass that drew upon his head the vengeance of Zeus was an order he gave to his troops to beat their swords against their shields all together, so as to drown out the noise of Jupiter's thunder. By way of punition for this sacrilege, he was struck dead by lightning and his whole house was submerged by Lake Albano, in the depths of which some columns and remains of constructions are said by Dionysius of Halicarnassus to be still visible during quiet weather.

The *Origo Gentis Romanae (Origins of Noble Roman Families)* reports the same story, but adds two diverging sources ("Aufidius" and "Domitius") according to whom the King was not struck by lightning but that his kingdom was precipitated, together with him, into the depths of Lago Albano by an earthquake.

Later historians pay the story little attention, Titus Livius only mentions *en passant* the death of the king from lightning, as does Ovid. Orosius adds a chronological clue by saying that the King was a contemporary of "Falaris." In the Chronicles of Girolamo (Barzano does not give the dates for these) it is mentioned that the King acceded to the throne in the "year 1142 after Abraham," and that his disastrous death occurred in the year 1161. This would be in our Iron Age.

One study in modern times has addressed itself to the story: K. F. Smith, "On a Legend of the Alban Lake told by Dionyius of Halicarnassus."[189] Smith tends to dismiss the story of the death by lightning, for which he finds suspicious similes, but he sees, in the tale of the submerged kingdom, the traces left by a very ancient event, for "the lake was in the habit of rising from time to time... (which is) abundantly shown by traces of its action upon the surrounding banks, and that it sometimes overflowed and did much injury to the adjacent slopes and lowlands is proved by the famous Emissarium by which, to this day, the lake is prevented from rising above its present level."

Much more recently, Giuseppe Chiarucci, director of the Civic Museum of Albano, has reported the discovery of the remains of human occupation dating to the Bronze Age under the waters of Lake Albano.[190] The archaeological site is situated "on the declivity in front of the ancient coastline." It is situated on a small promontory which rose several meters above the ancient beach (at a depth of ca 8 to 10 meters below present level).

Pieces of burned wood have been found, as well as black ashes, bone fragments and a great number of ceramic sherds. There were also found some wooden posts of ca 30cm of diameter standing vertically in the earth. Some of those are situated between two heaps of stones in the shape of truncated cones distant by about 8-10 meters, their base having a diameter of ca 3m, their height being about 1m50... Large vases have been found. The site is dated to the Middle Bronze Age, at a period estimated, in terms of absolute (conventional chronology) to ca 16th century B.C.E. It is conceivable that wooden posts, seen under the lake, can have been identified as "columns" and tumuli of stones as the "remains of constructions" to which Dionysius of Hallicarnassos is referring and could have been understood in antiquity to represent the ruins of the palace of the arrogant king.

Research done in the Basin of Lake Albano by E. Stella[191] confirms that the waters are exceptionally transparent, and allow a depth vision of 8 to 10 meters in very quiet weather (the very terms which Dionysius himself uses). The Lake itself is known for its treacherous vortexes, especially at midday, near the exit cone of its emissary, not only in the water but in the air above, to the point where they have supposedly caused (small) planes to crash... Also, following heavy rains, the north-east shores tend to become inundated... The gentle slope following the beaches is composed of very mixed, 'incoherent' geological material, tossed and rearranged by the water, which must often submerged its shores. It is therefore quite possible that constructions built along the shore could have been inundated and have remained covered by the water in consequence of a more or less gradual change in the level of the earth....

The catastrophic destruction of ancient Volsinium is preserved as a vague, but indeed frightening memory in literary sources. It was, of course, anterior to the fully historical age of Rome, which we may initiate with the coming to power of the Tarquin dynasty.

Yet, from the period preceding the Tarquins, it may be rewarding to fix our attention on the traditions connected with King Tullius Ostilius, especially those of his death and of the destruction, upon his order, of the city of Alba Longa.

The antique sources unanimously agree about the circumstances of his death: he died struck by lightning or, more precisely, in the fire of his house which had been struck by lightning. Dionysius of Halicarnassos reports that "he lost his life in the fire of his house [palace] together with his wife and children and all the great number of those who lived in his house and who were surprised by the fire." Dionysius adds that according to some, the fire had been set by Anco Marcio, in the hope that the kingship would pass to him as a result, but

Dionysius dismisses the rumor. The *Scriptores rerum mythicarum latini* add an interesting moralistic comment: fire had turned into a dangerous thing because of the evil use made of it by men.... Whereas Numa Pompilius was able to handle it without being punished, because he used it only in the sacred rites of the gods..." (This could be a reference to electric fire, induced on a device comparable to the electrostatic machine or Ark of Moses, which is extensively treated in my book, *God's Fire: Moses and the Management of Exodus.)*

Sicily

In Mycenean times Sicily maintained a prosperous civilization which carried on a busy trade with Greece. as well as with the Minoan empire of Crete. "This civilization disappears from view about the same time that the chief Mycenean centers were destroyed," and five centuries of darkness are said to have descended upon the island, according to L. B. Brea *(Sicily before the Greeks)*. In other words, it was part of the Phantom Age. The archaeological record of these five centuries is naught.

Yet, tholos tombs of the Mycenean type are found to the north of Agrigento, containing gold bowls and rings reminiscent of Mycenean objects - neither tombs nor objects can be dated earlier than the seventh century, supposedly the time of the founding of the first Greeks settlements - this dating being imposed by the find of geometric pottery inside the tombs. The Phantom Age had to be inserted only to keep apace with Egyptian conventional chronology.

Gela was said to have been the earliest Greek colony, with its migrants from Crete and Rhodes, and a date then considered to be 689 BCE. Its leader was remembered as a veteran of the Trojan War, Antiphemos. Scores of colonies and sub-colonies were set up within the next century. It is unknown how much of the large and thriving Sicilian people came from Siculi and Sicani survivors of the Mars Quantavolution and how many from Greece and Carthage. Moreover, Purcell and Snodgrass agree that the colonies were melting pots of Greeks, native Sicilians, and other foreigners. Between the end of the Mycenean Age and the first colonies there occurred the Phantom-500 Age, with its absolute lack of archaeological and cultural remains.

Snodgrass speculates that the Greek cities were too weak to launch strong colonizing expeditions and that groups of condottieri and adventurers may have been the initial settlers. Often, however, the party about to invade another people's country took pains to obtain the approval of oracles, especially the Apollo Oracle at Delphi.

Crete (Tarshish)

The removal of several centuries of "Phantom Ages" helped Velikovsky to identify Tarshish, a mysterious country famous for its seafarers and maritime traders, mentioned in three different instances in the Bible, and once in cuneiform tablets from Assyria. Velikovsky identified Tarshish with Crete, a location which fits what is said about it both in the Bible and in the Assyrian tablet of King Esarhaddon.

What kept this identification from being made earlier, was the fact that, in the conventional chronology, the end of Minoan Crete is put some four to six hundred years before the texts referring to Tarshish had been written, and that Crete was supposed to be plunged into the Phantom Age, without a high civilization and without the means for far-reaching trade by sea. (It is indeed absurd to imagine that Crete, which is at a strategic crossroads, could have been plunged into Phantom Ages while the countries around (Assyria, Palestine, Tyre, Egypt, Ionia...) were thriving... Surely, someone would have taken it over, established bases for trade, planted colonies, etc.

The Phantom Age has affected Crete, as elsewhere. The Minos Age of Thucydides combines the Early Minos, pre-Hellenic and Middle Minoan. King Minos is doubled: The first lived at the time of the wizard Daedalus, and pursued him to Sicily there to be himself killed by King Kokalos. The Greek Bronze Age Daedalus fathered the Daedalic School of sculptors. It was the second Daedalus who was the originator of sculpting statues standing in natural poses instead of having arms close to the sides and one foot forward.

The great Island of Crete, rich in all ways, was quite devastated during what is regarded as the latter decades of the Late Minoan Period, which we would label as already the beginning of Martia, the transition between the Bronze and the Iron Ages. "Nearly all major excavated sites in Crete reveal evidence of damage, desertion, or destruction." There are at least one and perhaps two horizons of fire destruction found to exist throughout Crete. The first at perhaps 1450 BCE might have been connected with the Venusian Quantavolution period beginning around 1500. The second occurred at the end of Late Minoan II probably, and would fit into the Martian scheme of events.

The strong similarities among the debris ceramics and other objects of localities all around the island go to prove that the destructions were probably simultaneous, or no more than a few years apart. (A useful survey is to be found in "The Emergence of Divergence.." contained in *Development and Decline in the Mediterranean Bronze Age.*) Herodotus claimed that after the Trojan War (but not caused by it) Crete suffered total famine and pestilence, becoming practically uninhabited.

The Bronze-Iron destructions and desertions included the towns of Nirou Khani, Amnisos, Gazi, Malia, Katsambas, Ayia Pelagia, Knossos, Archanes, Stamnio – these in the North, while in the East one counts Palaikastria and Gournia, in the West Chania, Perivolia, Stylos, Armenoi, and in the South Kalohorafites, Ayia Triadha, Kommos, Gallia, Hondros Viannu. These are not associated with volcanism, it is important to note, and are regarded as non-concurrent, so possibly in various Mars phases. Pomerance writing in 1970 attributed the general destruction to a huge tsunami following the Thera explosion that he locates in the 12th century.

On the present working model of this author, the Thera explosion is placed earlier, and although it caused great destruction within a thousand kilometer radius, it was not a cause great enough to be termed a major quantavolution. On the other hand, as I have already hinted, it is not impossible and in the emerging clarity of an improved chronology, that it followed not long after Akhnaton and the Amarna Letters, and in conjunction with the Quantavolution of Mars. Not to be ignored is the possibility that a great volcano burst or a meteorite fell in the southeastern Aegean, which has gone wholly buried and unrecognized up to the present time.

Less than a dozen settlements out of the hundreds of Middle Minoan ones provide any evidence of habitation in the Late-Late Minoan. Only Knossos had visible activity. "The decline of Minoan Crete is therefore something of an enigma. At the apparent peak of its powers, it suffers what seems – in archaeological terms – to be a sudden disaster and transformation. No antecedent process is clearly visible. For this reason, 'prime-mover' explanations have a long history. The LMIB destructions have thus been seen as the result of: the eruption of the Thera-Santorini volcano, or earthquakes, or a Mycenean invasion, or internal warfare."

The Dartmouth Classics site on the Web gives us the following lines about hill-top settlements:

> The 12th century in Crete appear to have been equally unsettled. It seems likely that there were influxes of Mainland Greek migrants to the island at various times during this period, and the unsettled nature of life on the island during the LM IIIC period is reflected in the appearance of refugee settlements such as Karphi (on a peak high above the Lasithi Plain of central Crete), Kavousi-Kastro, Chalasmeno, and Katalimata (on peaks and a virtually inaccessible ledge overhanging a ravine at the northeast end of the isthmus of Ierapetra), Erganos (on a steep acropolis in the southwestern foothills of Mt. Dikte), Kastro Kepahala (on a high ridge near the north coast and just west of Heraklion), Kastri (on a steep acropolis above the earlier LH IIIA-B settlement at Palaikastro in east Crete), and numerous other sites

explored and mapped during the 1980's and 1990's by K. Nowicki.

Recently several scholars, prominently Renfrew, have conceived of a systems collapse. It is rather like the theory of Roman Empire decline and collapse from overload. Or perhaps like the American and European Great Depression that came to a peak in the late twenties and went on remorselessly until it was ended only by the precipitation of World War II and its waste of resources and energy, and slaughter of millions. The same pre-war civilization persisted and its superstructure was rebuilt. The nations involved never crashed or depopulated, or even changed much of their social-political systems.

According to the theory, social costs and stresses rise to overburden the society; specialization and bureaucratizing take their toll by rigidities. But no, compared with Rome, the Cretan collapse came more suddenly. And it came when the region was at its highest state of development.

...It was the base of an increasingly large-scale, complex, hierarchical, and centralized, social, economic, religious, and political system through to the LMIB period. Knossos was, if anything, becoming more important with time. The last period, LMIB, appears the high point from most viewpoints. How then does one explain its sudden end? Yoffee, for example, argues that in reality no civilization collapses 'suddenly', nor across the board in all its facets (1988b) – ruling out comprehensive natural disaster.

The Azoria (NE Crete) Project is a million-euro project, multi-disciplinary, of several universities and research institutions, four years old by 2005 and concentrated upon a ten-hectare site with three aims in mind. Over a hundred Americans and Greeks worked each season, to study how in the Early Iron Age (1200-600 B.C.E. or our ~-800 to 600) a town center developed, with especial attention to changes in ecology. That is, paleoethnobiology and the formation of a state were the topics. Evidence of regional and overseas trade and other contacts were to be sought.

Although the site was rebuilt around -700, no explanation is afforded its destruction and ".. We must assume that remodeling was the motive , a reorganization of space that is physically unifying." That might signify a large sudden political change. An intriguing sentence in the 2003 report deserves quotation: "The kitchen in A2100 is very well preserved, exhibiting the evidence of the ubiquitous burnt destruction and late sixth-century abandonment phase."The *rapporteurs* feel duty-bound to mention destruction (doing so 5 times), burning (10 times), ashes (14 times) in three years of reporting, but make nothing of these (and in fact they are surprisingly few mentions), for generally they are gung-ho to reveal a progressive development of the hamlet into a good-sized town and do their best to fill up the Phantom-500 Age. By their eminence and top establishment sponsorship, the grand effort and brigade of diggers, and the pomposity and roundabout unintelligibility of the reporting thus far on their web site, it must be said that "the Center Holds!" as Professor William Mullen entitled an article forty years ago on the fate of Velikovsky's threat.

Thera-Santorini and the Cyclades

Some scholars have tried, as I mentioned earlier, to correlate the volcanic explosion of the Island of Thera in the Cyclades, whose effects were felt throughout a large part of the Eastern Mediterranean, with the destructive end of the Bronze Age. Others have essayed to demonstrate that Thera was the probable site of the fabulous continent of Atlantis and its destruction. Neither proposal is likely. Correlation is more probable with the tremendous catastrophes at the end of the Middle Bronze Age, attributable largely to the encounters of Earth with Planet Venus. Every 52 years, Venus would pass in close proximity to Earth and provoke disaster, notwithstanding every conceivable form of worshipful appeasement. If Thera did not explode in 1450 it would have exploded at 1400 or 1350, or some such anniversary until the Planet Mars became entangled and a new series of disasters began. But the analysis of debris around the region would suggest earlier rather later occasions of planetary encounter.

Some attention might be given to the possibility that a tsunami or flood running down from the North poured over and into the Thera volcano causing it to explode mightily. This water might have been connected with the catastrophes of the 1450 B.C.E. period (the Venusian Quantavolution) or the -800 disasters, in which latter event it would have been the Southern extension of the Hungarian Plain floods mentioned earlier, related, also, to the drowning of the Aegean Islands, to the breakthrough of the Bosphorus, and to the climatic changes of the Far North. Obviously geography, archaeology, and ecology have a large job of investigating ahead. Spyridon Marinatos left an important bequest of quantavolutionary research problems when he fell to his death at Akrotiri in Thera-Santorini.

As to the Atlantis connection, practically all of the fundamental mythical features of the setting and the occasion bespeak a culture far removed from the Aegean setting. Atlantis solutions have been often the work of men of genius, and what they have tried is more understandable and commendable than the immense efforts of Isaac Newton to prove the literal veracity of the Old Testament, or so it would seem to this author. Plato's story is precise and factual, and, as I indicate elsewhere in this book, it is relatively simple to project the course of Plato's story until it enters upon classical times. The best work on Atlantis has been that of Jurgen Spanuth, unattended to probably because his publisher became a neo-Nazi. He set the catastrophe in the extreme Northwest of Europe where the globally destructive comet Phaeton appears to have crashed. He followed the archaeological consensus, however, in basing his theory on events depicted invalidly and unreliably at Medinet Habu.

Invasions by mostly imagined Peoples of the Sea would have been incompetent to conquer and destroy the cities and towns and shrines all over Crete. The steep decline in population could hardly be the work of groups of invaders. In many places large conflagrations occurred. A need for fulminology is manifest here. What or who set the fires, and fed them? Too, drought, famine and plague rendered the Bronze-Iron transition in Crete more terrible.

The Archipelago of the Cyclades were part of the pattern of quantavolution that transformed Crete. Its towns and people disappeared in large part. Its distinctive and flourishing arts, especially the sculpture, vanished. Rising and sinking of lands occurred. Thereupon the islands followed the course of development into classical Greek culture. Thus, at one point, Thracian adventurers found the Island of Naxos uninhabited, raided Anatolia for women, suffered retaliation, profited from subsequent internecine warfare among their conquerors, and held on for 200 years until drought brought on abandonment. It was resettled by Carians who called it by their King Naxios.

There is no end to the case studies that could be made: Find the site and there you will find, almost invariably, the destruction level of the Iron Age Quantavolution. Robert Markot's *Black Pharaohs*, for example, provides a history of Nubia-Sudan. In the late -700's, the Sudanese invaded Egypt, established what has been called the 25th dynasty, and moved also into Palestine, where they fought to withstand the Assyrians. Conventionally, the events were put into the -1100's. But why could not the Sudanese also be called "People of the Seas," so typical of the Age was this set of events, as we are discovering, and consequently the defeat of Egypt registered as the result of invasion rather than of natural catastrophe? To answer our own question: Yes, it might be so classified, but, too, the Sudanese would be not only propelled by disaster but also drawn to the scene of a crippled nation.

Might not, too, this misfortune of Egypt have happened upon the downfall of the monotheistic Pharaoh Akhnaton, so hated by the Egyptian priesthood, and blamed for the natural disasters of Egypt. And could the erasure of his monuments and newly built city have been partly or all the work of natural forces rather than the deliberate grudge of his conservative enemies? Unlikely, to be sure; but we must someday eliminate its possibility.

Phrygians, Cimmerians, Scythians and Ethiopians

Speaking of the Phrygians,, Jan Sammer affirms that the eighth century - (starting in 776 BC) was, together with the beginning of the seventh (700-675 BC), a period of great natural upheaval, which moved entire nations to migrations towards hopefully undamaged lands.

The Phrygians appear in the Iliad as prominent allies of Priam and were assigned a determinant role in defending the citadel. They were first heard of from Thrace. Their presence in Asia Minor is confirmed by numerous ancient authors and by abundant archaeological remains. It may have been the Cimmerians who forced the Phrygians to move.

"It seems that in one of the earliest waves of the eight century migrations the Phrygians moved from Thrace... to Asia Minor." Xanthus the Lydian says they arrived after the Trojan War, but Strabo, leaning on Homer, believes they must have arrived some time before the Trojan War. "Then, Strabo writes, "after Troy was sacked, the Phrygians, whose territory bordered on the Troad, got mastery over it."

Arrian, biographer of Alexander, thinks that the Phrygians had been pushed into Asia Minor by the Cimmerians (which would make them come from another direction altogether).

According to Ekrem Arkugal (*Phrygische Kunst*, Ankara, 1954) "Phrygian art first originated at the beginning of the eighth century BC." He adds that there is no sign of the Phrygians or any other people in Central Asia Minor in the four centuries prior to -800. No Dark Age, that is.

The Phrygians, after moving into the central highlands, founded their capital at Gordion and an important religious center at "Midas City" in present-day Turkey. Phrygia formed the western part of a loose confederation of peoples (identified as "Mushki" in Assyrian records) that dominated the entire Anatolian peninsula. About 730 the Assyrians detached the eastern part of the confederation, and the locus of power shifted to Phrygia proper under the rule of the legendary king Midas.

Midas, the first King of Phrygia, built the new capital, Gordion. The rapid prosperity and power of the city were remarkable. According to Eusebius, Midas reigned from 742 to 696 BC. Gordion did not last long however, nor did the kingdom: about 676 BC it was razed to the ground by an invading army of Cimmerians. No more than three generations of kings can have ruled at Gordion between its founding and its destruction.

In 1953, a team from the University of Pennsylvania under Rodney Young excavated Gordion and brought to light "a large double gateway with a central courtyard belonging to the Phrygian period."[192] It was dated to some time in the eighth century. It strongly reminded the excavators of the fortifications of the sixth city at Troy -- dated five hundred years earlier...

"In their batter as well as their masonry," writes Young," the walls of the Phrygian gate at Gordion find their closest parallel in the walls of the sixth city of Troy... the masonry... recalls neither the cyclopean Hittite masonry of the Anatolian plateau in earlier times, nor the commonly prevalent contemporary construction of crude brick. The closest parallel is the masonry of the walls of Troy VI, admittedly very much earlier. If any links exist to fill this time-gap, they must lie in Western Anatolia rather than on the plateau."

If the legendary Hittite Empire had occupied the site of Gordion, its remains should be found below the Phrygian remains. But Prof. Young's team discovered the contrary, and pondered how an expansive layer of clay containing many Hittite sherds had come to overlay the Phrygian material. Young believed that the clay had been transported from a far location to provide a basis for new construction, granting that it involved much labor. How-much-labor was estimated by Velikovsky, given four meters as the depth of the layer; it would involve the portage of millions of tons of clay over a considerable distance, up hill and down hill. In any event, there would have to have been additional layers, above the Hittite or the Phrygian, whichever it was. Young held tenaciously to his position, despite there occurring other contradictions coming out of his excavation.

The Trojan-Hisarlik fortifications belong in the eighth century, according to the revised chronology, and are therefore roughly contemporary with the Phrygian. A little light is thus shed on the alliance between Phrygians and Trojans, and the date of the Trojan war should fall between the dates of 750 to 676 BC. We note that the Encyclopedia Britannica makes the destruction of Gordion by the Cimmerians contemporary with Sennacherib (died 681 BC) and Nineveh. The utter destruction by the Cimmerians may have demanded more than the hand of the conqueror -- possibly including before or after natural catastrophe. As for Nineveh, the *Britannica* says, "Fourteen years after the death of Ashurbanipal, however, Nineveh suffered a defeat from which it never recovered. Extensive traces of ash, representing the sack of the city by Babylonians, Scythians, and Medes in 612 BC, have been found in many parts of the Acropolis."

The great disturbances and movements of people of the 8th and 7th centuries brought the Scythians from the depths of Asia into contact and confrontation with Assyria, Egypt, Greece. Their first settlements in Southern Russia date from the 8th century. Their tombs in the Crimea bear striking resemblance to those of Mycenae and their animal art bears unmistakable resemblances to those of Mycenae and Crete, according to Gregory Borovka and Solomon Reinach.[193] Yet the accepted time tables would have them arrive in the Middle East five centuries after the end of the Mycenean civilization.

According to Homer the Cimmerians (who are mentioned in the Odyssey but not in the Iliad) live "shrouded in mist and cloud, and never does the shining sun look upon them, but deadly night is spread upon them."

The Cimmerians pushed the Phrygians towards the Bosphorus and ravaged the Greek cities of the coast of Asia Minor. According to Herodotus, the Cimmerians were originally displaced from the Asiatic steppes by the Scythians: the Scythians arrived on the scene of the middle east after 650 BC, decimated the Cimmerians with the help of the Assyrians, and pushed to the border of Egypt, engulfing Palestine.

> They were at the time worshipers of Mars, whom they represented as a sword... leaving their worship of Saturn in abeyance. They were called Unman-Manda, or 'People of Saturn' in Akkadian and in the so-called Hittite literary texts."

Among the allies of Priam are also mentioned the Ethiopians under their king Memnon.

> The Ethiopians fought repeatedly and sometimes successfully with the Assyrians for control over Egypt... Again and again we are brought to the same period - the time of Phrygian power in Asia Minor, of its destruction by the Cimmerian invasion, and of the Ethiopian rule in Egypt at the end of the eighth and beginning of the seventh century BC. Then this is the historical background of the Trojan War..

Egypt

Egypt is being continually mentioned. Its chronology sets a woefully false standard, but its presence is always felt, whatever the date. A troublesome attitude occurs often to us: we imagine somehow Egypt to be a singularly intact empire, almost eternal. Yet, when we start counting the years and the events, we discover that Egypt was often subjected to foreign rule. The Hyksos (Shepherd Kings, Amalekites, Arabs) invaded and ruled for several centuries of the Late Bronze Age. Time afterwards has to be allotted to Libyan and Ethiopian Dynasties, to Assyrian domination, then to the Persian rule and finally to

Alexander – all of these in the first Millennium BCE, in other words, in the Iron Age of Mars.

Are we permitted to ask, when did the Quantavolution of Mars strike Egypt? The answer must be: simultaneously with the other catastrophes of the Greater Mediterranean Region.

Egypt of the First Millenium BCE – or, let us say, the Iron Age – was more often than not in deep trouble. The country was already in decline, according to Finkelstein, at the time of David and Solomon. Every manifestation of a quantavolution was experienced. Having decided that we shall use Velikovsky's chronology for the period, we can outline the situation at a glance. The first century or two were the peak of an exceedingly well developed Late Bronze Age. The famous visit of the Queen of Sheba, most likely Queen Hatshepsut of Egypt and Ethiopia, to the Court of Solomon at Jerusalem, seems ironic in view of the destructive phases of history that followed in both countries, first in actual war, then in successive 'sky wars.'

The Pharaoh Akhnaton came to the throne of Egypt from abroad, somewhere in the Syrian-Palestine or possibly from Western Arabia. He introduced what is said by many scholars to have been the first official monotheism of the world. He put aside, indeed persecuted, other religions, including even the worship of the dominant God Amen [Jupiter] of Egypt. He built a new city and moved his Capital there, calling it Akhetaten.

The new god was drawn, painted and sculpted as a bright disk like the sun with a band of rays extending from part of its circumference. This could readily portray a comet by its brilliant head and flaming tail. Ordinarily this disk has been conceived of as the Sun, and therefore the new cult not much more than a cult of the sun. We should not forget, however, that still moving elliptically in the sky of the age was the new planet Venus, and this could have been named Aten. The Hymn to Aten resembles the Babylonian Hymn to Ishtar (Venus). Velikovsky wondered whether the name Aten was cognate with the Greek goddess Athena, whose ending was non-Greek and whose identity and behavior bespoke the Planet Venus. The planet, was, by evidence brought forward by Velikovsky, orbiting on a 50- or 52-year calendar, producing what was termed a Jubilee Year and was observed with heavy rites at such intervals by peoples as diverse as Mexicans and Jews.

We have written that the introduction of Mars into the fray of Earth and Venus was occasioned by a near encounter of the planets Mars and Venus, with the latter and larger of the two sending Mars into a near-Earth ellipse, while it altered its orbit as well. This three-way movement, the next to last of Venus before it took up its present near-circular orbit around the sun, might have been the occasion for the promotion of and official adoption of Venus-Athena to the supreme status accorded it by Akhnaton as the pure supreme abstract God Aton.

Perhaps Egypt had even been spared on this occasion great destruction only to experience such fifteen years later at the hands of Mars, which thus demonstrated Mars' (and Amen's) superior prowess over the God of Akhnaton. A merest hint that something of significance may lie there is the naming by Akhnaton of one of the numerous monumental structures "The House of Rejoicing for the Aten in the Island 'Exalted in Jubilees.'"

The revolution of Akhnaton, preaching and practicing in its own way nature and truth and peace, seems first to have been spared natural destruction and other quantavolution effects, but then ended more expectedly with the outbreak of famine and pestilence, disturbed skies, and the downfall of the Pharaoh who was blamed by the priests of Amon whom he had removed and impoverished for the sad state of the realm. Akhnaton was implored often to send aid to his revolt-ridden, invaded, plagued and hungry vassals of Palestine; his failure to respond to them would indicate not only an other-worldly idealism that colored his regime, but also an inability on the part of the Great Protector Egypt to take care of its own people and land.

Akhnaton removed himself and his Capital from

Thebes to set up an ideal new religious-cultural complex. Queen Tiy, his mother, who had called for his return upon the death of her husband Amenhotep III, became in time his wife and his wife Nefertiti appears to have been in time exiled. Neither his (to us) grotesque appearance, of vastly extended head and hips, nor his new religion, nor his pacifism, nor his monotheism to a material kind of god whom many modern commentators regard as the first genuine monotheism – none of these policies brought anything but antagonism, and finally removal and exile – under circumstances of which we know little.

Not long after his disappearance and the short reign of Tutankhamen, there came a period of foreign rule by Libyans,~-800 to 700, and then a half century under a new conqueror, the Ethiopians. During these dynasties (which we may be permitted to suspect as accidents of turbulence – as Martian delegations, so to speak), great floods swept over Egypt. Under the Libyan Pharaoh Osorkon, all the Nile dikes crumbled. Under Shabaka, the towns of Egypt hastily put up earthen walls against the water.

Cambyses, 525 BCE, brought Persian rule. Disordered relations with vassals, delegations of large powers to priestly fiefs, struggles against new invasions, and rebellions led by Egyptian generals and princes marked the centuries until the conquest of Egypt by Alexander the Great in 325 BCE.

Ramses III (Nectanebo I), of whom I speak in several places, finds his prominent place inside this Persian period. Much less important players to follow him were Ramses IV (Tachos) down through a Ramses XII.

Thus, the coming of the Persians did not bring full peace and stability. Finally it was the Greeks of Alexander who did so. Yet only to a degree so far as old Egypt was concerned, for, as Velikovsky has pointed out, practically every tomb and grave in the Empire that could be found and that showed some elegance was broken into. Little respect for the dead: it was a greatly changed Egypt.

The Founding of Carthage

The Phoenicians, who are credited with imparting the alphabet to the Greeks, did not themselves leave important documents, yet we know that they nurtured historians and kept chronicles. We are left to rely on testimony from their enemies, the Greeks and the Romans.

Carthage, a Phoenician colony, was annihilated by Rome in 146 BC. Roman historian Appian said it had existed for "seven hundred years." From the Greek chronographer Timeus, we infer 814 BC as the date of its founding by Dido or Elissa. From Josephus we infer the date of 826 BC for the escape of Dido from Tyre, which led her to found Carthage. A Sicilian chronographer, Philistos, places Carthage's founding "a man's life-length" before the fall of Troy. Appian himself places the founding of Carthage "fifty years before the capture of Troy." Therefore, in his opinion, the capture of Troy must have happened around 800 BC.

(We recall that according to Eusebius, Sanchunjaton is supposed to have lived just before the events at Troy, at the time of Queen Semiraris of Babylon, who, herself, had lived just before, or during, Exodus. This last is a coincidence that we do not accept but can see that Eusebius might have thought so, as does, we know, indeed, a contemporary group of Biblical historians.)

Yet archaeology does not support such a date for the founding of : the most ancient foundation structure - a chapel to the Goddess Tanit - has been dated to 725-700 BC by means of sherds of Greek vases found there. Then, says the author of the article, the destruction of Troy would have to be placed, if one follows Philistos and Appian, to about 675 BC. That would bring Homer down to two or three generations before Heracleitus - born ca 450 BCE - at most... Not to mention what it would do to Exodus and the Bible, following Eusebius *et al.*)

Central and Celtic Europe

"The twelfth century B.C. (~-800) was a time of profound culture change in central and southeastern Europe." There were abundant contacts between Europeans and peoples of the Eastern Mediterranean region. So asserts Peter S. Wells, who also would absolve groups from Europe of blame for the collapse of the southern cultures. He is, as we would guess, remarking about events of the close of the Bronze and the beginning of the Phantom Age, that is, the Iron Age in reality.

Rhys Carpenter comments that incomplete evidence shows an immense flooding of the river basins of the Hungarian plain in the early first millennium, which would be our early Iron Age, about ~-800. The rich Bronze Age in the region comes to an abrupt end, desolation, abandonment.

Gordon Childe tells, in *The Danube in Prehistory* (1929) of the "fierce controversy" about dating the Hungarian urnfields. They would be Late Bronze Age (~-1100, our ~-750) according to some, or they belong to the Iron Age and Hallstatt culture (~- 800) according to others.

The Hungarian Urnfield culture is supposed to have been spread from the Villanovan in Italy and be roughly its contemporary, which precludes it from being any earlier than -1100. In fact, we would place it in the 9th century.

Yet the earlier Urnfield finds show a connection with Mycenean pottery, as well as Hittite and Minoan, and to the Macedonian Bronze Age. Gordon Childe reluctantly agrees to the long dating, hoping for later excavations to settle the matter. He notes a "striking correspondence" between the key Vattina site of Hungary (the later phases of which should be placed between -700 and -400) and the pottery of Troy VIa (later identified as Homer's Troy by Blegen, and dated by him to ca 1250 BC (!) Doerpfeld had dated the same stratum earlier to slightly before 700 BC, and we would agree.

I find few works on the Iron Age destructions in

France. I note that the Depot de Vénat near Angoulême in Charente preserves over 2000 objects illustrating all aspects of life as the Bronze Age ended and the Iron Age began: weapons, tools, harnesses, jewelry, etc. They had been hidden and were never recovered, then ultimately discovered by shepherds in what was in 1893 an abandoned quarry. We are led to suspect here as in other cases stretching around the greater region a hurried flight and abandonment, with a hope to return that was to be frustrated.

Dorothea Kenny, noting the neglect of Celtic mythology, turned to the story *Togail Bruidne Da Derga,* and found there what amounts to a holospheric destructiveness, masked, as expected, in mythic language. Gods and heroes act out the forces of fire, flood, earth movements, human wars and migrations. The time is uncertain but appears to have been the Iron Age.

Perhaps the prolonged aftermath of the Atlantis destruction had still new effects upon the Martian period. These will be dealt with in the next chapter.

Enkomi - Building 18

In 1896 Dr. A. S. Murray conducted excavations on behalf of the British Museum at a burial ground on the site of Enkomi in Cyprus. In the 1960's Claude Schaeffer returned to the scene of his pre -WWII triumphs in the same area. We shall comment on the work of both men. Murray uncovered many varieties of objects that he could readily place in the Mycenean palace syndrome, and connect to Greek, Phoenicians, Etrurian and Assyrian counterparts of ~-850 to ~-600. But he was compelled by the pressures of the Petrie Egyptological chronology working through the Museum and British Establishment to carry back his datings to the epoch of Amenhotep III and Akhnaton, around 1400 B.C.E. [~-850].

For example, a white-dotted figural vase common at Encomia had also been found at Caere in Etruria and at

Cameras, Rhodes and assigned to the -600s. An ivory carving showing a man with helmet and chin-strap was nearly identical to the design on a common metal bowl and on ivories whose provenance was Phoenicia, all of the period ~-850 to ~-700. A pair of bronze greaves unmentioned in Homer were most likely of ~-700. The same date had been assigned to a complicated pendant whose patterning and technique of gold soldering also occurred on pendants from Cameras in Rhodes. Many comparable cases were discovered and disclosed by Murray.

Although Murray was Curator of Greek and Roman Antiquities at the British Museum, or perhaps for that reason, he had to go along with the Museum authorities, with Flinders Petrie, with Arthur J. Evans, excavator of Knossos on Crete, with H.R .Hall, Curator of Egyptian and Assyrian antiquities, and assign his finds to around 1400 B.C.E. in Egypt [~-850].

Murray was accused of insinuations against his colleagues, of not judging properly the relative age of graves, and Evans, later on, himself to be later justly criticized for manipulating data improperly, wondered how "views so subversive" could come from so high an authority on classical studies.

If Claude Schaeffer were disturbed by the Murray case he did not express any doubts and went along with the British view in his pre-War excavations and in a return excavation of the 1960's. He was, publicly at least, impervious to the protestations of Velikovsky, who drew up finally in 1974 a memorandum on the Murray case that he called "The Scandal of Enkomi," and which there is no sign of having been read by Schaeffer.

Schaeffer in the 1960's was referring to Enkomi as Enkomi-Alasia and placed its special prosperity in the Late Bronze between -1600 and -1200 [~-1100 to ~-800]. We shall formulate from his larger study of the 1960's a synopsis of the phases of the history of a construction called simply Building 18. Building 18 as constructed originally was a large exceptionally well-built mansion of cut stone with a beautiful floor. Its original occupants must not have occupied it for more than a century, maybe much less. The following phases took place, concentrated in the early stages of the Martian Quantavolution.

1. "The departure of the original occupants is connected with an event which has left only slight traces in the structural parts of the building. It seems that they were not aware of the imminence of the danger for otherwise they would not have failed to attempt to entrust valuables to hiding places under the floor or in the walls as inhabitants of Enkomi have done so often…

If the total absence of signs of fire or destruction in the corresponding layers excludes the hypothesis of an occupation of the building by a barbaric and destruction force, one must nevertheless not underestimate the seriousness of the event."

2. The new inhabitants seem to have lower living standards…

In the layers corresponding to these first reoccupation, Mycenean pottery, which had been so abundant on Cyprus and particularly in Enkomi for the preceding two centuries, is entirely absent.

"On the other hand, it seems that this period of transition from the end of the Bronze (or Final Mycenean) to the Iron Age has been at Enkomi, of a relatively brief duration…" A great fire ensued.

A small number of remains were found in the ash layer of the fire. There is however one item, an exceptionally beautiful vase, the type of which is extremely rare at Enkomi (which has otherwise furnished museums all over the world with thousands of ceramics) and points to the fact that this type of pottery and those who used it were only an ephemeral presence at Enkomi.

3. "This first period of reoccupation of bldg 18 ended in a catastrophe the violence and extent of which are illustrated by the thick mattresses of ashes which cover floors everywhere where digging has occurred, as well as by numerous traces of black smoke found at the foot of the

facade and on most of the walls."

It seems that only the strongly built walls were left standing. The debris or the rest was later evacuated into the street, the level of which was raised by 50 to 60cm at one fell swoop.

4. Then the atelier of a bronze foundry emplaced itself in the ruins, as well as other workshops.

"The great fire of bldg 18 and its transformations coincide with a change in the character of the pottery used at Enkomi. From all evidence, this was an occurrence, or a series of incidents, which affected the whole site (of Enkomi.)" .... The new type of pottery "appears (at Enkomi) with all its characteristics fully developed and in a sudden manner, following the grave events which are responsible for the destruction of bldg 18 and probably of a large part of the city during Cypriot Iron I.

"The last occupants of bldg 18 - those who had used the beautiful rare *close style* ceramic were taken by surprise and chased or exterminated by people who conquered Cyprus."

4a. "The working population of the city, otherwise, does not seem to have deserted it during the hostilities, or then it must have returned soon after the events, for the industrial activity of this part of the city was intense, as early as the time of floor IV, the first that was fashioned on top of the ruins of bldg 18. Indeed, in addition to the founder's atelier mentioned above, we have found in it two more workshops with large fires and crucibles in place..."

5. These workshops moved after a time, and the building was taken over by modest dwellings.

6. "From floor II onward... all the archaeological layers present an astonishing poverty of stratification and a confused aspect. In many places, these upheavals are due to the activity of tomb raiders or, concerning the upper layers, to agricultural work. But these causes cannot suffice to explain the upheavals observed in places which have remained intact and without any changes since the site was abandoned at the beginning of the Iron Age.... Yet, we

have observed a great confusion as far as regards the layers situated immediately above the level of floor II. It seems to us that the best hypothesis which can be advanced here is an earthquake...an earthquake which seems to have hit the city hard, and whose effects have been noticed also at Sinda, 16km from Enkomi, and even at Curium, some 120km away in a straight line."

"...I admit that the dwellings brought to light among the ruins of bldg 18, corresponding to floor II, were laid waste by a seismism and that they were replaced, probably immediately, by the construction of which exists still only floor I and some remains of a wall of rough-hewn stone situated immediately under the actual surface. All these events seem to have already occurred before the end of the 12th century.[~-800]

7. The last catastrophe. "...everywhere on our dig of bldg 18 where this (last) level was found discovered in situ, we were struck by the quantity of archaeological material it contained. It is true that the architectural aspect is rather poor... But the great number of ceramic fragments which we retrieved and which can be counted literally by the thousands, as well as the presence of hiding places containing bronze objects of good quality clearly bear witness that the city was not abandoned at the end of a long agony, but in full activity and full prosperity, struck by a brutal event.

"The nature of this event is revealed by the numerous hiding places which have been found... which attest that the events responsible for the final abandonment of the city did not occur without warning, as would have been the case, for instance, of an earthquake, or destruction in an accidental fire.

"Alerted by the harbingers of the looming danger, Alasiotis were able to entrust to the floors of their dwellings their precious objects and, particularly, the statues of their divinities, profanation of which they must have feared. The fact that they did not take them back shows that the threat was real and that the owners of these objects were forced to exile themselves or that they perished during the unfolding of the events. The distribution over the whole extent of the site of these hiding places indicates, moreover, that the catastrophe struck the whole of the city.

"No other hypothesis seems to better agree with the clues collected during the investigation of the last level of bldg 18 than the invasion of an armed force which seized and destroyed the city and cast out forever its inhabitants."

I would ask Schaeffer: "Why didn't the invaders then take over the city? And if they did not reoccupy the city, why did none of the former inhabitants go back - or any of their descendants - to retrieve some of the objects? Does this means that everybody died shortly after the takeover of the city? Also, the inventory of the bronze treasure shows that many of the 37 pieces were small pieces of jewelry, like bracelets and rings which could easily have been carried away by the fleeing inhabitants. The statuette of the god itself was only 0,55m tall, according to Schaeffer. Certainly easily transportable. So why, if they knew about the danger, did the inhabitants choose to leave without these objects? Also, how was the city destroyed by the invaders? There is no "mattress of ashes" this time. Why did nobody, ever, build there again? If so many archaeological remains of the last inhabitants are found, why are there no remains left by the invaders - arrowheads, weapons etc.? How long did it take for the left-over structures to disappear from sight under layers of cultivable earth?

I would conclude this account of the early and later work at Enkomi with a quotation from the hand of Vassos Karageorghis, Head of Cyprian Archaeology:

"The short period before and after 1200 B.C. [~- 800] is of crucial importance for the political and cultural development of Cyprus. Already established towns are destroyed, abandoned, or rebuilt and various novelties appear in religious, domestic, and military architecture, in weaponry and objects of everyday use."

He joins Muhly in feeling that the collapse was not

total, that the crises have various causes here and there and did not occur simultaneously. [Here I need to repeat my position, that the collapse was practically total, in Cyprus as everywhere else, but, since the catastrophic incursions of Mars and his heavenly host came several times at intervals of about 15 years, this series would lead to the double misunderstanding that the disasters were unconnected, and that the Phantom Age of 400 years gave plenty of time to fit in any number of disasters, keeping them meanwhile comfortably apart.]

There remains one point to make respecting events in Enkomi-Alasia, one that brings us back to the skies. Claude Schaeffer reports that his team found in Enkomi-Alasia a statuette of Phoenician aspect, a god wearing a conical hat with bull's horns. This is unquestionably the god Reseph, worshipped throughout the Eastern Mediterranean and around the world, actually, as planet Mars. Everyone then and there knew that the equivalent gods were Nergal, Mars, Apollo, and also Apollo-Reseph (or Reshef) who continues to be worshipped well after the destruction of the city, under the name of Apollo Alasiotas, which, in Phoenician is read Reshef Alahyotas. Cochrane has traced this pestilential god well, not only as doppelganger of Mars, but as possessing his own planetary identity, and a widespread cult in the Near East.

Ugarit

A few miles across the sea, on the Syrian shore, we find the ruins of the important city-state of Ugarit, whose connections with Enkomi-Alasia were always close. Marguerite Yon writing of "Monuments and habitations coming to light at the surface of the tell of Ras Shamra," site of ancient Ugarit, capital of the kingdom of the same name of the 2nd millenium BC) are precisely those of the ultimate phase (of the Late Bronze Age) preceding the final catastrophe, which ended around 1185 [-800] with the brutal destruction of the city and the definitive abandonment of the site. During this phase, a great number of documents coming from Cyprus appear in Ugarit... comprising texts written in cypro-minoan, as well as a correspondence in Akkadian between Ugarit and Alice (Cyprus). (...) Cypriot objects found at Ugarit comprise bronze objects like tripods, and a large amount of ceramics. Sherds of it are found in the ruins of the houses as well as in the tombs underneath, so that one cannot tell if they were part of the furnishings of the house or of the tombs..."

A generation earlier Velikovsky had called attention to numerous 500-year discrepancies in the site, both in the precious literary relics found there, and in the uncovering of numerous vaulted tombs that could be twins of tombs found on Cyprus, only a few miles away by sea, but supposedly centuries away when designed, constructed, and destroyed or buried. Actually, in Carthage, and supposedly a full Phantom Age later in time, the most ancient tombs were reproduced again.

Again, as we conclude this chapter, we confess to a state of bemusement. We have to applaud Prof. J.D. Muhly when he writes: "Scientific field work, often highly detailed in nature, finds itself held hostage by an often naive interpretation of a literary text that, at best, is of questionable historical value." But, I think, is not the opposite at least as true? Scientific literary investigation, often detailed in nature, finds itself held hostage by an often naive interpretation of an archaeological report that, at best, is of questionable historical value." What he says of the one is true of both: "We must come to recognize this problem, and take steps to deal with it."

Chapter Eighteen

An Atlantis Connection

Thousands of works - over 20,000 titles, according to one count - have been written to prove or deny the existence and culture of an ancient continent called Atlantis, a subject first introduced by Plato. As Hans Bellamy

Thousands of works - over 20,000 titles, according to one count -have been written to prove or deny the existence and culture of an ancient continent called Atlantis, a subject first introduced by Plato. As Hans Bellamy once wrote: "So the German ethnologist Frobenius sought Atlantis in Nigeria; the Anglo-Spanish archaeologist Whishaw placed it in Andalusia; the German Schulten found it at Tartessos at the mouth of the Guadalquivir; the Germans Borchardt and Herrmann, and the French Count de Prorok, suggested North Africa; Colonel Fawcett looked for Atlantean vestiges in the Amazon Valley; and Central America and the West Indies have also been mooted".

Jürgen Spanuth put it in the North Atlantic off of Denmark. Marinatos and other modern Greek scholars have thought to locate it as the greater Island of Thera-Santorini before it exploded, Peter James finds it in Anatolia, and Emilio Spedicato in the Caribbean. Siegfried and Christian Schoppe derive Atlantis from the vast sunken civilization on the slopes of the Black Sea. Judging by the score of papers offering new sites at a conference on the Island of Milos, Greece, in July 2005, we are far from exhausting the list of candidates. For there, besides a

Schoppe presentation, we had Atlantis placed in Algeria, at Helike (Anatolia), in Morocco, Malta, India (the Tamils), the Aegean Sea (the Cyclades), Ireland, Gibraltar (Spartel Bank), Guadalquivir River Delta at Tartessus (Spain), the Atlantic Ocean (between the Canaries and British Isles), Lake Guatavita (Guatemala), and Israel *(sic)*. A few meters away from the site of the conference there is a fascinating mining museum in which is displayed a well-preserved tree trunk of cedar, 2.5 meters long and 50 centimeters thick, dated by C14 to somewhat older than 2,000 years, and it was found by miners 28 meters under the surface in a layer of bentonite. Mysteries near at hand; Atlantis, thousands of kilometers away: common to both, catastrophe.

My Earlier View to be Amended

I included a few words on the subject of Atlantis in a book of two decades ago and may repeat them here:

> My position is that the megalithic cultures of Spain, France, Ireland, England and Scandinavia are survivors of the larger realms of Atlantis. [I should have added Northwest Germany, the Netherlands, and Denmark at the least.] Atlantis sank in a day of furious trembling and flood, it was told. Portions of the sialic continents that had remained above the oceans were deluged, not only at Atlantis but throughout the world. Total destruction came upon the large part of the Earth's population which was living on the continental margins. For these suddenly became the vast continental slopes and shelves of the oceans... The multiple kingdoms of Atlantis that Plato described may have been of the political and social order of Saturnia. Atlantis was a set of kingdoms of related cultures. It was perhaps Celtic or Germanic (one should adopt regularly the prefix 'priori-' for all cases where the modern geographical name confuses history, giving, for example 'priori-Denmark..), and in close touch with the Tethyan-Mediterranean culture. [It might also have been proto-Mycenaean.]

> Its survivors may have been the Stonehenge and megalithic builders of Western Europe. They remained under the influence of the Minoans, Phoenicians, and Mycenaeans... Atlantis can be best defined by a line enclosing all of the European northwestern continental platform from the Bay of Biscay to Scandinavia on the north, from the

western banks of Ireland into Denmark and France. It is difficult to decide whether the Pillars of Hercules that led to the several kingdoms were at Gibraltar, or whether the "Pillars" referred to the innumerable megalithic dolmens that later lined the shores in honor of Hercules, perhaps even in conjunction with a precursor to the English Channel.

In general, what I was saying permits the notion that survivors of Atlantis were to be found in Scandinavia, the North Sea coasts, and the Baltic region. The Atlantis treatise of Hans Spanuth (edition of 1975) allows this designation; he has them settling throughout the North and then spreading south and into the Balkans. There is much evidence of catastrophe and of Iron Age culture in the civilization of Northwestern Europe. Peat beds evidencing layers of dessication, flood and ashes are tell-tale phenomena. I have discussed the case of Philippi in Chapter Six. The archaeological study of Eastern and Central Europe has lagged behind the study of the Mediterranean region. But the Martian quantavolution is to be readily discovered there too.

Helgoland, the Crash Scene of Phaethon

But let me return to the possible capital of the region of Atlantis, off the coast of priori- Schleswig-Holstein, Denmark. Spanuth could not have known of my theory (1982) of the drowning of the continental shelves in the prelude to the Saturnian epoch around -4000. In dating the Atlantis event, and like Velikovsky, he placed the Phaethon event in the Second Millennium. He visualized the comet going down after its disastrous flight from the South-East, by Helgoland, off Denmark, and he dated Phaethon at ~-1200, combining the Venusian and Martian periods, which we separate by seven hundred years following Velikovsky. Thus he accepted the conventional date for the transition from the Bronze Age to the Iron Age, and combined the catastrophes of both Venusian and Martian quantavolutions. (The year -1200 became a shibboleth for all events, as we have shown throughout my work. In my book here alone the -1200 has appeared 47 times, and has just as often been printed and at the same time corrected by me to dates later than of -850. I would like to have replaced them all. Many dates between 1300 and 1200 have also been assigned to events that I should put into the Iron Age.)

Alternatively, I have argued for a Venusian peak at around -1450 and a Martian peak around -750. I would then vote for the Phaethon event occurring during the Venus regime, and a further Martian disaster at the beginning of the Iron Age. So I am concerned with separating the two quantavolutions, and I therefore interpret both Spanuth and Vinci to conform to this scheme. Phaethon, boastful son of Helios, badgered his father until he was let drive the chariot of the Sun, which he lost control of and destroyed a goodly portion of the Earth and its inhabitants. In 1902 a Sun Chariot was dug up in the Trundholm Moor of Denmark, its position 55° 11 . N by 11° 37' E. This is incredibly near the location where Spanuth calculated that Phaethon had crashed his chariot of the sun. It is in bronze, and yet similar chariots were not made until Etruscan 6th century Iron Age times.

After a long archaeological hiatus in Northwest Europe, exploration started up on a large scale, and many rich bronze Age finds have been reported. At Nebra in Northwest Germany, a bronze disk with gold images of sun, moon, stars (including the Pleiades group), and boats was discovered, hard evidence, unless it had been made and carried up from the far South, that both artisanship and astronomy were preoccupying the priori-Germanic population. The Nebra disk was dated at 3600 years ago, not far from the Venusian Period boundary of ~ -1450.

But there was no doubt about the provenance of the troy-town that was brought to light near Goseck by aerial spotting followed by digging. In 1991 aerial images indicated the presence of humanoid mounds. The concentric circles uncovered are much larger than Stonehenge. The gates appear to be positioned toward marking the summer and winter solstice. Goseck circles were dated at ~-5000 y, considerably earlier than the Nebra

Disk. A full Bronze Age thus would seem to have passed in the region.

At the same time, I was led toward the idea of Northern lands of the Hyperboreans as the source of heavy migrations southwards into the Mediterranean Region. This idea came with the book of Felice Vinci, *Homer in the Baltic (2000)*, which places the origin of the Homer epics mostly in the Baltic Sea regions to the East. He argues that the climatic crises of the end of the Ice Ages forced the Greek-speaking inhabitants there to migrate South to Greece and Anatolia to found the Mycenaean and related cultures, to adopt the alphabet, and to sing and write down modified versions of the story of the Trojan War. Vinci applies toponymics to show how the geography of the North went South, so to speak. Many Greek towns, places, landmarks, and personal names seem to be of Baltic origin.

He speculates that the later Iron Age Greeks mistakenly claimed the setting and the events for themselves, acting in the South. Their Northern origins and history were mostly forgotten. Mistaken, too, Schliemann 'discovered' the ruins of Troy near the modern Turkish village of Hisarlik, a site recommended as early as 1822 for the site of Homer's Troy by Charles Maclaren. Many scholars have disputed Schliemann's claim, but, not finding a plausible alternative, have for the most part accepted it. It is convenient to point to some site where the Trojan War happened that would be within the reach of Hellenes of a second stage of the Iron Age.

I was beset by the need to integrate the potent work of Vinci and Spanuth with my own general theory of quantavolutions composed in the 1970's, notably in *Chaos and Creation* and *The Disastrous Love Affair of Moon and Mars*. I decided that there must have occurred a sinking of Atlantis in connection with the Phaethon event. Culturally and linguistically, the Atlanteans and/or their neighbors of Northwest Europe would have been priori-Greeks. Some of those who survived remained in the Baltic region, stretching from priori-Denmark to priori-Finland; other survivors migrated south to Greece and elsewhere, constituting the priori-Mycenaean civilization especially.

The Atlantis (Venusian Age) disaster did not change radically the climate of the Baltic region. But the Martian quantavolution brought on, with all of its other disasters, a sudden worsening of the climate in the Baltic region. Half of the area that today is within the Arctic Circle had been of a temperate climate, with a thriving biosphere, including human cultures. It now became insufferably inhospitable. Both Vinci and Spanuth, citing many experts, have built a strong case for this event.

The Eddas and Fenris-Wolf

Spanuth adopts the Eddas' myth of the monster Fenrir, pointing out that Fenrir, like Phaethon supposedly, fell to earth, near the mouth of the river Asgard, after a destructive sky-voyage. He also brings in here Fenris-wolf, which I incline to identify with Mars, who holds the wolf identity in ancient Rome and other places such as China, Mexico, Russia, and Babylonia. In the Eddas Fenris-wolf kills the daylight and rains blood over the earth, as myths of the Finns and Tartars confirm.[194] That the Edda was revised after the Mars Quantavolution seems confirmed by the battles between what appear to be giant sky bodies, in our estimation Venus and Mars, blotting out the sun at one time, raining blood upon the sea and land, drowning the earth, setting fires that climb into the sky.

The word 'Tys' is an ancient runic sign designating the ancient Indo-European god who is originally identified with Zeus and gives us the weekday Tuesday, and then, like the Roman Jupiter-to-Mars emphasis, switches to an identity with Odin, who is generally identifiable with Mars. This change may have occurred before the Martian quantavolution, as happened with the god Thor, also Nordic.

Felice Vinci's Troy in Finland

A number of those peoples who had survived the Mars

destructions might have gotten together to seek new homes to the South. An alliance was formed of Baltic Danaans, in a major instance, who fought for control of the routes leading south down the Dnieper River, especially since the 'priori-Cretan' and 'priori-Libyan' territories of the German-Polish coast were more heavily defended. The Trojans were not ancient sworn enemies of the Greeks, but, on the contrary, related to them in some ways culturally and possibly ethnically; this might explain why, in the epics of Homer, they are treated in an objective even-handed manner that should shame many historians of modern nations at war.

The campaigns of the legendary and later Homeric Trojan War were fought on the coast of Finland, claims Vinci, where the topography and names of places correspond to those of Homer's Iliad. (It is hard to accept the location of the famous Troy at a removed site in Finland. One is driven to speculate whether this Troy was a Troy-town, pursuing the model of the primordial circles and labyrinth. The root of Troy is *tr*, which stands for 'turning'. Possibly Hisarlik was the same, a troy-town, with a proper circle, wall, and moat arrangement. Too, one might even nominate Atlantis itself as Troy of the Trojan War(s). After all, it was designed as a Troy-town, maybe the prototype thereof, with its circles of walls, moats and embankments. In the Gylfaginning 9 passage of the Eddas, it is said, 'They made for themselves in the middle of the world a city which is called Asgard; men call it Tr_ja.'[195]

Then, as Plato's story goes, the warfare may have occupied several seasons, to the accompaniment of celestial bombardments, earthquakes, floods and fires, until the overwhelming catastrophe occurred. However, bringing the setting back to Finland, where Vinci would place it, the victors, after putting the Trojans to flight, would then have led their decimated families down to the South, as the Sons of Hercules (identified with the planet Mars or Ares), Heraclids, Dorians, Achaeans, Danaans.

Reaching the Black Sea via heavily flooded waters of Southeast Europe, these Baltic priori-Greeks could have proceeded through the Bosporus, and begun to fan out in small groups until they had reached as far as Epirus to the West and Crete to the South, settling also in Western Anatolia. Everywhere they had to fight with similarly displaced groups.

Wherever they settled they were prone to name the place after the home town from which they had come. Often they insisted upon changing the old place names. Where they failed to conquer, the old names remained. Many places of the North never did find a place and name in the South, whether because their champions had died or had to compromise with those already in place. Many more toponyms of the Iliad are to be found in the Baltic area today than in the Aegean region in historical times. Occasionally they had to confront a people, desperate conquerors like themselves, such as the Thebans of Cadmus (who was perhaps Nikmed and had come from a devastated Levantine kingdom of Phoenicia). Cadmus brought the alphabet to Greece, the new Danaan Greece that had been analphabetic in the North, and Greek became a written language.

The devastated peoples whom the victors of Baltic Troy encountered were Mycenaeans, speaking a variety of Greek, too. Numerous dialects were to be found. The Mycenaean towns, however, were everywhere devastated. Where new settlements stood on old ruins, their debris mingled with the old culture's debris, so that, for example, geometrical designs from Northwestern Europe mixed with Mycenaean designs.

The elapsed time for: a) the global natural destruction (accompanied by the frenzied human destruction that accompanied chaos), b) the Trojan War events, c) the migration southwards, d) the collapsing together of Mycenaean and Dorian cultures, e) the revision and recomposition of epic poetry, f) the adoption of the epics as the hallmark of Greek culture, and g) the creation physically of a proto-classical culture and literature, took up about two centuries. There had been no gap to speak of between Mycenaean and Dorian Greece. The long-accepted 500 years of Dark Ages of Greece, we need to repeat, were a concoction to keep Greek chronology in line with an equally mistaken Egyptian chronology.

Bards came down with the Dorians. They chanted of the Baltic (or Atlantean) Trojan war and of the wanderings of the victors, such as Odysseus. A polymath bard, probably of Western Anatolia, where writing systems and a literature were well-known and quickly reestablished after the Martian catastrophes, was a compiler and publisher, named Homer. He assembled on behalf of all Greek-speaking peoples traditional epics that mixed North and South, with a frequent disregard for reality and congruency, making up a kind of national anthem, in thousands of lines, that was spread immediately by means of other bards and by written copies, and that was greeted and adored by a highly receptive new elite of letters, culminating in the Golden Age of Greek arts and sciences, an age that still was enchained to the Iron Age of migrants and vagrants, wars, storms, and clashing theocracies.

The surviving Baltic Trojans would perhaps have been let pass by their continental allies and journeyed down westwards of the descending Greeks, ending in Italy at Latium and Gela in Sicily, among other places. Finding, expectedly, the Etruscans, a people who bore the same relationship to them as the Dorians to the Mycenaeans, the Baltic Trojan Romans-to-be, worshipers of Mars, whose planet was still threatening the world, adopted the language of their Latin neighbors. The time was also the 8th century.

The Etruscans, whose culture-complex paralleled that of the Mycenaeans, had, like the Mycenaeans, possibly descended from Northernmost Europe, but conceivably from the region of Finland, that had now recently supplied Baltic Troy and the Baltic Trojans to the world. Its language, still mainly undeciphered, neither proto-Latin nor proto-Greek, might have been of the Eastern Baltic region.

Speculating, then, at a low level of probability, I would maintain a scenario whereby the final act has the proto-Greeks descending perforce from the far North, recreating somewhat fantastically their mythologies, legends, and struggles in a Mediterranean setting, and training a generation of poets worthy of chanting about their history and writing it down. The Atlantean generation, which had composed the Mycenaean civilization, themselves having miscegenated with the priori-Greek Pelasgians, was absorbed by their distant cousins from the Baltic region after several centuries of separation.

The Amber Trade

Jürgen Spanuth, in his scholarly work on Atlantis, affords us evidence that makes sense in the Bronze Age-Iron Age transition. He demonstrated how the trade in amber had been abruptly halted in the Iron Age. He showed from where new populations descended into the Mediterranean Region. He confirmed the destruction to be found everywhere both outside and within the region. He demonstrated an affinity between the older Mycenaean Civilization and the Atlantis culture. He traced many small and large artifacts, costumes, and religious practices.

No one has bettered the dedicated German pastor, who, like practically everyone who engages himself fully in a cause, grew too warm in crediting a proto-Germanic people for too much in the way of providing the culture of the Bronze and Iron ages. (We hardly know whence came the denizens of his Northwest Europe, but we can be sure that they did not behave in the exemplary manner of Plato's Atlanteans or Homer's Phaeacia.) Yet his work exposed, just as Velikovsky's for the Jews, a certain recalcitrance of the historical establishment of Europe and America in circulating and accrediting many useful German studies pertaining to Atlantis and ancient history.

I find one of Spanuth's conclusions, after his accomplishing a detailed comparison, probably true:

> So the Eddas are a kind of Germanic Atlantis document; that is to say, an account of the site of the 'holy island' in the amber region in the Bronze Age; of its 'Golden Age', of its destruction in a worldwide conflagration in flood, and of its reemergence at a later time.

Spanuth's Work Attracts Disgraceful Support

But both the Eddas and Atlantis partake liberally of the legendary and the romantic. Both are complimentary to their original authors, myth-making ancient Germans and Plato's Athenians, and those promoting the authors, German nationalists and Germanophiles, Greek nationalists and Hellenists.[196]

Spanuth survived the Second World War, published his work, and then was faced with the circumstances that his publisher now began bringing out work of neo-Nazi inclination, as for example, a book denying the holocaust. Spanuth did not denounce him nor pursue him for a release from his contract. For that he was probably wrongly accused of Nazi sympathies. He sued for defamation and won an ambiguous judgement. The charge seems to have been reckless and exaggerated, but, as has occurred often, sufficed to damage Spanuth's reputation as a scholar.

In any event, we might bear in mind the case of the American poet, Ezra Pound, where the poetry should be appreciated in its own right, even though with care, and even if the poet is properly incarcerated for treason or confined for madness or hanged. Pound was comfortably imprisoned in an insane asylum for some years and then released and retired to his beloved Italy. The matter requires further study, which we cannot manage to do here; but we indicate something of the nature of the problem in a chapter to come.[197]

Chapter Nineteen

A Society in Shock

From the earth sciences and archaeology, we move to the social and psychological effects of the Martian Quantavolution.

Speaking of the aftermath of catastrophe, Plato declares of the survivors: "At first, they would have natural fear ringing in their ears which would prevent their descending from the heights into the plain." I suppose that he is speaking of actual experiences. A rush of terror that would make one's ears ring? A change in atmospheric pressure? Survivor shock, in any event: the post-traumatic stress disorder or syndrome: PTSD

Moving from low to high pressure into a miasma of dirty foul air, aftermath of the soils and settlements being roiled up by turbulence beyond measure, and the horror of the wreck and the reek of death: but how long could they rest up, or down? The ringing of ears could be not only from fear, but from lightning and thunder, and fierce winds.

Authorities such as Aristotle and Cicero insisted upon the unchanging order and beneficence of the sky bodies, and the Church followed them. There was always a strong current of catastrophism and apocalytic belief in the Church's mass of believers, and there were occasional scholars who disagreed with the Church -- Bruno, Galileo, and Whiston, for example. Thus, Galileo wondered at men who believed the heavenly bodies immutable. "These men who so extol incorruptibility, inalterability, etc, speak thus, I believe, out of the great desire they have to live long and for fear of death..."[198]

But it was not until the Eighteenth Century

Enlightenment that a clear voice, that of Nicolas-Antoine Boulanger, brought forward the full idea of an ancient history of quantavolutions, outlining even dire psychological effects.[199] He based his work upon legend and cosmogonies from around the world. (Professor Frank Manuel brought his work to the attention of Stecchini, who brought it to the attention of Velikovsky and myself, so that it could be publicized.) I quote two passages of Boulanger:

> We still tremble today as a consequence of the deluge and our institutions still pass on to us the fears and the apocalytic ideas of our first fathers. Terror survives from race to race.... The child will dread in perpetuity what frightens his ancestors....[200]

> (The catastrophe is...) the origin of the terrors which throughout the ages have alarmed the minds of men always possessed by ideas of the devastation of the world. There we shall see generated the destructive fanaticism, the enthusiasm which leads men to commit the greatest excesses against themselves and against their fellows, the spirit of persecution and intolerance which under the name of zeal makes man believe that he has the right to torment those who do not adore with him the celestial monarch, or who do not have the same opinion he does about His essence or His cult.[201]

Q-Schock

Granted that the multiplicity of and interaction of spheres, the holosphere, indicate quantavolution shock, then we should be able to speculate with some validity on what kind of human mind results from one, then another, then still another, and how long it will take for first effects, secondary effects, equilibrium effects until the next Q shock.

How does Q shock cause different effects on different cultures (after the primordial creative shock of humanization that my scenario of humanization calls for)? Etruscan, Hebrew, Greek, Egyptian, Celtic -- all societies, that is to say, had differentiated long before the Iron Age, so that the new quantavolution would not only fall differently upon them, but they would also react and respond differently.

If their character as social entities would change differently, so would their relations with other peoples and a new kind of international order would come about.

Once again we ask ourselves: "Did the Iron age bring creativity and inventiveness because of some transient, albeit lengthy (as much as 300 years') span of experience with changes, or did the heavy blows of quantavolution change some constant of the environment or the human genome to provoke altered behavior?"

Every year, in our time, the camera and recorder register for our eyes and ears some collective shock somewhere in the world: the survivors of massacre, a tsunami, a volcano eruption, a hurricane, an earthquake, a gas explosion. The people of Bhopal, India, which I investigated shortly after the accident.[202] are still in large numbers in a state of shock and physical illness from the explosion two decades ago of a pesticide factory near their city.

How long will they or their descendants recall the event? Probably for some generations. The same is true of the people subjected to the Indonesian tsunami of 2004. By what we know and can calculate and imagine, we realize that a quantavolution affects severely a large proportion of the population of a very large area, extending over the whole world. Too, we contemplate perforce every natural machine of destruction being in motion – the holosphere in sudden, drastic change.

Iron Shortens Life Variously

Let me estimate demography. If the population of the Late Bronze Age of the Greater Mediterranean Region consisted of two hundred million persons, the Iron Age Quantavolution would perhaps have reduced this number to five millions. In three succeeding centuries, ~-650, the population might have arisen to fifty millions, and by the time of Alexander the Great to 100 millions, reaching a maximum until modern times, of 150 millions at the height of the Roman Empire ~-100. Not until ~ 1900 would the population arrive at its Late Bronze Age numbers.

There appears to have been a prior quantavolution 700 years earlier, ~-1450, associated particularly with the planet Venus, which seems to have been considerably worse than the Martian Quantavolution. If so, and if the major desiccation of the Sahara and of Arabia occurred then, ending thus the Middle Bronze Age, my estimate of the Mediterranean Region's population of ~-850 most likely would be too high, reducible therefore to one-half, say, or 100 millions. In each quantavolution, one may guess that the Earth's viability for humans is rendered less.

Hesiod wrote that the Age of Iron was unhealthy, subsistence difficult. He was not alone in this view. Thus, the Rabbi Jehudah the Holy gave an ancient Jewish stricture against plastering the altars with an iron trowel, lest it might touch and defile. For iron was created to shorten the days of man, and the altar is created to lengthen the days of man.[203]

It was Velikovsky's hunch that every 700 years the human race (and the holosphere) must revive its Venusian-Martian memories. In that case, we would expect two statistical humps in the curves of societal and physical re-enacting and reacting to the anniversary of ~-1450 and ~-750. The hypothesis has not been studied and I shall say no more of it here. Furthermore, we would expect the mnemological event to be farther off the statistical norm than the physical norm. That is the PTSD index would significantly rise , while the physical Q index, given the present technology and practice of observations show little or no glitch or hump on the curve.

Psychiatry is well aware of physical and mental trauma, of its symptoms, effects, and therapeutic possibilities. It deals almost entirely with personal traumas, leaving collective, group, or mass traumas to politicians and social welfare specialists. However, Sigmund Freud extended his treatment of individuals symptoms into a theory of collective trauma. In *Totem and Taboo*, Freud speculated that there must be an underlying catastrophic incident in the history of the race that people suppress and which continues nevertheless to function subconsciously, manifesting itself in disguise in a major way with the Oedipus complex.

He conjectured a primordial scene in which the brothers of a first human family killed their father, who had been monopolizing sexual relations with the females of the family. This terrible deed had been suppressed in the memory of all humans who came afterwards. The wish to enjoy sex with the mother has possibly (most Freudian psychologists were sure of this) created a wide display of neurotic symptoms, indeed a normal possession of the symptoms in a suppressed form.

Not many accepted Freud's theory, although precious few had a theory of their own to explain the symptoms. Velikovsky, once he was onto the hypothesis of historical and pre-historical quantavolutions, searched for reasons to explain why mankind recalls little or nothing distinct about quantavolutions. What is recalled is put into sacred literature, as with the Deluge of Noah in the Bible. Modern science, until lately, has denied that great catastrophes occurred, resorting to an ever more gradual evolution of everything on earth including the human race.

Velikovsky thought that he might eliminate the large problem presented by the lack of data concerning quantavolution by postulating a massive amnesia affecting whole populations and continuing forever, or until a sufficient portion of mankind experienced psychoanalytic therapy. The prescribed therapy consisted of learning to recover memory to the point at which people would actually recall the sensations and terror of the actual catastrophe. Then recovery would come quickly, inasmuch as the patient would be able to control and erase untrue and improper connections.

Ultimately, *Mankind in Amnesia*,[204] left practically

complete upon his death, was published, and there he expounded his theory: great cataclysms cause universal trauma, which had to be suppressed because unendurable, and were seemingly forgotten, but yet not really forgotten, but went on to create much mischief – being a principal cause of hyper-aggressiveness hence personal conflicts and wars, further that all mankind needed to be placed on the psychoanalytic couch, there to recall finally the full nature of the trauma, whereupon a cure would take place, and a peaceful and neighborly people would ensue, cleansed of this neurosis of collective amnesia.

I was well acquainted with the sources of these ideas when I came upon Velikovsky's publications in quantavolution, for I had taught for many years courses in international politics and personal and group psychology. My first publications in quantavolution thereafter were a study of "The Reception System of Science" in *The Velikovsky Affair* (1963) and a theory of mnemonology.[205] Even while appreciating the fundamental theory of subconscious motivation and non-rational behavior, however, I could accept neither Freud's nor Velikovsky's theories. Both men were Darwinists and at the same time added a Lamarckian sidecar. That is, they both believed in the persistence very possibly in the germ plasm, that is, the genes, of the effects of the original trauma of family behavior in the one case, of collective catastrophe in the other case.

I moved on to develop a model of the sudden evolution or quantavolution of mankind, called *homo sapiens schizotypus* rather than *homo sapiens sapiens*.[206] *Homo schizo* (for short) is a new species who suddenly came into being upon the event of a quantavolution. He (actually a female) did have a memory of its creation, in a period not long ago that I called Urania, associating the primary event as the nova of the Sun and the production of the binary, super-Uranus, the primordial god of the Greeks.

The instant humanization, which I termed a gestalt, was brought on by a mechanism that delayed for a microsecond the transmission of messages across the corpus callosum which divides the left from the right hemisphere of the brain. The two hemispheres are nearly identical in that they possess each the same message content as the other (even subsisting individually in the case of an accident or operation necessitating the excision of a complete hemisphere). This instinct delay cast humans into eternal doubt about controlling themselves because they were now conscious that, having two identical messages about everything that happened to them internally and externally, they were two selves at least, and had to coordinate the mass of practically identical messages of the two hemispheres.

In transmission of all messages there would be slight leakage into strictly speaking irrelevant cell centers and therefore a possibility, an inevitability, that an iota at least of every message would go into enlarging the domain of the not-quite true, mythology and legends and incorrectness. The human, it was theorized, had to cope with two personages, closer than identical twins, which, when subjected to trauma would diverge rather more from each other than would be normal" or "healthy."

This was the normal condition of *homo schizo* and there was no way of avoiding it. We all live with our plural selves, some more than other, depending on minor gene differences and distinctive impressive experiences, and including a mass of repressed memories, ancient and recent. Although it was conceivable, as Velikovsky would have it, that sheer terror could be inherited, I thought that no amount of exposure and awareness of the original terrors of mankind (except the moment of the gestalt of creation) could cure humankind of his essential doubleness and anxieties over the need to control himself (himselves). The basic human nature, then, is of a mild case of schizophrenia, and the major normal tendencies of the human species are those which when acute bring on the illness called schizophrenia.

When subjected to collective trauma such as natural turbulence, but especially under the stresses of a quantavolution, the new human race and the present human race acted and act in a more schizoid manner. The whole society would become schizoid, as I have been attempting to show in this book. All the schizoid tendencies would be exhibited in a collective as well as individual form. The new form would endure until stabilized and accommodated to a changed environment

Internally the ethnic composition would transform frequently as vagrant and migrant elements agglomerated. The elite and the different classes would likewise differentiate in peculiar modes. Economic and gender components of societies would change differently, too. And, emphatically, religious practices would change, even exchanges of gods, as well as, delusory though they might be, the relations of humans and the gods that they project. Certainly, with all of this, our knowledge about the age, if not largely mistaken, is bound to be highly tenuous at best.

Still, we continue to speculate. In another work, I offered a model of Homeric man in the early Iron Age. Restating it here might be a useful way of getting into the other major question of the chapter, viz., what kinds of trauma were suffered. The "Love Affair of Aphrodite and Ares," the song of Demodocus, to be found in The *Odyssey* portrays an astral and earthly disaster that had recently occurred, and is the theme of my book on *The Disastrous Love Affair of Moon and Mars*. It shows us how the religion of the older society was emplaced on the new society by way of myth. Let us call this model, "The Crazed Survivors of Disaster."

There have been successors to my defined model, or, at least, shoves of thought in the correct direction. Thus, we find James J. Muhly writing about Greece and Anatolia in the Early Iron Age, to say:[207]

> What followed the breakup of palace structures? Into the vacuum stepped a number of ruthless warlords, warrior princes determined to create something new out of the wreckage of the old: warriors with the drive, energy, and ambition to seize everything they could and fashion some sort of power base for themselves. There was no one to stop them. Opportunities for plunder were everywhere, and they apparently acted as quickly as possible.

Our model stands in contrast to the conventional "Phantom Age" model, which holds that the Mycenaean Age collapsed over the period of a century because of barbarian invasions and that these barbarians in the course of centuries acquired the mentalities and facilities of a civilized people. Once more, I should allude to the confusing role played by divergent chronologies. As Hallo has indicated,[208] experts who believe that a discontinuity occurred between the Ages, can use this idea to explain the bizarre amnesia between peoples of the two Ages, but the same amnesia can be explained as the result of a displacement of one people by a culturally different people. Was the discontinuity one of time or of cultures? I say it was of cultures stressed by amnesia incurred by both old and new peoples.

The "Crazed Survivors" model is constructed from the theory that a general catastrophe involving great ecological and cultural damage is followed by a shocked society. The shocked society would exhibit a complex of expected behaviors that distinguish it from stable or moderately changing or even revolutionary societies, or more significantly, from a society that is slowly evolving from a "primitive" to a "civilized" culture. In the societies of crazed survivors, personal and mass self-destructiveness and destructiveness of others and of culture increase as terror and guilt interact on a complex and massive scale. Depending upon the extent of the disaster, a totally amnesiac and stupefied society of cultural degenerates may ensue or a more furious cultural coping that may eventuate in a flowering of religious institutions, crafts, and arts.

The Homeric heroes, Odysseus and Achilles among them, typified the bands of survivors of the extensive Mycenaean civilization that was largely destroyed in the catastrophic interventions of the planets Mars and Venus in the Earth-Moon system in the 8th century. The plots of the *Iliad* and *Odyssey*, despite 2700 years of trying to make something else of them, clearly point to the skies as the source of the disruptive and awful events that produced the crazed heroes of the dark times. Western civilization has treasured and imitated the posturings of these mad warriors, hardly ever realizing what they were and how the docile mind of later generations would be affected when this madness was presented to it as normality and for inspiration. We shall proceed now to enumerate and describe briefly a number of psychological and social indications that we are dealing with human beings behaving in the aftermath of catastrophe.

The Homeric Greeks developed a pantheon of sky-gods and assumed that these gods would continuously manifest themselves by thunderbolts, showers of arrows, tidal waves, earthquakes, meteorites, and so on. They venerated all sky signs and objects from the sky, such as meteoric iron and stones. The earth itself was a living animal and thoroughly animated in its parts. A number of gods and demi-gods contributed to a continual geological and ecological restlessness. Animals, plants, and rocks changed readily into humanoid forms and vice versa. Ovid's *Metamorphoses* elaborates this theme interminably.

By the time of Thucydides, free will and controlled change were accredited to mankind, but the Homeric Greeks were yoked to *moira*, fortune, destiny, lot - the law of chance that determines human fate. Uncontrolled license and little self-discipline were ascribed to (projected upon) the gods. Well-developed priesthoods had dissolved, just as other specialized occupations crumpled into individuals. (Finley calculates that over 100 occupations discernible in the linear B tablets dropped to a mere dozen in Homer. Nevertheless there were ritual guardians and diviners with prodigious memories, aides to kings but not members of kingly families. Priests, bards, and madmen were possessed by gods.

The priests "were guardians of ritual and of the forms and language of the sacramental songs; preservers of the motions and rhythms for the due observance of ceremonial; interpreters of those signs and often obscure sayings by which the gods manifested their decrees, desires or warnings; and, lastly they were the custodians of the science of precedents in all domains."

The preceding Mycenaean bureaucratic and feudal order had broken down. Finley and other experts have described an *oikos* (household) system as a kind of feudal plantation system that survived the collapse of bureaucratic urban centralism. It is true that the *oikos* system prevails, but it is really a piratical or ship-wreck system in which people gathered around surviving leaders. A great many expatriates, outcasts, outlaws and refugees were to be found among the community. There is a remarkable lack of the stable assignment of social, economic, and political rights to the types of people who clustered in these strongholds.

Practically all of the titles of hierarchical officialdom disappeared. The chiefs of households (that it would be a mistake to call "clans") ruled a mixed community as judge and religious-political protector.

The "Argive Kings" and the kings who were supposed to have developed *from* and *after* the Homeric heroic age were actually the same traditional kings whose Greco-Mycenaean kingdoms had come tumbling down in the disasters of the 8th and 7th centuries. The warlords and oligarchies followed. Alcinous of Phaeacia rules like Agamemnon. We quote Denys Page:

> When history dawns on the island of Lesbos in the seventh century B. C., we discover there a mode of government hardly distinguishable from that of Agamemnon at the siege of Troy. The will of the sovereign power, Agamemnon himself, is not absolute: he must first summon a council of elders, and whatever they approve must be declared to an agora, an assembly of all lesser noblemen. In the seventh century BCE, at Lesbos, the political constitution is exactly the same; and it happens that the sovereign power is still in the direct line of descent from the family of Agamemnon.

This startling claim is followed by one even more sweeping:

In this place certainly, and in other places presumably, the royal family survived throughout the dark ages from beginning to end." We cannot grant either the Lesbos presumption or the general presumption. It is rare in the annals of history to find a genuine 400-year old dynasty, and hard to imagine one that would have suffered 400 to 500 years of the so-called Dark Ages. If the family of Agamemnon of Troy still ruled Lesbos in the seventh century, it is simply because the Trojan War took place less than a century beforehand.

Indeed, Agamemnon himself had probably an upstart pedigree like most of the Homeric heroes. The heroes spoke of home frequently but there is a lack of definition of their homes, Nestor's account being exceptional in the *Iliad* and those of the *Odyssey* being largely mythical and savage. The heroes boasted in the names of their parents, some of their grandfathers, and usually stopped at this point; some lapsed into claims of divine forebears in the second generation. Glaukos and Diomedes, in a famous encounter in the *Iliad,* discovered while bragging of their antecedents that their grandfathers were guest-friends and decided not to fight each other . The absence of "family trees" among self-assertive "nobles" raises doubts that they either knew their ancestors or, if they did, could claim any distinction on their behalf.[209]

The Dark Ages, as a catastrophic century, found ancestors in short supply. So also communities. Homer "does not talk a great deal about tribes and groups and clans and sects and varieties of idealistic associations, whether pacific or belligerent. What Homer does is to confine himself to the immediate family of the warrior in question." Only a short paternal link is stressed, along with guest-friends. This is exceedingly strange. It is not at all like "primitive peoples" whose lives are bound into communities of blood served by totems. Nor like a bureaucratic society. But by the "dawn of history," in the next century, we find definite blood lines as the basis of organization of the Greek polis. Apparently, though missing in Homeric times, they are quickly reestablished in the succeeding generations.

The warriors stayed away from their "homes" so long that we could question whether they had any. They remind us of Vandals and Vikings who left home never to return. Of all of Ithaca's warriors, only Odysseus ever reached home. Odysseus played the pirate - looting, killing, raping. For the sake of Athena, he had to be brought home, there to face and slay a horde of suitors of his "long-suffering" wife. His shepherd slave, Eumaeus, was armed against other shepherds and wild beasts. Marauding was frequent, if not from one's neighbors then from pirates and foreign warriors. Slaves abounded, of various nationalities, one may note. It was a society where every man's hand was raised against his neighbor. *Homo lupus homini.* "The bearing of arms, particularly lance and sword, on all solemn occasions of civil life, was the distinguishing feature which, more than any other, marked the separation of classes in Homer's time."

In battle one encounters a frenzied behavior whereby fear is whipped up in order to gain courage. Eliade's words apply to the heroes: "The frenzied *berserker,* ferocious warriors, realized precisely the state of sacred fury... of the primordial world."[210] In a famous scene of the *Iliad,* Achilles went so berserk that he battled the river, the River-God and the gods themselves. Ajax went mad and finally committed suicide.

A frank, hollow, extreme bragadoccio characterized the best and the worst of the fighters. The glorification of destructiveness seems interminable. Apart from a chosen few, the women are subjects of aggressive degradation and measured by head of livestock; yet some time before, in Minoan, if not Mycenaean, civilization, women had achieved high position and status. More information about Mycenaean women is needed before we can claim what we guess to be true: that the degradation of women was not a trait of the Indo-European but was the outcome of catastrophically induced aggression.

Certain undercurrents of attitude haunt the passages of Homer. The boasts of the warriors are often about the conquests and destruction of towns. The similes of Homer are overwhelmingly rural and pastoral. May we surmise that the heroes sacked many a half-destroyed town? There is a pervading sense of splendors of the past being gone and citations of armies, cities, and wealth appear to be grossly exaggerated. This pretentiousness is not that of nobles, or of a people who had lost something they once knew, did not own, but had given them their character.

One senses also the general lack of awareness, a "mind-blown" stupidity, a calloused morality. Am I reading feelings into Homer's poetry that are not there? Perhaps. But the interpellations of morality in the *Iliad* and/ *Odyssey* are mostly those of the poet. Are these traits not typical of "primitive man" ? Definitely not. It is only by getting one's concept of primitive man from Homer that one can believe so, for usually modern "primitive man" is gentle, aware, and only occasionally "possessed" or obsessed. The Homeric warriors are not primitive types.

The "guest-stranger" concept of Homeric times is intriguing too. The Homeric peoples had an ambivalence towards outsiders. Deep mistrust alternated with sometime hysterical acceptance. Apparently, a person entering the precincts of an unknown community, one such as Odysseus, for example, would not know whether he would be maltreated or well-treated. This ambivalence appears to have gone beyond logic or normal behavior. Odysseus was warned by Nausicaa that he should avoid being seen in Phaeacia because of the general mistrust of strangers. Yet she also assured him, that if all went well, he would be royally treated. And so he was.

The forms of human relations, like the world itself, were shaky. Augeas, "the king of the Epeians, treacherous to his very guest-friends, not long thereafter saw his own rich city, under stark fire and the stroke of iron, settling into the deep pit of destruction. Augeas was himself dragged to the edge of steep death, nor escaped it." It was for double-dealing over the cleaning of his stable that Augeas incurred the wrath of Hercules which destroyed his city and him.

We should say that this same Hercules is an active participant in many of the events of the dark times and we have come close to confirming him as alter ego of the planet Mars. He destroyed Troy once before its destruction by the Achaeans of Homer. He destroyed Nestor's Pylos once. He is often berserk, a paragon of the crazed survivor, and was deified upon death.

Hercules (or Heracles) had progeny, the Heraclids. They were so many that they seemed to be whole bands of people. More than that, they have been identified with the Dorians whom scholars believe to be the Greek ethnic strain that devastated the Mycenaean kingdoms and carried on their primitive development during the so-called "Dark Ages." For example, Rhys Carpenter is to be discovered on a magnificent *tour de force* aimed at proving that long term intense climatic change from wet to dry caused the Mycenaean civilization of the "14th century" literally to collapse and permitted the starving country folk to sack and burn the centers of civilization in search of necessities. The country and islands were practically abandoned, and only with time did a better acclimated population begin its rise.

Carpenter encounters many obstacles, only three of which need be mentioned here. He is confronted by *sudden* disaster; yet it is apparent from his own words and in meteorology that climatic disaster can only be sudden and quite destructive if an immense external source produces it. Second, everywhere he turns he sees terrible incendiarism (or, rather, he turns everywhere to avoid seeing the terrible incendiarism that destroyed Mycenaean civilization). Third, it may even be more likely that the city folk, in the imagined case, would raid and ruin the countryside than the obverse.

We cannot help but thank him, however, as one must thank practically every strainer and stretcher of the Dark Ages. For he describes in many an incident the takeover of Mycenaean areas by the Heraclids, whom he obligingly postulates as Mycenaean refugee families returning a couple of generations later at the head of mixed bands of other ethnic Greeks, especially Dorians. The Heraclids, in our theory, are crazed survivors, sons, naturally, of Hercules, who is identifiable in myth with Ares or Mars, even though he sometimes fights Ares. The Heraclids are borne down in the name of the God who destroyed their kin and culture.

"How unsettled and mobile were all these heroes," writes Mireaux,[211] after he has devoted a book, like Finley, to discovering a social order that would make sense. "The heroic world of the epics appears in our eyes as something mobile, effervescent and tumultuous."

They depended upon the seas but were bad sailors.

There was no class of specialized sailors. Everyone was a "sailor." Maritime ventures were not materially distinguishable from piratical excursions. We can imagine what confusion and fear drove them over the seas to found their many colonies, for the period 750-600 B. C. was the great period of colonial expansion. The journey from Crete to Egypt took five days and nights, "a terrifying venture for such poor navigators as were the Greeks of Homer's time."

They were meat-eaters: cattle, sheep, and wild game, animals of the uplands. "For Homer fish is a detestable food, while Hesiod does not even deign to mention it. Never is fish eaten at the Homeric repasts."

They traveled by ship, and ships were more and more pictured in their art. There is "sudden popularity of ships" from "a "surprisingly wide variety of sites that depict ships.". If we look for contrasting instrumental themes from Bronze to Iron Ages, we can contemplate the changes in weaponry. In the palatial culture warriors carried the tower-type or figure-of-eight body shields with horned helmets; in the Iron Age, they wore hedgehog smallish helmets with a horsehair or smaller horns, with small shields and spears. The sword is shorter and more common, with a possible connection to the sword that Mars seems to be wielding in the sky. The Dartmouth group alludes to changes in warfare, "especially taken in combination with the prevalence of hilltop refuge sites in both the island and on Crete."[212] Surely the two go together, hilltop settlement to protect against raids from the sea. Conceivably, too, the combination may be related to the kind of catastrophe that people lived in fear of, one that had flooded them and would flood them again.

Probably ~-680 Gyges, King of Lydia, overthrew the Heraclids of Maeonia in Asia Minor, and struck the first coins. Actually they were not the first coins, but the Greeks had largely abandoned coinage. Homer mentions a gold talent of fixed value, reports Mireaux, but exchange was almost entirely in kind rather than in money.

Gift-giving was often a spectacular affair. It was more a system of exchange than a pleasant supplement to normal exchange like bonuses or birthday presents. The things given seem often to be for re-giving, to be untouched and unused, even homely objects like linens, and the metal gifts seem all too frequently to have semidivine or divine "makers" which, as false pedigrees conceal humble origins, may have concealed their origins in loot and theft. Their description, too, conveys an awesomeness, as if they were not familiar objects to the childhoods of the gift-exchangers. They are described as pirates would speak of their misunderstood loot of pots and laces.

Altogether there is an incongruous mixture of ethnic names, events, artifacts and practices in the works of Homer. Names that are "centuries old," and not to be heard again in history, occur. Chariots are used, not as battle-wagons, but to convey warriors to places where they would descend and fight. Their use was partly forgotten or had not been familiar to the types who owned them.

T. B. L. Webster shows that Homer is indebted to Minoan and near East influences in plots, style, and references. He is influenced by the archaic Mediterranean culture. He is very Mycenaean, Webster concludes.[213]

But in all of his speculations, Webster does not speculate upon the important chronological puzzle: If it is proper to imagine that all of these influences happened so "early" and Homer came so late, why not speculate as well that all of these similar bits actually existed almost within the living grasp of the poet?

At one time, many scholars believed that Troy or Ilium, as Homer called it, and the Trojans were poetic inventions. Then Schliemann discovered "Troy" or something that corresponded to indications found in the poetry. His site at Hisarlik has revealed in successive excavations a number of "Troys." It appears now that the Troy of levels VI and VIIa may have been more clearly like an archaic town that underwent destruction, ergo Homer's Troy. It also appears now that the Trojans were akin to the Greeks and that the Trojan War(s) pitted Greek against Greek. Homer probably stressed differences between Greeks and Trojans as a splendid device, first, to convey the battle of the gods, and, second, to give the disarrayed and scattered Greek communities a common *weltanschauung* - a common religious, political and cultural outlook on the world.

Moreover, now we permit ourselves another conjecture: The besieged Troy was a congress of allied forces containing Greek and non-Greek forces, clustered survivors, who could be called Greek or Anatolians, who might provide characters with connections as far away as Etruria, and send an Anatolian like Aeneas to seek kin in Italy after the wars (as Virgil says).

The Trojan Wars were plural, most likely, during the Martian period. Armies may have come and gone; the occupants of Troy may have changed several times. The artifacts dug up could be interpreted as coming from a melange of cultures - Greek and Anatolian. The revolution of heaven and earth is the heart of the primordial myth and the epic poem. The Homeric epics are no exceptions to the rule. An old era was being destroyed and a new one was arising.

The *Iliad* and the *Odyssey* used various dialects of Greek blended by the genius of the bard. Homer used metaphors of the clearest and most ordinary kind, to the exclusion of far-flown and fancy comparisons. Words expressing "fire" abound, for example. His poetry seems to be addressing audiences of low verbal ability; or they might have understood a melange of dialects and phrases, a *lingua greca* like a *lingua franca* or both. On the other hand, his similes are prolonged and complicated, dealing with rural and pastoral comparisons. Obviously Homer was not primitive, nor inexperienced, nor bereft of imagination; nor were the poets of his confraternity, nor their audiences.

Why should this melange be used, and not, say, a single preferred dialect like the Tuscan that Dante's genius made to become the preferred Italian tongue? A reasonable answer would be that there was then only a gathering of tongues: the audiences were related, widespread, itinerant, and diffused.

Mycenean Linear B script was, of course, found to be a Greek dialect. There is no use of a sacred, liturgical language. If there had been a Mycenaean dead language, like classical Greek is to modern Greek, or Latin to Italian, then would not that have been the basis for portions of the epic poems? But it was not, not even for prayers. Therefore it did not exist. Mycenaean Greek was probably a living and related set of dialects whose standard expression had disappeared with its ruling class and scribes.

It gives cause for bewilderment. If there were a sacred language employed or said to be employed or said to be not understood, this could place the old civilization far into the past. There are many also tie-ins of Homeric and Mycenaean cultures. This situation might indicate that the memorialized civilization was either foreign (which it was assuredly not) or largely destroyed (which we think was the case).

The linguistic melange (with its numerous catch-phrases from various Greek sub-cultures), which was Homeric Greek, was "instant prosody." There had been no time, no more than a couple of generations, to build an epic language. Yet several of such epic languages would surely have evolved smoothly and uniformly over the several centuries of any "Dark Ages," to the point where no single language would be understood by many varied linguistic audiences. (It would be like trying to find a popular audience everywhere for an epic in Latin, or in Italian, or in Greek, 500 years after the final collapse of the Roman Empire.) What emerges therefore is a people and culture exploding in space and time, whose language, that of Homer, had not yet caught up with its expanding front.

The Greeks of Homer, to conclude, did not come as an invasion from afar. They consisted of all kinds of Greeks. They were survivors, largely from the rural areas and the interior highlands. From personal experience and hearsay, they knew of the centers of their societies that had been destroyed. They often lacked kith and kin; they lacked communal security; they lacked law and order; they lacked education; they trembled upon the often trembling earth.

Experts commonly remark on the unabashed juxtaposition of knowledge and ignorance in the epics. Mireaux has said, "There was decidedly nothing primitive about Homeric civilization."[214] The very sophistication of the poets, like Homer and Hesiod, who told about them, indicates an age whose savagery could easily be penetrated by civilized forms.

For a grandly disciplined, informed, and stylized poet like Homer to write so sympathetically of his subjects, he had to be of their age, and to be of their age required that *their* age be the eighth century. I quote Finley:

> The massive destruction of Mycenaean civilization fully attested in the archaeological record, was accompanied by a complete social transformation, in which all the institutions by which men organized their existence were refashioned to met the new situation... When Mycenae fell, the surviving Greeks, in their new kind of society, had no need for records or for scribes; in fact, on the evidence we have at present, they had no need for the art of writing and they lost it altogether, improbable as that may seem to modern men.

What seems "improbable" to me is that anything but abrupt catastrophe could cause "the massive destruction" in so many places - Crete, Mycenae, and elsewhere. The Homeric scribes, working with new dialects and a new alphabet, did not need centuries of time to accumulate material on the chaotic life that followed.

Homer did his best to reassure the survivors and to set them on their way again. The incongruence and inconsistencies of material culture, nomenclatures, customs, and attitudes found in his works are not sloppy artistry; they are of the essence of the people whom he was describing. And his work was not an oral conglomerate of centuries, but a description, from two main sources, those he used in the *Iliad* and the *Odyssey,* with as much consistency as he could import to them, of the suddenly produced cultural chaos of the eighth and seventh centuries. He took as his task the assembly of plots dealing with erratic and fear-driven survivors and inspiring these folk to become "one nation under the gods."

Can one maintain, holding to what has been said in the last several pages, that, yes, this all happened, but much of it, up to and including the Trojan War, took place, not in Anatolia or even in European Greece, but in the region of the Baltic Sea, as Felice Vinci has set up his scenario? It is possible but unlikely. I see no reason why ancient historiography cannot carry along both scenarios, the Baltic and the Anatolian, until more and more evidence accumulates and decisively tips the scales on behalf of the one or the other.

Isaiah and the Hebrew Prophets

We come upon a second highly important controversy of scenarios, this one whether the nation of Israel formed and acted its history in the region of Palestine or in West Arabia. Again as with Troy, research in abundance and perspicacious can bring ultimately an answer. Astonishingly our interpretation of the Prophets is the same whether they happen to be in Palestine or Arabia.

Isaiah is a critical figure in explaining events of the Iron Age in Judah (whether in Palestine or West Arabia), and by extension to the whole Near East. He actually existed. He is credited with a prolonged set of pronouncements, running to 66 chapters (a score of the later chapters and several others being denied his authorship, however). His subjects exceed by far the topics engendered from the ruins of a city, for he boldly characterizes many types of Jews, from kings to beggars, as they take part in events. He testifies to the regimes of Uzzi'ah, Jotham, Ahaz, and Hezeki'ah. He predicts the downfall of Assyria and Babylonia.

If only he were a controlled historian instead of a madman! As it is, if one were to eliminate all statements laying claim to the voice and authority of the Lord, one would be left with a set of scorching denunciations of the morality and conduct of the population, of descriptive statements about the state of affairs, psychically, environmentally, celestially. Repetitions are countless. A psychiatrist would have no trouble whatsoever in categorizing him as a megalomaniac projecting shame and blame for all manner of evil (dietary, ritual, sexual, disobedience, corruption, blasphemy, cowardice, etc.) onto whosoever comes to mind, but especially other Jews..

When I wrote and published two volumes on '*Homo Sapiens Schizotypus,*' I denied the ordinary meanings of normality and rationality and instead perceived a model of the human being that included tendencies toward an omnipresent fear, guilt, aversion to strangers or even familiars, paranoia, catatonism, and obsession-compulsion. These all emerged from the basic inability to control oneself, in fact, one's-selves, inasmuch as the distinctive essence of mankind is a practical duplication of mental operations in both the right and left brain hemispheres.

In a sense, the prophets of Israel are intended to be psychiatrists as well as seers, for they spend most of their time lecturing the Jews and seeking to focus their minds properly. The people of Israel can practically do no good, to hear their prophets. So much terror occupies their lives, there would hardly be time to do good. Once in a long harangue, the Prophet will urge charity upon his wicked people. But times beyond number Yahweh is offended, so often so, that there is scarcely a pause to say how people should behave to avoid offending him.

From another modernist aspect, the Prophets were nothing more than "Superman" comic artists. It is no wonder that, wherever one goes, the more stupid Christians, not all red-necks or untutored blacks by any means, but Cabinet Secretary, even perhaps a President or two, are ready for the Last Great Day, and meanwhile they help Hollywood to smear the wide world with films of violent nonsense. They are madmen who persuade some people of scenarios that have actually happened, but they lack a language to describe events soberly and measurably. Therefore the effects of their prophecies have been to misguide people in the mass to let them live in a punitive horrible world as God's world most of the time . Only if we consider the circumstances of the Martian Iron Age can we tolerate their jabberings, and only then if we apply scientific and psychological insight into what stands behind their exclamations.

Yahweh as Superman spends much time in darkness or thick clouds. Contrary to Jewish-Christian-Muslim doctrine Yahweh is pictured in animations and many anthropomorphisms. He (and there is no question of his gender) is the center of far more cherubs, angels and the host of heaven numberless than there are Catholic saints, and none of them with more character than a stone (which, in astral fact, they were).

The hosts of heaven are myriad. "The Lord from Sinai rose up from Sieir unto them.. He came with 10,000 saints" *(Deut.33.2)*They are almost certainly the maruts of the Hindus. On the rarest of occasions, a line of an accidental Psalm *(2:4)* "He that siteth in the Heavens shall laugh. The Lord shall have them in derision." (Note the unpleasant laugh specified.) The same Lord "rode upon a cherub and did fly."

But mostly he is smiting his devotees.

What this animated scenario gives us is truly a set of natural disasters, however, and owing to the absence of historiography, then and later, the reconstruction of the scenario in scientific images and terms (most of which are available for other and less important purposes) are simply not employed. Yahweh and His Heavenly Host are to have no competition, but are to live in their never-never land forever and ever.

The only great nation that sought to rid itself of the incubus of the Bible collapsed ignominiously, of other causes, we hasten to say; I mean the Soviet Union. Priests and parishioners sprang up magically and scurried in upon its unworkable structure to recast their olden times religion. Nor is this a proof of the Bible's durability. The Chinese have a respected book called the *I Ching: the Book of Changes,* and is a Bible of Changes, while the Hebrew Bible is a "A Book against Changes."

A threatening people of the world today may be the fundamentalist orthodox Jews of Israel and abroad, and their realpolitik cohort in Israel and the United States of America. In the back of their minds is the thought: "If half the Jews of the world could be tortured and murdered while the world's government and people looked on, half the world with all its people might now be destroyed with no greater compunction." No one openly expresses this logic, but men in critical positions have this kind of mentality, perforce. They have chalked up a bad record over the past 60 years, and have enough nuclear bombs to destroy or cripple any nation in the world. ("Nuclear stockpiles could create 300,000 bombs," reads a *New Scientist* headline of 7 September 2005.)

Neither Velikovsky nor his heirs and followers could swallow his own logic when he explicated what he regarded as his great contribution to the peace of humankind, the collective amnesia or scatoma and its subsequent diseased outbreak, a true PTSD – for his logic and his appeals

Two aspects of Isaiah and by extension his co-adjutant prophets impress us. They are preserved, of course, as monotheists, notwithstanding that during the time they lived, most of the population was practicing polytheism. They were specially recruited as monotheists. A scrutiny of all of the scriptures, argumentation and lore of the Jews would probably give them additional reason for the hatred of their people, not alone other tribes of Jews, and of their own tribe.

No Jewish prophet until Jesus -- and then he not completely so – made of the Lord of Hosts a likeable figure. Is it possible that the Jewish God was so terrible simply because he was the representative of the history of the Jews? And those who believed in this one god had nowhere else to go to distribute blame for their sufferings, as the Greeks could do with their gods who were often in conflict with one another. A wound by one god could be cured by another.

Correctly, the damage to the Greater Mediterranean Region in the Iron Age was such as to give a god a bad reputation insofar as protecting and indulging his flock were concerned. A single god would carry all the blame, except that he would be believed to have discovered that the full blame belonged to his chosen people. In the Hebrew case, the Lord of Hosts employed even the enemies of the Jews to punish them, dissatisfied apparently with the sufficiency of natural disaster, internal justice and injustice, and conscience to do the job.

But let us revert to the heart of the matter. The prophets claim to have witnessed or to have reliable promises of celestially provoked and all other manner of natural catastrophes. Isaiah has claimed to witness the sun stayed for hours on one occasion, and then a few years later to have caught up its lost hours. Two contrary tilts of the Earth, it would seem.

Granted that we have pictured a kind of madness typical of prophets of all times and places, are we entitled to believe the statements of Isaiah as to the occurrences in the New East in the early Iron Age? Can a madman describe truly what has happened in the world about him? The law of evidence in a court of law puts restrictions upon accepting testimony of a mentally deranged person. The main restriction is that he not be believed on a matter where he is sole witness, where there is no supporting hard or material evidence, and where the testimony is precisely the kind denied credence, because it is precisely the material that has served to define mental instability in the first instance. That is, if a man is examined for sanity because he went about lifting the skirts of little girls, he should not be trusted to testify whether this is common practice.

Humanity Shocked Beyond Recall

Now we may turn to the general question of humanity in a state of shock. Given all that has happened, the human is probably shocked beyond recall. It comes from the gestalt of creation, as I term the phenomenon in *Homo Schizo I and II*, the books that search the origins of mankind and find it in a splitting of personality as a consequence of quantavolutionary environmental, and therefore internal physiological, brain change in the direction of double-thought processes (the hemispheres right and left interrelate closely, but not identically, and slow up by a fraction of a second a communication within the brain and therefore spread out the communication so that it can affect plural identities, emotions and ideas simultaneously. The split selves gives the human, Homo Schizo, the aforesaid normal tendencies to paranoia, apathy and personal aversion, obsession and compulsion, displacement and projection

These unsteady poly-selves norms are easily destabilized. When shocked, traumatized, direly threatened in body or mind, he or she reacts with several or more symptomatic indicators. One psychotherapist, Terry Larimore, has listed over sixty physical and emotional indicators for adults, noting that some of them can occur without severe emotional trauma, and depend upon what stage or how remote a recapitulation is involved, or whether the shock is sympathetic or parasympathetic. Many of the behaviors seem normal and pass muster day by day. Others are odd and call attention to the person. Many are disabling, many not. (See www.terrylarimore.com/SignsOfShock.html)

The personal behaviors have names that do not lead directly nor are obviously subsumed under the social or collective behaviors that are the result of the shock of a number of persons of a group at the same time. (The shocks are never identical for all persons, which complicates the effect and the exact knowledge of the effect.

To determine the effects on human populations of a catastrophe or quantavolution, we would also have to discover how many high energy forces were operative, to what degree of intensity, over how long a period of time, and what were the cultural traits of the affected people.

This is an impossible menu except within the widest margins of error. But, presuming it done, we would have to guess at some degree of diminution of effects, negatively exponential to be sure, but with wide margins of error once again. Decades, centuries, millennia would elapse with ever-diminishing effects, we might presume, but then we would be losing the measure of the original quantavolution in the morass of determinants, happening before the Q under examination, and after it, and then effects of less than Q-scale catastrophes (such as sun-spot storms) or continuous warfare, and medical intervention in the constitution of the population.

King Nabopolassar's Stress and Shock

The archaeologist and historian must think and act upon hints and legend. Like the hero of *The Mikado*, "A wandering minstrel I, a thing of shreds and patches..." See here what Velikovsky once picked up, employed by him in a different connection but not for my usage here. (Especially in ancient and pre-history, useful scraps are so few that they need often be employed gratefully in several contexts. It is the inscription of a great king of Neo-Babylonia, Nabopolassar-Hattusilis, who ruled for 21 years, who described his reign honestly, who managed his empire successfully, and who examined and described his symptoms of illness:

"I was on the road to Til-Kunnu. Stormy weather broke loose, the God of Storm did thunder dreadfully. Inside my mouth the word became scarce, and the word came out somewhat stumbling."

"And the years came and went and this condition began to play a part in my dreams. And god's hand struck me in the time of a dream, and the ability of speech I lost entirely."

Soon thereafter he died. We note this happened in the full Iron Age. Hemon, god of noise, was raging and thundering. (Hemon is Hamon in Hebrew, meaning noise.) Hemon is also Nergal who is Mars and Ares and the Archangel Gabriel. The King suffered a stroke, and became partially mute. He suffered in his dreams from the same incident and finally after such a dream he became speechless.

A brief hint is all we can offer here. Only if it jibes with Homo Schizo and Q theory, and with clinical psychopathology, and then with scores of parallel or supporting hints and bits of evidences, can we add this case history to our building blocks of the Martian Q..

Collective Shock-Response

Let us turn from individual to collective responses, as happened in two recent catastrophes, the tsunami of December 2004, which struck Indonesia and all the countries around it, and the hurricane (Katrina) and flood that devastated New Orleans and adjoining Gulf Coasts areas, USA, in September 2005.

The great Indonesian regional wave killed over 200,000 persons, wiped out sores of towns and villages, disrupted several national economies, and counted its victims in the millions. We have noted the occurrence of many tsunamis in ancient times. We cannot know of most of them. If the Indonesian disaster were to have happened two centuries earlier, the world beyond a thousand-mile radius would scarcely have heard about it and would have forgotten it in a few years.

Scarcely anyone has a recollection whether direct or suppressed of the explosion of Tambora Volcano , Indonesia, in 1815, which grew three miles tall in three years, which then blew its top, killing 100,000 people and polluting the world's atmosphere with 100 cubic km of gases, dust and debris. In Europe at that moment, most eyes were turned upon the Congress of Vienna, which was settling the fate of Napoleon Bonaparte, and, almost incidentally, bring an end to the British-American War of 1812. (The War's total casualties were less than the dead of the Tambora explosion.

Two experts from the National Center for Post-Traumatic Stress Disorder have written: "If the rate of psychological problems turns out similar to previous natural disasters studied (e.g., Armenian earthquake, mudslides in Mexico, Hurricane André in the United States) 50% of those affected could suffer from clinically significant distress or psychopathology."[215] This bespeaks clinical cases upwards of a million, then.

Rates of mental illness could be higher here, too, because of individuals suffering multiple stresses that may also continue. We speak not alone of pre-traumatic stressors such as extreme poverty and police repression, but especially of factors in the disaster such as bereavement, injuries to self and kin, life threat, panic during the disaster, feelings of hopelessness and helplessness, separation from family, loss of all belongings, and displacement.

High-Energy Shocking Forces

Yet people could come from afar to help, such as would not be possible in other times and when the scope of catastrophe was greater. Moreover the number of hi-energy forces operative was quite limited. Inserted here is a list of the hi-energy forces that a quantavolution such as of 2300 BCE, 1500 BCE, and 2700 BCE would call out. Most of them are treated in my book, *The Lately Tortured Earth*. Asterisks denote occurrences also in the Indonesian 2004 disaster. Number symbols (#) denote occurrences also in the New Orleans disaster.

1. Tsunami *
2. Ash falls
3. Meteorite or comet crash*?
4. Spectres *#
5. Civil chaos (revolution, mob violence) #
6. Tilt of the Earth
7. Catatonism (mutism, analphabetism) *#
8. Avalanche
9. Changed sky bodies owing to Earth tilt
10. Atmosphere heat-up
11. Changing positions and appearance of sky bodies (also 'gods')
12. Grotesque huge auroral displays
13. Flood *#
14. Changes in geographical morphology *#
15. Edible fall-out (manna, ambrosia, *et al.*)
16. Amnesia *#
17. Gas clouds (methane and others)
18. Major depression (considered as a major nervous system force) *#
19. Acute anxiety, panic (a major rush of physiological forces) *#
20. Post-traumatic stress disorder (a varying set of psychosomatic symptoms) *#
21. Armed assault

22. Destruction of public records #
23. Water and soil pollution #
24. Forced evacuation of population *#
25. Tornado
26. Hunger, thirst #
27. Apocalyptic mental aberration #
28. Fall-out of tektites, stones
29. Sheet flames from above or horizontal
30. Lightning storms, mega-lightning, clusters
31. Thunder, acoustics, loud voices #
32. Invading army, pirate, brigand bands *#
33. Darkness #
34. Hurricane #
35. Massacre
36. Animal plague (rabbits, grasshoppers, lemmings, mice, snakes)
37. Biological plague (viral or bacterial)
38. Blasts of wind (often laden) #
39. Fire #
40. Quick-Freeze
41. Dust falls (including arsenic, iron, chemicals) #

The Indonesian disaster brought on many cases of deep depression, acute anxiety, panic, and seems to have produced cases of catatonism, of extreme apathy and muteness. It was provoked by an earthquake of a strength sufficient to shift minutely the crustal plates involved. Hundreds of kilometers of coastline were altered, but by meters rather than kilometers. Bearing in mind the paucity of evidence from ancient catastrophes and quantavolutions, still I am tempted to venture a figure to compare the Indonesian disaster of 2005 with the Martian

Quantavolution of the eighth-seventh centuries BCE. Seven of the 41 forces that I listed above managed the scenario of disaster of Indonesia. In the Martian Quantavolution that I have studying, all 41 of the high energy forces came into play. The total short-time effect (~-850 to -700) was at least 5,000 times the 2004 Indonesian effect. Further, the after-effects were a great many years more prolonged.

A second report of the National Center, this one by Fran H. Norris,[216] assembled the findings of 121 sampling studies of 52,061 persons that in all had experienced 62 different natural disasters around the world in this generation. The forces at play consisted of earthquakes, hurricanes and cyclones, floods and volcanoes.

In the 37 samples that dealt with developing (i.e. poor) countries only, these results were obtained: Minimal impairment (transient stress reactions) was scored in only one sample but that was a study among rescue workers. One third of the samples showed moderate impairment, with prolonged but sub-clinical distress. In the case of somewhat under half the samples, from 25% to 49% of the people suffered from clinically significant distress and psychopathology. In a quarter of the samples, over 50% of the respondents suffered clinically significant distress and psychopathology.

From these and other studies it could be reported that pre-disaster predispositions inclined many to more serious disorders arising from the disaster, and similarly slowed recovery. A high level of individual morale (self-efficacy, mastery, perceived control, self-esteem, hope, and optimism) stemmed the effects of disaster and made for more prompt recovery. Also, strong social and political support from the outside as well as inside helps markedly to restore victims. Normal and naturally occurring environmental and social supports are superior to professional and interventional methods often. Assignments of blame and blotting out of memories are strategies not to be recommended in therapy, whether group or individual.

Did God Call in Katrina to Destroy New Orleans?

The New Orleans regional disaster unquestionably initiated very many cases of Post-Traumatic Stress Disorder. Only preliminary indications have been reported as of this date, September 30, 2005 after Hurricane 'Katrina' struck the area, on September 1. Although the number of lives lost was only a small fraction of the heavy losses in the greater Indonesian region, the complications of 'normal' life in the U.S. Gulf State area affected are incomparably greater and therefore 'simple' solutions will be a great deal more rare; millions of persons will never find living formulas thereafter, not for many years, if at all. Their lives will remain forever de-structured. Many institutions infiltrate an ordinary American's life; a much greater proportion of Americans than of Malayans and East Indians is normally neurotic, hence on the verge of intensified psychoneurotic symptoms.

Costs are a rough measure of neurotic potential: Katrina will cost directly well over a hundred billion dollars, whereas the costs of the Indonesian tsunami several billions. I am not comparing human worth, I would emphasize, but the complex and prolonged messes of hi-tech disasters when compared with lo-tech events, and therefore the simpler and shorter ways out of the messes in lo-tech societies. The American effects will be artificially enlarged and stretched out over time.

The religious cults of the victims play a larger role in America than in Indonesia. The latter disaster was not accompanied by a wave of guilt and psychic punition of the self and others. By contrast, at the very crisis of the New Orleans disaster, apocalyptic voices were telling the victims that they had gotten what they deserved for their sins.

One popular web site (www.realtruthmag.org) was letting it be known that New Orleans and the region in general had gone so far into wickedness -- gambling, prostitution, atheism, corruption, drunkenness, homosexuality, sexual promiscuity, bastardy, moral relativism, murderousness, tolerance, 'political correctness,' lawlessness, hypocrisy, un-godlike pastors, wicked entertainments, falsifying media, and more, that God had to step in and correct matters catastrophically. "Consider.. an annual Labor Day festival for homosexuals had to be canceled because *Katrina* destroyed New Orleans... Was this mere coincidence, or was it by the hand of God? Remember Sodom and Gomorrah." Needless to say, the diatribe was studded with passages from Isaiah, Ezekiel, Deuteronomy, *et al.* -- the usual cast of characters.

Blame and shame are hallmarks of Judeo-Muslim-Christian religious sects. The Chief Mufti of Palestine, the Chief Rabbi of Israel, and others of their ilk have in times not too recent to believe praised Hitler or called him the instrument of the Lord in punishing the Jews for their sins. Priesthoods played a large role in the governing of ancient societies and we should conjecture, though we can scarcely learn or know, how cult and catastrophe met.

Elsewhere, I have developed the point that the basis for all historical religions was a punishing set of gods, and moreover that religions based upon the Hebrew Bible (especially when enforced by rabbinical controls) are particularly prone to use blame and shame as tools of organizing and directing human behavior. Can we go so far as to claim that a secular society can undergo and endure and recover from catastrophe and develop the positive potential of a quantavolution better than a society founded upon a godhead, scripture and ritual?

Why Societies Collapse

Actually we could investigate the records of historical and recent disasters and organize the materials of the studies at hand so as to frame a respectable hypothesis about this most important question. One might separate the societies struck by the recent disasters, such as are included in the cited studies, into three levels of religious structure and practice and then probe the individual records to determine whether religious differences provides a useful variable, and perhaps detect significant difference even between the religious and non-religious societies as a whole.

Let us go back to our earlier concerns with the Mycenean Palace Culture Collapse and look into its causes. The Dartmouth College Classics Department prepared a note on various theories as to the reasons for the Mycenean Palace System Collapse. I have added several to their list and present the list here, with keywords and the name of a prominent exponent.

1. Extreme social unrest and revolt, class struggle, Andronikos, 1954, Dever and Sader (1990).

2. Piracy and marauding , Vermeule, 1960.

3. Invasion and immigration from the North, Desborough, 1964.

4. Many different local causes, Mylonas, 1966.

5. Extended drought, Carpenter, 1966.

6. Cutting of trade routes by Sea Peoples, Iakovides, 1974.

7. Climate change (hitherto underestimated), von Storch, 2004.

8. Deconstruction of Complex Societies, Tainter.

9. Population explosion and migration, Hallo

10. Decline, bottom social takeover, and invasion, Rutter 1990, Walberg 1976, Degr-Jalkotzy 1083, Small, 1997, Pilides 1994, Bankoff, Meyer and Stefanovitch 1996.

11. Anonymous invaders adapting to low culture elements, Winter 1977.

12. Topheavy specialization tips over and brings down other elements, Betancourt 1976

13. Warfare changes from chariots to infantry, Drews

1993.

After describing the essences of these theories, the Dartmouth professors make clear that a number of factors interacted: economic, climatic, revolutionary, outside invaders, and changes in warfaring. None of the theorists argued that their preferred causes had to do originally or concurrently with Mars, religious crisis, or exo-terrestrial events. At the same time, the authors grant that several important questions have not been answered withal: Why the palace systems were not rebuilt, whether there were general shocks of some kind that undermined the whole civilization, how unstable was the social system to begin with, why were areas everywhere so depopulated and was this the effect of plague, famine, warfare, or and/or out-migration?

Several of the theories blame aggressive warfare for the omnipresent destruction. I have stipulated this also whenever it seemed to be a critical force in the devastation. Conquering troops often set fire to settlements, cut down orchards, burned crops. How often, we cannot say. Shalmaneser, King of Assyria, ruler of the Hatti Region, said of himself, repeating it as if it were his motto: "I destroyed, I devastated, I burned with fire." Again, after his sixteenth march into Syria, "Countless cities I destroyed, I devastated, I burned with fire."*(Ages in Chaos, 314)* When did such practices start? Was they peculiar to his domain? Was it peculiarly Assyrian; were the Assyrians especially notorious for their wickedness? Yes, would appear the answer to these several questions. But we are not sure about the normality of such practices, over time and among cultures.

Here we wish that archaeology would be more informative. Possibly the Bronze Age was less brutal. If so we must by all means know it. Lest this sound absurd – "Invaders are always the same," I can deny this view from extensive personal experience and specifically we should recall the evil reputation possessed by the Iron Age among all those who, such as Hesiod, compared it with prior ages. We believe there to have been a real distinction among the ages. And even in these solarian times, when men run amok against their enemies, as did the German Nazis and their enlisted supporters, there were years of intense propaganda preparing Germans to behave ruthlessly and brutally in warfare, especially against those peoples whom they termed "racially inferior," such as Eastern Europeans. This propaganda contained a full measure of ancient symbols (such as the swastika) and catastrophic mythology of their ancient pagan gods.

This being so, we should expect the terrible destructions wrought by nature to have a telling effect on the conduct of humans, setting for them an insane example. The wild burnings by war parties and invading hordes of towns that were not already afflicted by disaster were imitations of the red and fiery planet Mars-Nergal-Hercules and its associated Marut fragments. Its sheets of flame and thunderbolts terrorized innumerable places. Many invaders had, previous to their taking to the route of invasion, seen their own towns and lands lacerated and scorched by the high energy forces of nature.

By now, considering how many hundreds of sites have been explored, library-research archaeologists should have begun to carry in their breast pockets a master chart, continually updated, of the lethal statistics of settlements. Its variables would include approximations of dates, type of culture, marks of an invading presence or natural destruction with degrees of intensity of the effect and a rating of the confidence on the conclusion arrived at. We might in time find ourselves satisfied that we are answering the question, "What came first, the chicken or the egg?"

Inventiveness in the Iron Age

I have written in some pages above about the striking inventiveness of the Iron Age, so that I need here mention the subject again mainly to emphasize the positive side of quantavolutions. "Iron ores are widely distributed...Now there is a massive amount of archaeological and anthropological evidence, which suggests that iron served to reinforce and reconfigure existing political and economic structures," quoting Peter Magee.[217] (Bryn Mawr *Class. Rev.* 2003.02.27). I will interject three more examples of inventiveness, set in Arabia, a land whose contributions to the ancient world have been long neglected.

The *falaj* system of irrigation, it is now shown, began, not in Iran, but in Arabia and Oman, with a beginning date in the early Iron Age. (Peter Magee) Further, domestication of the camel, it appears now, was an early Iron Age achievement of southeast Arabia. A legend of West Arabia gives credit to Judaic Arabs of the same time for the same complex cultural invention.

As already affirmed, we could claim more inventions and discoveries for Arabia. The Iron Age brought a desperate spurring of energies. One could connect it with the omnipresence of warfare and violence: "War is the parent of invention." (Heraclitus) The index of invention rises with desperation and desperation with conflict.

Underground irrigation on the one hand, various innovations in underground water systems on the other hand. With some adjustments of chronology, as usual, we can relate deep wells to stone pipes carrying water to distant citadels in the center of towns. This to begin with, we find done in Mycenae, in Judah, in Tiryns, in Athens, and no doubt in other places. In many places later on, like the *falaj*. Appropriately, the excavated wells show that they were of Bronze-Iron transitional construction.

Unquestionably a highly promising field of research is opening up here in the Greater Mediterranean Region Iron Age Quantavolution. Employing the hypothetical model presented in this book, for instance, a large research project might address the question: What forms of energy emerging in what spheres of existence affected what different civilizations in what ways? The cultures submitted for comparison could be the Egyptian, Phoenecian, Hebrew-Judaic, Greek, Mede-Persian, Italic, Sicilian, Iberian, Assyrian, Chaldean, Syrian, Philistine,

Canaanite, Gallic, Ethiopian, Cyrenaic, Etruscan, Roman, Arabic, and Hallstadt.

The component spheres of the holosphere were elaborated earlier – biosphere, astrosphere, anthroposphere, theosphere, et al. The high energy forces have also seen some discussion – earthquakes, wind, flood, volcanism, fire, lightning, acoustical shock, and so on. We have also discussed *en passant* the subtle but perhaps highest forms of energy that alter the human constitution and mentality, and with this their social habits and systems.

Changes, in Greek and Jewish Societies, and in General

As part of the study, we would expect, for example, to throw light upon how changes in Greek, as compared to Judaic behavior, mentation, and cultures, took place. With the help of the Bible, retentive, tenacious, legalistic, authoritarian, and aggressive traits were fostered among ancient Jews as they developed the Yahweh cult, and became characteristic of Jews in Palestine where only a majority of them dwelled, and, once the principal Diaspora followed the rebellion against Roman rule, a small minority hung on. (Actually a continuous diaspora had been taking place ever since they began to leave Western Arabia for Palestine, then in the last centuries before Christ from Palestine to many other places of the Roman Empire and beyond. The Jewish state proper, Judaea, did not pull itself together in Palestine until about 250 years before it was taken apart by the Romans in the late first century after Jesus Christ. The diaspora was continuous and often flourishing – conceivable as a bedouin state adapted successively over three thousand years of world change until it arrived at 2005 with an actual residential State of Israel, competing and cooperating with and partially financed by and well-connected to the continuing and prospering Diaspora Jews around the world.

Greek ideology and conduct, by contrast, became

flexible, polytheistic, rationalistic, colonizing, self-governing by secular rule, inventive and artistic. The Greek character blended into the Roman, and after centuries dominated politically as well as culturally the Eastern Roman Empire, then Byzantium, and via the Greek Orthodox Church and the bureaucratic suppressive Ottoman Empire, altered its own original traits. When the West was overcome and revived by the Italian Renaissance, the Classical Greek ideals suffused it, and the consequent Western European civilization even penetrated and modified the Roman Catholic Church.

The Jews in Diaspora were already much different from those of ancient Judah and Israel. I speak of those centered in Spain, the Islamic lands and elsewhere. And with the Enlightenment and their liberation from pariah restrictions in Western Europe, they became a leading element in cultural, financial and cosmopolitan life everywhere in the West. Finally, with emigration to America and Soviet communism, they broke out from the *shtetls* in Russia, and were assimilated into the wide reaches of Russian culture as a whole. Ultimately, secular and religious Jews, no matter how intricately related and held together by outside prejudice as much as by internal cohesion, were as disparate as gentile fundamentalists and religious libertarians. Some element of collective amnesia respecting the Martian Quantavolution may possibly be present, then, in everyone, along with the marks of prior quantavolutions. The value of extensive further investigation lies in the catastrophes and even a possible quantavolution that might come upon the world at some future time.

Most Americans, Christians, Muslims, and Jews believe in an afterlife. Except for a small minority who believe that they will go to a hell for unforgivable sins, this great majority look upon life after death as pleasant and interminable. A large number, too, regard a prospective annihilation of the world as a prelude to their ascendence to heaven. Therefore they are not, one would imagine, prone to suppress long ago memories of catastrophe, for the intimation of the end of the world holds for them a comfortable promise. Recalling past catastrophe, then, is not terribly alarming, as it was in the story of Noah, to whom his god promised that he would never again call upon a Deluge to drown all other but a single family and a pair of all species. The flood had been a bad experience, granted humanity deserved it. And a double protection was afforded by Sheol, a word that occurs 65 times in the Old Testament.

However, despite their confidence in Heaven, most people are uneasy, to say the least, about undergoing a universal catastrophe that eradicates the living. Perhaps with the past near-extinctions deep in mind, they cannot but wonder why these test cases had to occur and whether the next quantavolution will also be only a test case.

The utility of the disciplines that explore the ancient world is considerable. We may reasonably ask for a large increase in synthesis and eclecticism in archaeology. This would require changes in the typical curriculum in ancient history and archaeology, going beyond traditional methodology, and the chronometric tests and classificatory procedures, and even the most helpful new techniques such as satellite soil exploration and topology. Social and individual psychology should occupy a respectable place in the full curriculum. Every sign and symbol is a product of human mentation. It illuminates a mind, a social group, a history.

Chapter Twenty

A Neurosis of Concerned Scholars

In his dialogue, *Laws*, Plato, though himself quantavolutionary, as attested by his propagating the story of Atlantis in the *Critias* and *Timaeus* as a true catastrophe (preceded by disordered heavens), moves in a drastically opposed direction. "The ruler of the universe has ordered all things with a view to the excellence and preservation of the whole."[218] The rules call for the heavenly bodies to operate today as they have for "time beyond understanding," and not to change their nature or wander, changing their orbits.

A person who upholds the contrary view, to wit, that everything exists "by nature or chance," including the heavenly bodies, is to be imprisoned and brainwashed in a "House of Better Judgement." Whereupon, after five years, if still recalcitrant, he is to be put to death.[219] (We can note the remarkable pre-play of the fate of Giordano Bruno, imprisoned for denying the eternal Heavenly order, defiant, ultimately burnt at the stake by the Catholic authorities. The Church has recently confessed that it was in error.)

Could there be among archaeological and historical scholars similar forms of mentation, that is, a terrible fright, a deeply suppressed memory, that in consequence of its suppression brings about a heightened intensity of group cohesion, a projection of hostility and aggression against quantavolutionary history and its paradigm, such that its proponents are dealt with intolerantly? The answer to this question is fairly obvious, and more of an answer is forthcoming.

The most educated and scientific public is most vulnerable mentally to Q-shock because it lacks the religious conviction of a saving god who provides a heaven in the end. Moreover, it denies that anybody should deserve dire punishment. At all events, it cannot discover any god who is famous for giving a fair trial to the accused.

At the age of 83, Velikovsky was still fighting the scientific establishment that had treated him cruelly and frustrated the acceptance of his theories. Rationalizing nicely his private and public motives, he referred their behavior to a collective amnesia that goes back to the ancient quantavolutions. Resistance to the recall of mankind's intense traumas, he wrote at the end of his last book, "made the scientific community go through all the facets of self-degradation in order not to face and not to let others face what was our common past."[220]

Has this phenomenon, this neurosis, this scatoma, afflicted archaeologists since 1950, at which time his book about the rampant planets Venus and Mars and their cohorts appeared? His well-documented book called *Stargazers and Gravediggers*, lends him support; it was essentially ready for publication in 1962, when I read the manuscript and it was published posthumously. It is a simply written book, without psychoanalytic jargon, letting documents speak for themselves for the most part. I need not use the material evidence of *Mankind in Amnesia* either; anyhow that work is dedicated to the general problem of collective amnesia rather than especially to the psychology of archaeologists and historians.

Professional Hazards

It is for me to take the occasion, perhaps, to indicate that specialists are vulnerable to the diseases that they treat.

1. A person chooses one's occupation for psychological reasons, in part. An historian will often derive his indulgences from the control that he exercises over the substance of history. He wants to write history, sometimes to bury it, and his motives are as hidden as he can make them.

2. The training of an archaeologist is usually incomplete in view of the outstanding problems of his field.

3. The credence given to the highly vulnerable Egyptian chronology is so automatic that it must happen under a kind of mesmerism, with roots for acceptance in the unconscious.

4. The wishful denial, often, that earthquakes might occur as a general and simultaneous phenomenon, is suspect, as is the neglect of the works of Claude Schaeffer.

5. Also psychologically suspect is the obdurate, though kindly spoken, resistance of Claude Schaeffer himself to going beyond his earthquake theory, even if to help strengthen it by closing the Dark Age phantom gap.

6. Then, also, Schaeffer and every other establishment archaeologist refused to consider the skies as a source of trouble for the universal destruction. Even those who believed in a god as author of all things would venture into the heavens only under the scriptural guidance of their cult.

7. We can detect a noticeable late trend among archaeologist to find in the Dark Ages a promising "grey age" where change was taking place gradually, and happens not to be too noticeable. This despite an imposing array of destructions and desolations.

8. Starting off on the wrong railroad line, all the stations were wrong. Ramses III in the Fourth Century boasted of repelling some "Peoples of the Isles," which "Peoples of the Sea" became a catchword for every eruption of peoples by land or sea, even when lacking all evidence of their presence. The error came from a non-existent Ramses III probably being wrongly placed in the fourteenth century. The hasty conclusion was to be followed by all the other unexplainable Sea

Peoples, who were actually Martian Iron Age creations, of the 9th to 7th centuries.

9. Mircea Eliade in his Myth of *The Eternal Return*[221] writes of the impulse of cultures around the world to invent a set of rites that are believed to permit them to go back to the beginning of all things, their creation and origins. Velikovsky speaks of the impulse to repeat the act, return to the scene, fixations – often sexual – or "selection of an occupation offering a regular substitute for an act repressed from the conscious memory." And Freud's *Beyond the Pleasure Principle* is quoted to the effect that a patient will repress a significant part of his experience and it lurks in him like a torturing demon, a dark anxiety over awaking something that should be left asleep.

The Zionist Dilemma of the Western Scientist

Velikovsky could not solve this specific problem, and, although it was uppermost in his mind, it hardly found mention in his books. Ultimately the blame or sin, if one wishes to use this decrepit ancient Hebrew concept, is to be assigned to whichever cause, immediate or remote, in the infinite progression of causes, that we feel may be most useful... even the planets Venus and Mars, or to the causes of their eccentric behavior.

Embarrassing as this dilemma was, another was even more so. Velikovsky possessed a passion for the Jewish people second to no one's. His father was a Zionist pioneer. Immanuel stood off from Zionism, but was intensely pro-Israel. In the middle of the most strenuous research , during and after World War II, he wrote under a pseudonym on behalf of the Jewish claims and against the British and Palestinian obstacles to a full realization of "the Promised Land."

Try as he might to appear objective or aloof, clues to his feelings can be detected in details of his work, and as

I pointed out long ago, his heartfelt dedication to his two early pamphlets containing his *Theses* for the reconstruction of ancient Near East history and the astrophysics and history of the solar system evolved from the happy marriage of his Jewish traditionalism to his discoveries in natural science, which, amazingly, raised the cause of Hebrew (and Israeli) history to the secular skies.

Satisfied that his major scientific theories suited his political theories, he nevertheless had still to contend with his psychoanalytic theory. Here, the concept of collective amnesia was once more getting him into trouble. For if it appeared that the Israeli government were displacing most Palestinians from their own country forever, and, too, if those Palestinians, who were disposed to make a Palestinian nation on the same ground as the Israelis or on separate grounds, were subjected to innumerable and increasing discriminations that diminished day by day their already minuscule rights to welfare, justice and education, then the analogy to Nazi behavior was becoming increasingly appropriate.

(One needs to read, apropos, Professor Victor Klemperer's astonishingly detailed and stupendously honest Dresden diary, 1933 to 1945, for the minutiae of persecution increasingly applied to Jews from one day to the next in the Third Reich of Adolf Hitler. He ended his diary in 1959 two weeks before dying. Susie Ehrmann, reviewing the first volume, 1933 to 1941, for the Australian Holocaust Commemoration Centre in 1999, said, "He hated Nazism, and could see little benefit in Zionism.. 'Anyone who goes to Palestine,' he wrote, 'exchanges nationalism and narrowness here for nationalism and narrowness there... it is just like the Nazis, with their nosing after blood and their ancient cultural roots.'" Klemperer was faithful to his chosen field of the French Enlightenment until his death.)

We need simply to go back to Velikovsky's own words to picture his second deep embarrassment, for, of course, he would never admit Nazism to be applicable to the situation in the Middle East -- preferring to become a vulnerably bad historian, if needs be. The Nazis, he had to let one believe, though he would not say it, possessed a unique quality of free will. Therefore, they might legitimately be punished. (When one reflects upon this exception, it devolves into flattery of the enemy.)

The analogous conduct of the Jews could show them also to be victims of PTSD, reinforced by the Nazi terrors of the Shoah. Should their PTSD go unrecognized or denied, or should it also be treated, though granted that their conduct toward the Palestinians, however despicable it was, fell far short of the "total solution" pursued by Hitler and Himmler.

So we should conclude, I suppose, by also forgiving all bad historiographers, "for they know not what they do." Velikovsky himself, we see, had the same kinds of problems, but in a different field. He was as neurotic and incurable as the typical archaeologist. "Physician, heal thyself!"

What makes a Yalie into an Egyptologist?

It is bemusing, under the circumstances, to read a description of what it takes to be an Egyptologist, as given in the *Yale Bulletin* (Jan.17, 2000), by staff writer Dorie Baker: "An Egyptologist is a specialized archaeologist, a field that embraces a number of disciplines, including geology, geography, anthropology, history and chemistry . In addition, an Egyptologist must draw heavily on philology, the study of language, and paleography, the science of dating and decoding ancient forms of writing. A student of ancient Egypt also has to master a full gamut of hands-on skills, from wielding a pick and shovel with surgical dexterity to dealing with sophisticated photographic technology. Finally to trace the origins of a particular finding, an Egyptologist must display the cunning and deductive imagination of a detective."

Unforgivable gaps in the recital are the theosphere, astrosphere, and psychosphere, all three of which were flagrant preoccupations of the ancients of Egypt and every place else in the world. We shall take the present occasion to contribute to the aforesaid wondrous list of cultural achievements a few generalities on the need for and prescription of psychiatric self-analysis, so as to expose tendencies toward authoritarianism, psychic denial, and complacency.

Archaeologists' denial of and indifference to the theosphere portion of the catastrophes of the Iron Age and of the ~400-year gap in chronology of the same period is tantamount to a neurosis. Can there be such a thing as a collective neurosis and a professional neurosis? Our answer is Yes. Are archaeologists prone to the neurosis? Yes. Can the neurosis be named? Yes. Can its symptoms be discerned? Yes. Can the causes of the symptoms be discovered? Yes. Have we a therapy in mind for the neurosis? Yes. Can the therapy and cure be applied? Doubtful. As I said earlier, specialists are often vulnerable to the diseases that they treat.

Velikovsky did not escape contradiction for all his pains and broad theory. He was caught up in a conflict of deep feelings. Following the lead of Sigmund Freud, "The victim of amnesia caused by traumatic experiences lives under the urge to repeat the experience, often reversing the roles, himself becoming the aggressor and inflicting punishment on a new victim." The shock that is followed by diminished memory , then seeks to heighten the memory, which can be most conveniently done by targeting a third party for punishment.

Anxieties Peculiar to Archaeology

Let us move on from his attitude, which certainly suggested that therapy was in order. We admit to a certain reluctance to apply the term neurosis to colleagues. But we feel relieved to use the adjective "collective", ergo "collective neurosis." A mental illness should basically be assigned to an individual, a person. Then, if it can be observed to be contagious or developing out of a source common to a number of persons or the totality of a population, it can be called a collective neurosis.

Possibly a cause in common can be surmised: a heavy concentration on the ruins of civilizations and communities, especially on death as so frequently is the original suggestive force, the inspiration for the most common surviving objects in tombs and burial practices. This can stimulate the collective unconscious to regurgitate ancient quantavolutions. This makes for predisposition and reinforcement, at work and in their special education. So those symptoms that are normal tendencies of humans and of professions: authoritarianism, dogmatism, and hierarchical fixation become extraordinarily active.

Archaeologists need more self-protection than is normal for the population, especially the young ones among them. Therapy for the profession might consist of a heavy revision of admission standards, of educational curriculum, of training in the field, of reporting methods. and of the system of rewards, grants, etc. This is practically everything, therefore a revolution most difficult to accomplish. And all the more difficult since archaeologists also ride on the corpus of the society which is already endemically ill with the same post-traumatic stress disorders, plus other PTSD reinforcements in a great many individual cases and in some collective diseases. Modern life, like ancient life, is studded with threats and fears, with horrible happenings or simulations thereof.

The neurosis of archaeology begins with the variety of behaviors popularly familiar today as post-traumatic stress disorder (PTSD). It is not at all new, except as people believe it to be so, and agree on a new term for it. For it has been with Homo Schizo since the beginning of time and recognized by the earliest shamans.

If I have set up the idea that the human behaves badly by virtue of an uncontrollable mind, which is additionally stressed by the terrors of quantavolution, I trust that I have also succeeded in bringing out the beneficial effects upon creativity that it has upon the same Homo Schizo, all the more so when he is stressed by the traumas of quantavolution. To explain further what I mean, I should point back to the Greek natural philosophers of the Iron Age, and to the invention of many artifices and systems, such as the underground reservoirs and irrigation systems of a number of countries. To explain farther what I mean, I would pause to delineate how the whole concept of aesthetics and the behavior connected with it are associated with quantavolutions.

Aesthetics Respond to Quantavolution

Aesthetics denotes the theory, standards and databases of the arts. Included as arts are the planning of settlements, housing design and practice, modeling, poetics, graphics, photography, singing, reciting, music, the crafts (especially in their non-routine aspects), etc. Indeed, all human activity may be considered to have an aesthetic element, in that it can be judged to be pleasing according to vague but essential notions of artistry.

So one encounters in science "the elegant theory," in labor, "the neatly dug ditch," as well as "the masterpiece of sculpture" or the "beautifully-shaped woman's shoe." One can have "a well-written report on sewage," and a "marvelously-drawn map of the heavens."

Even a horror can be beautiful, as the explosion of a volcano or the sight of a tornado. All drawing of lines to exclude any human activities whatsoever from the reach of aesthetic theory is illogical and probably anti-utilitarian.

What is the underlying basis of the so-called "aesthetic sense."? It is little known and understood. No one has been able to sample randomly the full range of mankind and subject it to interview, get it to fill out a questionnaire, and obtain a history of its behavior, such that one could analyze the data and emerge with a set of propositions denoting the extent of common standards and how they are applied in thought and practical life.

It is likely that humans derive their basic

aestheticism from a catastrophized outer and inner setting and experience. That is, every human is genetically induced or heavily trained by genetic types to sublimate the totality of his perception and cognition of the world such that one cannot "take the world as it is." One must make something of it, and that "something" is cloaked in thoughts and symbols, communicating interpersonally, which brings about a set of perceptions and representations and productions reflecting the aesthetic standards of one and all. The one never escapes the all, and the all must tolerate the one, no matter how uneasy the relationship between the artist and his groups.

A principal problem or dilemma facing aesthetics and the artist of every kind is how to confess his catastrophied mind and at the same time deny it. So a poet like Ovid will write of frightful metamorphoses of humans and at the same time cloak them in beautiful settings of brooks, flowers, dells, and lovers. Or, contemporary furniture designers (the best of which might be Eames), in a permissive society urging them to express their libido frankly, devise chairs that, as Benjamin Nelson said, "force us to suffer because of how they hated their mothers."

The quantavolutionist would say that a large part of all artistic production, especially that which need not be routinely functional, is the displacement upon art and one's audience of the essential schizoid fear of losing control over one's selves (*sic*) so as to get the comfort of the others' sharing the fear and even converting it into enjoyment.

Catastrophe as a theme in itself is a vivid engrossing portion of all artistic production, especially in sacral art everywhere, for it is the "function" of religion to manage catastrophic fear by dispensing controlled suffering -- including art that depicts or enacts suffering. The flight from the suffering and openly expressed fear (of damnation, etc.) that religion provides often takes bizarre forms in which artists unconsciously reveal their denial of primal fears or express them in shapes and structures that, it sometimes would seem, everyone but themselves can grasp.

What is beautiful, good, true, satisfying, and useful all at the same time would be the ideal aesthetic form or thing. And, in a strict sense, nothing can be aesthetically perfect by just being "beautiful," for it cannot be such, that is, this is a contradiction in terms. It must have elements of all the other traits to qualify at a decent level. (This is not to say that many aestheticians and artists have not denied the need of anything but "beauty." Their position usually ends up absorbing the other qualities in the process of denying them.)

Perhaps one needs to say that the "best" art is that which helps oneself and the most others control the mind, letting out its energies in satisfying, constructive ways. The aesthetic dimension of existence is so huge that endless opportunities to develop and practice the "best art" are available to all.

The Broad-Gauged Archaeologist

Archaeology needs intellectual and cultural breadth to appreciate the roundness of events, the holosphere. No matter that its tasks consist often of sheer manual labor, which, while necessary and even sometimes exhilarating, can depress the mind, if, weighing against this force, is the force of well-anchored and continuously reinforced learning. (Socrates was remembered by a friend as standing sentry, stolid and uncomplaining, during a freezing night before a critical battle.)

Referring back to the calcinology of Troy, all the work of the excavators, including their failure to detect any physical sign of abandonment, their belief that Troy VII ended immediately before Troy VIII began (i.e., sometime around 700 B.C.), their detection of continuity of culture, their discovery of a house that seemed to span the ghost years, their finds of "12th-century" pottery just beneath or mixed in with 7th-century strata, their finds of 7th-century pottery in and sometimes under "12th-century" layers which seemed undisturbed (a situation quite similar to but more disturbing than what we saw for the stratified section just inside Mycenae's Lion Gates), the opinions they held, the problems that upset them -- all became secondary to the forcing of evidence to fit the accepted chronology. Archaeological facts were made to fit a historical theory.

Then a new theory was needed. If there was indeed a 400-year gap, something must have caused it. The cause for the end of layer VII b2 was unknown when no gap was seen, but when the gap became necessary, it was decided that Troy VII b2 must have perished by fire and sword more terrible in their effect than the Trojan War which ended Troy VIIa. Why else would people too stubborn to leave, despite 2000 years of great hardships, abandon their site now? Once more we conclude that only a revision of the Egypto-Mycenaean dates can resolve the "still unexplained" problems at Hisarlik. Only then will they cease to be "perplexing."

Excuses, rationalizations, avoidance, denial, etc. – there are too many labels to pin on psychological problems, and too many seem so normal as to be passed over ordinarily. Too, being a matter of degree, all these symptoms, if we use the term, vary in intensity from one to another individual, over the years, and from one group to another. We have no discipline with which to analyze the plethora of stumbles of mind. If Person K always uses "all" when he should use "some" he can be said to require therapy; it is not only a habit out of ignorance; it connects to a basic mental weakness in coping with interpersonal relations, a perpetual illusion.

Paradigm Paralysis

The Paradigm Paralysis of archaeologists is indicated by many arguments, most of which we can list here. Numerous principal figures going back over a century have been contributors to the persistence of and victims of Paradigm Paralysis in Archaeology: Petrie, Dorpfeld, Griffith, Blegen, Albright, Coldstream, Young, Schaeffer,

Frankfort, Evans, Caskey, Wooley, Hallo, and many another. In most cases, these scholars sacrificed their personal discoveries derived from their own excavations for the sake of the uniformitarian and authoritative paradigm.

As with the crushing suppression of quantavolution by conventional theory, the professional and popular media have played their part in spreading and advertising the Paradigm Paralysis in archaeology – the *National Geographic Magazine, Nature, Science, Antiquity, Biblical Archaeology*, and many others.

The list of ways by which they operated to preserve the old paradigm is too long for total recall. (With the help of Velikovsky, I once listed all the ways in which his extinction was furthered in the literature, such as by denial of requisite citation, misquotation, etc. They were several dozens in number.) The incomplete list here will serve for illustrative purposes, however. It might persuade us that something like a collective neurosis is hovering about.

1. Extending a false finding to other settings to bolster a weak point. On page 207 of *Ramses II and His Times,* speaking of the Osorkon House of Samaria, Velikovsky complains that "scarabs found in Palestine – and elsewhere, too – are regularly denied their chronological value on a variety of pretexts – but a few, definitely unacceptable cases are elevated to the representative role of verifiers of the conventional order of things."

2. Using material from a dump heap to prove an *a priori* position (*Ramses II,* p245*).* Two pages earlier, he notes a "fragment of the [Sosenk] stela came from one of the old surface dump heaps, or the refuse of earlier excavations."

3. Using a scarab to prove correctness of a stratum claim already pronounced to be correct. He points out the scarabs that carry Thutmose III upwards in time by 500 to 600 years, and again alleges that any

remote possibility of an occasional scarab giving credence to the conventional early dating is turned into the hardest evidence.

4. Claiming that earlier sherds had percolated upwards in the strata levels is a technique of forcing the evidence, that Schorr has exposed at Pylos.[222]

5. Sheer suppression of inconsistencies has often happened and again been noted by Schorr.

6. Claiming that a young stratum find naming a ruler is celebrating an old King. In *Ramses II,* Velikovsky indicates how seals in the name of Thutmose III and found in an Early Iron Age context were excused from consideration as contemporary evidence of the Pharaoh; they were alleged be a commemoration of the King as of five centuries earlier.

7. Hasty digging is alleged to excuse an inconsistent set of finds. This report by Watzinger at Tell el-Mutesellim is quoted again by Velikovsky in RII, 243.

8. Claiming that oral traditions can persist and recover their identical material form after centuries of desuetude.

9. Using a chronology dogmatically. "There is no scrap of evidence and no reason whatever to assume that the art of writing was practiced in Greece between the end of the Mycenean era and the eighth century B.B..." So says Denys L. Page[223] in *History and the Homeric Iliad* (1959, p122). Yet he also believes that oral tradition would suffice to keep the details alive, as did Rhys Carpenter.

10. An Age without records is impossible, to my view. Now here, now there, dogs and other mammals compulsively mark various spots as their own. Man is genetically prone to leave a record of himself wherever he has found himself. To locate a human presence when and where no deliberate record exists or has existed is impossible. Because he is

human, and unlike, say, a dog, man must raise the level of sophistication of his markings, such that he excretes signs and symbols.

In the years of World War II, an unknown American soldier somewhere scrawled "Kilroy was here" on a wall, and soon in thousands of cases around the world, wherever Americans troops went, we would find the same ludicrous yet meaningful message that "Kilroy was here."

Recording is a mode of conduct, moreover, that comes hologenetically with the event of humanization. According to Homo Schizo theory, a step-by-step acquisition of humanness was impossible. Every basic trait would have the capability of branching out in many directions, often, as in much of sublimatory conduct, quite disguising its origin. Both by definition and by observation, to say 'human' is to say 'symbolizer.'

11. And, once begun, recording or symbolizing does not stop, because it cannot stop. Hence it is all the more suspicious when writers claim to have discovered an ongoing settlement where "no record is to be found over several centuries of human existence." We need to investigate what would happen were the gap to be a phantom and the two ends were brought together, which is to say that the bringing together of the edges of the phantom age lights up more brilliantly the disjunction of the Bronze and Iron Age.

12. Conjuring useful surrogate methods of survival. Alan J.B.Wace opined that "... Letters or Literary texts may well have been on wooden tablets or some form of parchment or even papyrus; some fortunate discovery will some day reveal them to us."[224]

13. The great differences between Bronze and Iron Ages is proof in itself that a long time had to pass for the one to devolve into the other age. Finkelstein may have been under this

misapprehension when forming his idea that the Hebrews were stuck in the boondocks and hills of Eastern and Southern Palestine for a long time before finally filtering down by mostly peaceful means into Canaan.[225]

14. Simplistic interpretation is common, and serves to avoid dangerous hypotheses. Thus, Finkelstein comes upon a heavy scattering of arrowheads in a ruined village, which he interprets as a sign of intense struggle. But why would not the victors collect these reusable weapons? Or the defenders for that matter? If subsequently reoccupied, the village would be swept for such objects by men, women and children. If heavy ash or debris would have fallen, they would be explainable. If natural destruction occurred, they would be left in place. Or perhaps a plague or storm might have forbidden searching the ruins. Let us say that the archaeologist, limited in wordage permitted to him, might simply have let pass other considerations. Still, the choice of warfare is significant.

15. Weird assumptions of human behavior.

"The burial circumstances inside the temple complex reminded Desborough of the situation encountered by C. Tsountas at another spot inside the western extension of the citadel walls. To the northeast of the Lion Gate Tsountas excavated some LH III houses and discovered six cist tombs datable sometime within the eleventh-ninth centuries. The tombs lay *under* a deposit over six feet thick of LH III pottery and other remains, which by the accepted chronology should be older than the graves. To explain why LH III material lay over the graves, rather than the graves lying above it or cutting through it, Desborough speculated that even after tremendous fires supposedly flattened the city in the late thirteenth and mid-twelfth centuries, a few houses survived the conflagrations, remained intact for centuries until people entered their ground floors, not to inhabit them, but only to bury their dead, and that only sometimes thereafter the upper stories, still filled with LH III goods, which had somehow withstood earthquakes, fires and the ravages of time, then collapsed onto the graves."

16. Lacking an absolute chronology (actually, such a thing is nowhere in the universe), prominent scholars such as Hall, Breasted, and Gardiner continued to use (and others still use) the ragged King list of Manetho, abetted by Eratosthenes and Ctesias. Nor could switching back to Herodotus, Hellenicus, and Hecathaeus help, for these men also relied upon the fallacious Egyptian calculations. One may wonder whether the frustration at being deprived of a reliable time scale will give a permanent irritability to a historian.

17. Fear of a looming monster date of catastrophe – if a Q date – whether a single date or a cluster of 15-year dates within a 150- year period that fits into the disordered years of a real time, would be determined to replace the 500 years of phantom time.

18. Sites where Greek temples were built promptly upon Mycenean ruins, "unused for 500 years," and thereupon were revived for religious practices.

19. Dishonesty is not unknown to science, and usually is associated with neurotic symptoms. In many instances, embarrassing finds are hidden or go undisclosed. Violations of professional ethics take many forms.

    I may quote Kamal Salibi, who gives us an example, this involving the famous American Professor Albright, who was transliterating, we can be sure, with great eagerness, so as to find the site of Lachish., Ostracon VI: "In the case of Ostracon VI, the reading of the name 'Jerusalem' is nothing short of dishonest. On a fragment of this broken potsherd, the letters *slm* can be discerned. As a Hebrew word, this can be read in a variety of ways to yield various meanings, such as 'spark', 'peace', 'good health', 'agreement', 'completeness', or 'reward'. It can also be the word of Semitic greeting (Hebrew *shālōm*) or any of a number of personal or place-names. Nothing, on the other hand, justifies reading *slm* as the name of 'Jerusalem'. ... "There are certainly no 'signals of Lachish' involved in the whole statement" of which this is a crucial part. And renders the identification of Lachish "untenable."[226]

20. The taboo of citing any work by Velikovsky in the archaeological literature is immaculately observed, and is an obvious symptom of collective neurosis. There is even a quasi-taboo against citing Schaeffer except on the narrowest of grounds. His great idea of concurrent destructions at the end of the several Bronze ages is blotted out. The 80 studies in his honor, I have already pointed out, do not go into his work notably, no thought being given why he should have become a quantavolutionist in fact.

I shall go on now without citations, using actual quotations that reveal the path of a fallacy.

21. Allusions are common: "..shape of [object like shard] seems to foreshadow..", or "anticipates in an uncanny way the ...," or .."a long step from... to..," "the flow was interrupted, only to be resumed..,".

22. "A shortage of raw materials ended the practice..."

23. ..."a lack of funds.."

24. "Diminished skills... "

25. "A resumption of rites, after cleaning out intervening debris.."

26. Leaving the puzzle for others to solve (which rarely happens).

27. This destruction "was a unique isolated event, not a cause for the end of the Late Bronze Age.."

28. "At this point something happens and the basic

structure collapses."

29. Final publication of the expedition results was completed twenty years later (but not really complete). Reference is to the famous Blegen studies of Troy.

30. Ignoring links between cultures of two settlements "500 years apart."

31. "Clung to their customs and traditions through the troubled period from 1100 to 800 or later," (said in regard to transmitting a Gray Minoan Pot).

32. "Possibility of a contrary view exists" (but not discussed).

33. Pious descendants tossed their ritual objects through a broken ceiling onto 500-year old ritual objects of their ancestors.

34. Late ritual votive offerings were squeezed through a hole in a tomb to resume the cult of the dead of 500 years before.

35. A cult surrounds Mycenean tombs abandoned 500 years earlier.

36. The practically identical Lion Gates of Phrygia (assuredly ~-800 to ~-700) and Mycenean (supposedly~1400) are forced into Mycenae. Flinders Petrie saying, .."now we have a wooden lion, in exactly the same attitudes, dated to 1450 in Egypt [his chronology, of course].." So therefore Egypt originated the idea for Mycenae. Cretan lions dutifully follow suit.

37. Moving items of Geometric Age of Greece back by centuries to Mycenean Age instead of doing the opposite (Dőrpfeld) to reconcile their obvious contemporaneity, which is the opposite of the usual way of reconciling them to get rid of the Phantom Gap, but which brought only ridicule to him. (Both methods are ridiculous.)

38. Explaining the reversal of Hittite and Phrygian layers, it is conjectured that millions of tons of clay

had been carried up and down a hill to form the basis for a temple, and there it would be said that the many sherds found in the clay that are Hittite had actually preceded the Phrygian layer and the reversal is not real. (This was the Young expedition, as ironically exposed by Velikovsky.)

The "Peoples of the Sea" exemplified "slogan slinging," an absurd merry-go-round. Yet, the weakness of thought among archaeologists becomes as nothing when bolstered by the strength of numbers.

Thus, many a work that attempts to bridge the gap of five centuries between the end of the Bronze Age and the apparently uncouth civilizations that follow, which credibly can be shown to evolve into the Classical Age, wallows in half-truths, ellipses of logic, incomplete statements, and "gaposis".

Not every slip in scholarship is a sign of a neurosis. I would be hard put, or at least would need another volume, to analyze them in context, classify them, and make of the syndrome a *Psychopathology of Everyday Archaeology* (to parody Sigmund Freud's *Psychopathology of Everyday Life* and Harold Laswell's *Psychopathology and Politics*).

In the thousands of pages of archaeology of the Iron Age and its boundaries that I have perused, I have found only one sentence connecting social and earth events to unusual motions and matter of the sky, and it is dismissive. There must be more -- 5, 10, 20, 50? Besides denying immense events of the heavens, archaeologists have been clueless with regard to what brought on the Iron Age and accompanied it. They have also refused to invite, much less to consider, alternative theories.

Chapter Twenty-One

Near and Far Future Defenses

The paradigm of quantavolution intimates what to do next with the subject of the Iron Age and religion. It also lends itself to our scheme for 1) obtaining welfare, justice and new experiences for humankind, while (2) at the same time encountering apocalyptic natural events of the millennia ahead.

Please recall, however, that this is a book of speculations and that I am departing from this work without claiming to have finished it. It has evolved beyond my capacities. Nor is it a one-man job. Finally I am quite skeptical about any possibility of knowing the "true universe" by one method.

Within these limits, I hope that I have established the importance of understanding the ancient history of the first millennium B.C.E. and the methodology of quantavolution studies. I hope, also, to have shown the persistence and pertinence of the Iron Age in the ideology of modern times, whether we speak of one or all of the spheres of existence. This has come about by applying the concept of quantavolution to all manner of data. It seems, too, that the paradigm of quantavolution may lend itself to the appreciation of the role and possibilities of the religious experience.

A Radical Approach to Applied Science

I would suggest that our radical approach to science and existence is in order. Archaeology has had a surfeit of pretensions that meaningful facts will pop up from a dig, willy-nilly, and assemble themselves into a fine theory. It seems often to resemble a religious cult, that expects truth to burgeon from an endless iteration of dogma and rite.

Iron Age history teaches us about the religious experience and can teach us much more. I have come to believe that all the world's sacred scriptures need to be replaced. The forthcoming scriptures should then lead on the sciences, not be set aside from them or fight with them. The sciences are being cracked open and spread out by powerful diversifying concepts and tools. So now is a good time to undertake a fresh and useful religiousness that would take everything into account.

What is probably needed next is the collaboration of a group of specialized quantavolutionary scholars, one or more to each of the major spheres of existence – a mythologist, a geologist, an astronomer, a psycho-social historian, an archaeologist, a meteorologist, a theologian, a chronologist, and so on to the number of a score. Were each to pursue the Iron Age of Mars through the method and substance of one's own discipline and regularly communicate questions and findings to one's colleagues, they might bring to focus in time an unprecedented extensive and profound view of the interaction of humans and the cosmos. The paradigm of quantavolution would guide them well, until something better comes along.

Ill-controlled as he is by his nature, man can yet selfishly perceive methods by which he can control the world environment and protect himself from himself. He can "lift himself by his own bootstraps," agonizingly and part-ways. Adam and Eve are the same people that they were during the Iron Age and before, but they can scarcely be recognized or recognize themselves as the same people. And they act significantly differently. To tell how different they could possibly become is impossible to say, but can be figured from experience, pragmatically, as we move along.

In a second phase, the new science would move out upon the world. Man alone of all species self-consciously proposes to control the world. He says as often as he fails, that "Man proposes and God disposes," meaning that man is both helped and deterred in reaching his goals by a supernatural operator. We do not think and work by this theory. More simply and directly we know what we should like to see happen; we realize that this is most likely impossible; yet we feel that, for lack of better, we should go ahead with our schemes. One can call this Existentialism. So our philosophy of action is both pragmatic and existential.

In the last couple of centuries, man has at first sneakily and then more and more proudly asserted his claims to control nature laws and events. He has developed a state of mind that has made of Earth's history a uniformly proceeding series of happenings, which appeared amenable to deliberate controls and plans. Presumed endless and equal units of time enhanced the feelings of being at the controls. Our intellectual elite is still in this state of mind.

However, the mass of people have become more aware that what they have always believed – the deluges, the world conflagrations, the near-total destructions of man and his environment – but were beginning to suppress and sublimate as imaginary creations, have actually occurred. Therefore, the mass is increasingly nervous and frightened, paranoid, obsessed with violence – in short tinctured more darkly with the schizotypical tendencies that are its genetic heritage.

The priests of the modern world of control, the scientific professions and their true believers, have themselves become worried that they will not be finally able to control the mass of people, and, what is more striking, have begun to turn their own minds around in the direction of the mass, acknowledging that quantavolution is in fact a more accurate version of earth history than uniformitarianism.

As this process is occurring, secular social and natural scientists find themselves facing two alternatives. The first is to join the enemy, so to speak, to accept and go along with old-fashioned religion. Thus let science play its games and let religions play theirs. This bifacial resolution is Scientific Religious Creationism. It turns over the Quantavolution Paradigm to religion.

The preferable alternative is to renew the secular scientific challenge of the universe, in a changed spirit and with the different paradigm as its basis.[227] Very few have done this. Many denounce any turning-around of their minds. But also many are discovering that they are already quantavolutionary without having realized it: they can see, if questioned directly, that they subscribe to most of the principles of a world beset by occasional sudden, intense, wholesale changes whose effects are catastrophically bad, yet are also productive of some advances in achieving what they have always said they wanted: welfare, justice and education.

Providing for Short-Run Defense

I see, therefore, that to end my book, I must at least postulate several major steps that can achieve our human goals for the short run. Provided that we will have achieved these immediate goals, I can suggest, then, several large moves that we can make, that would help our quality of existence in the long run. What I have in mind is maximizing human chances for happiness for the longest term possible, leaving it up to the future, the far future, I hope, to continue to extend the human future and possibilities of happiness.

There is no question but that we can provide every last person on Earth with generous portions of the three universal human needs: justice, welfare, and invigorating experience.

We must begin with justice, whose basis is good government. The obvious means to this end is a world government representative of the people of the world and ruled by councils whose members must have been pre-qualified for psychological normalcy and expertness in one or more fields of applied science.

Justice would include its instruments – police, courts, and punition officers – and an independent inspectorate to guarantee the process.

By welfare we mean a decent subsistence and personal care and comfort from conception to death. Superstitious extravagances and diversions, time and material wastes, and costs of conflicts add up to several times the effort and costs of arranging for universal welfare.

It is needless and dangerous to promise and provide less than a decent welfare for all the world's people. Working time should be universally required and minimized.

A limit to world population must be fixed at a comfortable figure, such as three billions, to which every fertile woman who is genetically healthy is given an equal chance to contribute.

A world budget should be prepared biennially and every person of all ages should be taxed equally to pay for its costs. Each person would have a Life Account that would balance taxes against tax payments. It is pre-figured that most people would be in arrears, many until death.

New experiences are vitally important because they include by definition all education, and then beyond that the arts and entertainment, and travel. This is the sphere of paedeia. From rich and directed experience would emerge the abilities to control ourselves and, so far as humanly possible, the universe.

Cut-backs in military and less generally beneficial expenditures of government are absolutely necessary. The returns would be paid half into Far Future Sky Defense and half directly into the welfare budget. A direct transfer is recommended, rather than going out of the account books with the savings, and afterwards trying to come back into the grand scheme by newly legislated spending.

Far-Future Sky Defense

In lock-step with the Near Future, we proceed to Far Future Sky Defense. This involves those several kinds of design and readying of technologies that are most likely to block or limit harm to the Earth and its people from the heavens. Engendering this program would be most difficult, as would be to keep it alive and flourishing, and ultimately to utilize it. Its heavy costs would be difficult to legislate: people are used to being staggered with the costs of military defense and warfare, but to use the same money for welfare and the far future will appear to be too radical and difficult an engagement.

Sky Defense, to be fully useful for the predictable occasions of threat, would cost about one half of the present world expenditures on armaments and warfare. If these are now $700 billions then we would have to use $350 billions for welfare, as stated above, and $350 billions for Sky Defense. The difficulties of taking funds from established military programs are notorious. But we shall have to mobilize the masses for the Welfare benefits and the intelligentsia for the Future Sky Defense. If we cannot stop killing and wrecking one another, it is unlikely that we can put together the requisites for a Far Future Sky Defense.

Sky defense would be required should there be a chance of invasion from beings of outer space, other worlds. Thus far, there is no indication that this is a ponderable risk. The types of disaster most likely to occur would be bolide and meteorite fragmental impacts, with extremely varied energies and effects. Secondly, the drop of liquids would be a threat, water but also ice and solidified gases like methane. A third form of disaster from outer space would be gases and radiation. Obviously we must be thinking in broad terms already.

There are more threats. The sun is not reliable; no one can tell how extreme solar storms can be, and therefore what transformations of the solar wind that passes through and around the Earth are potentiated. It is also feared that gamma rays could arrive at some intervals from other star systems and galaxies, with deadly effect.

Upon such preliminary considerations would be based our first organizational chart. Probably the best structure for a Far Future Sky Defense would be a World Department of Future Sky Defense, headquartered in a basaltic or artificial cave, alternatively operated from a movable outer space station. Its divisions might well be the Holosphere and spheres of existence that were mentioned above and discussed in Chapter 3, the geosphere, psychosphere, astrosphere, *et al.*

Each sphere would be concerned with those elements of the sky threats falling within its scope. The Holosphere Division attached to the Headquarters would coordinate the work of all the others. Within the organization of each sphere would be a Department of Theory, Planning and Exploration, and a Department of Prediction, Applications, and Engineering. I think that the descriptions already given the spheres will suggest the requirements of Sky Defense in their regard.

I have already discussed the various intensities and scope of quantavolutions, the vast differences, for instance, between the Iron Age catastrophes of this book and the Indonesian tsunami or Tunguska bolide explosion. Mention has been made of their supposed frequencies of occurrence.

A question arise whether the lower level Q's are not disastrous enough for their prediction and relief to be included in the scope of the Far Future Sky Defense. Should they be cared for by another world agency? If the Indonesian tsunami was to be protected in some ways by our prospective Far Future Defense system, some billions of dollars and most deaths would have been prevented. Valid arguments can be made, however, that the quantitative difference between the damages provoked by a sky event and the subterranean event are great and the two operations should not be confused.

On the other hand, we must assume that the essentially space-threat Defense Divisions in all the Spheres would not refuse to come to the aid of a locale of a terrestrially provoked event. (Actually it may well have been a space-provoked event of the distant past or the sunspots of today that engendered the slight plate movement near Indonesia.) Another hypothetical case would be a discharge, accidental or deliberate, of a volley of nuclear weapons. Obviously the Far Future Sky Defense should be called upon to help in the case of such accidents or aggressions.

No doubt a first task is to set up definitions of the intensity and scope of the Q-event and to plan what part of the defense effort should be put into the response to the several categories. Once we have begun planning, it will become apparent that even the totally destructive impact or radiation storm, whose incidence is estimated at once in 100,000 years , should be responded to. Demography at a certain point becomes philosophy. If 5 persons survive a quantavolution, they might become millions in a few centuries. If a billion persons survive a #7 event out of ten orders of intensity, say, in the longer run, the two populations will be equalized in numbers.

Therefore, should we not be as concerned with the survival of the 5 as of the billion? For that matter, should we not start our protective preparedness with regard to the penultimate Q, and work downwards into the less destructive events to, say, the 1,000 - year or 300 - year probability.

Perhaps we shall be spared such niceties of policy-making if it happens that the same types and measures of defense can be designed to take effect against quantavolutions of all sizes. There will, of course, be plenty of such all-occasions measures.

Obviously the modest history of past catastrophes that we possess will not give us ready answers to such questions. Discussions will be interminable. We shall be lucky if a helpful resolution of the future defense problem occurs before the first significant bolide makes it mark upon Earth.

Figures

Fig. 1: Responses to Q Test

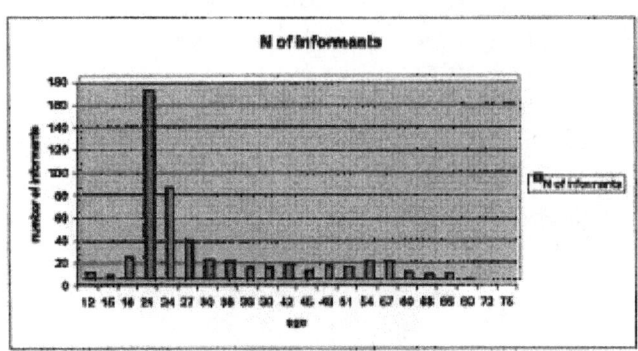

Ques.#	C answers
1	62,92%
2	45,03%
3	75,84%
4	21,56%
5	84,63%
6	75,85%
7	65,57%
8	69,94%
9	24,16%
10	82,87%
11	41,80%
12	3,99%
13	80,66%
14	74,16%
15	43,82%
16	35,34%
17	59,83%
18	46,63%
19	67,98%
20	58,43%

Tot.Score	Informants
1–5	358

Ques.#	Q answers
1	92,00%
2	42,33%
3	19,26%
4	77,90%
5	11,36%
6	20,79%
7	27,75%
8	25,16%
9	70,02%
10	13,26%
11	31,29%
12	91,47%
13	16,41%
14	22,22%
15	49,23%
16	35,01%
17	33,60%
18	46,06%
19	27,79%
20	35,67%

Tot.Score	Informants
–15	451

Q score	Informants
1–5	457

Fig. 2: Atmospheric Electric Events

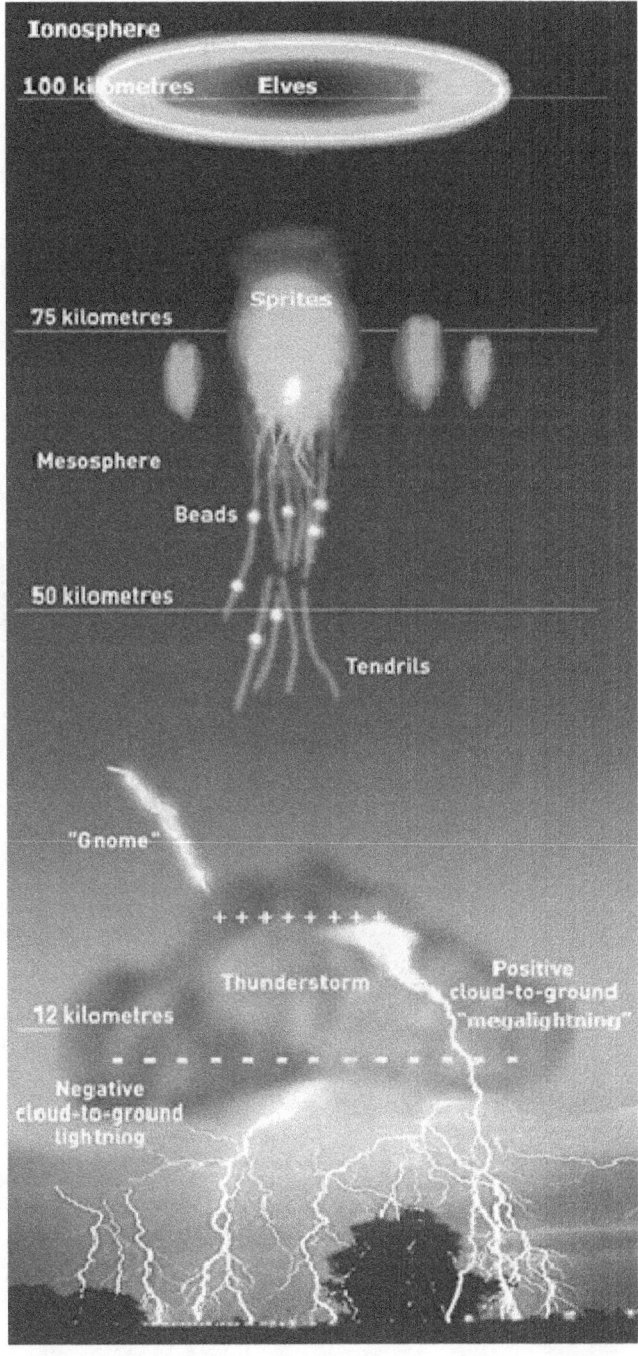

Fig. 3: Shatter-cones typical of Impact structure

Shatter cones; small, well-developed. Small, finely sculptured shatter cones, developed in fine-grained limestone from the Haughton structure (Canada). The cone surfaces show the typical divergence of striae away from the cone apex ("horsetailing"). Photograph courtesy of R. A. F. Grieve.

Fig. 4: Typical simple impact crater

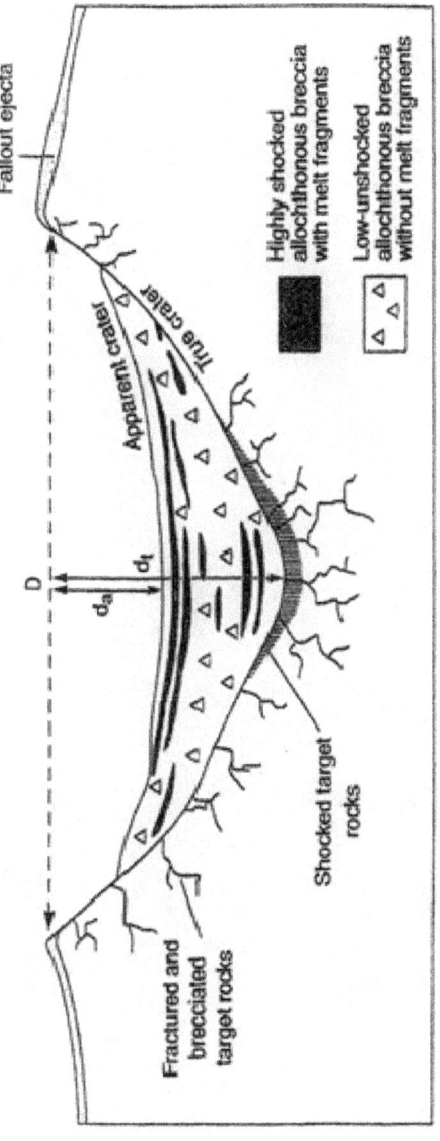

Simple impact structure: locations of impactites: Schematic cross section of a typical simple impact structure, showing the simple bowl shape and the locations of various types of impactites in and around the structure. The parautochthonous rocks below the true crater floor are fractured and brecciated but generally show no distinctive shock effects, except in a small zone (fine vertical ruling) in the center of the structure. The crater is filled, to approximately half its original height, with a variety of allogenic breccias and impact melts, which forms the crater-fill units or the breccia lens. A thinner layer of ejected material (fallout ejecta) overlies the uplifted crater rim and surrounds the crater. This unit is easily eroded and is present only in the youngest and best-preserved structures. D = final crater diameter, which is 10–20% greater than the diameter of the original, premodification transient crater; d_t = true depth of the final crater, which is approximately the depth of the original transient crater; d_a = apparent depth of the crater, or the depth from the final rim to the top of the crater-fill units. The diagram represents the state of the final crater before any subsequent geological effects, e.g., erosion, infilling. The model is based on drilling studies at Barringer Meteor Crater (Arizona) (Roddy et al., 1975; Roddy, 1978), Brent Crater (Canada) (Dence, 1968; Grieve and Cintala, 1981), and similar structures (e.g., Masaitis et al., 1980; Garvin and Garvin, 1991). (From Grieve, 1987, Fig. 1.)

Fig. 5: Philippi Peat basin, Greece

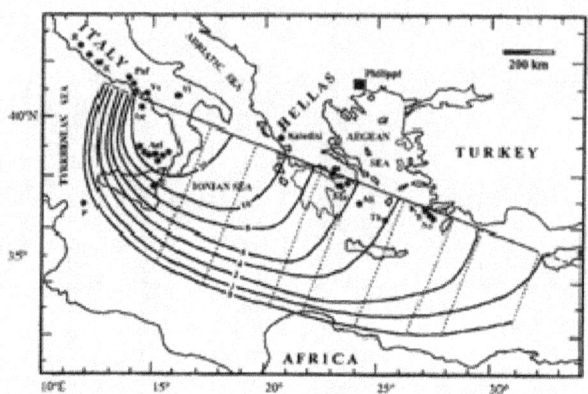

Location of Philippi peatland, Heallas. Map has superimposed isopaches of the Y-5 ash layer derived from distribution of piston cores. Isopachs are in centimeters (adapted from Cornell et al., 1983). Main Quaternary volcanoes: Th, Thera; Mi, Milos; Me, Methana; K, Kos; Y, Y'ah; Ns, Nisyros; R, Roman; PhF-Vs-Isc-VI, Campanian Province Volcanoes (Phlegrean Fields, Vesuvius, Ischia, Vulture, respectively); Ael, Aeolian Island; E, Etna; P, Pantelleria.

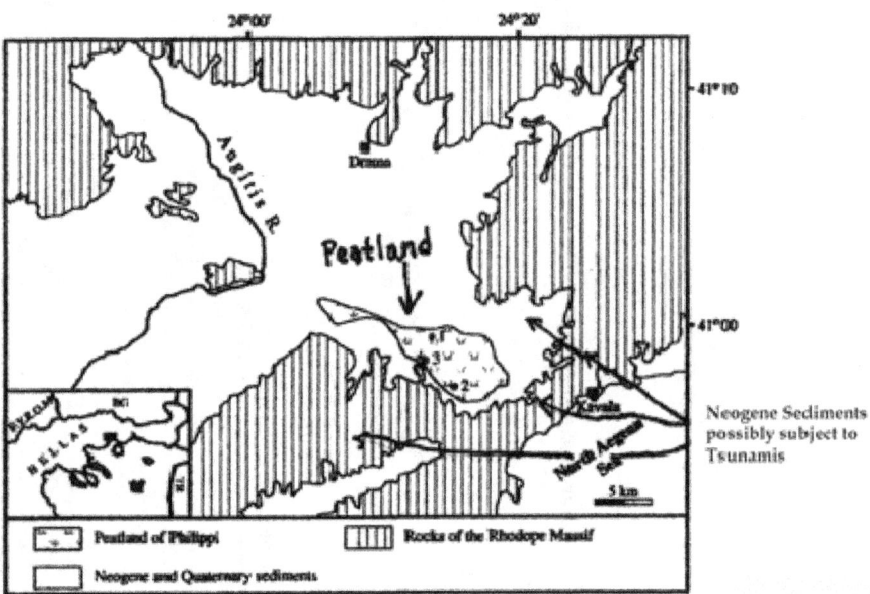

Fig. 6: Letter, Schaeffer to Velikovsky, 19/9/56, facsimile

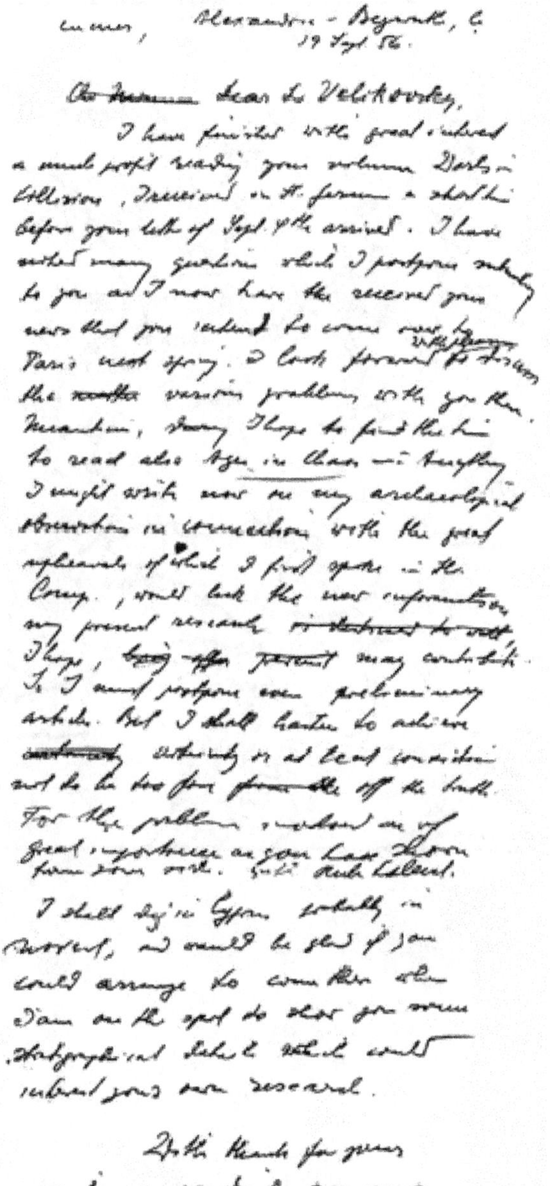

Fig. 7: Routes of ancient amber trade

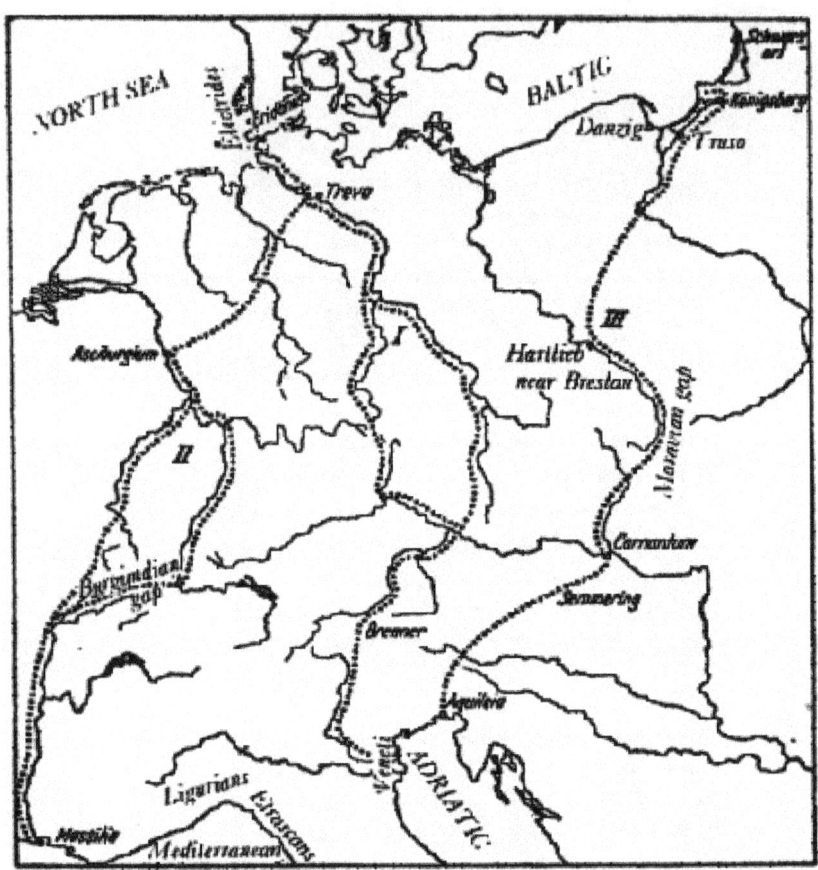

Fig. 8: The agricultural migration virtualized

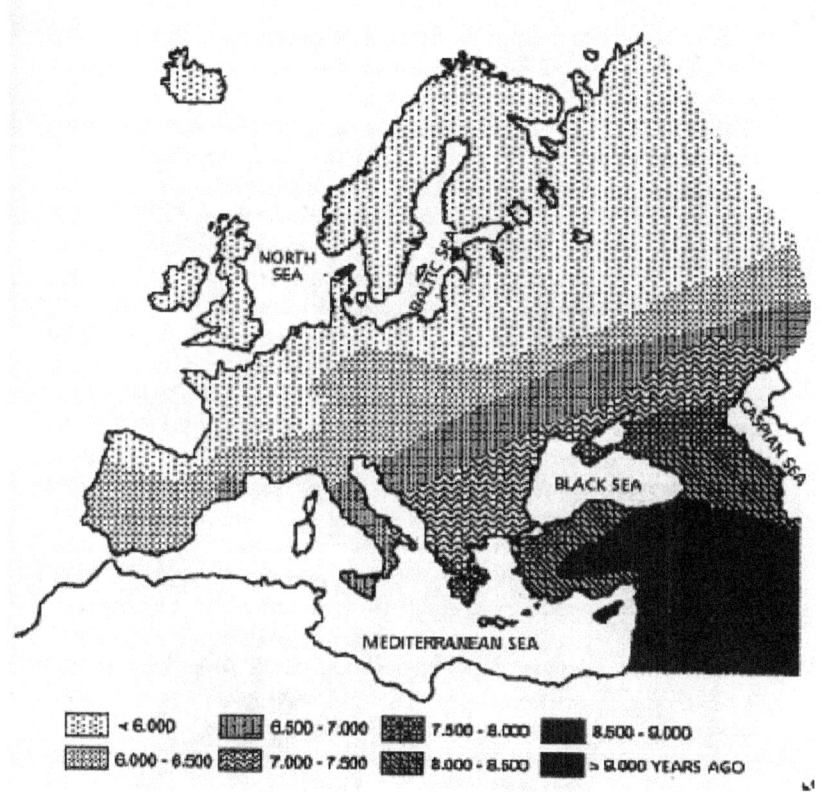

Fig. 9: The migration of blood and gene types, Asia to Europe

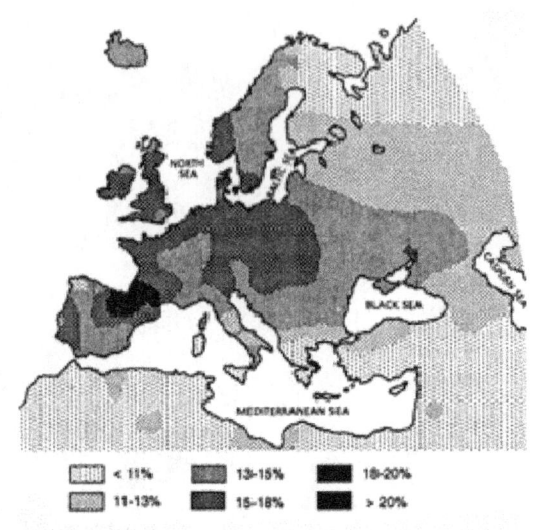

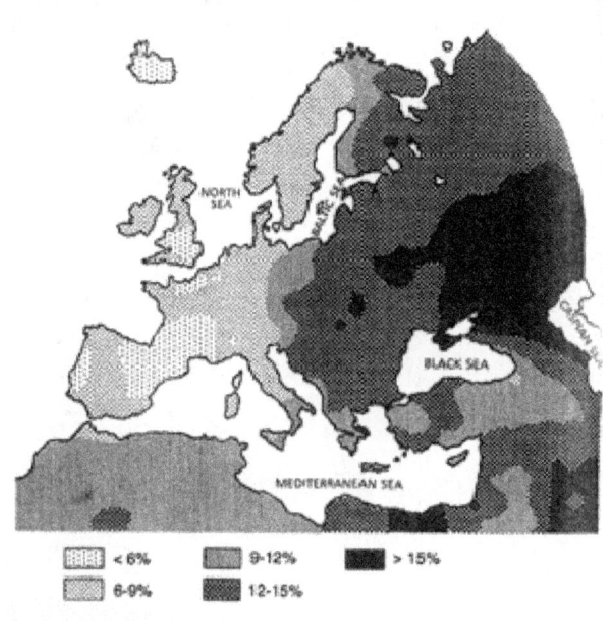

Fig.10: Bronze Age routes around the Middle-East

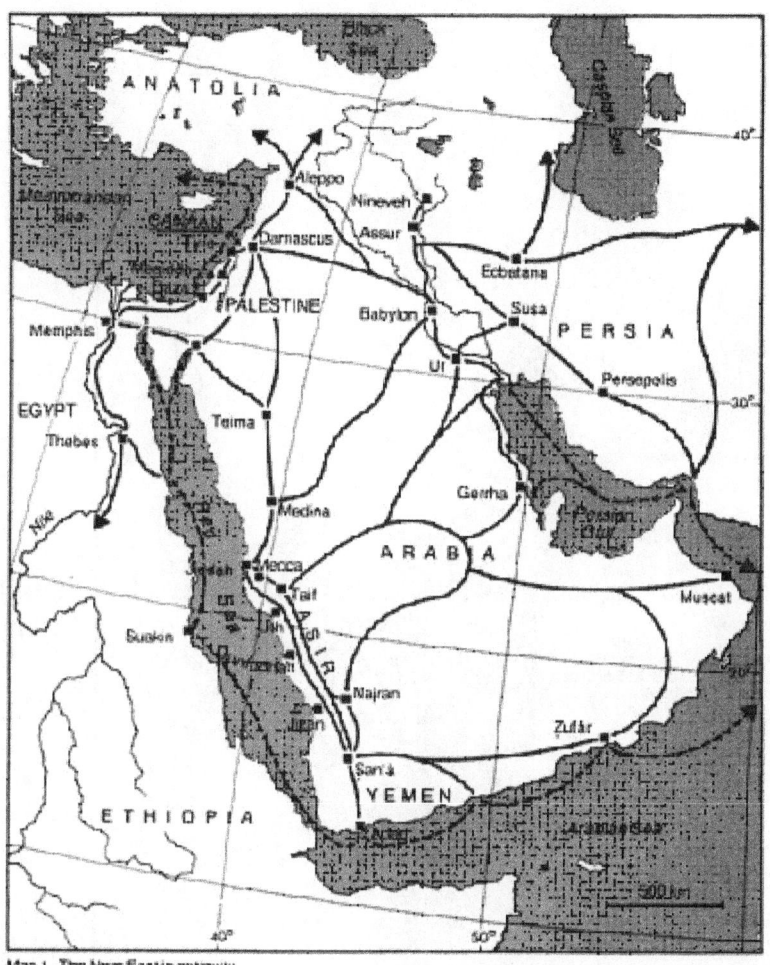

Map 1 The Near East in antiquity

Fig. 11: Settlements of West Arabia today

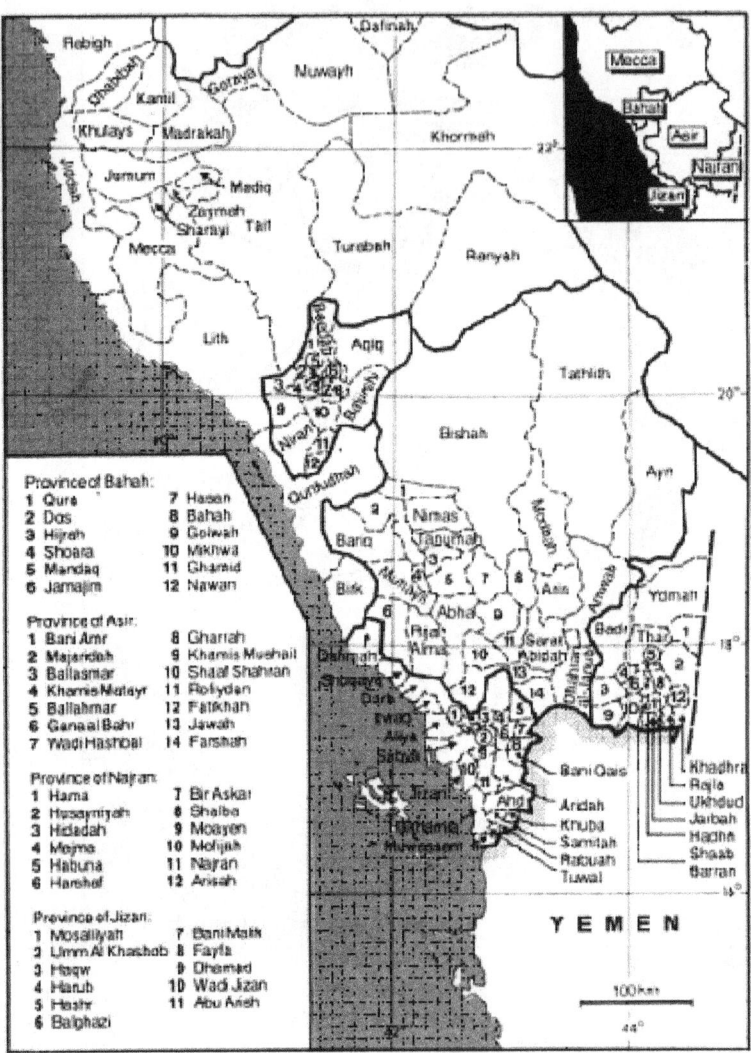

Asir: administrative areas (provinces and districts), 1978

Fig. 12: The Promised Land of Abraham and Mose

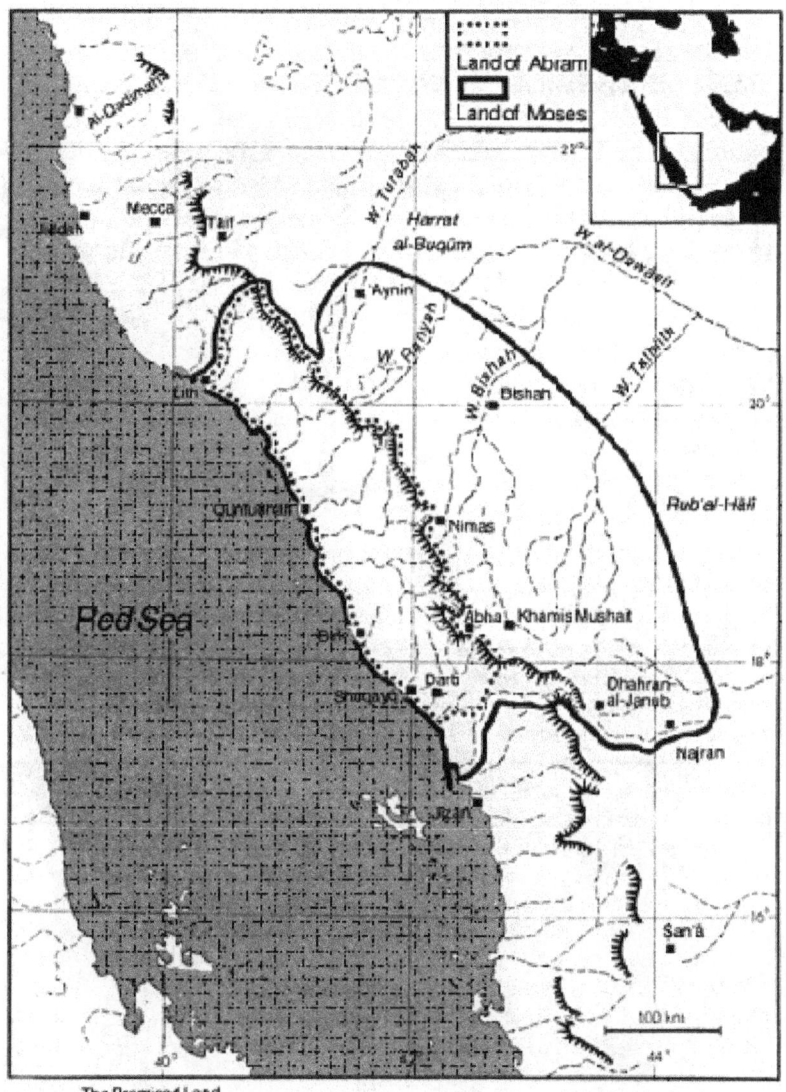

The Promised Land

Fig. 13: Maps of contrasting expeditions of Thutmoses III

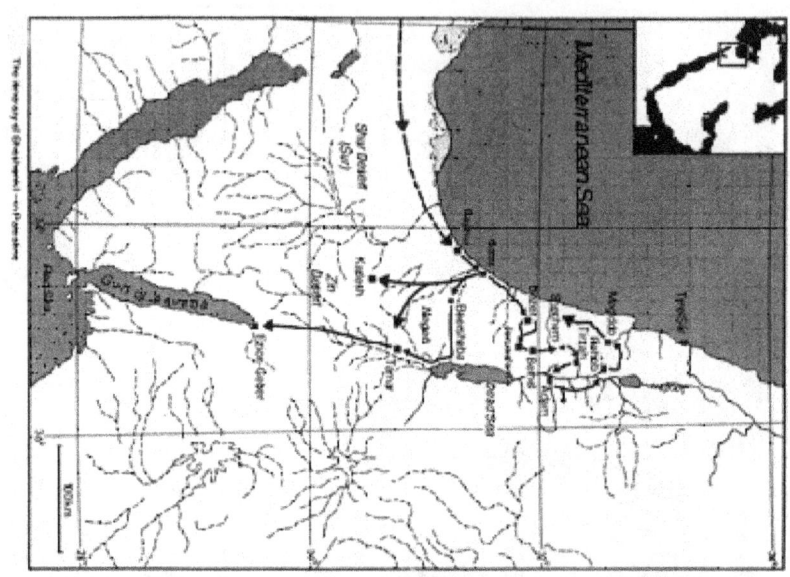

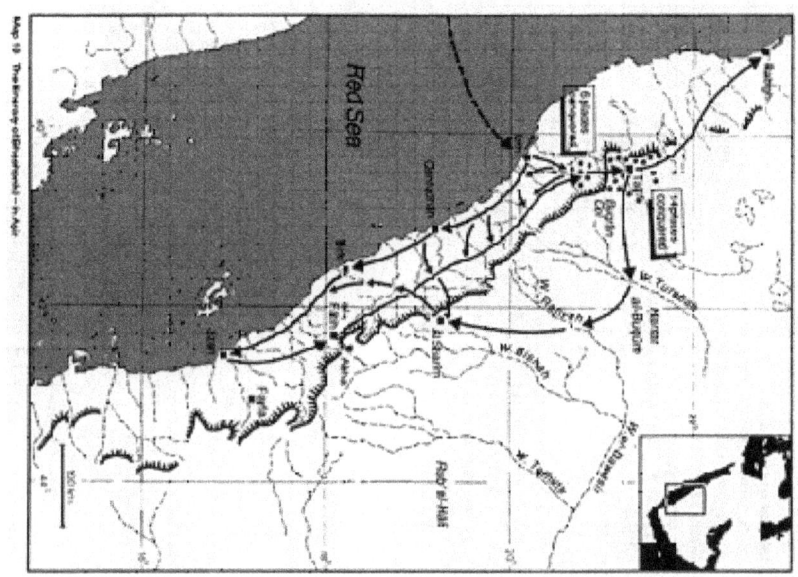

Fig. 14: The God Ganesh with a gerbil

Fig. 15: Banded iron formation

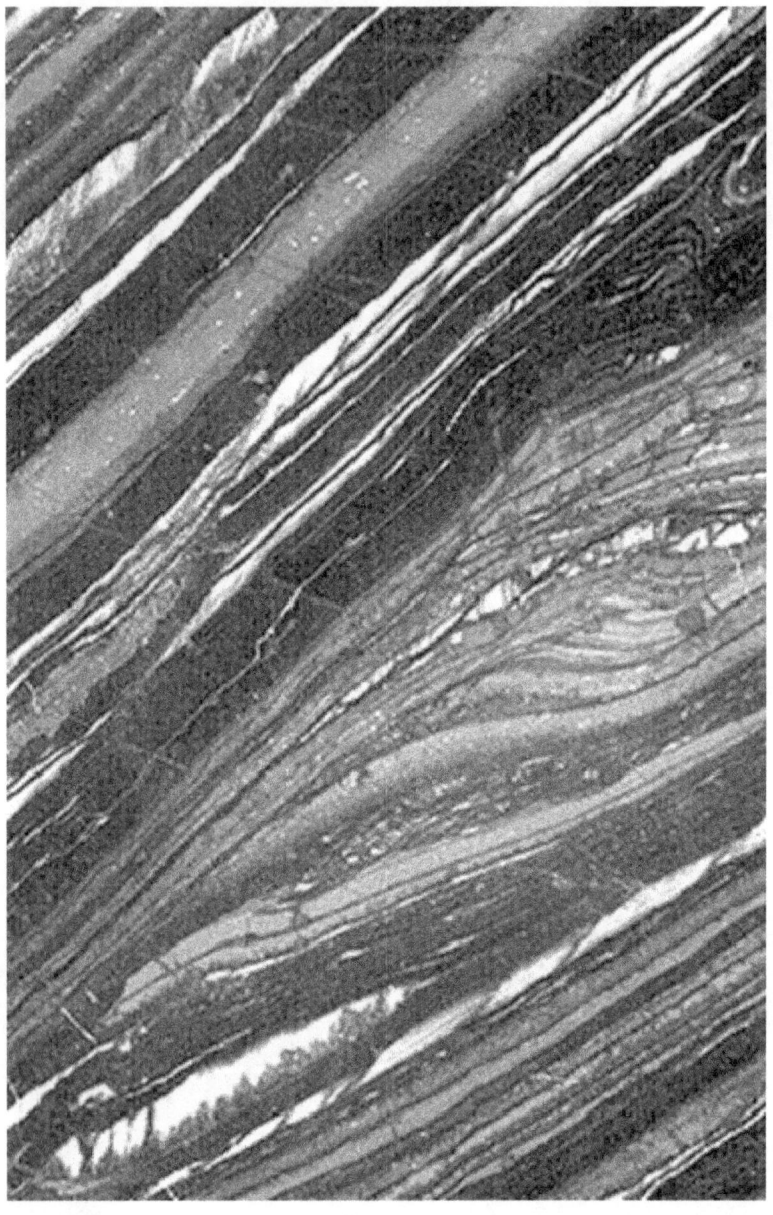

Fig. 16: Early Iron Age oven: Italy

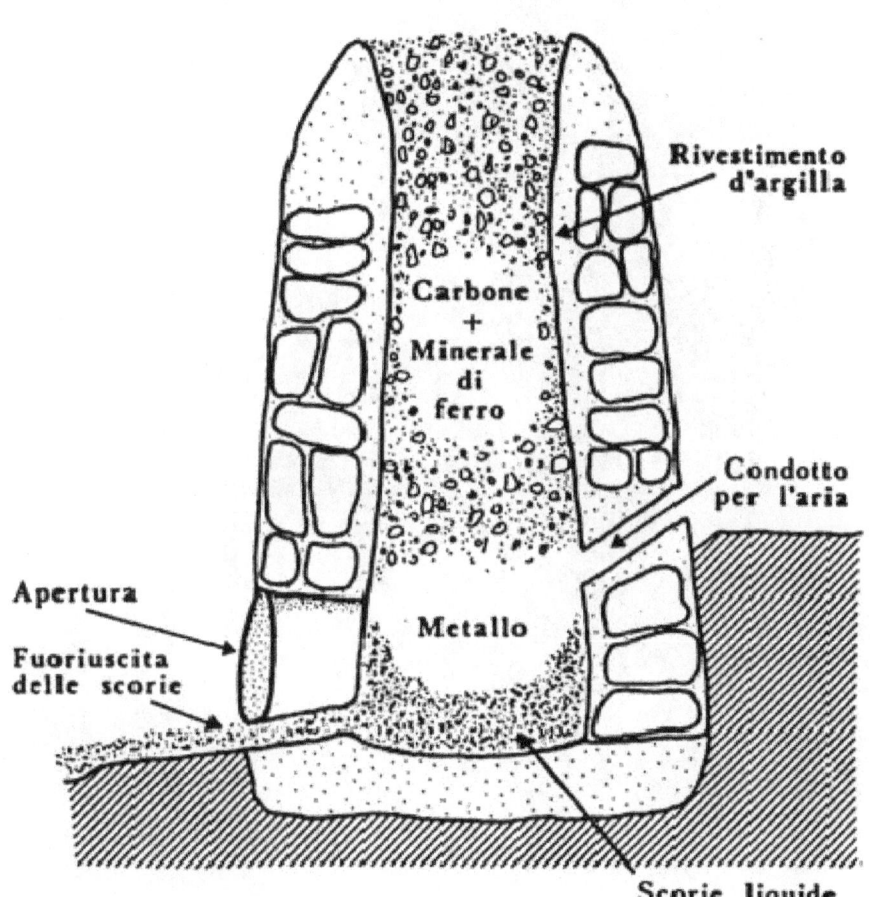

Fig. 17: Early Iron Age smelter: Rwanda

Excavated slag pit iron-smelting furnace, Ngoma I, Rwanda, dated to the Early Iron Age. The pits are very noticeable features, sometimes still containing the plugs of slag that settled into them and, as here, the clay coil super structure of the collapsed furnace.

Fig. 21: Hieroglyph of the Eye of Horus

Fig. 22: Valles Marineris on Mars

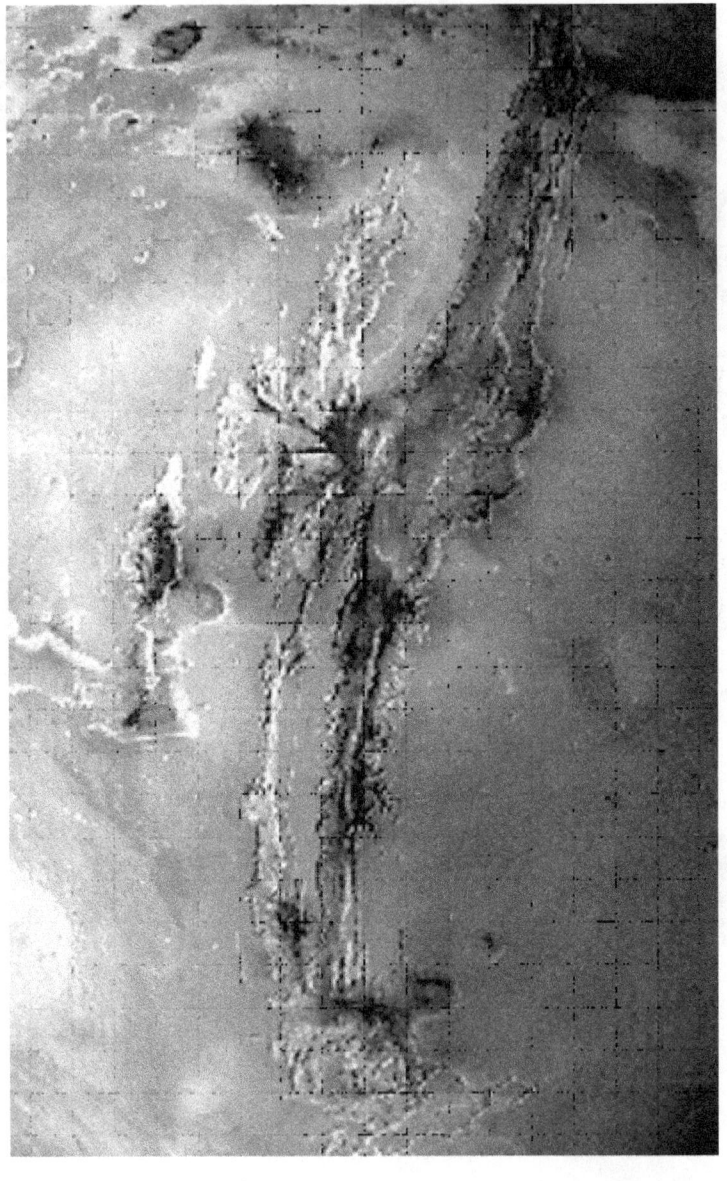

Fig. 23: Upper-Red-Sea - Mediterranean satellite map

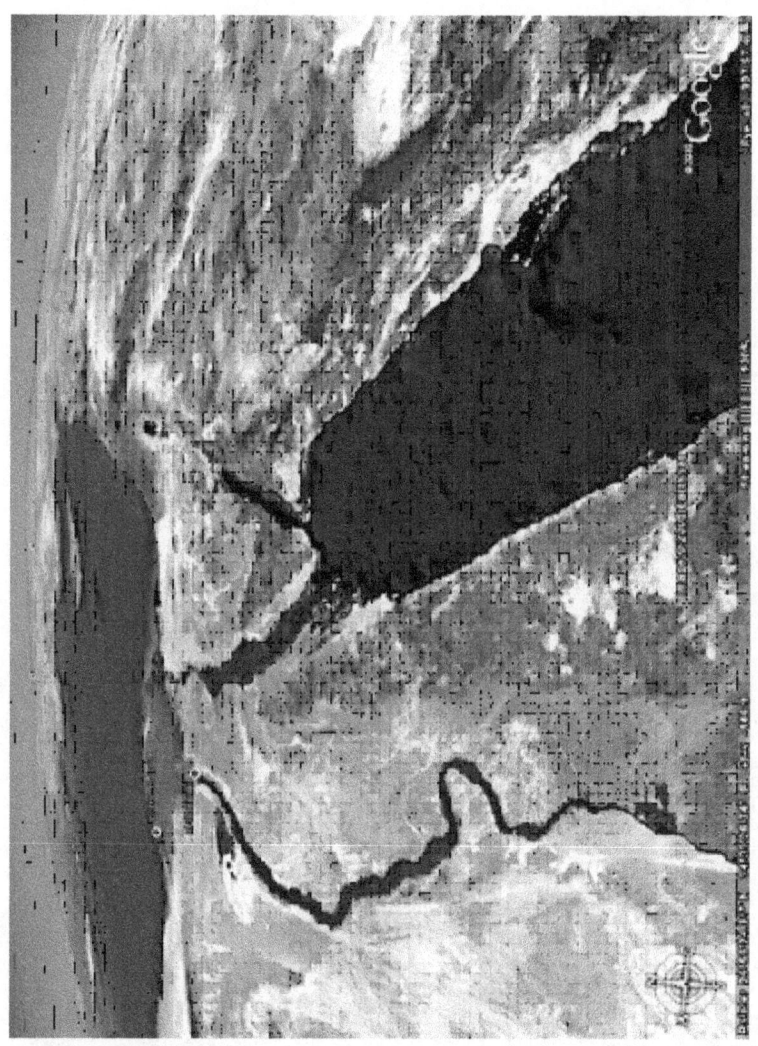

Fig. 24: West Arabian Biblical source region

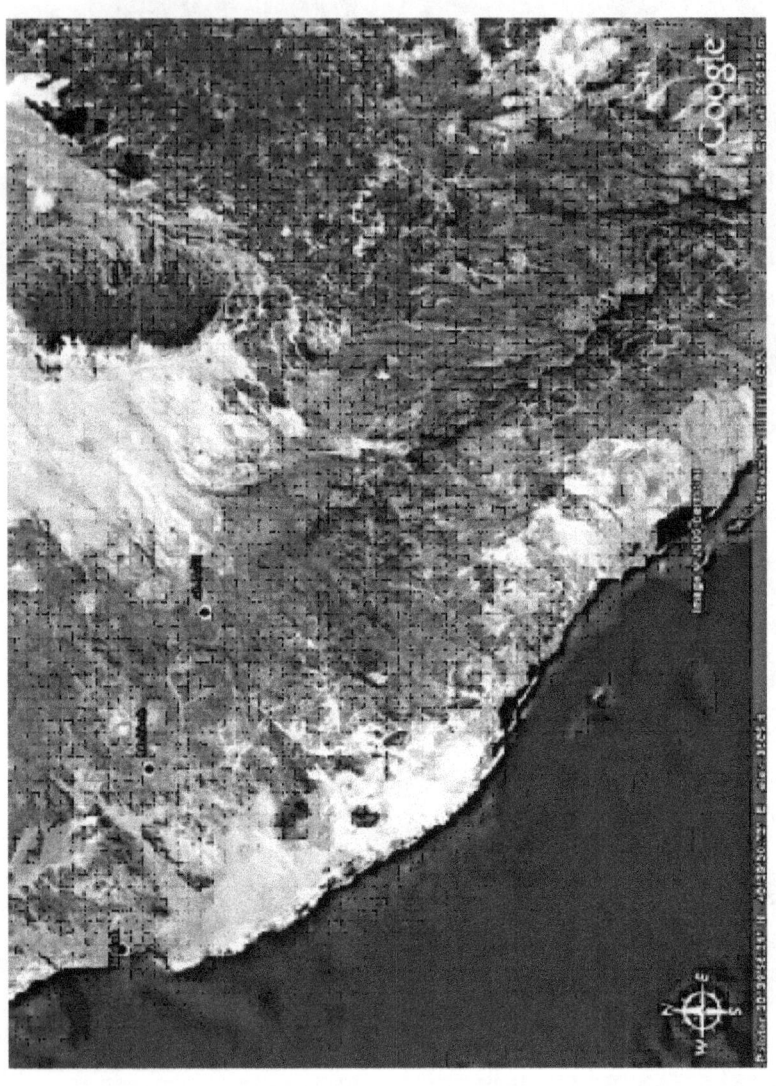

Fig. 25: The South-Arabian African connection

Fig. 26: Volcanism of the Red Sea region

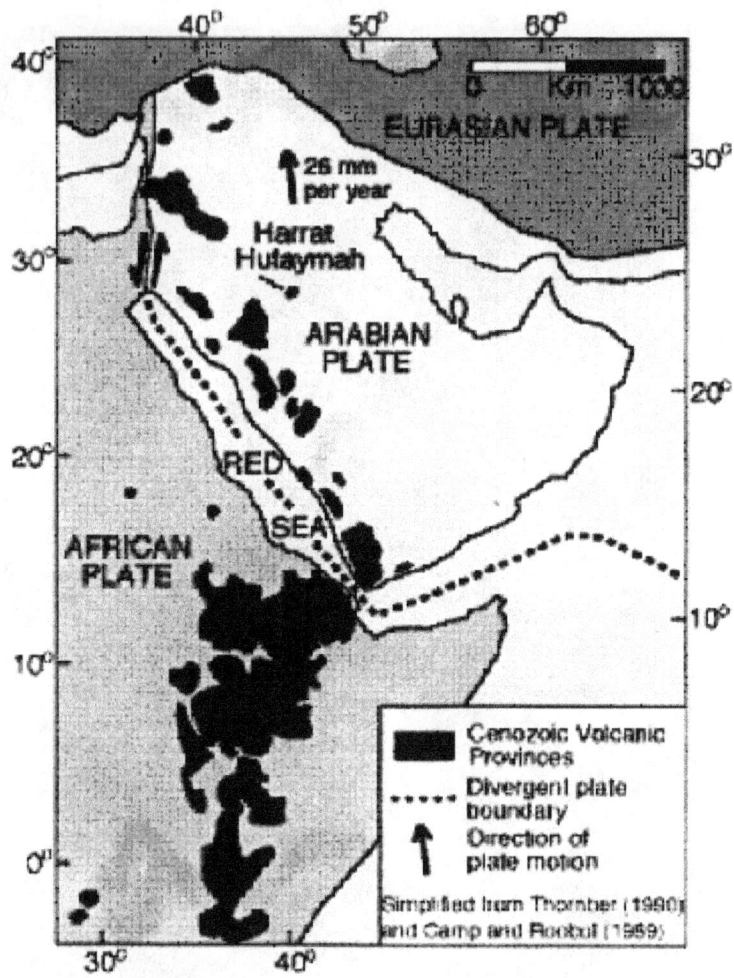

Fig. 27: Perspectives from Palestinian "Mount Nebo"

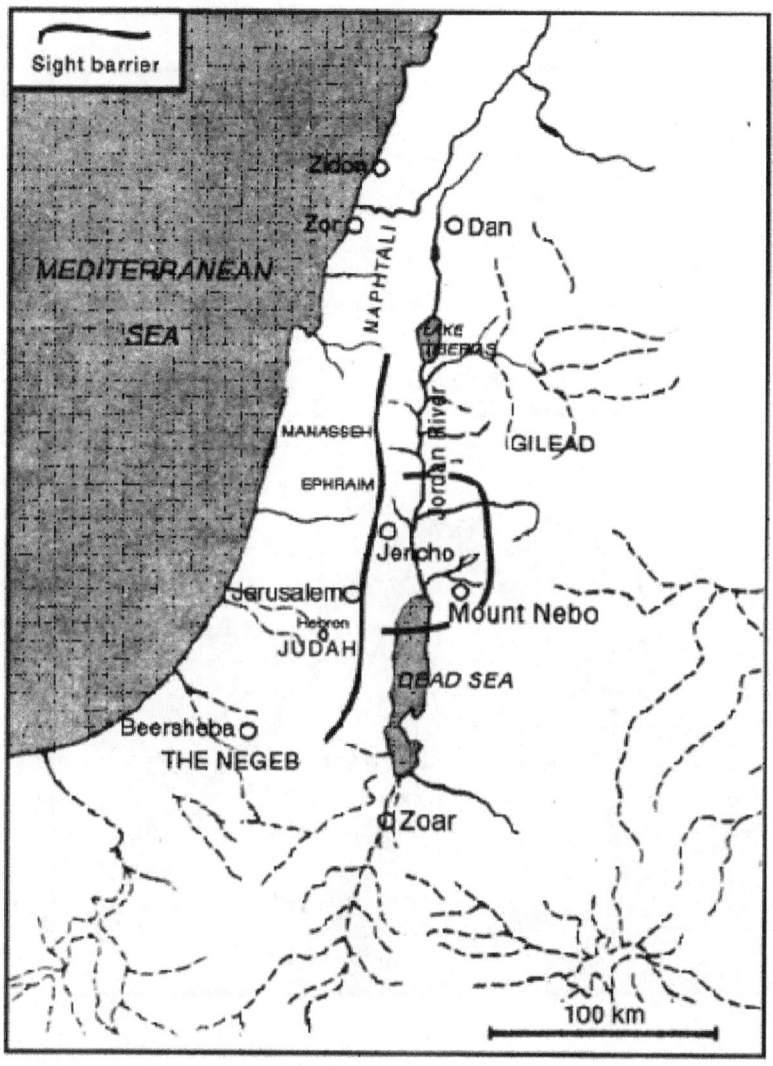

Fig. 28: Perspectives from Arabian "Mount Nebo"

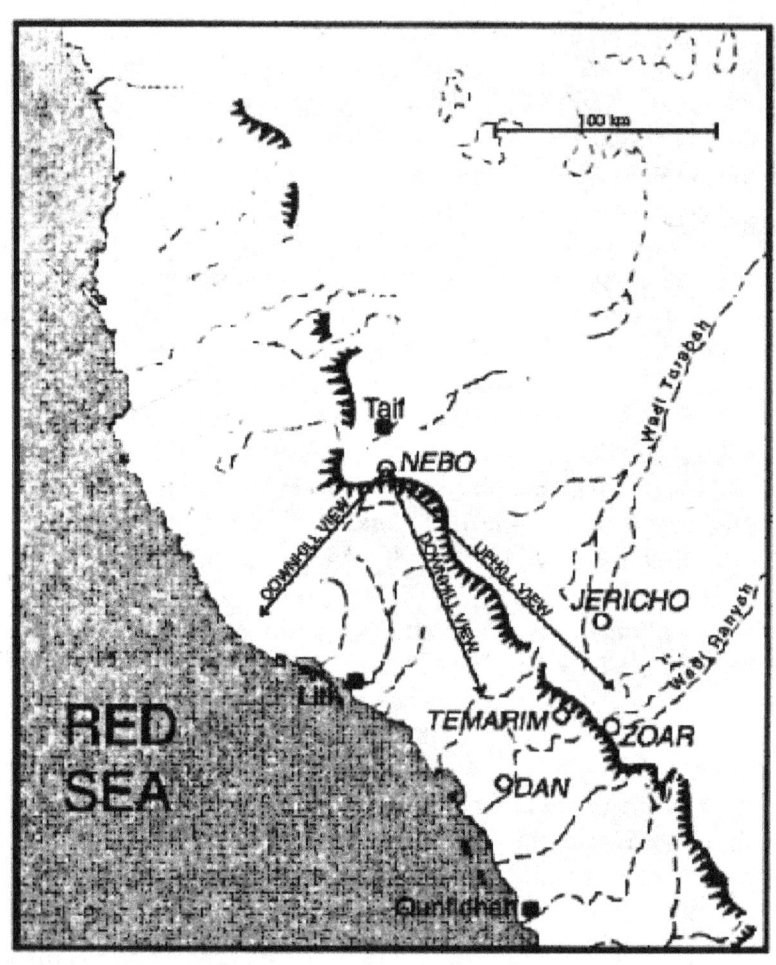

Fig. 29 Geological sketch of Bolsena region

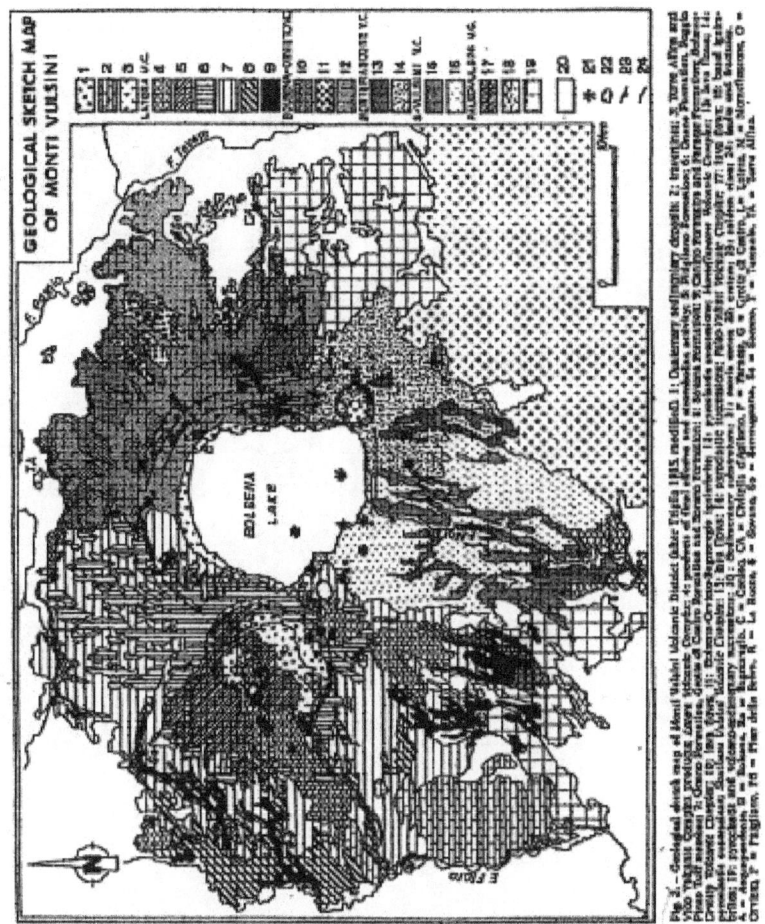

Fig. 30: Geological sketch of Lake Bolsena

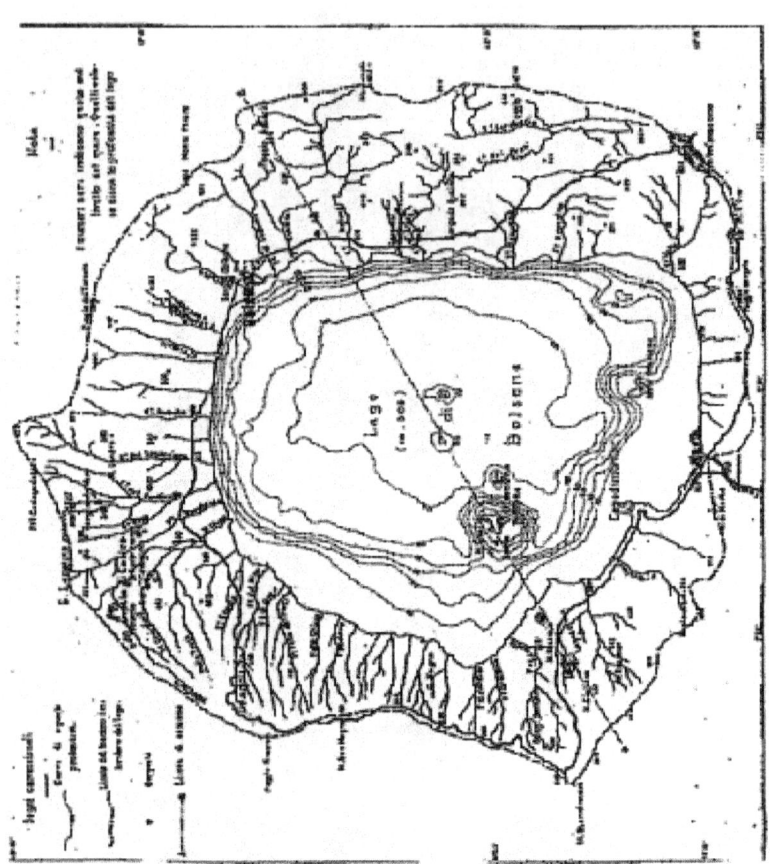

Fig. 31: Satellite photo of Lake Bolsena

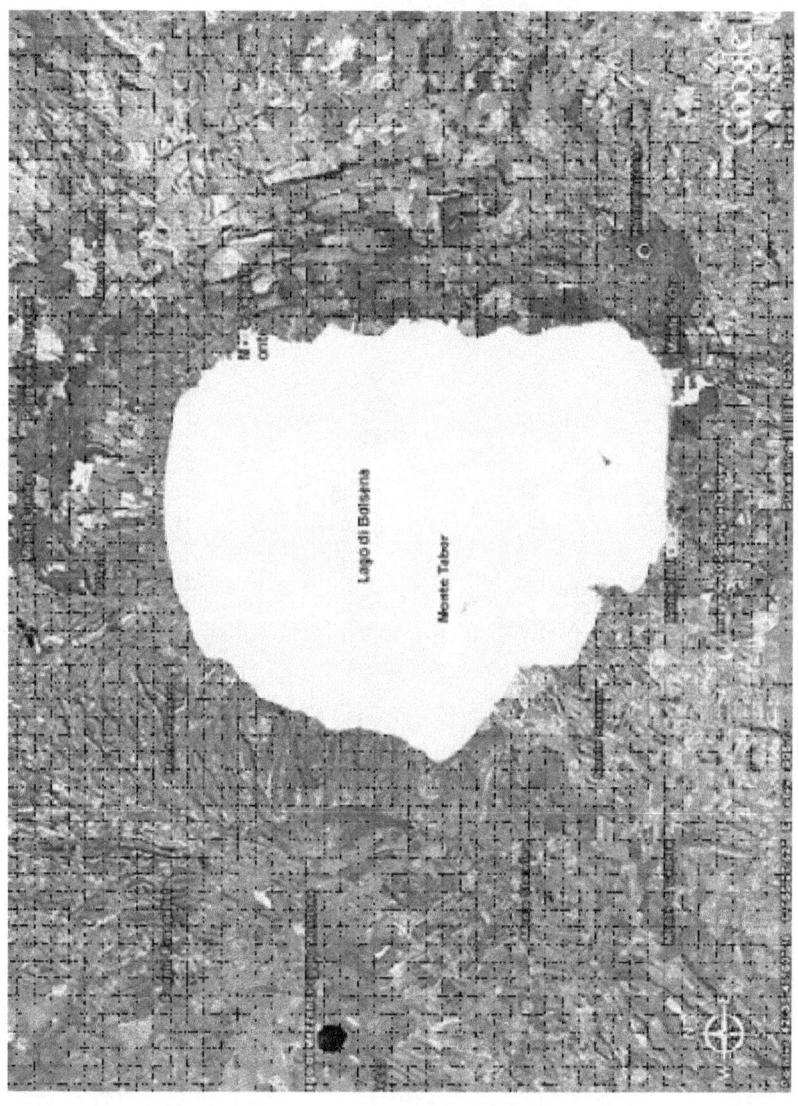

Fig. 32: Profile of Lake Bolsena

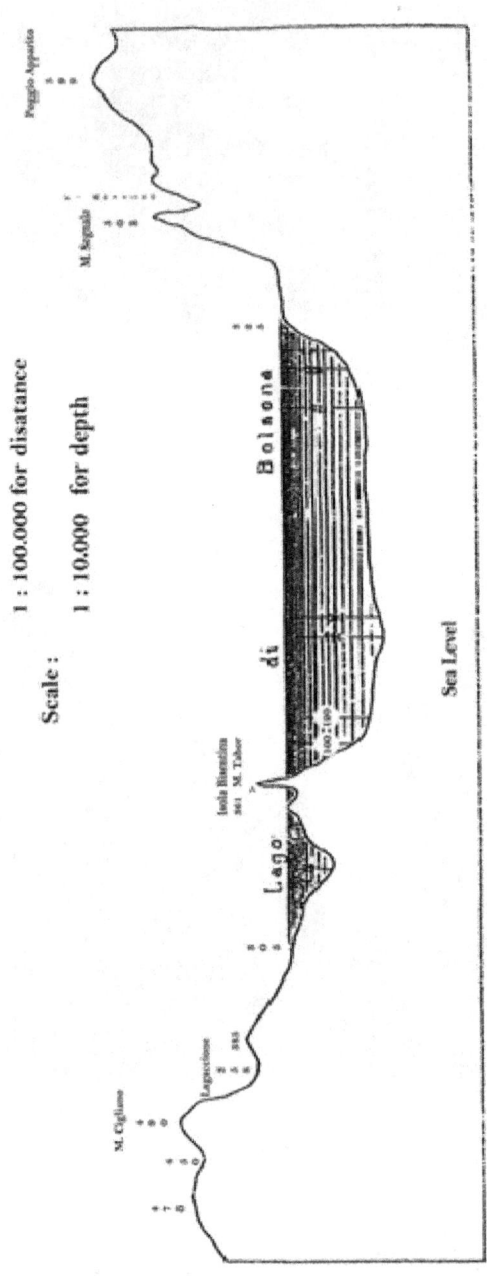

Fig. 33: Paucity of Etrurian fossils of the Phantom Age

TABELLA 2.1
Tabella dei resti faunistici dell'insediamento di Narce

Fase/Contesto Data approssimativa (secolo) Numero/percentuali	I XIII/XII a.C. N.	%	II XII a.C. N.	%	III XI a.C. N.	%	IV X a.C. N.	%	V IX a.C. N.	%	VI VIII a.C. N.	%	VII VIII a.C. N.	%	VIII VII/VI a.C. N.	%	IX IV/III a.C. N.	%	X II/III a.C. N.	%	Saggio M XI/VIII a.C. N.	%
Ovini e Caprini	27	44·3	174	53·6	242	47·2	357	49·7	218	51·7	124	46·3	6	66·6	3	27·2	29	49·2	15	53·7	55	64·8
Bovini	20	32·8	97·	29·3	146	28·5	122	22·7	89	21·1	57	21·3	2	22·2	3	27·2	8	13·5	9	32·1	15	17·6
Cani	1	1·6	6	1·8	5		9	1·6	9	2·1	10	3·7	1	11	1	9·2	1	1·7	2	7·1	1	
Cavalli							12	2·3	18	3·3	6	1·4	4	1·5				3·4	1		2	2·3
Suini	12	19·7	49	14·8	103	20·3	122	22·7	93	22·3	70	26·1	1	11·1	3	27·2	14	23·7	2	7·1	13	15·3
Cervi	1	1·6			2																	
Roditori			3		2		8	1·4	5	1·2	3	1·1					4	6·8				
Caprioli					1		2															
Tartarughe			1		3		2								1		1	1·7				
Lupi					1		2															
Totale identificabile	61	26·7	331	22·8	513	28·8	539	24·9	422	27·3	268	21·7	9	100	11	91·7	59	53·6	28	100	85	19·3
Totale non identificabile	167	73·3	1,118	77·2	1,265	71·2	1,618	75·1	1,122	72·7	964	78·3			1	8·3	51	46·4			355	80·7
Totale	228		1,449		1,778		2,157		1,344		1,232		9		12		110		28		440	

Fig. 34: Temple of Medinet Habu

Fig. 35: Roman Via Appia on top of a Volsinium wall

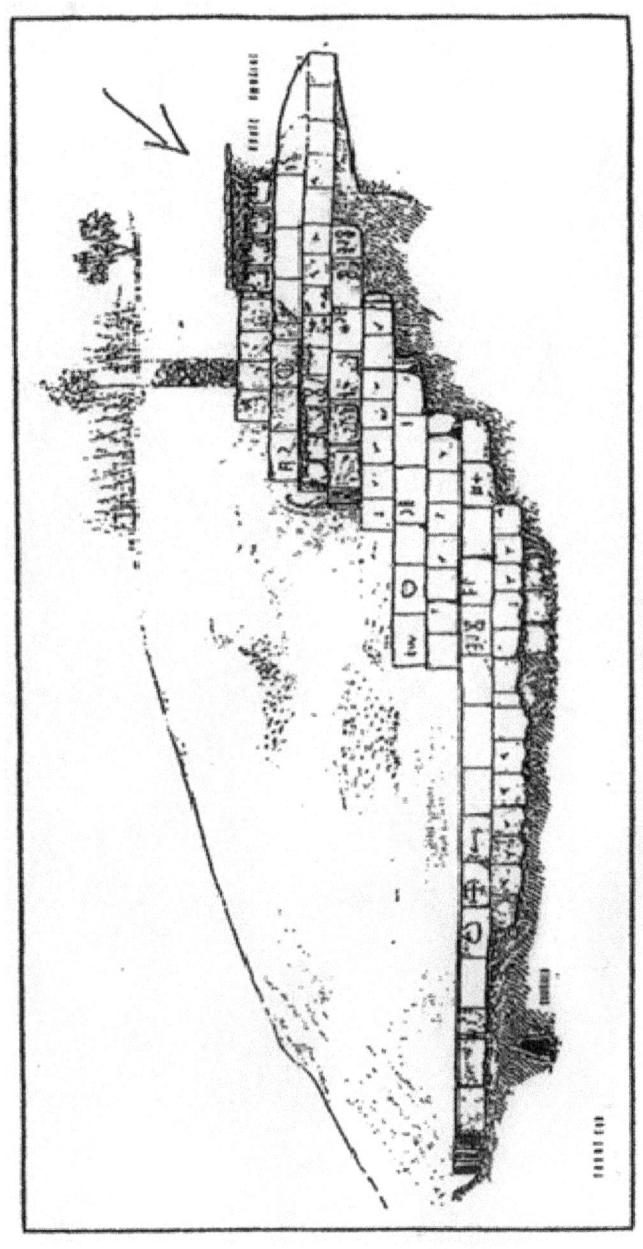

Fig. 36: Routes of migration from Spanuth's "Atlantis"

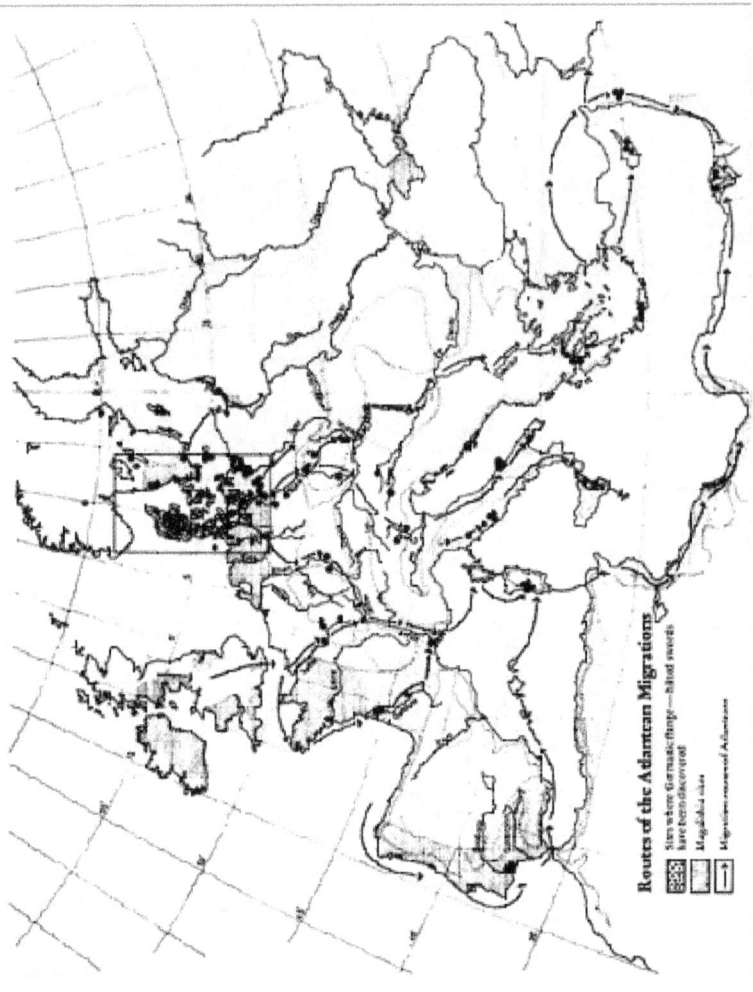

Fig. 37: A Northwestern European "troy-town" of the Early Bronze Age

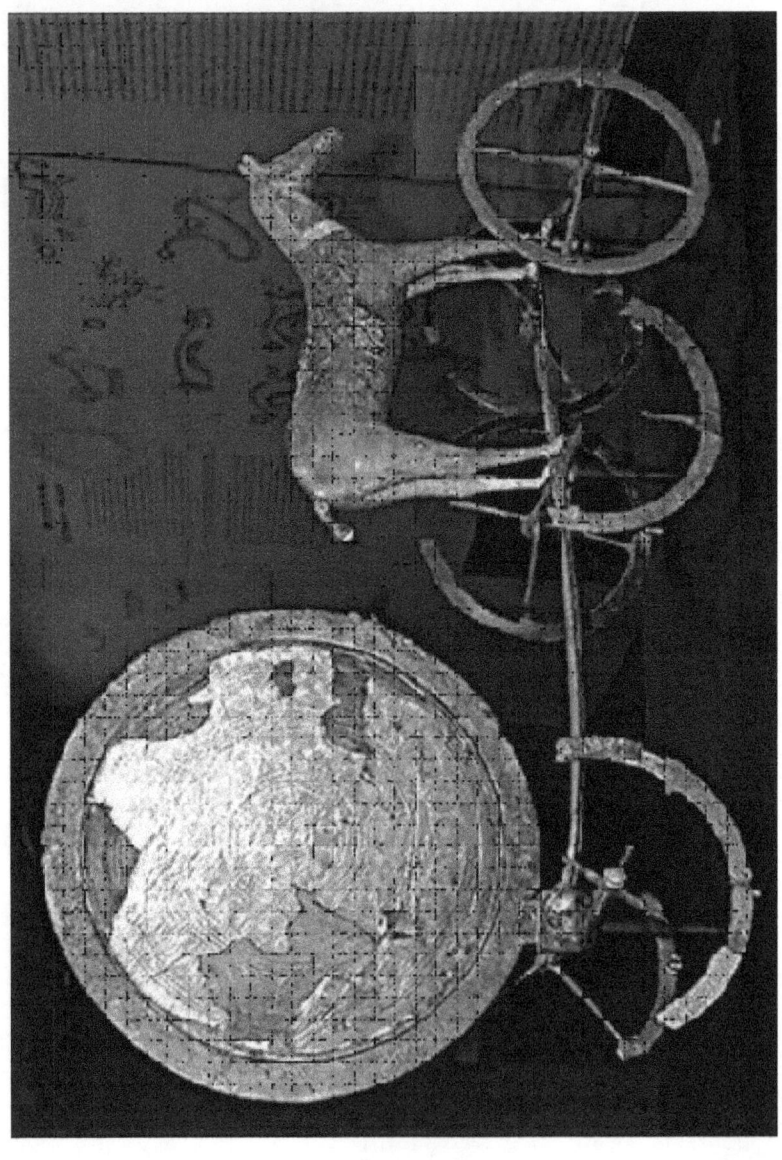

Fig.: 38: Chariot of the Sun, conceivably Phaethon

Fig. 39: Ramses III cartouche copy of Darius statue

Red dot glyphs common to lt side

Rt side glyphs all in common except blue dot

Cartouche of Ramses III
(enlarged from below)

The Persian king Darius (521-485 BC) sits on a throne carried by figures representing 28 subjected peoples.
[Insert] The artists of Ramses III seemed to have imitated the layout of this relief in their rendition of the "divine" Pharaoh.

Bibliography

Acta, First International Scientific Congress on the Volcano of Thera. Athens, Greece, 1969.

Adams, Robert McC.: "From Sites to Patterns," *Univ. of Chicago Magazine,* Winter, 1975.

Adey, Walter H.: "Coral Reef Morphogenesis: A Multidimensional Model," 202 *Science* No. 4370, pp. 831-7, November 24, 1978.

Ager, Derek V.: *The Nature of the Stratigraphical Record,* John Wiley, New York, 1973.

Ager, Derek V.: *The Great Alaskan Earthquake of 1964*, U.S. Government Printing Office, Washington, D.C., 1970.

Albright, W. F.: *Archaeology and the Religion of Israel,* 2nd ed., Baltimore, 1946.

Albritton, Claude C.: "Uniformitarianism," 18 *Encyclopedia Brittanica*, 1974.

Albritton, Claude C.: *Philosophy of Geohistory, 1785-1970,* Dowden, Hutchinson and Ross, Stroudsburg, Pa., 1975.

Alfven, Hannes: "Plasma Physics, Space Research, and the Origin of the Solar System," 172 *Science* pp. 991-4, June 4, 1971.

Allchin, F. R.: "The Stone Alignments of Southern Hyderabad," 56 *Man,* 150:133-59, 1956.

Alter, Dinsmore: "A Critical Test of the Planetary Hypothesis of Sun Spots," 57 *Monthly Weather Review,* April, 1929, 143-6. (Repr. in *Corliss,* A2, 190-5.)

Allen, Richard H.: *Star Names, their Lore and Meaning,* Dover

Publications, New York, 1899, repr. 1963.

Ambraseys, N. N.: "The Value of Historical Periods of Earthquakes," 232 *Nature* Aug. 6, 1971.

Anderson, John Lynde & George W. Spangler: "Radiometric Dating: Is the 'Decay Constant' Constant?" 4 *Pensée,* No. 4, 31-33, 1974.

"Argon in Mars' Atmosphere," 49 *Sky and Telescope*, May, 1975.

"Ash," IV *Kronos,* Winter, 1978.

"Ash," IV *Pensée,* Winter, 1973-4.

Aspden, Harold: "Galactic Domains, Geographic Fluctuations, and Geometric Reversals," 2 *Catas. Geo.* 2, 42-7, 1977.

Atharva-Veda, transl. Maurice Bloomfield, Greenwood Press, New York, 1969.

Atkinson, R. J. C.: *Stonehenge,* Pelican Books, London, 1960.

Asimov, Isaac, et al.: *Scientists Confront Velikovsky,* Cornell U. Press, Ithaca, N.Y, 1977.

Avery, T. E.: *Natural Resources Measurements,* McGraw-Hill, New York, 1975.

Babcock, William H.: *Legendary Islands of the Atlantic:A Study in Medieval Geography,* American Geographic Society,New York, 1922.

Bader, Otto N.: *La Caverne Kapovaia: Peinture Paléolithique,* Moscow, 1965.

Bailey, James R. A.: *The God-Kings and the Titans,* Hodder & Stoughton, London, 1973.

Baity, Elizabeth Chesley: "Archaeoastronomy and Ethnoastronomy Thus Far," 14 *Current Anthropology* No. 4 389-449, October, 1973.

Baker, Howard B.: "The Atlantic Rift and Its Meaning," mimeograph, Detroit, 1932.

Baker, Howard B.: "The Earth Participates in the Evolution of the Solar System," *Detroit Acad. Nat Sci.,* 1954.

Barbeau, Marius: "The Old-World Dragon in America." in Sol Tax, ed., *Indian Tribes of Aboriginal America,* Cooper Square Publ., New York, 1967.

Bargmann, Valentine & Lloyd Motz: "On the Recent Discoveries Concerning Jupiter and Venus," 138 *Science* 1350-2, December 21, 1962.

Barnes, Thomas: "Recent Origin and Decay of the Earth's Magnetic Field," II *S.I.S.R.* No. 2, 42-6,

December, 1977.

Barnes, Thomas: "A Response to Dr. Milsom," II *S.I.S.R.* No. 4 110-1, Spring, 1978.

Bass, Robert W.: "Did Worlds Collide?" 4 *Pensée* No. 3 8-20, Summer, 1974.

Bass, Robert W.: "Proofs of the Stability of the Solar System," 4 *Pensée* No. 3, 21-26, Summer, 1974.

Bass, Robert W.: "Can Worlds Collide?" 1 *Kronos* No. 3 (Fall), 59-72, Fall, 1975.

Bathurst, G. B.: "The Earliest Recorded Tornado," 19 *Weather,* 202-4, 1964.

Baudouin, Marcel, "La Préhistoire des Etoiles au Paléolothique. Les

Pléiades à l'Epoque Aurignacienne et le Culte Stello-Solaire Typique au Solutréen," ser. VI *Bull. et Mémoires de la Société d'Anthropologie de Paris,* Tome VII, 25-103, 274-317, 1916.

Beaumont, William C. (under pseudonym of Appian Way): *The Riddle of the Earth,* Chapman & Hall, London, 1925.

Beaumont, William C.: *The Mysterious Comet,* Rider & Co., London, 1945.

Beaumont, William C.: *Britain, the Key to World History,* Rider & Co., London, 1949.

Bell, Barbara: "The Dark Ages in Ancient History: Part I, Egypt," 75 *American Journal of Archaeology,* 1-26, 1971.

Bellamy, H. S.: *Moons, Myths and Man,* Faber & Faber, London, 1936.

Bellamy, H. S.: *Built before the Flood,* Faber & Faber, London, 1943.

Bellamy, H. S.: *The Atlantis Myth,* Faber & Faber, London, 1948.

Bellamy, H. S.: *A Life History of our Earth,* Faber & Faber, London, 1951.

Bellamy, H. S. & P. Allan: *The Calendar of Tiahuanaco.* Faber & Faber, London, 1956.

Bender, Barbara: *Farming in Prehistory,* John Baker, London, 1975.

Benedict, R.: "Zuni Mythology," *Contributions to Anthropology* No. 21, Columbia University, New York, 1935.

Bentley, John: *A Historical View of the Hindu Astronomy, from the Earliest Dawn of that Science in India to the Present Time (Part I & Part II),* Smith, Elder & Co., London, 1825.

Bernal, Ignacio: *Olmec World,* tr. D. Heyden and F. Horcasitas, U. of California, Berkeley, 1969.

Berndt, Ronald M.: "A Wonguri-Mandzikai Song Cycle of the Moon-Bone," XIX *Oceania* 16-50, September, 1948.

Bibby, Geoffrey: *Looking for Dilmun,* New American Library, Mentor Books, New York, 1969.

Bidez, Joseph: *Eos: ou Platon et l'Orient,* M. Hayes, Brussels, 1945.

Bimson, John J.: "Rockenbach's 'De Cometis,' and the Identity of Typhon," I *S.I.S.R.* No. 4, 9-10, Spring, 1977.

Bimson, John J.: "An Eighth Century Date for Merneptah," III *S.I.S.R.* 2, 57-9, Autumn, 1978.

Birgham, Francis: "The Discovery of Organic Remains in Meteoric Stones," 20 *Popular Science,* 83-7; repr. in *Corliss* AIAMB001, 25-8, 1881.

"Black Sea Issue: From Meter to Centimeter to Micron and Finally to Angström Units," XV *Oceanus* No. 4, Woods Hole Oceanographic Institution, July, 1970.

Blinkenberg, Christian S.: *The Thunderweapon in Religion and Folklore,* Cambridge University Press, Cambridge, 1911.

Bloch, R.: *Gli Etruschi,* Il Saggitore, Milan, 1962.

Blumer, M. & W. W. Youngblood: "Polycyclic Aromatic Hydrocarbons in Soils and Recent Sediments," *Science,* 53, April 4, 1975.

Bord, Janet: *Mazes and Labyrinths of the World,* Latimer New Dimensions, London, 1976.

Borst, Lyle B.: "Megalithic plan Underlying Canterbury Cathedral,"

163 *Science,* discussion with Frank K. E., Feb.7, 1969.

Boulanger, Nicolas-Antoine: "Deluge," in *L'Encyclopédie,* D. Diderot, ed., Briasson, Paris, 1751-65.

Boulanger, Nicolas-Antoine: *L'Antiquité Dévoilée par ses Usages ou Examen Critique des Principales Opinions, Cérémonies et Institutions Religieuses et Politiques des Différents Peuples de la Terre,* 4 vols, Amsterdam, 1766.

Brandon, S. G. F.: *Creation Legends of the Near East,* Hodder & Stoughton, London, 1963.

Brasseur de Bourbourg, Charles-Etienne: *Histoire des Nations Civilisées du Mexique et de l'Amérique Centrale,* A. Bertrand, Paris, 1857-59.

Brasseur de Bourbourg, Charles-Etienne: "S'il Existe des Sources de l'Histoire Primitive du Mexique dans les Monuments Egyptiens, etc.," Extrait du Volume *Relations des Choses de Yucatan,* de Diego

Maisonneuve, Paris, 1864.

Bray, J. R.: "Volcanism and Glaciation during the Past 40 Millennia," 252 *Nature,* 679-80, December 20-7, 1974.

Breuil Henri: "Le Bison et le Taureau Céleste Chaldéen," XIII *Revue Archéologique,* series IV, 250-4, March-April, 1909.

Briffault, Robert: *The Mothers, A Study of the Origins of Sentiments and Institutions,* 3 vols, Hamilton, New York, 1927.

Brooks, Charles Ernest Pelham: *Climate Through the Ages,* McGraw Hill, New York, 1949.

Brown, E. W.: "The Age of the Earth from Astronomical Data," *Bull. National Res. Council,* No. 8, 460-6, June, 1931.

Brown, Hugh A.: *Cataclysms of the Earth,* Twayne Pub., Inc., New York, 1967.

Brown, John Macmillan: *The Riddle of the Pacific,* Small, Maynard & Co., Boston, 1924.

Brown, W. Norman: "Mythology of India," in Samuel N. Kramer, ed., *Mythologies of the Ancient World,* Doubleday Anchor, New York, 1961.

Bruce, C. E. R.: "The Role of Electrical Discharges in Astrophysical Phenomena," 95 *The Observatory* No. 1008, 204-10, October, 1975.

Bruno, Giordano: D. W. West, ed., *His Life and Thoughts,* 1950.

Bumstead, A. P.: "Sunspots and Lightning Fires," 43 *Forestry Rev.,* 134-44, 1943.

Burkert, Walter: *Lore and Science in Ancient Pythagoreanism,* trans. E. L. Miner, Harvard University Press, 1972.

Burtt, E. A. *The Metaphysical foundations of Modern Science,* rev. ed., Doubleday, Garden City, New York, 1954.

Butzer, K. W. *Environment and Archaeology: an Ecological Approach to Prehistory,* Aldine Press, Chicago, 1971.

Cadogan, Gerald, with the collaboration of R. K. Harrison & G. E. Strong, "Volcanic Glass Shards in Late Minoan I Crete," 46 *Antiquity,* 310-3, 1972.

Cambridge Ancient History, Cambridge, Eng., University Press, vol. II., 1973.

Campbell, Joseph, *The Hero with a Thousand Faces,* Princeton University Press, Princeton, 1949.

Cardona, Dwardu: "The Pyramids and Earth's Axis," letter, 4 *Pensée* No. 1, 66-7, 1973-4.

Cardona, Dwardu: "Tektites and China's Dragon," I *Kronos* No. 2, 35-47, 1975.

Cardona, Dwardu: "The Problem of the Frozen Mammoths," I *Kronos* No. 4, 77, 1976.

Cardona, Dwardu: "On the Origin of Tektites," II *Kronos* No. 1, 38-44, 1976.

Cardona, Dwardu: "The Sun of Night," III *Kronos* (Fall), 31-37, 1977.

Cardona, Dwardu: "Let There be Light," III *Kronos* (Spring), 34-54, 1978.

Cardona, Dwardu: "The Mystery of the Pleiades," III *Kronos* (Summer), 24-44, 1978.

Cardona, Dwardu: "The Stones of Ballochry" and "The Cairns of Kintraw," IV *Kronos*, No. 3 (Spring), 23-55, 1979.

Carli, Giovanni-Rinaldo (also Carli-Rubbi): *Lettres Américaines,* 2 Vol., Buisson, Paris, 1788.

Carpenter, Rhys: *Discontinuity in Greek Civilization,* Cambridge University Press, Cambridge, England, 1966.

Cicero, M. T.: *De Natura Deorum,* H. Rackham transl., G. P. Putnam's Sons, New York, 1933.

Chinnery, Michael A. & Robert G. North: "The Frequency of Very Large Earthquakes," 190 *Science*, 1197-8, 19 December, 1975.

Clark, D. H., W. H. McCrea & F. R. Stephenson: "Frequency of Nearby Supernovae and Climatic and Biological Catastrophe," 265 *Nature,* 318-9, 1977.

Cobine, J. D.: *Gaseous Conductors -- Theory and Engineering Applications,* Dover Press, New York, 1958.

Coe, Michael D., R. A. Diehl & M. Stuiver: "Olmec Civilization, Veracruz, Mexico: Dating of the San Lorenzo Phase," 155 *Science,* 1399-1401, 1967.

Coe, Michael D.: "Native Astronomy in Mesoamerica," in Anthony F. Aveni, ed., Archaeoastronomy in Pre-Columbian America, University of Texas Press, Austin, Texas, 1975.

Cohane, John Philip: *The Key,* Crown Publishers, New York, 1967.

Coleman, P. J.: "Tsunamis as Geological Agents," 15 *Journal Geol. Soc. Australia,* 267-73, 1967.

Cook, Arthur B.: *Zeus, a Study in Ancient Religion,* Biblo & Tannen, New York, 1964.

Cook, Melvin A.: "Where is the Earth's Radiogenic Helium," 179 *Nature,* 213, January 26, 1957.

Cook, Melvin A.: "The Radio-Carbon Method," 39 *Utah Academy Sci. Arts Letters Proceedings,* 115-5, 1961-62.

Cook, Melvin A.: "Evidence for Recent Rupture of Continental Crust," 40 *Utah Academy of Sciences, Arts and Letters,* Part I, 74-77, 1963.

Cook, Melvin A.: "Continental Drift: Is Old Mother Earth just a Youngster?" *The Utah Alumnus,* 10-12, September, 1964. (Critiques and Debate, Nov., 1963; Oct., 1964; Nov., 1964).

Cook, Melvin A.: "Uranium-Thorium-Lead 'Time Clocks'," University of Utah, Depart, of Metallurgy, Salt Lake City, Utah, 1964.

Cook, Melvin A.: *Prehistory and Earth Models,* Max Parrish, London, 1966.

Cook, Melvin A.: "Carbon 14 and the Age of the Atmosphere," *Creation Research Society Quarterly,* June, 1970.

Cook, Melvin A.: "Rare Gas Adsorption on Solids of the Lunar Regolith," 38 *Journal of Colloid and Interface Science* No. 1 12-18, January, 1972.

Corliss, William R., compiler, *Sourcebook Project,* Glen Arm, Maryland, 9 Vols, 1974-X.

Courville, Donovan A.: "Limitation of Astronomical Dating Methods," 1 *Kronos* No. 2, 49-72, 1975.

Cox A. & R. R. Doell: "Paleomagnetic Evidence Relevant to a Change in the Earth's Radius," 189 *Nature,* 45, 1956.

Crew, E. W.: "Lightning in Astronomy," 252 *Nature* No. 5483, 539-42, December 13, 1974.

Crew, Eric (1976-7): "Electricity in Astronomy," in four parts, *Soc. Interdiscip. Studies Rev.* Vol. I, No. 1, 2, 3; Vol. II, No. 1, 1976-7.

Dachille, Frank: "Interactions of The Earth with very Large Meteorites," 24 *Bull. S. Carolina Acad. Sci.,* 1-19, 1962.

Dachille, Frank: "Axis Changes in the Earth from Large Meteorite Collisions," 198 *Nature,* 176, April, 13, 1963.

Dachille, Frank: "Meteorites-Little and Big," 46 *Earth and Mineral Sciences,* No. 7, 42-52, April, 1977.

Daly, R. A. (1923): "The Earth's Crust and its Stability: Decrease of the Earth's Rotational Velocity and its Geological Effects," V *Amer. J. of Sci.,* 349-77, May, 1923.

Damon, P. E., A. Long, E. I. Wallick in W. G. Mook, et al.: *Proceedings* 8 International Conf. RC Dating (Wellington, N.Z., October 1972), mimeo, University of Delft, G. W. van Oosterhout, Neth, 1976.

Däniken, Erich von: *Chariots of the Gods,* trans., Bantam Books, New York, 1971.

Däniken, Erich von: *The Gold of the Gods,* Putnam, N.Y., 1973.

Danjon, André: "On the Change in the Rate of Rotation of the Earth Occurring During the Month of July 1959." 250 *Comptes Rendus des Séances de l'Academie des Sciences,* 1399-1402, February 22, 1960.

Danjon, André: "On the Continued Variations of the Rotation of the Earth," Series 8, 254, *Comptes Rendus des Séances de l'Academie des Sciences,* 2479-82, April 2, 1962.

Danjon, André: "The Rotation of the Earth and the Quiet Sun," Series 8, 254 *Comptes Rendus des Séances de l'Academie des Sciences,* 3058-61, April 25, 1962.

Darwin, Charles: *Journal of Researches,* D. Appleton, New York, 1845.

de Grazia, Alfred: *Chaos and Creation,* Metron Publications, Princeton, 1981. http://www.grazian-archive.com/

de Grazia, Alfred: *The Lately Tortured Earth,* Metron Publications, Princeton, 1982. http://www.grazian-archive.com/

de Grazia, Alfred: *Homo Schizo I.* Metron Publications, Princeton, 1983. http://www.grazian-archive.com/

de Grazia, Alfred: *Homo Schizo II.,* Metron Publications, Princeton, 1983.
http://www.grazian-archive.com/

de Grazia, Alfred: *God's Fire: Moses and the Management of Exodus,* Metron Publications, Princeton, 1982. http://www.grazian-archive.com

de Grazia, Alfred: *Solaria Binaria,* Metron Publications, Princeton, 1983. http://www.grazian-archive.com/

de Grazia, Alfred: *The Disastrous Love-Affair of Moon and Mars,* Metron Publications, Princeton, 1983. http://www.grazian-archive.com/

de Grazia, Alfred: *The Burning of Troy,* Metron Publications, Princeton, 1984. http://www.grazian-archive.com/

de Grazia, Alfred: *The Divine Succession,* Metron Publications, Princeton, 1983.

http://www.grazian-archive.com/

de Grazia, Alfred: *The Cosmic Heretics,* Metron Publications, Princeton, 1984.

http://www.grazian-archive.com/

de Grazia, Alfred: *The Way of 'Q',* Eumetron Naxos, Naxos, Greece, 2005.

de Grazia, Alfred: "The Coming Cosmic Debate in the Sciences & Humanities," From Past to Prophesy: Velikovsky's Challenge to Conventional Beliefs, *Proceedings* of the Symposium held at the Saidye Bronfman Centre, Nahum Ravel, ed., Montreal, Quebec, January 10-12, 1975.

de Grazia, Alfred: "Paleo-Calcinology: Destruction by Fire in Pre-Historic and Ancient Times," I *Kronos,* 25-36, April, 1976; II *Kronos,* 63-71, August, 1976.

de Grazia, Alfred: "Catastrophic Finale of the Middle Bronze Age," Proceedings IX International Prehist. and Protohis. Cong., Nice, France, Sept. 1976.

de Grazia, Alfred: "Ancient Knowledge of Jupiter's Bands and Saturn's Rings," 2 *Kronos,* 64-9, February, 1977.

de Grazia, Alfred: "Palaetiology of Memory" in *Recollection of a Fallen Sky,* Symposium 1974, Earl Milton, ed., Lethbridge University Press, Lethbridge, Canada, 1978.

de Grazia, Alfred, Ralph Juergens & Livio C. Stecchini: *The Velikovsky Affair,* New York University Books, New York, 2nd ed. (1967) Lyle Stuart. Second ed., Sphere Books, London, 1978.

de Leonard, Carmen Cook: "A New Astronomical Interpretation of the Four Ballcourt Panels at Tajin, Mexico," in A. F. Aveni, ed., *Archaeoastronomy in Pre-Columbian America,* U. of Texas, Austin, 263-83, 1975.

de Santillana, Georgio and Hertha von Dechend: *Hamlet's Mill: An Essay on Myth and the Frame of Time,*

Gambit, Boston, 1969.

The Devi-Mahatmyama, trans. by S. Jagadisvarananda, Madras India, 1953.

Donnelly, Ignatius: *Ragnarok: The Age of Fire and Gravel,* D. Appleton & Co., New York, 1883.

"Don't Rock the Ark," n.a., III *Kronos* (Fall), 68-71, 1977.

Dorsey, G. A.: *Traditions of the Skidi Pawnee,* Houghton Mifflin & Co., Boston, New York, 1904.

Douglas, Mary: *Natural Symbols, Explorations in Cosmology,* Pantheon, New York, 1970.

Doumanis, George A. & William E. Long: "The Ancient Life of the Antarctic," 207 *Scientific American* No. 3, September, 1962.

Doumas, Christos: "The Minoan Eruption of the Santorini Volcano," XLVIII *Antiquity,* 110-115, 1974.

Driscoll, E.: "Bonanza from the Highlands," *Science News,* 12-3, July 1, 1972.

Duran, Diego: *Book of the Gods and Rites of the Ancient Calendar,*

Transsl., ed. and annot. by Fernando Horcasitas and Doris Heyden, U. of Oklahoma Press, Norman, 1971.

Duxbury, T. C. & J. Veverka: "Deimos Encounter by Viking," 201 *Science,* 812-14, September 1, 1978.

"Ebla, the Plain Dealer," II *S.I.S.R.* No 4, (unsigned note), Spring, 1978.

Eddy, John A.: "The Maunder Minimum," 192 *Science,* 1189-1202, June 18, 1976.

Eddy, John A.:"The Case of the Missing Sunspots," 236 *Scientific American,* 80-92, May, 1977.

Eddy, John A., P. A. Gilman & D. E. Trotter: "Anomalous Solar Rotation in the Early 17th Century," 198 *Science,* 824-29, November, 1977.

Ehrich, Robert W. Ed.: *Chronologies in Old World Archaeology,* 4th impression 1971, U. of Chicago Press,

Chicago & London, 1965.

Einstein, Albert: "Letter to I. Velikovsky," repr. in 2 *Pensée* 2, 39, 1955.

Eisler, R.: *Weltenmantel und Himmelszelt,* C. H. Beck, München, 1910.

Eliade, Mircea: Trans. By Trask (1954), *The Myth of the Eternal Return,* Princeton U. Press, Princeton, N.J., 1949.

Eliade, Mircea: *Myth and Reality,* Harper & Row, New York, 1963.

Eliade, Mircea: *Traité d'Histoire des Religions,* Payot, Paris, 1964.

Eliade, Mircea: *Gods, Goddesses, and Myths of Creation,* Harper & Row,

New York, 1974.

Emery, W. B.: *Archaic Egypt,* Baltimore, Penguin Books, 1961.

Eratosthenes: C. Robert ed., *Catasterismorum Reliquiae,* 1878.

Everhart, Edgar: "Close Encounter of Comets and Planets'" 74 *Astronomical Journal,* 735-50, June, 1969.

Fairbridge, Rhodes W.: "Holocene Epoch," 8 *Encyclopaedia Britannica,* 998-1007, 1974.

Fauconnet, Max: " Mythology of the Two Americas," *New Larousse Encyclopedia of Mythology,* Hamlyn London, 1968.

Fell, Barry: "Etruscan," V, *Occasional papers,* No. 100, Harvard Univ., Cambridge, Mass, 1977.

Ferte, Thomas: "A Record of Success," II *Pensée* No. 2 11-15, May, 1975.

Finney, John W.: "Slowing of Jupiter's Rotation Reported by Radio Astronomer," *New York Times,* April 27, 1965.

Fitzgerald. C. P.: *China: A Short Cultural History,* New York, 1965.

Flammarion (1880): *Astronomie Populaire,* C. Marpon et. E. Flammarion, Paris (repr. 1955).

Fontenrose, Joseph: *Python, A Study of Delphic Myth and Its Origins,* U. of California Press, Berkeley, 1959.

Fox, Hugh: *Gods of the Cataclysm,* Harper and Row, New York, 1979.

Francis, Wilfrid: *Coal: Its Formation and Composition,* Arnold, London, 1961.

Francis, Wilfrid: "Velikovsky on the Origin of Coal," 2 *Pensée* 19-21, Fall, 1972.

Frankfort H. et al.: *The Intellectual Adventure of Ancient Man,* U. of Chicago Press, Chicago, 1946.

Frankfort H.: *The Art and Architecture of the Ancient Orient,* Penguin Books, Harmondsworth, Middlessex, 1954.

Frazer, James G.: *Folk-Lore in the Old Testament,* 1919.

Frazier, Kendrick: "When the Sun went strangely Quiet," *Science News,* March 6, 1976.

Frickenhaus, August H.: *Tiryns,* vol. I Athens, 1912.

Furneaux, Rupert: *Krakatoa,* Prentice Hall, Englewood Cliffs, N.J., 1964.

Galanopoulos, Angelos & Edward Bacon : *Atlantis: The Truth behind the Legend,* Bobbs-Merrill Co., Indianapolis & New York, 1969.

Galilei, Galileo: *Dialogue on the Great World System,* Giorgio de Santillana, ed., U. of Chicago Press, Chicago, 1953.

Gallant, René L. C.: "Meteorite Impacts, Lunar Maria, Lopoliths, and Ocean Basins," 197 *Nature,* 38-9, January 5, 1963.

Gallant, René L. C.: *Bombarded Earth, An Essay on the Geological and Biological Effects of Huge Meteorite Impacts,* John Baker, London, 1964.

Gardiner, A. H.: *Admonitions of an Egyptian Sage from a Hieratic Papyrus in Leiden* (Papyrus Ipuwer), 1909.

Gaster, Theodor H.: *Myth, Legend, and Custom in the Old Testament,* Harper & Row, New York, 1965, repr. (1969); Harper Torchbooks, 1975.

Gibson, John: "Saturn's Age," pre-publication interview with author David N. Talbott, Research Communication Network, Portland, Oregon, October, 1977.

Gillispie, C. C.: *Genesis and Geology, A Study in the Relations of Scientific Thought, Natural Theology, and*

Social Opinion in Great Britain, 1790-1850, Harper, New York, 1951, 1959.

Gimbutas, Marija: *The Gods and Goddesses of Old Europe: Myths, Legends and Cult Images,* U. of California

Press, 1974.

Ginzberg, Louis: *The Legends of the Jews,* trans. by H. Szold, The Jewish Publication Society of America,

Philadelphia, 1909-1939.

Glass, Billy: "Microtektites in Deep-sea Sediments," 214 *Nature,* 372-4, April 22, 1967.

Glass, Billy & B. C. Heezen: "Tektites and Geomagnetic Reversals," 214 *Nature,* April 22, 1967.

Glass, Billy & B. C. Heezen: "Silicate Spherules from Tunguska Impact Area: Electron Microprobe Analysis," 164 *Science,* May 2, 1969.

Goblet, Count d'Aviella: *The Migration of Symbols,* New York U. Books, New York, repr., 1956.

Goff, Beatrice L.: *Symbols of Prehistoric Mesopotamia,* Yale U. Press, New Haven, 1963.

Gold, T.: "Instability of the Earth's Axis of Rotation," 175 *Nature,* 526-9, 1955

Gold, T.: "Irregularities in the Earth's Rotation -- Part I," 17 Sky and Telescope, 216-8 March, 1958; "Part II," 284-6, April, 1958.

Golonetsky, S. F., V. V. Stepanok & E. M. Kolesnikov: "Signs of Cosmochemical Anomaly in the Area of the 1908 Tunguska Catastrophe," 11 *Geoktrimiya,* 1635-45, 1977.

Goneim, Zakaria: *The Buried Pyramid,* 1956.

Gordon, Cyrus H.: *Before Columbus -- Links between the Old World and Ancient America,* Crown Publishers, New York, 1971.

Gordon, Cyrus H.: *Riddles in History,* Crown Publishers, New York, 1974.

Gössmann, P. F.: *Das Era-Epos,* Augustinus-Verlag, Würzburg, Germ., 1955.

Graves, Robert: *The Greek Myths,* Vol. 1 & 2 Penguin, Baltimore; 1955, repr. 1959.

Gray, L. H. ed.: *The Mythology of all Races,* Cooper Square Publishers, New York, 1964.

Greenberg, Lewis M.: "The Papyrus Ipuwer," III *Pensée* 36-7, Winter, 1973.

Greenberg, Lewis M.: "Atlantis," VI *Pensée,* 51-4, Winter, 1973-4.

Greenberg, Lewis M.: "A Concordance of Disaster," I *Kronos* Summer, 1975.

Greenberg, Lewis M. & Warner B. Sizemore: "Jerusalem--City of Venus," III *Kronos* No. 3, 56-90, Spring, 1978.

Gribbin, J. & S. Plagemann: "Discontinuous Change in Earth's Spin Rate Following Great Solar Storm of August 1972," 243 *Nature,* May 4, 1973.

Gribbin, J. & S. Plagemann: *The Jupiter Effect: The Planets as Triggers of Devastating Earthquakes,* Vintage Books, New York, 1974.

Griffiths, J. G.: "Archaeology and Hesiod's Five Ages," XVII *J. Hist. Ideas* No. 1, 109-19, January, 1956.

Grove, David C.: *The Olmec Paintings of Oxtotitlan Cave, Guerrero, Mexico,* Harvard U. Studies in Pre-Columbian Art and Archaeology, No. 6, 1970.

Guerrier, E.: "Le Forgeron venu du Ciel," 17 *Kadath,* 30-6, 1976.

Guirand, F.: "Greek Mythology," *Larousse World Mythology,* 85-198, Putnam, 1968.

Gundel, (1894-1941), "Kometen," in Pauly-Wissowa, XI *Real Encyclopädie* (also "Planeten.")

Gunkel, H.: *Schöpfung und Chaos in Urzeit und Endzeit, Eine Religionsgeschichtliche Untersuchung über Gen. I*
und Ap. Joh. 12, Vandenhoek und Ruprecht, Göttingen, 1895 & 1921.

Goodrich, Luther C.: *A Short History of the Chinese People,* Allen & Unwin, London, 1957.

Haliburton, R. G.: "Primitive Traditions as to the Pleiades," 25 *Nature,* 100-101, December, 1881; repr. in W. R. Corliss, Compiler, *Strange Artifacts,* M-1, MLW-003, Glen Arm, Md., 1974.

Hapgood, C. H.: *Maps of the Ancient Sea Kings,* Chilton Books, Philadelphia, 1966.

Hapgood, C. H.: *The Path of the Pole,* Chilton Books, Philadelphia, 1970.

Harris, T. M.: "Forest Fire in the Mesozoic," 46 *J. Ecology* No. 2, 447-453, 1958.

Hartmann, William K.: "The Smaller Bodies of the Solar System," 233 *Scientific American* No. 3, 142-59, September, 1975.

Harwit, M.: "Spontaneously Split Comets," 151 *Astrophysical Journal,* 789-90, February, 1968.

Hatfield, G. B. & M. J. Camp: "Mass Extinction Correlated with Periodic Galactic Events," 81 *Bull. Geol. Soc. Amer.,* No. 3, 911-14, 1970.

Hawkes, Jacquetta: *Atlas of Ancient Archaeology,* McGraw Hill, New York, 1973.

Haymes, Robert C.: *Introduction to Space Science,* John Wiley and Sons, New York, 1971.

Heide, Fritz: *Meteorites,* Edward Anders & Eugene Du-Fresne, transl. U. of Chicago Press, Chicago, 1964; *Kleine Meteoritenkunde,* Springer Verlag, Berlin, 1957.

Heninger, S. K. Jr.: *A Handbook of Renaissance Meteorology,* Duke U. press, Durham, N. Ca., 1960.

Hentig, Hans von: *Ueber den Zusammenhang von Kosmischen, Biologischen und Sozialen Krisen,* Ernst Klett

Verlag, Stuttgart.

Herr, Richard B.: "Solar Rotation Determined from Thomas Harriot's Sunspot Observations of 1611 to 1613," 202 *Science,* 1079-81, December 8, 1978.

Hesiod: *The Homeric Hymns,* and *Homerica,* H. G. Evelyn-White, trans. 1936.

Hild, J. A.: "Saturnus," IV-2 *Dict. Antiq. Grecque et Rom.,* 1083-90, 1919.

Hirschberg, Walter: "Die Plejaden in Afrika und ihre Beziehungen zum Bodenban," 60-1 *Zeitscrift für Ethnologie,* 1928-29.

Hitching, Francis: *Earth Magic,* Morrow, New York, 1977.

Hoch, Roy: *God in Greek Philosophy,* Princeton U. Press, Princeton. N.J., 1969.

Holbrook, John: "The Revised Chronology," 3 *Pensée* No. 2, centerfold, Spring-Summer, 1973.

Homer: Richmond Lattimore trans. (1951), *The Iliad,* U. of Chicago Press, Chicago; 19th impression, 1967.

Homer: *The Odyssey,* A. T. Murray, trans., 2 vol. Putnam's Sons, New York, 1919.

Homer: *The Odyssey,* E. V. Rieu, trans., Penguin Books, Baltimore, 1955.

Honeyman, James R.: "Sinking Continents," 13 *Creation Res. Q.,* 58, 1976.

Hooqkaas, Reijer: "Catastrophism in Geology, Its Scientific Character in Relation to Actualism and

Uniformitarianism," 33 *Koninklijke Nederlandse Akademie van Wetenschaften Letterkunde,* No. 7, 271-316, 1970.

Hope-Simpson, R. E.: "Sunspots and Flu: a Correlation," 275 *Nature* 86, 1978.

Hopkins, Clark: "The Canopy of Heaven and the Aegis of Zeus," *Bucknell Review,* March 29, 1965.

Hoyle, Fred & N. C. Wickramasinghe: "Does Epidemic Disease Come From Space," *New Scientist,* Nov. 11, 1977.

Humboldt, A. von: Engl. transl., *Researches concerning the Institutions and Monuments of the Ancient Inhabitants of America,* Vol. II, Longman, etc. Hurt, Rees, Orme & Broung J. Murray & H. Colburn, London, 1814.

Inglis, D. R., "The Shifting of the Earth's Axis of Rotation," 29 *Review of Modern Physics,* 9-19.

Isaacson, Israel M.: "Carbon 14 Dates and Velikovsky's Revision of Ancient History: Samples from Pylos and Gordion," 3 *Pensée* No. 2, Spring-Summer, 1973.

Isaacson, Israel M.: "Applying the Revised Chronology," 4 *Pensée* No.4 Fall, 1974.

Isaacson, Israel M.: "Some Preliminary Remarks about Thera and Atlantis," 1 *Kronos* No. 2, 1975.

Jacobsen, Thomas W.: "17,000 Years of Greek Prehistory," 234 *Scientific Amer.,* 76-87, 1976.

James, E. O.: *Seasonal Feasts and Festivals,* Barnes & Noble, New York, 1961.

James, Peter: "Aphrodite--The Moon or Venus?" I *S.I.S.R.,* No. 1, 2-7, 1976.

James, Peter: "Aphrodite," Letters, I *S.I.S.R.,* No. 3, 1976.

James, Peter: "Peoples of the Sea?" II *S.I.S.R.,* No. 1, 4-6, 1977.

James, Peter: "Metallurgy and Chronology," III *S.I.S.R.,* No. 4, 81-3 1979.

James, Williams: *The Will to Believe,* Longmans Green, London, 1937 ed., 1896.

Jastrow, M.: *Religion of Babylon and Assyria,* 1898.

Jaynes, Julian: Houghton-Mifflin, Boston, 1977.

Jeans, J. H.: *Astronomy and Cosmology,* Cambridge, Eng., 1928.

Joseph, P.: *The Dravidian Problem in the South Indian Culture Complex,* Orient Longman, Ltd., New Delhi, 1972.

Josephus, Flavius: *The Works of Flavius Josephus,* trans. Whiston, 1895 ed., J. B. Lippincott, Philadelphia.

Juergens, Ralph: "Reconciling Celestial Mechanics and Velikovskian Catastrophism," 2 *Pensée* No. 3, Fall, 6-12, 1972.

Juergens, Ralph: "Juergens Replies," letter, 4 *Pensée,* No. 1 Winter, 62-64, 1973-4.

Juergens, Ralph: "Electricity Absent from Sagan's Astrophysics," 4 *Pensée,* No. 2, Spring, 38-43, 1974.

Juergens, Ralph: "Electrical Discharges and the Transmutation of Elements," 4 *Pensée,* No. 3, Summer, 45-6, 1974.

Juergens, Ralph: "Of the Moon and Mars, Part 1," 4 *Pensée,* No. 4 Fall, 21-30, 1974; "Part 2," 4 *Pensée,* No. 5 Winter, 27-39, 1974-5.

Juergens, Ralph: "Radiohalos, and Earth History," III *Kronos,* Fall, 3-17, 1977.

Juergens, Ralph: "Geogullibility and Geomagnetic Reversals," III *Kronos,* Summer, 52-63, 1978.

Justin (3rd century A.D.): *The History.*

Kaiser, T. R.: *The Incident Flux of Meteors and the Total Meteoric Ionization,* Pergamon, London, 1955.

Kelley, Allan: *Continental Drift: Is It a Cometary Impact Phenomenon ?*, Carlsbad, Calif., 1963, rev. ed. 1966.

Kelley, Allan: *Gravitational Disruption of Mars: Speculation, Theory or Fact?* (privately printed) Carlsbad, Calif., 1974.

Kelley, Allan & Frank Dachille: *Target: Earth, the Role of large Meteors in Earth Science,* Carlsbad, Calif., 1953.

Kennedy, G. E.: "Early Man in the New World." 255 *Nature,* 274-5, 1975.

Kerenyi, Karl: *Hermes, Guide of Souls,* Spring, Zurich, 1976.

Kerr, Richard A.: "Isotopic Anomalies in Meteorites: Complications Multiply," 202 *Science,* 203-4, 1978.

Kofahl, Robert E.: "Could the Flood Waters Have Come from a Canopy or extraterrestrial Source?" 13 *Creation Res. Q.,* 202, 1976-7.

Komarek, E. V., Sr.: "Fire Ecology--Grasslands and Man," *Proceedings,* 4th Annual Tall Timber Fire Ecology Conference, March 18-19, 169-220, 1965.

Kolata, Gina Bari: "Catastrophe Theory: The Emperor Has No Clothes," 996 *Science,* April 15, 287, 1977.

Kondratov, Alexander: *The Riddles of Three Oceans,* Progress Publishers, Moscow, U.S.S.R., 1974.

Kopal, Z.: *Close Binary Systems,* Wiley, New York, 1959.

Kramer, Samuel Noah, ed.: *Mythologies of the Ancient World,* Anchor, Doubleday, Garden City, 1961.

Krinov, E. L.: *Giant Meteorites,* Pergamon Press, Oxford. London, Edinburgh, New York, 1966.

Kronos, Editors: *Velikovsky and Establishment Science,* Kronos Press, Glassboro, N.J., 1977.

Kronos, Editors: IV "Scientists Confront Scientists who Confront Velikovsky," 2:2-79, 1978.

Kroeber, Alfred L.: *The Nature of Culture,* U. of Chicago Press, Chicago, 1952.

Kruskal, Martin, Ralph Juergens, C. E. R. Bruce, Eric W. Crew: "On Cosmic Electricity, Supplement," III *Pensée,* No. 3 Fall, 42-50.

Kugler, Franz Xavier: *Sybillinischer Sternkampf und Phaëton in Naturgeschichtlicher Beleuchtung,* Munster, 1927.

Kuong, Wong Lee: "The Synthesis of manna," III *Pensée,* Winter, 45-6, 1973.

Kuper, Charles G. & Asher Peres, eds.: *Relativity and Gravitation,* Gordon and Breach, New York, 1971.

Lamberg-Karlovsky, C. & M.: "An Early City in Iran," *Scientific American,* June, 102-11, 1971.

Lane, Frank W.: *The Elements Rage,* Chilton Co. Publ., Philadelphia and New York, 1965.

Langdon, Stephen H.: *Enuma Elish, The Babylonian Epic of Creation,* Clarendon Press, Oxford, 1923.

Langdon, Stephen H.: *Babylonian Menologies and the Semitic Calendars,* Oxford U. Press, Milford, 1935.

Laville, Henri: *Climatologie et Chronologie du Paléolithique en Périgord,* Laboratoire de Plaentologie, U. de

Provence, France, 1935.

Lederer, Wolfgang: *The Fear of Women,* Harcourt Brace Jovanovich, Inc., New York, 1968.

Legget, Robert R. ed.: *Glacial Till: An Interdisciplinary Study,* Royal Society of Canada, 1976.

Leglay, Marcel: *Saturne Africain,* Boccard, Paris, 1966.

Leighton, Robert G.: "The Surface of Mars," 222 *Scientific American,* May, 27-40, 1970.

Lessing, G.: *Laokoon,* trans. by E. C. Beasley, G. Bell and Sons, London, 1888.

Lewis. Gilbert N.: "The Genesis of the Elements," 46 *The Physical Review,* November 15, 897-901, 1934.

Libby, W. F.: "The Radiocarbon Dating Method." 3 *Pensée* No. 2, Spring-Summer, 7-12, 1973.

Libby, L. M. & H. R. Lukens: "Production of Radiocarbon in Tree Rings by Lightning Bolts," 78 *J.*
Geophysical Res., No. 26, September 10, 5902-3, 1973.

Lichtenberg, Georg C.: *The Lichtenberg Reader:* Beacon Press, Boston, 1959.

"Lightning Superbolts Seen from Space:" *New Scientist* October 20, 150, 1977.

Lockyer, J. N.: *Dawn of Astronomy,* M.I.T. Press, Cambridge, Mass., 1965.

Long, Charles H.: *Alpha: The Myths of Creation,* G. Braziller, New York, 1963.

Long, Charles H.: "Myths and Doctrines of Creation," 5 *Encyclopedia Britannica,* 240-1, 1974.

Lowery, Malcolm: "Father Kugler's Falling Star," II *Kronos,* No. 4, Summer, 3-28, 1977.

Lowery, Malcolm: "Some Notes on Senmut's Ceiling," II *S.I.S.R.,* No. 1 Autumn, 7-10, 1977.

Lowery, Malcolm: "Dating the 'Admonitions': Advance Report," II *S.I.S.R.,* No. 3, 54-7, 1977-8.

Lowery, Malcolm: "The Sybil and Dr. Stecchini," III *S.I.S.R.,* No. 2, Autumn, 32-4, 1978.

Lucretius: *De Rerum Natura,* trans. by R. C. Trevelyan, The University Press, Cambridge, Eng., 1937.

Maccoby, Hyam: "Ebla," a note, I, *S.I.S.R.,* Spring, 3

McCall, G. J. H., ed.: *Meteorite Craters,* Wiley, New York, 1977.

McCrea, W., D. H. Clark, F. R. Stephenson: "On possible cosmic event of last several thousand years bombarding Earth by cosmic radiation," 265 *Nature,* 318, 1977.

McDonnel, J. A. M., ed.: *Cosmic Dust,* Wiley-Interscience, New York, 1978.

MacKie, Euan W.: "Megalithic Astronomy and Catastrophism," 4 *Pensée* No. 5, Winter, 5-20, 1974.

MacKie, Euan W.: "Science and Society in Prehistoric Britain."

MacKie, Euan W.: "Radiocarbon Dates for the Eighteenth Dynasty," II *S.I.S.R.,* No. 2-3, 95-6, 1977-8.

MacKinnon, Roy: "Cenomanian Sync.," I *S.I.S.R.,* No. 2, Spring, 1976.

MacKinnon, Roy: "The Inexact Science of Radiometric Dating," I *S.I.S.R.,* Summer, 8-19, 1977.

Mac Neish, Richard S.: "The Origins of New World Civilization," 11 *Scientific American,* November, 29-37, 1964.

Macrobius: P. V. Davies, trans., *Saturnalia,* Columbia U. Press, 1969.

Mainwaring, A. Bruce: "Final Report, Foundation for Studies of Modern Science Radiocarbon Project," *Project* conducted by the Museum Applied Science Center for Archaeology of the Museum of the University of Pennsylvania, Philadelphia, Pa., 1973.

Manuel, Frank E.: *Isaac Newton: Historian,* Harvard U. Press, Cambridge, 1963.

Maringer, Johannes: *The Gods of Prehistoric Man,* trans. by Mary Ilford, Weidenfeld and Nicholson, London; Knopf, New York, 1960.

Marsden, Brian G.: "One Hundred Periodic Comets," *Science,* 10 March, 1207-13, 1967.

Marsden, B. G. & A. G. W. Cameron: *The Earth-Moon System,* Plenum, New York, 1966.

Marshack, Alexander: *The Roots of Civilization. The Cognitive Beginnings of Man's First Art, Symbol And Notation,* Weidenfeld and Nicolson, London; McGraw Hill, New York, 1972.

Marshall, Sir John: *Mohenjo-daro and the Indus Civilization,* 3 vols., London, 1931.

"Martian Poles Shift, Say Polar Drift Theorists," 43 *Science Digest,* June, 74-5, 1973.

Martin, P. S. & H. E. Wright, eds.: *International Association for Quaternary Research, Pleistocene Extinctions,*
The Search for a Cause, Yale U. Press, New Haven, 1968.

Martineau, LaVan: *The Rocks Begin to Speak,* KC Publ., Las Vegas, Nev., 1973.

Mavor, J. W. Jr.: *Voyage to Atlantis,* Putnam's Sons, New York, 1969.

Mead, G. R. S.: *Thrice Greatest Hermes,* J. M. Watknis, London, 1906.

Meggers, Betty J.: "The Transpacific Origin of Meso-American Civilization: A Preliminary Review of the Evidence and Theoretical Implication," 77 *Amer. Anthro.,* 1-27, 1975.

Mellaart, James: *Catal Huyuk, a Neolithic Town in Anatolia,* McGraw Hill, New York, 1967.

Mercer, S. A. B.: *The Pyramid Texts,* Longmans, Green, New York, 1952.

Mergell, M. et al.: "A City Plagued by Noise..." *Environment Report* (November 27), I. National League of Cities, Washington, D.C., 1978.

Michell, John: *The View Over Atlantis,* Ballantine Books, New York, 1969.

Michelson, Irving: "Mechanics Bears Witness," 4 *Pensée,* NO. 2, 15-22, 1974.

Michelson, Irving: "Tide's Tortured Theory,' 30 *Science and Public Affairs* No. 3, March, 31-4, 1974.

Miller, Molly: *The Sicilian Colony Dates: Studies in Chronography I,* State U. of New York Press, Albany N.Y., 1970.

Miller, Robert D.: *The Origin and Original Nature of Apollo,* Ph.D. Dissertation. U. Of Pennsylvania. Philadelphia, 1939.

Milsom, John: "A Commentary on Barnes' Magnetic Decay.' II *S.I.S.R.,* No, 2, December, 46, 1977.

Milton, Earl: *The Planets Bear Witness,* Dept. of Physics and Astronomy, Lethbridge, Canada, 1975.

Milton, Earl: *Recollections of a Fallen Sky.* Lethbridge U. Press, Lethbridge, Canada, 1975.

Mireaux, Emile: *Les Poèmes Homériques et l'Histoire Grecque,* 2 Vols. Albin Michel,, Paris, 1948.

Mishra, D. P.: *Studies in the Proto-History of India.* W. H. Patwardhan, Orient Longman, New Delhi, 1971.

Misner, Charles W., K. S. Thorne & J. A. Wheeler: *Gravitation,* W. H. Freeman, San Francisco, 1973.

Mowles, Thomas: "Radiocarbon Dating and Velikovskian Catastrophism," III *Pensée,* Spring-Summer, 19-25, 1973.

Mulcaster, Geoff: Letter on the "Maunder Minimum," II *S.I.S.R.,* December, 31-2, 1977.

Mullen, William: "A Reading of the Pyramid Texts," 3 *Pensée,* No. 1, Winter, 10-17, 1973.

Mullen, William: "The Mesoamerican Record," 4 *Pensée,* No. 4 Fall, 34-44, 1974.

Müller, Rolf: *Der Himmel über dem Menschen der Steinzeit, Astronomie und Mathematik in den Bauten der*

Megalith-kulturen, Springer, Berlin, 1970.

Munch, Peter A.: *Norse Mythology,* Am-Scand. F., New York, 1926.

Munk, W. H. & G. J. F. Mac Donald: *The Rotation of the Earth,* Cambridge U. Press, Cambridge, 1960.

Murdock, George P.: "The Common Denominator of Cultures" in S. C. Washburn & P. C. Jay, eds. *Perspectives on Human Evolution,* Holt, Rinehart & Winston, New York, 1968.

Murray, Bruce C.: "Mercury," 233 *Scientific American,* No. 3, September, 58-69, 1975.

National Academy of Sciences, Astronomy Survey Committee, *Astronomy and Astrophysics for the 1970's,* Washington, 1972.

News Report, excerpts: "Cosmic Violence," National Academy of Sciences. National Research Council, National Academy of Engineering (June-July). In 2 *Pensée,* No. 3, 39, 1972.

Newton, Robert R.: *Ancient Astronomical Observations and the Acceleration of the Earth and Moon,* John Hopkins Press, Baltimore, 1970.

Niederberger, Christine: "Early Sedentary Economy in the Basin of Mexico," 203 *Science,* 4376 January 12, 138, 1979.

Nilsson, Martin P.: *Primitive Time-Reckoning,* Oxford U. Press, London, 1920.

Niniger, Harvey H.: *A Comet Strikes the Earth,* Palm Desert Press, Palm Desert, Calif., 1953.

Niniger, Harvey H.: *Out of the Sky,* Dover Publ., New York, 1959.

Ninkovich, P. & B. C. Heezen: "Santorini Tephra" in *Submarine Geology And Geophysics,* W. F. Whittard & R. Bradshaw, eds. Butterworth, London, 413-52, 1965.

Ninkovitch D. & W. L. Donn: "Explosive Cenozoic volcanism and Climatic Implications," 196 *Science,* January 10, 1231-4, 1977.

Occidens, Stella: "Moon Lore and Eclipse Superstition," 11 *Knowledge,* January 2, 51-2; repr. in Corliss, Compiler, *Strange Universe,* Vol. AI-13-14, Source Book Project, Glen Arm, Md., 1888.

O'Gheoghan, Brendan: "Cosmic Imagery from the Time of Joseph," *S.I.S. Newsletter,* No. 2 July, 8-9, 1978.

O'Keefe, John A.: "The Origin of the Moon and the Core of the Earth" in B. G. Marsden & A. G. W. Cameron: *The Earth-Moon System* Plenum, New York, 224-33, 1966.

O'Keefe, John A.: "After Apollo: Fission Origin of the Moon," 29 *Science and Public Affairs,* November, 26-29, 1973.

O'Keefe, John A.: "The Tektite Problem," 239 *Scientific American,* August, 116, 1978.

Olson, E. A.: "Dating, Relative and Absolute," 5 *Ency. Britannica,* 496-13, 1974.

Olsson, Ingrid V., ed.: *Radiocarbon Variations and Absolute Chronology,* Wiley & Sons, New York, 1970.

Oosterhout, Gerard W. van, & Wouter van der Lek: "Radiocarbon Dates of Samples of Known Age Suggest that the Length of the Solar Year Did Change," unpublished. xerox, 18pp. August, 1972.

Opik, E. J.: "The Martian Surface," 153 *Science,* 3733 July 15, 255-65, 1966.

Otto, Walter: *The Homeric Gods,* M. Hadas, trans., Pantheon, New York, 1954.

Ovid: *Metamorphoses,* Rolfe Humphries, trans., U. of Indiana Press, Bloomington & London, 1971.

Owen, Nancy K.: "The Dresden Codex and Velikovsky's Catastrophe Dates," III *S.I.S.R.* 3, Spring, 88-93, 1979.

Oyama, V. I. et al.: "Venus Lower Atmospheric Composition," 203 *Science,* 23 Feb., 802-5, 1979.

Oyama, V. I. et al.: "Could Paleomagnetism Be Wrong?," 227 *Nature,* August 22, 776, 1970.

Parker, David & Martin Sieff: "Joseph and the Pyramids," letter and reply. I *Newsletter of the Interdisciplinary Study Group,* No. 2 September, 18-19, 1975.

Parker, L. N.: "The Sun," 233 *Scientific American,* No. 3 September, 42-57, 1975.

Paterson, A. M.: "Giordano Bruno's View of the Earth without a Moon," III *Pensée* Winter, 25-6, 1973.

Patten, Donald W.: *The Biblical Flood And the Ice Epoch: A Study in Scientific History,* Pacific Meridian Publ. Co., Seattle, 1966.

Patten, Donald. W. & Windsor, Samuel R.: *The Flood of Noah,* Pacific Meridian Publ., Seattle, n.d.

Patten, Donald W., Ronald R. Hatch & Loren C. Steinhauer: *The Long Day of Joshua and Six Other Catastrophes,* Pacific Meridian Publ., Seattle, 1973.

Patten, Donald. W. & Windsor, Samuel R.: *The Mars-Earth Wars,* Pacific Meridian Publ., Seattle, 1996.

Pauly-Wissowa: *Real-Encyclopädie der Klassischen Alterumswissenschaft,* J. B. Metzlen, Stuttgart, 1894-1919.

Pawley, G. S. & N. Abrahamsen: "Orientation of the Pyramids," 181 *Science,* July 6, 7-8, 1973.

Pawley, G. S. & N. Abrahamsen: "Do the Pyramids Show Continental Drift?" 179 *Science,* March 2, 892-3, 1973.

Payne-Gaposchkin, Cecilia: "Fifty Years of Novae," 82 *Astronomical J.,* No. 9, 665-73, 1977.

Pearce, Joseph Chilton: *The Crack in the Cosmic Egg,* Julian Press, New York, 1971; Pocket Books, New York, 1973.

Pearl, R. M.: "World of Lakes: Meteorite Lakes," 31 *Earth Science,* March 1978, 75-6, 1976.

Pensée (Magazine), ed.: *Velikovsky Reconsidered,* Doubleday, New York, 1976.

Piddington, J. H.: *Cosmic Electrodynamics,* Wiley, New York, 1969.

Plato's Cosmology: The Timaeus of Plato, trans. F. M. Cornford, Harcourt, Brace & Co., New York, 1937.

The Epinomis of Plato, J. Harward, trans. with intro. and notes, Clarendon Press, Oxford, 1928.

Pluche, Noel-Antoine: *Histoire du Ciel, Où l'on Recherche l'Origine de l'Idolâtrie et les Méprises de la*

Philosophie sur la Formation et sur les Influences des Corps Célestes, Veuve Estienne, Paris, Trans. J. B. De Freval as *The History of the Heavens,* Osborn, London, 1740.

Plutarch: trans. *Miscellanies and Essays,* Little Brown, Boston, 1818.

Pollack, James B.: "Mars," 233 *Scientific American,* No. 3 September, 106-117-129, 1975.

Popol Vuh: The Sacred Book of the Ancient Quiche Maya, English version by Delia Goetz and Sylvanus G. Morley from the translation of Adrian Recinos, U. of Oklahoma Press, Norman, 1950.

Posnansky, Arthur: *Tiahuanaco, the Cradle of American Man,* J. J. Augustin, New York, 1945; 2nd ed., 1958.

Possehl, Gregory L.: "The Mohenjo-daro Floods: A Reply," 60 *Amer. Anthrop.,* No. 1, 32-40, 1967.

Price, George M.: *The New Geology,* 1934.

Pritchard, J. B.: *Ancient Near Eastern Texts,* 2nd ed., Princeton, 1955.

Proclus Parmenides nec non Procli Commentarium in Parmenidem, eds., R. Klibansky and C. Labowsky, London,
1953.

Raikes, R. L.: "The Mohenjo-daro Floods," 39 *Antiquity,* 196-203, 1965.

Raikes, R. L.: "Kalibangan: Death from Natural Causes," 42 *Antiquity,* 268-91, 1968.

Raikes, R. L.: "The Ecological Role of Extreme but Predictable Climate Events on Prehistory..." *Ninth International Congress of Pre-Historical and Proto-Historical Sciences* (Nice, France), 15 pp mimeo, 1976.

Ransom, C. J.: "How Stable is the Solar System?" II *Pensée,* May, 16-7, 35, 1972.

Ransom, C. J.: The Age of Velikovsky, *Kronos Press,* Glassboro, N.J., 1976.

Rawlinson, H. G.: *India: A Short Cultural History,* New York, 1965.

Reade, M. G.: "Manna as a Confection," I *S.I.S.R.,* No.2, 9-13, 25, 1977.

Reade, M. G.: "Senmut and Phaeton," II *S.I.S.R.* No. I Autumn, 10-

18, 1977.

Rich, Vera: "The 70-year-old Mystery of Siberia's Big Bang," 274 *Nature,* 207, 1978.

Richardson, Emeline: *The Etruscans: Their Art and Civilization,* U. of Chicago Press, Chicago, 1964.

Richter, N. B.: *The Nature of Comets,* Methuen & Co., London, 1963.

Riley, Carroll J., J. Charles Keller, Campbell W. Pennington & Robert L. Rands: *Man Across the Sea: Problems of Pre-Columbian Contacts,* U. of Texas Press, Austin & London, 1971.

Rilli, Nicola: *Gli Etruschi a Sesto Fiorentino, Tipografia Giuntina,* Firenze, 1964..

Rittmann, A.: *Volcanoes and Their Activity,* John Wiley & Sons, New York, 1962.

Rix, Zvi: "King-Shepherds or Moloch Shepherds?' unpubl. manus. 11 p., 1974.

Rix, Zvi: "The Great Terror," I *Kronos,* No. I Spring, 51-64, 1975.

Rix, Zvi: "Note on the Androgyne Comet," I *S.I.S.R.,* 5, 17-19, 1977.

Robins, Don: "Isotopic Anomalies in Chronometric Science," II *S.I.S.R.,* Spring, 108-10, 1978.

Rock, Fritz: "Die Götter der 7 Planeten in Alten Mexico und die Frage eines Alten Zusammenhanges Toltekischer Building mit einem Altweltlichen Kultursystem," *Anthropos.*

Rose, Lynn: "Could Mars have been an Inner Planet?" with a note by Lynn Rose and Raymond Vaughan, 2 *Pensée,* No. 2 May, 42-3, 1972.

Rose, Lynn: Babylonian Observations of Venus," 3 *Pensée* No. 1 Winter, 18-22, 1973.

Rose, Lynn: "The Length of the Year," 4 *Pensée,* No. 3 Summer, 35-7, 1974.

Rose, Lynn: "Just Plainly Wrong: A Critique of Peter Huber," III *Kronos,* NO. 2 Winter, 102-12, 1977; IV *Kronos,* 2:33-69, 1978.

Rose, Lynn & R. C. Vaughan: "Velikovsky and the Sequence of Planetary Orbits," 4 *Pensée,* No. 3, 27, 1974.

Rowland, B.: *The Art and Architecture of India,* Penguin Books, London, Baltimore, 1953.

Runcorn, S. Keith, Leona Marshall Libby, and Willard F. Libby: "Primeval Melting of the Moon," 270 *Nature,* 22 Dec., 676-81, 1977.

Ruzic, Neil P.: "The Case for Returning to the Moon," *Industrial Research* July, 48-54, 1973.

Sagan, Carl: "The Solar System," in *The Solar System,* W. H. Freemann, San Francisco, 3-11, 1975.

Sanford, Fernando: *Terrestrial Electricity,* Stanford U. Press, Milford, Oxford, U. Press. London, 1931.

Santillana, Giorgio de, & Hertha von Dechend: *Hamlet's Mill: An Essay On Myth and the Frame of Time,* Gambit Inc., Boston, 1969.

Sarvajna, D. K.: "Orbits Of Charged Bodies," 6 *Astrophysics and Space Science,* 258-62, 1970.

Schaeffer, Claude F. A.: *Stratigraphie Comparée et Chronologie de l'Asie Occidentale,* Oxford U. Press, London, 1948.

Schaeffer, Claude F. A.: *Ugaritica V,* Imprimerie Nationale, Paris,

1968.

Schaeffer, O. A., ed.: *Potassium-Argon Dating,* Springer-Verlag, Berlin, New York, 1969.

Schindewolf, Otto H.: "Neocatastrophism?" 114 *Zeitschrift Deutsche Geol. Ges.,* No. 2, 430-45, 1963; trans. in 2 *Catastrophist Geol.* No. 2 December, 9-21, 1977.

Schultz, Gwen: *Ice Age Lost,* Doubleday Anchor, New York, 1974.

Semple, Ellen C.: *The Geography of the Mediterranean Region: Its Relation to Ancient History,* Constable, London, 1932.

Shafer, R.: *Ethnography of Ancient India,* Harrassowitz, Wiesbaden, 1954.

Shapiro, Irwin I.: "Resonance Rotation of Venus," 157 *Science* July 28, 423-5, 1967.

Shelly-Pearce, Derek P.: "The Catastrophic Substructure of the Samson and Delilah Myth," *S.I.S. Newsletter* No. 2 July, 9-11, 1978.

Sherrerd, Chris: "Venus' Circular Orbit," 2 *Pensée,* No. 2 May, 43, 1972.

Sieff, Alvin, et al.: "Structure of the Atmosphere of Venus up to 110 Kilometers," 203 *Science* 23 Feb., 787-90, 1979.

Sieveking, Gale: "The Migration of the Megaliths," in Edward Bacon: *Vanished Civilizations,* McGraw Hill Book Co., London, 1963.

Siever, Raymond: "The Earth," 233 *Scientific American,* No. 3, 82-91, 1975.

Simpson, John A.: "Journey to Jupiter," 66 *U. of Chicago Magazine,* November-December, 6-11, 1973.

Simpson, G. G.: *Life of The Past,* Yale U. Press, 1953.

Simpson, G. G.: "Uniformitarianism, An Inquiry into Principle, Theory, and Method in Geohistory and Biohistory," 43-96 in M. K. Hecht and W. C. Steere, *Essays in Evolution and Genetics in Honor of Theodosius Dobzhansky,* Appleton-Century-Crofts, New York, 1953.

Slosman, Albert: *Le Grand Cataclysme,* Laffont, Paris, Stockholm, 1976.

Sugden, David: *Glaciers and Landscapes,* E. Arnold, London, 1976.

Suhr, George: *The Spinning Aphrodite,* Helios Books, New York, 1969.

Sullivan, Walter: *Continents in Motion,* McGraw Hill, New York, 1947.

Sutherland, Carter: "China's Dragon," 4 *Pensée,* No. 1 Winter, 47-50, 1973-4.

Sykes, N. J. G.: "An Investigation of Isotope Decay Constancy," III *S.I.S.R.,* No. 2 Autumn, 43-5, 1978.

Tacitus : *De Germania,* trans., George Stuart, ed., Eldredge & Brother, Philadelphia, 1885.

Talbott, David N.: "Saturn: Universal Monarch and Dying God," *Report,* Research Communications Network, Portland, Oregon, 1977.

Talbott, George R.: "The Cabots, the Lowells and the Temperature of Venus." IV *Kronos,* 2:2-25, 1978.

Talbott, Stephen: "Mystery of the Radiohalos," Res. Communications Network (February 10), Portland, Oregon, 3-6, 1977.

Temple, Robert K. G.: *The Sirius Mystery,* Sidgwick and Jackson, London, 1976.

Thom, Alexander: *Megalithic Sites in Britain,* Clarendon Press, Oxford, 1967.

Thom, René: "Topological Models in Biology," *Topology,* No. 2, 1968.

Thom, René: "Catastrophe Theory," 270 *Nature,* 658, and 270, *letters,* 381-4, 1977.

Thomas, P., et al.: "Origin of the Grooves on Phobos," 273 *Nature,* 282-4, 1978.

Thompson, J.: *Maya History and Religion,* U. of Oklahoma Press, Norman, 1970.

Thompson, J.: *Rise and Fall of the Mayan Civilization,* U. of Oklahoma Press, Norman, 1977.

Thompson, Win J. III: "Catastrophic Origins for Asteroids and Rings of Saturn," 13 *Creation Res. C.,* 82, 1976-77.

"Scientists Protest denial of research on plague origins in space," Times Higher Education Supplement, *The Times* of London, April 14, 1978; in Corliss, Compiler, A Source Book Project, *Strange Artifacts* MES-006, Glen Arm (Md.)

Turekian, K. ed.: *The Late Cenozoic Glacial Ages,* Yale U. Press, New Haven, 1971.

Uman, M. A.: *Lightning,* McGraw Hill, New York, 1969.

Umgrove J. H. F.: *The Pulse of the Earth,* Nijhoff, The Hague, 1947.

Underwood, Guy: *The Pattern of the Past,* Abacus ed. London, 1969.

Urey, Harold: "Meteorites and the Moon," 147 *Science* March 12, 1262-5, 1965.

Urey, Harold: "Cometary Collisions and Geological Periods," letter, 242 *Nature,* March 2, 32-3, 1973.

Vaihinger, Hans: *The Philosophy of "As If",* Harcourt Brace & Co. Inc., New York, 1924.

Vail, Isaac N.: *Selected Works,* Annular Publications, Santa Barbara, Calif., 1972.

Van Allen, James A.: "Interplanetary Particles and Field," 233 *Scientific American,* No. 3 September, 160-73, 1976.

Van Buitenen, J. A. B.: "Manu, Ut-Napischtim, and Noah," *U. of Chicago Magazine,* Winter, 10-3, 1975.

Van Deventer, T. R.: "Holocene Woodlands in the Southwestern Deserts," 198 *Science,* 182-92, 1977.

Van Seters, John: 50 *J. Egyptian Archeology,* 13-23, 1964.

Velikovsky, Immanuel: "Theses for the Reconstruction of Ancient History," *Scripta Academica Hierosolymitana,* New York, 1945.

Velikovsky, Immanuel: "Cosmos Without Gravitation," *Scripta Academica Hierosolymitana,* New York, 1946.

Velikovsky, Immanuel: *Worlds in Collision,* MacMillan (April), Doubleday (June), New York, 1950.

Velikovsky, Immanuel: "Hoerbiger's Theory," *New York Times,* Sect. IV, p. 8, col. 6 (June 25), 1950.

Velikovsky, Immanuel: "Answer to Professor Stewart," 200 *Harper's Magazine* (June), 63-6, 1951.

Velikovsky, Immanuel: *Ages in Chaos: A Reconstruction of Ancient History from the Exodus to King Akhnaton,* Doubleday, New York, 1952.

Velikovsky, Immanuel: *Earth in Upheaval,* Doubleday, New York, 1955.

Velikovsky, Immanuel: *Oedipus and Akhnaton: Myth and History,* Doubleday, New York, 1960.

Velikovsky, Immanuel: "Venus -- A Youthful Planet," XLI *Yale Scientific Magazine,* No. 7 (April), 8-11. Lloyd Motz: "Velikovsky -- A Rebuttal," Immanuel Velikovsky: "A Rejoinder to Motz", 1967.

Velikovsky, Immanuel: "When was the Lunar Surface Last Molten?" 2 *Pensée,* No. 2 (May), 19-20, 1972.

Velikovsky, Immanuel: "On Decoding Hawkins' 'Stonehenge Decoded,'" 1972, 2 *Pensée,* No. 2, 24-28.

Velikovsky, Immanuel: "Astronomy and Chronology," 3 *Pensée,* 2 (Spring-Summer), 38-40, 1973.

Velikovsky, Immanuel: "Metallurgy and Chronology." 3 *Pensée,* 3 (Fall), 5-9, 1973.

Velikovsky, Immanuel: "Eclipses in Ancient Times." 3 *Pensée,* 3(Fall), 20-1, 1973.

Velikovsky, Immanuel: "The Orientation of the Pyramids," 3 *Pensée* , No. 1 (Winter), 17, 1973.

Velikovsky, Immanuel: "Earth without a Moon," 3 *Pensée* , 1 (Winter), 25-6, 1973.

Velikovsky, Immanuel: "The Lion Gate at Mycenae," 3 *Pensée* , 1 (Winter), 31-2, 1973.

Velikovsky, Immanuel: "Tiryns," 4 *Pensée* , No. 1 (Winter), 45-6, 1973.

Velikovsky, Immanuel: "Venus' Atmosphere," 4 *Pensée*, 4 (Winter), 31-6, 1973-74.

Velikovsky, Immanuel: "My Challenge to Coventional Science," 4 *Pensée*, 2 (Spring), 10-4, 1974.

Velikovsky, Immanuel: "The Scandal of Enkomi," 4 *Pensée* 5 21-23, 1974-75.

Velikovsky, Immanuel: *Peoples of the Sea,* Doubleday, New York, 1977.

Velikovsky, Immanuel: "Khima and Kesil," III *Kronos,* (Summer), 19-23, 1978.

Velikovsky, Immanuel: *Ramses II,* Doubleday, New York, 1978.

Venturi, Franco: *L'Antiquitá Svelata e l'Idea Del Progresso in N. A. Boulanger, 1722-1759,* La Terza, Bari, Italy, 1947.

Vermeule, Emily: "The Promise of Thera: A Bronze Age Pompeii." CCXX *The Atlantic Monthly,* December, 83-4, 89-94, 1967.

Vico, Giovanni Battista: *The New Science,* trans. T. G. Bergin and Max H. Fish, 1937; *Scienza Nuova,* A. Miliani, Padova; Doubleday, Garden City, N.Y., 1961.

Viemeister, Peter E.: *The Lightning Book,* Doubleday, New York, 1961.

Vikentiev, V.: "The God 'Hemen,'" *Recueil de Travaux Faculté des Letters,* Université Egyptienne, Cairo, 1930.

Vilks, Gustavs & Peta J. Mudie: "Early Deglaciation of the Labrador Shelf," 202 *Science,* December 15, 1181-3, 1978.

Visher, S. S.: "Tropical Cyclones and The Dispersal of Life from

Island to Island in the Pacific," *Smithsonian Institution Report,* Washington, D.C., 1925.

Vita-Finzi, Claudio: *The Mediterranean Valleys: Geological Changes in Historical Times,* The University Press,
Cambridge, 1969.

Vita-Finzi, Claudio: *Recent Earth History,* John Wiley & Sons, Halsted Press Division, New York, 1973.

Vitaliano, Dorothy B.: "Plinian Eruptions, Earthquakes, and Santorin. A Review," *Acta of First International Scientific Congress on the Volcano of Thera,* 1969.

Vitaliano, Dorothy B.: *Legends of the Earth: Their Geologic Origins,* Indiana U. Press, Bloomington & London, 1973.

Vitaliano, C. & D.: "Volcanic Tephra on Crete," 78 *Amer. J. of Archaeology,* No. 1 January, 19-24, 1974.

Vsekhsviatskii, S. K.: (1962), "Comets, Small Bodies, and Problems of the Solar System," 74 Publications of the Astronomical Society of the Pacific, 106-15.

Vsekhsviatskii, S. K.: "New Evidence for the Eruptive Origin of Comets and Meteoric Matter," *AJ Soviet Astronomy,* No. 11 (November-December), 473-84; trans. from 44 *Astronomicheskii Zhurnal,* (May-June), 595-609, 1967.

Vsekhsviatskii, S. K.: "The Origin and Evolution of the Comets and other Small Bodies in the Solar System," II *Kronos,* (November), 46-54.

Wainwright, G. A.: "The Teresh, the Etruscans and Asia Minor," 9 *Anatolian Studies,* 197, 1959.

Wallis Max K.: "Comet-like Interaction of Venus with the Solar wind," 3 *Cosmic Electrodynamics,* (April), 45-59, 1972.

Warlow, P.: "Geomagnetic Reversals," II *J. of Physics,* 2107-30, 1978.

Watson, David L.: *Scientists are Human,* Kegan Paul, London, 1938.

Weber, Joseph: "Evidence for Discovery of Gravitational Radiation," 22 *Physical Review Letters,* No. 24. (June 16), 1320-1324, 1969.

Webre, A. L. & P. H. Hess: *The Age of Cataclysm,* G. Putnam's Sons New York, 1976.

Weinstein, G. A. & H. N. Michael: "Radiocarbon dates from Akrotiri, Thera," 20 *Archaeometry,* ,203-9, 1978.

Wells, Dr. Calvin: *Bones, Bodies and Diseases,* Praeger, New York, 1964.

Westropp, Hodder & C. Staniland Wake: *Ancient Symbol Worship : Influence of the Phallic Idea in the Religions*

of Antiquity, J. W. Bouton, New York, 1875.

Whiston, William: *Astronomical Principles of Religion, Natural and Revealed,* London, 1717.

Whiston, William: *New Theory of the Earth,* Tooke, 3rd ed., London, 1722.

White, J. P. & J. F. O'Connell: "Australian Prehistory," 203 *Science,* (January 5), 21-8, 1979.

Whitehead, Alfred N.: *Science and the Modern World,* New York, 1925.

Whitehouse David & Ruth: *Archaeological Atlas of the World,* Freeman, San Francisco, 1975.

Wilkins, Harold T.: *Mysteries of Ancient South America,* Citadel Press,

Secaucus, N.J., 1956.

Wilson, A. T.: "Origin of Petroleum and the Composition of the Lunar Maria," *Nature* (October 6), 11-13, 1962.

Wilson, Clifford: *Crash Go the Chariots,* Lancer, New York, 1972.

Wilson, J. Tuzo: "Static or Mobil Earth: The Current Scientific Revolution," 112 *Amer. Philos. Soc.,* No. 5 (October 17), 309-20, 1968.

Winchester, James H.: "Safe Havens for Sea Life," in *Marvels and Mysteries of the World Around Us,* Reader's Digest Assn., Pleasantville, New York, 1972.

Wissler, C. and H. J. Spinder: "The Pawnee Human Sacrifice to the Morningstar," 16 *Amer. Museum J.,* 49-56, 1916.

Wolfe, Irving: "The Catastrophic Substructure of Shakespeare's Anthony and Cleopatra'," I *Kronos.* No. 3, 31-45; I No. 4 37-54, 1975-76.

Wolfe, Irving: "'Worlds in Collision' and the Prince of Denmark," II *S.I.S.R.* (Spring), 104-8, 1978.

Wolfe, John H.: "Jupiter," 233 *Scientific American,* No. 3 (September), 130-141, 1975.

Wood, John A.: "The Moon," in *The Solar System,* Freeman, San Francisco, 69-77, 1975.

Woronow, Alexander: "Origin of the Martian Chaotic Terrains," 178 *Science,* (November 10), 649-50, 1972.

Wright, G. Frederick: "The Idaho Find," 11 *Amer. Antiquarian* 379-81, 1889; repr. in Corliss, W. R. Compiler, *Ancient Man: A Handbook of Puzzling Artifacts,* Source Book Projects, 458-60, Glen. Arm., Md., 1978.

York, Derek: "Lunar Rocks and Velikovsky's Claims," 2 *Pensée,* No. 2 (May) 18-19, 1972.

Young, A. T.: "Are the Clouds of Venus Sulfuric Acid?" 18 *Icarus,* 564-82, 1973.

Young, Andrew & Louise: "Venus," 233 *Scientific American* No. 3 (September), 70-81, 1975.

Zahan, Dominique: "Etudes sur la Cosmologie des Dogons du Soudan Francais," 80 *Notes Africaines,* 108-11, 1958.

Zammit, Sir T.: "The Prehistoric Remains of the Maltese Islands," IV *Antiquity,* 55-9, 1930.

Zeuner, Friedrich E.: *Dating the Past,* London, 1946.

Zeylik, B. S. & E. Y. Scytmuratova: "Giant Impact Structure in Central Kazakhstan and its Magma and Ore-Controlling Significance," *Dok. Akad. Nauk, SSSR,* 218:1, 167-70, 1974.

Ziegler, Jerry: *YHWH,* Star Publishers, Morton, Illinois, 1977.

Ziegler, Jerry: *Indra Girt by Maruts,* unpubl. Manuscript, 1978.

Zimmer, Heinrich: "Myths and Symbols in Indian Art and Civilization," ed. by Joseph Campbell, Bollingen Foundation, Washington D.C., 1946.

Zubrin, Robert: *Entering Space: Creating a Space-Faring Civilization,* Putnam, New York, 1999.

Zubrin, Robert; Wagner, Richard: *The Case for Mars,* Simon & Schuster, New York, 1996.

About the Author:

Alfred de Grazia (b 1919, Chicago, Illinois, USA). After receiving a PhD from the University of Chicago, he taught political sociology and social invention at the University of Minnesota, Brown University, Stanford University, New York University, and the University of Bergamo, lecturing also at various universities in the USA and abroad. He has been continuously active also as educator and consultant, soldier, politician and playwright. His personal archive on the web (www.grazian-archive.net) holds presently about 500 megabytes and counts some two million visits annually, including hundreds of his works on political science and social psychology, quantavolution, world governance, theatre, poetry, autobiography, and warfare. With Jill Oppenheim de Grazia (deceased), he fathered and raised seven children. He lives mainly on the island of Naxos, Greece, with his wife, the French novelist and translator, Ami Hueber de Grazia, and in the rural country south of Paris, while maintaining his connection with the University of Bergamo (Italy) as Professor in the Department of Mathematics, Statistics, Computer Science and Applications. An abridgement of his Quantavolution Series is now available with an introduction by Ami de Grazia under the title of *The Way of Q* (Eumetron, Naxos, GR). He produced two films from his plays *Sisyphus* and *The Gene of Hope*. In 2009, he published his book proposing a 51st State solution to the Israel-Palestine strife, entitled *The American State of Canaan* (Metron Publications.)

Appreciation and Acknowledgement

The author has quoted by name scores of scholars and scientists to whom he wishes here to give general acknowledgements and thanks. He has drawn especially upon the facilities of the Claude Schaeffer Library and CAARI at Nicosia, Cyprus; the work of Israel Finkelstein and the Archaeological Circle at the University of Tel Aviv, the Velikovsky Archives at the Hebrew University of Jerusalem and the Mudd Library Archives at Princeton University, the books and the assistance of Kamal Salibi of the American university at Beirut, the remarkable journalism of *Der Spiegel* Magazine, and the archival genius and personal advice of Ian Tresman of the Society for Interdisciplinary Studies at London.

Endnotes

1. It is fairly safe to assume that an ancient date is approximate and relative, but some are more so than others. I often use the sign (~) to designate an approximation, as here, and I often use the minus sign (-) as here to signify "before Christ" (whose birth year is actually somewhere around "0," that is, "~- or +0") instead of BC, B.C., BCE, or B.C.E. Dates are especially messy questions in this book. For instance, calling centuries by a name referring to the preceding or succeeding numeral has balked me all of my life; hence I often now call the Nineteenth Century "the Eighteen Hundreds," and the Seventh Century B.C.E., "the -600's," and so on. There is nothing I can do about the dates going backwards in this book, because they are referred to as the "late seventh century" when they mean "~-630 to 600." So to understand a date often required several boggles of mind.

2. These works are listed in the Bibliography. I suggest perusing *The Cosmic Heretics* at first. The books are on the Web, all of them.

3. *Festschrift für Claude Schaeffer,* Neukirchener Verlag, 1980.

3. His works are listed in the Bibliography and on CD. Throughout this book our footnote references, which are numbered consecutively from first to last, are most biref, but are more fully indited in the Bibliography. My related works are *The Velikovsky Affair, Cosmic Heretics,* etc.

4. De Grazia, *Disastrous Love Affair...,* 59*ff.*

5. Cf. Martin Sieff on the end of the Bronze Age and Peter James on "Centuries of Darkness."

6. The author thanks Anne-Marie de Grazia for managing the study, Richard Stern and Argeo Magi of the University of Bergamo and Professor Stefan Stefanov of the Dept. Of Physics, University of Sofia, Bulgaria, for his analysis. The study and its reports are continuing.

7. *Copyright © 2001 by Alfred de Grazia*

8. Schaeffer, Claude F. A., *Stratigraphie Comparée et Chronologie de l'Asie Occidentale (III. et II. millénaires),* Oxford University Press, London, 1948.

9. 1928, quoted by Spanuth, *176.*

10. *Science,* April 3rd, 1936.

11. See Bibliography for their works.

12. Velikovsky, Patten and de Grazia are among those who cite these passages. Isaiah describes a holosphere of quantavolutionary effects.

13. *Textes Taoistes,* C. De Harlez trans. 1891. *Cf* Velikovsky, *Worlds in Collision,* 256.

14. Cited in Velikovsky, *Worlds in Collision,* p.142.

15. *The Library,* Epitome 2.

16. From the Legge Edition of the Chinese Classics, quoted by Velikovsky in *Worlds in Collision,* p.235.

17. Cf. *Metamorphoses.* Also, Fasti, Frazer trans. 1931, II, *II,* 489*ff.*

18. *Nature* 434, 14 Apr. 05, 873.

19. Http://www.universetoday.com/am/publish/planet_dragging_star.ht

20. See the works of Vladimir Damgov in the Bibliography.

21. *Proc. Nat. Acad. Sci.,* 30/1/01.

22. *Astronomy,* 2 Feb. 2005

23. *Cf.* Spedicato, 1999.

24. Baltensperger, Walter: "On the geographical displacement of poles after close passage of a body of planetary size," (abstract) *SIS,* 1, 2002.

25. Warlow, P. (1978), "Geomagnetic Reversals," *II J. of Physics,* 2107/30.

26. Barbiero, Flavio: "Changes in the rotation axis of Earth after asteroid/cometary impacts and their geological effects," (abstract) *SIS,* 1, 2002.

27. *Oceanographia Sinica,* II:1, from an unpublished note of I. Velikovsky.

28. Damgov, Vladimir: "A megaquantum model, instabilities and chaos," (abstract) *SIS,* 1, 2002.

29. Discussed in L. Stecchini, "Astronomical Theory," de Grazia, ed. *The Velikovsky Affair.*

30. *Cf.* Stecchini, *op. cit.*

31. Stecchini, *op. cit.*

32. Greenberg, Lewis M., & Sizemore, Warner B.: "Jerusalem - City of Venus," *III Kronos,* N° 3, 56/90, Spring, 1978.

33. *Cf.* their works by name in the Bibliography, and, too, his book, *Stargazers and Gravediggers,* and my work, *Cosmic Heretics.*

34. All cited in the Bibliography.

35. The author wishes to thank CAARI (The Cyprus American Archaeological Research Institute) for their hospitality in Cyprus and permission to reproduce the letter of Professor Schaeffer.

36. See the Bibliography for his published works.

37. A summary of the book by Geoffrey Gammon is to be found in the *Review of the Society for Interdisciplinary Studies,* (UK), V3 (1980-1).

38. Velikovsky's *Oedipus and Akhnaton* is a detective work of genius, superior to the best of detective fiction, such as Conan Doyle and Simenon wrote. It is most likely true as well.

39. p .192

40. Spanuth, p.152

41. Spanuth, p.153

42. Chang, Kenneth: "Composition of a comet poses puzzle for scientists," *New York Times,* September 7, 2005.

43. *Quaternary International* 121 (2004), 53-65, "Tephrostratigraphy and tephrochronology in the Philippi peat basin, Macedonia, Northern Hellas (Greece): Karen S. Seymour, Kimon Christanis, Antonis Bouzinos, Stephanos Papazisimous, George Papatheodorous, Ernesto Moranc, Gerge Denesc, Department of Geography, Concordia University, Montreal.

44. These authorities were gathered by Spanuth, *op. cit.*

45. Åström, P.: "Continuity, discontinuity, catastrophe, nucleation - some remarks on terminology," *The Crisis Years: the 12th Century B.C.,* Dubuque, 1992.

46. Weinstein, James: "The collapse of the Egyptian empire in the Southern Levant," *The Crisis Years: the 12th Century B.C.,* Ward, Wm A. And Joukovsky, M.S., eds, Dubuque, 1992.

47. Hallo, William W.: "From bronze age to iron age in Western Asia: defining the problem," *The Crisis Years: the 12th Century B.C.,* Ward, Wm A. And Joukovsky, M.S., eds, Dubuque, 1992.

48. *Chaos and Creation* carries my charts on conventional and quantavolutional ages.

50 Karageorghis, V., Muhly, J.D.: *Cyprus at the Close of the Late Bronze Age,* A.G. Leventis Foundation, Nicosia, 1984. Karageorghis, V.: E: "End of Late Bronze Age in Cyprus," *CS HIS.* Karageorghis, V.: "Cyprus," *The Cambridge Ancient History: The expansion of the Greek world, eighth to sixth century B.C.,* Boardman, J., Hammond, N.G.L. eds, Cambridge University Press, Cambridge. Karageorghis, V., Demas, M.: Acts of the International Archaeological Symposium "Cyprus between the Orient and the Occident," Department of Antiquities, Nicosia, 1986.

50. Luigi Cavalli-Sforza: *Genes, Peoples and Languages,* University of California Press, Berkeley, 2000.

51. Bryan Sykes, *The Seven Daughters of Eve,* Bantam Press, 2001.

52. Childe, Gordon: *The Dawn of European Civilization,* 6th ed., Routledge, London, 1957.

53. Muhly, J.D., "The role of the sea-peoples in Cyprus during the LC III period," *The Crisis Years: the 12th Century B.C.,* Ward, Wm A. and Joukovsky, M.S., eds, Dubuque, 1992.

54. Gordon, Cyrus: "The Mediterranean Synthesis," *The Crisis Years: the 12th Century B.C.,* Ward, Wm A. and Joukovsky, M.S., eds, Dubuque, 1992.

55. Thucydides: *History of the Peloponnesian Wars,* Hobbes transl., http://oll.libertyfund.org/Texts/Hobbes0123/Works

56. Http://www.kronia.com/library/journal/method.txt *Cf.* Martian Metamorphoses: the Planet Mars in Ancient Myth and Religion.

57. In his books, *Chaos* and *Firmament*. He also publishes a newsletter on the web as www.Chaos-Firmament.com

58. *Cf.* Bibliography, of which *The Mars-Earth Wars* (1992) is most pertinent here.

59. In *Chaos and Creation*.

60. Hoyle, Fred and Wickramasinghe, N.C.: "Does epidemic disease come from Space?" *New Scientist,* Nov. 11, 1977.

61. www.astrobiology.com/news Carnegie Institute press release, Oct. 4, 2005

62.

63. Ackerman, *Chaos,* 206

64. Bellamy, *Moons,* p.84

65. Velikovsky, *Ramses II.,* 221-47

66. Heide, *Meteorites,* p.44

67. *Ibid.* p.16

68. Cook, *Prehistory...*

69. *Sci. American Suppl.,* 1876, p.510

70. Bellamy, in de Grazia, *Lately Tortured Earth,* p.131

71. Bellamy, *Life Hist.,* p.196

72. In *Ancient Celtic Mining in America,* (5th International Mining History Congress, September 2000, Milos, Greece), P.281

73. Http://geology.about.com

74. *Ramses II.,* p.225

75. *Ibid.,* p.234-5

76. Velikovsky, Immanuel (1973a), "Metallurgie and Chronologie," 3 *Pensée,* N°3 (Fall), 5?9

77. See fn52 of Ackerman's *Firmament*

78. *Indian J. Hist. Sci.* 39, 1, 2004, 11-49 INSA, New Delhi

79. Simon and Schuster Publ., 1997, p.200

80. Source NASA, http://images.spaceref.com.news.2004-20004.06.20.R1401823.gif and ibid.views.html_pid'13176

81. *New Scientist,* Sept. 24, 2005

82. *Chaos and Creation,* pp.210-6

83. *Missile of the Creator,* 1979, privately published; revised in mss unpublished as "Earth's Encounter with a Comet" (1980's)

84. Juergens, Ralph: "Electrical Discharges and the Transmutation of Elements," 1 *Penséo,* N°3, Summer, 15 6, 1971

85. *Materials,* Elsevier, 45, 2000, 353-63

86. Ackerman, *Firmament,* p.134

87. *Ibid.,* p.129

88. Http://www.scientificamerican.com/2000/0900issue/0900sci.cit5.html

89. Http://www.tau.ac.il/humanities/archaeology/megiddon/chronology.html

90. Finkelstein, Israel: *The Bible Unearthed,* pp 119-20

91. Finkelstein, *Ibid.,* pp280-1

92. *Ibid.,* p134-5

93. *Cf.* Chapter 17 on Helice, below

94. Finkelstein, Israel, *Ibid.,* p135

95. *Ibid.,* p203

96. *Ibid.*

97. *Ibid.,* p118

98. *Ibid.,* p102-3

99. *Ibid.,* p107

100. *Ibid.,* Chapter Four

101. *Ibid.,* p101

102. *Cf.* www.sacred-texts.com

103. Ginzberg, *Legends of the Jews*

104. This voluminous work was published by Forrest himself and finely bravely republished by the Society for Interdisciplinary Studies on its web site by Ian Tresman (q.v.)

105. Pp294-7

106. De Grazia, Alfred: "Palaetiology of Fear and Memory," in *Recollections of a Fallen Sky,* Symposium 1974, Earl milton, ed., Lethbridge University press, Lethbridge, Canada, 1978

107. A useful map positioning Elephantine is at http://www.specialtyinterests.net/map_nile2nubia.html

108. Finkelstein, Israel: *The Bible Unearthed,* p287

109. *Ibid.,* p281

110. P.v of Acknowledgements

111. *Ibid.,* pp1-2

112. *Ibid.,* p3

113. *HBI,* 87-8, I claim that the Ark was a producer of static electricty, a "scorcher," in *God's Fire*

114. "La Mecca, la Ka'aba e le Origini del Islam," p295 in Emilio Spedicato e Adalberto Notarpietro, eds, *Nuove Scenari sulla Evoluzione del Sistema Solare: Consequenze sulla Storia della Terra et del' Uomo,"* Università degli Studi di Bergamo, 7-9 June, 1999

115. *H of BI,* p32-3

116. A forthcoming publication by the polymath Bergamo mathematician, Professor Emilio Spedicato, traces intricately the probable path of Phaethon.

117. p17

118. John Ackerman: *Newsletter,* www.firmament-chaos.com, January, 2003

119. "Effet Mars," les Sceptiques du Québec, http://www.sceptiques.qc

120. Mullen, William C.: "The Agenda of the Milesian School: the post-catastrophic paradigm shift in Ancient Greece," privately published.

121. "Cultural novelties..."

122. *Encyclopedia Britannica,* "Gods, mythology and world view."

123. See geological sketch map of the Monti Vulsini and satellite photo of Lake Bolsena.

124. I am using a 1-th century translation

125. Uman book, *All About Lightning,* pp145-9, and C.C. Delwiche, "The Nitrogen Cycle," *Sci. American,* 223:3 137-46, Sept. 1970

126. Cater, Joseph H., 1998, *The Ultimate Reality,* Pomeroy, WA: Health Research, 83ff

127. *Enea nel Lazio,*1981, p92

128. Supplied in personal conversation at Orvieto

129. *Per. Mineral,* 1987, 56, 89-110

130. "Dating the Aegean Bronze Age without radiocarbon," 20 *Archaeometry,*(1978), p212

131. *Worlds in Collision,* p238-9

132. *Legends of the Jews,* Vol. VI, p280

133. *Enea nel Lazio: archaeologia e Mito,* (Milano: Fratelli Palombi, 1981), p5

134. Ogilvie, R. L., *Early Rom and the Etruscans,* New York: Humanities Press, 1976, 16

135. *Enea nel Lazio,* p107

136. *Ibid.,* quoting Alessandro Guidi, p94

137. *Ibid.,* p88

138. *Ibid.,* p92

139. *Ibid.,* p157

140. *Ibid.,* p158

141. *Ibid.,* p157-8

142. Somella, P., *Rediconti 44: Atti di Pontificio Accademia di Archaeologia,* (1971-2), 47-74; *Enea nel Lazio,* p157-8, 172-7

143. *Aeneid III,* 94-6 (Humphries trans.), 64-66

144. *Histories I,* 94, Penguin Edition, 1954, 80-1

145. Claude F.A. Schaeffer, *Stratigraphie Comparée et Chronologies de l'Asie Occidentale* (London: Oxford U. Press, 1948), p7

146. J.W. Mayor, Jr summarizes the work of Marinatos and Galanopoulos in "A mighty Bronze Age Volcanic Explosion," *XII Oceanus* (Woods Hole, Mass.), 3 April 1966, and *Voyage to Atlantis* (New York: Putnam's Sons, 1969). Christos Doumas summarizes the latest "official" theory of the succession of events at Thera in *Antiquity XL* VIII (1974), 110-15, plates. Also, *cf.* D. Ninkovich and B.C. Heezen, "Santorini Tephra," Colston Research Society Papers, 17 (1965), p415-53; the papers of J. Keller, D.L. Page, and C. And D. Vitaliano in *Acta of the First International Scientific Congress on the Volcano in Thera, Greece,* 1969 (Athens, 1971); and C. And D. Vitaliano, "Volcanic Tephra on Crete," *Amer. Jrnl Archaeology,* Vol.78, n°1, Jan. 1974, pp19-24

147. *IX Anatolian Studies* (1969)

148. This and the following quotations are from pp 16-17, 348 and 325 of H. Schliemann, *Troy and Its Remains* (1875)

149. *Ibid.,* p330. Schaeffer, *op. cit.,* 223-4 claims that he saw no evidence of flame-exposure (feu d'un incendie) on the objects exhibited at the Berlin Museum from the treasure, and suggests chemical fusion. Also, radiative heat would be an alternative to "chemical fusion" if one must be sought.

150. Schliemann, *op. cit.,* p333

151. *Ibid.,* p334-5

152. *Ibid.,* p340

153. *Ibid.,* p302; *cf.* p347. The walls and gates of ancient cities had usually an orientation to the cardinal direction points. The "dealignment" of successive Trojan escarpments is itself cause for suspecting and investigating a possible reorientation of the hill.

154. Communication of March 7, 1984. Bruce V. Ettling and Mark F. Adams accelerated combustion of woods, cotton cloth, and plastics by hydrocarbons (fuel oil, gasoline, etc.) and discovered by gas chromatography that accelerate hydrocarbons could be distinguished from the natural hydrocarbons in the char. ("The Study of Accelerate Resudies in Fire Remains," N.D. offprint, Washington State University, College of Engineering Research).

155. Allan O. Kelly and Frank D'Achille, *Target: Earth, The Role of Large Meteors in Earth Science* (Carlsbad, Calif.: the authors, 1953), p192

156. *Loc. cit.*

157. Blegen, *Troy and the Trojans* (London: Thames and Hudson, 1963), pp161-4. Troy II g is presently dated to ca 2200 BC by the conventional chronology.

158. *Ibid.,* p69. There is a contradiction here with other reports as to how many bones were found

159. *Ibid.,* p70

160. *Op. cit.,* p17

161. It is well to stress that an influential school of experts on Troy consider the Trojan War(s) to have been essentially a struggle for the command of the Dardanelles, through which heavy commerce funneled. *Cf.* Emile Mireaux, *Les Poèmes Homériques et l'Histoire Grecque,* 2 vol. (Paris; Albin Michel, 1948), ch. II, XIV, *et passim.* A strategic city that had to be put to good economic use might be thoroughly destroyed, short-sightedly, and another later on built on the site. Even if this were true of Troy VII, would it also have been true of the earliest Troys, a habitual shortsightedness?

162. Chandler, *loc. cit.*

163. Rupert Fornix, *Krakatoa* (1964)

164. Communication from Prof. Jorg Keller, Institute of Mineralogy, Univ. Of Freiburg, June, 1974

165. Israel M. Isaacson (E.M.S.), "Some Preliminary Remarks about Thera and Atlantis," *Kronos I,* 2 (Summer, 1975) pp93ff

166. *Iliad* (Latimeria trans., 1951), p405

167. "Lightning and Fire Ecology in Africa," *Proceedings Annual Tall Timbers Fire Ecology Conference* (Apr. 22-23, 1971), pp473-511, 475

168. Quoted by I. Velikovsky, *Worlds in Collision* (N.Y., 1950) p218

169. Fornix, *op. cit.,* pp73, 97, *et passim*

170. A. Rittmann, *Volcanoes and their Activity,* trans. By E.A. Vincent (1962) pp12-3, 218

171. *Worlds in Collision,* especially "The Hail of Stones," "Naphta," "Ambrosia," "Rivers of Milk and Honey," "Samples from the Planets."

172. Harold Urey, "Cometary Collisions and Geological periods," 242 *Nature* (March 2, 1973), P32; Velikovsky, *Earth in Upheaval* (1955), pp147-53

173. *Troy* (Princeton NJ: Princeton U. Press) Vol 1; pp325, 363

174. *Ibid.,* p373

175. *Cf. Worlds in Collision,* pp48-51, "The Red World"

176. *Cf.* Nicola Rilli, *Gli Etruschi a Sesto Fiorentino* (Firenze: Tipograpfia Giuntina, 1964). Also, Michel D. Coe, R.A. Diehl, and M. Stulver, "Olmec Civilization, Veracruz, Mexico: Dating of the San Lorenzo Phase," 155 *Science* (1967), 1399-1401 (the authors report that many pieces of asphalt litter the excavated ruin level). F. Wendorf, *et al.,* "Egyptian Prehistory,3 169 *Science* (18 Sept. 1970), n°3951, pp1163-9 and figure 43, speak of widespread bush fire in reference to a bed of ash in the Nile Valley. Geologist Louis Lartel, in his first studies of Cro-Magnon man near Les Eyzies de Tayec, Dordogne, in 1968 uncovered five archaeological layers covered with ash. And so forth.

177. *Op. cit.,* p700

178. Vol. I, p17

179. E.C. Baily, "Archaeoastronomy and Ethnoastronomy Thus Far," 14 *CurrentAnthropology* (October, 1973), 389-449

180. *Legends of the Earth* (Bloomington: Indiana U. Press, 1973)

181. J. Lawrence Angle, *Troy: The Human remains* (Princeton, N.J.: Princeton U. Press, 1951)

182. Site visit with Arthur Brown, geologist and technical consultant, Athens metro project, September 11, 1974

183. Communication of April 24, 1974 from K.F. Huff, Manager, Exploration Division, Exxon

184. M. Blumer and W.W. Youngblood, "Polycyclic aromatic Hydrocarbons in Soils and Recent Sediments," *Science* (April 4, 1975), p53

185. W. Gentler, B.P. Glass, D. Storzer and G.A. Wagner, "Fission track Ages and Ages of Deposition of Deep-Sea Microtektites,3 168 *Science* (17 April, 1970) pp359-61

186. *Ibid.*

187. www.knowledge.com See also references in Concordance Bibliography.

188. (See also *The Restless Nisyros Caldera , Greece: Probing Subsurface Dynamics via a New GPS and Gravity Network,* by the Institute of Earth Science Jaume Almera, Barcelona. The caldera has undergone increased seismicity and inflation of more than 10cm in the past decade.)

189. in *AJPh* 16 [1895] pp. 203-210

191 "Materiali dell' etá del Bronzo nelle acque del lago Albano," in *ArchLaz 7: QuadAEI 11 (1987), pp 34-9*

191. "Risultati di Ricerche zoogeografiche nel Lago di Albano," in *RSGI* 1954, pp 275-283

192. R. Young, "Gordion 1953," *American Journal of Archaeology* (1954)

193. http://www.varchive.org/dag/mas.htm

194. Spanuth, pp200ff; Velikovsky, *Worlds in Collision,* pp264-5

195. Quoted in Spanuth, p210

196. *Cf.* Anthony D. Smith, *Theories of Nationalism* (1983) and Hans Kohn, *The Idea of Nationalism* (1944)

197. This author's play on the treason of Pound can be downloaded at www.grazian-archive.com

198. *Dialogue on the Great World System,* G. de Santillana, ed., Chicago, 153, pp68-9

199. Boulanger, Nicolas-Antoine: "Déluge," in *l'Encyclopédie,* D. Diderot, ed., Briasson, paris, 1751-65. Boulanger, Nicolas-Antoine: *L'Antiquité Dévoilée par ses Usages* ou *Examen critique des Principales ioinions, Cérémonies et Institutions Religieuses et Politiques des Différents Peuples de la Terre,* 4 vols, Amsterdam, 1766

200. N. A. Boulanger: *Op. cit.,* III, p316

201. N. A. Boulanger, *Op. cit.,* III, p48-9

202. De Grazia, Alfred: *A Cloud Over Bhopal,* Popular Prakashan, Bombay, 1985

203. Philologus, "Sketches of Jewish Social Life," at http://philologus.org/_eb-sjs

204. Velikovsky, Immanuel: *Mankind in Amnesia,* New York, Doubleday, 1982

205. De Grazia, Alfred: *The Disastrous Love-Affair of Moon and Mars,* Metron publications, Princeton, 1983

206. De Grazia, Alfred: *Homo Schizo I,* and *Homo Schizo II* Metron Publications, Princeton, 1983.

207. Muhly, James D.: "From Bronze Age to iron Age in western Asia: Defining the Problem," *The Crisis Years: the 12th century B.C.,* Ward, Wm. A. And Joukovsky, M.S., eds, Dubuque, 1992

208. Hallo, W.W.: "From Bronze Age to iron Age in Western Asia: Defining the Problem," in *The Crisis Years: the 12th century BC,* Ward, WM A. And Joukovsky, M.S., eds, Dubuque, 1992

209. *History and the Homeric Iliad,* 1959, p122

210. Eliade, Mircea: *The Myth of the Eternal Return,* Princeton U. Press, Princeton, NJ, 1949; *Myth and reality,* Harper and Row, New York, 1963; *Traité d'Histoire des Religions,* Payot, Paris, 1964; *Gods, Goddesses and Myths of Creation,* Harper and Row, 1974.

211. Mireaux, Emile: *Les Poèmes Héroïques et l'Histoire Grecque,* 2 vols, Albin Michel, Paris, 1964, p30

212. "Post-Palatial Twilight," Dept. Of Classics, university of Dartmouth, http://projectsx.dartmouth.edu/history/bronze_age/lessons/les/29.html

213. Webster, T.B.L.: *From Mycenae to Homer,* New York, 1964

214. Mireaux, Emile: *The Poèmes Héroïques et l'Histoire Grecque,* 2 vols, Albin michel, Paris, 1964

215. Stevens, Susie, and Stone, Laurie: "Tsunami and Mental health: what can we expect?" *A national Center for PTSD Fact Sheet,* http://www.ncptsd.va.gov/facts/disasters/fs_tsunami_research.html

216. Norris, Fran H.: "Psychological Consequences of Natural Diasasters in developing Countries: what does past research tell us about the potential effects of the 2004 tsunami?" *A National Center for PTSD Fact Sheet,* http://www.ncptsd.va.gov/facts/disasters/fs_tsunami_research.html

217. Magge, Peter: Review of: Robert G. Hoyland: *Arabia and the Arabs - From the Bronze Age to the Coming of Islam,* Routledge, New York, 2001, in Bryn Mawr College Classical review, 02/27/2003

218. X, 903c

219. X 909a

220. Velikovsky, I.: *Mankind in Amnesia,* p208

221. Eliade, Mircea, 1954, Princeton NJ, Princeton U. Press, 1949

222. Edwin Schorr: "Pylos," file://G/_Tresman archive/root/data/pubs/websites/varchive/schorr/pylos.htm

223. Page, Denys L.: *History and the Homeric Iliad,* 1959, p122

224. Wace, Alan J.

225. Finkelstein, Israel; Silberman, Neil Asher: *The Bible Unearthed: archaeology's new vision of ancient Israel and the origin of its sacred texts,* Simon and Schuster, New York, 2002

226. Salibi, Kamal: *La Bible est Née en Arabie,* Grasset, Paris, 1985

227. *Cf.* with my work *The Divine Succession* and also *Kalos: Construction of a New World Order.* A recent book by Dean Hamer, an illustrious research official and geneticist, entitled *The God Gene,* fumbles in a bag of genomes for "spirituality" but cannot emerge with a constructive program, or indeed a definable genetic inheritance that can be educated to specific universal behaviors and a course of action. One may compare it with a whacky play of this author of less recent vintage, *The Gene of Hope,* that has been produced as cinema on DVD.